care-free plants

care-free

Reader's Digest

plants

Hundreds of trouble-free winners for a beautiful garden

Published by
The Reader's Digest Association, Inc.
LONDON • NEW YORK • SYDNEY • MONTREAL

contributors

Consultant
Daphne Ledward

Writers
Peter Barnes
Richard Rosenfeld
Alexa Stace

Photographers
Sarah Cuttle
Debbie Patterson
Jason Smalley

Illustrators
Ian Sidaway
Rudi Vizi

Botanist
Sarah Wilson

Indexer
Hilary Bird

visit our web site at
www.readersdigest.co.uk

contents

How to use this book

Dip into this book at any point and you will find hundreds of care-free solutions for any garden. The first section helps you to decide what sort of site you have and which plants will thrive in it, while the second lists the most care-free varieties of more than 250 plants.

• From choosing tools to choosing plants, putting them in, and keeping them trim and disease-free, turn to the essential gardening techniques explained on pages 8–19.
• The borders are not the only thing in the garden. Pages 328–339 give inspiration and practical advice for care-free lawns and ground cover, water gardens and containers.
• A directory of plants on pages 340–344, listed by season of interest and linked to the Plant Profile entries, will help you to make your selections.

What sort of site?

Test your soil (see pages 9–10), make a plan of your garden to identify sunny, shady or soggy spots (see page 22) then turn to this section for advice and planting suggestions for trees, flowers and shrubs that will be care free and vigorous in your conditions.

• Once you have identified the different conditions you have in your garden – from dappled tree shade with light soil to a windy inland bed with heavy soil – turn to the relevant pages of this section for all the advice you need to plan a care-free garden.

• Planting illustrations give an idea of how to group a collection of the expert's suggested plants to create a flourishing and attractive bed for each of the sites in the section.

SYMBOLS USED IN THE BOOK

✿ Flower colour
∅ Leaf colour
◁ Fruit, berry or nut colour
♀ Royal Horticultural Society Award of Garden Merit (see opposite page)
h. Height *s.* Spread (or *h.&s.* if height and spread are equal)

2 *G. pilosa* 'Vancouver Gold' Ideal for a rockery, this dwarf variety forms a neat mound.
✿ Golden yellow • Early summer
h.&s. 45cm (1½ft)

THE NAMING OF PLANTS The first part of a plant name is the genus, *Genista*; after its first mention on a page, it is abbreviated to its initial letter. A genus may have several different natural species, such as *G. lydia* and *G. pilosa*, for example. When plant breeders cultivate even more new varieties they are given a cultivar name, always listed within inverted commas: *G. pilosa* 'Vancouver Gold'. Often a plant is better known by its English name, such as **Broom**, which is listed beneath the main heading.

32 WINDY MARITIME SITE
LIGHT SOIL

At the back of the beach, behind the dunes, sand has stabilised into the lightest of soils. Here, tamarisks filter the sea breezes to protect colourful dahlias, gladioli, red-hot pokers (*Kniphofia*) and cornflowers (*Centaurea*) that glow in the clear sunlight that bathes on a coastal garden.

In the sunny, even climate of a seaside site, where the soil is light and free-draining, the care-free gardener can sit back and watch normally tender plants, such as *Osteospermums*, flourish.

At the coast the difference between summer and winter temperatures is less pronounced than it is inland, and there is rarely a severe frost.

The soil may be laden with salt, making it alkaline (with a pH higher than 7), but there are many lovely plants that are tolerant of such conditions, and many more, like *Tamarix* and *Escallonia*, that can easily tolerate being battered by the fierce salty gales that blow inland during foul weather.

The crimson flowers of Escallonia 'C.F. Ball' last all summer long. The bush grows vigorously, even in the face of salty sea breezes, and several planted together will soon merge to make an excellent care-free hedge.

Give your garden a head start
Choose wisely, by picking plants that thrive in the specific conditions of a coastal location, and you are more than half way to enjoying a beautiful garden. Give the plants a little help and success should be guaranteed: stake tall or soft-stemmed varieties, like *Gladioli*, that may be bent or broken by the wind, for example.

Be firm when planting, and check the garden after strong winds to be sure that none of your precious plants has been shaken loose or uprooted. Spreading a generous blanket of organic mulch over the soil every so often will help to lock in moisture and lower the soil's pH, making it less alkaline. It will also improve the texture of the soil, giving plant roots a firmer bed.

Expert's Selection

Herbaceous perennials

The thistle-like heads of *Centaurea*, *Echinops* and *Eryngium*, and the flaming pokers of a tall *Kniphofia* make striking shapes in a border. In this light soil, traditional wild flowers often do well.

Centaurea hypoleuca '**John Coutts**' ✿ Pinkish red • Mid–late summer • *h.&s.* 60cm (2ft) ►p.104
Echinops ritro ♀ ✿ Steel-blue Late summer • *h.* 1.2m (4ft) *s.* 30cm (1ft) ►p.111
Eryngium variifolium ✿ Silvery blue Mid–late summer • *h.* 40cm (16in) *s.* 25cm (10in) ►p.114
Kniphofia '**Early Buttercup**' ✿ Yellow • Late spring–early summer *h.&s.* 60cm (2ft) ►p.138

Wild grasses are first to colonise when sand turns to soil. Plant ornamental species (see pages 126–127) with alliums (see page 306), lavender, osteospermums and wallflowers (*Erysimum*) for a seaside summer bed.

Climbers & shrubs

A low profile and narrow leaves help to keep salt-tolerant shrubs thriving even in brisk sea breezes.

Artemisia arborescens ∅ Silvery grey • *h.* 1m (3ft) *s.* 50cm (20in) ►p.184
Brachyglottis '**Sunshine**' ♀ ✿ Yellow Midsummer • *h.* 1m (3ft) *s.* 2m (7ft) ►p.189
Cytisus x *praecox* ✿ Yellow • Spring *h.* 1.2m (4ft) *s.* 1m (3ft) ►p.202
Escallonia '**C.F. Ball**' ✿ Crimson Summer ∅ Dark green *h.&s.* 3m (10ft) ►p.204

SALT-TOLERANT SHRUBS SHRUG OFF SEA SPRAY

Every coastal garden should include at least one tamarix to act as a windbreak against the salt-laden winds that blow in from the sea. Harsh northerly winds blow onto the front of this exposed border, which makes an attractive shelter for the garden and house behind it.

Plan shows garden in early summer

Tamarix tetranda
Dahlia 'Arabian Night'
Escallonia 'C.F. Ball'
Spartium junceum
Pinus sylvestris 'Chantry Blue'
Cytisus x praecox
Gladiolus communis subsp. byzantinus
Brachyglottis 'Sunshine'
Artemisia arborescens
Eryngium variifolium
Gladiolus communis subsp. byzantinus

Lavandula angustifol... Muffet ✿ Lilac-blue • ... midsummer ∅ Silver-... *h.&s.* 30cm (1ft) ►p.2...
Pinus sylvestris 'Cha... ∅ Blue-grey ◁ Yellow... to brown • *h.* 4m (13... ►p.234
Rosa pimpinellifoli... Early summer • *h.* 1... *s.* 1.2m (4ft) ►p.242...
Solanum laxum '...' Midsummer–autumn... *s.* 60cm (2ft) ►p.2...

A–Z plant profiles

For an exhaustive list of plants that will be care free in the right situation turn to this section. 255 main entries and five features covering groups of plants, such as grasses, mean that there is something for even the most challenging growing conditions.

- The **Expert's Selection** lists plants from the A–Z Plant Profiles section that will thrive in each particular site.

- Each entry in the Expert's Selection lists flower, leaf or berry colour, season of interest and size. Turn to the page indicated for the main entry in the following section for more detailed information.

- The section is divided into herbaceous perennials; climbers, shrubs, sub-shrubs and conifers; trees; annuals, biennials, bedding and container plants; and bulbs, corms, tubers and rhizomes.

- For easy reference, plants in each section are listed alphabetically by their botanical (latin) name.

- Each entry highlights a **'Star Performer'** for sure success.

- The **Expert's Selection** ranks varieties in order of ease of care. Look out for the RHS Award of Garden Merit symbol, ♀, for plants that are particularly hardy and disease resistant.

- **The Essentials** lists the key planting and care information for each plant: site demands, planting practice, flowering time, pruning needs (if appropriate), the main pests and diseases to look out for and a bonus point.

- **Take a Fresh Look** boxes focus on new or unusual plant varieties that are worth trying out for a different effect.

CLIMBERS &

208

Garrya

Silk tassel bushes earn their keep with spectacular male catkins, which appear at the start of the year. They grow quickly, are easy going, and will flourish in sun or shade.

Expert's Selection

1 *G. elliptica* 'James Roof'♀ Showy catkins are 35cm (14in) long, over twice the length of those on its parent plant, *G. elliptica*.
☆ Silver-green catkins • Winter–early spring • *h.&s.* 2.5m (8ft)

2 *G. x issaquahensis* 'Glasnevin Wine' Wine-red catkins turn lime-green in spring.
☆ Red, then green catkins • Winter–early spring
h.&s. 2.5m (8ft)

3 *G. x issaquahensis* 'Pat Ballard' Has spectacular, 20cm (8in) long, mauve catkins.
☆ Mauve catkins • Winter–early spring • *h.&s.* 2.5m (8ft)

4 *G. elliptica* 'Evie' Wavy-edged leaves and 30cm (1ft) long catkins add interest.
☆ Grey-green catkins • Winter–early spring • *h.&s.* 2.5m (8ft)

> **STAR PERFORMER**
> *G. elliptica* 'James Roof'♀ In mild winters this garrya bush will be festooned with a stunning display of silvery green catkins.

The Essentials

Site demands Any well-drained, fertile soil, in shade, or, for the best catkins, in full sun. Place by wall for shelter in windy, northerly gardens.
Planting practice Plant in autumn or spring.
Flowering time Winter to early spring.
Pruning needs Just remove dead wood, and trim after flowering.
Pests and diseases Trouble free.
Bonus point Thrive even in city pollution and salty, seaside air.

Spartium junce...
Early summer–ea...
h.&s. 3m (10ft) ▸...
Tamarix tetran...
Spring–early sum...
h.&s. 4m (13ft) ▸...

Trees

...ing
Plant open-crown...
)
not be felled by...

...White
Acer pseudopla...
...eft)
'Brilliantissimu...
Spring • *h.&s.* 3m...

Genista

Broom actually thrives in poor soil, like that on the heaths and moors where it grows naturally. Plant in full sun, and it will reward you with masses of golden yellow flowers.

Expert's Selection

1 *G. lydia*♀ A spreading shrub with arching stems and clusters of flowers.
☆ Golden yellow • Late spring–early summer • *h.&s.* 60cm (2ft)

2 *G. pilosa* 'Vancouver Gold' Ideal for a rockery, this dwarf variety forms a neat mound.
☆ Golden yellow • Early summer *h.&s.* 45cm (1½ft)

3 *G. hispanica* Good as ground cover, the spiny Spanish gorse is especially tolerant of dry, hot sites and poor soil.
☆ Golden yellow • Early summer *h.* 60cm (2ft) *s.* 1m (3ft)

4 *G. tinctoria* The flowers of 'dyer's greenweed' make a golden yellow dye. The shrub grows erect or prostrate.
☆ Golden yellow • Summer *h.* 30cm–2m (1–7ft) *s.* 45cm–1m (1½–3ft)

G. hispanica

planted to cascade over a wall or down a bank, while, *G. tinctoria*, when prostrate, will form a low-growing mat, making it ideal in a rockery or to fill gaps in a border.

The Essentials

Site demands Best in a light sandy soil in full sun.
Planting practice Plant in early autumn.
Flowering time Early summer.
Pruning demands Prune lightly in late winter; only trim new wood.
Pests and diseases Trouble free.
Bonus point Bright colour for difficult gardens.

Brooms make attractive shrubs, with their wiry stems and masses of golden yellow flowers. They are stars in difficult spots, because they actually flower best in poor soils.
Low-growing varieties such as *G. lydia* can be

> **STAR PERFORMER**
> *G. lydia*♀ Each flower is small, but there are so many that the effect of a broom in bloom is stunning.

Hebe

Not all hebes are hardy but these selections are all frost-resistant, and flower over a long season. They range in habit from low ground cover to bushy border varieties.

Expert's Selection

1 *H. pimeleoides* 'Quicksilver'♀ Silvery leaves set off a mass of violet flowers.
☆ Violet • Mid–late summer ∅ Silver *h.* 60cm (2ft) *s.* 1m (3ft)

2 *H.* 'Autumn Glory' This medium-sized bush produces heavenly violet-blue flowers.
☆ Violet-blue • Summer–late autumn *h.* 60cm (2ft) *s.* 75cm (2½ft)

3 *H.* 'Nicola's Blush' Enjoy two waves of flowers a year.
☆ Pink, fading to white • Spring–midsummer and autumn–winter *h.&s.* 75cm (2½ft)

4 *H. cupressoides* 'Boughton Dome'♀ Rarely flowers, but forms a neat, green dome, packed with scale-like leaves.
∅ Green • *h.* 60cm (2ft) *s.* 1m (3ft)

5 *H.* 'Red Edge'♀ The delicate flowers are a subtle violet; the leaves have a red edge.
☆ Pale violet • Summer ∅ Grey-green with red edge *h.&s.* 60cm (2ft)

6 *H.* 'Youngii' Also called 'Carl Teschner', its flowers fade as summer wanes.
☆ Violet, fading to white • Summer *h.* 20cm (8in) *s.* 60cm (2ft)

7 *H.* 'Wingletye' A lilac, low-growing variety.
☆ Lilac • Summer *h.* 20cm (8in) *s.* 30cm (1ft)

TAKE A FRESH LOOK

H. ochracea 'James Stirling'♀ 'Whipcord' hebes, like this one, look similar to cypresses. Its flat top is covered with white flowers in spring.

8 *H. pinguifolia* 'Pagei'♀ This hardy, prostrate variety makes excellent ground cover.
☆ White • Mid–late spring ∅ Grey *h.* 20cm (8in) *s.* 60cm (2ft)

The Essentials

Site demands Plant in any well-drained soil, preferably in full sun.
Planting practice Plant in autumn or spring.
Flowering time From spring to autumn, depending on variety.
Pruning needs Cut back large or leggy plants in spring.
Pests and diseases Look out for downy mildew in damp autumns.
Bonus point Tolerant of salt-laden winds, they are perfect for providing easy seaside colour.

Hebes are versatile, evergreen shrubs, noted for their stunning flower displays. Many stay in bloom all summer and well into autumn. Mix the pinks, whites and purples of 'Nicola's Blush', 'Pagei' and 'Quicksilver', for a pretty, layered pastel display.
Some of the low-growing hebes, such as 'Youngii' and 'Wingletye', make good ground cover or rockery plants. Another compact variety is 'Boughton Dome', which forms a rounded dome of bright green.

Hardy beauty
Choose a hebe from this list, and you should have no trouble with frost. However, as a general rule of thumb, the larger the leaf, the more tender a hebe will be, so if you live in a very exposed site, choose a 'whipcord hebe', like 'James Stirling'. They are easy to grow and will tolerate gusty, salty winds, making them ideal for seaside gardens.

Testing & improving your soil

The first step in planning a care-free garden is to find out what kind of soil you have so that you can pick plants that suit the conditions. But there are also a few simple ways to improve your soil that will widen your planting options and save you time and energy in the future.

Light and stony soil

Boggy heavy soil

What sort of soil do you have?

Ask yourself the following questions about your garden and you will quickly be able to make a rough analysis of the kind of soil you have.

• Is the surface covered with stones, and do you bring more up when you dig? Stony ground like this is probably also light and free-draining.
• Do cracks appear in the surface and the soil sets as hard as concrete in dry weather? Does the earth stick to your boots at the first sign of a shower? If so, then your soil is heavy.
• Can you sink the whole blade of your spade or fork easily into the earth, or do you soon strike rock, shale or gravel? If the latter is the case, your soil is likely to be thin, impoverished and shallow.
• Look at the plants that are already doing well in your garden and the gardens around. Most soils have a roughly neutral pH, but if rhododendrons, camellias and heathers are flourishing, the soil is almost certainly acid. If carnations, pinks, wallflowers, stocks and clematis do well, your conditions are probably alkaline.

The easiest way to confirm your observations is with a water test (see box, right) and soil pH testing kit. If you notice a lot of plants with yellowing foliage, or downward pointing leaves with brown, brittle edges – this indicates deficiency disorders – and it may be worth buying a more comprehensive soil-testing kit. This will check for nitrates, phosphates and potash as well. Alternatively ask a commercial soil analyst to test it for you.

A soil pH testing kit

Rhododendrons will only thrive on acid soil

The jam jar test

A good way to determine your soil's conditions is with a water test. This will quickly show you the texture and give you an idea of how much organic matter it contains.

• Quarter-fill a screw-topped jar with garden soil. Top it up with water, replace the lid and shake vigorously for 2 minutes. Leave it to settle for a few hours.
• Coarse soil particles will have sunk to the bottom of the jar first, followed by progressively finer ones. With an average soil, you should be able to see distinct layers of different sized particles.
• An even balance of coarse to light particles denotes a medium loam, suitable for a wide range of plants.
• A thick layer of coarse particles indicates a light sandy soil.
• Very fine particles will still be in suspension in the water, so if the liquid is still cloudy, the soil is heavy clay or silt.
• Humus (organic material) will be floating on the top. If there is very little of this, your soil needs more.

Use a jam jar with a lid

Heavy soil (left) and light soil

Improving the soil

All soil benefits from digging to loosen weeds so that they can be removed and to improve the texture. This can be done at any time of year, but if your ground is heavy, digging in autumn will allow winter frosts to break up the soil and make it much easier to manage the following spring. If possible, never walk on heavy soil when it is wet, as this will destroy your work to improve its texture.

Adding compost

Digging in organic material, such as farmyard or stable manure, garden compost or spent hops (from a local brewery), and mulching the soil regularly with the same things will improve a soil's texture and help it to retain moisture and nutrients.

Most garden waste, except for perennial weed roots, can be used as compost ingredients. Uncooked vegetable waste from the kitchen, such as vegetable parings, tea leaves and coffee grounds, can also be used, as can the hay, straw and sawdust bedding from pets, such as hamsters and rabbits. Avoid meat bones and scraps, which will attract vermin.

The larger the heap or bin, the hotter the compost gets and the quicker it will rot down. Shred tough items, such as shrub prunings to speed the process and add them to the heap in layers, mixed with finer material, such as grass mowings. The compost will be ready in around three months in hot weather, but will take longer during cooler periods. When ready to use, compost should be sweet-smelling, crumbly, and look rather like coarse peat.

Feed with fertilisers

Heavy soils are usually rich in nutrients, but they soon wash out of free-draining ones. Adding sustained manure or garden compost provides some nutrients, but not enough to keep plants vigorous and healthy over a long period. Concentrated fertilisers are longer-lasting.

• Sulphate of ammonia and its organic equivalent, dried blood, provide nitrogen, which promotes rapid, healthy top growth.
• Superphosphate or bone meal boosts phosphates, needed for good root development.
• Compounds, such as blood, fish and bone, provide a balanced feed, including plenty of potash for good flowering, fruiting and hardening of juvenile growth in trees and shrubs.

It is a good idea to incorporate a fertiliser when you are planting. In spring and summer, a compound, such as blood, fish and bone, will provide all the necessary nutrients for growth and flowering. If you are planting in autumn and winter, use a slow-release feed such as bone meal, to get the young specimens off to a good start.

Good compost is crumbly and sweet

Blood, fish and bone enriches soil

Tools to make light work

It is better to spend money on a few good-quality tools than a large number of inferior ones. Badly made tools will often bend or break, or poor design may turn the easiest of jobs into really hard work. Follow these tips to choosing wisely for a well-stocked tool shed.

Useful
hand tools

Basic toolkit essentials

Spade Unless your garden is little more than a window box, a spade is vital. A border spade is not as wide as a digging spade, so is a good choice for small gardens and for densely planted borders; it is also lighter and will be less tiring to use for long periods.

Many spades have a 'turnover' at the top of the blade where you place your foot for digging. This makes the tool more comfortable to use and prevents your instep being bruised as you push the spade into the ground.

A spade
'turnover'

Fork If your ground is very heavy or stony you may find a fork easier to use than a spade. A digging fork, which has four narrow sharp tines, has the most all-round use, but if you

Choose a fork
to suit your soil

have very solid ground, you may find a flat tined, or potato fork easier. A small border fork is useful in confined areas and when weight is a consideration.

Rake You will need a rake for levelling ground after digging. It is also handy for clearing up leaves and rubbish with minimal bending. Look for one with a rubber or plastic hand grip for comfort.

Trowel You can use a trowel for planting small things, and for loosening stubborn weeds. A hand fork is also useful. The neck of such tools is often weak, so always check that it is strongly constructed. The most versatile trowel has a medium width blade.

Secateurs For trimming plants and light pruning jobs you will need a pair of secateurs. There are several different designs available, but providing the blade is kept sharp, they will all work satisfactorily.

Bucket A bucket is useful for all kinds of jobs in the garden. Those made of recycled rubber or plastic are light and durable.

Watering can A watering can is the most precise watering tool. It is helpful to have both a coarse rose with a few, large holes, and a fine one, with many tiny holes, for watering different sized plants.

Hand shears Trimming back plants and clipping shrubs is easiest with hand shears. Some have telescopic handles to save bending and stretching.

Keeping your tools clean Your tools are only as good as the care they receive. Clean them after use, wipe metal parts with oil and lubricate any working parts, treat wooden handles periodically with linseed oil, and keep them dry, and they should last you a lifetime. Stainless steel tools are easy to clean, do not rust and do not need wiping with an oily rag before putting away. Carbon steel blades may stay sharper for longer, but only if they are well cared for.

Take care of
your tools

More advanced tools

Loppers When you need to cut back thick branches, loppers are the best tool. They work like secateurs, but are more substantial and some have a ratchet system on the blade, requiring less effort for cutting. All have handles about an arm's length for reaching into shrubs and some have telescopic handles for an even longer reach.

Tree pruners have very long or telescopic handles, and enable you to work right into the crown of a tree from ground level.

A pruning saw Removing unwanted branches from trees and shrubs is easy with a pruning saw. A narrow blade reaches between shoots and often works on the back stroke only for easy use. A small version with a folding blade is ideal for carrying with you as you work.

Hoe A long-handled hoe will help you to control weeds without getting on your hands and knees. The Dutch hoe, or D-hoe, has a sharp blade which severs young weeds from their roots as you push it over the soil. Some hoes have a sharp edge on either side of the blade and are operated with a push-pull action. The swan neck, or draw hoe is also available, and removes weeds with a chopping motion; it can also be used to make seed drills in fine soil.

Sprayer A sprayer is useful for controlling pests and diseases or for applying foliar feeds. If you only have a small area, you may find a hand-operated trigger sprayer adequate, but with a larger garden, the pneumatic (pump-up) type is much more practical. Bigger sprayers require less frequent refilling, but are heavier when full.

Hoes have different actions

Machinery

Mower
- Unless your lawn is very small, your mower will need power. Mowers can be powered by electricity, petrol or a 'two-stroke' mixture of oil and petrol.
- A two-stroke mower is best for sloping lawns, as a petrol engine can cut out in these situations.
- Electric mowers are ideal for small gardens. Rechargeable battery versions remove the danger of accidentally cutting the cable and electrocuting yourself.
- A traditional cylinder mower will ensure a striped finish, but many rotary mowers are also fitted with a roller, to give the same effect.
- If your lawn is not perfectly even, a rotary mower or hover mower is less likely to 'scalp' the surface.

Hedge trimmer
- A hedge trimmer will make short work of keeping hedges neat. Petrol tools are heavy, so an electric or battery-powered model is more convenient for trimming shrubs and small hedges.

Spin trimmer
- A trimmer that uses a nylon line or metal blade for cutting, may be worth while if you have rough areas around trees, dry ditches, or 'wild' areas.
- Petrol or two-stroke trimmers are best for large areas. Electric ones need a long cable, but battery-operated ones will cut for only around 20 minutes.

Safety warning
All electrical garden equipment should be connected to the mains via a residual current device (RCD), that shuts off the power instantly if a cable is cut or a problem occurs that could cause an electric shock.

Test handles for comfort

Handles Tools are made with 'D' or 'T'-shaped handles and come in wood or plastic. Take time to decide which is more comfortable for you. Handles also vary in length, and it is important to choose one that is right for you – too short or too long and the tool will be uncomfortable to use for more than a short period and may give you backache.

If you have limited storage space for garden tools, it is worth considering a 'snap-in' type of tool system. Choose one or two handles of different lengths and they will fit a whole range of tool heads.

One handle, many tools

Buying & choosing for success

If you buy healthy plants and give them the best possible start by planting them correctly, you will cut down on the care they subsequently need. You will make a lot of work for yourself if you start with unhealthy plants and put them in the ground the wrong way or at the wrong time of year.

Where to buy plants

Friends and neighbours may sometimes offer you plants or cuttings from their gardens. But before you accept, it is worth checking that they are suitable for the conditions in your garden, and that they are not showing signs of pests or diseases.

Nurseries or garden centres are a better source (nurseries generally raise their own plants and sell little else). The Royal Horticultural Society's annual publication, *Plant Finder*, lists suppliers for each plant and is useful for tracking down unusual varieties.

Mail-order shopping from catalogues or the Internet is also worth considering if you are looking for something special.

Choosing healthy plants

Plants worth buying should look healthy, not long and straggly or weak and stunted. And avoid buying a plant just because it has a flower: a bushy plant without flowers will establish itself faster than a scrawny one with a few blooms. But if both the flowering and non-flowering specimens are equally good, it may pay to take the one with flowers, then you can be sure you have the plant you wanted.

From late autumn to early spring, some nurseries sell bare-root (not container-grown) plants. Make sure the roots are damp and plant them as soon as you can. If these plants dry out they may not recover.

Look out for moss and weeds

A plant should feel firm in the pot

Inspect the shoots

Use this checklist to help you to choose the best specimens on offer in the garden centre.

• Make sure the compost is free of weeds, moss and algae: these indicate that a plant has been neglected.
• Pick the plant up – if it has rooted into the bed, it has been there too long and will probably be stressed.
• However, a few roots poking out of the base of the pot are not necessarily a bad sign, but show that the plant is established and ready for planting.
• Check that the plant is firm in its pot: if it lifts out of the compost with a gentle tug, it has been recently repotted and needs time to settle down, or is lacking water and may be stressed.
• Feel the compost: it should be moist.
• Inspect the shoots for pests and disease.

Planting advice

The best time to plant is when the ground is moist. Plants grown and sold in containers can be planted at any time, but if you do it in summer you will need to water them regularly until they are established. The planting times given in this book refer to bare-root plants, seeds or seedlings.

Between autumn and mid spring is the best time to plant, as most plants are dormant then and can devote their energies into making good roots. Check that new plants do not dry out in windy weather or dry spells. Plant Mediterranean, sun-loving subjects such as lavenders in spring, because these need higher temperatures and better light to re-establish.

It is a good idea to trim the roots of bare-root plants by about a third at planting time. This will remove any damaged parts which might rot, and encourages the plant to produce a spurt of new hair roots. These will help it to establish itself quickly.

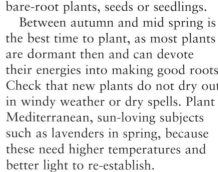

❶ Check the size of the hole

❷ Add fertiliser

❸ Back-fill with soil and compost

❹ Make sure the plant is firm

How to plant

How to plant Whether you are putting in a tree or a small bedding plant, follow these simple steps to give your plants their best possible chance of success.

❶ **Dig a hole** wide enough to leave room to spare around the sides of the rootball and deep enough so that the plant will be at the same depth as it was in its pot. Break up the soil in the base of the hole then fill it with water and allow it to drain away.

❷ **Place the plant in the hole** so it is upright. If the roots had filled the pot, carefully tease a few of them out from the edge of the rootball. If the roots are wrapped in sacking or net, place the plant in the hole with the wrap intact, then loosen it with a knife. Add a little fertiliser (see page 9) to the base of the hole: blood, fish and bone in spring or summer, bonemeal in autumn and winter.

❸ **Back-fill the hole** with a mixture of good garden soil and peat substitute, such as well-rotted garden compost, old potting compost or leaf-mould.

❹ **Firm in** so you cannot pull the plant out if you tug at it gently. Water the new plant well, unless the ground is already very damp.

Staking tall plants for support

Young trees, shrubs that are trained on a single stem, and other top-heavy plants will need to be supported with a stake. Place the stake so that it is close to the plant, but not touching, and make sure the trunk and stake are kept separate when tying.

Tree straps (below) are supplied with a separating device and can be loosened as the plant grows.

Support floppy bushy plants (right) with a ring of three or four stakes, with soft string or old nylon tights run round the outside. Do this when the plant is young and it will hide the supports as it grows.

Use string to support bushy plants

Keep the trunk and stake apart

Watering, feeding & weeding

Even the most care-free garden will need a little care and attention every now and then if it is going to look its best in every season. Follow these tips to ensure that the time you spend watering, fertilising and controlling weeds is kept to a minimum, but with maximum results.

How to water

To get the best results from your plants and to avoid wasting precious water, particularly during hot dry spells, follow these watering tips:

- Water in the evening. This will reduce evaporation and the ground will stay damp overnight.
- Water only when necessary. New plants may need daily watering in hot weather. Container plants need watering at least once a day when in full growth in summer; more if it is hot or windy.
- Water young plants in winter if they grow against a wall or fence or if the weather has been very dry.
- Apply water in a ring round the base of the plants to reach the outer edges of the roots, not just at the bottom of the stems.
- Give plants a good soaking. A dribble does more harm than good as it brings roots to the surface. Unless plants are wilting, it is often better not to water at all, to encourage them to produce a wide-ranging, deep root system.
- Do not overwater early and late in the season – it may cause root rot.
- Do not wet foliage and flowers in bright sunlight. During dry, hot spells, misting the leaves with a fine spray when not in full sun is beneficial.
- Use a perforated hose to leak water gently onto the soil near the roots, rather than onto the foliage.

Choose a fertiliser that best suits you and your plants. Water in soluble feeds ❶, dig pellets ❷, granules ❸ and powders, such as bone meal ❹, into the soil, and push slow-release tablets ❺ and pellet clusters ❻ into container compost.

Water at the base

Conserving water

Soils that are rich in organic material retain water well. A sunny area will dry out faster than one that receives some shade, so create shelter on the sunny side of your garden for moisture-loving plants.

Planting through a semi-permeable membrane, sometimes called landscape fabric (below), is a good way to conserve moisture. It allows water to soak through, but reduces evaporation from the surface and has the added benefit of keeping out weeds. Rid the area of weeds, lay the membrane and cut holes to plant through. Finally, add a mulch of bark chippings or gravel to hide the fabric.

A membrane keeps moisture in

Feeding

Improving your soil by adding fertilisers before and when you plant (see page 9) will cut down the amount of feeding your plants subsequently need. However, most plants benefit from a regular feed, too. Look out for the letters **P, N** and **K** (see below) on fertiliser packaging to give your plants what they need.

- **All plants**, but particularly newly planted ones, benefit from phosphates (**P**) in autumn, to help them to establish strong roots.
- **Grass and other foliage plants** need nitrates (**N**). Use a slow-release lawn fertiliser for ornamental grasses and bamboos.
- **Plants grown for flowers** require more potash (**K**) and phosphates, and less nitrogen.
- **Tomato feeds** have high levels of magnesium and also stimulate flowering and fruiting.
- **Rose fertilisers** contain high levels of potash, iron and magnesium.

• **Compound fertilisers** contain all the elements required for healthy growth.
• **Quick-release fertilisers** encourage good overall performance early in the season and generally need renewing at least once during summer.
• **Slow-release fertilisers** such as container plant feeds and lawn feeds will last all year if they are applied in spring.
• **Foliar feeds** are sprayed onto leaves for instant effect. They are best used as a 'pick-me-up' for plants stressed by moving or drought, for example.
• **Organic fertilisers** are derived from various natural substances, including chicken manure and the by-products from slaughterhouses and fisheries, such as bone meal or blood, fish and bone. Occasionally, they are mixed with other substances, such as spent hops. They come in the form of either bulky manures or concentrated powders, and may be slow or quick in effect.

Dealing with weeds

Weeds not only look untidy, they also steal vital moisture and nutrients from the plants you really want in your garden, and can encourage pests and diseases. Keeping them at bay from the outset makes weeding much easier and may save a lot of other problems later on.

Hoeing This is the cheapest and easiest way to remove young weeds, as it severs the top of the weeds from their roots, so neither can re-grow. Hoeing also breaks up the surface of the soil, and can help to reduce water loss.

Hand-weeding In closely planted beds where there is no room for a hoe, and between young seedlings that may be damaged by hoeing it may be easier to weed by hand and this is the only way to tackle perennial weeds effectively. Remove all weeds once they have been pulled up, as some may continue to flower and seed.

Mulching A layer of mulch will prevent weeds growing, by not giving them chance to root. Composted bark, shredded prunings, well-rotted compost, cocoa shells, farmyard manure and spent hops are all suitable, but you could also lay a semi-permeable membrane (see left). For best results, apply a mulch in spring or early autumn, when the soil is warm and damp, and make sure that it is at least 5cm (2in) deep.

Hoe out weeds

Ground cover blocks weeds

Spread chemicals evenly

Ground cover Spreading plants are among the most care-free ways to prevent weeds growing and have the bonus of being far more attractive than areas of bare soil. Low-growing evergreens are the best choice, as they soon merge together and stop weed seeds germinating. Good examples are *Euonymus fortunei*, *Hypericum calycinum*, *Cotoneaster dammeri*, *Senecio* 'Sunshine', *Bergenia* or *Vinca* (periwinkle) shown left.

Chemical weedkillers If you have a large area of weeds to clear, chemicals will save you time and effort. A number of different preparations are available. Make sure you read the instructions or take the advice of a knowledgeable salesperson before you buy, to make sure you have the right one for the job. Use a spreader to ensure even coverage.

• Paraquat, diquat and certain fatty acids kill the top of the plant almost instantly on contact, but perennial weeds will generally re-grow in time.
• Glyphosate and some broad-leaved herbicides designed to be used as grass weedkillers are a better choice for perennial and difficult-to-control weeds. They do not affect the soil, so replanting can take place immediately the weeds have died.
• Some chemicals poison the surface of the soil, so new seeds cannot germinate and any dormant plants die as they reach the poisoned layer. Some are suitable for use around existing plants, but others can only be used on paths and bare ground.

Easy-care maintenance

Follow these simple guidelines to make light work of keeping your garden neat, tidy and in excellent health. Cutting back, pruning and training correctly, and at the right time, will help you to get maximum value from your plants.

Pinch off soft-stemmed dead flowers

Cut back after flowering

Thin out at the base

Simple plant care

Most plants will benefit from a little light maintenance to keep them looking tidy and in peak condition.

Deadheading

Removing spent flowers can also prolong a plant's display by encouraging a second flush of blooms. If they cannot set seed, plants have more energy for producing robust, disease-resistant growth.

- **Soft-stemmed plants** such as pansies and petunias can be deadheaded by snapping off the fading flowers by hand.
- **Shrubs and herbaceous plants** have tougher stems, and you may need to use scissors or secateurs.
- **Do some light pruning** as you deadhead, by trimming back the flowering stem to a leaf joint or bud pointing in the direction in which you want the stem to continue growing.
- **Leave dead heads** on plants that produce attractive seed heads, berries, fruits or nuts.

Cutting back

Many herbaceous perennials, like hardy geraniums, benefit from cutting back after flowering and may produce vigorous new foliage from the base to fill an otherwise blank space in the border. Cut back the flowering stems and a little of the foliage. The harder you cut many plants, the more they re-grow.

Thinning out

You will reduce the likelihood of pests and diseases if you thin out overcrowded plants to allow air to circulate through them. Remove cluttered stems from the centre of a plant as close to the base as possible (see above).

Pruning

There is often no need to prune a plant unless it gets out of hand, but young plants can benefit from cutting down low to encourage them to make plenty of new shoots, while other plants may need shaping.

Follow the pruning advice given for each plant in the A–Z plant profiles section of this book or, if you are not sure what kind of shrub you have, wait a year to see how it grows and if and when it flowers, then use these simple tips.

Climbers and wall shrubs

- **Evergreen climbers**, such as *Akebia* and *Hedera* (ivy), are best cut back in spring. It may be necessary to trim long new growths in late summer.
- **Flowering evergreen wall shrubs**, such as *Pyracantha*, are pruned after flowering and again later in the season if they need tidying. Be careful not to cut back any developing berries.
- **Climbers flowering in winter and early spring** need cutting back after flowering to the main branch framework.

• **Climbers flowering in late spring and early summer** should be cut back after flowering to their main branch framework. Remove some older branches to encourage young growth.
• **Climbers flowering in late summer and autumn** should be cut back in spring.

Free-standing shrubs
• **Evergreens** such as *Aucuba, Elaeagnus* and *Ilex*, do not need regular pruning. Trim them while they are in full growth to keep them neat and to remove dead or diseased wood, but no later than the end of August, otherwise new shoots may be frost-prone.

Early-flowering deciduous shrub

Late-flowering deciduous shrub

• **Early-flowering deciduous shrubs** that flower in spring on wood produced the previous year, such as *Forsythia* and *Ribes*, and those that flower in early summer on old and new wood, such as *Philadelphus* and *Deutzia*, should be pruned after flowering. Remove all the old flowered shoots (blue, above) and cut back any young ones to encourage vigorous new growth.
• **Late-flowering deciduous shrubs** that bloom in summer and autumn on the new year's wood, such as *Buddleja*, should be cut back in spring to two or three buds of the old wood (blue, above). Do the same with shrubs grown for their winter bark.

Plant supports can be a feature

Make a show of trellis

Vine eyes and wire

Roses
• **Young bushes** should be cut back hard in spring, so plenty of new branches are produced.
• **Large-flowered** (hybrid tea) and cluster-flowered roses are best pruned in spring. Shorten strong branches by a third, to an outward-pointing bud and remove any dead or badly placed branches.
• **Shrub roses** only need deadheading. Prune overgrown bushes like large-flowered roses (above) and cut back very old, woody bushes hard in winter.
• **Miniature roses** need clipping with shears in spring and again after the first flush of flowers.

Trees
• **Young trees** should have badly placed branches removed when dormant. Do not cut a *Prunus* from autumn to spring: they are vulnerable to infection.
• **Low branches** may need to be removed from young trees to encourage a straight, clear trunk.
• **Trees with coloured bark** or interesting leaves on their young wood, such as *Acer negundo* 'Flamingo', should be cut back to their main branch framework every 3–5 years.

Training and supports
Naturally trailing or climbing plants need a support to scramble up or through. It is easier and less likely to harm the plant, if you provide this at the outset.
• **Wires** can be attached to a wall or fence with vine eyes that are hammered in, or screws and plugs. They are unobtrusive, but are most effective with bushy evergreen plants.
• **Ornamental trellis** is a better choice for deciduous climbers, because the trellis provides decoration when the plant is dormant.
• **Self-clinging climbers,** such as *Parthenocissus*, need no support. Do not grow them on walls that need regular painting: they are difficult to detach.
• **Arches, pergolas and obelisks** can be enhanced by growing a climbing plant over them.

Dealing with pests & diseases

The simplest way to avoid pests and diseases is to ensure that your plants are strong and growing in suitable situations. All the plants in this book are as resistant as possible; the Royal Horticultural Society's Award of Garden Merit, denoted by a ♀ after the plant name, is another good endorsement.

Recognising pests

To limit the chemicals you put on your garden, it is preferable to deal with pests when you see them, rather than spray liberally on the chance that you may later have a problem. There are a few common pests that can be found in most gardens at some time – look out for these tell-tale signs so that you can catch them early on.

- **Aphids** are sap-sucking insects, and may spread disease. They cluster on stems, and often attract ants with the sticky honeydew they secrete. Wash them off with a jet of water. If you see them in the garden, cover plants you want to protect with horticultural fleece until the infestation has passed.
- **Leaf miners and thrips** may spoil the appearance of your plants, by taking bites out of the leaves or clustering on flowers, but they are not damaging to the plant's health.
- **Caterpillars** chew through leaves and are best picked off by hand.
- **Vine weevils** take bites out of leaves, but their grubs are more damaging, as they destroy roots. They thrive in overwet soils, so be careful not to overwater. If you see the adults on a plant, take steps to destroy the grubs.

Pest control

- **Contact pesticides** are the easiest way to get rid of pests once you spot them. Most are based on derris or pyrethrum, which are natural plant derivatives, or on synthetically manufactured pyrethroids and kill the pest on contact.
- **Organic gardeners** may prefer to use insecticides based on natural fatty acids or plant oils.
- **Disfiguring insects** such as leaf miners and thrips are difficult to control, unless you can spray them directly with contact pesticide.
- **Barrier controls**, such as covering plants with fleece, are particularly successful with pests which have definite seasons, such as sawflies.
- **Mulching** with polythene, planting membrane or even old carpet underlay, will deter soil-borne pests, such as cabbage root fly, which also attacks wallflowers and stocks.
- **Hoeing** around vulnerable plants can control some early pests, such as narcissus fly.

Cover plants to keep off pests

Wash off aphids

Nature's pest control

Encourage insects into your garden and they will help to keep pests in check for you.

Avoid using chemicals and you will find that ladybirds, lacewings, hoverflies and wasps will move in. You can even buy insect larvae to introduce. All these predatory insects have big appetites for damaging pests, such as aphids.

Ladybirds are helpful predators

Vine weevils do their damage underground

Pick off caterpillars

Beer trap for slugs

Slugs and snails The most common garden pests are slugs and snails. They can destroy a plant overnight or stop its development by eating young shoots and buds. Slug pellets are effective, but short-lived, so try these alternatives.

• **Beer traps** sunk into the ground attract slugs and, less frequently, snails, which fall in and drown. It is best to use a purpose-designed trap (above) rather than improvise, as homemade traps can catch beneficial beetles as well.

• **Sprinkle powdered kaolin** around susceptible plants. This dries the pest's mucus and prevents it from moving across the soil, but it may need renewing after heavy rain.

• **Nematodes** watered into the soil infest slugs and kill them, but are less effective with snails. However, they are expensive so are best used for really special plants.

• **A nightly patrol** is the most effective form of control. Pick off any slugs and snails you find and dispose of them.

Recognising diseases

Modern plant breeding has ensured that many newer varieties are more disease resistant than their ancestors. However, there are a few diseases to which many plants are susceptible.

• **Powdery mildew** is most common in warm, dry weather and leaves a dusty white 'bloom' on leaves.

• **Honey fungus** shows itself as toadstools growing at the base of a plant's stem, but these are a clear sign that the fungus is also growing beneath the bark and in the roots. If you suspect you have an infestation, seek specialist advice.

• **Rust** is also caused by a fungus and can be difficult to eradicate. If you know from experience that you have a vulnerable plant, it is a good idea to prevent infection by spraying new shoots in spring.

• **Black spot** is particularly common on many roses, and leaves rusty blemishes on the foliage. When you spot any affected leaves remove them and spray the whole plant with a suitable fungicide.

• **Grey mould** is a velvety mould commonly found on flowers, leaves and fruit, often where they join the main stem. Leaving water on leaves in dull weather can encourage it. Remove affected parts to stop it spreading.

• **Fireblight** leaves shrubs looking as though they have been scorched. Remove and burn diseased shoots or dig up the whole plant if necessary.

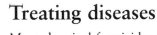

Powdery mildew

Honey fungus

Rust

Treating diseases

Most chemical fungicides work by being absorbed by the plant to make its new young growth disease resistant. They do not usually cure diseases that are already present, such as rose black spot, so cut out diseased wood and leaves before you spray. However, if they are used when the foliage appears in spring and once or twice thereafter during the growing season, the likelihood of disease will be greatly reduced in susceptible plants.

Sulphur is an old remedy and is still widely used as a fungicide by organic and non-organic gardeners alike. It is very effective on most of the most common plant diseases. However, some varieties may be damaged by sulphur, so test a few leaves before you spray the whole plant.

Black spot

of site?

Care-free gardening is easy once you get to know your growing conditions. This section gives you planting suggestions and advice for every situation: windy, shaded, sunny, sloping or flat, and type of soil.

• **Draw a plan of the garden,** including buildings, walls, fences or hedges, paths and patios and trees.

• **Note how the sun moves** through the garden and how long it stays on each spot. Also identify areas with specific conditions: windy, sloping or wet, for example.

• **Test the soil** to see whether it is fine and heavy or coarse and light, and whether it is strongly acidic or alkaline.

• **Use your findings** to identify which of the pages in this section match your site most closely then turn to them to find the best care-free planting solutions.

On squared paper, draw a scale plan of your garden, showing it at midday in midsummer if possible. This is when the sun is at its highest and conditions are at their most extreme. As the garden progresses you can do the same thing for other seasons to help you to refine your planting plans.

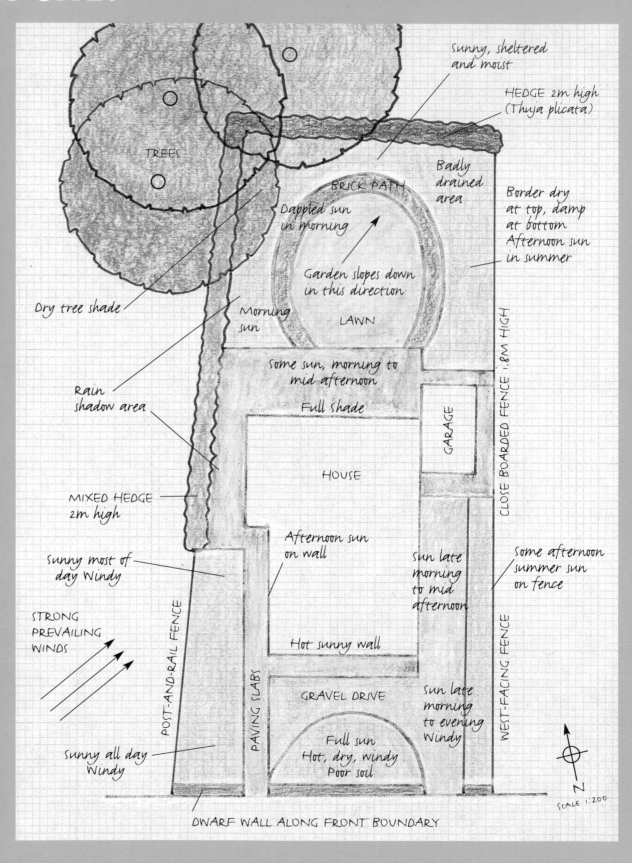

TREES

sunny, sheltered and moist

HEDGE 2m high (Thuja plicata)

Badly drained area

BRICK PATH

Dappled sun in morning

Border dry at top, damp at bottom Afternoon sun in summer

Garden slopes down in this direction

Dry tree shade

Morning sun

LAWN

Some sun, morning to mid afternoon

Rain shadow area

Full shade

GARAGE

HOUSE

MIXED HEDGE 2m high

CLOSE BOARDED FENCE 1.8M HIGH

Afternoon sun on wall

sunny most of day Windy

sun late morning to mid afternoon

some afternoon summer sun on fence

STRONG PREVAILING WINDS

Hot sunny wall

POST-AND-RAIL FENCE

PAVING SLABS

GRAVEL DRIVE

sun late morning to evening Windy

WEST-FACING FENCE

sunny all day Windy

Full sun Hot, dry, windy Poor soil

N

SCALE 1:200

DWARF WALL ALONG FRONT BOUNDARY

With most plants, it is essential to know whether they prefer a wet or dry position. Many will rot in permanently wet soil, others shrivel and die if they do not receive abundant moisture. However, there are a few, such as *Hosta* and *Hemerocallis*, which will thrive in any soil, from bone-dry to permanently damp and soggy.

Are there trees and hedges?

Trees, large shrubs and hedges have a big impact on a garden. They cast shade, and most have far-reaching roots, which suck moisture and nutrients from the soil. There are many plants that will grow happily beneath trees and shrubs and tolerate the dryness and impoverished growing conditions without trouble. These are much more care free than those demanding constant watering and feeding.

Plot a diagram of your site

Once you have a sketch of the garden you can use it to make a more detailed plan for the plants you would like to grow (see page 85). Draw a scale plan, indicating permanent features, such as a driveway or large trees, marking which way is north and whether the garden slopes. Then ask yourself the following questions and note your findings on the plan.

Where is the sun and shade?

Most gardens will have a mixture of full sun and deep and partial shade, determined by the proximity of trees and buildings. Count the number of hours an area is in sun during high summer on a cloudless day. Open sites will receive full sunshine virtually all day, but most will move in and out of the shade as the sun moves throughout the day.

The time of year also has an effect. Tall trees and buildings may cast little shade in summer, when the sun is high in the sky, but leave areas in total shade in midwinter, when the sun is at its lowest.

Shade cast by a building, fence or thick hedge will be complete, while some light will filter through the branches of most trees, so make a note of whether your shade is tree shade or non-tree shade.

Is it wet or dry?

Can it take days before you can walk on the ground after heavy rain? Are there always damp spots, even in summer? This may indicate that you have heavy soil – try a water test (see page 8) to be sure. Or you may find that water drains readily – a clear indication that your soil is light.

Where the wind whips through a site and the sun beats down, conditions range from dry, baking heat to freezing gales. Such open and exposed sites demand a particular kind of tolerant plant.

The shade cast by a building is solid and hard-edged. As the sun moves throughout the day, parts of the garden may move into or out of the shadow – these areas are categorised as partial shade.

Is there a slope?

Most gardens slope a little, but unless the gradient is very steep, it will not restrict your choice of plants. On steep sites, however, the top of the slope will be free-draining, while the lower half will be damp. On a long bank, the top may be in full sun while the bottom is in almost total shade. You may also find that soil slips from top to bottom. This can largely be prevented by planting through semi-permeable membrane or using plants that bind the soil.

Is it exposed or sheltered?

Strong winds batter gardens in exposed sites all year round. Wind chill can appear to lower the temperature significantly, so that plants may be slow to come into bloom. Give shelter to an exposed site by erecting a windbreak, such as a hedge, or a trellis covered with suitable climbers.

Is it inland or coastal?

Seaside gardens have a much more even climate than those further inland, as the sea tends to keep the air temperature higher in winter and cooler in summer. Extremes of weather, particularly severe frosts, are less likely, but strong, on-shore winds which can contain damaging levels of salt, are frequently a problem.

You will be repainting the house every year

if the whole garden is exposed to baking sun, window-rattling gales, and freezing rain and winds in winter. Many gardens, especially on high ground or in the north, have a section that is wide open to the weather, bearing the full heat of the summer sun and winter wind.

Blasts of strong wind are just as likely to scorch plants as hours of unrelenting sunshine. Wind strips leaves and soil of moisture, leaving evergreens brown around the edges in winter and new shoots vulnerable to freezing in spring. In wet weather, when the ground is soft, or on light soil when it is dry, a tugging wind can loosen or even uproot taller plants overnight, so keep an eye on any saplings and bushes and tread them in if they start to wobble.

The alpine columbine, **Aquilegia alpina,** *produces bright blue flowers that nod in the brisk breezes of late spring.*

Relax in the sun

The upside of having an open garden comes in the summer months, when there is nothing to block out the sun. You can sit in the garden at almost any time of day and have the perfect situation for growing sun-loving perennials, such as a *Potentilla* or the blue grass, *Festuca glauca*. Open gardens like these are unlikely to have frost pockets and you will not have the drought problems that come from buildings or trees casting rain shadows over an area.

However, with no buildings or fences to offer shelter, planting a few sturdy trees and shrubs, such as a mountain ash, *Betula alba*, or a spreading *Rosa rugosa* 'Alba' as a first line of defence will widen your options for the rest of the plot. Protect these living windbreaks with temporary fencing or netting until they are well established and they will add a lifetime of structure and shelter to your garden.

Follow a good health regime

Make sure that you buy only the most robust specimens and keep them in tiptop condition so that they will withstand the rigours of your site. Maintaining the soil is a good first step to keeping your plants healthy. Plants root best in a soil that is rich in humus, so dig in some well composted plant matter if your soil is thin, and spread on a blanket of mulch to trap precious moisture inside.

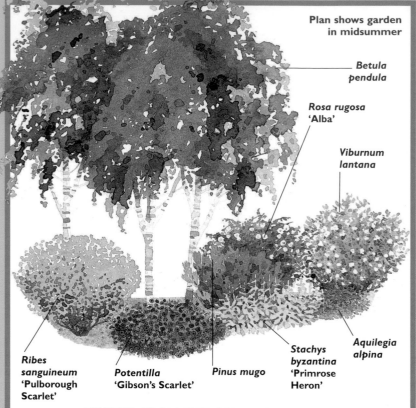

Plan shows garden in midsummer

- Betula pendula
- Rosa rugosa 'Alba'
- Viburnum lantana
- Aquilegia alpina
- Stachys byzantina 'Primrose Heron'
- Pinus mugo
- Potentilla 'Gibson's Scarlet'
- Ribes sanguineum 'Pulborough Scarlet'

SHELTER FROM THE COLD NORTH WIND

Cold northerly winds blow into this site from the left, but are filtered out by three silver birches (*Betula alba*), clustered above a tough Ribes bush. In spring, short varieties of daffodils and tulips surround the evergreen shrubs, where they shelter from the worst of the wind.

Expert's Selection

Herbaceous perennials

Blue-grey foliage reflects sunlight to keep plants cool in the hot sun that beats down onto an open garden at the height of summer.

Aquilegia alpina ❀ Bright blue
Late spring–early summer
h. 45–60cm (1½–2ft) s. 30cm (1ft)
➤p.93

***Festuca glauca* 'Elijah Blue'**
⌀ Blue • Early summer
h.&s. 30cm (1ft) ➤p.127

***Potentilla* 'Gibson's Scarlet'** ♀
❀ Bright red • Early summer
h. 45cm (1½ft) s. 60cm (2ft) ➤p.160

***Rudbeckia* 'Herbstsonne'** ❀ Yellow

Midsummer–early autumn
h. 2m (7ft) s. 60cm (2ft) ➤p.164

***Sedum kamtschaticum* 'Variegatum'** ♀ ❀ Yellow • Mid–late summer • h. 10cm (4in) s. 25cm (10in) ➤p.167

***Stachys byzantina* 'Primrose Heron'** ⌀ Grey tinged yellow
h. 60cm (2ft) s. 1m (3ft) ➤p.170

Climbers & shrubs

Glossy, waxy leaves help to make shrubs and climbers tolerant of harsh conditions, such as baking sun and moisture-stripping winds.

***Cotoneaster salicifolius* 'Gnom'**
❀ White • Summer ❧ Red • Autumn
h. 30cm (1ft) s. 2m (7ft) ➤p.201

Ilex aquifolium 'Ferox Argentea'♀
∅ Dark green and white ❧ Red
Autumn–winter • h. 8m (27ft)
s. 4m (13ft) ➤p.217

Pinus mugo ∅ Dark green ❧ Black-
brown cones, ripen to yellow-brown
h.&s. 1m (3ft) after 10 years ➤p.234

Pyracantha 'Orange Charmer'
❧ Dark orange • Autumn ❀ White
Early summer • h.&s. 3m (10ft)
➤p.236

**Ribes sanguineum 'Pulborough
Scarlet'**♀ ❀ Deep red • Mid spring
h.&s. 2m (7ft) ➤p.237

Rosa rugosa 'Alba'♀ ❀ White • All
summer ❧ Orange-red hips • Autumn
h.&s. 1–2.5m (3–8ft) ➤p.242

Viburnum lantana ❀ White • Late
spring–early summer ❧ Black
Autumn • h. 5m (16ft) s. 4m (13ft)
➤p.258

Trees

Choose only the toughest varieties
of trees if you want to plant them
where gales frequently blow through.

Acer negundo 'Flamingo'♀
∅ Variegated green with white and
pink • Spring and summer
h. 6m (20ft) s. 4m (13ft) ➤p.264

Betula pendula♀ ∅ Yellow
Autumn • h. 14m (46ft) s. 5m (16ft)
after 20 years ➤p.265

**Sorbus aucuparia 'Sheerwater
Seedling'**♀ ❀ White • Late spring
❧ Orangey red • Autumn
h. 8m (27ft) s. 3m (10ft) when fully
mature ➤p.273

Bulbs

Tall flowers may be felled by high
winds, particularly in spring, when
there are few surrounding plants, so
choose short varieties for success.

Narcissus 'Tête-à-tête'♀ ❀ Yellow
Early spring • h. 15cm (6in) ➤p.320

Tulipa 'Red Riding Hood'♀ ❀ Red
with black base inside • Early spring
h. 20cm (8in) ➤p.324

*Airy grasses (see pages
126–127), such as the tall
Miscanthus and fluffy
Pennisetum, make the
most of a wind-blown
site. The panicles rustle
in the breeze, but the
flexible plants remain
unaffected by even the
strongest winds. Golden
rudbeckias add colour.*

WINDY INLAND SITE
LIGHT SOIL

Bright and breezy can be a mixed blessing. Strong winds can do more damage than frost and in light soil the buffeting breeze can shake plants loose. Take a tip from nature and plant wind-resistant, drought-loving plants.

The golden hop, Humulus lupulus 'Aureus' (above right) smothers fences, walls and pergolas with yellowy green foliage, and female plants produce clusters of pale green fruits.

A light windy site has many benefits. The crumbly soil is easy to work and weed, and warms up fast in spring. Waterlogging is unlikely, and pests and diseases hate fresh breezes.

On the downside, the ground can dry out during periods of low rainfall, and wind exacerbates the problem. But there are still plenty of care-free choices that will work well. Fill beds with stocky, wind and drought-resistant plants, firming and staking the taller ones. For spring colour, plant drifts of **alliums** and **scillas**. Attract summer butterflies with **buddlejas**, and plant clumps of pretty **veronicas** and **feverfew**.

When it does rain, nutrients are washed away, and you have to keep a close eye on new plants to make sure that they do not blow clean out of the ground on windy days. Dig in lots of organic material and feed plants with slow-release fertilisers to keep them vigorous, and heap on a thick mulch after a rainy spell to lock in all the moisture you can.

After food, offer plants shelter

A trellis or loosely planted hedge will filter rather than block the wind, but if your garden is big enough, plant a 'first line of defence' of tough **hawthorns** or *Caragana* on the windy boundary. A solid fence or wall is the worst kind of shelter for a site like this: the wind will eddy over the top chilling everything on the side you are trying to protect.

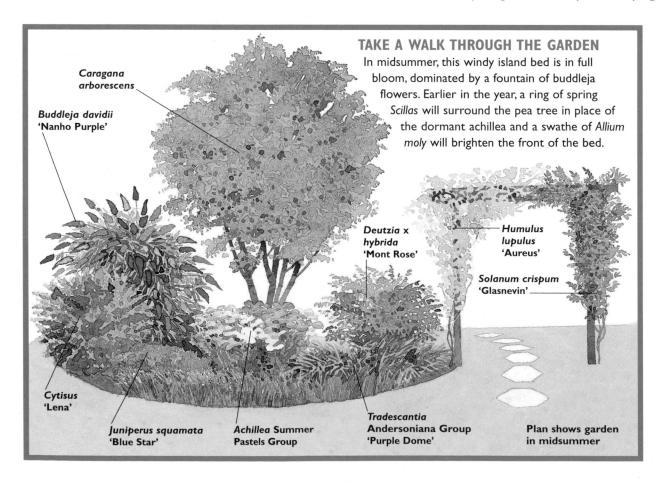

TAKE A WALK THROUGH THE GARDEN

In midsummer, this windy island bed is in full bloom, dominated by a fountain of buddleja flowers. Earlier in the year, a ring of spring *Scillas* will surround the pea tree in place of the dormant achillea and a swathe of *Allium moly* will brighten the front of the bed.

Caragana arborescens

Buddleja davidii **'Nanho Purple'**

Deutzia x hybrida **'Mont Rose'**

Humulus lupulus **'Aureus'**

Solanum crispum **'Glasnevin'**

Cytisus **'Lena'**

Juniperus squamata **'Blue Star'**

Achillea **Summer Pastels Group**

Tradescantia **Andersoniana Group 'Purple Dome'**

Plan shows garden in midsummer

Expert's Selection

Herbaceous perennials

Silvers, whites and blues reflect the sun, keeping plants cool in open sites. Spiky foliage with limited surface area is also a way to conserve moisture in windy gardens.

***Achillea* Summer Pastels Group**
❀ White, cream, yellow, pink, salmon or pale purple • Summer
h. 75cm (2½ft) s. 60cm (2ft) ➤p.88
***Kniphofia* 'Atlanta'** ❀ Orange-red
Late spring–late summer
h. 1m (3ft) s. 75m (2½ft) ➤p.138
***Tanacetum parthenium* 'Aureum'**
❀ Yellowish white • Late spring
h. 45cm (1½ft) s. 30cm (1ft) ➤p.172
Thymus serpyllum* var. *coccineus♀
❀ Crimson pink • Midsummer
h. 5cm (2in) s. 30cm (1ft) ➤p.174
***Tradescantia* Andersoniana
Group 'Purple Dome'** ❀ Purple
Early summer–early autumn
h. 60cm (2ft) s. 45cm (1½ft) ➤p.176
***Veronica gentianoides*♀** ❀ Blue
Summer • h. 30cm (1ft)
s. 40cm (16in) ➤p.178

Climbers & shrubs

Sun-loving helianthemums bask on this open site, while moorland *Cytisus* and *Genista* stand up to the wind.

***Buddleja davidii* 'Nanho Purple'**
❀ Purple • Midsummer–early autumn
h.&s. 2m (7ft) ➤p.190
***Cytisus* 'Lena'**♀ ❀ Yellow with red
Spring • h. 1.8m (6ft) s. 1.2m (4ft)
➤p.202

The **Genista lydia** *in the centre of this bed will keep its flowers in the briskest of breezes. Around it, a spiky-leaved Kniphofia, a silvery Phlomis, and woody, white-flowered Hebe all have their own survival strategy for a dry, sunny and windy site.*

***Deutzia* x *hybrida* 'Mont Rose'**♀
❀ Deep pink • Early summer
h.&s. 1.8m (6ft) ➤p.203
Fuchsia magellanica ❀ Crimson and purple • Summer–autumn
h.&s. 1.2m (4ft) ➤p.207
***Genista lydia*♀** ❀ Yellow • Early summer • h.&s. 60cm (2ft) ➤p.208
***Hebe* 'Nicola's Blush'** ❀ Pink and white • Spring–midsummer, and autumn winter • h.&s. 75cm (2½ft) ➤p.209
***Helianthemum* 'Fire Dragon'**♀
❀ Orange-scarlet • All summer
h. 20cm (8in) s. 40cm (16in) ➤p.213
***Humulus lupulus* 'Aureus'**♀
❀ Greeny yellow hops • Autumn
⊘ Yellow-green • Summer
h. 6m (20ft) s. 4m (13ft) ➤p.214
***Juniperus squamata* 'Blue Star'**♀
⊘ Silvery blue • h. 60cm (2ft)
s. 1m (3ft) ➤p.219
Phlomis bovei* subsp. *maroccana
❀ Purple-pink • Summer
h.&s. 1.5m (5ft) ➤p.232
***Solanum crispum* 'Glasnevin'**♀
❀ Blue–purple • Late spring–autumn
h. 4m (13ft) s. 1m (3ft)➤p.251

Trees

Pea trees (*Caragana*) and hawthorns (*Crataegus*) both grow vigorously in sunny, well-drained spots.

Caragana arborescens ❀ Yellow
Late spring ⊘ Green • Spring–summer • h.&s. 1.5m (5ft) ➤p.265
***Crataegus laevigata* 'Paul's Scarlet'**♀ ❀ Red • Spring ⊘ Dark green • h.&s. 5m (16ft) ➤p.266

Bulbs

Short-stemmed bulbs are best for a site where there is little shelter.

***Allium moly*♀** ❀ Yellow • Early summer • h. 15–25cm (6–10in) ➤p.306
***Scilla siberica* 'Spring Beauty'**
❀ Vivid blue • Early spring
h. 15cm (6in) ➤p.323

WINDY INLAND SITE
HEAVY SOIL

Wind can be the enemy of many planting schemes, drying the ground and felling or up-rooting tall treasures. But if you combine it with a moist fertile soil and a sunny aspect, and make the most of its good points, you can have a garden brimming with colour and fragrance throughout the year.

The windiest plots are often on steep slopes, where gravity pulls moisture, nutrients and soil down and away from your plants. But if you are lucky enough to have a good heavy soil and only the gentlest of slopes you can make the wind work in your favour.

Although 'wind rock' can disturb tall plants, resist the urge to tread them in hard, or you will trample out the air pockets in your heavy soil. Instead, grow tough **hawthorns** as windbreaks and stake tall plants firmly, checking them in windy spells for movement.

However, once new plants are established, heavy soil provides all the moisture and nutrients they need to grow strongly. What's more, the sun in this open site encourages them to flourish and the wind whisks away pests and diseases before they can take hold.

Clusters of purple flowers smother Campanula glomerata in early summer. A vigorous spreader, it will stop soil setting solid in dry spells or 'panning' to smooth clay in heavy rain.

From puddles to pavement

Your plants may take longer to get started in spring than those at the other side of the house or on the more sheltered side of the street. A strong wind can lower the temperature by several degrees and strip moisture from the ground, making even soggy soil set solid at the surface so that rainwater runs off and new shoots have to struggle to nudge through.

To avoid your soil 'panning' in heavy rain to the finish of smooth clay, try to keep off wet ground until the wind has whipped through and dried it out. It is also a good idea to break up the surface from time to time, so that it does not dry pavement-hard.

A thick mulch is quick to lay and will lock in moisture and keep the texture of the soil free, but dense planting is just as effective and far more attractive. Experiment through the year with carpets of spring bluebells, clumps of nodding *Campanulas*, fiery autumn *Berberis* or hardy evergreen *Thujas*.

Cornus earns its keep in winter with its vivid bare stems. This red-barked dogwood glows like a flaming bush in the border.

Herbaceous perennials

Short perennials stand up best in windy sites. Choose dwarf varieties, such as the *Aster* 'Flora's Delight' or stake tall blooms, like the *Helenium*.

Aster x frikartii 'Flora's Delight'
❀ Lilac • Autumn
h.&s. 45cm (1½ft) ➤p.97
Campanula glomerata ❀ Violet
Early summer • *h.* 40cm (16in)
s. 50cm (20in) ➤p.103
Erigeron 'Dimity' ❀ Pink • Summer
h. 30cm (1ft) *s.* 40cm (16in) ➤p.113
Helenium 'Moerheim Beauty'
❀ Copper • Early summer–autumn
h. 1m (3ft) *s.* 30cm (1ft) ➤p.128
Thalictrum aquilegiifolium
❀ Pink • Midsummer
h. 1m (3ft) *s.* 30cm (1ft) ➤p.173

Climbers & shrubs

Tough leaves, low stature and a firm root structure are the most essential attributes for shrubs to survive in a windy garden like this. If you have a sturdy fence or wall, use climbers, like ivy or a climbing rose to add vertical interest, and tie them securely to trellis panels or wires.

Berberis x ottawensis 'Superba'♀
❀ Yellow • Spring ∅ Purple
h.&s. 1.5m (5ft) in five years 2.5m
(8ft) in ten years ➤p.188
Cornus alba 'Sibirica Variegata'
∅ Crimson leaves and bark
h.&s. 1.5m (5ft) ➤p.200
**Hedera colchica 'Dentata
Variegata'**♀ ∅ Variegated
h. 10m (33ft) *s.* 5m (16ft) ➤p.212
Philadelphus x lemoinei ❀ White
Early–midsummer • *h.&s.* 1.8m (6ft)
➤p.232
Rosa 'Geranium'♀ ❀ Bright red
Early summer • *h.* 2.5m (8ft)
s. 2m (7ft) ➤p.242
Rosa 'Compassion'♀ ❀ Salmon
pink • All summer • *h.&s.* 3m (10ft)
➤p.244
Thuja occidentalis 'Smaragd'♀
∅ Olive green • *h.* 2.5m (8ft)
s. 50cm (20in) after 10 years ➤p.256

Trees

Pollard your trees every two years to keep their crowns low, and with a firm, wide root system they should be able to stand strong against any winter gales.

Crataegus persimilis 'Prunifolia'♀
❀ White • Early summer ∅ Dark
green ⫟ Dark red • Autumn
h.&s. 3m (10ft) ➤p.266
**Salix alba subsp. vitellina
'Britzensis'**♀ ∅ Orange-red stems
Late autumn • *h.* 1.5m (5ft)
s. 3m (10ft) ➤p.272

Bulbs

Soft bulbs, such as daffodils and tulips, may rot over winter in boggy ground, but snowdrops and bluebells thrive in heavy soil to bring cheer to dull days.

Galanthus ❀ White • Late winter
h. 20cm (8in) ➤p.314
Hyacinthoides ❀ Blue • Spring
h. 40cm (16in) ➤p.316

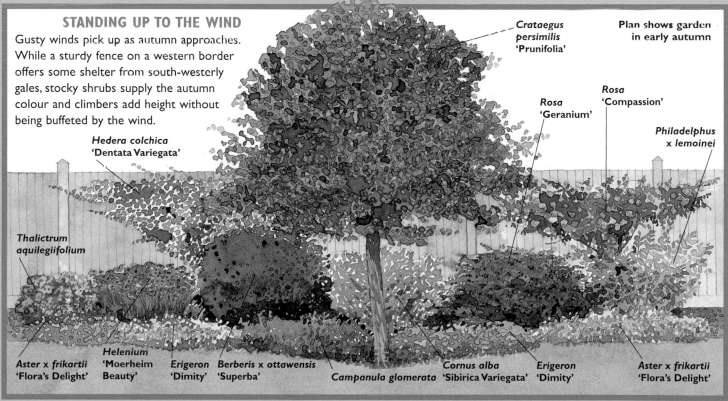

STANDING UP TO THE WIND

Gusty winds pick up as autumn approaches. While a sturdy fence on a western border offers some shelter from south-westerly gales, stocky shrubs supply the autumn colour and climbers add height without being buffeted by the wind.

Crataegus persimilis 'Prunifolia'

Plan shows garden in early autumn

Rosa 'Geranium'

Rosa 'Compassion'

Philadelphus x lemoinei

Hedera colchica 'Dentata Variegata'

Thalictrum aquilegiifolium

Aster x frikartii 'Flora's Delight'

Helenium 'Moerheim Beauty'

Erigeron 'Dimity'

Berberis x ottawensis 'Superba'

Campanula glomerata

Cornus alba 'Sibirica Variegata'

Erigeron 'Dimity'

Aster x frikartii 'Flora's Delight'

WINDY INLAND SITE
POOR SOIL

A house with a fine view is something to cherish. But a view comes at a price, namely that you are probably high on a hill or ridge, with a fairly meagre layer of topsoil. You have the wind to contend with, threatening to blow away your precious light soil, but you have sunshine, too, warming the ground and encouraging buds to open.

If you garden on a site like this, you will be all too familiar with the chink of metal on stone, accompanied by a painful jarring jolt to your knee or ankle. You do not have to dig far before you hit stone, gravel or sand.

However, this sunny, breezy garden will be relatively unaffected by pests and diseases. Its thin soil will always drain well, and can be easily improved. The sunny aspect also means that the garden warms up quickly in spring, allowing you to plant and sow early in the year and enjoy the blooms of a *Hebe* or the bobbing heads of **thrifts** over a long summer season.

Beef up the topsoil

Before you start work in your garden, look at what is already growing. Some plants may show signs of deficiency disorders (see page 10). Others may be wind-scorched. And some naturally deep-rooted plants may be stunted because they have difficulty in establishing a good root run. Take note of your neighbours' gardens, too, and learn about your soil from the signs above ground.

The most important thing you can do for this garden is to improve the quality of the topsoil by heaping on plenty of compost or manure and letting the worms work it through. Although it may be back-breaking work, and take several years to achieve, you will reap the benefits in the long run if you try to break up the hard layer beneath the topsoil, removing any large stones as you go.

The plants you choose can also improve the site. Plant sturdy hedging such as **beech**, quickthorn and hornbeam, and tough **silver birches**, twiggy *Potentillas* and **rock roses**, and **lavender** to protect more fragile plants against the wind. Lay a good layer of mulch to retain moisture and prevent wind erosion. And put up temporary windbreaks while new plants get established, being careful not to create frost pockets (see page 40).

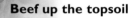

Bearded irises, like 'Blue Shimmer' are easy to grow, given full sun and good drainage and will make a splendid early summer display in a site like this.

The pompom heads of a tall Allium, like A. hollandicum 'Purple Sensation', are held on robust, leafless stems so that they seem to rise out of the surrounding plants, such as these richly scented French lavender (Lavandula stoechas).

Expert's Selection

Herbaceous perennials

Seaside plants, such as thrifts (*Armeria*), do well on impoverished soils, but there are plenty of other colourful perennials you can use to brighten a windy border.

Armeria alliacea ❀ White to purple Summer • *h.&s.* 40cm (16in) ➤p.94
***Centranthus ruber* 'Albus'** ❀ White Summer • *h.&s.* 60cm (2ft) ➤p.104
***Iris* 'Blue Shimmer'** ❀ White and blue • Early summer • *h.* 75cm (2½ft) ➤p.137
Lysimachia punctata ❀ Yellow Mid–late summer *h.* 1m (3ft) *s.* 60cm (2ft) ➤p.146
***Sempervivum* 'Commander Hay'**♀ ❀ Dark pink • Midsummer ∅ Red and green • *h.* 10cm (4in) *s.* 20cm (8in) ➤p.168

Climbers & shrubs

It is best to avoid tall shrubs in windswept gardens, but the loose stems of a *Leycesteria* let the breeze whistle through. Train climbers over sturdy frames to add height.

***Hebe* 'Wingletye'** ❀ Lilac • Summer *h.* 20cm (8in) *s.* 30cm (1ft) ➤p.209
***Helianthemum* 'Fire Dragon'**♀ ❀ Orange-scarlet • All summer *h.* 20cm (8in) *s.* 40cm (16in) ➤p.213
Hypericum androsaemum ❀ Yellow All summer ◁ Purple ∅ Green *h.&s.* 1m (3ft) ➤p.216
***Lavandula angustifolia* 'Hidcote'**♀ ❀ Deep blue • Summer ∅ Silver-grey • *h.&s.* 45cm (1½ft) ➤p.221
Leycesteria formosa ❀ Wine and white ◁ Red-purple • Early summer–autumn • *h.* 1.8m (6ft) *s.* 1m (3ft) ➤p.223

Passiflora caerulea♀ ❀ White with a purple-blue corona • Midsummer–early autumn ◁ Orange • Autumn *h.* 10m (33ft) *s.* 1m (3ft) ➤p.231
***Potentilla fruticosa* 'Abbotswood'**♀ ❀ White • Summer ∅ Dark green • *h.* 75cm (2½ft) *s.* 1m (3ft) ➤p.235

Trees

A whitebeam (*Sorbus*) or silver birch (*Betula pendula*) will spread shallow roots just below the surface, and their leaves will rustle in the wind.

Betula pendula♀ ∅ Yellow Autumn • *h.* 14m (46ft) *s.* 5m (16ft) after 20 years, ultimately 20m (66ft) ➤p.265

Sorbus* x *hostii ∅ Red, orange and yellow ◁ Bright red • Autumn ❀ Pink Early summer • *h.* 4m (13ft) *s.* 1.5m (5ft) ➤p.273

Bulbs

For early spring flowers choose species tulips and plant swathes of crocuses. For summer splendour, try stately *Alliums*.

Allium christophii♀ ❀ Purple Midsummer • *h.* 30–60cm (1–2ft) ➤p.306
Crocus ❀ Various • Autumn–early spring • *h.* 5–18cm (2–7in) ➤p.310
Tulipa turkestanica♀ ❀ Creamy white • Winter–early spring *h.* 30cm (1ft) ➤p.324

A SUNNY SPOT WITH THIN SOIL

When the sun beats down in midsummer, silvery foliage and pale flowers reflect light, keeping plants cool and conserving water. *Hebes* and lavenders are ideally suited to this kind of exposed garden, where sun, wind and poor soil all mean that moisture is in short supply.

Sorbus x *hostii*
Passiflora caerulea
Lavandula angustifolia 'Hidcote'
Lysimachia punctata
Iris 'Blue Shimmer'
Armeria alliacea
Hebe 'Wingletye'
Potentilla fruticosa 'Abbotswood'
Centranthus ruber 'Albus'
Hypericum androsaemum f. *variegatum* 'Mrs Gladis Brabazon'
Plan shows garden in early–midsummer

At the back of the beach, behind the dunes, sand has stabilised into the lightest of soils. Here, tamarisks filter the sea breezes to protect colourful dahlias, gladioli, red-hot pokers (*Kniphofia*) and cornflowers (*Centaurea*) that glow in the clear sunlight that bathes on a coastal garden.

In the sunny, even climate of a seaside site, where the soil is light and free-draining, the care-free gardener can sit back and watch normally tender plants, such as *Osteospermums*, flourish. At the coast the difference between summer and winter temperatures is less pronounced than it is inland, and there is rarely a severe frost.

The soil may be laden with salt, making it alkaline (with a pH higher than 7), but there are many lovely plants that are tolerant of such conditions, and many more, like *Tamarix* and *Escallonia*, that can easily tolerate being battered by the fierce salty gales that blow inland during foul weather.

The crimson flowers of Escallonia 'C.F. Ball' last all summer long. The bush grows vigorously, even in the face of salty sea breezes, and several planted together will soon merge to make an excellent care-free hedge.

Give your garden a head start

Choose wisely, by picking plants that thrive in the specific conditions of a coastal location, and you are more than half way to enjoying a beautiful garden. Give the plants a little help and success should be guaranteed: stake tall or soft-stemmed varieties, like *Gladioli*, that may be bent or broken by the wind, for example.

Be firm when planting, and check the garden after strong winds to be sure that none of your precious plants has been shaken loose or uprooted. Spreading a generous blanket of organic mulch over the soil every so often will help to lock in moisture and lower the soil's pH, making it less alkaline. It will also improve the texture of the soil, giving plant roots a firmer bed.

Expert's Selection

Herbaceous perennials

The thistle-like heads of *Centaurea*, *Echinops* and *Eryngium,* and the flaming pokers of a tall *Kniphofia* make striking shapes in a border. In this light soil, traditional wild flowers often do well.

***Centaurea hypoleuca* 'John Coutts'** ❀ Pinkish red • Mid–late summer • *h.&s.* 60cm (2ft) ➤p.104
Echinops ritro ♀ ❀ Steel-blue Late summer • *h.* 1.2m (4ft) *s.* 30cm (1ft) ➤p.111
Eryngium variifolium ❀ Silvery blue Mid–late summer • *h.* 40cm (16in) *s.* 25cm (10in) ➤p.114
***Kniphofia* 'Early Buttercup'** ❀ Yellow • Late spring–early summer *h.&s.* 60cm (2ft) ➤p.138

Wild grasses are first to colonise when sand turns to soil. Plant ornamental species (see pages 126–127) with alliums (see page 306), osteospermums and wallflowers (Erysimum) for a seaside summer bed.

Climbers & shrubs

A low profile and narrow leaves help to keep salt-tolerant shrubs thriving even in brisk sea breezes.

Artemisia arborescens ⌀ Silvery grey • *h.* 1m (3ft) *s.* 50cm (20in) ➤p.184
***Brachyglottis* 'Sunshine'** ♀ ❀ Yellow Midsummer • *h.* 1m (3ft) *s.* 2m (7ft) ➤p.189
Cytisus x praecox ❀ Yellow • Spring *h.* 1.2m (4ft) *s.* 1m (3ft) ➤p.202
***Escallonia* 'C.F. Ball'** ❀ Crimson Summer ⌀ Dark green *h.&s.* 3m (10ft) ➤p.204

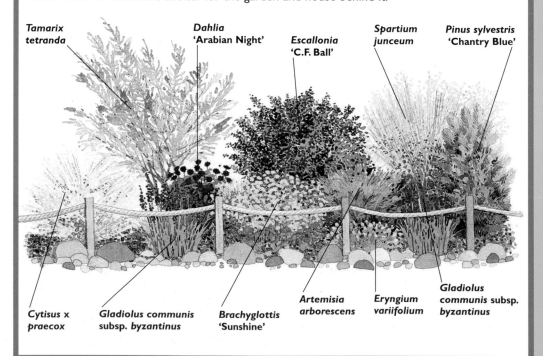

SALT-TOLERANT SHRUBS SHRUG OFF SEA SPRAY

Plan shows garden in early summer

Every coastal garden should include at least one tamarix to act as a windbreak against the salt-laden winds that blow in from the sea. Harsh northerly winds blow onto the front of this exposed border, which makes an attractive shelter for the garden and house behind it.

Tamarix tetranda
Dahlia 'Arabian Night'
Escallonia 'C.F. Ball'
Spartium junceum
Pinus sylvestris 'Chantry Blue'
Cytisus x praecox
Gladiolus communis subsp. byzantinus
Brachyglottis 'Sunshine'
Artemisia arborescens
Eryngium variifolium
Gladiolus communis subsp. byzantinus

Lavandula angustifolia 'Miss Muffet' ❀ Lilac-blue • Early–midsummer ∅ Silver-grey
h.&s. 30cm (1ft) ➤**p.221**

Pinus sylvestris 'Chantry Blue'
∅ Blue-grey ⚘ Yellow cones; ripening to brown • h. 4m (13ft) s. 2m (7ft)
➤**p.234**

Rosa pimpinellifolia ❀ White
Early summer • h. 1m (3ft)
s. 1.2m (4ft) ➤**p.242**

Solanum laxum 'Album'♀ ❀ White
Midsummer–autumn • h. 3m (10ft)
s. 60cm (2ft) ➤**p.251**

Spartium junceum♀ ❀ Yellow
Early summer–early autumn
h.&s. 3m (10ft) ➤**p.252**

Tamarix tetranda♀ ❀ Pale pink
Spring–early summer ∅ Pale green
h.&s. 4m (13ft) ➤**p.254**

Trees

Plant open-crowned trees that will not be felled by strong winds.

**Acer pseudoplatanus
'Brilliantissimum'**♀ ∅ Pinky yellow
Spring • h.&s. 3m (10ft) ➤**p.264**

Eucalyptus gunnii♀ ∅ Silvery blue
h. 15m (50ft) s. 6m (20ft) ➤**p.266**

Annuals

Let sun and rain encourage a mass of annuals to bloom and spread.

Erysimum Bedder Series ❀ Red, orange or yellow • Late spring–early summer • h.&s. 30cm (1ft) ➤**p.279**

Osteospermum Springstar Series
❀ White, pink or purple • Late spring–autumn • h. 45cm (1½ft)
s. 60cm (2ft) ➤**p.291**

Bulbs

A scattering of these hardy, care-free bulbs will bring welcome splashes of extra colour all summer long.

Dahlia 'Arabian Night' ❀ Blackish crimson • Summer–autumn
h. 1m (3ft) ➤**p.313**

**Gladiolus communis subsp.
byzantinus**♀ ❀ Magenta • Early summer • h. 1m (3ft) ➤**p.315**

Ornithogalum umbellatum
❀ White and green • Late spring–early summer • h. 30cm (1ft) ➤**p.322**

A maritime climate can be a challenge to any gardener. If the soil is heavy it can set as hard as concrete in summer, or be flooded in winter with saltwater. However, there are care-free plants that will thrive, even in these unpromising conditions.

Most maritime gardens enjoy plenty of sunshine, but even plots slightly inland will suffer to some extent from salt-laden gales. Heavy soils are usually fertile and support strong growth once plants are established; they also offer better moisture-retention than the sandy soils in many coastal sites. Heavy clay is also less likely than light soils to retain the salt thrown at it in spray, since it absorbs very little water unless it is flooded, so it can be a bonus when you live at the coast.

The colourful dangling blooms of Fuchsia 'Riccartonii' are remarkably resistant and trouble free, and will thrive even in the demanding conditions of a maritime garden.

Earth, wind and fire

Even though the warming influence of the sea means that severe frosts and snow are rare, heavy soils are slow to warm up and clay will be fairly cold until late spring – an inhospitable environment for young plants. Try to avoid planting until the weather improves and the temperature rises and always buy the most robust specimens you can find in the garden centre (see page 12).

Wind-rock, and wind and salt burn can also damage plants, so choose stocky specimens, such as a sturdy *Garrya* that will not get badly blown about and seek out salt and wind-tolerant plants, such as *Erigeron*, *Miscanthus* and *Olearia*. The wind has benefits, too, whisking away germs and pests so that disease is rarely a problem in coastal sites.

Lighten the soil and break up the wind

Before embarking on a major planting project, add plenty of organic material to the beds to lighten the soil and improve its texture: if you spread well-rotted manure over the surface in autumn, worms will do the work of incorporating it into the soil for you. If the ground is really heavy, dig in sharp sand or fine grit to improve the drainage.

Once your plants are in place surround them in a thick mulch of compost, manure, forest bark or cocoa shells to help to prevent the wind drying out the soil and to keep down wind-borne weeds.

Expert's Selection

Herbaceous perennials

Daisy-like flowers work well with grasses to create textural interest in a windswept coastal site.

Echinacea purpurea 'Robert Bloom' ✿ Bright purple Midsummer–early autumn • h. 1.2m (4ft) s. 50cm (20in) ➤p.110

Erigeron karvinskianus 'Profusion' ✿ White, pink • Spring–summer h. 30cm (1ft) s. 40cm (16in) ➤p.113

Gaillardia 'Dazzler' ♀ ✿ Orangey red and yellow • Midsummer–early autumn • h. 60cm (2ft) s. 45cm (1½ft) ➤p.121

Hosta 'Wide Brim' ♀ ✿ Lavender ⊘ Green and cream • Summer h. 60cm (2ft) s. 1m (3ft) ➤p.135

Miscanthus sinensis 'Morning Light' ✿ Reddish • Autumn ⊘ Green with white edging • h. 1.2–1.5m (4–5ft) s. 1.2m (4ft) ➤p.127

Rudbeckia 'Goldquelle' ♀ ✿ Yellow Midsummer–early autumn h. 1.5m (5ft) s. 1m (3ft) ➤p.164

Shrubs & climbers

Choose wind and salt-proof shrubs such as a hardworking *Elaeagnus* to soften the force of sea gales.

Elaeagnus x ebbingei 'Limelight' ⊘ Green and gold • h.&s. 3m (10ft) ➤p.204

Euonymus japonicus 'Ovatus Aureus' ♀ ⊘ Green and gold h.&s. 1.5m (5ft) ➤p.205

Fuchsia 'Riccartonii' ♀ ✿ Crimson and purple • Summer–autumn h. 2m (7ft) s. 1.2m (4ft) ➤p.207

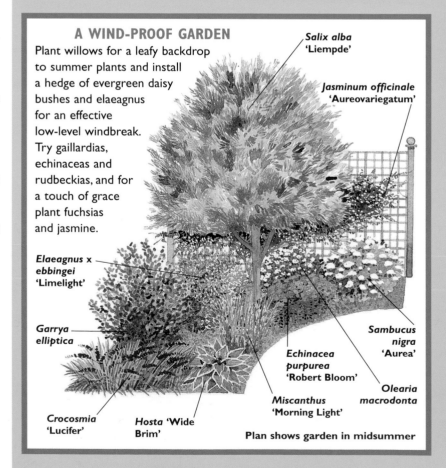

A WIND-PROOF GARDEN

Plant willows for a leafy backdrop to summer plants and install a hedge of evergreen daisy bushes and elaeagnus for an effective low-level windbreak. Try gaillardias, echinaceas and rudbeckias, and for a touch of grace plant fuchsias and jasmine.

Salix alba 'Liempde'

Jasminum officinale 'Aureovariegatum'

Elaeagnus x ebbingei 'Limelight'

Garrya elliptica

Crocosmia 'Lucifer'

Hosta 'Wide Brim'

Miscanthus 'Morning Light'

Echinacea purpurea 'Robert Bloom'

Sambucus nigra 'Aurea'

Olearia macrodonta

Plan shows garden in midsummer

Garrya elliptica 'James Roof'
❀ Silver-green catkins • Winter–early spring • h.&s. 2.5m (8ft) ➤p.208

Jasminum officinale 'Aureovariegatum' ♀ ❀ White ∅ Grey-green and cream Midsummer–early autumn h. 9m (30ft) s. 3m (10ft) ➤p.218

Olearia macrodonta ♀ ❀ White Mid–late summer ∅ Green and white • h.&s. 6m (20ft) ➤p.228

Rosa pimpinellifolia syn. Rosa spinosissima ❀ White • Early summer • h. 1m (3ft) s. 1.2m (4ft) ➤p.242

Sambucus nigra 'Aurea' ♀ ❀ White Early summer ∅ Gold • h. 6m (20ft) s. 4m (13ft) ➤p.248

Trees

The whippy branches of a *Salix* make a great windbreak to shelter the garden from strong breezes.

Salix alba 'Liempde' ∅ Silver-grey Spring–summer • h. 12m (40ft) s. 5m (16ft) ➤p.272

Sorbus aria 'Lutescens' ♀ ∅ Red and brown • Autumn ◂ Orange h. 6m (20ft) s. 4.5m (15ft) ➤p.273

Bulbs

Crocuses and hycinths in unusual shades add interest to the border.

Crocosmia 'Lucifer' ♀ ❀ Vivid red Summer • h. 1m (3ft) ➤p.309

Hyacinthus 'City of Haarlem' ♀ ❀ Primrose-yellow • Mid spring h. 20cm (8in) ➤p.316

The vivid daisy flowers of Erigeron glauca 'Sea Breeze' are an ideal choice for this kind of site. Here they are complemented by starry lilac Campanulas.

WINDY MARITIME SITE
POOR SOIL

In the teeth of a sea breeze, a clifftop garden can present a challenge. Salt-laden winds lash the site in winter, while the sun beats down in summer, threatening to burn delicate leaves. But rise to the challenge and plant drought-resistant succulents, shrubs that will shrug off salt and low-growing plants that thrive beneath the gales.

Windswept seaside gardens often suffer from impoverished soil. The relentless onslaught of salt, from crashing waves or windy spray can make the site very alkaline, and wind and rain can whisk away topsoil, or what little nutrients and organic material there is in the ground. Buy a pH testing kit to check the alkalinity of your soil so that you can tailor your planting to suit, and shake a handful of soil in a jar of water to see how rich it is (see page 8). Spread organic mulches over your beds as often as you can to lower the pH (make the soil more acid), retain water and feed the soil, and sprinkle on slow-release fertilisers as you wander round the garden on fine days throughout the year, to replenish nutrients leached away through the thin soil by rain.

A carpet of white Campanula carpatica makes a pretty and wind-resistant addition to a blustery seaside garden.

A thin and uncomfortable bed

As you plunge your fork through the meagre layer of soil you may be jolted by rocks or hard sub-soil not far beneath. If you are feeling energetic you could try to free up this layer of rock. A more care-free option is to choose plants that can grow over it, such as *Campanula carpatica* and *Parahebe catarractae*, which both have shallow roots.

Plant a windbreak for shelter

The climate at the coast varies, depending on which part of the country you are in, but you can rely on there being plenty of wind, long periods of sunshine and little likelihood of frost or prolonged coverings of snow. Choose plants that are resilient to salt and windburn, and stake spindly or new plants until they are well established.

Trellis will offer shelter without casting dense shade or being blown down by the first sea gale, but robust *Olearias*, **hollies** or a **service tree** all make attractive green windbreaks instead.

Aloe vera, and other succulents, like sedums, thrive in a sunny, gritty, seaside garden – safe from frost – storing their own moisture for when the soil is dry.

Expert's Selection

Herbaceous perennials

Low, spreading perennials crouch happily beneath the worst of the wind. Their shallow roots also help to bind the thin soil, preventing erosion.

Campanula carpatica♀ ✿ Blue or white • Early–late summer
h. 15cm (6in) s. 40cm (16in) ➤p.103
Dianthus plumarius ✿ White and pink • Midsummer
h.&s. 30cm (1ft) ➤p.107
Eryngium bourgatii 'Oxford Blue'♀ ✿ Silvery violet-blue
Mid–late summer • h. 60cm (2ft) s. 50cm (20in) ➤p.114
Geranium macrorrhizum ✿ White, pink or magenta • All summer
h. 25cm (10in) s. 60cm (2ft) ➤p.123
Limonium bellidifolium ✿ Blue or pinkish blue • Midsummer–early autumn • h. 20cm (8in) s. 10cm (4in) ➤p.142
Sedum kamtschaticum 'Variegatum'♀ ✿ Yellow • Summer–early autumn ∅ Green and gold
h. 10cm (4in) s. 60cm (2ft) ➤p.167
Tradescantia Andersoniana Group 'Purple Dome' ✿ Purple Early summer–early autumn
h. 60cm (2ft) s. 45cm (1½ft) ➤p.176
Veronica peduncularis 'Georgia Blue' ✿ Deep blue • Summer
h. 10cm (4in) s. 60cm (2ft) ➤p.178

Climbers & shrubs

Small, waxy or glossy leaves retain moisture, do not absorb salty sea spray, and are not blown off their bushes in windy gales.

Aloe vera♀ ∅ Grey-green
h. 60cm (2ft) s. indefinite ➤p.336
Berberis thunbergii f. atropurpurea ∅ Purple-red ❧ Bright red • Autumn
h. 1.8m (6ft) s. 2.5m (8ft) ➤p.188

Hebe 'Wingletye' ✿ Lilac
Summer • h. 20cm (8in) s. 60cm (2ft) ➤p.209
Ilex aquifolium 'Golden Milkboy'♀ ∅ Green and gold ❧ Red Autumn–Winter
h. 6m (20ft) s. 4m (13ft) ➤p.217
Juniperus communis 'Hibernica'♀ ∅ Silver-blue • h. 6m (20ft) s. 60cm (2ft) ➤p.219
Olearia x haastii ✿ White Mid–late summer ∅ Green and grey
h.&s. 1.8m (6ft) ➤p.228
Parahebe catarractae ✿ Blue • All summer • h.&s. 25cm (10in) ➤p.230
Pyracantha 'Teton' ✿ White • Early summer ❧ Yellow-orange • Autumn
h. 5m (16ft) s. 3m (10ft) ➤p.236
Rosa rubiginosa♀ ✿ Rose-pink Summer • h.&s. 2.5m (8ft) ➤p.242

Trees

An open crown of swaying branches filters the sea breezes and creates a windbreak without the risk of the tree being blown over.

Sorbus cashmiriana♀ ✿ Pale pink Spring ❧ Pink or white • Autumn
h. 4m (13ft) s. 3m (10ft) ➤p.273

Bulbs

These two bulbs do not mind poor soil and their delicate petals stand up surprisingly well in this windy site.

Nerine bowdenii♀ ✿ Pink • Autumn
h. 45cm (1½ft) ➤p.321
Ornithogalum narbonense ✿ White • Late spring–early summer
h. 60cm (2ft) ➤p.322

A WINDBREAK FOR SALTY GALES

By midsummer the worst of the gales will have abated, but a clifftop garden like this could be washed with salty spray all year round. Robust shrubs like the *Berberis* and *Juniperus* bear the brunt of winds blowing in from the back of the border, but the other plants are salt-resistant, too.

Plan shows garden in early to midsummer

Juniperus communis 'Hibernica' · Berberis thunbergii f. atropurpurea · Nerine bowdenii · Rosa rubiginosa · Olearia x haastii · Nerine bowdenii · Veronica peduncularis 'Georgia Blue' · Veronica peduncularis 'Georgia Blue' · Eryngium bourgatii 'Oxford Blue' · Ornithogalum narbonense · Ornithogalum narbonense · Parahebe catarractae · Tradescantia Andersoniana Group 'Purple Dome'

SLOPING SITE
NORTH OR EAST FACING WITH FROST POCKETS

During the winter months a hilly, north-facing garden is an uninviting place for gardeners. The weak rays of the sun may never reach some dark corners and frost may persist in these gloomy sunless areas all day long. But even in these difficult conditions you can find care-free plants that will bring colour and texture to your garden.

North and east facing slopes are exposed to biting northerly winds, and months can pass at the bleakest times of year when the frost never seems to clear. A garden at the base of such a slope is often in a frost pocket, as the cold air drifts downhill and collects at the lowest point, creating challenging conditions for gardening.

Challenge the difficult conditions

Instead of dismissing this inhospitable environment as a lost cause, look at its advantages. A garden at the top of a slope, for instance, is usually well drained and perfect for spring bulbs or **geraniums**, while one at the base is great for moisture-lovers and shade-loving plants, like **hostas**. All you need to do is choose suitable plants, avoiding frost-tender species, and swaddle them in a thick blanket of insulating mulch.

A cotoneaster will shrug off icy blasts. Against the bright red berries and glossy dark green leaves fingers of silvery frost have a decorative appeal.

Keep plants low to the warming ground

Even the early morning sun on slopes facing east can scorch buds that have been frozen over night or tender young leaves in spring. Choose plants with tough or waxy leaves, like **cotoneaster** or **juniper**, and spreading varieties that hug the ground, which will retain some warmth. Make sure you don't make things worse by trying to provide too much shelter: if a garden is enclosed with fences or thick hedges, these will tend to trap frost and freezing air, and may block out any sun that tries to break through.

In the cold shade, a frost-hardy berberis adds interest with its purple leaves. A broad-leaved hosta and easy-going Alchemilla mollis also thrive in this difficult spot.

Expert's Selection

Top of slope
Herbaceous perennials

In well-drained soil near the top of a slope, lamiums and geraniums will spread low and wide.

Brunnera macrophylla ♀ ❀ Bright blue • Spring • *h*. 45cm (1½ft) *s*. 60cm (2ft) ➤p.101

Epimedium perralderianum
∅ Bronze-red, dark green and copper • All year ❀ Yellow • Spring *h*. 30cm (1ft) *s*. 45cm (1½ft) ➤p.112

Geranium macrorrhizum ❀ White, pink or magenta • All summer *h*. 25cm (10in) *s*. 60cm (2ft) ➤p.123

***Lamium maculatum* 'Beacon Silver'** ❀ Purplish • Late spring *h*. 15cm (6in) *s*. 1m (3ft) ➤p.139

Climbers & shrubs

Only the hardiest climbers survive in frosty sites. Choose a low spreading juniper or woody berberis instead.

Berberis darwinii ♀ ❀ Yellow • Spring ✦ Purple • Autumn *h*. 2m (7ft) *s*. 1.5m (5ft) ➤p.188

Cotoneaster salicifolius ❀ White • Late spring–early summer ✦ Bright red • Autumn • *h.&s.* 2.5m (8ft) ➤p.201

***Euonymus fortunei* 'Coloratus'**
∅ Dark green; purple-red in winter *h.&s.* 1.5m (5ft) ➤p.205

***Juniperus horizontalis* 'Emerald Spreader'** ∅ Bright green *h*. 30cm (1ft) *s*. 3m (10ft) ➤p.219

Bulbs

Plant bulbs where the ground is dry and let their blooms cheer you after the cold, dark winter months.

Hyacinthoides non-scripta ❀ Violet blue • Spring • *h*. 30cm (1ft) ➤p.316

***Narcissus* 'Vulcan'** ♀ ❀ Yellow with vivid orange cup • Mid spring *h*. 45cm (1½ft) ➤p.320

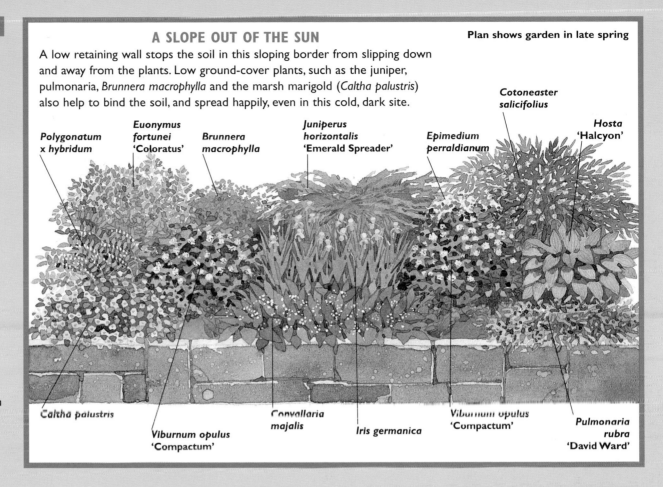

A SLOPE OUT OF THE SUN

Plan shows garden in late spring

A low retaining wall stops the soil in this sloping border from slipping down and away from the plants. Low ground-cover plants, such as the juniper, pulmonaria, *Brunnera macrophylla* and the marsh marigold (*Caltha palustris*) also help to bind the soil, and spread happily, even in this cold, dark site.

Polygonatum x hybridum — *Euonymus fortunei 'Coloratus'* — *Brunnera macrophylla* — *Juniperus horizontalis 'Emerald Spreader'* — *Epimedium perraldianum* — *Cotoneaster salicifolius* — *Hosta 'Halcyon'*

Caltha palustris — *Viburnum opulus 'Compactum'* — *Convallaria majalis* — *Iris germanica* — *Viburnum opulus 'Compactum'* — *Pulmonaria rubra 'David Ward'*

Base of slope
Herbaceous perennials

The damp soil near the base of a north or east-facing slope makes the perfect conditions for these shade-loving perennials.

Alchemilla mollis ♀ ❀ Yellow-green Early summer ∅ Lime green *h*. 45cm (1½ft) *s*. 75cm (2½ft) ➤p.90

Caltha palustris ♀ ❀ Yellow • Spring *h*. 45cm (1½ft) *s*. 75cm (2½ft) ➤p.102

***Hosta* 'Halcyon'** ♀ ❀ Pale mauve ∅ Blue-green • Midsummer *h*. 60cm (2ft) *s*. 45cm (1½ft) ➤p.134

Iris germanica ♀ ❀ Blue-purple and white • Mid–late spring *h*. 70cm (28in) ➤p.137

Polygonatum x hybridum ♀ ❀ White • Late spring *h*. 1.2m (4ft) *s*. 1m (3ft) ➤p.159

***Pulmonaria rubra* 'David Ward'**
❀ Reddy pink • Late winter– mid spring ∅ Green with cream edges • *h*. 45cm (1½ft) *s*. 1m (3ft) ➤p.163

Waldsteinia ternata ❀ Yellow • Late spring–summer • *h*. 15cm (6in) *s*. 60cm (2ft) ➤p.179

Climbers & shrubs

Berries, leaves and even bare stems offer glorious autumn and winter colours, with this choice of shrubs.

***Cornus sanguinea* 'Midwinter Fire'** ❀ White • Summer ∅ Yellow, orange and red stems • Winter *h.&s.* 2.5m (8ft) ➤p.200

***Sambucus nigra* 'Black Beauty'**
❀ Rose pink • Early summer ∅ Deep purple • *h.&s.* 6m (20ft) ➤p.248

***Viburnum opulus* 'Compactum'** ♀ ❀ White • Early summer ✦ Bright red Late summer–autumn ∅ Red Autumn • *h.&s.* 1.5m (5ft) ➤p.258

Trees

The Kilmarnock willow's weeping branches make a good windbreak, to shelter less sturdy plants.

***Salix caprea* 'Kilmarnock'** ♀ ❀ Greeny yellow catkins • Spring *h*. 1.5m (5ft) *s*. 2m (7ft) ➤p.272

Bulbs

Many bulbs rot in the soggy soil at the base of a slope, but lily-of-the-valley loves damp sites and flowers reliably, even in shady corners.

Convallaria majalis ♀ ❀ White Spring • *h*. 23cm (9in) ➤p.309

Swinging from suntrap to freezer, a south or west-facing slope catches the sun all day long – and in fine weather is a joy to the gardener – but offers no protection to plants when the wind blows. At northerly latitudes and high altitudes, cold snaps bring the threat of frost.

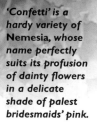

'Confetti' is a hardy variety of Nemesia, whose name perfectly suits its profusion of dainty flowers in a delicate shade of palest bridesmaids' pink.

A slope facing south or west will always be slightly warmer than one facing north or east. Whatever the time of year, frost will be unlikely to linger beyond lunchtime as the sun will warm the soil during even the months with the shortest days.

Resist the temptation to plant windbreaks or put in other kinds of shelter to protect your plants, because you will probably create exactly the opposite effect, trapping cold air in damaging frost pockets. There will be winds in a garden like this, but nothing as brisk as the north-easterly gales that bring with them the chills of Siberia.

Water flows down the slope

When you live on a slope you will find that conditions in your garden vary widely. The top of the slope will drain freely, leaving light, crumbly soil that is easy to work. However, as the water drains away to the bottom of the garden it takes with it valuable nutrients and, if there are areas that are not planted, the soil itself may start to slide away.

Make the most of these varied conditions by growing a variety of plants, from a golden yellow *Hypericum* or white-flowered mountain *Anaphalis triplinervis* at the top of the slope to the wafting, pink, moisture-loving **loosestrife** (*Lythrum*) and **snakeweed** (*Persicaria*) closer to the base.

Choose frost-hardy plants for cold spots

Where frost is most likely – at the base of the slope where cold air settles, or in corners shaded from the sun – plant frost-hardy species. Cover the ground with a thick blanket of mulch in early autumn to retain the summer's heat in the soil and encourage plants to start growing again in spring, despite the low temperatures above ground.

If spring frosts are forecast, the tender young shoots of even the hardiest plants will benefit from a protective layer of horticultural fleece.

If you view your garden from above, make it a patchwork of low-growing plants, like Dianthus, thyme and dwarf irises, and add a few sturdy taller species, such as Euphorbias and bushy Santolinas for interest.

Expert's Selection

Top of slope
Herbaceous

The hot dry conditions near the top of a south or west-facing bank suit these sun-loving perennials.

Anaphalis triplinervis ♀ ✿ White Summer–autumn ⊘ Grey-green *h.&s.* 60cm (2ft) ➤p.90
***Aster novi-belgii* 'Climax'** ✿ Lavender blue • Autumn *h.* 1.2m (4ft) *s.* 60cm (2ft) ➤p.97
***Dianthus* 'Gran's Favourite'** ♀ ✿ Pink and white • Early–midsummer *h.* 35cm (14in) *s.* 25cm (10in) ➤p.107
Euphorbia griffithii ⊘ Green Early spring ✿ Orangey red • Early summer • *h.* 1m (3ft) *s.* 75cm (2½ft) ➤p.119
***Nemesia denticulata* 'Confetti'** ✿ Pink • Summer • *h.* 30cm (1ft) *s.* 75cm (2½ft) ➤p.150
***Thymus vulgaris* 'Silver Posie'** ✿ Pink or white • Early summer *h.* 23cm (9in) *s.* 40cm (16in) ➤p.174

Climbers & shrubs

Compact or low-lying shrubs will withstand the prevailing winds.

***Hypericum* 'Hidcote'** ♀ ✿ Golden yellow • All summer ⊘ Dark green *h.* 1.5m (5ft) *s.* 1.2m (4ft) ➤p.216
***Juniperus* x *pfitzeriana* 'Gold Sovereign'** ⊘ Golden yellow *h.* 60cm (2ft) *s.* 1.2m (4ft) ➤p.219
***Santolina chamaecyparissus* 'Lambrook Silver'** ⊘ Silver ✿ Deep yellow • Mid–late summer *h.&s.* 60cm (2ft) ➤p.249
***Weigela* 'Victoria'** ✿ Red • Summer ⊘ Purplish • *h.&s.* 1m (3ft) ➤p.259

Bulbs

Red tulips stand sentinel in spring.

***Tulipa praestans* 'Fusilier'** ♀ ✿ Brilliant red • Early spring *h.* 30cm (1ft) ➤p.324

Base of slope
Herbaceous perennials

Rich moist soil, combined with an open sunny site, makes the base of a slope a very good place to grow these thirsty perennials.

Aruncus aesthusifolius ✿ Creamy white • Midsummer *h.* 25cm (10in) *s.* 30cm (1ft) ➤p.95
***Erigeron* 'Dunkelste Aller'** ♀ ✿ Purple • Spring–summer *h.* 75cm (2½ft) *s.* 45cm (1½ft) ➤p.136
***Iris siberica* 'Emperor'** ✿ Purple-blue • Early summer *h.* 1m (3ft) *s.* 30cm (1ft) ➤p.136
***Lythrum salicaria* 'Feuerkerze'** ♀ ('Firecandle') ✿ Rosy pink Mid–late summer • *h.* 1.2m (4ft) *s.* 45cm (1½ft) ➤p.147
***Persicaria bistorta* 'Superba'** ♀ ✿ Pink • Summer–autumn *h.* 1m (3ft) *s.* 60cm (2ft) ➤p.156

Climbers & shrubs

Choose one or two large shrubs, like a lilac (*Syringa*) to add interest, but use spreaders for ground cover.

***Rosa* 'Flower Carpet'** ♀ ✿ Pink, white or yellow • All summer *h.* 1m (3ft) *s.* 1.2m (4ft) ➤p.245
Spiraea thunbergii ♀ ✿ White Early spring • *h.&s.* 1m (3ft) ➤p.252
***Syringa microphylla* 'Superba'** ✿ Rosy pink • Late spring and early autumn • *h.&s.* 1.8m (6ft) ➤p.254
***Taxus baccata* 'Summergold'** ⊘ Golden green • *h.* 50cm (20in) *s.* 1.5m (5ft) ➤p.255

Bulbs

Large goblet-shaped flowers make an unusual sight in autumn.

***Colchicum speciosum* 'Album'** ♀ ✿ White • Autumn • *h.* 23cm (9in) ➤p.308

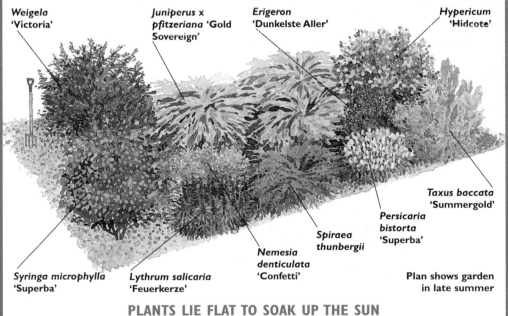

Weigela 'Victoria' • Juniperus x pfitzeriana 'Gold Sovereign' • Erigeron 'Dunkelste Aller' • Hypericum 'Hidcote' • Taxus baccata 'Summergold' • Persicaria bistorta 'Superba' • Spiraea thunbergii • Nemesia denticulata 'Confetti' • Lythrum salicaria 'Feuerkerze' • Syringa microphylla 'Superba' • Plan shows garden in late summer

PLANTS LIE FLAT TO SOAK UP THE SUN

The spreading rosettes of three golden junipers make a splash of colour that lasts all year. Other prostrate varieties of *Taxus* and *Spiraea* help to stop soil slipping down this bed, as it slopes towards the front. Even as summer draws to a close, this warm sunny site is still blooming with a colourful combination of shrubs and perennials that will withstand frost.

On a cold, dark hill the winds are chilly, and the sun shines only in the morning – and hardly at all in winter. You may despair of plants thriving here, but the shade means that the soil retains moisture better than on many sloping sites, and there is no chance of scorching by searing sun.

Anyone with a sloping garden will know that soil tends to migrate downwards. Rainwater also runs downhill over the surface, meaning that during periods of low rainfall the top of the slope can dry out and in wet weather, the bottom of the slope can become soggy.

Rain is not the only weather factor to consider when you are choosing plants and deciding where to put them. Strong cold winds may shred or scorch tender leaves, and flowering shrubs may burn after frost if they catch the early morning sun, making plants that flower early in the year an unwise choice for a north or east-facing slope.

You can improve conditions for your plants very easily by planting a row of fast-growing trees or hedging to provide shelter on the windward side of the garden. If you are on a very steep slope, you might consider constructing a series of terraces and retaining walls. This will not only give you a flat place to sit on fine days, but will help to stop the soil from sliding away.

Pools of easy-care colour in a carpet of green
However, there are planting techniques that require much less effort than terracing, but are as effective at preventing soil erosion. Work the soil as little as possible and try planting through a semi-permeable membrane (see page 14) which, while inhibiting weeds, will still allow spreading plants to grow and root.

Choose plants with running stems – blue **periwinkles** (*Vinca major*) and pale pink **cranesbills** (*Geraniums*) – or those which root where they touch, such as creeping **cotoneaster** as the basis for your planting scheme. These will all help to bind the soil while acting as attractive ground cover. Give the foliage a lift with a few bold patches of colour, such as a **rose of Sharon** (*Hypericum calycinum*), with its brilliant golden cup-shaped flowers.

Plants with variegated foliage, striking stems or abundant berries will bring welcome brightness to dull corners, particularly during winter.

Cranesbill geraniums, such as Geranium macrorrhizum 'Album', with its delicate white summer blooms, will spread in a shady site to cover the ground in a pretty carpet.

The bright sunny yellow of a clump of trollius, feathery white plumes of astilbes and variegated foliage of a cornus in the background brighten a dark north-facing slope.

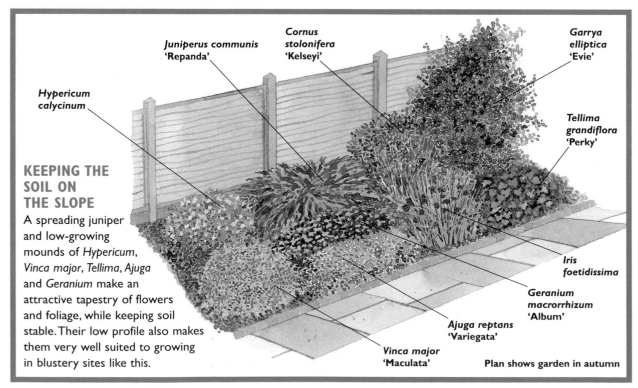

KEEPING THE SOIL ON THE SLOPE
A spreading juniper and low-growing mounds of *Hypericum*, *Vinca major*, *Tellima*, *Ajuga* and *Geranium* make an attractive tapestry of flowers and foliage, while keeping soil stable. Their low profile also makes them very well suited to growing in blustery sites like this.

Juniperus communis 'Repanda'

Cornus stolonifera 'Kelseyi'

Garrya elliptica 'Evie'

Hypericum calycinum

Tellima grandiflora 'Perky'

Iris foetidissima

Geranium macrorrhizum 'Album'

Ajuga reptans 'Variegata'

Vinca major 'Maculata'

Plan shows garden in autumn

Expert's Selection

Herbaceous perennials

Early flowering species are vulnerable where late frosts are likely to occur, so choose evergreens or summer-flowering perennials for success.

Ajuga reptans 'Variegata' ∅ Grey-green and cream • *h.* 15cm (6in)
s. 45cm (1½ft) ➤p.89

Astilbe simplicifolia♀ ✿ Pale pink
Summer • *h.&s.* 23cm (9in) ➤p.98

Geranium macrorrhizum
'Album'♀ ✿ White • All summer
h. 25cm (10in) *s.* 60cm (2ft) ➤p.123

Hukonechloa macra 'Aureola'♀
∅ Yellow with green stripes • Spring
∅ Pinkish red • Early autumn
h. 30cm (1ft) *s.* 60cm (2ft) ➤p.127

Iris foetidissima♀ ❧ Orange-red
seeds in pods • Autumn • *h.* 50cm
(20in) ➤p.136

Tellima grandiflora 'Perky' ✿ Red
Early–midsummer • *h.* 75cm (2½ft)
s. 30cm (1ft) ➤p.172

**Trollius chinensis 'Golden
Queen'**♀ ✿ Orangey yellow • Early–
midsummer • *h.* 75cm (2½ft)
s. 45cm (1½ft) ➤p.177

Climbers & shrubs

Low-spreading shrubs or climbers that are happy to sprawl horizontally are good choices for steep slopes.

Cornus stolonifera 'Kelseyi'
∅ Yellow-green shoots • Autumn–winter • *h.&s.* 75cm (2½ft) ➤p.200

**Cotoneaster x suecicus 'Coral
Beauty'** ✿ White • Summer
❧ Orange • Autumn • *h.* 60cm (2ft)
s. 1.5m (5ft) ➤p.201

**Euonymus fortunei 'Emerald 'n'
Gold'** ∅ Green and gold, turning
pink • *h.* 3m (10ft) *s.* 2m (7ft) ➤p.205

Garrya elliptica 'Evie' ✿ Grey-green catkins • Winter–early spring
h.&s. 2.5m (8ft) ➤p.208

Hypericum calycinum ✿ Bright
yellow • All summer ❧ Bronze
h. 30cm (1ft) *s.* 1m (3ft) ➤p.216

Juniperus communis 'Repanda'♀
∅ Grey-green • *h.* 30cm (1ft)
s. 2m (7ft) ➤p.219

Rosa x jacksonii 'Max Graf'
✿ Pink • All summer • *h.* 1.2m (4ft)
s. 2.5m (8ft) ➤p.242

Vinca major 'Maculata' ✿ Pale blue
All summer • *h.* 35cm (14in)
s. indefinite ➤p.259

On a sun-drenched slope, even ground near the base of the hill is dried by long hot days to a friable soil that is a joy to work. This garden is a gift for the care-free potterer because the right plants will thrive with the bare minimum of attention to create a stunning display.

A Potentilla will spread without any attention in a sunny spot, making a terrific choice for ground cover in a south or west-facing sloping garden.

If it faces due south, a sloping garden can be a very hot place, where the sun beats down all day long in summer. While this unrelenting heat is perfect for sunworshippers, it can scorch plants that are not designed to cope. Living in parched soil can also mean that young plants lack the moisture they need to get established. A west facing slope has all the south-facing benefits of warm prevailing winds and protection from frost, and basks in the sun just a little later in the day.

A hot dry home for Mediterranean plants

The key to success on a site like this is to choose drought-resistant species such as the sun-loving *Helianthemum*. Mediterranean-type plants, such as aromatic **lavender** and **sage** (*Salvia*), will be particularly at home at the top of a sunny slope. *Artemisia* and others with narrow silvery grey or furry leaves are also well equipped to survive in harsh sun (see above right).

Washing away the goodness

A slope allows rainwater to drain freely through the soil, so stroll round the garden with a watering can during long, dry spells and admire your summer display as you water. It is also a good idea to apply a general fertiliser periodically to replace nutrients washed out of the soil by rain. Of course, any water or feed you apply will gradually run down the slope, so be sparing with fertiliser at the top of the garden to make sure that the bottom does not get overfed.

Heavy rain can even wash the soil itself down the slope, particularly after a dry spell – and wind and gravity also play their parts. You can help to stem the loss by choosing ground-cover plants, such as the pretty spreading *Aurinia* (**yellow alyssum**) to help to bind the soil. Planting through a semi-permeable membrane (see page 14) in the most precipitous sections of the garden will also help to keep the soil in place and conserve moisture.

The filigree foliage of a silvery artemisia and the furry leaves of a grey stachys make these plants perfect for a sun trap. Narrow leaves have a small surface area, which minimises the amount of water lost through evaporation, while a furry coating traps a layer of cool moist air next to the leaves.

Expert's Selection

Herbaceous perennials

Plant spreading ground-cover plants, like a *Potentilla*, to stop soil slipping down a steep slope.

***Artemisia* 'Powis Castle'**♀ ⊘ Silver
h. 60cm (2ft) s. 1m (3ft) ➤p.94
Aurinia saxatalis♀ ❀ Yellow
Early summer • h. 20cm (8in)
s. 30cm (1ft) ➤p.99
Campanula portenschlagiana♀
❀ Deep lavender-blue • Summer
h. 15cm (6in) s. 50cm (20in) ➤p.103
Potentilla alba ❀ White
Midsummer • h. 10cm (4in)
s. 15cm (6in) ➤p.160
Scabiosa graminifolia ❀ Lilac
Late summer • h.&s. 30cm (1ft)
➤p.166

***Sedum kamtschaticum*
'Variegatum'**♀ ❀ Yellow • Mid–late summer • h. 10cm (4in)
s. 25cm (10in) ➤p.167
***Stachys byzantiana* 'Silver Carpet'**
⊘ Silver-grey • h. 60cm (2ft)
s. 1m (3ft) ➤p.170

Climbers & shrubs

Silver or grey-leaved shrubs keep their cool in sun-baked spots by reflecting the bright light.

***Hebe* 'Youngii'** ❀ Violet • Summer
h. 20cm (8in) s. 60cm (?ft) ➤p.209
***Helianthemum* 'Fire Dragon'**♀
❀ Orange-scarlet • All summer
h. 20cm (8in) s. 40cm (16in) ➤p.213
Lavandula stoechas♀ ❀ Dark
purple • Early summer ⊘ Silver-grey
h.&s. 45cm (1½ft) ➤p.221

***Rosa* 'Flower Carpet'** ❀ Pink, white or yellow • All summer
h. 1m (3ft) s.1.2m (4ft) ➤p.245
***Salvia officinalis* 'Kew Gold'**♀
⊘ Golden yellow • h. 60cm (2ft)
s. 1m (3ft) ➤p.247
Santolina pinnata ❀ White
Mid–late summer • h. 60cm (2ft)
s. 30cm (1ft) ➤p.249

Bulbs

Add a splash of exotica to the garden border with clumps of airy autumn flowering *Nerines* and gaudy summer *Gladioli*.

Gladiolus ❀ Various • Early
summer–autumn • h. 1m (3ft)
➤p.315
Nerine bowdenii♀ ❀ Pink • Autumn
h. 45cm (1½ft) ➤p.321

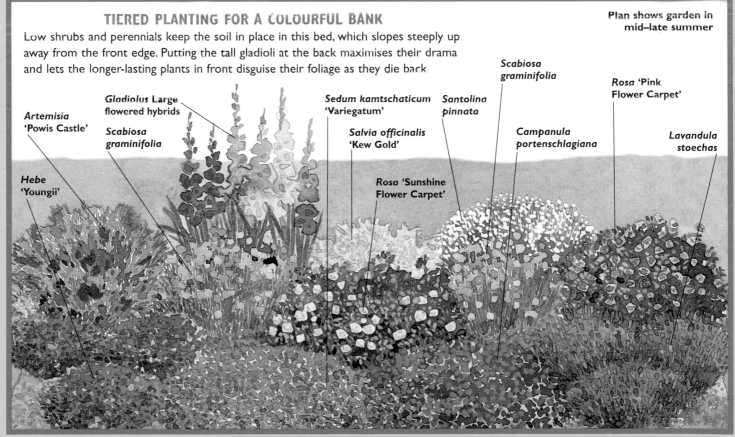

TIERED PLANTING FOR A COLOURFUL BANK

Low shrubs and perennials keep the soil in place in this bed, which slopes steeply up away from the front edge. Putting the tall gladioli at the back maximises their drama and lets the longer-lasting plants in front disguise their foliage as they die back.

Plan shows garden in mid–late summer

Artemisia 'Powis Castle'

Gladiolus Large flowered hybrids

Scabiosa graminifolia

Hebe 'Youngii'

Sedum kamtschaticum 'Variegatum'

Salvia officinalis 'Kew Gold'

Santolina pinnata

Scabiosa graminifolia

Rosa 'Sunshine Flower Carpet'

Campanula portenschlagiana

Rosa 'Pink Flower Carpet'

Lavandula stoechas

The easiest soil in the world is a light and sandy one on flat open ground. You can pull weeds out without resorting to a fork, can walk on bare earth after rain without your boots doubling in weight, and if you pick up a handful, it will crumble and run through your fingers.

Lighter soils warm up quickly in spring, allowing early sowing and planting and helping new plants to establish quickly. Sometimes you may think that the drainage is just too good – nutrients tend to be quickly washed away, and the ground dries out rapidly in sunny or windy weather. But a good heap of compost or well-rotted manure forked in with a general-purpose fertiliser a couple of times a year will replenish lost nutrients and help to make the soil better at retaining water.

More than any other, a flat garden needs trees to add shape and height. For clouds of spring blossom and colourful fruit in autumn, one of the best is the **Japanese crab apple**, *Malus floribunda*. Or for striking copper foliage and large white blooms, choose an ornamental cherry, *Prunus* 'Taihaku'.

Tough shrubs and herbs thrive on neglect
Mediterranean herbs are a good choice in this environment as they thrive in hot dry weather. Grey or silver, often woolly, foliage is a good indication of a plant that will do well here. A spiky **yucca** will add a more exotic hothouse touch.

Old-fashioned species roses are tougher than modern varieties and *Rosa* 'Stanwell Perpetual' will reward you with a series of blush pink double blooms and spread like mad. Underplanted with campanulas and daisies, it will give a pretty cottage-garden look and require minimum attention.

A sunny spot on light, well-drained soil is the perfect place to grow a herb garden. This sunken gravelled area would be a haven for bees and butterflies, as well as a sensory delight for gardeners.

Malus floribunda

Acer platanoides 'Drummondii'

Celastrus scandens

Aster x frikartii

Kniphofia 'Fiery Fred'

Prunus 'Taihaku'

Kniphofia 'Fiery Fred'

Jasminum nudiflorum

Perovskia 'Blue Spire'

Hypericum x moserianum

Yucca gloriosa

Phlomis fruticosa

Plan shows garden in autumn

FRUITS, LEAVES AND FLOWERS GIVE AUTUMN COLOUR
Complementary yellows and blues – in the *Hypericum* flowers, *Acer* leaves, *Celastrus* fruits and *Perovskia* flowers and foliage – give this border a different autumn look from the traditional shades of bronze. The trees are underplanted with a swathe of white daffodils, which bloom until the perennials begin to emerge.

⌀ Green • h.&s. 75cm (2½ft) ➤p.216

Jasminum nudiflorum♀ ❀ Bright yellow • Late autumn–early spring h. 4.5m (15ft) s. 1.8m (6ft) ➤p.218

***Lavandula angustifolia* 'Twickel Purple'**♀ ❀ Purple • Midsummer ⌀ Grey-green • h. 60cm (2ft) s. 45cm (1½ft) ➤p.221

***Perovskia* 'Blue Spire'**♀ ❀ Deep blue • Midsummer–early autumn ⌀ Silvery blue-green • h. 1.2m (4ft) s. 1m (3ft) ➤p.231

Phlomis fruticosa♀ ❀ Yellow All summer ⌀ Silvery grey h.&s. 1m (3ft) ➤p.232

***Rosmarinus officinalis* 'Sissinghurst Blue'**♀ ❀ Deep blue Early spring–autumn h.&s. 1.2m (4ft) ➤p.246

***Salvia officinalis* 'Purpurascens'**♀ ❀ Purple • Summer ⌀ Purply green h. 60cm (2ft) s. 1m (3ft) ➤p.247

Yucca gloriosa♀ ⌀ Dark green h.&s. 1.5m (5ft) ➤p.261

Trees

Colour, shape and year-round interest are important for a tree in a small or medium-sized garden.

***Acer platanoides* 'Drummondii'**♀ ⌀ Green and white • h. 10m (33ft) s. 5m (16ft) ➤p.264

Malus floribunda♀ ❀ Pale pink Spring ❧ Yellow • Autumn • h. 1.5m (5ft) s. 1.2m (4ft) ➤p.269

***Prunus* 'Taihaku'**♀ ❀ White • Spring ⌀ Coppery green • h. 2.7m (9ft) s. 1.5m (5ft) ➤p.270

Herbaceous perennials

On a site like this you can have your pick of plants. This list offers a range of colour and flowering season.

Aster x frikartii ❀ Pink-lilac Autumn • h.&s. 45cm (1½ft) ➤p.97

***Campanula lactiflora* 'Pouffe'** ❀ Mid blue or pink • Summer–early autumn • h.&s. 60cm (2ft) ➤p.103

***Kniphofia* 'Fiery Fred'** ❀ Orange-red • Midsummer h. 1m (3ft) s. 60cm (2ft) ➤p.138

***Oenothera fruiticosa* 'Fyrverkeri' ('Fireworks')**♀ ❀ Golden yellow Early summer–autumn • h. 30cm (1ft) s. 40cm (16in) ➤p.152

***Tanacetum parthenium* 'Aureum'** ❀ Yellowish white • Late spring h. 45cm (1½ft) s. 30cm (1ft) ➤p.172

Climbers & shrubs

Choose plants with a long flowering season to minimise your work.

Celastrus scandens ⌀❧ Yellow Autumn • h.&s. 2.5m (8ft) ➤p.195

Cytisus battandieri♀ ❀ Golden yellow • Late spring–early summer h.&s. 4m (13ft) ➤p.202

Hypericum x moserianum♀ ❀ Yellow • All summer ❧ Purple

Bulbs

Spring comes quickly on light soil, so bulbs may bloom earlier than usual.

***Narcissus* 'Geranium'**♀ ❀ White with orange cup • Late spring h. 40cm (16in) ➤p.320

Ornithogalum umbellatum ❀ White and green • Late spring– early summer • h. 30cm (1ft) ➤p.322

If your soil sticks to your shoes in wet weather, but dries to a crust when the sun shines, you will know the pitfalls of this kind of site. However, sticky clay is very fertile, and a flat open plot lends itself to a textured blend of trees, shrubs and pretty perennials.

With foliage in burnished shades of purple and clusters of glossy red berries, a barberry, like this Berberis thunbergii 'Rose Glow' makes an impact on heavy soil in autumn.

In many ways, heavy soils are ideal for the care-free gardener. Digging can be an energetic workout and new plants may struggle to find a foothold in or push through the solid ground, but once established, they will thrive in conditions that are generally moist and fertile. Even the poor drainage comes with the benefit that, in an average summer, you will be spared the task of daily watering.

Easy ways to improve your soil
Dig thoroughly to break up the soil before you plant and, if heavy rain often leaves the garden under water, improve the drainage at the same time by incorporating some sharp sand or grit.

It is worth spending a little time in autumn, too, to maintain the natural fertility of your soil. Spread plenty of well-rotted manure or compost over the surface and let the worms work it through. Three months later scatter on lime to encourage the fine particles of clay to clump together and loosen the texture. Pick a fine day for this job: walking in the garden when it is wet or frosty will only compound the heavy soil and undo all your good work.

Reap the benefits of groundwork
Look ahead as you labour and remember that the less waterlogged your soil is, the faster it will warm up in spring and the sooner you will be able to enjoy the dripping blossom of a **wisteria** or the exotic beauty of a clump of **oriental poppies**.

From its slow cool start in spring, heavy soil soaks up the heat that beats down onto an open site all summer and retains it, like a storage heater, well into autumn and winter. This warm bed gives late flowering shrubs and perennials, such as *Helenium* and *Lysimachia*, a chance to shine.

PLANT A BED FOR ALL-ROUND COLOUR
If grass does not thrive on your heavy soil, dig up a section of lawn and plant an island bed instead. In midsummer, the plants – a pair of hybrid tea roses surrounded by an assortment of bright summer-flowering perennials – will make a colourful centrepiece for the garden.

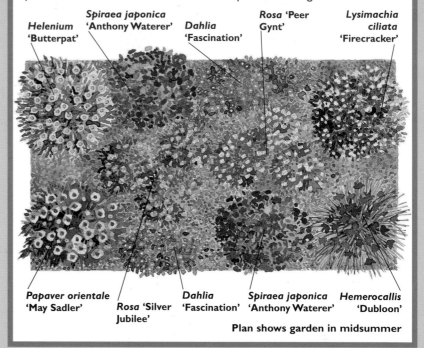

Helenium 'Butterpat'
Spiraea japonica 'Anthony Waterer'
Dahlia 'Fascination'
Rosa 'Peer Gynt'
Lysimachia ciliata 'Firecracker'
Papaver orientale 'May Sadler'
Rosa 'Silver Jubilee'
Dahlia 'Fascination'
Spiraea japonica 'Anthony Waterer'
Hemerocallis 'Dubloon'

Plan shows garden in midsummer

Expert's Selection

Herbaceous perennials

Plant sun loving flowering perennials, such as *Achilleas*, bright *Heleniums* and poppies, and they will flourish in a heavy soil that is rich in nutrients.

***Achillea filipendulina* 'Gold Plate'** ⚐ ✿ Yellow • Summer
h. 1.5m (5ft) *s.* 1m (3ft) ➤p.88

***Anemone hupehensis* 'Hadspen Abundance'** ⚐ ✿ Dark pink • Late summer–early autumn
h. 75cm (2½ft) *s.* 45cm (1½ft) ➤p.91

***Brunnera macrophylla* 'Aluminium Spot'** ✿ Clear blue Late spring • *h.* 45cm (1½ft) *s.* 60cm (2ft) ➤p.101

***Helenium* 'Butterpat'** ✿ Rich yellow • Mid–late summer
h. 1m (3ft) *s.* 60cm (2ft) ➤p.128

***Hemerocallis* 'Dubloon'**
✿ Deep orange • Mid–late summer
h.&s. 75cm (2½ft) ➤p.132

***Lysimachia ciliata* 'Firecracker'** ⚐
✿ Pale yellow • Mid–late summer
h. 1.2m (4ft) *s.* 45cm (1½ft) ➤p.146

***Miscanthus sinensis* 'Morning Light'** ✿ Reddish • Autumn
⌀ Green and white • *h.* 1.2–1.5m (4–5ft) *s.* 1.2m (4ft) ➤p.127

***Papaver orientale* 'May Sadler'**
✿ Orange-pink • Early summer
h. 75cm (2½ft) *s.* 45cm (1½ft)
➤p.155

Climbers & shrubs

Tough-leaved, thick-stemmed, these will withstand winter wind and rain.

***Berberis thunbergii* 'Atropurpurea Nana'** ⚐ ⌀ Purple-red • Autumn
❦ Bright red • Autumn
h.&s. 60cm (2ft) ➤p.188

***Cornus alba* 'Sibirica Variegata'**
⊘ Crimson with red stems
Autumn–winter • *h.&s.* 1.5m (5ft)
➤p.200

Paeonia suffruticosa ❀ White, pink,
red or purple • Late spring–early
summer • *h.* 2m (7ft) *s.* 1.5m (5ft)
➤p.229

***Potentilla fruticosa* 'Elizabeth'**♀
❀ Canary-yellow • Summer ⊘ Mid
green • *h.* 1m (3ft) *s.* 1.2m (4ft)
➤p.235

***Rosa* 'Peer Gynt'** ❀ Bright yellow
All summer • *h.* 75cm (2½ft) *s.* 60cm
(2ft) ➤p.241

***Rosa* 'Silver Jubilee'**♀ ❀ Pink • All
summer • *h.* 1m (3ft) *s.* 60cm (2ft)
➤p.241

***Sambucus racemosa* 'Sutherland
Gold'** ❀ Yellow • Early summer
⊘ Gold • *h.&s.* 4m (13ft) ➤p.248

***Spiraea japonica* 'Anthony
Waterer'**♀ ❀ Red • Mid–late
summer ⊘ Yellow • *h.&s.* 1m (3ft)
➤p.253

***Wisteria floribunda* 'Multijuga'**
❀ Violet • Early summer
h. up to 9m (30ft) ➤p.260

Trees

Heavy soil provides a secure footing
for mature trees. For year-round
interest and colour, choose a mix of
specimens for their eye-catching
blossom, foliage and berries.

***Eucalyptus pauciflora* subsp.
niphophila♀** ⊘ Grey-green
h. 15m (50ft) *s.* 6m (20ft) ➤p.266

***Robinia pseudoacacia* 'Frisia'**♀
❀ White • Spring ⊘ Golden yellow
h. 9m (30ft) *s.* 8m (27ft) ➤p.271

***Sorbus aria* 'Lutescens'** ⊘ Red and
brown ✧ Orangey red • Autumn
h. 6m (20ft) *s.* 4.5m (15ft) ➤p.273

Bulbs

Purples and pinks make a vibrant
addition to a summer planting.

***Dahlia* 'Fascination'**♀
❀ Pinky purple • Summer–autumn
h. 60cm (2ft) ➤p.313

*In an open garden with
heavy soil the spires of
Lysimachia, shown here
with Joe Pye weed
behind (Eupatorium
purpureum, see page
115) and bright pink
coneflowers in front
(Echinacea purpurea
see page 110), have the
sun, food and moisture
they need to soar.*

OPEN SLOPING SITE
LIGHT SOIL

Defy the force of gravity by using carefully selected plants to stop soil migrating from the top to the bottom of a slope. This site combines the best and worst of gardens: you are blessed with a sunny spot and an easily worked friable soil, but water and nutrients drain quickly through, while sun and wind dry up any moisture left behind.

With some careful planning, a hillside garden can have a truly theatrical feel, with banks of shrubs and flowers. There are, however, obstacles to overcome. Light soil will gravitate downwards, especially in very wet weather. And rain and wind can erode the soil at the top of the slope, leaving it thin and lacking in nutrients. The steeper the slope, the worse the erosion, so be sure to keep this area well fertilised.

The thin soil near the top of a slope dries out quickly in warm or breezy weather, but it will not seem a chore to water in summer if your garden is packed with colours, textures and fragrances for you to enjoy.

One advantage of gardening at the top of a sunny slope, however, is that the soil warms up quickly in spring, giving your plants a head start on those growing in colder spots. What is more, waterlogging is most unlikely, even in the wettest spells of weather.

Planting for stability

Careful planting can solve many of the shortcomings of a hilly site and will give you a rewarding garden without the hard work of landscaping to create flat terraces in your slope. Be lazy with your digging and you will actually help to prevent erosion by breaking up the soil as little as possible.

Covering beds with plant matting (see page 14) and planting through this will also help to retain soil, but for a more attractive natural method, choose ground-cover plants that will bind it. For a cool colour scheme, *Hebe pinguifolia* **'Pagei'** has pretty bluish foliage which makes a complementary backdrop for the lavender flowers and furry silver leaves of *Nepeta* x *faassenii*. If you prefer sunny golds, try planting **rose of Sharon** (*Hypericum calcyinum*), with its large yellow buttercup-shaped flowers, amid a sea of golden *Lysimachia nummularia* and variegated ivy (*Hedera helix*).

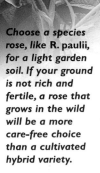

Choose a species rose, like R. paulii, for a light garden soil. If your ground is not rich and fertile, a rose that grows in the wild will be a more care-free choice than a cultivated hybrid variety.

Expert's Selection

Herbaceous perennials

A light well-drained soil is perfect for herbs like thyme and *Nepeta*, which grow best in dry sunny spots.

Artemisia vulgaris 'Oriental Hybrids' ∅ Gold-green • Spring–autumn • *h.* 60cm (2ft) *s.* indefinite ➤p.94

Fragaria 'Red Ruby' ❀ Red Summer–early autumn
h. 10cm (4in) *s.* indefinite ➤p.120

Leucanthemum x superbum 'Snowcap' ❀ White • Early–midsummer • *h* &*s.* 45cm (1½ft) ➤p.141

Lychnis chalcedonica ♀ ❀ Bright red • Early summer
h. 1m (3ft) *s.* 40cm (16in) ➤p.145

Melissa officinalis 'Aurea' ♀ ❀ White • Summer ∅ Green
h. 1m (3ft) *s.* 40cm (16in) ➤p.149

Miscanthus sinensis 'Morning Light' ❀ Reddish • Autumn ∅ Green with white edging
h. 1.2–1.5m (4–5ft) *s.* 1.2m (4ft) ➤p.127

Nepeta x faassenii ❀ Lavender Midsummer ∅ Silver-grey
h.&*s.* 60cm (2ft) ➤p.151

Prunella grandiflora 'Blue Loveliness' ❀ Lilac-blue • Summer
h. 23cm (9in) *s.* 1m (3ft) ➤p.162

Thymus vulgaris 'Silver Posie' ❀ Pink or white • Early summer
h. 23cm (9in) *s.* 40cm (16in) ➤p.174

Climbers & shrubs

Keep light soil in place by growing shrubs and climbers as ground cover.

Cotoneaster damerii ♀ ❀ White Early summer ⬩ Red • Autumn
h. 20cm (8in) *s.* 2m (7ft) ➤p.201

Euonymus fortunei 'Emerald Gaiety' ♀ ∅ Green and cream ∅ Bronze-edged • Winter
h. 1m (3ft) *s.* 1.5m (5ft) ➤p.205

Hebe pinguifolia 'Pagei' ♀ ❀ White • Mid–late spring ∅ Grey
h. 20cm (8in) *s.* 60cm (2ft) ➤p.209

Hedera helix ∅ Green or variegated
h. 10m (33ft) *s.* 5m (16ft) ➤p.212

Hypericum calycinum ❀ Yellow All summer ⬩ Bronze • Autumn
h. 30cm (1ft) *s.* 1m (3ft) ➤p.216

Rosa paulii ❀ White • Early summer
h. 1.2m (4ft) *s.* 1.5m (5ft) ➤p.242

Trees

A small tree is less vulnerable to winds on an open slope than a tall swaying variety.

Prunus 'Talhaku' ♀ ❀ White • Spring ∅ Coppery green • *h.* 2.7m (9ft) *s.* 1.5m (5ft) ➤p.270

Dense planting is an attractive way of stabilising soil on a slope. Here, silvery Lychnis and Nepeta in the foreground, tall white Shasta daisies (Leucanthemum), and low-growing thymes jostle for position in a garden where every inch of space is planted.

Rosa paulii

Miscanthus sinensis 'Morning Light'

Nepeta x faassenii

Hebe 'Pagei'

Fragaria 'Red Ruby'

Euonymus fortunei 'Emerald Gaiety'

Artemisia 'Oriental Hybrids'

Melissa officinalis 'Aurea'

Plan shows garden in midsummer

FLOWERS AND FOLIAGE FOR A SUNNY SLOPE

The evergreen *Miscanthus*, *Hebe* and *Euonymus* create a backbone of foliage for a bed next to a path that is used all year round, while a rose and a clump of *Nepeta* offer summer fragrance and colour. A low wall stops the soil slipping down onto the paving during heavy rain.

OPEN SLOPING SITE
HEAVY SOIL

Heavy soil is a boon at the top of a sloping garden. Rainwater washes through lighter soils, leaching away much of the goodness – and some of the soil – but the heavier the earth, the more nutrients and moisture it retains, providing food and water for hardy plants. Of course, the base of the slope is an altogether soggier place.

If your garden sits at the bottom of a hill you will know how wet it gets underfoot during periods of unrelenting rain. As the gradient levels out, rainwater from the rest of the slope collects in puddles and muddy swamps, full of soil washed down from above.

Plant easily established **willows, dogwoods, loosestrife, water figworts** and other waterside species that like to get their feet wet – and that look after themselves in winter – so that you can keep off the garden as much as possible and admire it from the warm dry house.

The cerise blooms of the double-flowered Dahlia 'Fascination' make a vibrant addition to the top of a sloping garden towards the end of summer.

A garden of extremes
Take advantage of the range of conditions a sloping garden offers by growing a wide variety of plants, from **cranesbill geraniums** that enjoy sun and good drainage at the top to *Hostas* that thrive in damp shade lower down the slope.

Although the top of the slope may set hard in summer, heavy soil holds moisture and nutrients well. Because it retains cold winter water, the soil can be slow to warm up in spring – more so at the base of the slope – and bulbs and new shoots will take longer to appear than in more hospitable sites.

Stopping the soil slipping
Planting fast-spreading ground cover, such as **dead nettles, creeping blueblossom** or **periwinkles**, or growing plants through a layer of soil matting (see page 14), will help to bind the soil and stop it being washed away during heavy rain. Terracing your slope or building low retaining walls will also help, but make sure the foundations are deep and secure.

An annual scattering of fertiliser at the top of the slope will compensate for nutrients washed away by winter rain, but there is no need for digging: heavy soil will naturally stick together, but if you break it up it will be more likely to slip down the slope.

Expert's Selection

Top of slope
Herbaceous perennials
Rich foliage tones and bright flowers make a feature of the top of a slope.

Epimedium perralderianum
⌀ Bronze-red, dark green and copper • All year ✿ Yellow • Spring
h. 30cm (1ft) *s.* 45cm (1½ft) ➤p.112
***Geranium sanguineum* var. *striatum* 'Splendens'** ✿ Pink • All summer • *h.* 30cm (1ft) *s.* 45cm (1½ft) ➤p.122
***Lamium garganicum* 'Golden Carpet'** ✿ Pink and white Midsummer • *h.&s.* 45cm (1½ft) ➤p.139
Linum narbonense ✿ Blue Midsummer • *h.* 50cm (20in) *s.* 30cm (1ft) ➤p.143

Climbers & shrubs
Low-growing shrubs and climbers left to spread will bind the soil on slopes.

Ceanothus thyrsiflorus* var. *repens ♀ ✿ Lilac blue • Spring–early summer • *h.* 45cm (1½ft) *s.* 2.7m (9ft) ➤p.194
***Cotoneaster salicifolius* 'Gnom'** ✿ White • Summer ⚘ Red • Autumn *h.* 30cm (1ft) *s.* 2m (7ft) ➤p.201
***Euonymus fortuneii* 'Blondy'** ⌀ Green, gold and white *h.&s.* 45cm (1½ft) ➤p.205
***Rosa* x *jacksonii* 'Max Graf'** ✿ Pink • All summer • *h.* 1.2m (4ft) *s.* 2m (7ft) ➤p.242
***Vinca major* 'Maculata'** ✿ Pale blue • All summer ⌀ Green-gold *h.* 35cm (14in) *s.* indefinite ➤p.259

Bulbs
Few bulbs tolerate the wet, so keep them near the top of a soggy slope.

***Dahlia* 'Fascination'** ♀ ✿ Pinky purple • Summer–autumn *h.* 60cm (2ft) ➤p.313

Bottom of slope
Herbaceous perennials

Even with sour, heavy soil, you can still enjoy these easy-going perennials that do not mind difficult conditions.

Astilbe ✿ White, pink, red • Summer h. 30cm–1.2m (1–4ft) s. 30cm–1m (1–3ft) ➤p.98

Hosta **'Ginko Craig'** ✿ Deep purple • Summer ∅ Dark green and white • h. 25cm (10in) s. 45cm (1½ft) ➤p.135

Lysimachia clethroides ♈ ✿ White Mid–late summer • h. 1m (3ft) s. 60cm (2ft) ➤p.146

Prunella grandiflora **'Blue Loveliness'** ✿ Lilac blue • Summer h. 23cm (9in) s. 1m (3ft) ➤p.162

Scrophularia auriculata **'Variegata'** ∅ Blue-green and cream Spring–summer • h.&s. 1m (3ft) ➤p.167

Solidago **'Goldenmosa'** ♈ ✿ Bright yellow • Late summer–early autumn h. 75cm (2½ft) s. 45cm (1½ft) ➤p.169

Climbers & shrubs

Grow a cornus for its vividly coloured bare winter stems and a flowering quince (*Chaenomeles*) for its profuse blooms.

Chaenomeles speciosa **'Simonii'** ✿ Bright red • Winter–early spring h. 1m (3ft) s. 2m (7ft) ➤p.197

Cornus stolonifera **'Flaviramea'** ♈ ∅ Red or orange, followed by yellow-green stems • Autumn–winter h.&s. 2.5m (8ft) ➤p.200

Salix repens var. argentea ♈ ✿ Yellow catkins • Late spring ∅ Silver-grey • h. 75cm (2½ft) s. 1.2m (4ft) ➤p.247

MAKING THE MOST OF MOISTURE

On a gentle slope, like this one, which slopes down and away from the front of the bed, the problems of gardening on a hill are less pronounced. The ground will be more evenly rich and damp and you can mix summer-flowering plants suited for the base of a slope, such as hostas, with ones that are happier at the top, like a vivid blue ceanothus.

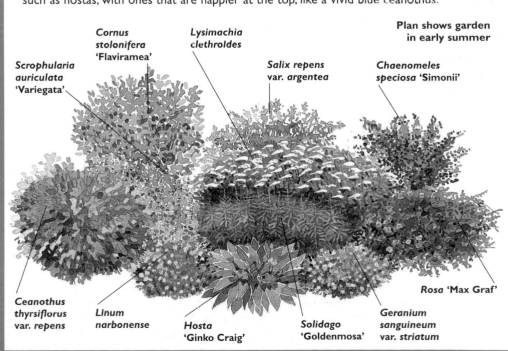

Plan shows garden in early summer

Cornus stolonifera 'Flaviramea'

Lysimachia clethroides

Salix repens var. argentea

Chaenomeles speciosa 'Simonii'

Scrophularia auriculata 'Variegata'

Ceanothus thyrsiflorus var. repens

Linum narbonense

Hosta 'Ginko Craig'

Solidago 'Goldenmosa'

Geranium sanguineum var. striatum

Rosa 'Max Graf'

In the deep shade of a spreading tree, light is not the only thing in short supply. A dense canopy can stop rain reaching the soil, and the tree makes great demands on the ground water, leaving other plants struggling to find enough food and moisture.

The leaves of Hedera helix 'Goldchild' are bright green with a paler centre and yellow margin when young, but take on a blue-green hue as they mature.

If you have conifers in your garden, you will find that the earth beneath them remains dry all year round. Any rain that does get through is slow to soak through the waterproof layer of fallen pine needles, and then drains quickly away through the coarse, light soil.

Even deciduous trees cast dense shade when they are in full leaf, so that the soil beneath may only see sunlight at midday on a clear winter day.

Plant blocks of evergreen colour

The choice of plants that will thrive here is limited, but those that are suitable will soon spread to fill your space with interesting flowers and foliage. The key to success is to choose a few drought-loving plants that do not need sunshine or rich soils, and to plant them in blocks (see plan, far right), rather than embarking on an ambitious, complex planting plan.

Variegated, ground-covering, foliage plants, such as **arums** and **ivies** (*Hedera*), are good space-fillers, and you can introduce spots of colour in the form of autumn berries on a *Ruscus*, spring bulbs such as blue *Muscari* and, in summer, purple *Violas* and periwinkles (*Vinca*) and bright yellow *Lamium*.

Trees scatter a natural mulch

A network of tree roots just beneath the surface may make it almost impossible to dig or even hoe the soil, but the tree will do the work for you, applying its own annual mulch to enrich the soil beneath as the leaves fall. Rake up pine needles, which are slow to decompose, but leave other leaves to rot, just clearing away any that are smothering young plants.

One great advantage of this environment is that weeds find it very difficult to get established. Wind-blown seeds are unlikely to penetrate the dense canopy, and once any established weeds are uprooted, they are reluctant to reappear.

Flowers and variegated leaves add colour and light in shady corners. The yellowy foliage of this elaeagnus complements the bright early spring blooms of the mahonia.

Expert's Selection

Herbaceous perennials

Berries and seedpods have a robust appeal and do better than flowers in deep shade. Plant *Iris foetidissima* near the back of the border where you will not crush its stinking leaves.

***Arum italicum* 'Marmoratum'**♀
❀ Cream spathe • Early summer
❧ Red • Late summer
h. 40cm (16in) s. 20cm (8in) ➤p.96
***Iris foetidissima*♀** ❧ Orange-scarlet
seeds in pods • Autumn–winter
h. 50cm (20in) ➤p.136
***Lamium galeobdolon*
'Florentinum'** ∅ Green and silver
∅ Purple • Winter ❀ Yellow
Spring–summer • h. 60cm (2ft)
s. 75cm (2½ft) ➤p.139

***Viola cornuta*♀** ❀ Lilac or white
Midsummer • h. 15cm (6in)
s. 30cm (1ft) ➤p.178

Climbers & shrubs

Variegated foliage lights up a dark corner, adding colour and texture. Choose shrubs with autumn and winter interest, such as a *Ruscus* or a *Mahonia*, that will have their chance to shine when the tree above is bare.

***Elaeagnus* x *ebbengei* 'Gilt Edge'**♀
∅ Green and gold • h.&s. 3m (10ft)
➤p.204
***Euonymus fortunei* 'Coloratus'**
∅ Dark green ∅ Purple-red • Late
autumn–winter • h. 3m (10ft)
s. 2m (7ft) ➤p.205
***Hedera helix* 'Goldchild'**♀ ∅ Blue-
green, grey-green and yellow
h.&s 1.2m (4ft) ➤p.212

***Mahonia aquifolium* 'Apollo'**♀
❀ Golden yellow • Late winter–late
spring ∅ Dark green ∅ Greenish
purple • Winter • h. 1m (3ft)
s. 60cm (2ft) ➤p.227
Ruscus aculeatus ∅ Light green
❧ Bright red • Autumn
h.&s. 1m (3ft) ➤p.246
Vinca major* var. *oxyloba ❀ Dark
violet • Spring–early summer
h. 35cm (14in) s. indefinite ➤p.259

Bulbs

The traditional spring woodland is ablaze with colourful bulbs, but many demand sun. Muscari will thrive in all but the very deepest shade.

***Muscari armeniacum* 'Blue Spike'**
❀ Blue • Spring • h. 15–20cm (6–8in)
➤p.319

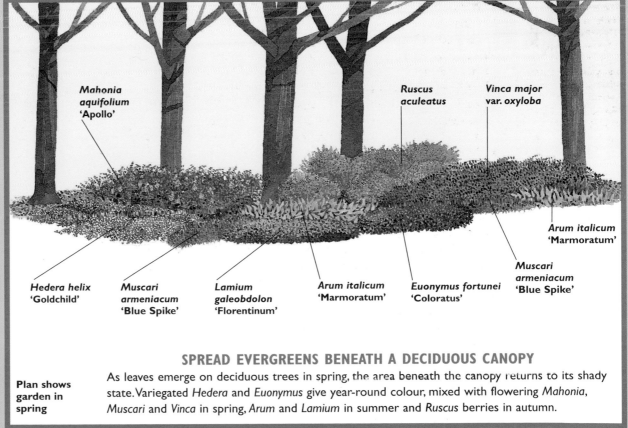

Mahonia aquifolium 'Apollo'

Ruscus aculeatus

Vinca major var. oxyloba

Arum italicum 'Marmoratum'

Muscari armeniacum 'Blue Spike'

Hedera helix 'Goldchild'

Muscari armeniacum 'Blue Spike'

Lamium galeobdolon 'Florentinum'

Arum italicum 'Marmoratum'

Euonymus fortunei 'Coloratus'

Plan shows garden in spring

SPREAD EVERGREENS BENEATH A DECIDUOUS CANOPY

As leaves emerge on deciduous trees in spring, the area beneath the canopy returns to its shady state. Variegated *Hedera* and *Euonymus* give year-round colour, mixed with flowering *Mahonia*, *Muscari* and *Vinca* in spring, *Arum* and *Lamium* in summer and *Ruscus* berries in autumn.

Rock hard and riddled with roots, parts of your garden may seem utterly hopeless for some or all of the year. Not a ray of sunlight penetrates the leaf canopy above. The heavy clay soil is often so dry and hard that even weeds struggle to grow. And no matter where you attempt to plunge a fork, you always hit a tree root.

Under trees, the ground is often very dry, hard, and crowded with roots. The leaf canopy can act as a barrier to rainfall and sunlight. With deciduous trees, this is only really a problem in summer, but evergreens such as conifers provide cover all year round, often leaving the soil beneath constantly dry. Also, pine needles do not rot quickly, and cannot be incorporated into the earth; in fact, they act as a barrier against any moisture trying to trickle through. Heavy soil absorbs few nutrients, too, so it is likely to be impoverished.

A low-maintenance woody glade
Do not despair. It is possible to create a glorious, woodland garden. The secret lies in preparing your site well before planting. Once established, your plants will make few demands. What is more, weeds will never be a problem – they simply will not grow.

Do the groundwork
It is worth taking the time to prepare this kind of site properly. Start by breaking up the soil, removing small, surface tree roots if necessary. Then dig in plenty of organic material. Household compost is ideal. Fertilise the site regularly with both quick and slow-release feeds. In autumn, gather up fallen leaves, and dig in those too, along with plenty of heavy, wet manure – pig is the best.

Your plants will settle in quicker in really damp ground, so ideally plant them after heavy rainfall. If you have the time and patience, plant through plant membrane or black polythene covered with bark chippings to conserve moisture. New growth should be well watered throughout its first season.

Inevitably, in such a challenging environment, some plants take a while to become established. Select the right combination from the suggestions here, and you will be surprised how easy it is to turn a dull patch into a haven of tranquil beauty.

Viburnum davidii

Polygonatum biflorum

Aucuba japonica f. 'Longifolia'

Polypodium vulgare

Symphytum grandiflorum 'Hidcote Pink'

Geranium phaeum

Prunus laurocerasus 'Otto Luyken'

SMALL INVESTMENT YIELDS RICH REWARDS
Dense, ground-covering perennials, and a mix of contrasting shrubs are the choices for a shaded area of heavy clay soil. Once established, they will provide years of beauty and interest, particularly in the summer months.

Plan shows garden in midsummer

The striking coppery leaves of a Heuchera bring warmth and contrast to a mass of varied greens, while flowers, such as Primulas, splash eye-catching colour across this woodland glade.

Expert's Selection

Herbaceous perennials

Blend ground-covering perennials to create a backdrop for the dots of flower colour that arrive in spring.

Geranium phaeum ❀ Purplish red
Spring–autumn • *h.* 60cm (2ft)
s. 45cm (1½ft) ➤p.122
***Heuchera micrantha* var. *diversifolia* 'Palace Purple'**♀
❀ Creamy white • Early–midsummer
∅ Copper-purple • Autumn–winter
h. 60cm (2ft) *s.* 30cm (1ft) ➤p.133
Polygonatum biflorum ❀ White
Late spring • *h.* 2m (7ft)
s. 75cm (2½ft) ➤p.159
Polypodium vulgare ∅ Green
h. 40cm (16in) *s.* 60cm (2ft) ➤p.117
Primula pulverulenta♀ ❀ Dark pink
Spring • *h.* 80cm (32in)
s. 20cm (8in) ➤p.161
***Symphytum* 'Hidcote Pink'**
❀ Pink and white • Late spring
h.&s. 45cm (1½ft) ➤p.171

Climbers & shrubs

A mix of evergreen shrubs give the site a framework. Those with bright autumn and winter berries provide colour when flowers are long gone.

***Aucuba japonica* f. 'Longifolia'**
∅ Pale green ❧ Bright red
Autumn • *h.&s.* 2m (7ft) ➤p.185
***Ilex crenata* 'Convexa'**♀
∅ Dark green ❧ Black, white or
yellow • Autumn–winter
h. 5m (16ft) *s.* 4m (13ft) ➤p.217
***Prunus laurocerasus* 'Otto Luyken'**♀ ❀ White • Mid spring
❧ Purple • Early autumn ∅ Dark
green • *h.* 1.2m (4ft) *s.* 1.5m (5ft)
➤p.235
Viburnum davidii♀ ❀ White • Early
summer ❧ Iridescent blue • All
winter • *h.&s.* 1.5m (5ft) ➤p.258
***Vinca minor* 'Atropurpurea'**♀
❀ Purple • Spring–early summer
h. 20cm (8in) *s.* indefinite ➤p.259

Along the leafy woodland margin, the ground is dappled with sunlight, filtering through the outer branches of the trees. If you are lucky enough to have such a patch that is blessed with light workable soil, it will make an ideal site for some of the loveliest plants around.

Crocuses and winter **aconites** that brighten the gloom of late winter; arches of **Solomon's seal**, bearing elegant, bell-shaped flowers from early spring well into summer; shade-loving, bushy evergreens, some dotted with bright berries in late autumn and winter – all will thrive readily in light soil with just a gentle trickle of light spilling through the edge of the leaf canopy. The right mix, selected for variety and timing of foliage and flower can create a care-free edge-of-the-wood garden, alive with eye-catching colour throughout the year.

Sweet perfume wafts from the flowers of Lonicera periclymenum 'Serotina' all summer long.

Plants easily become rooted in light soil, so are quick to settle in. But moisture, along with nutrients, can slip through such soil fairly rapidly as well. Before you plant, therefore, work your site over as thoroughly and deeply as possible. Then dig in plenty of organic material, such as compost and manure, and water well, especially if rainfall is low.

Keeping plants happy

For an easy time later on, get them off to a good start by planting through a water-retaining membrane, covered with bark or wood chippings. This type of mulch will hide the membrane and help to conserve moisture. Check all new plants regularly to make sure they do not dry out, and fertilise at fairly frequent intervals.

Once they are established, your plants will make few demands. Keep an eye open, however, for a sooty mould that may form on foliage – this is caused by honeydew dropping from aphids in overhead branches. And watch out, too, for falling leaves in autumn. Too many can smother new or small plants, so pick them off where necessary.

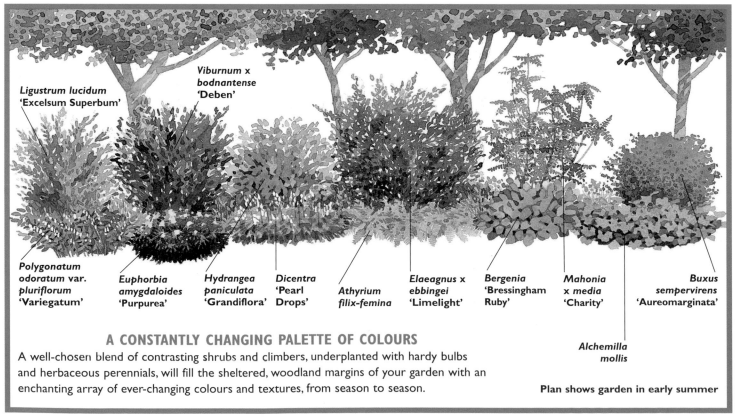

Ligustrum lucidum 'Excelsum Superbum'

Viburnum x bodnantense 'Deben'

Polygonatum odoratum var. pluriflorum 'Variegatum'

Euphorbia amygdaloides 'Purpurea'

Hydrangea paniculata 'Grandiflora'

Dicentra 'Pearl Drops'

Athyrium filix-femina

Elaeagnus x ebbingei 'Limelight'

Bergenia 'Bressingham Ruby'

Mahonia x media 'Charity'

Buxus sempervirens 'Aureomarginata'

Alchemilla mollis

A CONSTANTLY CHANGING PALETTE OF COLOURS

A well-chosen blend of contrasting shrubs and climbers, underplanted with hardy bulbs and herbaceous perennials, will fill the sheltered, woodland margins of your garden with an enchanting array of ever-changing colours and textures, from season to season.

Plan shows garden in early summer

Expert's Selection

Herbaceous perennials

Illuminate your site with a range of low to medium height perennials to form a blanket of floral colour.

Alchemilla mollis♀ ❀ Yellow-green Early summer ∅ Lime-green *h.* 50cm (20in) *s.* 75cm (2½ft) ➤p.90

Athyrium filix-femina♀ ∅ Green Spring–early summer • *h.* 30cm (1ft) *s.* 40cm (16in) ➤p.117

Bergenia 'Bressingham Ruby' ❀ Reddish pink • Spring ∅ Beetroot-red • Winter *h.&s.* 35cm (14in) ➤p.100

Corydalis flexuosa 'Purple Leaf' ❀ Blue • Late spring–midsummer *h.&s.* 30cm (1ft) ➤p.106

Dicentra 'Pearl Drops' ❀ White Late spring–summer • *h.* 30cm (1ft) *s.* 45cm (1½ft) ➤p.108

Euphorbia amygdaloides 'Purpurea' ∅ Maroon-red • Early spring ❀ Lime-green • Late spring–early summer • *h.&s.* 45cm (1½ft) ➤p.118

Hosta 'Gold Standard'♀ ❀ Lavender ∅ Green • Summer *h.* 50cm (20in) *s.* 1m (3ft) ➤p.135

Polygonatum odoratum var. pluriflorum 'Variegatum' ❀ White Late spring • *h.* 60cm (2ft) *s.* 30cm (1ft) ➤p.159

Cimbers & shrubs

Climbers and bushy shrubs shape the site. Focus on creating an interesting blend of leaf colour and texture.

Buxus sempervirens 'Aureo-marginata' ∅ Dark green with yellow edge • *h.&s.* 4m (13ft) ➤p.191

The woodland edge bursts into life in spring, when the arching stems of Polygonatum are fringed with white, and Corydalis carpets the earth with colour.

Clematis montana var. rubens 'Mayleen' ❀ Pink • Late spring *h.* 8m (27ft) *s.* 4m (13ft) ➤p.198

Elaeagnus x ebbingei 'Limelight' ∅ Green and gold • *h.&s.* 3m (10ft) ➤p.204

Hydrangea paniculata 'Grandiflora'♀ ❀ Whitish pink Late summer–early autumn *h.* 3m (10ft) *s.* 1.5m (5ft) ➤p.215

Ligustrum lucidum 'Excelsum Superbum'♀ ∅ Variegated *h.* 1.5m (5ft) *s.* 1.2m (4ft) ➤p.224

Lonicera periclymenum 'Serotina'♀ ❀ Purple, red and white • Mid–late summer • *h.* 1.8m (6ft) after 5 years ➤p.225

Mahonia x media 'Charity'♀ ❀ Yellow • Late autumn–early spring *h.&s.* 3m (10ft) ➤p.227

Viburnum x bodnantense 'Deben' ❀ White • Winter • *h.* 3m (10ft) *s.* 1.8m (6ft) ➤p.258

Bulbs

Planting a selection of bulbs will guarantee a sea of colour in your garden, even in the short, dark days of late winter and early spring.

Crocus cartwrightianus 'Cream Beauty'♀ ❀ Clotted cream • Late winter • *h.* 10cm (4in) ➤p.310

Crocus pulchellus♀ ❀ Pale lilac Mid–late autumn • *h.* 18cm (7in) ➤p.310

Eranthis hyemalis♀ ❀ Yellow Early spring • *h.* 5–8cm (2–3in) ➤p.314

Eranthis hyemalis Tubergenii Group 'Guinea Gold'♀ ❀ Yellow Early spring • *h.* 8cm (3in) ➤p.314

Scilla bifolia♀ ❀ Violet-blue • Early spring • *h.* 15cm (6in) ➤p.323

Scilla siberica 'Spring Beauty' ❀ Vivid blue • Early spring *h.* 15cm (6in) ➤p.323

SHADED SITE UNDER TREES
DAPPLED SHADE, HEAVY SOIL

Moist and fertile, heavy soil provides an excellent growing medium, even in the shade cast by a tree. Dappled sunlight filters through loosely open trees or branches at the edges of the canopy providing light shade, where many garden plants will thrive. With very little trouble, you can soon have a care-free garden, packed with flowers.

The gentle light that reaches the soil beneath a tree is perfect for woodland plants, such as **hellebores** and **bluebells** (*Hyacinthoides*, see page 316) but, more surprisingly, can also make just the right spot for a **rose** or **ornamental currant** (*Ribes*). Variegated shrubs, like an *Aucuba japonica*, **euonymus** or upright **holly** will stand out in the shade and many are evergreens, so provide bold clumps of colour when the trees above are bare.

The first time it rains in your new garden you will know if you have heavy soil, because it will clump together and stick to your boots the moment you walk outside. You can free up the texture of the soil by digging in plenty of organic material before you plant, and heaping on mulch on a regular basis.

This will widen the variety of plants that will thrive in the garden, but be prepared for some hard work. Digging heavy soil can be tough and you may find yourself battling against tightly packed roots. You can remove any fibrous surface roots that are in your way without damaging the tree, but working with the situation you have will be much easier.

Let the soil work hard for you

Heavy soils, particularly in shade, can be relied on to retain moisture and nutrients for a long time, so they will minimise the task of feeding and watering. Even so, in the heat of summer, with the demands of mature trees in full leaf, the ground may set dry and hard. Planting through a layer of water-retaining membrane, weighed down with a layer of chippings, will seal in moisture and keep down weeds, too.

Hungry trees will also take more than their fair share of nutrients, so add a top-dressing of slow-release fertiliser in spring to give the soil a boost.

Puschkinias, which are commonly known as 'squills', will naturalise in short grass or spread freely in a border. Their spikes of flowers appear in spring.

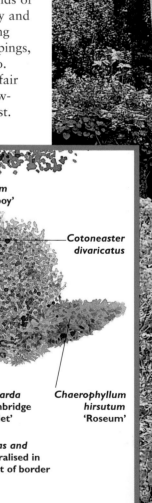

This multi-hued, evergreen backdrop is punctuated by a splash of seasonal colour from the lavender blue, summer blooms of a trailing Campanula (see page 103).

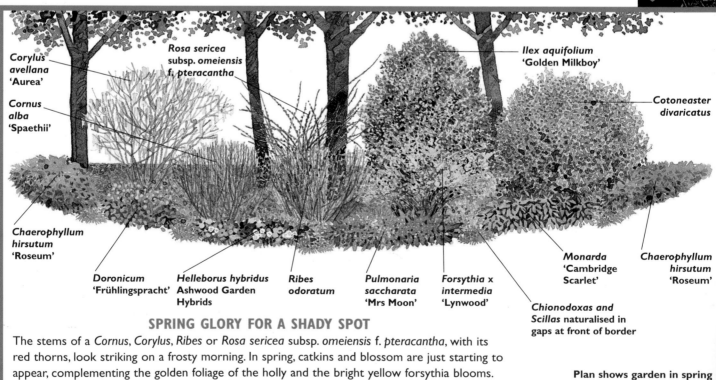

Corylus avellana 'Aurea'

Cornus alba 'Spaethii'

Rosa sericea subsp. omeiensis f. pteracantha

Ilex aquifolium 'Golden Milkboy'

Cotoneaster divaricatus

Chaerophyllum hirsutum 'Roseum'

Doronicum 'Frühlingspracht'

Helleborus hybridus Ashwood Garden Hybrids

Ribes odoratum

Pulmonaria saccharata 'Mrs Moon'

Forsythia x intermedia 'Lynwood'

Chionodoxas and Scillas naturalised in gaps at front of border

Monarda 'Cambridge Scarlet'

Chaerophyllum hirsutum 'Roseum'

SPRING GLORY FOR A SHADY SPOT

The stems of a *Cornus*, *Corylus*, *Ribes* or *Rosa sericea* subsp. *omeiensis* f. *pteracantha*, with its red thorns, look striking on a frosty morning. In spring, catkins and blossom are just starting to appear, complementing the golden foliage of the holly and the bright yellow forsythia blooms.

Plan shows garden in spring

Expert's Selection

Herbaceous perennials

Heavy soil is rich and fertile. Many perennials will thrive in it, even when light levels are low.

***Brunnera macrophylla* 'Langtrees'** ✿ Clear blue • Late spring *h.* 45cm (1½ft) *s.* 60cm (2ft) ➤p.101

***Chaerophyllum hirsutum* 'Roseum'** ✿ Lilac-pink • Early summer • *h.* 75cm (2½ft) *s.* 35cm (14in) ➤p.106

***Doronicum* 'Frühlingspracht'** ✿ Rich yellow • Late spring *h.* 40cm (16in) *s.* 1m (3ft) ➤p.109

***Euphorbia amygdaloides* 'Purpurea'** ⊘ Maroon-red • Early spring ✿ Lime-green • Late spring– early summer • *h.* 45–75cm (1½–2½ft) *s.* 45–60cm (1½–2ft) ➤p.118

***Helleborus hybridus* Ashwood Garden Hybrids** ✿ White, yellow, red and green • Spring *h.&s.* 45cm (1½ft) ➤p.130

***Hosta* 'June'** ✿ Greyish lavender to near white ⊘ Yellow/Blue-green Midsummer • *h.* 50cm (20in) *s.* 1m (3ft) ➤p.135

***Lamium galeobdolon* 'Hermann's Pride'** ✿ Yellow • Spring–summer *h.* 60cm (2ft) *s.* 75m (2½ft) ➤p.139

***Monarda* 'Cambridge Scarlet'**♀ ✿ Scarlet • Midsummer–autumn *h.* 1m (3ft) *s.* 45cm (1½ft) ➤p.149

***Pulmonaria saccharata* 'Mrs Moon'** ✿ Pink–violet • Spring ⊘ Spotted pale green *h.* 30cm (1ft) *s.* 60cm (2ft) ➤p.163

Climbers & shrubs

Shrubs with variegated, evergreen foliage or good late-season colour will brighten even a dull winter day.

***Aucuba japonica* 'Picturata'** ⊘ Greeny gold ❧ Bright red Autumn • *h.&s.* 2m (7ft) ➤p.185

***Clematis* 'Madame Julia Correvon'**♀ ✿ Wine-red Midsummer–early autumn *h.* 3m (10ft) *s.* 1.5m (5ft) ➤p.199

***Cornus alba* 'Spaethii'**♀ ⊘ Green and gold; Red stems • Winter ❧ Black Autumn • *h.&s.* 1.5m (5ft) ➤p.200

***Corylus avellana* 'Aurea'** ❧ Brown cobnuts • Autumn • *h.* 3m (10ft) *s.* 2.5m (8ft) ➤p.201

***Cotoneaster divaricatus* ✿** Pinkish white • Summer ❧ Red • Autumn *h.* 2.5m (8ft) *s.* 3m (10ft) ➤p.201

***Euonymus fortunei* 'Emerald 'n' Gold'**♀ ⊘ Green and gold; pinkish in winter • *h.* 3m (10ft) *s.* 2m (7ft) ➤p.205

***Forsythia* x *intermedia* 'Lynwood'**♀ ✿ Yellow • Early spring ⊘ Dark green • Late spring *h.&s.* 3m (10ft) ➤p.206

***Hydrangea paniculata* 'Grandiflora'**♀ ✿ Whitish pink Late summer–early autumn *h.* 3m (10ft) *s.* 1.5m (5ft) ➤p.215

***Ilex aquifolium* 'Golden Milkboy'**♀ ⊘ Green, gold ❧ Red • Autumn– winter • *h.* 6m (20ft) *s.* 4m (13ft) ➤p.217

***Lonicera japonica* 'Halliana'**♀ ✿ White • Mid–late summer *h.* ultimately 10m (33ft) ➤p.224

***Ribes odoratum* ✿** Yellow • Spring ⊘ Purple • Autumn • *h.&s.* 2m (7ft) ➤p.237

***Rosa sericea* subsp. *omeiensis* f. *pteracantha* ✿** White • Late spring *h.&s.* 2.5m (8ft) ➤p.242

Bulbs

Make the most of the months when the sheltering trees are bare by planting spring and autumn bulbs.

***Chionodoxa* ✿** Pink, blue or white Spring • *h.* 10–20cm (4–8in) ➤p.308

***Puschkinia* ✿** White or blue • Spring *h.* 15cm (6in) ➤p.323

***Scilla* ✿** Blue, violet, or lilac Spring–early summer; autumn– winter • *h.* 10–30cm (4–12in) ➤p.323

Deeply shaded by a tall wall, this part of the garden may never see the sun, even at the height of summer. When the soil is thin and shallow the challenge to find plants that will thrive without light, many nutrients and plentiful water is even greater. However, a little tender loving care is all it takes for the right plants to create a flourishing garden.

Tall buildings not only cast shade, but block out wind, making air in the garden stagnant. If your lawn is more moss than grass, if algae spread over uncultivated ground and your plants are prone to pests and diseases, you probably have a site like this. Choose shade-loving plants and look out for signs of sickness and you are already half way to success.

In the 'rain shadow' close to the wall the ground is likely to be very dry, but where the rain does wet the ground the light soil will retain its moisture better than in sunny gardens, allowing you to grow plants that may not normally be suitable for light soil. Avoid sun-lovers, though – they will strain to reach the light and may become weak and leggy.

Expert's Selection

Out of the rain shadow
Herbaceous perennials
Choose perennials that will provide a range of colours and textures.

Acorus calamus ∅ Bright green
h. 1.5m (5ft) s. 60cm (2ft) ➤p.334
Aruncus dioicus ❀ Creamy white
Midsummer • h. 1.8m (6ft)
s. 1.2m (4ft) ➤p.95
Astilbe x arendsii 'Fanal'♀
❀ Scarlet • Summer • h. 60cm (2ft)
s. 40cm (16in) ➤p.98
Astilbe x arendsii 'Brautschleier'♀
❀ White • Early summer
h. 75cm (2½ft) s. 40cm (16in) ➤p.98
Astrantia major ❀ White
Midsummer • h. 75cm (2½ft)
s. 45cm (1½ft) ➤p.99
Bergenia 'Bressingham Salmon'
❀ Salmon-pink • Spring ∅ Dark red
Winter • h.&s. 35cm (14in) ➤p.100

Polystichum setiferum♀ ∅ Pale green • Autumn–winter
h. 1.2m (4ft) s. 1m (3ft) ➤p.117

Climbers & shrubs
Stems and berries in strong colours add a dramatic touch to a border.

Cornus alba 'Sibirica'♀
∅ Coral-pink stems • Winter
h.&s. 1.5m (5ft) ➤p.200
Humulus lupulus ❀ Pale green hops
Autumn • h.&s. 6m (20ft) ➤p.214
Hydrangea anomela subsp.
petiolaris♀ ❀ White • Summer
h. 5m (16ft) s. 3m (10ft) ➤p.215
Sarcococca hookeriana var.
humilis ❀ Pinky white • Winter
◄ Black • Summer
h.&s. 60cm (2ft) ➤p.249
Skimmia japonica 'Veitchii'
❀ White • Late spring ◄ Bright red
Winter ∅ Bright green
h.&s. 1.5m (5ft) ➤p.250

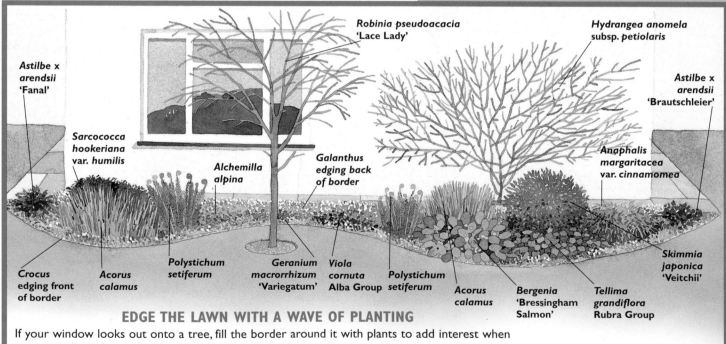

Robinia pseudoacacia 'Lace Lady'

Hydrangea anomela subsp. petiolaris

Astilbe x arendsii 'Fanal'

Astilbe x arendsii 'Brautschleier'

Sarcococca hookeriana var. humilis

Alchemilla alpina

Galanthus edging back of border

Anaphalis margaritacea var. cinnamomea

Crocus edging front of border

Acorus calamus

Polystichum setiferum

Geranium macrorrhizum 'Variegatum'

Viola cornuta Alba Group

Polystichum setiferum

Acorus calamus

Bergenia 'Bressingham Salmon'

Tellima grandiflora Rubra Group

Skimmia japonica 'Veitchii'

A hop inches over an archway towards a late-flowering clematis (see pages 198-199) on the other side. Geraniums and Astrantia fill the foreground of this shady summer bed.

EDGE THE LAWN WITH A WAVE OF PLANTING
If your window looks out onto a tree, fill the border around it with plants to add interest when the tree is bare. *Crocus* and snowdrops (*Galanthus*) have their moment of glory, edging the border in spring before the *Alchemilla*, *Geranium* and *Viola* grow up, and supersede them.

Plan shows garden in spring

Anaphalis margaritacea* var. *cinnamomea ❀ White • Late summer–early autumn ∅ Silvery grey
h.&s. 60cm (2ft) ➤p.90

***Geranium macrorrhizum* 'Variegatum'** ❀ Soft pink • All summer ∅ Grey-green
h. 25cm (10in) s. 60cm (2ft) ➤p.123

Polypodium vulgare ∅ Green All year • h. 40cm (16in)
s. 60cm (2ft) ➤p.116

***Tellima grandiflora* Rubra Group** ❀ White • Early–midsummer ∅ Reddish • Winter • h. 75cm (2½ft)
s. 30cm (1ft) ➤p.172

***Viola cornuta* Alba Group**♥ ❀ White • Midsummer
h. 15cm (6in) s. 30m (1ft) ➤p.178

Climbers & shrubs

Cover the ground with a prostrate Cotoneaster or train an ivy over an arch for evergreen interest.

Cotoneaster horizontalis♥ ❀ Pink-white • Late spring ◄ Red • Autumn
h. 1m (3ft) s. 1.5m (5ft) ➤p.201

***Hedera colchica* 'Sulphur Heart'**♥ ∅ Yellowish green • h. 10m (33ft)
s. 5m (16ft) ➤p.212

Ligustrum japonicum ∅ Dark green • h. 3m (10ft) s. 2.5m (8ft)
➤p.224

Trees

An acer will thrive in a shady spot like this, with light, well-drained soil.

***Acer platanoides* 'Drummondii'**♥ ∅ Variegated • Spring and summer
h. 10m (33ft) s. 5m (16ft) ➤p.264

Bulbs

Plant drifts of muscari at the front of your border for their short, but dense spikes of colour in spring.

Muscari ❀ Blue or white • Spring
h. 15–30cm (6–12in) ➤p.319

Trees

Plant these trees where they will catch the falling rain and they will be happy in the shade of a building.

***Robinia pseudoacacia* 'Lace Lady'** ❀ White • Late spring ∅ Lime-green
h. 2.5m (8ft) s. 3m (10ft) ➤p.271

***Salix babylonica* 'Tortuosa'**♥ ❀ Green-yellow catkins • Early spring
h. 10m (33ft) s. 7m (23ft) ➤p.272

Bulbs

Spring bulbs will grow even in areas of dense shade, lighting them up.

Crocus ❀ White–yellow, purple and mixed colours • Late winter–spring
h. 5–13cm (2–5in) ➤p.310

Galanthus ❀ White • Late winter–spring • h. 10–23cm (4–9in) ➤p.314

Scilla ❀ Blue • Spring or autumn
h. 10–30cm (4–12in) ➤p.323

In the rain shadow
Herbaceous perennials

In the dry soil by a wall, drought-tolerant species are the best choice.

Acanthus spinosus♥ ❀ White-mauve • Early summer • h. 1.2m (4ft)
s. 60cm (2ft) ➤p.88

Alchemilla alpina ❀ Yellow-green Midsummer ∅ Dark green
h. 15cm (6in) s. 45cm (1½ft) ➤p.90

If you have a north-facing plot of sticky clay, you will know the meaning of damp and heavy shade. Even in high summer some plants will never feel the warming caress of the sun, but do not despair: with a little effort and the right plants you can still create a garden to enjoy.

The shade of a building is unforgiving. The rain shadow, the sheltered ground next to the structure, is permanently dry, while farther away, ground becomes wet, but is slow to dry out without the help of the sun, becoming waterlogged below and hard and slimy on top.

Walking on this ground when it is wet or frosty will only compact the soil further, so plant a backbone of variegated shrubs, such as *Aucuba* or *Euonymus*, and admire their golden tones from inside the house during autumn and winter.

Heavy soils retain moisture and nutrients well, and many lovely plants will thrive here, despite the gloom. Woodland flowers, such as *Crocus* and *Chionodoxa* will add a splash of colour under your shrubs, but be careful in your choice of perennials.

Even with constant attention a lawn is unlikely to thrive, so lay hard landscaping and give it style with a few sculptural plants in containers (see page 336).

Drumstick primulas, P. denticulata, bear clusters of flowers on tall stems. Group them at the front of a bed on moist ground.

Expert's Selection

In rain shadow
Herbaceous perennials

Softly muted colours in flowers or foliage work well in heavy shade.

Helleborus foetidus♀ ❀ Pale green
Late winter–early spring
h. 75cm (2½ft) *s.* 60cm (2ft) ➤**p.130**

Hosta undulata var. albomarginata ∅ Green with white edge ❀ Lavender • Early–midsummer
h. 35cm (14in) *s.* 45cm (1½ft)
➤**p.134**

Persicaria campanulata ❀ Pink
Summer–autumn • *h.&s.* 1m (3ft)
➤**p.156**

Primula denticulata♀ ❀ Mauve
Early spring–early summer • *h.* 40cm (16in) *s.* 20cm (8in) ➤**p.161**

Climbers & shrubs

Smother a shade-casting wall with climbers tolerant of low light and plant drought-hardy shrubs nearby.

Hypericum x inodorum **'Elstead'**
❀ Yellow • All summer ❧ Pinkish red
∅ Green • *h.&s.* 1.2m (4ft) ➤**p.216**

Ilex x altaclarensis **'Belgica Aurea'**♀ ∅ Grey-green
h. 12m (40ft) *s.* 5m (16ft) ➤**p.217**

Lonicera pileata ∅ Dark green
❀ White • Late spring • *h.* 60cm (2ft)
s. 2.5m (8ft) ➤**p.225**

Parthenocissus henryana♀ ∅ Deep scarlet • Autumn • *h.* 10m (33ft)
s. 6m (20ft) ➤**p.230**

Philadelphus **'Avalanche'** ❀ White
Early–midsummer • *h.* 1.5m (5ft)
s. 75cm (2½ft)➤**p.232**

Pleioblastus auricomus♀ ∅ Yellow and green leaves, purplish stems
h. 1m (3ft) *s.* 60cm (2ft) ➤**p.186**

Vinca minor **'Argenteovariegata'**♀
❀ Violet blue • Spring–early summer
∅ Green and yellow • *h.* 20cm (8in)
s. 75cm (2½ft) ➤**p.259**

Bulbs

Bring cheering splashes of colour to the front of a border by planting ranks of mixed bulbs.

Cyclamen hederifolium♀ ❀ Pink
Autumn • *h.* 13cm (5in) ➤**p.311**

Oxalis tetraphylla **'Iron Cross'**
❀ Reddish purple • Summer
h. 15cm (6in) ➤**p.322**

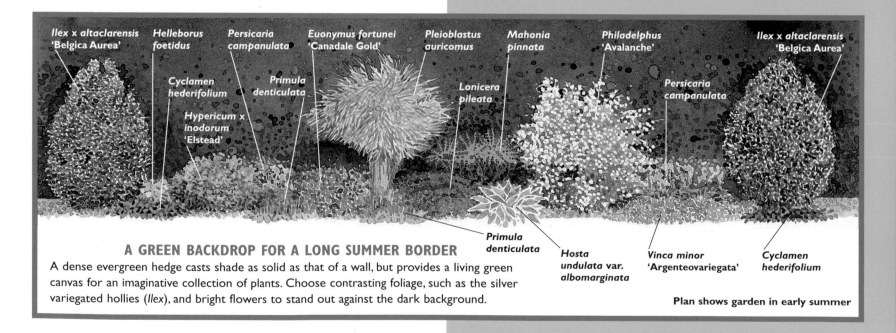

Ilex x altaclarensis 'Belgica Aurea' — *Helleborus foetidus* — *Persicaria campanulata* — *Euonymus fortunei 'Canadale Gold'* — *Pleioblastus auricomus* — *Mahonia pinnata* — *Philadelphus 'Avalanche'* — *Ilex x altaclarensis 'Belgica Aurea'*

Cyclamen hederifolium — *Primula denticulata* — *Hypericum x inodorum 'Elstead'* — *Lonicera pileata* — *Persicaria campanulata*

Primula denticulata — *Hosta undulata var. albomarginata* — *Vinca minor 'Argenteovariegata'* — *Cyclamen hederifolium*

A GREEN BACKDROP FOR A LONG SUMMER BORDER

A dense evergreen hedge casts shade as solid as that of a wall, but provides a living green canvas for an imaginative collection of plants. Choose contrasting foliage, such as the silver variegated hollies (*Ilex*), and bright flowers to stand out against the dark background.

Plan shows garden in early summer

An Elaeagnus, growing over the low wall, will thrive in rich, heavy soil, even in the dense shade of a house. Hostas and other woodland plants make excellent companions.

Out of rain shadow

Herbaceous perennials

Choose perennials that thrive in low light and are moisture lovers.

Geranium phaeum ❀ Purplish red Spring–autumn • *h.* 60cm (2ft) *s.* 45cm (1½ft) ➤p.123

Iris foetidissima ♀ ❧ Orange-scarlet seeds in pods • Autumn–winter *h.* 50cm (20in) ➤p.136

Lamium maculatum **'White Nancy'** ♀ ❀ White • Late spring *h.* 15cm (6in) *s.* 1m (3ft) ➤p.139

Climbers & shrubs

Variegated foliage or bright flowers and berries shine out in dull spots.

Aucuba japonica **'Crotonifolia'** ♀ ∅ Greeny gold ❧ Bright red Autumn • *h.&s.* 2m (7ft) ➤p.185

Berberis x stenophylla ♀ ❀ Yellow Spring ❧ Purple • Autumn *h.&s.* 2.5m (8ft) ➤p.188

Elaeagnus angustifolia ∅ Silvery green ❧ Orange • Autumn *h.&s.* 3m (10ft) ➤p.204

Euonymus fortunei **'Canadale Gold'** ∅ Dark green and gold *h.* 45m (1½ft) *s.* 60cm (2ft) ➤p.205

Mahonia pinnata ❀ Yellow • Early spring ∅ Bronze, turning to bright green • *h.&s.* 1m (3ft) ➤p.227

Trees

An acer will withstand the gloom in a garden of heavy shade.

Acer negundo **'Flamingo'** ♀ ∅ Green, pink and white variegated Spring–summer • *h.* 6m (20ft) *s.* 4m (13ft) ➤p.264

Bulbs

Most lilies prefer some shade; white ones are particularly dramatic.

Lilium speciosum var. *album* ❀ White • Late summer • *h.* 1.2m (4ft) ➤p.318

Sheltered and shaded by walls and fences, most gardens experience partial shade. Some parts will be in constant shade, or rain shadow, while others get all the light available but for differing periods during the day. If your garden has light, easily worked soil, you have additional potential for creating a flourishing display all year round.

A gentle climate of sunshine and shade, combined with light soil, gives you plenty to work with. Digging this type of soil is simple, and young plants establish easily, provided they have plenty of water. Usually moist, light soils dry out in summer, so your plants will need extra watering. Keep an eye on those at the tops of slopes, where moisture drains rapidly.

When planting against a wall or fence, check for rain shadows – areas of dry, poor soil, that get no rain. Demanding hedge roots also mean meagre soil. Before planting, dig in lots of organic material, and add slow-release fertilisers. You can minimise any water loss with a water-retaining membrane or a mulch, which will also boost humus levels.

If you want a lawn in your garden, choose a seed mixture suited to shady areas. Let your grass grow long to deter moss.

The frothy pink flowerheads of Filipendula purpurea stand elegantly above darker leaves.

Expert's Selection

Not in rain shadow
Herbaceous perennials

With water, light soil and a constant supply of light, perennials will flourish from spring to autumn.

Doronicum x excelsum 'Harpur Crewe' ❀ Rich yellow • Late spring h.&s. 1m (3ft) ➤p.109

Epimedium x youngianum ❀ Greenish white or pale pink • Mid –late spring • h. 20–30cm (8–12in) s. 30m (1ft) ➤p.112

Filipendula purpurea♀ ❀ Purple-red • Mid–late summer ∅ Bright green • h. 1.2cm (4ft) s. 60cm (2ft) ➤p.120

Hosta 'Sagae'♀ ❀ White Midsummer ∅ Green and cream h. 1m (3ft) s. 1.5m (5ft) ➤p.134

Lysimachia punctata 'Alexander' ❀ Bright yellow • Mid–late summer ∅ Green and cream, pinky in spring h. 1m (3ft) s. 60cm (2ft) ➤p.146

Matteuccia struthiopteris♀ ∅ Green • Autumn-winter h. 1.5m (5ft) s. 1m (3ft) ➤p.117

Persicaria amplexicaulis 'Inverleith' ❀ Dark red Midsummer–early autumn h.&s. Up to 45cm (1½ft) ➤p.156

Solidago cutleri ❀ Bright yellow Late summer–early autumn h. 45cm (1½ft) s. 30cm (1ft) ➤p.169

Climbers & shrubs

Bright foliage and lush blooms make an enticing, ever-changing formation.

Chamaecyparis obtusa 'Crippsii'♀ ∅ Greeny yellow • h. 10m (33ft) s. 3m (10ft) ➤p.196

Forsythia 'Golden Times' ❀ Yellow Early spring ∅ Golden yellow • Late spring • h. 1.8m (6ft) ➤p.206

Hebe 'Red Edge'♀ ❀ Pale violet Summer ∅ Grey-green, with red h.&s. 60cm (2ft) ➤p.209

Hypericum androsaemum 'Albury Purple' ❀ Yellow • Summer ◀ Cerise ∅ Green • h.&s. 1.2m (4ft) ➤p.216

Kerria japonica 'Picta' ❀ Golden • Mid–late spring ∅ Grey-green and cream • h. 1.2m (4ft) s. 2m (7ft) ➤p.220

Nandina domestica 'Richmond' ❀ Cream • Midsummer ∅ Reddish purple • Autumn and winter h. 2.5m (8ft) s. 1.5m (5ft) ➤p.227

Rosa 'Alberic Barbier'♀ ❀ Creamy white • Early summer • h. 4.5m (15ft) ➤p.244

Weigela 'Briant Rubidor' ❀ Red Late spring–early summer ∅ Yellow h.&s. 1.8m (6ft) ➤p.259

Trees

As beautiful close-up as from a distance, trees can bring intricate detail to a planting display.

Acer pseudoplatanus 'Nizetii' ∅ Pale green, white and purple h.&s. 12m (40ft) ➤p.264

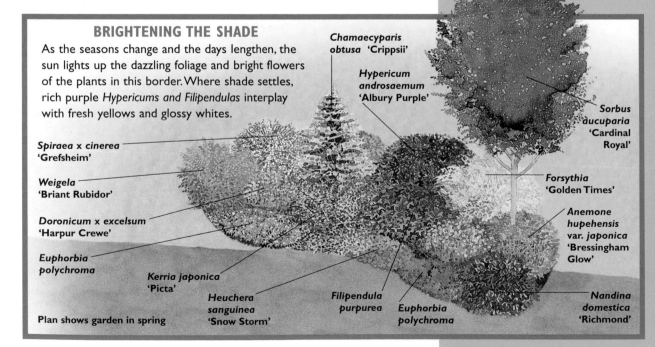

BRIGHTENING THE SHADE

As the seasons change and the days lengthen, the sun lights up the dazzling foliage and bright flowers of the plants in this border. Where shade settles, rich purple *Hypericums and Filipendulas* interplay with fresh yellows and glossy whites.

Chamaecyparis obtusa 'Crippsii'

Hypericum androsaemum 'Albury Purple'

Sorbus aucuparia 'Cardinal Royal'

Spiraea x cinerea 'Grefsheim'

Weigela 'Briant Rubidor'

Doronicum x excelsum 'Harpur Crewe'

Forsythia 'Golden Times'

Anemone hupehensis var. japonica 'Bressingham Glow'

Euphorbia polychroma

Kerria japonica 'Picta'

Heuchera sanguinea 'Snow Storm'

Filipendula purpurea

Euphorbia polychroma

Nandina domestica 'Richmond'

Plan shows garden in spring

A harmonious combination of Persicaria amplexicaulis 'Inverleith', Lysimachia punctata 'Alexander' (background) and a variegated Hosta – all plants that thrive in moist, shady conditions.

Crataegus 'Autumn Glory' ❀ White • Spring ∅ Dark green ⚘ Bright red • Autumn h.&s. 6m (20ft) ➤p.266

Bulbs

You can fill any bare patch with dazzling colour, and in light soil bulbs will grow with ease.

Cyclamen hederifolium ♀ ❀ Pale to deep pink • Autumn • h. 13cm (5in) ➤p.311
Hyacinthus ❀ Various • Early–mid spring • h. 20–30cm (8–12in) ➤p.316
Lilium pyrenaicum ♀ ❀ Bright yellow with purple spots • Early summer • h. 1.2m (4ft) ➤p.318

In rain shadow
Herbaceous perennials

The dryer, poorer soil found in a rain shadow can, with the right attention, be perfect for some flowering perennials.

Anemone hupehensis var. japonica 'Bressingham Glow' ❀ Purply pink Late summer–early autumn h. 1.2m (4ft) s. 45cm (1½ft) ➤p.91
Euphorbia polychroma ♀ ∅ Dark green, red, purple • Autumn ❀ Bright yellow • Mid spring h.&s. 60cm (2ft) ➤p.119
Geranium procurrens ❀ Dark pinky purple • Midsummer– autumn ∅ Green • h. 15cm (6in) s. 1m (3ft) ➤p.122
Hemerocallis 'Stella de Oro' ♀ ❀ Bright yellow • Midsummer h. 30cm (1ft) s. 45cm (1½ft) ➤p.132
Heuchera sanguinea 'Snow Storm' ❀ Red • Early summer ∅ Dark green, marbled with silvery white; flushed pink in winter. h. 45cm (1½ft) s. 30cm (1ft) ➤p.133
Prunella grandiflora 'Blue Loveliness' ❀ Deep lilac blue Summer ∅ Green • h. 30cm (1ft) s. 1m (3ft) ➤p.162

Climbers & shrubs

In darker spaces, bright flowers and variegated foliage draw the eye.

Garrya elliptica 'James Roof' ♀ ❀ Silver-green catkins • Winter–early spring • h.&s. 2.5m (8ft) ➤p.208
Hedera colchica 'Dentata Variegata' ♀ ∅ Bright green, grey and white • h. 10m (33ft) s. 5m (16ft) ➤p.212
Jasminum x stephanense ♀ ❀ Pale pink • Early–mid summer ∅ Olive h. 5m (16ft) s. 3m (10ft) ➤p.218
Ribes speciosum ♀ ❀ Deep red Mid–late spring • h.&s. 3m (10ft) ➤p.237
Rosa 'Golden Showers' ♀ ❀ Bright yellow • Summer h. 2.5m (8ft) ➤p.245
Salix integra 'Hakuro-nishiki' ∅ Pink and white • Late spring– autumn • h.&s. 1.5m (5ft) ➤p.247
Spiraea x cinerea 'Grefsheim' ♀ ❀ White • Mid spring ∅ Grey-green h.&s. 1.8m (6ft) ➤p.253

Trees

Pockets with only light rain can play host to wonderful autumn displays.

Prunus padus 'Purple Queen' ❀ Pale pink • Late spring ∅ Coppery purple-green • h. 6m (20ft) s. 3m (10ft) ➤p.270
Sorbus aucuparia 'Cardinal Royal' ❀ White • Late spring ∅ Red and yellow ⚘ Orange-red • Autumn h. 12m (40ft) s. 5m (16ft) ➤p.273

Bulbs

Line a path by a wall with ranks of rounded Alliums and graceful Irises.

Allium cernuum ❀ Rosy purple Early summer • h. 30–60cm (1–2ft) ➤p.306
Iris danfordiae ❀ Bright yellow Late winter–early spring h. 10cm (4in) ➤p.317

A little shade, but heavy-duty soil can be a combination that leaves the surface gluey and slippery when wet and rock-hard when dry. Adding some grit and humus works wonders to improve the texture of clay and can help to make the partial shadow of buildings or fences an inviting spot for a wide variety of care-free plants.

While a heavy soil can make it difficult for new plants to get established, it also holds moisture and nutrients well, so that mature plants thrive. In areas of shade, heavy soil retains its moisture all year round, although it may become over-wet during periods of high rainfall. At the bottom of a slope the soil may even have a tendency to become waterlogged. But this is never a problem in the 'rain shadow' of a building, fence or hedge, where rain seldom falls.

Resist the urge to rush out into the garden with tools and a load of new plants on the first fine day of spring. Heavy soil takes a long time to warm up sufficiently for planting, and walking on a still wet or frosty garden will only compact the soil and make it harder to work than it already is.

The opening petals of a tulip soak up the first rays of sun in spring.

Expert's Selection

Out of rain shadow
Herbaceous perennials

Some light and moisture keep these plants happy. Heavy, nutrient-rich soil provides plenty of food to grow well.

***Anemone x hybrida* 'Honorine Jobert'** ❀ White • Late summer–early autumn • *h.* 1.5m (5ft) *s.* 60cm (2ft) ➤p.91

Brunnera macrophylla ❀ Bright blue • Spring • *h.* 45cm (1½ft) *s.* 60cm (2ft) ➤p.101

Campanula persicifolia ❀ White–violet-blue • Midsummer • *h.* 1m (3ft) *s.* 40cm (16in) ➤p.103

Climbers & shrubs

Substantial shrubs create a backbone of planting in sites where flowering perennials find it hard to flourish.

Celastrus orbiculatus ∅ Yellow Autumn • *h.* 3m (10ft) in 5 years, ultimately 12m (40ft) ➤p.195

***Deutzia scabra* 'Plena'** ❀ White and rosy purple • Early summer *h.* 3m (10ft) *s.* 1.8m (6ft) ➤p.203

***Elaeagnus pungens* 'Goldrim'** ∅ Green and gold • *h.&s.* 3m (10ft) ➤p.204

***Kerria japonica* 'Pleniflora'** ❀ Golden yellow • Late spring *h.&s.* 3m (10ft) ➤p.220

***Osmanthus heterophyllus* 'Variegatus'** ❀ White • Autumn ∅ Variegated • *h.&s.* 3m (10ft) ➤p.228

***Philadelphus* 'Belle Etoile'** ❀ White • Early–midsummer *h.&s.* 1.5m (5ft) ➤p.232

***Rosa* 'Albertine'** ❀ Warm pink Early summer • *h.* 4.5m (15ft) ➤p.244

***Syringa vulgaris* 'Congo'** ❀ Deep pink • Late spring–early summer *h.* 1.8m (6ft) *s.* 1.5m (5ft) ➤p.254

GROWING IN THE SHELTER OF A WALL

An acer forms the centrepiece of this curved border, while a rambling rose smothers the wall behind. From autumn to spring, *Colchicums* and *Cyclamen coum* fill gaps between the shrubs, taking the colour and interest right through the year.

Rosa 'Albertine'
Acer negundo 'Flamingo'
Berberis thunbergii 'Harlequin'
Syringa vulgaris 'Congo'
Deutzia scabra 'Plena'
Heuchera 'Greenfinch'
Juniperus horizontalis 'Emerald Spreader'
Plan shows garden in midsummer
Iris sibirica 'Perry's Blue'
Crocosmia 'Emberglow'
Potentilla 'Gibson's Scarlet'
Tanacetum densum subsp. *amani*

The pink blooms of Potentilla nepalensis *'Miss Wilmott' complement the bursting buds of a Regal lily (see page 319), making this a delightful, cool and shady spot to sit in on a hot summer afternoon.*

Trees

Colourful leaves or autumn berries help a tree to earn its space in a small urban garden.

***Acer negundo* 'Flamingo'** ♀
⌀ Variegated • Spring–summer
h. 6m (20ft) s. 4m (13ft) ➤p.264
***Sorbus* 'Joseph Rock'** ♀ ⌀ Red, orange and yellow ♥ Creamy yellow turning orange • Autumn
h. 6m (20ft) s. 2.5m (8ft) ➤p.273

Bulbs

Most of the favourite spring bulbs will do well in this site; the ones listed below are also good choices.

Colchicum ❀ White–pink • Autumn
h. 10–23cm (4–9in) ➤p.308
***Crocosmia* 'Emberglow'** ❀ Deep red • Early summer • h. 60cm (2ft)
➤p.309
Cyclamen coum ♀ ❀ White or pink
Winter–early spring • h. 8cm (3in)
➤p.311
Eranthis hyemalis ♀ ❀ Yellow • Early spring • h. 5–8cm (2–3in) ➤p.314

In rain shadow
Herbaceous perennials

Even in areas of dry shade, you can create a colourful garden with this selection of pretty perennials.

***Heuchera* 'Greenfinch'** ❀ Yellowish
Early summer ⌀ Dark green
h. 1m (3ft) s. 30cm (1ft) ➤p.133
***Iris sibirica* 'Perry's Blue'** ❀ Blue
Early summer • h. 1m (3ft) ➤p.136
***Monarda* 'Beauty of Cobham'** ♀
❀ Pink • Midsummer–autumn
h. 1m (3ft) s. 45cm (1½ft) ➤p.149
***Potentilla* 'Gibson's Scarlet'** ♀
❀ Bright red • Early summer
h. 45cm (1½ft) s. 60cm (2ft) ➤p.160
Tanacetum densum* subsp. *amani
⌀ Grey • h. 20cm (8in) s. 30cm (1ft)
➤p.172

Climbers & shrubs

Deep or spreading roots help shrubs to find moisture in areas that the rain does not reach.

***Berberis thunbergii* 'Harlequin'**
⌀ Purple and pink ♥ Red • Autumn
h. 1.5m (5ft) s. 1.2m (4ft) ➤p.188
***Clematis* 'General Sikorski'** ♀
❀ Mauvish blue • Early–late summer
h. 3m (10ft) s. 1m (3ft) ➤p.198
***Juniperus horizontalis* 'Emerald Spreader'** ⌀ Bright green
h. 30cm (1ft) s. 3m (10ft) ➤p.219
***Lonicera* x *heckrottii* 'Goldflame'**
❀ Pink and yellow • Mid–late summer • h. 5m (16ft) ➤p.224
***Spiraea japonica* 'Candlelight'**
❀ Pink • Mid–late summer ⌀ Yellow
h.&s. 1m (3ft) ➤p.253
***Yucca flaccida* 'Golden Sword'** ♀
❀ Creamy white • Late summer
⌀ Green with yellow banding
h.&s. 75cm (2½ft) ➤p.261

Trees

Glorious spring blossom transforms a garden and sweeps away the winter gloom in an instant.

Malus transitoria ♀ ❀ White
Spring ⌀ Yellow-red ♥ Pale yellow
Autumn h. 7m (23ft) s. 4m (13ft)
➤p.269
***Prunus* 'Taihaku'** ♀ ❀ White • Spring
⌀ Coppery green • h. 2.7m (9ft)
s. 1.5m (5ft) ➤p.270

Bulbs

Heavy soil can cause bulbs to rot in wet winters, so dry 'rain shadow' beds make excellent sites.

***Iris* 'George'** ❀ Purple • Early spring
h. 15cm (6in) ➤p.317
Tulipa ❀ Various • Late winter–late spring • h. 15–35cm (6–14in) ➤p.324

Plenty of sunlight and a breezy aspect make an open site like this a dream for most gardeners. Some delightful plants, including camellias, rhododendrons and heathers, will all flourish in this kind of soil, so fill your beds with these and other acid-loving species.

The best-known acid soil type is peat – rich, dark and crumbly – but light, sandy soils and heavy clays can also be acid (with a pH lower than 7) in certain areas of the country. A quick check of the local weeds will give you a clue to the pH: buttercups, daisies, docks and thistles all thrive on roadside verges on acid soil, and you might also notice mosses, lichens and liverworts, growing on walls.

Choose acid-loving plants for success

If your soil is very acidic (pH 4 or 5), the range of tolerant plants is quite limited, and being in an open or exposed site will eliminate more varieties, too. However, bushy *Rhododendrons* and *Azaleas*, glorious *Magnolias*, *Camellias*, lupins, heathers (*Erica*) and heathland berries, such as bilberries, will all be happy in this site.

Choose your varieties carefully: a few **clematis**, for example, thrive in strongly acid soils, while others cannot tolerate it; similarly, only certain varieties of carnation (*Dianthus*) will do well. Sweetening the soil by adding powdered limestone or ground chalk once in a while will widen your planting possibilities with very little effort.

Stand up to the elements

The sunlight that fills an open garden is a blessing for most plants, but the wind that may come with it can be more of a problem. Plant firmly in peaty soils, treading in well to prevent 'wind-rock' lifting your plants out of the ground. Use stakes on heavy soil to avoid compacting the ground and leaving the surface as impenetrable as concrete.

Dig in grit and organic material to lighten heavy soil and try to fertilise regularly with quick-release feeds. Very acidic soil may 'lock up' the nutrients, leaving plants with deficiencies: look out for signs of discoloured or dropping leaves.

Grow a magnolia for its glorious waxy blooms and delicious fragrance. Some varieties, such as M. liliiflora 'Nigra' (above), have upright, goblet-shaped flowers, others are open and star-like.

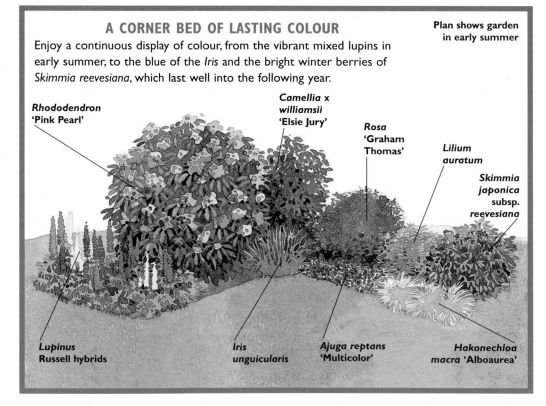

A CORNER BED OF LASTING COLOUR

Enjoy a continuous display of colour, from the vibrant mixed lupins in early summer, to the blue of the *Iris* and the bright winter berries of *Skimmia reevesiana*, which last well into the following year.

Plan shows garden in early summer

Rhododendron 'Pink Pearl'

Camellia x williamsii 'Elsie Jury'

Rosa 'Graham Thomas'

Lilium auratum

Skimmia japonica subsp. *reevesiana*

Lupinus Russell hybrids

Iris unguicularis

Ajuga reptans 'Multicolor'

Hakonechloa macra 'Alboaurea'

Iris setosa is the hardiest of all irises and grows brilliantly in acid soil, particularly if it is moist. The slate-blue to deep violet flowers of early summer stand tall amid the lance-like leaves, even in a windy spot.

Expert's Selection

Herbaceous perennials

Make the most of these colourful perennials by planting a selection for year-round interest.

***Ajuga reptans* 'Multicolor'** ❀ Dark blue • Early summer ∅ Variegated bronze • *h.* 15cm (6in) *s.* 45cm (1½ft) ➤p.89

***Dicentra* 'Adrian Bloom'** ❀ Dark red • Late spring–autumn *h.* 30cm (1ft) *s.* 20cm (8in) ➤p.108

Dryopteris erythrosora ♀ ∅ Pinkish red, then copper, then green, when mature • *h.&s.* 60cm (2ft) ➤p.117

Eupatorium cannabinum ❀ Pink, purple or white • Late Summer *h.* 2m (7ft) *s.* 1m (3ft) ➤p.115

***Hakonechloa macra* 'Alboaurea'** ∅ Green, white and yellow *h.* 30cm (1ft) *s.* 60cm (2ft) ➤p.127

Iris unguicularis ♀ ❀ Violet-blue Winter • *h.* 25cm (10in) ➤p.136

***Lupinus* Russell hybrids** ❀ Range of colours • Early summer *h.* 1m (3ft) *s.* 45cm (1½ft) ➤p.144

Climbers & shrubs

Some of the most decorative and glamorous of all the shrubs are acid lovers, including *Magnolia*, *Camellia* and *Rhododendron*.

***Calluna vulgaris* 'Beoley Crimson'** ❀ Crimson • Early autumn ∅ Dark green *h.* 30cm (1ft) *s.* 45cm (1½ft) ➤p.211

***Camellia x williamsii* 'Elsie Jury'** ♀ ❀ Deep pink • Early–late spring *h.* 2–3m (7–10ft) *s.* 1.2–2m (4–7ft) ➤p.193

***Erica cinerea* 'Alba Minor'** ♀ ❀ White • Early spring–early autumn ∅ Bottle green • *h.* 25cm (10in) *s.* 45cm (1½ft) ➤p.211

Magnolia grandiflora ❀ White Midsummer–autumn *h.&s.* 15m (50ft) ➤p.226

***Magnolia liliiflora* 'Nigra'** ♀ ❀ Deep purple • Spring–early summer • *h.&s.* 3m (10ft) ➤p.226

***Rhododendron* 'Pink Pearl'** ❀ Pink • Late spring–early summer *h.&s.* 4m (13ft) ➤p.239

***Rosa* 'Graham Thomas'** ♀ ❀ Golden yellow • Summer *h.* 1.5m (5ft) *s.* 1.2m (4ft) ➤p.243

***Rosa* 'Scarlet Fire'** ❀ Red Summer • *h.&s.* 1.8m (6ft) ➤p.242

Sarcococca ruscifolia ❀ Ivory Late winter–early spring ❧ Blood-red • Summer *h.&s.* 1.2m (4ft) ➤p.249

Skimmia japonica* subsp. *reevesiana ❀ Creamy white • Late spring ❧ Deep red • Late summer–winter • *h.&s.* 75cm (2½ft) ➤p.250

***Vaccinium vitis-idaea* Koralle Group** ♀ ❀ White to pink • Late spring–early summer ❧ Red Late summer • *h.* 30cm (1ft) *s.* 50cm (20in) ➤p.257

***Wisteria floribunda* 'Multijuga'** ♀ ❀ Violet • Early summer *h.&s.* up to 9m (30ft) ➤p.260

Trees

Strong-rooted trees are essential for creating shelter in an exposed site. Plant evergreens for year-round protection, and select deciduous trees for beautiful colour.

Betula pendula ♀ ∅ Yellow Autumn • *h.* ultimately 20m (66ft) *s.* 8m (27ft) ➤p.265

***Picea pungens* 'Koster'** ♀ ∅ Silver-blue needles • *h.* 3m (10ft) *s.* 1m (3ft) ➤p.233

Bulbs

A lily will add a touch of glamour to any garden, with its exotic-looking summer blooms and their heady fragrance in late afternoon.

Lilium auratum ❀ White and gold Late summer • *h.* 1.5m (5ft) ➤p.318

If you have a large birch tree growing robustly and casting shade over the garden, and if rhododendrons, heathers and lupins thrive all around, your soil is probably acidic. You could heap on lots of lime to neutralise it, but it is much simpler to choose acid-loving plants instead, then sit back and watch them thrive.

Boggy ground and rotting leaves will make soil acidic, so where a plot is shaded by a deciduous tree it is liable to have a low (acid) pH. Do a soil test to check the acidity (see page 8), and note the plants that thrive locally. Many plants struggle in very acidic soils, but woodland plants, like ferns, grow in this kind of situation in the wild and will fill the dark, dank and acidic area in the shadow of a tree with colour, texture and interest. Many of the best-suited plants are members of the *Ericaceae* family, such as heathers, so look out for plants that are described as 'ericaceous'.

Grass will not thrive without some sun and acidic soil just makes it harder, so do not try to grow a lawn. Plant beds and borders, or put in some hard landscaping instead, and choose decorative plants, including attractive ground cover, to fill the space.

An autumn fall of leaves may swamp young plants growing beneath the canopy. Sweep or pick up dead leaves regularly to avoid this. Mulching the ground with organic material can help to retain moisture if the soil is very light, but a tree's worth of leaves will probably be too thick a layer.

Greedy trees monopolise food and water

If your soil is thin or light, plants may need regular watering in dry spells, because a large tree will stop rain reaching the ground, and suck moisture out of it. It will also leach nutrients from the soil, so give growing plants regular doses of a good ericaceous feed. The roots of mature trees can be a problem too: they may undermine paving or block the spread of other roots. If this happens, you can make more space for nearby plants and improve soil quality at the same time by removing some of the offending roots and filling the gaps left with good top soil.

An early summer garden showcases the delicious pink-tinged blossoms of an acid-loving Rhododendron, a soft contrast to the detailed feather shapes of the bright green ferns beneath.

A Lamium will spread swiftly to cover bare ground under trees with attractive wrinkled leaves, often spotted or variegated and with spikes of pretty late-spring flowers.

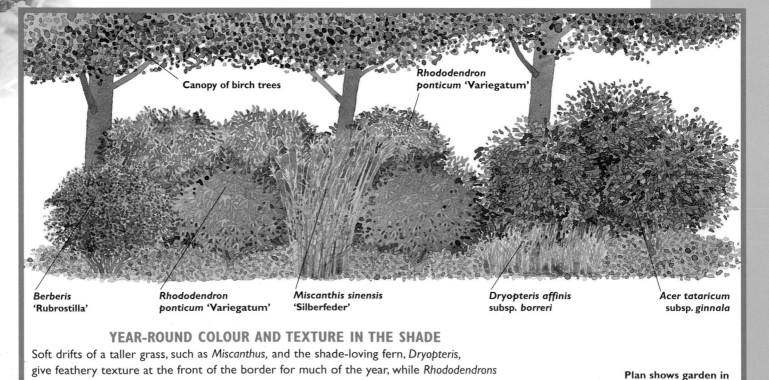

Canopy of birch trees

Rhododendron
ponticum 'Variegatum'

Berberis
'Rubrostilla'

Rhododendron
ponticum 'Variegatum'

Miscanthis sinensis
'Silberfeder'

Dryopteris affinis
subsp. borreri

Acer tataricum
subsp. ginnala

YEAR-ROUND COLOUR AND TEXTURE IN THE SHADE

Soft drifts of a taller grass, such as *Miscanthus,* and the shade-loving fern, *Dryopteris,* give feathery texture at the front of the border for much of the year, while *Rhododendrons* produce beautiful spring flowers, and an *Acer* gives vivid spring and autumn colour.

Plan shows garden in early autumn

Expert's Selection

Herbaceous perennials

Feathery ferns, soft grasses like
Miscanthus and ground-covering
Lamiums will thrive under the
canopy in this type of soil.

Asplenium scolopendrium
'Crispum' ∅ Green • All year
h.&s. 60cm (2ft) ➤p.117
Dryopteris affinis* subsp. *borreri
∅ Dark green • All year *h.* 1m (3ft)
s. 40cm (16in) ➤p.117
***Lamium garganicum* 'Golden
Carpet'** ❀ Pink and white
Midsummer ∅ Green and gold
h.&s. 45cm (1½ft) ➤p.139
***Miscanthus sinensis* 'Silberfeder'
(syn. 'Silver Feather')** ❀ Silver
pinkish brown • Autumn
h. 1.5–2.5m (5–8ft) *s.* 1.2m (4ft)
➤p.127

Shrubs

Azaleas and rhododendrons are
classics for acid conditions. *Berberis*
and *Salix* will give an appealing
display throughout the year.

***Berberis* 'Rubrostilla'** ♀ ❀ Yellow
Spring ∅ Pale green and silver, then
red ◀ Red • Autumn • *h.* 1.5m (5ft)
s. 2.5m (8ft) ➤p.188
Rhododendron ponticum
'Variegatum' ❀ Pinkish purple •
Late spring–midsummer ∅ Green
and white • *h&s..* 6m (20ft) ➤p.239
Salix cinerea ∅ Grey leaves and
stems • *h.* 1.5m (5ft) *s.* 2.5m (8ft)
➤p.247

Trees

The deeply lobed leaves of this low-
growing maple will turn from vibrant
green to a deep scarlet in autumn.

Acer tataricum* subsp. *ginnala ♀
∅ Green • Spring–summer; scarlet in
autumn • *h.* 5m (16ft) *s.* 3m (10ft)
➤p.264

FULL AND PARTIAL NON-TREE SHADE

Many town gardens are so well enclosed by tall fences, walls and nearby buildings that they rarely, if ever, see any direct sunlight. But it probably stays nice and damp all year round, and if the soil is acid, it will make a perfect home for rhododendrons and camellias.

Even suburban or rural gardens may have shady, moist corners that are worth exploiting. If **rhododendrons** and other ericaceous plants grow naturally in your area, you are probably sitting on acid soil; confirm it with a soil-testing kit (see page 8). Do not try to neutralise the soil's natural acidity – instead, create a care-free garden by making the most of what you have.

Your soil might be light and peaty, sandy, or heavy sour clay – whatever the type, if it is reasonably shaded, it will tend to remain moist except during long periods of drought. The only places likely to become dry are areas of rain shadow, such as at the bases of taller structures and beneath hedges, and in summer at the tops of slopes. The areas around well-established hedges may be impoverished, too, as mature hedging is greedy – for both nutrients and water.

Plant a warm orange Lilium davidii (Turk's cap lily) for its pendulous blooms, hung as if on a chandelier with upcurved petals and prominent ruddy stamens.

Beds, borders and somewhere to sit

Grass is usually not very happy on acid soils, nor does it like being in semi-permanent shade. All you end up with is a lot of moss and a redundant lawnmower. Instead, think about hard landscaping, such as decking, gravel or terrace, broken with colourful and scented beds and borders. You have a great opportunity to create an acid garden: just steer clear of lime lovers and go with the flow. As the list opposite demonstrates, there is an excellent choice of suitable plants to make your garden sparkle: **honeysuckles** and **lilies**, *Acers* and **azaleas**, *Hostas* and *Hellebores*.

Once you have prepared the planting areas, give them a soaking, preferably using soft water such as rainwater. Mulch to retain moisture (see page 14) and water new plants until they are established. Hoe the surface of the soil from time to time to get rid of algae, mosses and lichens, and when you fertilise, choose special ericaceous plant foods.

Expert's Selection

Herbaceous perennials

Mix winter-flowering *Hellebores* and sculptural *Hostas* for all-year appeal.

***Bergenia* 'Abendgut' (syn. *B.* 'Evening glow')** ❀ Rose red Early spring ∅ Maroon • Winter
h. 30cm (1ft) *s.* 60m (2ft) ➤p.100

Helleborus orientalis* subsp. *guttatus ❀ White • Winter–spring
h. 45cm (1½ft) *s.* 60cm (2ft) ➤p.130

***Hosta* 'Tall Boy'** ❀ Purple • Late Summer ∅ Mid green
h. 50cm (20in) *s.* 1m (3ft) ➤p.134

Shrubs

Evergreen shrubs with strong shapes such as *Ilex* and a shrubby *Lonicera* complement the lavish blooms of a *Rhododendron* or *Camellia*.

***Camellia japonica* 'Mikenjaku'** ❀ Red and white • Mid–late spring
h. 3m (10ft) *s.* 2m (7ft) ➤p.192

A vivid rusty red azalea
dominates the front of this
casual autumn border, offset
by a sprinkling of pale lilac
Colchicum (see page 308).

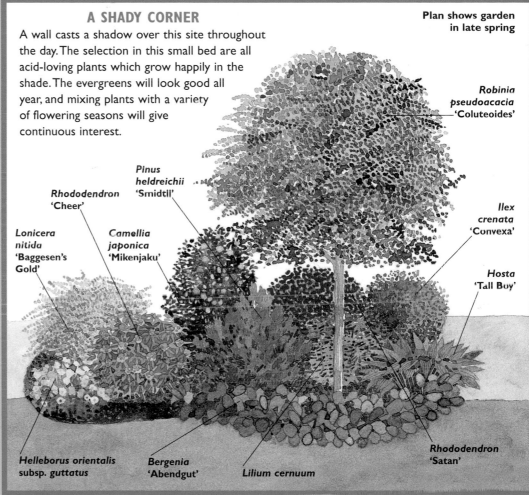

A SHADY CORNER

Plan shows garden
in late spring

A wall casts a shadow over this site throughout
the day. The selection in this small bed are all
acid-loving plants which grow happily in the
shade. The evergreens will look good all
year, and mixing plants with a variety
of flowering seasons will give
continuous interest.

*Robinia
pseudoacacia
'Coluteoides'*

*Pinus
heldreichii
'Smidtii'*

*Rhododendron
'Cheer'*

*Ilex
crenata
'Convexa'*

*Lonicera
nitida
'Baggesen's
Gold'*

*Camellia
japonica
'Mikenjaku'*

*Hosta
'Tall Boy'*

*Helleborus orientalis
subsp. guttatus*

*Bergenia
'Abendgut'*

Lilium cernuum

*Rhododendron
'Satan'*

Ilex crenata **'Convexa'**♀ ∅ Dark
green ❧ Black, white or yellow
Autumn–winter • *h.* 5m (16ft)
s. 4m (13ft) ➤p.217

Lonicera nitida **'Baggesen's
Gold'**♀ ∅ Green-gold
h.&s. 2.5m (8ft) ➤p.225

Rhododendron **'Cheer'** ✿ Shell
pink • Spring • *h.&s.* 1–2.5m (3–8ft)
➤p.239

Rhododendron **'Satan'**♀ ✿ Scarlet
Late spring ∅ Green; tinted bronze
in autumn • *h.&s.* 2m (7ft) ➤p.239

Pinus heldreichii **'Smidtii'**♀
∅ Green ❧ Blue cones; brown when
ripe • *h.* 3m (10ft) *s.* 1m (3ft) ➤p.234

Trees

A bright-leaved *Acer* gives a burst of
colour in spring and summer, while a
Robinia adds height and grace.

Acer negundo **'Flamingo'**♀
∅ Green, pink and white • Spring–
summer • *h.* 6m (20ft) *s.* 4m (13ft)
➤p.264

Robinia pseudoacacia
'Coluteoides' ✿ White • Late spring
∅ Pale green • *h.&s.* 6m (20ft)
➤p.271

Bulbs

Native to European and Asian
woodlands, lilies are happy in shady
sites. Many varieties are acid-lovers.

Lilium (most) ✿ Various • Early–late
summer • *h.* 60cm–1.5m (2–5ft)
➤p.318

ALKALINE SOIL
OPEN SITE

Wide open and windy, a garden near a clifftop, can be refreshingly breezy, but what is bracing for the gardener can make life difficult for tall plants, unless you give them shelter and support. If your soil is also chalky, plants will have to contend with very alkaline conditions too.

Chalky or limey soil is generally low in nutrients. However, it is usually free-draining with good air circulation, and in an open site this will be even better, keeping air and water-borne pests and diseases to a minimum. With just a little care, many delightful plants will thrive here.

A little support

Stake tall plants and plant hedging, such as *Berberis*, as windbreaks, erecting temporary brushwood or netting until the hedges are well established.

All the plants listed here will grow well in soil with a high pH, but will benefit if you dig in slow-release fertilisers or manure to raise the level of nutrients. Test your soil (see page 8) to see how alkaline it is, and if necessary neutralise it by forking in sulphur and by always watering with rainwater.

Expert's Selection

Herbaceous perennials

A good mix of perennials will sweep the ground with colour throughout summer, as the wind wafts their perfume across the garden.

Armeria maritima ❁ White, pink or red • Early summer • *h.* 20cm (8in) *s.* 50cm (20in) ➤p.94

Aurinia saxatilis ♀ ❁ Yellow • Early summer • *h.* 20cm (8in) *s.* 30cm (1ft) ➤p.99

***Dianthus* 'Doris'** ♀ ❁ Salmon-pink Midsummer • *h.* 35cm (14in) *s.* 25cm (10in) ➤p.107

***Fragaria* 'Pink Panda'** ❁ Pink Summer–early autumn *h.* 10cm (4in) *s.* indefinite ➤p.120

***Helianthus* 'Lemon Queen'** ❁ Pale yellow • Late summer–early autumn *h.* 1.5m (5ft) *s.* 1.2m (4ft) ➤p.129

Lathyrus vernus ♀ ❁ Purple Mid–late spring • *h.* 40cm (16in) *s.* 30cm (1ft) ➤p.140

***Leucanthemum* x *superbum* 'Snowcap'** ❁ White • Early–midsummer • *h.&s.* 45cm (1½ft) ➤p.141

Liriope muscari ♀ ❁ Violet • Late summer–autumn • *h.&s.* 45m (1½ft) ➤p.143

Lychnis chalcedonica ♀ ❁ Bright red • Early summer • *h.* 1m (3ft) *s.* 40cm (16in) ➤p.145

***Melissa officinalis* 'Aurea'** ❁ White Summer ∅ Green with yellow markings • *h.* 1m (3ft) *s.* 40cm (16in) ➤p.149

Nepeta sibirica ❁ Lavender-blue Midsummer ∅ Dark green *h.&s.* 1m (3ft) ➤p.151

***Scabiosa caucasica* 'Clive Greaves'** ♀ ❁ Lavender-blue • Late summer • *h.&s.* 60cm (2ft) ➤p.166

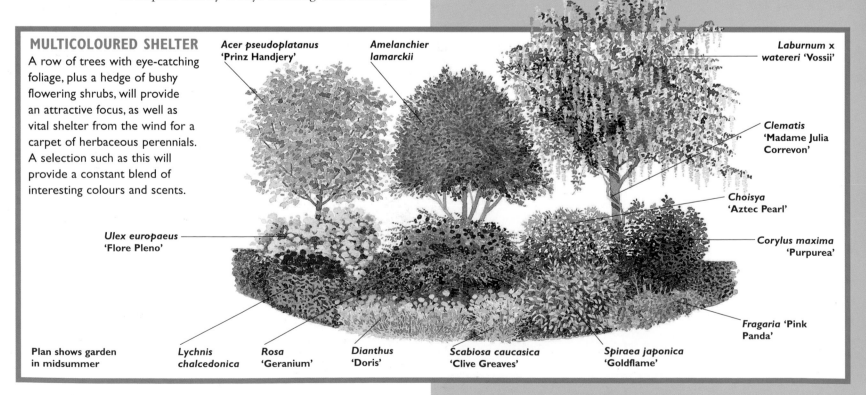

MULTICOLOURED SHELTER

A row of trees with eye-catching foliage, plus a hedge of bushy flowering shrubs, will provide an attractive focus, as well as vital shelter from the wind for a carpet of herbaceous perennials. A selection such as this will provide a constant blend of interesting colours and scents.

Acer pseudoplatanus 'Prinz Handjery'

Amelanchier lamarckii

Laburnum x *watereri* 'Vossii'

Clematis 'Madame Julia Correvon'

Choisya 'Aztec Pearl'

Corylus maxima 'Purpurea'

Ulex europaeus 'Flore Pleno'

Fragaria 'Pink Panda'

Plan shows garden in midsummer

Lychnis chalcedonica

Rosa 'Geranium'

Dianthus 'Doris'

Scabiosa caucasica 'Clive Greaves'

Spiraea japonica 'Goldflame'

In summer, this stony patch comes to life as hazy spikes of purple **Nepeta** appear, along with clumps of pink **Dianthus**, filling the air with their heavy perfume.

Climbers & shrubs

Shrubs and climbers not only bring their own colour, but when planted as hedging can give vital shelter.

Akebia quinata ❀ Maroon • Spring h.&s. 5m (16ft) ➤p.183

Amelanchier lamarckii♀ ❀ White Spring ∅ Red • Autumn h. 1.5m (5ft) s. 1.2m (4ft) after 5 years; ultimately 10m (33ft) ➤p.183

Berberis thunbergii 'Atropurpurea Nana'♀ ∅ Purple-red ❧ Bright red Autumn • h.&s. 60cm (2ft) ➤p.188

Berberis x media 'Parkjuweel'♀ ❀ Yellow • Spring ∅ Red • Autumn h.&s. 60cm (2ft) after 5 years; ultimately 1m (3ft) ➤p.188

Choisya 'Aztec Pearl'♀ ❀ White Late spring–autumn • h.&s. 2m (7ft) ➤p.197

Clematis 'Général Sikorski'♀ ❀ Mauvish blue • Early–late summer h. 3m (10ft) s. 1m (3ft)➤p.198

Clematis 'Madame Julia Correvon'♀ ❀ Wine-red Midsummer–early autumn h. 6m (20ft) s. 3m (10ft) ➤p.199

Corylus maxima 'Purpurea'♀ ❀ Purple catkins • Late winter–spring ∅ Purple • h.&s. 6m (20ft) ➤p.201

Lonicera periclymenum 'Red Gables' ❀ Red • Mid–late summer h.&s. 1.8m (6ft) after 5 years; ultimately 3.5m (12ft) ➤p.224

Osmanthus x burkwoodii♀ ❀ White • Spring ∅ Dark green h.&s. 3m (10ft) ➤p.228

Potentilla fruticosa 'Manchu' ❀ White • Summer ∅ Grey-green h. 75cm (2½ft) s. 1m (3ft) ➤p.234

Rosa 'Geranium'♀ ❀ Bright red Early summer ❧ Red-orange Autumn • h. 2.5m (8ft) s. 2m (7ft) ➤p.242

Spiraea japonica 'Goldflame'♀ ❀ Dark pink • Mid–late summer ∅ Reddish orange • h.&s. 1m (3ft) ➤p.253

Syringa vulgaris 'Charles Joly'♀ ❀ Dark purplish red • Mid–late spring • h. 3.5m (12ft) s. 3m (10ft) ➤p.254

Ulex europaeus 'Flore Pleno'♀ ❀ Yellow • Early–late spring h.&s. 60cm (2ft); ultimately 1m (3ft) ➤p.257

Trees

Select trees with striking foliage or a good floral display, such as the acers and laburnum suggested below.

Acer grosseri var. hersii♀ ∅ Orange • Autumn • h. 4m (13ft) s. 2m (7ft) after 20 years; ultimately 10m (33ft) ➤p.264

Acer pseudoplatanus 'Prinz Handjery' ∅ Purply yellow • Spring h.&s. 3m (10ft) ➤p.264

Laburnum x watereri 'Vossii'♀ ❀ Yellow • Early summer ∅ Pale green • h. 6m (20ft) s. 4m (13ft) ➤p.268

Pyrus salicifolia 'Pendula'♀ ❀ Creamy white • Mid spring h. 5m (16ft) s. 2.7m (9ft) ➤p.271

Bulbs

Planting a few bulbs will ensure that you can enjoy a scattering of flowers early in the year. Stately gladioli will take you through to autumn.

Chionodoxa luciliae♀ ❀ Blue and white • Early spring • h. 10–15cm (4–6in) ➤p.308

Gladiolus callianthus♀ ❀ White with purple throat • Late summer– early autumn • h. 1m (3ft) ➤p.315

Narcissus 'Tête-à-tête'♀ ❀ Yellow Early spring • h. 15cm (6in) ➤p.320

Tulipa urumiensis♀ ❀ Yellow, tinged with lilac • Early spring h. 15cm (6in) ➤p.324

FULL TREE SHADE

Beeches, hornbeams or wild cherries will grow into strong and handsome spreading trees on alkaline soil, casting shade on the ground beneath. Choose other lime-loving species to add colour to this shady spot and provide interest when the trees are not in leaf.

Any soil with a pH value higher than 7 is alkaline, but its texture may range from heavy and cold to shallow, light and stony. A simple pH testing kit (see page 8) will tell you just how alkaline your soil is, and help you to choose the most suitable plants.

Tree shade is another consideration. The heavy canopy of a deciduous tree will block out light in spring and summer; evergreens will cast dense shade all year round. However, if you have a heavy soil the shelter means that your garden will retain moisture and nutrients well, and creates an ideal cool and shady spot for foliage plants, such as a *Filipendula*.

Muscari will soon naturalise under a tree, carpeting the ground in blue or white in spring.

Make the best of challenging conditions

Extremely alkaline soils can be tough on even the hardiest of plants and you may notice signs of nutrient deficiency, such as yellowing of leaves. Add chelated trace elements (which are easily absorbed) to combat any problems like this (see pages 14–15), but if the soil is very alkaline, a scattering of sulphur once a year will help to neutralise it a little.

A tree may cast cooling shade, but its roots are very greedy of nutrients. This is a particular problem with very light sharply drained soils. Give plants under the tree a boost with an annual feed of slow-release fertilisers. The tree will also suck up moisture and the leaf canopy will stop all but the heaviest rain reaching the ground in summer. So water young plants well and spread a thick mulch over the soil to help to retain as much moisture as possible.

Pick up leaves and keep slugs in the cold

Watch that fallen leaves in autumn do not smother young plants in the beds below. Pick them off tender shoots, and clear the whole area regularly. Removing the leaves will also mean that there are fewer hiding places in the garden for slugs and snails. Choose a crisp day for this job – slimy wet leaves are more difficult to remove than dry ones.

Autumn leaf fall allows enough light to reach the alkaline soil under this apple tree for Asters and Astrantias to bloom.

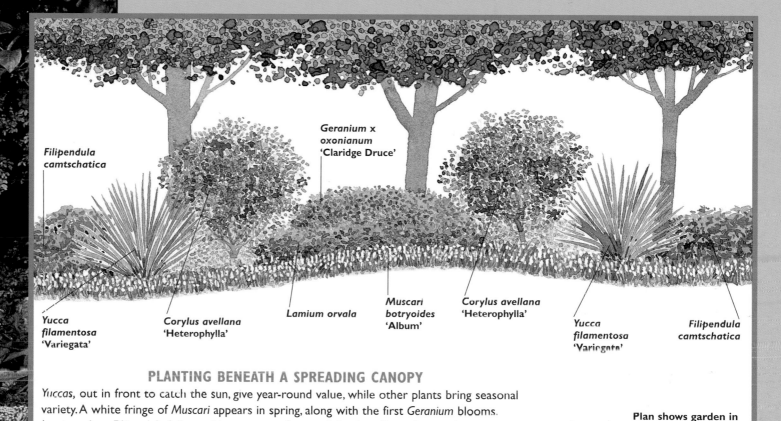

Filipendula camtschatica

Geranium x oxonianum 'Claridge Druce'

Yucca filamentosa 'Variegata'

Corylus avellana 'Heterophylla'

Lamium orvala

Muscari botryoides 'Album'

Corylus avellana 'Heterophylla'

Yucca filamentosa 'Variegata'

Filipendula camtschatica

PLANTING BENEATH A SPREADING CANOPY

Yuccas, out in front to catch the sun, give year-round value, while other plants bring seasonal variety. A white fringe of *Muscari* appears in spring, along with the first *Geranium* blooms. *Lamium,* then *Filipendula* follow with summer colour, and *Corylus* offers a burst of autumn gold.

Plan shows garden in late spring

Expert's Selection

Herbaceous perennials

Summer flowers lift the darkness beneath a tree. Choose from a pink palette for a harmonious scheme.

Aster x frikartii 'Flora's Delight'
❀ Lilac • Autumn • *h.&s.* 45cm (1½ft)
➤p.97
Astrantia major ❀ White
Midsummer • *h.* 75cm (2½ft)
s. 45cm (1½ft) ➤p.99
Filipendula camtschatica ❀ Pink or white • Late summer • *h.* 3m (10ft)
s. 1m (3ft) ➤p.120
Geranium x oxonianum 'Claridge Druce' ❀ Pink • Spring–autumn
h. 1m (3ft) *s.* 75cm (2½ft) ➤p.122

Lamium orvala ❀ Copper-pink
Early summer • *h.* 40cm (16in)
s. 50cm (20in) ➤p.139

Climbers & shrubs

Year-round foliage will keep interest in your borders even after the leaves on the trees above have fallen.

Artemisia arborescens ∅ Silver-grey • *h.* 1m (3ft) *s.* 50cm (20in)
➤p.184
Corylus avellana 'Heterophylla'
❀ Yellow catkins • Winter–late spring
∅ Golden ◀ Cobnuts • Autumn
h.&s. 5m (16ft) ➤p.201
Yucca filamentosa 'Variegata' ♀
❀ Creamy white • Late summer
∅ Green with cream and pink
h. 1m (3ft) *s.* 75cm (2½ft) ➤p.261

Trees

Create an area of tree shade in your garden with a striking red maple (*Acer*), and enjoy its flowers and glorious blaze of autumn foliage.

Acer rubrum 'Red Sunset' ❀ Red
Early–mid spring ∅ Orange-red
Early autumn • *h.* 8m (27ft)
s. 5m (16ft) ➤p.264

Bulbs

Scatter handfuls of muscari bulbs beneath a tree and leave them to naturalise and spread.

Muscari botryoides 'Album'
❀ White • Spring • *h.* 15cm (6in)
➤p.319

Lime-lovers' paradise, such as the chalky, alkaline ground found in areas like the South Downs, also tends to be quite dry, so plants that are happy in these natural conditions, including viburnums, narcissi and campanulas, will do well in the dry, partial shade of a fence or house.

Most plants are more tolerant of alkaline soils than acid, so even in the shade of a tall fence or a building, this is a reasonably care-free site. Your main concern will be to make sure that high levels of lime in your soil do not prevent plants from taking up certain vital nutrients. So if you notice them turning yellow, step in with a fast-acting remedy, such as a dose of plant tonic. It is also a good idea to keep the soil well nourished, with a good annual feed of slow-release fertiliser.

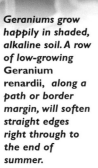

Geraniums grow happily in shaded, alkaline soil. A row of low-growing Geranium renardii, along a path or border margin, will soften straight edges right through to the end of summer.

Gardening in the dark

The solid shade cast by man-made structures can be more difficult to grow plants in than even the deepest shade beneath a tree, because areas in the shadow of a building are completely deprived of sunlight for at least some of the day.

It is a good idea to draw a plan of your garden before planting, and to record on it how the sun moves through the site. This will help you to decide where to position plants that need some sunlight so that they will get as much as possible. Reserve the darkest corners for total shade-loving varieties.

If you can't stand the heat

Ground closest to a building or structure will also be sheltered from rainfall to some extent, so you may need to water such areas from time to time. But soil just around the edge of the rain shadow does not only catch a fair sprinkling of moisture, it retains it well, since it avoids catching too much of the drying effect of the midday sun. Such ground will also remain fairly cool, and be generally fertile.

A spot like this should be perfect for a spreading *Pulmonaria* or for woodland spring bulbs, such as **crocuses** and **snowdrops**. Include a *Viburnum* or some other variegated or white-flowering shrubs to add a light note to the bed, and you will be guaranteed a beautiful, varied plot, brimming with an array of interesting, eye-catching colours.

Months before most other plants bloom, crocuses and snowdrops will bring a glow of life to even the darkest corners of your garden.

Expert's Selection

Herbaceous perennials

Choose perennials that will start to provide lively ground cover as soon as bulbs begin to die down.

Bergenia ciliata ✿ White • Early spring • *h.&s.* 45cm (1½ft) ➤p.100

Campanula 'Elizabeth' ✿ Cream, with reddish purple • Mid–late summer • *h.&s.* 40cm (16in) ➤p.103

Geranium renardii ♀ ✿ White with purple • Midsummer–early autumn *h.* 30cm (1ft) *s.* 25cm (10in) ➤p.122

Hemerocallis 'Glowing Gold' ✿ Orangey gold • Mid–late summer *h.&s.* 75cm (2½ft) ➤p.132

***Pulmonaria rubra* 'David Ward'** ✿ Red • Late winter–mid spring ∅ Green with cream edges *h.* 45cm (1½ft) *s.* 1m (3ft) ➤p.163

Shrubs & climbers

A selection of shrubs of varying height will help to give shape and structure to your plot and bring layers of interesting contrast.

***Pyracantha coccinea* 'Red Cushion'** ✿ White • Early summer ❧ Bright red • Autumn *h.&s.* 1.8m (6ft) after 5 years; ultimately 3.5m (12ft) ➤p.236

Spiraea prunifolia ✿ White Mid–late spring ∅ Yellow • Autumn *h.* 1.2m (4ft) *s.* 1m (3ft) after 5 years; ultimately 1.8m (6ft) ➤p.253

***Syringa x prestoniae* 'Elinor'** ♀ ✿ Pale lilac • Late spring–early summer • *h.* 1.2m (4ft) *s.* 1m (3ft) after 5 years; ultimately 5m (16ft) ➤p.254

Viburnum tinus ✿ Pinky white Winter–early spring ∅ Dark green *h.&s.* 3m (10ft) ➤p.258

Trees

If space permits, crown your garden with a tree or two, but take care that they do not add too much shade.

***Sorbus* 'Joseph Rock'** ♀ ∅ Red, orange and yellow • Autumn ❧ Orange-yellow • Autumn *h.* 6m (20ft) *s.* 2.5m (8ft) ➤p.273

Bulbs

Bulbs bring a spread of early colour. Dry chalky soil, means soft bulbs like *Narcissi*, are less susceptible to rot.

Crocus ✿ White, cream, yellow or purple • Late winter *h.* 5–13cm (2–5in) ➤p.310

Galanthus ✿ White • Late winter *h.* 10–23cm (4–9in) ➤p.314

Narcissus ✿ Yellow, cream and white Early–late spring *h.* 15–60cm (6–24in) ➤p.314

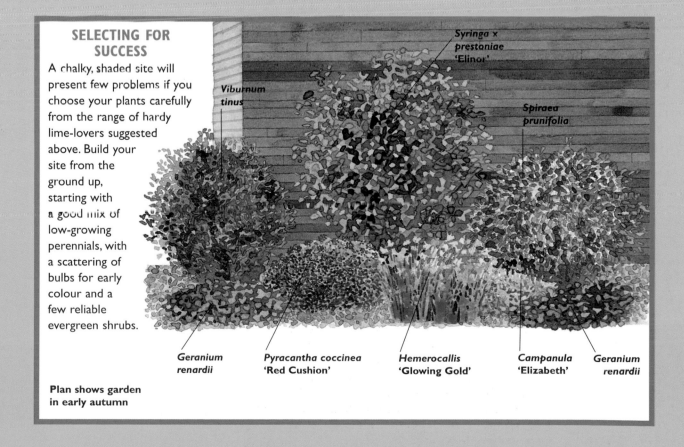

SELECTING FOR SUCCESS

A chalky, shaded site will present few problems if you choose your plants carefully from the range of hardy lime-lovers suggested above. Build your site from the ground up, starting with a good mix of low-growing perennials, with a scattering of bulbs for early colour and a few reliable evergreen shrubs.

Viburnum tinus

Syringa x prestoniae 'Elinor'

Spiraea prunifolia

Geranium renardii

Pyracantha coccinea 'Red Cushion'

Hemerocallis 'Glowing Gold'

Campanula 'Elizabeth'

Geranium renardii

Plan shows garden in early autumn

A–Z plant

profiles

A–Z PLANT PROFILES

One of the most exciting parts of starting a new garden or improving an existing one is choosing the plants. To help you, this section gives experts' selections of the most care-free herbaceous perennials, shrubs & climbers, trees, annuals, biennials & bedding plants, and bulbs, with advice on where they grow best.

- **Enjoy your plants** and relax. Do not worry about moving a plant to a new position if you think it will do better there.

- **See how other people garden.** Spend time visiting open gardens, both in your own area, which may have conditions similar to yours, and farther afield.

- **Visit gardens in spring and autumn,** and on wet, miserable days as well. Do not just go on fine summer days when everything is sure to be looking its best.

- **Avoid costly mistakes or disappointing displays** with some advance planning. Use the experts' selections listed here together with the planting suggestions for the sites in the first part of the book to make plans for flourishing care-free beds.

- **Fireside gardening in winter** – browsing through books, magazines and catalogues – is a lovely way to pass a wet afternoon when it is too cold to be outside.

Keeping a garden diary will help you to plan new plantings. Note down plants that have done well in a particular site, take photographs of the garden, and keep cuttings from magazines of plants you would like to incorporate.

Plan for growth

As you choose your favourite plants, make a note of their likely height and spread. The measurements given in this book are for ultimate size unless otherwise stated, and you can expect a plant to achieve that in around five years.

Design the garden on paper

It often helps to draw out a design (below), with circles to represent the space each plant will occupy once it is established. Buying more than you have space for is often a temptation and young specimens are deceptively small, so this is an easy way to see whether something will choke its neighbours when it is mature. If the garden looks a bit sparse for the first year or two, you can always fill it temporarily with annuals or 'cheap and cheerful' perennials, which can be removed when the permanent scheme begins to take effect.

Sales beds are designed to tempt

Many display beds in garden centres are positioned in full sun, but this is often more for the sake of good appearance than good plantsmanship. Just because something is in a certain position when it is offered for sale does not mean that these conditions are the most suitable in the long run. In fact, garden centres with the welfare of their plants at heart will provide shading from hot sun and shelter from cold winds for the plants which need it.

Mix and match

By shopping at a garden centre you can see exactly what you are getting. There is usually a full range of different types of plants, from annuals to trees and evergreen shrubs, so that you can try a plant to see how it looks against its likely neighbour before committing yourself.

However, you may prefer to choose plants from mail-order catalogues or the Internet. These are particularly good sources for the latest varieties of bedding plants and annual seeds.

Plant for year-round interest

The most interesting gardens are those packed with a diverse range of plants and designed to have something to catch the eye, whatever the time of year. This may not be flowers, but can be striking foliage, glossy berries, coloured bark or even bare branches in an attractive shape that are picked out by winter frosts. Think about what will look good in every season. Do not be seduced by plants that look great on the weekend you do your shopping – they may be largely without interest for the rest of the year.

Try out plant combinations at the garden centre before you buy to see how their colours, shapes and textures will work together when you get them home.

SYMBOLS USED IN THE BOOK

- ✿ **Flower colour**
- ∅ **Leaf colour**
- ⚜ **Fruit, berry or nut colour**
- ♀ **Royal Horticultural Society Award of Garden Merit**
- *h.* **Height**
- *s.* **Spread**

Once you have worked out your growing conditions (see page 22) turn from the What sort of site? section to this section to make your plant choices. Plan your beds – this is designed for a windy border – then make a list and go shopping.

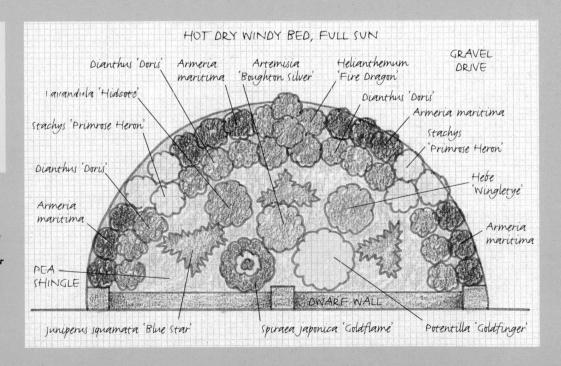

HOT DRY WINDY BED, FULL SUN

GRAVEL DRIVE

Dianthus 'Doris'
Armeria maritima
Artemisia 'Boughton Silver'
Helianthemum 'Fire Dragon'
Lavandula 'Hidsote'
Stachys 'Primrose Heron'
Dianthus 'Doris'
Armeria maritima
Dianthus 'Doris'
Armeria maritima
Stachys 'Primrose Heron'
Hebe 'Wingletye'
Armeria maritima
PEA SHINGLE
DWARF WALL
Juniperus squamata 'Blue Star'
Spiraea japonica 'Goldflame'
Potentilla 'Goldfinger'

herbaceous
perennials

Herbaceous perennials are the mainstay of most gardens, and with good reason. They are simple to grow in most situations, provide a great range of colour and variety of form, but ask very little in return. They are also easily moved around so it is possible to experiment with different plants and effects.

Although the word 'herbaceous' implies that they die down for winter, a few herbaceous perennials, such as **garden pinks** (*Dianthus*), retain their foliage in good shape throughout the year. For most, their deciduous nature, and changing seasonal appearance, is a bonus.

Make room for a traditional border

When choosing perennials, there are several aspects to bear in mind, including local climate and soil conditions, the space available, and the effect desired throughout the seasons.

The traditional herbaceous border seen in grand Edwardian country houses is most appropriate to very large gardens, since for best effect, it needs to be 2–3m (7–10ft) from front to back. However, you can create a most pleasing display with perennials in smaller gardens by grouping

them with shrubs, which will continue to provide interest when the perennials die down and will give them support and shelter in open sites.

Size matters, whatever the space

Herbaceous perennials range in height from a few centimetres to 3m (10ft) or more. The details in this section and labels in garden centres will give an indication of ultimate size, and perennials will generally reach this within a full season.

Spread is also important, because while many perennials form compact clumps others, such as *Helianthus* and *Solidago*, develop into spreading patches, and a few very vigorous spreaders, such as *Ajuga*, *Houttuynia* and *Lamium*, make useful, low-growing ground-cover plants.

Mix and match for best effect

Consider their different colours, textures and flowering seasons as well as size, as you decide which perennials to plant together. And think about whether you would prefer a simple colour scheme or a more relaxed 'cottage garden' effect.

Some gardeners buy single plants from a garden centre, to see how well they will grow before buying more, but this can result in a bitty-looking border. Planting in groups of three or five will give a much better result and, if you follow the site demands and planting advice given here, you can be sure of success. If a certain combination does not work, or a small plant is overwhelmed by a more vigorous one, simply move the plants around.

Use two forks to separate large clumps.

Time spent choosing a suitable site and preparing the soil will make plants more care free later on.

Wet or dry?
- Most herbaceous perennials do best in well-drained, humus rich soil.
- Some plants, such as *Astilbe* and *Caltha* demand moist conditions.

Test the soil's pH (page 8)
- Soils that are neutral (pH7) or only slightly acidic are the most accommodating for plants.
- Alkaline soils (with a pH greater than 7) suit only a few species.

Prepare the ground
- Dig the bed before you plant, removing all perennial weeds and working in plenty of organic matter.

Offer food and support
- Apply a general-purpose fertiliser in early spring and midsummer.
- Some taller perennials may need staking, especially in exposed sites.

At the end of the season
- Many gardeners cut dying foliage in late autumn, but in cold areas, it will protect slightly tender varieties.
- Only deadhead plants if they look untidy. Many seed heads, such as on *Acanthus* or *Arum*, are very attrctive.
- An exception is *Alchemilla mollis*, which may seed too freely if the fading flowers are not removed.

Lift and separate
- Most perennials, particularly those with spreading rhizomes, such as *Astilbe*, *Bergenia* and *Helianthus*, benefit from being divided every few years in autumn or early spring.

Acanthus

Bear's breeches are easily grown architectural plants. Short varieties shine at the front of a border, while at the back taller ones send summer spires soaring skywards.

Expert's Selection

1 A. mollis
A winner, with shoulder-high flower spikes and handsome, deeply cut, leaves, up to 60cm (2ft) long.
✿ **White-mauve • Midsummer**
h. 1.5m (5ft) **s.** 1m (3ft)

2 A. spinosus♀
Shiny, spine-tipped leaves, 1m (3ft) long, give this variety drama.
✿ **White-mauve • Early summer**
h. 1.2m (4ft) **s.** 60cm (2ft)

3 A. hungaricus
If you want an attractive medium-height acanthus, try this spine-free one.
✿ **Pink-white • Midsummer**
h. 1m (3ft) **s.** 60cm (2ft)

4 A. dioscoridis var. perringii This short variety blooms all summer long.
✿ **Deep pink and green • Summer**
h. 40cm (16in)
s. 60cm (2ft)

STAR PERFORMER
A. mollis White flowers with mauve hoods shoot up out of the border in July and August.

The Essentials

Site demands Any type of soil, provided it has good drainage. Need full sun to flower well.
Planting practice Plant in spring. For a good start, especially if your soil is chalky and free-draining, fill the base of the hole with humus.
Flowering time From early to late summer, depending on variety.
Pests and diseases Usually trouble free, but look out for slugs and snails.
Bonus point Acanthus are truly care free and positively thrive on neglect.

If you need a real showstopper in the border, go for a tall acanthus, such as *A. mollis*. A group of five will really grab the limelight, especially with a gap around them or low-growing plants to either side. Latifolius Group varieties of *A. mollis* have leaves up to 1.2m (4ft) long, but less flowers than their parent.

Winter care
If the first winter is severe, with freezing temperatures, protect the young plants with a mulch. Once they are fully established, they will survive without any problems.

Achillea

Yarrows are a staple of the cottage-garden border. Often evergreen, with ferny foliage, they display an array of tiny, daisy-like flowers in a range of bright summer colours.

Achilleas give an excellent show of flowers without any pampering. They stand out in a border, with their long-stemmed flowers and attract butterflies, bees and hoverflies. They are also long-lasting cut flowers and, dried, will keep their colour to make striking winter focal points.

Expert's Selection

1 A. Summer Pastels Group
These new hybrids come in a range of sugared-almond shades.
✿✿✿✿✿ **White, cream, yellow, pink, salmon or pale purple • Summer**
h. 75cm (2½ft) **s.** 60cm (2ft)

2 A. filipendulina 'Gold Plate'♀ Golden flowers make a great show at the back of a border.
✿ **Yellow • Summer**
h. 1.5m (5ft) **s.** 1m (3ft)

3 A. 'Moonshine'♀
For small gardens, choose this short, subtle yellow variety.
✿ **Pale yellow • Summer**
h. 60cm (2ft) **s.** 45cm (1½ft)

4 A. ageratum 'W.B. Childs'
A single-flowered achillea, it offers a daisy-like simplicity.
✿ **White • Summer**
h.&s. 75cm (2½ft)

5 A. chrysocoma
This short, but spreading variety is a cheerful addition to any rockery.
✿ **Sunny yellow • Summer**
h. 30cm (1ft) **s.** 40cm (16in)

The Essentials

Site demands Any sunny, well-drained site, but prolonged periods of drought will kill them.
Planting practice Plant in early spring; lift and divide every 3 years.
Flowering time All summer and sometimes into early autumn.
Pests and diseases Trouble free.
Bonus point Make good cut flowers, which can also be dried.

STAR PERFORMER
A. Summer Pastels Group
Flat-topped clusters of hazy, pastel flowers float on straight stems, above a cushion of soft fern-like leaves.

Ajuga

Bugle, a low, spreading evergreen, will provide stunning ground cover in any damp, lightly shaded spot. In late spring and early summer, it is adorned with lovely blue flowers.

Site demands Any moist site, except in baking sun. Dark-leaf varieties look best in a sunny site; variegated ones prefer shade.

Planting practice Plant in spring or autumn, and lift new offshoots after flowering.

Flowering time Short, blue flower spikes appear from spring to early summer.

Pests and diseases Trouble free.

Bonus point Also make an excellent container plant.

1 *A. reptans* 'Burgundy Glow'♀ A splendid edging plant, with creamy green and red leaves
⌀ **Variegated**
h. 15cm (6in) *s.* 45cm (1½ft)

2 *A. reptans* 'Atropurpurea'♀ Grow this for its striking dark purple leaves.
⌀ **Purple**
h. 15cm (6in) *s.* 45cm (1½ft)

3 *A. reptans* 'Catlin's Giant'♀ A tall variety, its large, bronze leaves have a hint of purple.
⌀ **Bronze**
h. 30cm (1ft) *s.* 45cm (1½ft)

4 *A. reptans* 'Multicolor' This is also known as 'Rainbow' because its bronzy leaves have red, pink and gold markings.
⌀ **Variegated bronze**
h. 15cm (6in) *s.* 45cm (1½ft)

5 *A. reptans* 'Variegata' Dense and slow-spreading, it forms a neat clump. The attractive grey-green leaves are rimmed and splashed with cream.
⌀ **Grey-green and cream**
h. 15cm (6in)
s. 45cm (1½ft)

Bugle can be an invasive plant, but it will seldom spread so fast that it becomes a nuisance. Several varieties have decorative foliage, and most give a great show of rich blue flowers in late spring and early summer, when there are few blues in the garden.

If you do find a patch of bugle is getting out of hand, be brutal: you will not harm the plant. Slice through the clump with a spade in spring, divide your discards and plant them in other parts of the garden that may need a lift.

Happy in the woods
If you have a part of the garden with a woodland feel, and rich damp soil, a bugle will thrive there. Make the most of it by planting it beside a light shady path, where you can fully appreciate the colourful leaves.

A. reptans 'Atropurpurea'

A. reptans 'Catlin's Giant'

STAR PERFORMER
A. reptans 'Burgundy Glow'♀ Grow this beautiful variegated cultivar around the edges of a small island bed, where its striking foliage will take centre stage and its blue summer flowers add a rich note to the border.

Alchemilla

Lady's mantle provides an airy mass of yellow-green flowers in summer, along with eye-catching leaves. Grow it to spill over a path, or as a foil for hothouse colours.

One of the easiest perennials to grow, lady's mantle is best seen at the front of a border, or edging a path. Its irregular, mounded shape, and wonderful flowery sprays, will soften the most rigid straight edges.

A. mollis always gives good results, especially when grown in large groups. But it does self-seed, and it can be irritating to have seedlings popping up where they shouldn't, so cut off flowers before they shed their seeds, if you don't want it to spread.

Expert's Selection

1 A. mollis♀
Good for ground cover. A mass of greenish yellow flowers appears on top of the clumps of hairy, lime-green leaves in early summer.
✿ Yellow-green • Early summer
⌀ Lime-green
h. 45cm (1½ft) *s.* 75cm (2½ft)

2 A. erythropoda♀
The blue-tinged, roundish leaves make this an attractive plant to place at the front of a border.
✿ Yellow-green • Midsummer
⌀ Blue-green
h. 20cm (8in) *s.* 30cm (1ft)

3 A. alpina
A low-lying creeper, the tops of its rounded, dark green leaves are shiny and smooth, while silvery hairs coat the underside.
Yellow-green • Midsummer
⌀ Dark green
h. 15cm (6in) *s.* 45cm (1½ft)

STAR PERFORMER
A. mollis The quintessential cottage garden plant, it is quite happy in hot dry spells. It forms clumps of lime-green leaves, with yellow flowers appearing from early summer.

The Essentials

Site demands Thrives anywhere, but plants will rot in boggy ground.
Planting practice Plant in spring or autumn.
Flowering time Flowers appear in early summer. For a second, autumn display: deadhead promptly.
Pests and diseases Problem-free, but hungry slugs and snails may nibble at new growth.
Bonus point A quick and easy-to-grow provider of good cover.

Anaphalis

Pearly everlasting excels in moist, sunny borders, producing clusters of pearly white flowers and a mass of silver-grey foliage – one of the best reasons for growing it.

Expert's Selection

1 A. triplinervis♀
Keep the soil moist to get a fine summer dome of grey-green leaves.
✿ White • Midsummer–autumn
⌀ Grey-green • *h.&s.* 60cm (2ft)

2 A. margaritacea var. cinnamomea Ideal for drier sites, producing a profusion of densely packed white flowerheads.
✿ White • Late summer–early autumn • ⌀ Silver-grey
h.&s. 60cm (2ft)

3 A. nepalensis var. monocephala Forms compact clumps, that work well in rockeries.
✿ White • Midsummer
⌀ Silver-grey • *h.&s.* 15cm (6in)

Anaphalis bears compact clusters of pearly flowers that glisten in the summer sun. It looks great planted in borders with a white colour scheme.

You will also find it perfect for offsetting patches of vivid reds, oranges and yellows, and it can be highly effective when it is combined with white, pink or mauve *Anemone* x *hybrida* (see opposite), that flower from late summer to early autumn, and also prefer moist soil.

STAR PERFORMER
A. triplinervis♀ **A mass of white flowers with yellow centres really brings this plant to life in late summer.**

The Essentials

Site demands Place in sun or light shade. Ideally, keep soil moist.
Planting practice From autumn to early spring in well-drained soil.
Flowering time Late summer and autumn.
Pests and diseases Trouble free.
Bonus point Blooms are also excellent for cutting and drying.

CUT FLOWERS Flowers will not last long, unless stems are trimmed quite short. They also make a very good central focal point in arrangements, especially dried ones.

Anemone

Windflowers come in over a hundred different varieties, at least one of which will suit most types of site. Choose a mixture with care, and you will get splashes of brilliant white, and bright pinks, reds and blues from early summer through to autumn, in nearly every part of the garden.

A. hupenhensis var. japonica 'Bressingham Glow'

A. rivularis

Expert's Selection

1 *A. hupehensis* 'Hadspen Abundance'♀ Long stems bear stunning flowers with two dark and three paler pink petals, and a rich yellow centre. It looks good in a border, adding colour, right up to the end of the season. The flowers of var. *japonica* 'Bressingham Glow' are semi-double, and have a deep purple-blue tinge.
✿ **Dark pink • Late summer–early autumn**
h. **75cm (2½ft)** *s.* **45cm (1½ft)**

2 *A.* x *hybrida* 'Honorine Jobert'♀ A spreading Japanese anemone with eye-catching, open white flowers with a yellow 'eye'. It should remain in bloom for a good 10 weeks.
✾ **White • Late summer–early autumn •** *h.* **1.5m (5ft)** *s.* **60cm (2ft)**

3 *A. rivularis*
Long, spreading stalks bear tiny, delicate white or blue flowers in early summer. A second flowering may appear in autumn.
✾✿ **White and blue • Early summer**
h. **1m (3ft)** *s.* **45cm (1½ft)**

Anemones are grown for their colourful saucer-like, or gently cupped, flowers. Smaller varieties are good planted at border edges or in rock gardens, while larger ones will help to keep beds flushed with colour well into the autumn.

They are hardy plants, and will grow readily wherever the soil is rich in nutrients. Add plenty of humus to the planting hole where necessary. This will ensure that they get off to an excellent start.

To propagate, divide plants in spring, before flowering, and replant immediately.

The Essentials

Site demands Best in sun or light shade, in rich soil, ideally moist and well-drained. Mulch well around the plants in spring to help conserve moisture.

Planting practice Anemones are best planted in autumn.
Flowering time Summer to early autumn, depending on type.
Pests and diseases Generally problem-free, but look out for grey mould, powdery mildew, and attacks by slugs and snails.
Bonus point The huge variety means there is an anemone suited to almost any site.

STAR PERFORMER
A. hupehensis 'Hadspen Abundance' **In rich soil that retains its moisture in summer, this lovely plant can grow up to around 75cm (2½ft) high.**

A. x *hybrida* 'Honorine Jobert'

Anthemis

These are perfect plants for borders and cottage gardens, with their pretty fern-like foliage and masses of fresh daisy-like flowers in white or yellow, with a yellow eye.

Expert's Selection

1 *A. punctata* subsp. *cupaniana* ♀ Silvery grey leaves and yellow eyed blooms.
❀ White • Early–midsummer
h. 30cm (1ft) *s.* 60cm (2ft)

2 *A. tinctoria* 'Grallagh Gold' Golden marguerites that flower for months.
✿ Bright yellow
All summer
h.&s. 60cm (2ft)

3 *A. tinctoria* 'E. C. Buxton' Tall and eye catching; 'Alba' is the white version.
✿ Pale lemon
All summer
h. 1m (3ft) *s.* 60cm (2ft)

4 *A. sancti-johannis* St. John's camomile provides a sharp flash of rich colour.
✿ Orange • Midsummer
h.&s. 60cm (2ft)

The Essentials

Site demands Position in full sun in a free-draining soil.
Planting practice Plant in spring.
Flowering time All summer.
Pests and diseases Trouble free.
Bonus point The foliage of *A. punctata* subsp. *cupaniana* is spicily aromatic.

PRUNING TIP Cut back the stems after flowering to force new growth and extend the life of the plant.

Anthemis need little encouragement to give a great show, and they get the summer garden off to a flying start. All they require is planting in a sunny, well-drained position, and you can forget about them until they have finished flowering, when you will need to cut the stems right back.

They are ideal in cottage-garden style borders, though *A. punctata* subsp. *cupaniana* is charming in a rockery. They all hate wet, heavy soils, so if your garden is badly drained or clay, it is best to grow them in tubs.

STAR PERFORMER

A. punctata subsp. *cupaniana* ♀ This sun-loving perennial sprawls in delightfully informal clumps at the front of a border.

Anthriscus

Cow parsley or **Queen Anne's Lace** is hugely underrated. It grows easily and gives a fantastic show in spring and early summer.

STAR PERFORMER

A. sylvestris Simple cow parsley, stalwart of countryside hedgerows, adds a light, wild touch to any garden, and looks superb when planted in long rows.

Expert's Selection

1 *A. sylvestris*
A native British plant best grown where its invasive habit is welcomed. The sprays of flowers are sweetly scented.
❀ Cream • Mid spring to early summer • *h.* 1m (3ft) *s.* 60cm (2ft)

2 *A. sylvestris* 'Ravenswing'
Brownish purple leaves provide a striking background for creamy, scented flowerheads.
❀ Cream • Mid spring to early summer • *h.* 1.5m (5ft) *s.* 60cm (2ft)

Cow parsley is not for the remorselessly neat and tidy. It is very easily grown and can be invasive: it might suddenly pop up in the middle of a semi-shady lawn. But when it grows in long grass among apple trees and roses it is the frothy epitome of early summer.

Ideally, you want to plant cow parsley and forget it, so try using it to line a driveway or path, or sow it in a wild-flower garden.

However, as it is so robust it is best planted once the other wild plants you choose have had a chance to establish themselves. Good planting companions include sweet cicely, bluebells, white stichwort and red campion.

The Essentials

Site demands A sunny or semi-shady position and moist soil.
Planting practice Plant in spring.
Flowering time From mid spring to early summer.
Pests and diseases Trouble free.
Bonus point Warmed by the sun it gives a sweet summery scent.

Aquilegia

Columbines are incredibly easy to grow, and give a superb display in early summer. The colours range from subtle to flashy.

A. vulgaris var. *stellata* 'William Guiness'

A. vulgaris var. *stellata* 'Nora Barlow'

A. flabellata

Expert's Selection

1 *A. McKana Hybrids*
Large flowers of mixed bright colours are abundant on this plant.
✿✿✿❀ **Various • Late spring–early summer**
h. 1m (3ft) *s.* 60cm (2ft)

2 *A. vulgaris* var. *stellata* 'Nora Barlow'♀ Pink pompom flowers are flecked with green and white. Another beauty is the purple and white 'William Guiness'.
✿ **Pink with white and lime green Early summer**
h. 75cm (2½ft) *s.* 45cm (1½ft)

3 *A. formosa*
The bright flashy flowers stand out.
✿ **Red with yellow inside Late spring–midsummer**
h. 1m (3ft) *s.* 45cm (1½ft)

4 *A. flabellata*♀
An excellent dwarf columbine.
✿ **Violet-blue • Early summer**
h. 30cm (1ft) *s.* 25cm (10in)

5 *A. coerulea*♀
Beautiful but short-lived.
✿ **Blue and white • Early summer**
h. 60cm (2ft) *s.* 30cm (1ft)

6 *A. alpina*
Delicate nodding flowers.
✿ **Bright blue • Late spring–early summer**
h. 45–60cm (1½–2ft)
s. 30cm (1ft)

The Essentials

Site demands Bright sun or light dappled shade, and any soil but clay.
Planting practice Plant in spring.
Flowering time Late spring to early summer, lasting a few weeks.
Pests and diseases Trouble free.
Bonus point Exciting new varieties appear regularly.

Aquilegias produce a marvellous show of shapely flowers on long thin stems that stand well clear of the leaves – and once they have finished flowering, the deeply lobed foliage remains decorative. The plants are easily grown and often self sow. They will happily spread around the garden by seed, and are good at cross-pollinating, so you may even find new colour combinations coming up.

Aquilegias tend not to be that long-lived – with one notable exception: the McKana Hybrids should survive for at least 10 years. You can extend the life of other sorts beyond two or three years by snipping off the flowerheads as they fade to stop the plants from setting seed.

STAR PERFORMER
A. McKana Hybrids **Raised in America and introduced to Europe in 1973, these exciting, vigorous, graceful plants have a great show of large flowers with long spurs and in bright colours.**

Armeria

Sea pink or **thrift** grows naturally on cliffs, seashores and mountains. At home, its white, pink and reddish pompom flowers stand erect in rock or gravel gardens in late spring.

Do not put armerias in a bed, because they will be swamped by taller plants. Instead, space them around in a well-drained rock garden or raised bed, where you will be able to see the flowers more clearly.

Gravel gardens

Armeria is also at home in gravel gardens or scree, and the smaller varieties, such as *A. juniperifolia*, look pretty grown in a trough filled with a gritty compost mix.

STAR PERFORMER
A. alliacea This variety makes a robust clump with large flowerheads.

Expert's Selection

1 *A. alliacea*
A low mound of dark green foliage forms a cushion below the flowers.
❀ **White to purple • Early summer**
h.&s. 40cm (16in)

2 *A.* **'Bees' Ruby'**♀ A clump of these or several scattered in gaps beside a path will look sensational.
✿ **Bright pink • Early summer**
h.&s. 25cm (10in)

3 *A. maritima*
Cushions of sea thrift will spread over a craggy rock garden.
❀✿✿ **White, pink or red • Early summer • h. 20cm (8in)**
s. 50cm (20in)

4 *A. juniperifolia*♀
A deservedly popular small thrift; the deep pink 'Bevan's Variety' cultivar is even more compact.
✿ **Deep pink to white • Early summer • h.&s. 10cm (4in)**

The Essentials

Site demands Thrifts don't like constant damp.
Planting practice Mulch around the plants with grit to protect crowns from excess winter wet.
Flowering time Spring and early summer.
Pests and diseases A trouble-free choice.
Bonus point Thrifts thrive in the most inhospitable spots.

Artemisia

Mugwort can be grown in the herb garden for its medicinal and moth repellant properties or in the border for its wonderful foliage. The best have fine, graceful silvery leaves, which, when dried, make an aromatic addition to a potpourri of other herbs and scented garden flowers.

A. lactiflora

A. ludoviciana

Expert's Selection

1 *A.* **'Powis Castle'**♀
Plant this variety in well-drained soil for the best display of wispy foliage over many years.
∅ **Silver • h. 60cm (2ft) s. 1m (3ft)**

2 *A. lactiflora*♀
White mugwort has large jagged leaves and huge plumes of flowers.
∅ **Deep green** ❀ **Creamy white Late summer • h. 1.8m (6ft)**
s. 60cm (2ft)

3 *A. ludoviciana* **'Silver Queen'**♀ Grow this for its striking finger-like silver-grey leaves.
∅ **Grey** ❀ **Yellow-grey • Summer h. 75cm (2½ft) s. 60cm (2ft)**

4 *A. alba* **'Canascens'**♀
For ground cover, try this bushy variety, with beautiful lacy leaves.
∅ **Silver** ❀ **Yellow • Midsummer h. 45cm (1½ft) s. 30cm (1ft)**

5 *A. stelleriana* **'Boughton Silver'** This prostrate Japanese form makes superb ground cover.
∅ **Silver** ❀ **Yellow • Late summer h. 15cm (6in) s. 45cm (1½ft)**

6 *A. vulgaris* **'Oriental Hybrids'** A new variety, often sold as a container plant, but excellent in a border.
∅ **Gold-green • Spring–autumn h. 60cm (2ft) s. indefinite**

The Essentials

Site demands Artemisias grow in all soils except for permanently wet ones. Plant the dwarf varieties in rockeries or raised beds.

Planting practice Dig plenty of humus and grit into heavy soils to improve drainage before you plant.

Flowering time Artemisias are primarily grown for their foliage. The flowers are largely insignificant, but appear in late summer.

Pests and diseases Rust can spot leaves, and look out for signs of aphid attack.

Bonus point Dry the aromatic leaves and use them in potpourri.

STAR PERFORMER
A. 'Powis Castle' ♥ **Its wispy texture and silvery grey foliage make this artemisia a great addition to a white garden.**

Silvery artemisias sparkle in a border of dark-leaved plants. The wispy foliage is the main draw of most varieties; the button-like flowers, which are mostly yellow, have less appeal and many gardeners cut them off.

You can encourage a burst of fresh new foliage by cutting back the plants in spring, just as they are starting into growth. This is also a good tip for keeping the more vigorous spreaders in check. For a taller display than these choices offer, try a shrubby variety instead (see page 184).

Herb gardens
Although it grows well beside most kitchen herbs, artemisia leaves are not edible. Dried and crushed, though, they are an effective moth repellent – without making your clothes smell unpleasant.

Aruncus

Goat's beard gives a prolific summer display with an erupting mass of leaves, topped by airy sprays of white or cream flowers.

Expert's Selection

1 *A. dioicus*
Stately plumes of creamy white feathery flowers shoot up from a graceful spray of broad horizontal leaves in summer.
✿ Creamy white • Midsummer
h. 1.8m (6ft) *s.* 1.2m (4ft)

2 *A. aethusifolius*
Divided leaves yellow in autumn after the flowers have faded. This can be hard to find, but is the only aruncus for a small space.
✿ Creamy white • Midsummer
h. 25cm (10in) *s.* 30cm (1ft)

3 *A. dioicus* 'Kneiffii'
If you have limited space, this slightly shorter variety of *A. dioicus* is a more suitable choice, without sacrificing the dramatic plumes.
✿ Creamy white • Midsummer
h. 1.2m (4ft) *s.* 60cm (2ft)

STAR PERFORMER
A. dioicus **Create a striking focal point in the border by including this stately specimen that tops 1.8m (6ft) tall.**

The Essentials

Site demands Aruncus will grow in most soils, ideally with only light shade, or sun.

Planting practice Dig in plenty of organic matter and water plants in sunny, free-draining ground during prolonged dry spells.

Flowering time One terrific show, around midsummer.

Pests and diseases Trouble free.

Bonus point Attractive foliage even when not in flower.

The largest and most popular goat's beard, *A. dioicus*, has tremendous impact when used as a big, bold architectural plant. However, it is not for the overcrowded or smaller garden.

If there is no room in the main part of your garden, but you have a wild area, try an aruncus there. They are particularly successful in the moist soil around a pond or near a stream.

Arum

Relatives of the Swiss cheese plant, arums offer beautifully patterned leaves, eye-catching, poisonous berries and large dramatic spathes. Even better, some unfurl their glossy leaves in late autumn when the garden needs a lift. Plant in a fertile, shady spot, and forget about them.

Expert's Selection

1 *A. italicum* 'Marmoratum'♀ Marbled arrow-shaped leaves appear in autumn. A spike of bright berries follows the early summer spathe.
❀ **Cream spathe • Early summer**
❧ **Red • Late summer**
h. **40cm (16in)** *s.* **20cm (8in)**

2 *A. pictum*
Thick, shiny green leaves have cream veins. Shelter from frost.
✿ **Purplish black spathe • Autumn**
h.&s. **20cm (8in)**

3 *A. maculatum*
Lords and ladies spread fast and are best grown in a wild area.
❀ **Cream spathe • Early summer**
❧ **Red • Late summer–autumn**
h. **30cm (1ft)** *s.* **20cm (8in)**

4 *A. creticum*
Plant for its amazing spathes in a mild, sheltered garden, or a pot.
✿ **Deep yellow, sweetly scented spathe • Late spring**
h. **40cm (16in)** *s.* **20cm (8in)**

The Essentials

Site demands
Fertile, humus-rich soil and partial shade.
Planting practice
Plant tubers in summer.
Flowering time Foliage appears before or after winter, followed by spathes in spring and berries in summer.
Pests and diseases Trouble free.
Bonus point Arums provide extraordinary year-round interest.

Arums are often sold as tubers. Look for plump tubers with just a couple of shoots – a lot of shoots may mean that a tuber has been damaged. Just place them in the ground, about 10cm (4in) deep, and scatter some small pebbles on the soil to remind you where they are.

Smells to tempt flies
In late spring or early summer, the eccentric looking arum spathe, which encloses the spadix (spike) and a cluster of minute flowers, emerges. On warm sunny afternoons the spike heats up and emits a noticeable smell of rotting meat to attract pollinating insects. Compared with some plants they don't smell too bad, and you will only detect a real pong up close, but it can cause some amusement. Be careful not to touch the plant.

Berry spikes appear in late summer

STAR PERFORMER
A. italicum 'Marmoratum'♀ **The striking leaves, perfect in flower arrangements, appear in autumn and last into spring or even the start of summer.**

SAFETY WARNING Arum berries are poisonous and the sap from the leaves and stems can irritate the skin.

A. pictum

A. creticum

Aster

Asters are the definitive autumn plants. They give glorious late season colour, attract bees and butterflies and end the year on a high. They come in a wide range of sizes, from low-growing ones for the front of the border to the classic tall Michaelmas daisies that stand at the back.

STAR PERFORMER

A. x *frikartii* 'Flora's Delight' **The aster with just about everything – abundant lilac flowers and pretty grey-tinged foliage, and stems short enough for it to be used at the front of the border.**

Use easy going asters to fill the gaps left by plants that have already finished flowering. They are easy to grow and like a sunny position. If you prefer the autumn to tiptoe out quietly, choose lilacs, pinks and light blues. And if you like snappy bright colours bursting out of the early morning mist, go for bright blues or even the vivid cerise *A. novae-angliae* 'Andenken an Alma Pötschke'.

If you can spare the space, plant a clump of asters especially for cutting. In a vase, they should give a good show for up to two weeks.

A. novae-angliae 'Andenken an Alma Pötschke'

A. lateriflorus 'Horizontalis'

A. amellus 'Veilchenkönigin'

The Essentials

Site demands They prefer slightly alkaline soil, in full sun, in ground that does not dry out completely.
Planting practice Plant in spring.
Flowering time Late summer to autumn.
Pests and diseases It is worth spraying against powdery mildew.
Bonus point Many make excellent autumn cut flowers.

Expert's Selection

1 *A.* x *frikartii* 'Flora's Delight' A dwarf aster with lilac flowers and greyish foliage.
✿ Lilac • Autumn
h.&s. 45cm (1½ft)

2 *A. turbinellus*♀
An American aster with abundant flowers on slender, wiry stems.
✿ Lilac • Mid autumn
h. 1.2m (4ft) *s.* 60cm (2ft)

3 *A. novae-angliae* 'Andenken an Alma Pötschke'♀ A terrific New England aster, in a stunning cerise.
✿ Cerise • Autumn
h. 1.2m (4ft) *s.* 1m (3ft)

4 *A. amellus* 'Veilchenkönigin'♀ Loose clusters of flowers are held on erect woody stems.
✿ Violet • Autumn
h. 45cm (1½ft) *s.* 60cm (2ft)

5 *A. lateriflorus* 'Horizontalis'♀ A compact, late flowering aster that forms a low bush with small purplish leaves and tiny flowers.
✿ Purple-and-white • Mid autumn
h. 60cm (2ft) *s.* 75cm (2½ft)

6 *A. novi-belgii* 'Climax' A terrific, tall, old-fashioned Michaelmas daisy, as popular now as at the start of the last century. Staking is not necessary.
✿ Lavender-blue • Autumn
h. 1.2m (4ft) *s.* 60cm (2ft)

Astilbe

With pyramids or spires of tiny flowers, astilbes make a fantastic summer show. Available in white, reds, pinks and lilac, they thrive in moist sites, and make even more impact when their dramatic shapes are reflected in water. Miniature versions can be just right for smaller gardens.

Astilbes are a gardener's dream. They have enormous presence and add lively colour to damp parts of the garden – which can often tend to be overly green in summer. Furthermore, the spent flower spikes with their fluffy seed heads give structure in winter, making them double value plants. First, enjoy their unmissable summer show of colour, with fine flower plumes held well above the mass of foliage, and then leave them to give a boost to the winter garden.

Winter tracery

Rather than cutting the spikes after flowering, leave them alone. This will ensure extra shape in the garden when so many plants are down and out. The tracery of stems and grainy seed heads look their best when frosty white. Cut them down before the new growth begins.

STAR PERFORMER

A. x *arendsii* 'Fanal'♀ **This spectacularly tall variety has really intense, crimson-red flowers and plenty of dark green foliage.**

TAKE A FRESH LOOK

A. *chinensis* 'Pumila'♀ For an astilbe with a difference, try this low, spreading variety. It has a 30cm (1ft) high mass of leaves topped by bright pinkish mauve flowers between late summer and early autumn.

When growing astilbes in drier soil, choose a spot with some shade so that the ground does not dry out in summer. A thick mulch of mushroom compost, for example, quickly applied after heavy rain, will really help to keep moisture locked in the soil.

Expert's Selection

1 A. x *arendsii* 'Fanal'♀
An excellent, medium-sized plant with plenty of impact. The vivid red flowers open in June and give a long show. 'Brautschleier'♀, or 'Bridal Veil', is white.
✿ **Scarlet • Summer • h. 60cm (2ft) s. 40cm (16in)**

2 A. 'Sprite'♀
Delightful pale-coloured flowers stand out against darker leaves. This small astilbe is a perfect choice for the front of a border.
✿ **Light pink • Early summer h. 45cm (1½ft) s. 30cm (1ft)**

3 A. *simplicifolia*♀
This short variety has a lovely display of fern-like leaves, which are excellent in cut flower arrangements. It looks particularly attractive dotted around a pond.
✿ **Pale pink • Summer h.&s. 23cm (9in)**

4 A. *chinensis* var. *taquetii* 'Purpurlanze' A late summer performer, this tall astilbe tolerates drier ground than most and gives a

A. chinensis 'Pumila'

A. 'Sprite'

colourful, attention-grabbing show. 'Superba' is bright mauve.
✿ **Purple-red • Late summer h. 1.2m (4ft) s. 1m (3ft)**

The Essentials

Site demands Fertile, moist soil. Keep damp in summer.
Planting practice Plant bare root specimens from autumn to spring; container-grown plants at any time the weather is favourable.
Flowering time The plumes are at their best in high summer.
Pests and diseases Powdery mildew can occur in dry spells.
Bonus point The robust stems never require staking.

Astrantia

Masterworts are one of the highlights of the summer garden with their white, pink or red pincushion flowers on tall thin stems. They are ideal for cottage gardens.

With their intriguing spikey blooms, astrantias are at their most striking in relaxed woodland-type gardens. In the right conditions they self-seed and spread, but if you prefer this not to happen, simply deadhead when the flowers are starting to fade.

Some red astrantias lack really vigorous growth. The best way to help them is by forking plenty of humus around the plant in spring. The reds are generally best placed in the border where they make a strong impact in bright sunshine.

Expert's Selection

1 A. major 'Shaggy' ♀
A creamy variety that looks terrific in light dappled shade.
❀ **White, tipped with green**
Early summer • h. 75cm (2½ft)
s. 45cm (1½ft)

2 A. major 'Ruby Wedding'
With its rich red flowers, this tall astrantia is stunning in the border.
✿ **Red • Midsummer**
h. 75cm (2½ft) s. 45cm (1½ft)

3 A. major
The petals are crisp and white with slivers of green and pink.
❀ **White • Midsummer**
h. 75cm (2½ft) s. 45cm (1½ft)

4 A. major var. rosea
Beautiful soft-coloured flowers.
✿ **Pink • Midsummer • h. 60cm (2ft)**
s. 40cm (16in)

The Essentials

Site demands A sunny or lightly shaded spot with fertile soil.
Planting practice Any time from late autumn to spring.
Flowering time Generally just before midsummer.
Pests and diseases Slugs and snails may attack new growth.
Bonus point They are great in flower arrangements, both fresh or dried.

STAR PERFORMER
A. major 'Shaggy' ♀ The best, big, bold astrantia, it has long white bracts tipped green, and flowers before midsummer.

Aurinia (Alyssum)

Yellow alyssum or **gold dust** is one of the brightest mid-spring sights, with its sprays of yellow. It grows best, and spreads fastest, on sunny walls and in rock gardens.

Expert's Selection

1 A. saxatilis ♀
This variety will soon thrive to form a spreading mat of flowers.
✿ **Yellow • Early summer**
h. 20cm (8in) s. 30cm (1ft)

2 A. saxatilis 'Citrina' ♀
A deservedly popular variety with soft lemon flowers.
✿ **Lemon yellow • Early summer**
h. 20cm (8in) s. 45cm (1½ft)

3 A. saxatilis 'Dudley Nevill Variegated' Striking variegated leaves combine with pale flowers.
✿ **Biscuit yellow** ⌀ **Green variegated**
Early summer • h. 20cm (8in)
s. 40cm (16in)

4 A. saxatilis 'Compacta'
A charming dwarf alyssum with bright golden blooms.
✿ **Gold • Summer • h. 10cm (4in)**
s. 30cm (1ft)

The Essentials

Site demands Excellent drainage and plenty of sunshine – the cracks in a wall or a rockery are ideal.
Planting practice Plant out seedlings from spring to summer.
Flowering time Late spring and early summer.
Pests and diseases Trouble free.
Bonus point Established plants often self-seed freely.

STAR PERFORMER
A. saxatilis
Long known as *Alyssum saxatile*, this aurinia is a great choice If you have a dull-looking crumbling wall: just plant it in the gaps between the stones and forget it.

Alyssum, now known as *Aurinia*, is a wonderful spreading plant for a sunny sheltered site or set against a wall or bank. It has been a staple in rock gardens and alpine schemes for many years, where its evergreen foliage makes low hummocks that are smothered in yellow flowers in early summer.

If you are building a wall or a craggy alpine garden, create a few planting pockets, fill them with soil, mixed with grit to improve drainage, and put in a few young plants. They can also soften the lines of a retaining wall in front of a raised bed: plant them at the front of the bed and allow them to tumble over the edge.

Bergenia

Elephant's ears make superb ground cover, and the evergreen leaves of many excel in winter when they flare up red or purple. With bold shapes, large often glossy foliage and gorgeous pink, red, white or mauve spring flowers on spikes, they provide year-round interest.

B. cordifolia 'Purpurea'   *B.* 'Baby Doll'

Bergenias add character to a border with their attractive, out-sized foliage. Steer clear of the very large-leaved kind, such as *B. ciliata*, in small gardens, where they will dominate. Plant elephant's ears beside straight-edged paths to soften the look, as a leafy frame around island beds, or around ponds where young frogs can hide under the leaves.

Winter focal points

Make an impact by growing a group on a south-facing bank, where drainage is good. If you are restricted to just one or two, go for winter performers, such as 'Bressingham Ruby', whose leaves redden up. Place them where they will catch the sun, and against a contrasting background.

STAR PERFORMER

B. 'Bressingham Ruby' In a family of stars, this bergenia is the best. Its mighty leaves, 18cm (7in) long are set off by reddy pink flowers in spring.

Expert's Selection

1 *B.* 'Bressingham Ruby' The glossy leaves turn a deep beetroot-red in winter. 'Bressingham Salmon' is similar, but with salmon-pink flowers.
✿ **Reddish pink • Spring**
∅ **Beetroot-red • Winter**
h.&s. 35cm (14in)

2 *B.* 'Eric Smith' Crinkled leaves point upward, showing their reddish undersides.
✿ **Pink • Late spring** ∅ **Bronze**
h.&s. 35cm (14in)

3 *B. cordifolia* 'Purpurea' ♀
Cabbage-like leaves – 30cm (1ft) long – gain a purple tinge in winter.
✿ **Dark pink • Early spring**
∅ **Purple • Winter • h.&s. 60cm (2ft)**

4 *B.* 'Baby Doll' Compared with other varieties, the leaves are tiny, just 10cm (4in) long.
✿ **Pale pink • Late spring** ∅ **Bronze**
h. 30cm (1ft) s. 60cm (2ft)

5 *B.* x *schmidtii* ♀
A big favourite, with bright, fresh green, toothed leaves.
✿ **Pink • Early spring**
h.&s. 30cm (1ft)

6 *B. ciliata* The hairy soup bowl-shaped leaves are 35cm (14in) long.
❀ **Rose white • Early spring**
h.&s. 45cm (1½ft)

7 *B.* 'Silberlicht' ♀
Vigorous white blooms develop an attractive pinkish tinge.
❀ **White • Early spring**
h.&s. 30cm (1ft)

8 *B.* 'Abendglut' Also called *B.* 'Evening Glow', its leaves turn maroon in winter.
✿ **Rose red • Early spring**
∅ **Maroon • Winter**
h. 30cm (1ft) s. 60cm (2ft)

The Essentials

Site demands Any soil, except the very dry or very wet. Full sun in winter gives the most striking leaf colour.

Planting practice Plant or divide in mid autumn or spring, or at any time in containers.

Flowering time From late winter to late spring.

Pests and diseases Slugs, snails and vine weevils may damage foliage.

Bonus point Bergenias are excellent at smothering weeds.

FOLIAGE FOR FLOWER DISPLAYS
Bergenia leaves add variety and impact to a floral arrangement. Soak them in cold water for a few hours before using them, or – if they have suffered in a frost – in a little luke warm water to perk them up.

Brunnera

With forget-me-not-like sprays of blue spring flowers, a clump of brunnera will spread to create a patterned carpet in any cool, damp, sheltered part of the garden with light shade. Only one species, *Brunnera macrophylla*, is available, but several excellent cultivars offer greater variety.

Expert's Selection

1 *B. macrophylla* 'Langtrees' Sometimes known by its previous name, 'Aluminium Spot', it spreads to make excellent ground cover.
✿ **Clear blue • Late spring**
h. 45cm (1½ft) *s.* 60cm (2ft)

2 *B. macrophylla* 'Hadspen Cream'♀ The blue flowers and cream-edged leaves create an appealing mix of colours.
✿ **Bright blue • Spring**
⊘ **Green, edged with cream**
h. 45cm (1½ft) *s.* 60cm (2ft)

3 *B. macrophylla* 'Betty Bowring' Plant this white-flowered variety for contrast in a clump of blue brunneras.
❀ **White • Spring**
h. 45cm (1½ft) *s.* 60cm (2ft)

4 *B. macrophylla*♀
Also called *Anchusa myosotidiflora*, it it the parent plant of all the varieties listed above.
✿ **Bright blue • Spring**
h. 45cm (1½ft) *s.* 60cm (2ft)

The Essentials

Site demands Plant in parts of the garden that are reliably moist, in light shade, or in sunnier spots, provided the soil does not dry out.
Planting practice Plant in spring or autumn. Fork humus into poor soil. Water new plants regularly over their first summer: established plants have longer roots and are better at finding moisture.
Flowering time Flowers appear from mid to late spring.
Pests and diseases Remarkably trouble free, so should present few problems.
Bonus point Will provide excellent ground cover, in all but the most shaded sites.

B. macrophylla 'Hadspen Cream'

B. macrophylla 'Betty Bowring'

Most gardens have a moist, lightly shaded area. It may be sheltered by a wall or fence for part of the day, or fall in the shade of a spreading tree.

Finding the right plants to fill the space could not be easier. Brunnera makes excellent ground cover in situations like this without getting out of hand. However, if you are tight for space, or if the plant threatens to be too invasive, cutting it back is simple. Divide large clumps in autumn and spread the resulting smaller plants around the garden.

Plants for the damp and shade

Brunnera is a pretty and informal plant that mixes well with other traditional ground-cover species. Try planting it with others that thrive in damp, dappled shade, such as the woodland **lily of the valley** (*Convallaria majalis*), a *Pulmonaria* or several *Hostas*.

Caltha

Marsh marigolds or **king-cups** give rich yellow, or sometimes white flowers in early spring and summer at the shallow edge of a pond or stream, or in a rock garden. Very striking, with shiny leaves, these excellent plants will contribute a sudden, surprise burst of colour.

Calthas belong to a group of plants that like growing in shallow water. If you wish to grow them beside a stream, plant them straight into the muddy soil, but avoid fast-flowing stretches that will immediately sweep new plants away. In bog gardens, too, marsh marigolds can be put straight into the ground. In ponds, however, you need a different approach.

STAR PERFORMER
C. palustris var. *palustris* **'Plena'** One of the largest of the marsh marigolds, it has bright yellow, double pompom flowers in spring. It is also well worth growing for its glossy rounded foliage. It will spread freely over wet ground.

Planting in a pond
You will need a special perforated plant holder, available from garden centres. Line the inside with hessian to stop the soil from seeping away. The special heavy pond loam is not the same as for pot plants, and is also sold at garden centres. Plant the calthas in the basket and put a handful of small pebbles on top of the soil. This will help to keep the soil and plants in place and stop fish from disturbing the surface of the soil.

Soak the basket thoroughly, and gently lower it into the pond. Pre-watering removes most of the air from the soil: otherwise, putting the basket in the water creates an upsurge of bubbles, which can loosen the plant.

The Essentials

Site demands Roots must be kept wet, so plant in a bog garden, pond or permanently moist border. Full sun needed for good flowering.
Planting practice Plant in spring or early summer; use a planting basket in ponds (see above).
Flowering time Early spring to early summer. Cutting back hard after flowering may lead to a second flourish.
Pests and diseases Usually trouble free.
Bonus point Glossy, dark green leaves form an attractive summer carpet.

CUT FLOWER DISPLAYS
The leaves bring variety and impact to flower arrangements. Soak them for a few hours first in cold water. Use warm water for leaves that have suffered slightly from frost.

C. palustris 'Alba'

C. palustris

Expert's Selection

1 *C. palustris* var. *palustris* **'Plena'** An excellent rock garden plant with double button flowers.
✿ **Yellow • Spring**
h. 45cm (1½ft) *s.* 75cm (2½ft)

2 *C. palustris* var. *alba*
Gold-eyed blooms in neat clumps.
❀ **White • Late spring**
h. 30cm (1ft) *s.* 35cm (14in)

3 *C. palustris* **'Flore Pleno'**♀
A superb showy plant with rosettes of double flowers.
✿ **Yellow • Late spring**
h.&s. 25cm (10in)

4 *C. palustris*♀
The variety found in the wild.
✿ **Yellow • Spring**
h. 45cm (1½ft) *s.* 75cm (2½ft)

Campanula

Bellflowers are synonymous with cottage gardens. Their delicate summer flowers feature all shades of blue, and sometimes white or pink. Some are tall enough to need staking, while others form low clumps which are ideal for the front of the border, or even tiny gaps in a wall.

With more than 300 species, there is a fantastic choice of bellflowers. Some form clumps, others have near vertical stems; some spread and others trail. Blues, whether pale lilac or rich dark hues, vary according to the brightness of the day. Although under a bright midday sun in the middle of summer, pale blue campanulas may look slightly washed out, the same blue in light shade will look far more vivid.

Cool down a hot bed

Choose paler shades for a cool, elegant style. They work well in formal designs with statues, pots and urns. Use them with soft pastels like pinks and cream. They are also good at framing or toning down hotter schemes with strong bright red and orange.

The Essentials

Site demands Any free-draining, moist, fertile soil, in either a sunny or lightly shaded site.
Planting practice Plant in spring or autumn, and divide every 3–4 years, after flowering, if necessary.
Flowering time Varies from early to late summer.
Pests and diseases Trouble free, but look out for slugs and snails.
Bonus point You may get a second flush of flowers if you cut back after blooming.

Expert's Selection

1 *C. glomerata* 'Joan Elliott'
Vigorous and with stunning, large blooms. *C. glomerata* has smaller flowers, but blooms all summer.
✿ **Violet • Early summer**
h. **40cm (16in)** *s.* **50cm (20in)**

2 *C. persicifolia*
Traditionally grown among Old Garden Roses, it reliably self-seeds.
❀ **White to violet blue • Midsummer**
h. **1m (3ft)** *s.* **40cm (16in)**

3 *C.* 'Burghaltii' ♀
Bell-like blooms on arching stems.
✿ **Pale lavender • Midsummer**
h. **60cm (2ft)** *s.* **40cm (16in)**

4 *C. carpatica* ♀
Low clumps of smooth leaves are topped by large bells.
✿ ❀ **Blue, white • Early–late summer**
h. **15cm (6in)** *s.* **40cm (16in)**

5 *C. lactiflora*
Support the tall stems of numerous pale flowers. 'Pouffe' has mid blue flowers on 60cm (2ft) stems.
✿✿ **Pale blue, pink**
Summer–early autumn
h. **1.2m (4ft)** *s.* **60cm (2ft)**

6 *C. portenschlagiana* ♀
This low spreader forms a floral 'carpet' in summer.
✿ **Deep lavender blue • Summer**
h. **15cm (6in)** *s.* **50cm (20in)**

7 *C.* 'Elizabeth'
Large bells – 5cm (2in) long – hang down from arching flower spikes.
✿ **Cream with reddish purple flush**
Mid–late summer • *h.&s.* 40cm (16in)

> ### STAR PERFORMER
> *C. glomerata* 'Joan Elliott'
> The sturdy stems are topped with striking clusters of lovely, large violet flowers.

C. persicifolia

C. 'Burghaltii'

Centaurea

Knapweed makes a marvellous summer show with thistle-like flowers in a range of colours from yellow and pink to purple and white, that attract bees and butterflies.

Knapweed adds reliable colour to wild flower gardens in summer. Its carefree nature – it spreads readily – means that some kinds can be invasive. Avoid *C. dealbata* unless you have room for it to spread; for a more controllable variety try '**John Coutts**' instead.

For a country cottage effect, try mixing colours. Cultivars of *C. montana*, for example, are available in three complementary colours – '**Alba**' (white), '**Carnea**' (pink) and '**Parham**' (light blue).

Expert's Selection

1 *C. montana*
Support the clear blue flowers of this vigorous mountain cornflower.
✿ **Blue** • **Late spring–summer**
h. **60cm (2ft)** *s.* **50cm (20in)**

2 *C. macrocephala*
Tall yellow flowers contrast with brown bracts beneath their petals.
✿ **Yellow** • **Midsummer**
h. **1m (3ft)** *s.* **60cm (2ft)**

3 *C. hypoleuca* '**John Coutts**' Enjoy two good crops of flowers: in June and September.
✿ **Pinkish red** • **Mid–late summer**
h.&s. **60cm (2ft)**

4 *C. dealbata*
A very vigorous spreader, giving an abundant supply of flowers.
✿ **Pink and white** • **Mid–late summer** • *h.* **1m (3ft)** *s.* **60cm (2ft)**

The Essentials

Site demands Free-draining, poor, chalky ground in full sun.
Pruning practice Cut back after flowering for a second flush.
Flowering time Summer.
Pests and diseases Look out for powdery mildew from midsummer.
Bonus point Knapweed makes fine cut flowers.

STAR PERFORMER
C. montana **The appealing wispy blue flowerheads are borne high above the leaves on tall, straight stems.**

Centranthus

Valerian pleases with plenty of red or white flowers through summer and into early autumn. Ideal for cottage gardens, it happily spreads and self-seeds.

Expert's Selection

1 *C. ruber*
Thick and fleshy grey-green leaves, up to 8cm (3in) long, set off the clusters of deep pink flowers.
✿ **Deep pinky red** • **All summer**
h.&s. **60cm (2ft)**

2 *C. ruber* '**Albus**'
This white valerian is the only widely available alternative to the more common red form, and makes a dramatic contrast.
✾ **White** • **All summer**
h.&s. **60cm (2ft)**

As long as you avoid wet soils, valerian will flourish in most situations. However, in fertile ground the stems can become floppy, and need staking.

Leggy plants will also need dividing every four years, so to make the most of their easy-going nature, only grow valerians if you have poor stony soil, or even a seaside garden. Then, valerian will thrive in tough, compact clumps. You can also grow it, or even better let it self-seed, on old walls and rocky banks, where it looks terrific.

Insect attraction
Besides its grow-anywhere, casual look, valerian is excellent at attracting butterflies and moths. Plant a clump near your favourite spot for sitting in the garden and watch the visiting wildlife all summer long.

The Essentials

Site demands Valerian is easy-going, but does best in poor soil.
Planting practice Sow seed or divide in spring. Cut back after the first flowers for a second crop.
Flowering time From early summer to early autumn.
Pests and diseases Completely trouble free.
Bonus point Their long flowering season makes valerians great value.

STAR PERFORMER
C. ruber **Red valerian produces a prolific supply of tiny, sweetly fragrant dark pink to dark red flowers, on tall stems. The blooms appear in late spring and last all summer.**

Chrysanthemum

Few plants have such garden impact in early autumn as a clump of chrysanthemums. Their flowers come in a range of colours from white to bright red, but are best known for their burnished tones. Not all are fully hardy, but this selection will survive all year in a well-drained spot.

D. 'Clara Curtis'

D. 'Brightness'

Any sunny garden on light soil will benefit from the splash of colour hardy chrysanthemums offer as summer draws to a close. In heavy soils they may need lifting for winter, but in the right situation all the care they require is pinching out as they start to grow, deadheading as the flowers fade and some support to keep their heads high.

Shape and colour
Ring the changes by growing different flower shapes as well as colours. Chrysanthemums range from open and daisy-like, such as 'Clara Curtis', through semi-double, with a round mass of outward pointing petals, like 'Brightness', to the pompoms of varieties like 'Hazy Days'.

Some types of chrysanthemum were classified as *Dendranthema* for a while, but are now known as *Chrysanthemum* once more.

The Essentials

Site demands Plant in full sun and well-drained soil, where the plants will not have to stand in boggy ground through winter.
Planting practice Dig in plenty of humus to improve poor soil. Water well in hot weather, but do not over water young plants.
Flowering time Late summer and early autumn.
Pruning needs Pinch out the growing tips to encourage bushy plants with plenty of flowers.
Pests and diseases Pick off slugs and snails and look out for signs of capsid bugs and red spider mites. Chrysanthemum leaf miners may nibble the leaves, but do no harm.
Bonus point Chrysanthemums make such good arrangements it is worth growing some just to cut.

Expert's Selection

1 *C.* 'Hazy Days'
Robust pompom blooms shrug off the wind and rain to add warm colour to the autumn border.
✿ Amber-bronze • Early autumn
h. 1.2m (4ft) *s.* 60cm (2ft)

2 *C.* 'Clara Curtis'
Masses of daisy-like flowers with a spicy scent appear in late summer on this hardy Rubellum hybrid. As the season fades to autumn, the green central eye turns yellow.
✿ Pink • Late summer–autumn
h. 1m (3ft) *s.* 45cm (1½ft)

3 *C.* 'Brightness'
The Korean hybrids, like this variety, give a beautiful spray of flowers that last all autumn.
✿ Red • Early–late autumn
h. 75cm (2½ft) *s.* 45cm (1½ft)

4 *C.* 'Pennine Flute' ♀
Hugely popular for its spray of open, daisy-like flowers with a yellow eye.
✿ Dark pink • Late summer • *h.* 1.2m (4ft) *s.* 75cm (2½ft)

5 *C.* 'Yellow Gingernut'
With its cheery flash of colour, this sunny yellow chrysanthemum will brighten up any display.
✿ Yellow • Autumn
h. 1.2m (4ft) *s.* 60cm (2ft)

6 *C.* 'Pennine Soldier' ♀
All the 'Pennine' chrysanthemums produce profuse sprays of flowers in free-draining ground.
✿ Red • Late summer
h. 1.2m (4ft) *s.* 75cm (2½ft)

7 *C.* Yoder series
A naturally short, bushy variety, which is ideal for patio cultivation.
✿ Bronze, red, orange, yellow, white
Late summer–autumn
h. 1.2m (4ft) *s.* 75cm (2½ft)

STAR PERFORMER
C. 'Hazy Days' This new variety produces an array of rich amber-bronze blooms, sturdy enough to withstand the worst of the autumn weather.

Chaerophyllum

Hairy chervil belongs to the same family as cow parsley and makes a sensational show in late spring with lilac-pink or white flowers against fern-like leaves.

STAR PERFORMER

C. hirsutum 'Roseum'
Dozens of tiny lilac-pink flowers cluster in rosettes at the top of each vertical, branching, hairy stem.

Chaerophyllum deserves a place in any garden. In damp ground it gives a superb show in early May, before self-seeding round the garden to give you a bigger display next year. It really stands out at a time of year when there is little else in bloom.

Planting companions
Chaerophyllum makes a lacy backdrop to more robust spring flowers, such as late-flowering **daphnes** or **tulips**. Or team it with plants with similar colours and textures, such as *Geranium maculatum*, or cranesbill, for a frothy border of lilac and pink.

Expert's Selection

1 *C. hirsutum* 'Roseum'
Pale flowers stand out against a mass of finely divided leaves.
✿ **Lilac-pink • Late spring**
h. 75cm (2½ft) *s.* 35cm (14in)

2 *Chaerophyllum aureum*
White flowers float above yellowy leaves. Though often called 'Golden chervil', do not confuse it with the similarly named culinary herb, *Anthriscus cerefolium*: it is not edible.
❀ **White • Late spring**
h. 1.2m (4ft) *s.* 45cm (1½ft)

The Essentials

Site demands Chaerophyllum thrives in damp soil. Plant it in sun or partial shade.
Planting practice Plant or divide in spring or autumn.
Flowering time The flowers bloom in late spring, with a second crop often appearing in August.
Pests and diseases Slugs and snails may seek out the succulent young plants.
Bonus point Use cut stems to add a lacy texture to floral displays.

Corydalis

There is room in every garden for at least one corydalis. They flower prolifically in spring in a wide range of colours, and some thrive and self-seed in old stone walls.

Expert's Selection

1 *C. flexuosa* 'Purple Leaf'
Delicate grey-green foliage grows in a tidy mound.
✿ **Blue • Late spring–midsummer**
h.&s. 30cm (1ft)

2 *C. lutea*
A graceful mass of bright flowers will quickly smother a stone wall.
✿ **Bright yellow • Summer**
h. 20cm (8in) *s.* 50cm (20in)

3 *C. solida* 'George Baker'♥
Deep green leaves, tinged bronze, are echoed by the rich flowers.
✿ **Deep brick-red • Spring**
h.&s. 20cm (8in)

4 *C. cheilanthifolia*
A clump of cheery yellow flowers gives a lift to any garden.
✿ **Yellow • Mid spring–midsummer**
h. 25cm (10in) *s.* 40cm (16in)

STAR PERFORMER

C. flexuosa 'Purple Leaf'
Clusters of fine blue flowers nod above rounded clumps of grey-green foliage.

The Essentials

Site demands Light shade and good drainage are essential.
Planting practice Plant in spring and divide clumps each year in early spring or autumn.
Flowering time Spring, with some carrying on into summer.
Pests and diseases Watch out for slugs, which will eat the leaves.
Bonus point Excellent easy-to-grow ground cover.

One of the best-loved plants recently introduced to Britain is *C. flexuosa*. It is easy to grow and produces marvellous vivid blue flowers above pretty, finely divided foliage.

Go crazy in paving
Corydalis do not demand deep soil for their roots. Plant them to fill gaps in paving and they will soon spread to soften the hard edges. Pull them out or split clumps if they become too invasive, or prevent them self-seeding by cutting back the flowers as they begin to fade.

Dianthus

Pinks are sensational cottage-garden plants, and come in a wide range of whites, pinks or reds. While some are charmingly simple, others look wonderfully blowsy. The best varieties also have a sweet clove scent and last well in water as excellent cut flowers.

For spectacular care-free pinks, choose the Modern, mostly large bloomed, varieties like 'Gran's Favourite'. These hybrids give a longer, often brighter show than pure dianthus. If you want a sweet fragrance, Old-fashioned pinks like '**Mrs Sinkins**' are best.

Alpine hybrids, such as '**Inshriach Dazzler**' are perfect for rock gardens. They thrive in free-draining soil and by raising them up you can intensify their scent.

Pinks grow very well in stone troughs, where you can give them the light soil they prefer, and help to ensure that they are at their most care free.

4 *D. plumarius*
Most hardy perennial pinks derive from this fragrant species.
❁ **White and pink • Midsummer**
h.&s. **30cm (1ft)**

5 *D.* '**Mrs Sinkins**'
This Old-fashioned pink is double-flowered and highly scented. It has a lovely ragged edge to the petals.
❁ **White • Midsummer**
h. **30cm (1ft)** *s.* **25cm (10in)**

6 *D.* '**Howard Hitchcock**'♀
With red edges and stripes, this Border carnation is unmistakable.
✿ **Yellow and red • Mid–late summer**
h. **60cm (2ft)** *s.* **45cm (1½ft)**

7 *D.* '**Inshriach Dazzler**'♀
Carmine blooms nestle in grey-green foliage. Turn over the petals and this Alpine pink is buff beneath.
✿ **Carmine red • Midsummer**
h.&s. **15cm (6in)**

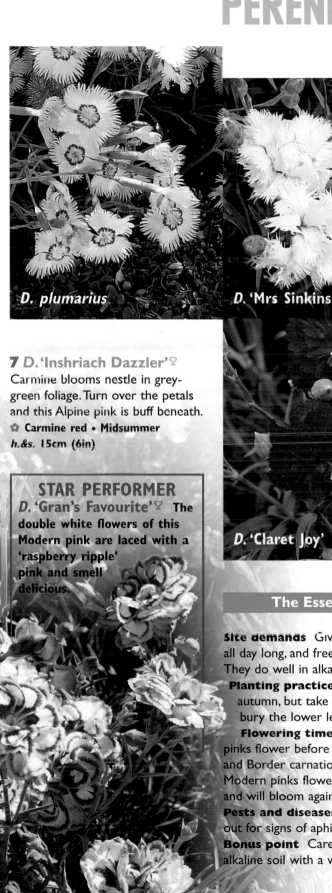

D. plumarius

D. 'Mrs Sinkins'

D. 'Claret Joy'

1 *D.* '**Gran's Favourite**'♀
A great value Modern pink that is vigorous and free-flowering.
❁ **White and pink • Early–midsummer**
h. **35cm (14in)** *s.* **25cm (10in)**

2 *D.* '**Claret Joy**'♀
Another Modern pink, this is an excellent, bright red cut flower.
✿ **Red • Midsummer**
h. **35cm (14in)** *s.* **25cm (10in)**

3 *D.* '**Doris**'♀
A beautiful Modern pink, combining salmon pink with a scarlet eye.
✿ **Salmon pink • Midsummer**
h. **35cm (14in)** *s.* **25cm (10in)**

STAR PERFORMER

D. '**Gran's Favourite**'♀ The double white flowers of this Modern pink are laced with a 'raspberry ripple' pink and smell delicious.

The Essentials

Site demands Give pinks full sun all day long, and free-draining soil. They do well in alkaline soil.
Planting practice Plant in early autumn, but take care not to bury the lower leaves.
Flowering time Old-fashioned pinks flower before midsummer, and Border carnations just after. Modern pinks flower for longer and will bloom again if deadheaded.
Pests and diseases Keep an eye out for signs of aphids.
Bonus point Care-free plants for alkaline soil with a wonderful scent.

D. spectablis

The Essentials

Site demands Bleeding hearts are not for hot gardens: they prefer partial shade and deep, rich, moist soil. Where they flourish, they can spread but they seldom become a nuisance.
Planting practice Improve thin soils by digging in organic matter.
Flowering time A big show in spring and early summer, with more flowers appearing as the season progresses.
Pests and diseases Keep an eye out for slugs and snails.
Bonus point Unusual shaped flowers add interest to a border.

Dicentra

Bleeding hearts are eyecatching and easy to grow in lightly shaded spots. The intriguing flowers, in white, yellow or characteristic red, which give the plant its descriptive common name, hang on arching stems, and put on their best show in spring, with later flowers opening in summer.

Expert's Selection

1 *D.* 'Adrian Bloom'
Large, dark red flowers dangle above grey-green foliage in spring, followed by subsequent flowerings through summer and into autumn.
✿ Dark red • Late spring–autumn
h. 30cm (1ft) *s.* 20cm (8in)

2 *D. spectabilis* ♀
Locket-like flowers hang from arching stems, their inner white petals protruding from the blood red 'heart'. For pure white flowers, choose the variety 'Alba'.
✿ Red and white • Late spring
h. 60cm (2ft) *s.* 45cm (1½ft)

3 *D. macrantha*
In a cool, sheltered part of the garden the jagged, ragged light green leaves of this variety spread into a ferny clump.
✿ Creamy yellow • Late spring
h. 60cm (2ft) *s.* 45cm (1½ft)

TAKE A FRESH LOOK

D. scandens Ring the changes with this unusual climbing dicentra. It clings with tendrils, like a clematis, to whatever gets in its way – from a strong open bush or shrub to wires strung across a wall. Its ultimate height varies from 1.8m (6ft) to 4m (13ft), so give it plenty of space and enjoy its late summer show of yellow flowers.

4 *D.* 'Pearl Drops'
For a dicentra in a different colour, try this low-growing variety with its attractive bluish foliage and pink-tinged flowers.
❀ White • Late spring–summer
h. 30cm (1ft) *s.* 45cm (1½ft)

5 *D.* 'Stuart Boothman' ♀
This very popular variety has richly coloured flowers. Also known as *D.* 'Boothman's Variety'.
✿ Dark pink • Mid spring–midsummer • *h.* 30cm (1ft) *s.* 40cm (16in)

Natural settings suit these compact mounds of fern-like foliage and their masses of small and delicate flowers. Few common names describe their plants as poignantly and aptly as bleeding hearts – *D. spectabilis* is unmistakable.

Most dicentras grow best in gardens with rich moist soil, but dig in plenty of organic matter before you plant and they will survive in lighter ground. Once the plants get established they die down soon after flowering, so it is worth marking the spot to make sure that you do not inadvertently disturb the roots.

STAR PERFORMER
D. 'Adrian Bloom' This variety makes an excellent clump with a long season of interest. Late spring brings clusters of large, carmine-red flowers up to 3cm (1¼in) long, that last in waves until early autumn, when the plant dies down.

Doronicum

Leopard's bane, with its bright, flashy yellow flowers, is a must for the spring garden. The flowers stand well clear of the foliage, giving a sensational show, and because they open in tulip time they can be used in all kinds of terrific combinations of colour, shape and texture.

D. 'Frühlingspracht'

D. x excelsum 'Harpur Crewe'

Leopard's bane grows wild in a wide variety of habitats, from lush meadows to scrubland and from woodland to craggy sites with thin soil – and anywhere from south west Asia to Siberia.

This flexibility makes it the perfect choice for the care-free gardener. Permanent damp or permanent drought will kill it, but otherwise this is among the most easy-going of spring plants.

Planting for contrasts

A clump of leopard's bane makes a marvellous backdrop to a display of different coloured tulips. Doronicum's daisy-like flowers, held on slender stems, and the small, heart-shaped, hairy leaves make a feathery foil for the tulips' robust leaves, stiff stems and large glossy petals.

One big care free advantage of growing leopard's bane is that it dies down quite quickly once the flowers have faded. This gives neighbouring plants a chance to come to the fore, but also means that you don't need to spend time cutting back the dying stems – or put up with them ruining the effect of your summer borders.

The Essentials

Site demands Avoid soil that is very dry or very wet. The plants do best in light shade, but will also tolerate bright sun.

Planting practice Divide clumps every four years between autumn and early spring. Stake tall varieties when they are flowering.

Flowering time Most flower in the second half of spring; some stay open until midsummer.

Pests and diseases Powdery mildew can be a problem, but otherwise vigorous and care free.

Bonus point Makes a bright splash of colour when few other plants are in flower.

Expert's Selection

1 *D.* 'Miss Mason' ♥
A single yellow flower blooms at the end of each stem from spring to early summer, smothering the clump of heart-shaped leaves.
✿ **Bright yellow** • **Mid–late spring**
h. **45cm (1½ft)** *s.* **60cm (2ft)**

2 *D. orientale* 'Magnificum'
For many, this vies for first place with 'Miss Mason'. At medium height with large, sunny flowers on slender stems, it is ideal for the front or middle of a border.
✿ **Rich yellow** • **Late spring**
h. **50cm (20in)** *s.* **1m (3ft)**

3 *D. x excelsum* 'Harpur Crewe' If you want a leopard's bane with more height and impact, this makes a stunning spring show.
✿ **Rich yellow** • **Late spring**
h.&s. **1m (3ft)**

4 *D. pardalianches*
This will spread happily in a light woodland garden. Its flowers make a great splash of colour between small trees, where they blow about atop slender, wiry stems.
✿ **Yellow** • **Early summer**
h.&s. **1m (3ft)**

5 *D.* 'Frühlingspracht'
Also known as 'Spring Beauty', this variety is covered by a mass of double flowers in late spring. It is particularly valued as a cut flower.
✿ **Rich yellow** • **Late spring**
h. **40cm (16in)** *s.* **1m (3ft)**

STAR PERFORMER

D. 'Miss Mason' A long-time favourite, especially in cottage gardens, 'Miss Mason' forms a mound of bright green foliage topped in mid and late spring by a mass of yellow daisy-like flowers.

Echinacea

Coneflowers are bright, bold additions to the late summer border. The large, striking, daisy-like flowers, up to 15cm (6in) wide, bloom for two months from July into early autumn, attracting bees and butterflies with the scent of honey. They look superb in flower arrangements.

Expert's Selection

1 *E. purpurea* 'Robert Bloom' Vibrant purple flowers and a deep orange central cone.
✿ **Bright purple • Midsummer–early autumn**
h. 1.2m (4ft) *s.* 50cm (20in)

2 *E. purpurea* 'White Lustre' A showstopper, with creamy petals around a green-yellow cone. Or try 'White Swan' that grows 50cm (20in) high.
❀ **Cream • Midsummer–early autumn**
h. 1.3m (4½ft) *s.* 50cm (20in)

3 *E. purpurea* 'Magnus' Enormous 18cm (7in) wide lance-shaped petals contrast strongly with a deep orange-brown cone.
✿ **Rich pinky purple Midsummer–early autumn**
h. 1.3m (4½ft) *s.* 50cm (20in)

4 *E. angustifolia*
The large, dark pink flowers have a central orange-brown cone.
✿ **Dark pink • Midsummer–early autumn**
h. 1.2m (4ft) *s.* 50cm (20in)

The Essentials

Site demands Average garden soil is fine but ensure adequate drainage and plentiful sunshine.
Planting practice Plant in autumn or spring.
Flowering time They bloom from late summer into the autumn.
Pests and diseases Slugs and snails may eat flowers and shoots.
Bonus point Attract beneficial insects, such as bees, to the garden.

STAR PERFORMER
E. purpurea 'Robert Bloom'
One of the most popular coneflowers, it has vivid flowers, which bloom resplendently from July to September, and sometimes even longer.

E. purpurea 'Magnus'

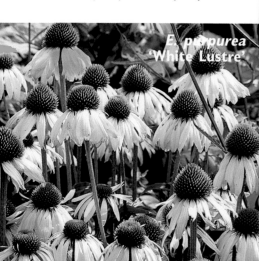

E. purpurea 'White Lustre'

Dynamic plants, native to North America, all of the readily available coneflowers are fully hardy in Britain. Their demands are minimal but ensure that they thrive by avoiding ground which may get waterlogged in autumn and winter as they will not thrive. The flowers bloom abundantly for a full two months in late summer and autumn: deadhead them frequently to keep them flowering well into autumn.

The most commonly grown coneflower is the sturdy and vigorous *E. purpurea*, but other varieties of the same species are available, and give a good mix of colours including white, yellow and pink. They look good with many other plants and, when planted by a pond, will make stunning reflections in the still water.

CUT FLOWERS
Coneflowers have dramatic flowers that look great in a vase. Add some greenery to set them off, or mix purple varieties with a few white penstemons and some cosmos.

Echinops

Globe thistles are ideal for hot sunny parts of the garden where the soil is poor and free-draining. They have good, strong shapes, jagged leaves and an architectural show of spherical flowers.

E. sphaerocephalus

Expert's Selection

1 *E. ritro* ♀
The pale grey stems bear a great stiff globe of deep blue flowers.
✿ **Steel-blue • Late summer**
h. 1.2m (4ft) *s.* 30cm (1ft)

2 *E.* 'Nivalis'
An excellent choice for a white garden. With its spiny greyish foliage and pale flowers, it can have a wonderful ghostly look.
✿ **Greyish white • Late summer**
h. 1.5m (5ft) *s.* 50cm (20in)

3 *E. sphaerocephalus*
A big, tough, coarse plant that is truly magnificent and has real presence in a border.
✿ **White • Late summer**
h. 2m (7ft) *s.* 1m (3ft)

The Essentials

Site demands All globe thistles need the same conditions, lots of sunshine and thin, dry soil.
Planting practice Plant in autumn or spring.
Flowering time Flowers appear in late summer and early autumn.
Pests and diseases Mildew may affect the shapely foliage but they are otherwise trouble free.
Bonus point Bristly seedheads provide architectural interest.

STAR PERFORMER
E. ritro ♀ **is a thrilling skeletal plant which is a magnet for bees and butterflies. It can reach 1.2m (4ft) in midsummer, with jagged, stiff, prickly leaves up to 20cm (8in) long and steel blue flowers. 'Veitch's Blue' with slightly darker blue flowers is an excellent alternative.**

Remember that globe thistles come from inhospitable, rocky parts of countries such as Turkey and Spain so do not try to grow them in radically different conditions.

Although they will certainly grow in slightly richer soil than in their native habitat, too many nutrients are counter-productive. The spiky foliage and stiff stems of echinops plants that grow too fast will lose their vigour and become soft and floppy.

Planting positions
The best place for globe thistles is in a gravel garden or positioned as focal points in the centre of smallish beds in a situation where children can not hurt themselves on the spiky leaves. The white blooms of **'Nivalis'** look even more striking if surrounded by rich colours, especially dark blues and deep purples.

Good companions
The range of good companion plants for globe thistles is huge. Other upright shapely plants include alliums, kniphofias and verbenas. Grasses (see pages 126–127) also work well with echinops, adding an extra element of height and shape to a mixed bed. They include *Stipa gigantea* with its 1.8m (6ft) high angled stems, and dangling spikelets.

Epimedium

Barrenwort is grown for its superb heart-shaped leaves and intriguing flowers. The foliage appears at the end of winter and can be tinged with bronze, pink or red. Many gain rich autumn colours. The mid-spring flowers vary from white, to yellow, to orange and red.

Forming low-lying leafy clumps, epimediums come in both deciduous and evergreen varieties, most of which, like those listed here, are fully hardy in well-drained, but moist soil, with shade from full sunlight. Use them for ground cover in dappled shade or in gravel borders or pots for their attractively-shaped leaves and enjoy a parade of changing foliage and flowers throughout the year.

Highlight spring flowers
Most evergreen epimediums are best sheared over in late winter to remove the foliage before the new growth starts. This removes tired growth and ensures that the new flowers will be more visible.

STAR PERFORMER

E. perralderianum The foliage has a hint of bronze-red at first, but turns dark green and then copper over winter. Small bright yellow early spring flowers perk up the mass of leaves.

Expert's Selection

1 *E. perralderianum*
The semi-evergreen, shiny foliage, provides a changing colour palette through the year.
⊘⊘⊘ **Bronze-red, dark green, copper • All year**
✿ **Yellow • Spring** *h.* **30cm (1ft)**
s. **45cm (1½ft)**

2 *E.* x *rubrum* ♔
A deciduous variety with pale leaf colour that changes seasonally and delightful early spring flowers.
⊘⊘⊘ **Brick red, pale green, yellow-orange** ✿ **Pale yellow • Spring**
h. **30cm (1ft)** *s.* **40cm (16in)**

3 *E. grandiflorum* 'Nanum Freya' The large, late spring summer flowers often appear again in late summer.
⊘ **Bronze • Spring, autumn**
✤✿ **White, rich pink • Spring**
h. **25cm (10in)** *s.* **30cm (1ft)**

4 *E.* x *versicolor* 'Sulphureum' ♔ The fresh new leaves have a wonderful reddish tinge, which they regain in autumn.
⊘⊘ **Reddish, green • Spring, autumn**
Yellow with reddish spur • Spring
h. **30cm (1ft)** *s.* **45cm (1½ft)**

5 *E.* x *youngianum*
Subtle spring flowers bloom amongst the mid-green leaves and red tinged leaf stalks.
⊘ **Green** ✤✿ **Greenish white or pale pink • Mid–late spring**
h. **20–30cm (8–12in)** *s.* **30cm (12in)**

FROST PROTECTION Once evergreen epimediums have been sheared back in late winter, provide a mulch to protect the new growth against frost damage.

E. grandiflorum

E. x *rubrum*

The Essentials

Site demands The ideal situation is a semi-woodland position with plenty of leaf-mould in the ground. Epimediums do not like their soil to dry out.
Flowering time Mid spring.
Planting practice Plant in early spring or autumn.
Pests and diseases Beware vine weevils. If the plants die back or lack vigour, weevil larvae are the most likely cause. Ensure too that slugs do not ruin the new foliage.
Bonus point Attractive and good at keeping down weeds, epimedium makes great ground cover.

Erigeron

Fleabanes, with their daisy-like flowers in delicate and vibrant shades, are available as both tiny tufts and much taller clumps. They appear from early to late summer, and some are quite exquisite. Hardy and easy to grow, there is room for at least one in every garden.

1 *E. 'Dimity'*
Gives a lively show of orange-eyed flowers above a mound of foliage.
✿ **Pink • Summer**
h. **30cm (1ft)** *s.* **40cm (16in)**

2 *E. karvinskianus*
'Profusion' Pink-tinged white flowers on a reliably hardy plant.
❁✿ **White, pink • Spring–summer**
h. **30cm (1ft)** *s.* **40cm (16in)**

3 *E. aurantiacus*
A medium-height fleabane with a flashy show of flowers.
✿ **Orange • Spring–summer**
h.&s. **30cm (1ft)**

4 *E. 'Dunkelste Aller'* ♀
Masses of deep purple blooms.
✿ **Purple • Spring–summer**
h. **75cm (2½ft)** *s.* **45cm (1½ft)**

5 *E. glaucus*
An unusually tall fleabane which grows happily in gaps in walls.
✿ **Violet-mauve • Spring–summer**
h. **40cm (16in)** *s.* **45cm (1½ft)**

If you are seeking a pretty plant for a wildflower or casual garden, why not choose a fleabane? These daisy-like plants will grow happily in quite inauspicious places, including walls, and a number will tolerate harsh winds and sea spray. Planted in well-drained soil in the sunshine, they will bloom from late spring into autumn with minimal attention.

Tidying up
To avoid an untidy spread, cut them back in March, at the start of spring, before the new growth begins. Do not wait any longer or you will cut into new growth and delay the onset of flowers.

A daisy for the lazy
E. karvinskianus is a delightfully reliable fleabane. Plant it in crevices in an old stone wall, in paving, and even in cracks in old stone steps and it will soon make a flowing spread of tiny flowers. To soften hard landscaping, buy seven or eight new plants and dot them around.

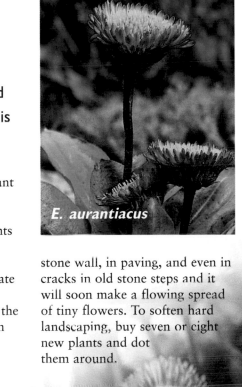
E. aurantiacus

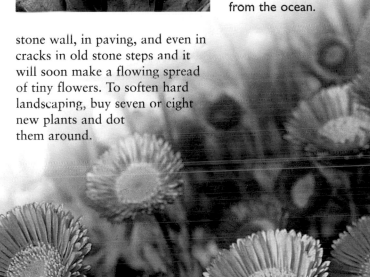

E. karvinskianus 'Profusion'

Eryngium

Sea hollies add a shapely wild touch to the garden. They have tough, thistle-like stems and often an array of short, sharp spines. The most striking have silvery or bluish flowerheads, sometimes in a true metallic blue. They also attract butterflies and bees, and are excellent for drying.

Expert's Selection

1 *E. 'Jos Eijking'*
Stunning, with brilliant blue stems, leaves and flowerheads.
✿ **Lavender-blue • Mid–late summer**
h. **60cm (2ft)** *s.* **50cm (20in)**

2 *E. variifolium*
Spiny rounded rosettes of rich green leaves are veined white. The tiny flowerheads are silvery blue.
✿ **Silvery blue • Mid–late summer**
h. **40cm (16in)** *s.* **25cm (10in)**

3 *E. bourgatii 'Oxford Blue'*♀ Silver-tinged flowerheads, spiny, curled leaves with wide white veins and lilac-blue stems.
✿ **Violet-blue • Mid–late summer**
h. **60cm (2ft)** *s.* **50cm (20in)**

4 *E. x giganteum*♀
Miss Willmott's ghost has robust stems and self-seeds freely.
✿ **Blue and silver • Mid–late summer**
h. **1.2m (4ft)** *s.* **75cm (2½ft)**

E. alpinum

5 *E. alpinum*♀
A fantastic spray of small flowerheads on wiry stems.
✿ **Lavender-blue • Late summer**
h. **1m (3ft)** *s.* **75cm (2½ft)**

The Essentials

Site demands Sea hollies demand full sun and free-draining soil. In heavier soil they will need plenty of horticultural grit so rain will flash through the ground.
Planting practice Plant in winter or early spring.
Flowering time Sea hollies flower from mid to late summer.
Pests and diseases To avoid rotting add grit and a spread of gravel around the base of the plant.
Bonus point Looks stunning in flower arrangements.

E. x giganteum

E. bourgatii 'Oxford Blue'

Native to coastal regions, sea hollies will grow happily in poor stony soils. Decide exactly where you want to place them as, once planted, they dislike being moved. Remember, too, that the spine-tipped leaves and bracts are quite sharp, so keep them away from the edge of a bed where a child might fall onto them. But do not hide them too far away. People love tapping the cones that stick out of the bracts.

Eupatorium

Big leafy plants for impressive informal borders and wild gardens, eupatoriums provide a highly impressive show of tiny tubular flowers rising above the foliage. Available as evergreen shrubs and herbaceous perennials, the perennial varieties are hardy and suitable for a care-free scheme.

STAR PERFORMER

E. cannabinum **White and pink-toned blooms tower above clumps of foliage in the second half of summer. The vertical stems have an appealing red tinge, and the leaves can be up to 10cm (4in) long.**

Substantial and sturdy, with light-hearted blooms and lance-shaped green leaves, hardy eupatoriums have few demands beyond reliable moist soil and a position in the sunshine. Deadhead as soon as the flowers have faded, and cut right back to the ground in the autumn.

Wild-flower schemes

Use eupatoriums to give height to a wild-flower garden or to create a more informal touch in a border. As moisture is so important, try growing them near ponds and streams.

Their big bold clumps work well if you are seeking to create a division between the more ordered, small-scale, flowery parts of the garden and a wild section where everything is that much bigger. *E. purpureum* is a big, robust plant, ideal for a wild-flower garden with a mass of purple-tinged stems and 30cm (1ft) wide flowerheads. It takes a few years to build up to a chunky clump, but once established combines well with other relaxed plants such as loosestrife (*Lythrum*) in informal schemes.

Expert's Selection

1 *E. cannabinum*
Hemp agrimony is a tall robust plant with scented white, pink or purple flowers. Give it plenty of space in which to thrive. The cultivar 'Flore Pleno' has rosy pink double flowers.
❀✿✿ **White, pink, purple • Late summer •** *h.* **2m (7ft)** *s.* **1m (3ft)**

2 *E. purpureum*
Joe Pye weed is another big plant. The purple-tinged stems are topped by a vivid show of purple-pink flowers in late summer and early autumn. *E. purpureum* subsp. *maculatum* 'Atropurpureum'♀ has richer purple-red flowers.
✿ **Purple-pink • Late summer–early autumn •** *h.* **2m (7ft)** *s.* **1m (3ft)**

3 *E. rugosum*
The North American snakeroot is a short, but extremely attractive eupatorium with plenty of long-lasting, flat heads of creamy flowers, and nettle-shaped leaves.
❀ **Cream • Late summer–early autumn •** *h.* **1.5–1.8m (5–6ft)** *s.* **60cm (2ft)**

The Essentials

Site demands Full sun and moist, but not boggy, soil are the twin requirements for success.
Planting practice Plant from autumn to spring.
Flowering time Flowers appear in summer, and may bloom well into early autumn.
Pests and diseases The damp soil makes a good venue for slugs and snails, but otherwise eupatorium should be largely trouble free.
Bonus point The flowers are attractive to bees and butterflies.

E. purpureum

E. rugosum

ferns

Dramatic shade plants

Ferns look superb in damp conditions in shady parts of the garden giving style and colour to otherwise unplanted sites. They can be grown along paths, in walls, around ponds and even in pots. The range of sizes is huge too: whether you want a low-growing fern for a small space or a tree fern to add drama to a larger garden. The fronds often have extraordinary shapes and their colour changes through the seasons from brilliant spring greens through warm rusts and yellows as they die back in autumn and winter.

Ensure that the conditions in your garden are suitable for growing ferns and you will be rewarded with lush foliage that will last throughout autumn and into winter.

A mild, warm, sheltered part of the garden with moist, acid soil is ideal. Dappled shade is fine; with most ferns the brighter the conditions then the more soil moisture is required, but choose a spot where they will not be buffeted by strong winds.

Though the majority of ferns prefer shade and damp soil, there are exceptions. Some ferns do like boggy ground and *Osmunda regalis* will thrive at the side of a pond. Others prefer bright situations: *Polystichum setiferum* will grow almost anywhere as long as the soil is moist.

A few will tolerate drier conditions: *Asplenium scolopendrium* will even grow among alkaline rocks in walls, though it also grows in rich border soil.

In summer, spread plenty of leaf-mould around the stems. This both feeds the soil and keeps moisture locked in the ground. The crowns of more tender ferns such as *Cyrtomium falcatum* should be protected over winter with a thick mulch.

Architectural ferns

For a theatrical effect, try one of the larger ferns such as the ostrich fern *Matteuccia struthiopteris* or the royal fern *Osmunda regalis*, whose feathery fronds can reach more than 1.5–2m (5–7ft) in height. Their graceful shapes look superb when mixed with plants such as hostas.

STUMPERIES Many grand Victorian gardens included a stumpery, where people came to look at extraordinary knarled roots which had become distorted to resemble amazing creatures. A small version of a stumpery can be re-created in modern gardens using old misshapen chunks of trees piled up and surrounded by ferns.

TAKE A FRESH LOOK

Dicksonia antarctica, the Australian soft tree fern is a big slow-growing architectural plant, with a great spread of fronds shooting out of a trunk which can reach 5m (16ft). As it is originally a tropical plant it does need a sheltered position, but should thrive in a temperate town garden.

STAR PERFORMER

Dryopteris erythrosora♀ **The superb copper shield fern is an evergreen. Young, triangular pinkish red fronds gradually darken from spring onward to a warm copper colour, ending up rich green. Cut away dying fronds in late winter so that new growth will stand out.**

Asplenium scolopendrium

Cyrtomium falcatum

3 *Woodwardia unigemmata* An ideal fern for warm, sheltered gardens, but it will not tolerate extreme cold.
⌀ **Green • All year**
h. 1m (3ft) *s.* 1.2m (4ft)

Tall ferns

Plant a taller fern for dramatic impact, either as a feature or as a stunning backdrop to other plants.

1 *Matteuccia struthiopteris*♀ The ostrich fern will thrive in rich, moist soil near ponds.
⌀ **Green • Autumn–winter**
h. 1.5m (5ft) *s.* 1m (3ft)

2 *Osmunda regalis*♀ The royal fern has elegant leaves with a varied seasonal colour.
⌀ **Green • Spring–autumn**
h. 1.5m (5ft) *s.* 1m (3ft)

Matteuccia struthiopteris

Small ferns

Try these smaller varieties as a lush backdrop or attractive ground cover in a compact space.

1 *Dryopteris erythrosora*♀ An evergreen Japanese/Chinese copper shield fern.
⌀⌀⌀ **Pinkish red, then copper, finally green • All year**
h.&s. 60cm (2ft)

2 *Asplenium scolopendrium* 'Crispum' The evergreen hart's-tongue fern has vertical strap-like fronds.
⌀ **Green • All year**
h.&s. 60cm (2ft)

3 *Cyrtomium falcatum*♀ Grow the evergreen Japanese holly fern in a mild, sheltered garden for its shiny, dark green fronds.
⌀ **Green • All year**
h. 60cm (2ft) *s.* 45cm (1½ft)

4 *Onoclea sensibilis*♀ Ideal for large bog gardens, this distinctive fern has erect fronds.
⌀ **Brown • Autumn**
h.&s. 60cm (2ft)

5 *Athyrium filix-femina*♀ The lady fern thrives in cool, moist parts of the garden.
⌀ **Green • Spring–early summer**
h. 30cm (1ft) *s.* 40cm (16in)

6 *Polypodium vulgare* A hardy fern which grows happily on rocks and tree stumps.
⌀ **Green • All year**
h. 40cm (16in)
s. 60cm (2ft)

Medium ferns

These mid-sized ferns all have beautifully shaped and coloured leaves.

1 *Polystichum setiferum*♀ The evergreen soft shield fern has light graceful fronds.
⌀ **Pale green Autumn–winter**
h. 1.2m (4ft) *s.* 1m (3ft)

2 *Dryopteris affinis* subsp. *borreri* An easy-to-grow fern which thrives by ponds and lakes.
⌀ **Dark green • All year**
h. 1m (3ft) *s.* 40cm (16in)

Woodwardia unigemmata

Osmunda regalis

Site demands Most ferns prefer shade and damp soil, but not waterlogged ground. Good drainage is important for most types of ferns.

Planting practice Plant in spring and keep well-watered during the first growing season.
Flowering time The colour comes from the fronds, especially the few with a pink or reddish hue; they do not flower.
Pests and diseases Trouble free.
Bonus point The back of the leaves bear the reproductive spores, many of which are arranged in attractive patterns.

Euphorbia

Spurges are found all over the world. They come in a huge range of sizes and their smart, often evergreen foliage, distinctive blooms and general hardiness means that there is a suitable variety for virtually every garden, giving interesting shape and unusual colour for most of the year.

A display of euphorbias with their brilliant lime green, yellow or rusty-red 'flowers' and sculptural leaves can make a scintillating counterpoint to more conventional plants and blooms. All the varieties selected here are fully hardy and are extremely easy to grow and maintain.

The unusual 'flowers' consist of two bracts protecting the very small male and female flowers. The true flowers have no petals. In some varieties, such as *E. × martinii* the nectar-secreting glands which form a ring around the true flowers are a prominent feature of the blooms.

For best results, choose a well-drained soil in full sun. Cut back the flowering shoots on varieties with biennial stems to ensure that the current season's shoots can flower the following year.

STAR PERFORMER
E. 'Charam' Still also known as 'Redwing', the new, spring growth is tinted red. The lime-green flowers appear in oversized spikes, almost doubling the height of the plant.

SAFETY WARNING
When pruning euphorbias do wear plastic, non-absorbent gloves because the cut stems leak a toxic, sticky white latex that can react badly with the skin, causing inflammation. Fish are particularly sensitive to this sap so plant euphorbias well away from ponds.

The Essentials

Site demands Most prefer full sun in a well-drained soil.
Planting practice Plant in spring.
Flowering time Usually spring and early summer, with some carrying on until autumn.
Pests and diseases Watch out for aphids and powdery mildew.
Bonus point Great variety in shape, size and colour.

Expert's Selection

1 *E.* 'Charam'
A stocky, bushy, evergreen plant, with dark green leaves with new, red growth in spring and pale green flowers.
⌀⌀ **Dark green, red • Early spring**
✿ **Pale green • Late spring**
h. 1m (3ft) *s.* 60cm (2ft)

2 *E. amygdaloides*
'Purpurea' Sometimes sold as *E. amygdaloides* 'Rubra', it has deep-coloured maroon red leaves. Unlike most euphorbias, it will grow happily in light shade.
⌀ **Maroon-red • Early spring**
✿ **Lime green • Late spring–early summer • *h.* 45–75cm (1½–2½ft)**
s. 45–60cm (1½–2ft)

E. characias subsp. *wulfenii* 'Lambrook Gold'

E. amygdaloides 'Purpurea'

E. x martinii

E. polychroma

E. griffithii 'Fireglow'

PRUNING NEEDS Certain varieties, *E. amygdaloides* and *E. x martinii* in particular, may be affected by a rash of powdery mildew in early summer. To get rid of it, simply cut back the affected leaves and fresh new growth will soon take its place.

3 *E. characias* subsp. *wulfenii* 'Lambrook Gold'♀
A vigorous evergreen with tall vertical or arching stems.
⊘ **Bluish-green • Early spring**
✿ **Yellow green • Late spring–early summer • *h.* 1.2m (4ft)**
s. **1m (3ft)**

4 *E. griffithii* 'Fireglow'
In bright sun it will develop brightly coloured flowerhead on large spreading clumps.
⊘ **Green • Early spring**
✿ **Orange-red • Early summer**
h. **1m (3ft)** *s.* **75cm (2½ft)**

5 *E. x martinii*♀
A superb evergreen euphorbia with visible nectaries which appear as a tiny red dot or 'eye' inside each cup-shaped, lime-green flowerhead.
⊘⊘ **Dark green, red • Early spring**
✿ **Lime green • Early summer**
h. **1m (3ft)** *s.* **75cm (2½ft)**

6 *E. polychroma*♀
A dome-shaped euphorbia with vivid yellow bracts in spring. The dark green leaves become tinged with red and purple in autumn.
⊘ **Dark green, often tinged with red and purple • Autumn**
✿ **Bright yellow • Mid spring**
h.&s. **60cm (2ft)**

7 *E. rigida*
A sculptural plant for a sheltered garden, it has spreading, near-prostrate stems with blue-green leaves topped with yellow flowerheads later in spring.
⊘ **Blue-green • Early spring**
✿ **Yellow, later red • Late spring**
h. **60cm (2ft)** *s.* **1.2m (4ft)**

8 *E. mellifera*
A magnificent plant for a temperate town garden with a delicious honey scent in springtime and lush, bright green leaves.
⊘ **Green • Early spring**
✿ **Yellowy-green and red • Late spring • *h.&s.* 1.2m (4ft)**

9 *E. schillingii*♀
This Nepalese native was only brought to the West in the late 1970s. It is a prolific flowerer, that keeps on going from midsummer into October.
⊘ **Green • Early spring**
✿ **Lime green • Midsummer to early autumn**
h. **1m (3ft)** *s.* **30cm (1ft)**

Filipendula

Meadowsweets, with their sweet summer scent and flattish, airy heads of white, pink or red flowers, will liven up any damp and shady corner of the garden.

Expert's Selection

1 *F. purpurea*♀
Elegant, deeply lobed leaves spread beneath flattish frothy heads.
✿ **Purple-red • Mid–late summer**
h. **1.2m (4ft)** *s.* **60cm (2ft)**

2 *F. ulmaria* 'Aurea'
A superb waterside plant that is best grown for its golden foliage. The flowers are very small.
⊘ **Golden** ❀ **White • Midsummer**
h. **1.2m (4ft)** *s.* **60cm (2ft)**

3 *F. camtschatica*
Tiny fragrant pink or white blooms cluster into flat frothy flowerheads.
✿❀ **Pink or white • Late summer**
h. **3m (10ft)** *s.* **1m (3ft)**

4 *F. rubra*
Profuse clusters of tiny blooms smother the queen of the prairie.
✿ **Pink • Midsummer**
h. **2m (7ft)** *s.* **75cm (2½ft)**

5 *F. vulgaris*
Dropwort has fern-like leaves; its tiny white flowers look pink in bud.
❀ **Creamy-white • Midsummer**
h. **1.2m (4ft)** *s.* **60cm (2ft)**

The Essentials

Site demands Damp and shady, though *F. vulgaris* likes dry, limy soil.
Planting practice Plant from autumn to spring.
Flowering time Midsummer.
Pests and diseases None.
Bonus point Great musky scent.

Meadowsweets are damp meadow or wild garden plants with lush, green growth and wonderful frothy displays of flowers. With 'Aurea', it pays to get rid of the flowers before they have a chance to open. The leaves noticeably fade when the flowers are out, and it is worth shearing off the flower stems to encourage the yellow foliage.

Besides damp, you need plenty of space to grow meadowsweets, especially *F. rubra* which spreads quickly. As the roots are near the surface unwanted plants can be easily dug up.

STAR PERFORMER

F. purpurea♀ **This big plant forms a superb clump, packed with hundreds of tiny purple-red flowerheads which bloom in July and August.**

Fragaria

Strawberries are not often grown in a decorative border, but a few earn their place for their beautiful flowers, and another for its striking variegated foliage.

STAR PERFORMER
F. 'Pink Panda'
It might not provide much in the way of fruit, but it certainly compensates with lovely pink flowers, instead of the strawberry's usual white, set off by fresh green foliage.

This versatile plant has a long flowering season. And, like the heavy cropping strawberry, it freely produces new young plants on runners. In the second half of summer these start weaving around neighbouring plants, but if they became too invasive, simply pull them out.

Placing the runners
Position new plants at the front of a border, so that as they spread you can turn one plant into several new ones. Fill small pots with multipurpose compost, and sink them in the soil around the plant. Push the runners that develop into the compost, and when they have developed roots and are growing well, sever each new plant from the parent. You can then lift the pots and plant your new strawberries around the garden. Since each plant develops several runners, you will certainly have more than enough.

Expert's Selection

1 *F.* 'Pink Panda'
Pretty flowers bloom into autumn.
✿ **Pink • Summer–early autumn**
h. **10cm (4in)** *s.* **Indefinite**

2 *F. vesca* 'Variegata'
A striking plant with white flowers and grey-green and cream foliage.
❀ **White • Summer–early autumn**
h. **30cm (1ft)** *s.* **Indefinite**

3 *F.* 'Red Ruby'
For red blooms, try this variety.
✿ **Red • Summer–early autumn**
h. **10cm (4in)** *s.* **Indefinite**

The Essentials

Site demands Well-drained soils.
Planting practice Detach rooted plantlets from runners from autumn to spring.
Flowering time Spring–autumn.
Pests and diseases Look out for powdery mildew and vine weevil.
Bonus point Good ground cover, which stays leafy all winter long.

Gaillardia

Blanket flowers add dash to any display and are gorgeous in cottage garden borders, where their stunning, often multicoloured blooms dazzle in a range of vivid shades. With their long flowering season, they add panache to the autumn border while other blooms fade.

Expert's Selection

1 *G.* 'Dazzler' ♈
A dark brown disc is bordered by orange-red petals with yellow tips.
✿ **Orangey red and yellow Midsummer–early autumn**
h. **60cm (2ft)** *s.* **45cm (1½ft)**

2 *G.* 'Kobold'
A dwarf plant, it shares the same flashy bright colours as 'Dazzler'.
✿ **Red and yellow • Midsummer– early autumn • *h.* 25cm (10in) *s.* 20cm (8in)**

3 *G.* 'Burgunder'
A glorious single-colour bloom in a deep burgundy red.
✿ **Dark wine red • Midsummer– early autumn**
h. **60cm (2ft)** *s.* **45cm (1½ft)**

G. 'Kobold'

Blanket flowers do have a bad reputation for being short-lived, especially when grown on heavier soil. The best way to keep up a good supply of plants is to propagate them every four years or so. Dig up the plants in spring, and divide them, making sure each clump has a decent growth of roots. Keep the newer, outer sections, and discard the old, inner growth. Replant immediately and water well.

The stems tend to be straggly and weak and may need some support. Twiggy sticks will keep them upright, and most importantly stop the vivacious brightly-coloured flowers from flopping forwards.

Adding annuals
If there are any gaps between the plants, especially in the early years before they get established, fill them up with annual blanket flowers which are easily grown from seed. One of the best varieties to choose is **'Red Plume'**. It has masses of double red flowers, and does not fade even in droughts. There are also mixed selections of seed, giving a range of colours from cream, through bright yellow to crimson.

STAR PERFORMER
G. 'Dazzler' ♈ **This marvellous plant is every bit as good as its name, with wide daisy-like flowers which flourish from June to September.**

Plant groupings
Sun-loving blanket flowers look great in a hot border, teamed with other brightly coloured, end-of-season plants that also thrive in poor, stony ground.

These include *Gypsophila* 'Rosenschleier' (see page 125) which has a late crop of small flowers, opening white and ending up pale pink; and *Bidens ferulifolia* (see page 277) which is usually grown as an annual, with its spreading mass of stems and small, bright yellow flowers.

The Essentials

Site demands Any soil, but they love a sunny, well-drained spot.
Planting practice Plant out in spring and support taller plants with twigs.
Flowering time All summer and through into early autumn.
Pests and diseases Slugs and snails may eat plants, and downy mildew may yellow the leaves.
Bonus point They add a splash of colour in early autumn when other plants have ceased flowering.

Geranium

Cranesbills add superb summer colours, including rich pinks, purples, whites and blues to any kind of site, from the relaxed cottage scheme to the highly organised and formal.

Expert's Selection

1 *G. sanguineum var. striatum* 'Splendens' The open flowers have darker pink veins offset by dark green leaves.
✿ Pink • All summer
h. 30cm (1ft) *s.* 45cm (1½ft)

2 *G.* 'Johnson's Blue'♀
A deserved favourite, it flowers throughout summer, makes excellent ground cover, and has attractive, finely cut foliage.
✿ Lavender-blue • All summer
h. 30cm (1ft) *s.* 45cm (1½ft)

3 *G. psilostemon*♀
One of the tallest geraniums, it has deep-toned flowers with a black eye and black veins. The leaves turn flaming orange-yellow in autumn.
✿ Magenta-purple • All summer
h. 1.2m (4ft) *s.* 50cm (20in)

4 *G. clarkei* 'Kashmir White'♀ Elegant, 'long-fingered' leaves are topped by lilac-veined flowers. It spreads well, but is easily kept in check by cutting back.
❀ White • All summer
h. 30cm (1ft) *s.* 45cm (1½ft)

5 *G. procurrens*
Long prostrate stems root as they spread to form new plants. It can also be trained through shrubs.
✿ Purple • Midsummer–autumn
h. 15cm (6in) *s.* 1m (3ft)

STAR PERFORMER
G. sanguineum var. striatum 'Splendens'
The parent plant of this marvellous pink-flowering geranium was found growing wild on Walney Island, in Cumbria. It makes a smallish clump, growing only about 30cm (1ft) high.

G. psilostemon

6 *G. x oxonianum* 'Wargrave Pink'♀ A tall pink geranium that flowers freely right through summer. 'Claridge Druce' has deep pink blooms with darker pink veins.
✿ Salmon pink • All summer
h.&s. 75cm (2½ft)

7 *G. himalayense*
The Himalayan geranium is a good ground-cover plant. 'Gravetye'♀ makes a neater, bushier clump and produces reddish flowers.
✿ Rich violet-blue • Summer–early autumn • *h.&s.* 45cm (1½ft)

8 *G. phaeum*
The purplish dusky cranesbill has small silky flowers with dark evergreen leaves.
✿ Purplish red • Spring–autumn
h. 60cm (2ft) *s.* 45cm (1½ft)

9 *G. sylvaticum*
An early flowering geranium. Try the pure white 'Album'♀ and 'Mayflower', with its white-eyed, soft violet-blue flowers.
❀✿ White, violet-blue
Spring–early summer
h. 45cm (1½ft) *s.* 40cm (16in)

10 *G. renardii*♀
A low-growing, clump-forming mountain plant with heart-shaped creamy petals striped with purple and soft, grey-green leaves.
❀ White with stripes
Midsummer–early autumn
h. 30cm (1ft) *s.* 25cm (10in)

(see pages 292–293)

TAKE A FRESH LOOK

G. 'Ann Folkard' has rich purple, midsummer flowers. Unlike many cranesbills it hugs the ground sending out trailing stems 1m (3ft) long. It will provide a perfect contrast to adjacent vertical plants, such as euphorbias, rich green grasses, and pink or yellow roses with bare lower stems. Or you can encourage it to scramble up through a shrub.

11 *G. sanguineum*

The bloody cranesbill forms a low mat of dark green foliage that turns orange and then red in autumn. 'Alan Bloom' produces a lively display of pink flowers.
✿ Magenta • All summer
h. 30cm (1ft) *s.* 40cm (16in)

12 *G. macrorrhizum*

An excellent ground-cover plant, it produces a dense tangle of scented foliage. 'Album' bears white flowers, 'Variegatum' is soft pink with grey-green leaves and 'Bevan's Variety' is magenta.
✿✿✿ White, pink, magenta
All summer
s. 25cm (10in) *s.* 60cm (2ft)

True geraniums or cranesbills are not to be confused with the *Pelargoniums* (see pages 292–293) which are often referred to by the same name. Bearing pretty rounded flowers with five petals, they are extremely versatile and can be used in a wide range of combinations in all kinds of sites.

As well as lovely summer blooms, geraniums often have good-looking circular leaves, finely divided into intricately cut lobes. Many varieties are evergreen but some of the deciduous kinds have brilliant autumn colour.

Once they have flowered, cut back larger plants to avoid reseeding and encourage them to produce new growth.

The right plant for your site
Typical geraniums are upright plants which reach a height of between 30cm (1ft) and 1.2m (4ft). Low-growing plants, suitable for ground cover grow to a compact 30cm (1ft).

Geraniums are extremely adaptable and certain kinds will even grow successfully in chalky soil. A larger geranium such as *G. psilostemon* will probably prefer a shadier site, while the low-growing varieties, such as *G. sanguineum* do best in well-drained soil in full sun.

Special effects
Since blue colours gain in intensity in the early morning and early evening, when light levels are low, the blue or violet toned cranesbills look superb in light shade. Low-growing geraniums are also ideal for planting along the side of straight paths where they will spill gracefully over the edge, softening the look of a more formal planting scheme.

G. sanguineum

G. clarkei 'Kashmir White'

G. x oxonianum 'Wargrave Pink'

CUTTING BACK Some geraniums can be left to flower, but get increasingly straggly during summer. Many are best cut back after their first flush of flowers. Cutting back low-growing varieties gives a brief period of baldness, but this is soon followed by more fresh new growth. And if the early flowering geraniums are cut back, they will also produce a good second show of flowers.

The Essentials

Site demands Most geraniums will grow in well-drained garden soil, in full sun or light shade.
Planting practice Plant in spring or autumn. Many can be grown from basal cuttings.
Flowering time Depending on the variety they will bloom from early spring onwards, with most at their best in late June.
Pests and diseases Geraniums are largely trouble free. Just look out for signs of vine weevil damage and mildew on the foliage.
Bonus point A terrific range of care-free varieties to choose from.

Geum

Avens are cheerful plants which will produce a mass of vibrant warm-toned flowers with bright green leaves and stalks to bloom perkily at the front of a border for most of the summer season. Available in yellows, reds, oranges and whites, there are also pastels for softer schemes.

Geums make few special demands of the care-free gardener. For guaranteed success, and an abundant display of blooms, give them plenty of sun, and a rich soil that is well drained, but slightly moist.

Even in winter it is essential that the roots do not dry out, but boggy sites are too wet for all geums except for *G. rivale*, which prefers cool conditions and damp soil. *G.* 'Borisii' will tolerate lighter, stonier soils.

Geums for boggy places
G. rivale and its cultivars, such as 'Lemon Drops' and 'Lionel Cox', is an ideal choice for bog gardens. A native of lowland marshes and water meadows in central Europe, and North America, it produces nodding flowers up to 60cm (2ft) tall in early summer.

G. rivale
'Leonard's Variety'

G. rivale
'Lionel Cox'

1 *G.* **'Mrs J. Bradshaw'** ♀
Plant this popular variety and look forward to a dense mass of vivid flowers against brilliant green stalks and leaves. 'Lady Stratheden' ♀ bears semi-double buttery blooms.
✿ **Brick-red • All summer**
h.&s. **60cm (2ft)**

2 *G.* **'Borisii'**
Bright green leaves mix with warm, rich, orange flowers. 'Coppertone' is shorter with apricot blooms.
✿ **Yellow, orange, apricot • Late spring–early summer**
h. **30cm (1ft)** *s.* **40cm (16in)**

3 *G. montanum* ♀
A low-growing variety with vivid flowers and rich green leaves, which spreads to form a mat.
✿ **Bright yellow • Early summer**
h. **15cm (6in)** *s.* **30cm (1ft)**

4 *G. rivale*
Excellent cultivars include 'Lemon Drops' (pale yellow), 'Leonard's Variety' (coppery orange), and 'Lionel Cox' (pale apricot).
✿✿ **Light yellow, orange, apricot**
All summer • *h.&s.* **45cm (1½ft)**

STAR PERFORMER
G. 'Mrs J. Bradshaw' ♀
A bright, brash, show of upright scarlet to brick-red flowers with yellow centres will flourish all summer long.

Site demands Rich, moist soil in the sunshine will suit most geums.
Planting practice Plant in autumn or spring.
Flowering time From early summer to midsummer.
Pests and diseases Trouble free.
Bonus point Tolerant of most situations in the garden.

Globularia

Globe daisies have appealing pompom flowerheads in shades of blue and lavender which bloom on dense, low mats of foliage. Plant in a raised bed or rock garden.

Globe daisies often occur naturally growing between rocks. These delightful alpines originate in the dry mountainous areas of central and southern Europe where their low habit and tough evergreen leaves are well adapted to the dry conditions.

Give them a sunny position in a well-drained, even stony soil, and you will be rewarded by a profusion of pretty, tufted flowers for the first half of summer.

The Essentials

Site demands Globe daisies need a sunny position in a well-drained soil. Add grit to improve drainage if necessary.

Planting practice Plant out in spring or sow seed in winter.

Flowering time From early to midsummer.

Pests and diseases Generally problem free when grown outdoors.

Bonus point Delicate-looking flowers that will survive in exposed or rocky situations.

STAR PERFORMER
G. meridonalis Lavender flowers stand up above a domed cushion of shiny leaves, which keep the plant cool in its native sunny spots of Italy and south-east Europe.

Expert's Selection

1 *G. meridionalis*
Single flowers spring out of a dense mat of leaves. Also known as *G. bellidifolia*.
✿ Lavender • Early–midsummer
h. 10cm (4in) *s*. 25cm (10in)

2 *G. cordifolia* ♀
A mini-shrub with single purplish blue flowers and lustrous leaves.
✿ Lavender-blue • Early–midsummer
h. 5cm (2in) *s*. 20cm (8in)

3 *G. nudicaulis*
Small flowerheads borne on stiff stems give a tufty appearance.
✿ Mauve blue • Early–midsummer
h. 10cm (4in) *s*. 25cm (10in)

4 *G. repens*
A good mat-forming evergreen.
✿ Lavender blue • Early–midsummer
h. 2.5cm (1in) *s*. 15cm (6in)

Gypsophila

Tiny blooms borne in lacey sprays are a soft contrast to bolder, more defined plants. They dry well and look good as cut flowers.

Expert's Selection

1 *G. paniculata* 'Bristol Fairy' ♀ Double white flowers stand out against darker foliage.
❁ White • Mid–late summer
h.&s. 45cm (1½ft)

2 *G.* 'Rosenschleier' ♀
Produces dense clouds of pale pink blooms in summer.
❁✿ White, pale pink • Mid–late summer • *h*. 50cm (20in) *s*. 1m (3ft)

3 *G. repens* 'Dorothy Teacher' ♀ Single white flowers turn pink as they age.
✿ White, then pale pink • Summer
h. 5cm (2in) *s*. 40cm (16in)

4 *G. cerastioides*
White flowers with purple veins cluster above hairy leaves.
❁ White • Late spring–midsummer
h. 10cm (4in) *s*. 25cm (10in)

The Essentials

Site demands Gypsophila does best in light, extremely well-drained alkaline soil. Avoid moist ground.

Planting practice Plant in spring.

Flowering time Most flower in summer; some from late spring.

Pests and diseases Generally trouble free but may be affected by stem rot.

Bonus point One of the staple plants for flower arranging.

STAR PERFORMER
G. paniculata 'Bristol Fairy' ♀
With the smallest white flowers, delicately threaded with pink, this is also known as baby's breath.

Dainty and pretty, but reliably hardy, gypsophila makes an airy backdrop for a border. The pinprick flowers look especially good in raised beds, or falling softly over a dry-stone wall.

Mats and cushions
The plants vary in size from some very low-growing mat-forming alpines to larger cushions. The blooms are exceptionally small, borne singly or in delightful sprays. There are also short-lived annual versions, some of which have deeper-coloured blooms.

Found naturally on stony slopes in mountainous or steppe regions, gypsophila prefers a dry, light and very well-drained soil. Most varieties, with the notable exception of **G.** 'Rosenschleier' will not thrive in moist soils.

grasses

Shape and texture

For exciting shape, unexpected colour and textural foliage throughout the gardening year, grasses are hard to beat. They can be used in all kinds of ways. The bigger clumps make focal points in a border. Those with rich autumn colours can be planted where they catch the late summer sun to bring out their beige or orange colours. And by not cutting back grasses until February, before new growth begins, you get wonderful winter shapes, with leaves and seed heads accentuated by hoarfrosts.

Grasses are wonderfully varied, offering displays ranging from brilliantly coloured foliage to beautiful airy sprays of flowers and great fluffy panicles borne high above the leaves, which will sway alluringly in the slightest breeze. They are also very easy to grow and add shape and texture even in winter.

A good-quality well-drained soil is necessary for success with most grasses but some will thrive in both drier and heavier soils as well as in an acid environment. Most grasses look best if they are trimmed in spring and once or twice during the growing seasons, but otherwise they are care free.

Drifts and pot plants

Shorter grasses can be used in swirling groups around feature border plants. *Festuca glauca* 'Elijah Blue' makes an eye-catching background. And for grasses in pots, one of the best is the self-contained, showy *Hakonechloa macra* 'Aureola'.

Colour contrasts

Grasses with tall sprays of silvery spikelets look terrific when highlighted against the darkish background of a winter beech hedge, for example, while cooler-toned plants can 'cool' a collection of extravagantly bright reds, oranges and yellows.

Calamagrostis x acutiflora 'Karl Foerster'

Pennisetum villosum

STAR PERFORMER

***Miscanthus sinensis* 'Morning Light'**
Only introduced to the West in the mid 1970s, it has fine, gracefully arching leaves and orange-red flowers, which need a very mild autumn in order to bloom.

The Essentials

Site demands Generally, provide rich, free-draining soil. There are grasses for almost every site from acid soil (*Molinia caerulea*) to dry ground (*Festuca glauca*), and heavy soil (*Deschampsia cespitosa*).
Planting practice Most grasses can be planted at any time except *Miscanthus* and *Stipa,* which should be planted in spring.
Flowering time Summer–autumn.
Pests and diseases Trouble free.
Bonus point Most grasses are easily raised from seed.

Short grasses

Plant the shorter grasses in clumps to add seasonal colour interest and texture to a planting scheme.

1 *Briza media*
Common quaking grass (or Doddering dickies) has loose panicles like oats that turn beige in late summer and autumn.
⊘ **Green • Late spring–midsummer**
h. **45cm (1½ft)** *s.* **35cm (14in)**

2 *Festuca glauca* **'Elijah Blue'** Blue festuca really does have blue foliage. Flower stems and seeds turn beige in late summer, which can mar the blue effect but these can easily be sheared off.
⊘ **Blue • Early summer**
h.&s. **30cm (1ft)**

3 *Hakonechloa macra* **'Aureola'**♀ A bright mound, with floppy green-striped yellow leaves, that flush red in summer. 'Alboaurea' has green, white and yellow leaves. Red spikelets appear on both in late summer.
⊘ **Yellow with green stripes Spring** ⊘ **Pinkish red Summer •** *h.* **30cm (1ft)**
s. **60cm (2ft)**

4 *Leymus arenarius*
Blue lyme grass naturally grows on sand dunes. Flat leaves are grey-blue, topped by summer spikelets.
⊘ **Grey-blue**
h.&s. **60cm (2ft)**

5 *Pennisetum villosum* Abyssinian fountain grass bears white bottlebrush plumes on mid green leaves in midsummer.
⊘ **Mid green •** *h.* **60cm (2ft)**
s. **45cm (1½ft)**

Medium height grasses

The selections given here will form large good-looking clumps, some topped by glorious plumes.

1 *Miscanthus sinensis* **'Morning Light'** Forms a smart upright clump of slender leaves with white edging. Other good varieties are 'Silberfeder' (syn. 'Silver Feather'), which has silver to pinkish brown panicles, while 'Variegatus' has leaves striped with creamy white and pale green.
✿ **Reddish • Autumn** ⊘ **Green with white edging •** *h.* **1.2–1.5m (4–5ft)**
s. **1.2m (4ft)**

2 *Deschampsia cespitosa*
Tufted hair grass makes a beautiful clump. The dark green leaves grow to 60cm (2ft) high, with airy panicles that turn purple or yellow.
⊘ **Silver-green • Mid–late summer**
h. **1.2m (4ft)** *s.* **60cm (2ft)**

3 *Panicum virgatum* **'Rubrum'** Switch grass makes good-sized clumps of medium height. In autumn it produces sprays of tiny flowers, and the foliage starts to ripen to a rich reddish colour.
⊘⊘ **Green, red • Late summer–autumn •** *h.* **1m (3ft)** *s.* **1.2m (4ft)**

4 *Calamagrostis x acutiflora* **'Karl Foerster'** This makes a terrific display with smartly erect, rich green foliage. Foaming red-bronze panicles are at their best during midsummer and fade with the season to a softer buff colour.
⊘ **Green • Late summer**
h. **1.8m (6ft)** *s.* **60cm (2ft)**

Tall grasses

Beautiful great big plants will rustle in the breeze and give ravishing golden and orange tones to an autumnal garden.

1 *Molinia caerulea* **subsp. arundinacea** A superb autumn plant, tall moor-grass makes an impressive, imposing show. The panicles are held high above the foliage on thin vertical stems, giving a see-through effect. The swaying foliage turns a fierce sugary orange in autumn.
⊘⊘ **Purple, orange Early summer–early autumn**
h. **2m (7ft)** *s.* **40cm (16in)**

2 *Stipa gigantea*♀
Lofty stems bear large dangling spikelets that turn golden brown, high above the tall green foliage making a marvellous airy show.
⊘ **Purple • Early–late summer**
h. **1.8m (6ft)** *s.* **1.2–1.8m (4–6ft)**

Briza media

Stipa gigantea

Festuca glauca 'Elijah Blue'

Helenium

Sneezeweed was grown by early American colonists as a substitute for snuff, but grow it just for the colours and you won't be disappointed. In a damp border, bronze, orange, red and yellow daisy-like flowers make a terrific show at the end of summer, just when the garden needs a boost.

STAR PERFORMER
H. 'Moerheim Beauty'
Warm coppery red flowers emerge in early summer. Deadhead them as the flowers fade for a second flush of blooms that will last from late summer into autumn.

Expert's Selection

1 *H.* 'Moerheim Beauty'
The truly stunning flowers have coppery red petals surrounding a domed, velvety, brown centre.
✿ Copper • Early summer to autumn
h. 1m (3ft) *s.* 30cm (1ft)

2 *H.* 'Pumilum Magnificum'
Its 8cm (3in) wide flowers will take centre stage in late summer.
✿ Yellow • Late summer
h. 1m (3ft) *s.* 30cm (1ft)

3 *H.* 'Bruno'
A long-stemmed variety for the back of a border.
✿ Mahogany red • Late summer
h. 1.2m (4ft) *s.* 30cm (1ft)

4 *H. autumnale*
This late season, clump-forming variety bears clusters of flowers.
✿ Yellow • Autumn
h. 1.5m (5ft) *s.* 45cm (1½ft)

5 *H.* 'Coppelia'
Start the sneezeweed season with this rich coloured variety.
✿ Orange-red • Mid to late summer
h. 1m (3ft) *s.* 30cm (1ft)

6 *H.* 'Butterpat'
The rich yellow petals of its large flowers radiate like spokes from a darker yellow centre.
✿ Rich yellow • Mid to late summer
h. 1m (3ft) *s.* 60cm (2ft)

Sneezeweeds gradually spread into clumps without ever becoming invasive. They have long been staples of the traditional herbaceous bed, but their bright colours are increasingly giving them a more flamboyant appeal.

Their daisy-like petals splay back from a central button, in the shape of a shuttlecock, making the flowers look as though they are pointing straight at the sky.

Set the border on fire
Burning reds, oranges and yellows add a blast of 'heat' to the garden as the late summer sun wanes. Unlike most hot-coloured plants, they do not need a warm, sunny site to thrive, but do better in the damp.

Heleniums also set the scene for the coming autumn: the coppery '**Moerheim Beauty**', for example, tones with the russets of autumn leaves and the burnished reds of chrysanthemums.

Bring the flowers indoors
Stiff-stemmed heleniums work well in flower arrangements. Strip the leaves from the lower part of the stem and arrange them with other late season performers like yellow *Rudbeckia*, red *Fuchsia* and white **Japanese anemones**.

TAKE A FRESH LOOK
H. '**Autumn Lollipop**' This new variety is unusual, but short-lived. Its central brown boss is surrounded by short, downward pointing, yellow petals that almost seem to be hanging underneath.

H. 'Bruno'

H. 'Pumilum Magnificum'

The Essentials

Site demands They do best in moist, though not constantly wet, soil. Avoid very hot, sunny borders, where their roots may dry out.
Planting practice Plant anytime; lift and divide clumps every 2–3 years, after flowering, if necessary.
Flowering time They flower in the second half of summer, for a colourful link into autumn.
Pests and diseases Mostly trouble free, but slugs sometimes attack leaves, stems and flowers.
Bonus point Bring fiery colour to cooler parts of the garden.

Helianthus

Sunflowers are a hit in the late summer garden. Many of the giants are annuals, but these perennial varieties have impact year after year. Their open faces stretch up on strong stems and bask in the sun, attracting insects and, later in the season, finches, which eat their seeds.

Expert's Selection

1 *H.* 'Capenoch Star' ♀
A bushy spreading plant with a mass of giant, daisy-like blooms.
✿ **Lemon yellow**
Late summer–autumn
h. 1.5m (5ft) *s.* 75cm (2½ft)

2 *H.* 'Lemon Queen'
Keep these soft coloured flowers, 10cm (4in) across, upright by supporting the stems.
✿ **Pale yellow • Late summer–early autumn • *h.* 1.5m (5ft) *s.* 1.2m (4ft)**

3 *H.* 'Monarch' ♀
A splendid sunflower with a difference, it has 15cm (6in) wide, open, outward-pointing petals, and a dark inner eye.
✿ **Pale yellow • Late summer–early autumn • *h.* 2m (7ft) *s.* 1.2m (4ft)**

4 *H. salicifolius*
If you want a giant perennial sunflower, this is the one. The flowers are relatively small, just 7.5cm (3in) across, but are held high above the ground. Wonderful, drooping, shiny leaves 20cm (8in) long are an added bonus.
✿ **Bright yellow • Early autumn**
h. 2.5m (8ft) *s.* 60cm (2ft)

5 *H.* x *laetiflorus* 'Miss Mellish' Give this sunflower plenty of space in a large garden: it grows as wide as it does tall, and makes a big display of flowers.
✿ **Orange-yellow • Late summer–autumn • *h.&s.* 1.8m (6ft)**

Perennial sunflowers make a more reliable addition to the garden than the single stem, see-how-high-they-can-get annuals. Instead, they make tall, chunky clumps – ideal for informal flowering hedges – and produce plenty of late summer and autumn flowers.

Plant perennial sunflowers where they will catch the sun and use them to support a late-flowering deep red **clematis** or the Flame **nasturtium** (*Tropaeolum speciosum*), which has vivid red flowers through summer and into early autumn. The red and yellow makes a bold combination.

Hit the roof
If you prefer the more traditional 'sky-high' variety of sunflower, then *H. salicifolius*, with its 2.5m (8ft) stems, is the star choice. It has willow-like leaves, and long before the flowers appear makes an attractive feature. This variety also flowers later than the others, and only begins to bloom in early autumn. Dot several around the garden and leave the stems uncut over winter to make interesting architectural totem poles on frosty mornings.

The Essentials

Site demands Grow anywhere, in full sun or partial shade.
Planting practice Plant in early spring. Support stems where windy.
Flowering time Late summer to early autumn.
Pests and diseases Largely trouble free, though slugs may attack any tasty new shoots.
Bonus point The seeds attract birds to the garden.

H. 'Lemon Queen'

STAR PERFORMER
H. 'Capenoch Star' ♀ **Lemon-yellow, saucer-sized flowers, 12cm (5in) across, do best in moist soil, but relish the gentle rays of the late summer and autumn sun. Pick out the seeds from the centre of the flowers in autumn, and save to plant in spring.**

Helleborus

Hellebores are top of every gardener's wish list for their exquisite saucer-shaped flowers, which add glamour to the garden from winter to spring. They are ideal for brightening up borders in light shade, where they prolifically self-seed, sometimes even creating exciting new variants.

H. niger

Expert's Selection

1 *H. atrorubens*
Saucer-like, dusky violet flowers open before the leaves in spring on this neat, deciduous hellebore.
✿ **Violet • Early spring**
h. **30cm (1ft)** *s.* **45cm (1½ft)**

2 *H. lividus*♥
The three-fingered, evergreen leaves are brightened with silvery veins. It needs a warm sheltered spot to thrive.
✿ **Green-purple • Late winter**
h.&s. **45cm (1½ft)**

3 *H. argutifolius*
Clusters of small, pale green flowers open among the dark, prickly, evergreen leaves in winter.
✿ **Green • Winter–early spring**
h. **1.2m (4ft)** *s.* **60cm (2ft)**

4 *H. hybridus* **Ashwood Garden hybrids** A group of semi-evergreen hybrids, with a wide range of flower colours from pastels to deeper tones.
❀✿✿✿ **White, yellow, red and green**
Spring • *h.&s.* **45cm (1½ft)**

5 *H. niger*♥
Known as the 'Christmas rose' it has beautiful white flowers which open in early January to reveal long golden stamens.
❀ **White • Late winter**
h. **30cm (1ft)** *s.* **45cm (1½ft)**

H. lividus

6 *H. foetidus*♥
Known as stinking hellebore, its leaves give off an unpleasant scent when crushed, and can cause a skin irritation. The clusters of nodding, bell-shaped flowers stand high above the foliage.
✿ **Pale green**
Late winter–early spring
h. **75cm (2½ft)** *s.* **60cm (2ft)**

7 *H. hybridus* 'Garnet'
Dramatic flowers in a rich, regal purple, shot through with black veining, make this one of the most desirable hellebores.
✿ **Purple-red • Winter–early spring**
h.&s. **45cm (1½ft)**

H. hybridus 'Garnet'

8 *H. orientalis* **subsp. *guttatus*** The beautiful white flowers, patterned with dozens of tiny maroon spots will ensure this variety stands out in any mixed border. *H. orientalis* is also known as the Lenten rose.
❀ **White • Winter–spring**
h. **45cm (1½ft)** *s.* **60cm (2ft)**

Just one hellebore is seldom enough. The unusual greens and dusky pinks and purples of their flowers would make them appealing at any time of year, but in winter and very early spring they offer a glamour that no other plant can match.

Some of the most striking hellebores are the hybrids, like 'Garnet'. They come in a wide colour range from white to green, pink, red and almost black, and many gardeners with an area of moist shade get hooked on collecting different varieties.

The one downside of these exquisite plants is that many of them grow flowers that hang down. Plant breeders are now trying to create more plants with upward or outward-facing flowers, so that the shades of green or white inside the saucer-shaped blooms, with their rosy red speckling are not hidden from view. Double-flowered plants are also becoming increasingly available. You can make the most of the blooms by removing the plant's old foliage in early winter.

Start a collection

Because hellebores flower at a time of year when there is little else available, they are often best planted with more of the same. There are many irresistible varieties that are easy to find, but it is well worth a little effort to seek out a few more unusual colours and varieties, too, from winter garden shows and specialist nurseries.

H. *hybridus* 'Ballard's Black', for example, is very dark purple, and makes a stunning contrast to brighter colours or pastel shades. Or try the **Kochii Group** which consists of small, white, early flowering plants.

Hellebores cross pollinate freely, so if you grow a mixed batch of hybrids in various colours, you may find that you inadvertently develop your own interesting new variants.

The Essentials

Site demands Best in rich, moist soil with some shade. The ground beneath a deciduous tree or shrub is perfect – and any fallen leaves will provide a fertile, annual mulch.
Planting practice Plant in autumn or winter. Lighten the texture of heavy clay by adding mushroom compost and grit. On fast-draining chalk, dig in plenty of organic material deep down to feed the long roots.
Flowering time From mid winter into spring.
Pests and diseases Generally trouble free, but look out for greenfly in late spring and early summer, and signs of black spot, especially in cold wet winters.
Bonus point Glamorous flowers in the depths of winter.

STAR PERFORMER
H. atrorubens
The violet to purple flowers, often tinged green within, face outwards rather than down, as with many hellebores, making a fine display in light shade in February and March.

H. argutifolius

H. orientallis subsp. guttatus

Hemerocallis

Day lilies are available in a marvellous choice of shapes and colours, with plant breeders offering newer, brighter kinds every year. They come in almost all colours from white to near-black. The flowers only last one day, but new blooms open continuously all through the summer.

Day lilies are care-free plants, at home in almost any garden. Besides the wonderful star-shaped flowers, sometimes with extravagantly frilled edges, they have arching, rich green, strap-like foliage, often evergreen, that complements the lustrous blooms perfectly. In addition, they are fully hardy and can be planted in a wide range of conditions, including windy sites, both inland and on the coast. They look superb planted near water, by the side of a stream or pond.

Rejuvenating old clumps
If an old clump of day lilies is no longer performing too well, dig it up in the spring (especially the evergreens) or autumn. Discard the older, central portion and replant the outer sections.

The Essentials

Site demands Any soil, except very poor and dry, in full but not burning sun.
Planting practice Plant in spring.
Flowering times All summer. Deadhead daily for the best show.
Pests and diseases Usually trouble free, but a new pest is the Hemerocallis gall midge, which causes the buds to swell but not open. Remove and destroy any affected buds promptly.
Bonus point Flower reliably over a long season, with almost no care.

Expert's Selection

1 *H.* 'Catherine Woodbery'
A graceful pink and yellow-toned lily with bright green leaves.
✿ **Light pink • Mid–late summer**
h. 75cm (2½ft) *s.* 60cm (2ft)

2 *H. lilioasphodelus*♲
An old-fashioned beauty with star-shaped flowers and a rich scent.
✿ **Yellow • Early summer**
h.&s. 1m (3ft)

3 *H.* 'Glowing Gold'
Flowers like large, golden trumpets bloom from July to September.
✿ **Orangey gold • Mid–late summer**
h.&s. 75m (2½ft)

4 *H.* 'Stafford'
Shaped like a star fish, with red petals and a greeny-yellow centre.
✿ **Red • Midsummer**
h. 70cm (28in) *s.* 1m (3ft)

5 *H.* 'Cartwheels'♲
Gives a bright, flashy show of brilliant star-shaped flowers.
✿ **Sharp orange • Midsummer**
h.&s. 75cm (2½ft)

6 *H.* 'Stella d'Oro'♲
A shorter evergreen lily with big rounded bright yellow blooms.
✿ **Bright yellow • Midsummer**
h. 30m (1ft) *s.* 45cm (1½ft)

7 *H.* 'Dubloon'
Subtly beautiful flowers glow above a central clump of rush-like leaves.
✿ **Deep orange • Mid–late summer**
h.&s. 75m (2½ft)

STAR PERFORMER

H. 'Catherine Woodbery' **A delicately coloured, star-shaped flower, with a greeny yellow centre and stamens, and an arresting scent. It starts flowering from midsummer.**

H. 'Cartwheels'

H. 'Stafford'

H. 'Red Spangles'

Heuchera

Alum roots or **coral bells** are a first-rate addition to a border. They have extremely attractive foliage, and some are grown for that alone. The best flowering varieties bear an airy mass of tiny bright flowers, held high above the leaves.

Expert's Selection

1 *H.* **'Chocolate Ruffles'**
Glorious, ruffled, brown leaves are tinged with purple beneath.
⌀ **Brown/purple** • **Autumn–winter**
h. 40cm (16in) *s.* 30cm (1ft)

2 *H.* **'Red Spangles'**♡
Superb, bright coloured, summer flowers contrast beautifully with the mound of dark green foliage.
✿ **Crimson** • **Early summer**
⌀ **Dark green**
h. 60cm (2ft) *s.* 30cm (1ft)

3 *H.* **micrantha var. diversifolia 'Palace Purple'**♡
The jagged foliage, 15cm (6in) long, is a wonderful coppery purple.
⌀ **Copper-purple** • **Autumn–winter**
h. 60cm (2ft) *s.* 30cm (1ft)

4 *H.* **'Pewter Moon'**
The purple foliage has highly distinctive silver markings.
✿ **Pale pink** • **Summer** ⌀ **Purple**
h.&s. 30cm (1ft)

5 *H.* **sanguinea 'Snow Storm'** Has bright summer flowers, and shapely, rounded dark green leaves, marbled with silver.
✿ **Red** • **Early summer** ⌀ **Dark green**
h. 45cm (1½ft) *s.* 30cm (1ft)

6 *H.* **cylindrica 'Greenfinch'**
Yellowish flowers rise above dark green, heart-shaped leaves.
✿ **Yellowish** • **Early summer** ⌀ **Dark green** • *h.* 1m (3ft) *s.* 30cm (1ft)

Coral bells look best planted towards the front of a border or island bed, where you can fully appreciate the tiny aerial flowers, on top of the tall thin stems, contrasting with the dark coloured foliage.

Give new life to old plants
While heucheras could not be easier to look after, they do need a small amount of attention every few years or so. If the plant is completely ignored for several years, the stems will get woodier and the flower show increasingly insignificant. Simply dig up the plant carefully, with all its roots, and then divide the clump. Replant the separated, more vigorous, outer sections, and discard the older, woodier, inner portions. Do this is late summer or early autumn. Refresh the soil with plenty of humus.

The Essentials

Site demands Any rich, fairly moist soil, in sun or light shade.
Planting practice Plant in early autumn, and mulch annually.
Flowering times Early summer; some flower again in late summer.
Pests and diseases Generally trouble free, but may be infected by leafy gall or vine weevil grubs.
Bonus point Makes excellent, good-looking ground cover.

STAR PERFORMER
H. 'Chocolate Ruffles'
The latest heucheras are being bred to produce superb winter foliage, and this American cultivar has quickly become a winner, with good-looking, purple-brown leaves that stay on the plant throughout the winter.

H. micrantha var. diversifolia 'Palace Purple'

Hosta

One of the finest foliage plants around, hostas will provide superb ground cover. Their sculptural leaves may be large and rounded, or more slender and pointed, in shades from blue to dramatically variegated green and yellow, in a range of textures from dull and waxy, to a glossy shine.

Hosta flowers are borne above the leaves

Not only beautiful, hostas are also undemanding. They are tolerant of all soil conditions except bone dry, but grow best in moist, slightly shaded sites. Add plenty of organic matter to the hole when you plant and mulch well to retain the soil's moisture.

Garden hostas

Hostas can be used in all kinds of contrasting ways. The bright yellowish green leaves of **'Gold Standard'** can be emphasised by placing darker colours behind.

The depth of colouring of blue-tinged hostas is enhanced when they are grown in light shade. The lush rounded leaves look particularly effective around ponds, where their shapes reflect in the water, and they give hiding places for frogs and toads. They also provide a good contrast for the lofty grace of *Irises*, and mix well with shade-loving plants, such as *Pulmonarias*.

Hostas in a pot

Growing shapely, elegent hostas in containers can help to highlight their beautiful foliage. The large-leaved varieties, such as the exotic *H. plantaginea*, look particularly striking when planted in pots.

H. sieboldiana var. *elegans*

Expert's Selection

1 *H.* 'Halcyon'♀
A beautiful cultivar with elegant blue-green foliage and light purple flowers in summer.
✿ Mauve ∅ Blue-green • Midsummer
h. 60cm (2ft) *s.* 45cm (1½ft)

2 *H.* 'Hadspen Blue'
This robust variety forms neat dense clumps of thick bluish, heart-shaped leaves.
✿ Lavender ∅ Green-blue • Summer
h. 60cm (2ft) *s.* 45cm (1½ft)

3 *H.* 'Big Daddy'
This impressive cultivar has large, rounded, bluish leaves.
❀ Off white • ∅ Blue • Midsummer
h. 75cm (2½ft) *s.* 1m (3ft)

4 *H.* 'Krossa Regal'♀
Forms a clump of upward-pointing, lance-shaped leaves.
✿ Pale lavender ∅ Grey-blue • Mid-summer • *h.* 1.4m (4½ft) *s.* 1m (3ft)

5 *H. sieboldiana* var. *elegans*♀ Sumptuous crinkled leaves, 30cm (1ft) long and wide.
✿ Pale lavender ∅ Silvery blue Midsummer • *h.* 60cm (2ft) *s.* 1.2m (4ft)

6 *H.* 'Colossal'
A real giant of a spreader with rounded green leaves.
✿ Lavender ∅ Green • Midsummer
h. 1m (3ft) *s.* 1.5m (5ft)

7 *H.* 'Honeybells'♀
An extremely vigorous hosta with light green, shiny leaves.
❀ White ∅ Light green • Mid-summer • *h.* 60cm (2ft) *s.* 1.2m (4ft)

STAR PERFORMER

H. 'Halcyon' A blue-green leaved hosta, with few rivals. The elegant, pointed foliage becomes more heart-shaped as it unfurls. In midsummer, pale mauve flowers appear on the top of straight bare stems.

H. 'June'

H. 'Gold Standard'

Houttuynia

In moist, lightly shaded sites, houttuynias are an excellent choice for ground cover. They have appealing heart-shaped leaves, which have a delicate citrus fragrance when crushed.

8 *H. plantaginea*
The shiny heart-shaped leaves with wavy edges have deep veins.
❀ **White** ∅ **Light green** • **Mid-summer** • *h.* **45m (1½ft)** *s.* **1m (3ft)**

9 *H. 'Gold Standard'*
Broad, glossy leaves turn from dark green to golden yellow, then beige.
✿ **Lavender** ∅ **Green** • **Early summer** *h.* **50cm (20in)** *s.* **1m (3ft)**

10 *H. 'Sagae'* ♀
The long olive-green leaves have irregular creamy-yellow markings.
❀ **White** ∅ **Olive-green** • **Midsummer** *h.* **1m (3ft)** *s.* **1.5m (5ft)**

11 *H. 'June'*
The graceful heart-shaped leaves are edged with a dark blue green.
❀ **Greyish lavender to near-white** ∅∅ **Yellow/blue-green** • **Midsummer** *h.* **50cm (20in)** *s.* **1m (3ft)**

12 *H. undulata* var. *albomarginata* Also known as 'Thomas Hogg', it needs full shade.
✿ **Lavender** • ∅ **Green, with white margin** • **Early–midsummer** *h.* **35cm (14in)** *s.* **45cm (1½ft)**

13 *H. 'Ginko Craig'*
White edges define dark leaves.
✿ **Deep purple** ∅ **Dark green and white** • **Summer** • *h.* **25cm (10in)** *s.* **45cm (1½ft)**

14 *H. 'Tall Boy'*
This large hosta bears flowers on stems up to 1m (3ft) tall.
✿ **Purple** ∅ **Mid green** • **Late summer** • *h.* **50cm (20in)** *s.* **1m (3ft)**

15 *H. 'Wide Brim'* ♀
Satiny mid-green leaves have a wide and uneven cream margin.
✿ **Pale lavender** ∅ **Green and cream** **Summer** • *h.* **60cm (2ft)** *s.* **1m (3ft)**

The Essentials

Site demands Light shade and moist soil give the best results.
Planting practice Plant in spring or autumn. Add plenty of humus before planting, keep well watered, and feed and mulch in autumn.
Flowering time Small flowers on long graceful stalks will appear from June onwards.
Pests and diseases Slugs and snails are the main problem – set beer traps (page 19) to keep them at bay or pick them off at night.
Bonus point Hostas flourish from early spring to the first frost.

Expert's Selection

1 *H. cordata* 'Chameleon'
With attractive creamy yellow, green and red leaves, this cultivar is also known as 'Tricolor'.
∅ **Green with yellow and red** • **Late spring** • *h.* **23cm (9in)** *s.* **Indefinite**

2 *H. cordata* 'Flore Pleno'
The heart-shaped green leaves have a bluish tinge and are thinly edged with red. In spring it bears densely packed spikes of white flowers.
❀ **White** ∅ **Blue-green** • **Late spring** *h.* **23cm (9in)** *s.* **Indefinite**

The Essentials

Site demands Cool conditions and damp soil in sun or partial shade are ideal.
Planting practice Plant pieces of underground stem in autumn.
Pests and diseases Houttuynia is remarkably trouble free.
Bonus point Tolerant of having its roots submerged, houttuynia can also be grown in a pond.

The most popular form and most easily obtained cultivar is *H. cordata* 'Chameleon', though others with names like 'Joker's Gold' and 'Boo-Boo' are sometimes available.

It needs to be grown in light, dappled shade rather than darker shade as the attractive red tinting on the leaf becomes muted with insufficient light.

Planting positions
Do not be tempted to put the smart foliage in the border as under ideal conditions it may spread too rapidly. Instead, grow it as ground cover or at the margins of a pond.

STAR PERFORMER
H. cordata 'Chameleon'
The vividly marked, ornamental foliage of 'Chameleon' makes a striking ground cover. It grows about 23cm (9in) high, and the small white spring flowers are in the shape of a small cross, with yellow in the middle.

Iris

There is an iris for just about every part of the garden, and for almost every season. Irises look stunning at the edge of a pond but also thrive in the hot summer sun. As well as the classic violet-blue, colours include delicate pink, ice-blue, yellow, purple, bronze, near-black and white.

Expert's Selection

Beardless water irises

1 *I. sibirica* 'Emperor'
Richly coloured and with an exquisite shape, it grows in large clumps with thin, grassy foliage. 'Perry's Blue' is a clearer blue.
✿ **Purple-blue • Early summer**
h. **1m (3ft)**

2 *I. pseudacorus*♀
The native British flag iris colonises stream sides and pools, and needs a large space to thrive. Its strap-like leaves are marked with yellow on 'Variegata' in spring, but fade when the flowers open.
✿ **Yellow**
Early summer
h. **1–1.5m (3–5ft)**

3 *I. versicolor*♀
The blue flag comes from North America and is good for small ponds. 'Kermesina' is claret and 'Rosea' pinkish purple.
✿ **Blue**
Early summer
h. **60cm (2ft)**

4 *I. laevigata*♀
Robust and tolerant, it gives a superb show at the edge of a pond. Sometimes there is a second

flush of flowers in early autumn. 'Alba' is white.
✿ **Purple–blue • Midsummer**
h. **75cm (2½ft)**

5 *I. ensata*♀
The Japanese flag iris has given rise to myriad superb cultivars, many with Japanese names like 'Haru-no-umi'. 'Moonlight Waves' is white.
✿ **Deep purple • Early summer**
h. **60cm–1m (2–3ft)**

6 *I. setosa*♀
Native to Siberia and Alaska this is one of the hardiest irises.
✿ **Slate-blue to violet • Early summer • h. 15–75cm (6in–2½ft)**

Among the most striking of all flowers, irises add beauty and drama to any garden. Some irises grow from bulbs (see page 317), but those listed here grow from rhizomes, and are divided into two main groups. Bearded irises have fluffy hairs on the outer petals which, in the wild, may attract pollinating insects, whereas beardless irises do not. The distinction is important when it comes to planting.

Growing bearded irises
Plant bearded border irises in a sunny position, ideally in soil which is free-draining and either neutral or slightly alkaline, like chalk and limestone. Rhizomes should be half above the soil level. Make sure they are well watered for the first few weeks.

Growing beardless irises
Rhizomes of beardless irises need to be planted 4cm (1½in) deep. *I. laevigata* and *I. pseudacorus* are set 5–25cm (2–10in) deep in water, although *I. pseudacorus* prefers slightly acid conditions. *I. ensata* likes to stand in water in summer, and in drier ground over winter. *I. sibirica* goes 2.5cm (1in) deep in moist soil. As they are heavy feeders, spread compost or manure around the plants.

AUTUMN AND SPRING IRISES
For a show of irises right through the later part of the year, try these varieties. Plant *I. foetidissima*♀, which has lilac-green summer flowers and striking, orange autumn seeds (that look superb with cut flowers). Then follow with *I. unguicularis*♀, which will bloom from December to March in a mild winter. It has large, wide, violet-blue flowers, that are fragrant.

Pond-side planting
Use a magical summer display of water irises to blend an ordinary-looking pond into the surrounding garden. The tall, thin, strappy foliage of the beardless water irises, from the little blue-toned *I. laevigata* at 40cm (16in) to the 1m (3ft) high *I. pseudacorus*, will add a degree of lushness to the side of the pond.

In addition, shallow water packed with rhizomes also provides a perfect egg-laying site for frogs. When new shoots emerge, the area will also offer protection for the thousands of tadpoles before they swim off.

I. versicolor

I. pseudacorus 'Variegata'

I. laevigata

Bearded border irises

1 *I.* **'Peach Frost'**
A tall iris, whose ruffled flowers
have a dash of white and peach.
✿ **Yellowish pink • Spring–early
summer • *h.* 1m (3ft)**

2 *I.* **'Stepping Out'**♀
Another tall iris with lovely
patterned flowers edged with blue.
❀ **White • Mid–late spring
h. 1m (3ft)**

3 *I.* **'Brown Lasso'**♀
Slightly shorter than the other
bearded irises, this is fun and flashy.
✿ **Yellow and violet • Mid–late spring
h. 60cm (2ft)**

4 *I.* **'Raspberry Blush'**♀
A luscious pink iris, ideal
for the end of spring.
✿ **Lilac pink
Mid–late spring
h. 50cm (20in)**

5 *I.* **'Jeremy
Brian'**♀ The smart
flowers of this dwarf
iris are enhanced with
white and cream.
✿ **Pale blue • Late spring
h. 25cm (10in)**

6 *I. pumila*
The earliest of the bearded irises
with flowers that grow on almost
non-existent stalks.
✿✿❀ **Blue, yellow or white
Early spring • *h.* 10cm (4in)**

7 *I.* **'Blue Shimmer'**
Pale flowers shimmer in full sun.
❀ **White and blue • Early summer
h. 75cm (2½ft)**

8 *I. germanica*♀
This purple flag iris flowers freely.
✿ **Purple • Mid–late spring
h. 70cm (28in)**

STAR PERFORMER
I. sibirica **'Emperor'** **This rich
purple-blue beardless iris is a typical
Siberian iris (the species originated
in central Europe and moved east). It
grows best in moist ground, and the
small, delicately veined and speckled
flowers emerge in early summer.**

I. 'Stepping Out'

I. 'Rasberry Blush'

The Essentials

Site demands Irises grow in a
range of sites, in dry borders or
ponds, and in sun or half-shade.
Planting practice See main text.
Flowering time Most bloom in
early summer, and a few in winter.
Pests and diseases Slugs, snails
and caterpillars may eat shoots.
Bonus point Architectural foliage
remains throughout summer, after
the flowers fade.

Kniphofia

Red-hot pokers are some of the most exciting and dramatic border plants. The strong, sturdy flower spike is packed with short, bottlebrush-type flowers in both quiet pastels or outrageously loud combinations of red and orange. Follow our suggestions for care-free pokers.

Red-hot pokers are among the most extraordinary flowers. Their outrageous flowerheads, and sometimes extravagant size add an exotic touch to any garden, perk up borders that need a lift, and will attract bees.

Easy-grow pokers

Pokers are remarkably drought-resistant and are an ideal easy-to-grow plant for gravel gardens and other well drained sites. They do not need pampering, and actively dislike rich, overworked soil.

Container-grown plants can be planted in summer, when the flowering plants are looking their most tempting in garden centres.

Months of display

If you are a fan of red-hot pokers, you can create a display of these eye-catching plants that will stay in flower for up to seven months of the year. Choose a succession of different varieties that flower from spring ('Early Buttercup') right through summer and into mid autumn ('Mount Etna').

Expert's Selection

1 *K.* 'Atlanta'
The enormous, dramatic orange-red flowers slowly fade to yellow over the summer months.
✿ **Orange-red • Late spring–late summer • h.** 1m (3ft) **s.** 75cm (2½ft)

2 *K.* 'Samuel's Sensation' ♀
A striking plant, its long spikes of brash red flowers add late summer impact, then gradually turn yellow.
✿ **Red • Late summer**
h. 1.3m (4½ft) **s.** 75cm (2½ft)

3 *K.* 'Mount Etna'
Though the buds are red, the flowers are a serene yellow-green.
✿ **Yellow-green • Late summer–early autumn • h.** 1m (3ft) **s.** 60cm (2ft)

4 *K.* 'Early Buttercup'
Blooms earlier than most varieties.
✿ **Yellow • Late spring–early summer h.&s.** 60cm (2ft)

5 *K.* 'Strawberries and Cream' A soft-coloured variety ideal for the early autumn garden.
✿ **Cream • Late summer**
h. 60cm (2ft) **s.** 45cm (1½ft)

6 *K.* 'Bressingham Comet'
The flowers of this small, flashy variety are tipped with orange.
✿ **Bright yellow • Autumn**
h. 40cm (16in) **s.** 23cm (9in)

7 *K.* 'Fiery Fred'
An aptly named, hot-coloured type.
✿ **Orange-red • Midsummer**
h. 1.1m (3½ft) **s.** 60cm (2ft)

K. 'Bressingham Comet'

The Essentials

Site demands Pokers are very trouble free. They need free-draining soil which is not too rich, and plenty of sun.
Planting practice Plant either in early autumn or in spring.
Flowering time There are red-hot pokers which flower in spring, summer and autumn.
Pests and diseases The main culprits are thrips which can strike during drought. Otherwise, they are trouble free.
Bonus point Just a few pokers will spice up the border.

STAR PERFORMER

K. 'Atlanta' Get summer off to a flying start with a burst of orange-red flowers that gradually calm down and fade to yellow. The flowerhead is well clear of the pale green leaves. This evergreen will stand out in any display, making a wonderful focal point.

Lamium

Dead nettles may sound like a strange choice for a care-free garden but they make excellent flowers for spring and summer, and many double as effective ground cover. They are ideal grown in a natural setting, with damp ground in shade, and even poor soil, under trees.

L. orvala

L. maculatum 'Beacon Silver'

Dead nettles are so-called because they do not sting. The spreading varieties are excellent at keeping down weeds, and at creating an array of flowers in shady spots. Those with variegated leaves are good for adding colour to shady areas.

Companions and control

Dead nettles thrive at the edge of a woodland area, but the spreaders must be planted among other robust plants because they will smother anything small and less vigorous.

Good companions include other woodland plants such as bluebells (*Hyacinthoides non-scripta*), daffodils (*Narcissus*), foxgloves (*Digitalis purpurea*) and Solomon's seal (*Polygonatum multiflorum*). When buying dead nettles, choose three or four kinds in order to create different effects.

If the spreaders do get over-vigorous they can easily be reined in, by slicing off unwanted growth with a spade. Another way of making sure that the spreaders do not get out of hand is to ensure that they are planted in relatively poor soil.

Shady passages

To add a touch of colour to a long, narrow, paved side passage, dig up the whole of one edge, to create a long, thin stretch of soil. Plant this with a few dead nettles, and they will soon spread to add interest to an otherwise dull and unappealing space.

Expert's Selection

1 *L. galeobdolon* **'Hermann's Pride'** A striking dead nettle with intricately patterned variegated foliage. 'Florentimum' has green leaves splashed with silver, that turn purple in winter.
✿ Yellow • Spring–Summer
h. 60cm (2ft) *s.* 75cm (2½ft)

2 *L. orvala*
A non-invasive dead nettle, this beautiful variety flowers all summer long, often starting in late spring. It thrives in dappled shade.
✿ Copper-pink • Early summer
h. 40cm (16in) *s.* 50cm (20in)

3 *L. maculatum* **'White Nancy'**♀ The silvery leaves have green round the edges. Other good cultivars, with variable coloured flowers, include 'Beacon Silver', 'Red Nancy' and 'Sterling Silver'.
✿ White • Late spring
h. 15cm (6in) *s.* 1m (3ft)

4 *L. garganicum* **'Golden Carpet'** Another non-invasive dead nettle, this variety has gold markings on the leaves and attractively striped flowers.
✿ Pink and white • Midsummer
h.&s. 45cm (1½ft)

The Essentials

Site demands Damp, but not boggy ground, and any degree of shade except the very darkest.
Planting practice Plant pot-grown plants at any time, but otherwise in spring or autumn.
Flowering time The flowers appear in spring and early summer.
Pests and diseases Dead nettles are virtually trouble free.
Bonus point The patterned foliage provides an excellent backdrop for a range of plants.

STAR PERFORMER
L. galeobdolon **'Hermann's Pride'** Often found growing wild in woodlands, 'Hermann's Pride' has bright yellow summer flowers. It also has good looking variegated foliage, with dark veins standing out against the paler, silvery green background. It makes excellent ground cover, and spreads so well in suitable sites you may need to keep it under control.

Lathyrus

Perennial sweet peas give gardens a summery boost, with beautiful coloured flowers, growing in abundant bushy clumps or on romping, climbing stems that never get out of hand. Often deliciously fragrant, they will grow in most soils in sites with a modicum of sun and a little daytime shade.

L. latifolius 'White Pearl'

L. nervosus

Expert's Selection

1 *L. latifolius* 'Rosa Perle' ♥
A rampant climber, it blooms for several months, well into early autumn. Also known as 'Pink Pearl', other colours include 'White Pearl' and 'Red Pearl'.
✿ **Reddish-pink • Summer–early autumn • h. 1.8m (6ft) s. 1m (3ft)**

2 *L. vernus* ♥
Quickly forms a low bushy clump, with dozens of tiny flowers, tinged with a hint of red and maroon. 'Alboroseus' is less vigorous, with pink and white flowers.
✿ **Purple • Mid–late spring**
h. 40cm (16in) s. 30cm (1ft)

3 *L. grandiflorus*
A classic climber, reminiscent of old-fashioned cottage gardens, it has beautiful large flowers.
✿✿ **Blue and purple • Midsummer**
h. 1.8m (6ft) s.1m (3ft)

4 *L. rotundifolius*
The Persian everlasting pea grows vigorously, its flowers varying from deep pink to brick red.
✿ **Deep pink • Midsummer**
h.&s. 1m (3ft)

5 *L. nervosus*
Lord Anson's blue pea has a lovely sweet scent, with beautiful sprays of flowers on long stalks.
✿ **Bright blue • Midsummer**
h. 1.5m (5ft) s. 1m (3ft)

The Essentials

Site demands They thrive in almost any well-drained soil in full sunlight, though a little shade is appreciated during the day.
Planting practice Sow seeds in early spring in pots, or at the flowering site. Or plant out ready grown small plants a little later.
Flowering times Most flowers appear in high summer.
Pests and diseases Generally trouble free though slugs and snails can chew through new stems. Set beer traps (page 19).
Bonus point Sweet peas are excellent as cut flowers.

Perennial sweet peas are more care free than their annual counterparts in one significant respect: they do not need to be re-planted every year and once established will produce a delighful display for a number of years. Though easy to grow, perennial peas do benefit from a helping hand. When the new growth is about 15cm (6in) high and there are three pairs of leaves up the stem, pinch off the tip of the growing shoot. This will encourage the plant to put out new stems lower down, and create a bushier, more prolific plant with many more flowers. If you forget, the show of flowers will not be quite as impressive.

A summer-long show
All sweet peas produce many more flowers if the old, dead flowers are constantly removed. The plant will then put its energy into making new blooms rather than producing seed.

Supporting climbers
Climbing sweet peas, which can reach 1.8m (6ft), do need some support. Attach wires to a wall, or allow the plants to clamber over an adjacent shrub.

Although many perennial sweet peas are luxuriant climbers, others, and especially the wonderful *L. latifolius*, can be also used as ground cover or to sweep down a bank, creating a flamboyant carpet of flowers.

STAR PERFORMER
L. latifolius 'Rosa Perle' ♥
This perennial pea is a fantastic climber, which will flower all summer. It makes a high impact show with up to 15 folded flowers carried on each stalk.

Leucanthemum

Shasta daisies offer a wonderful, free-flowering display from June to September. These sturdy, single-stemmed plants, which come either with white petals and a central yellow eye, or double flowers in all-white, will brighten up borders and flower arrangements alike.

The well-defined white or cream flowerheads and dark shiny leaves of shasta daisies are a crisp counterpoint to a wide range of border plants. They are fully hardy and will grow easily in most soils, both in full sunshine and partial shade, giving a good display all summer long.

Planting for success

Young plants of *L. × superbum* that have been bought in can be planted out in spring. For best results it is a good idea to add lime to acid soils to ensure the moisture these daisies love. Once the flowering season is over, remove the faded heads and cut stems down below the old flowerheads. In autumn cut the old stems down to the ground.

Border contrasts

Shasta daisies are such excellent, all-purpose plants that it is worth buying four or five to dot around the border where they will give reds, blues and yellows a strong contrast. They also look pretty in long grass where buttercups are left to flower, and free-flowering around the edges of a pond.

Expert's Selection

1 *L. × superbum* **'Snowcap'** A classic yellow-centred white daisy with thick petals and dark green leaves on strong medium-tall stems.
✿ **White • Early–midsummer**
h.&s. **45cm (1½ft)**

2 *L. × superbum* **'Wirral Supreme'**♀ One of the tallest of the shasta daisies, it has a circular pale boss like a ruff, instead of the usual yellow eye.
✿ **White • All summer**
h. **1m (3ft)** *s.* **75cm (2½ft)**

3 *L. × superbum* **'Phyllis Smith'** Fine, individually separated petals, give a carefree, informal, slightly tousled look.
✿ **White • All summer**
h.&s. **75cm (2½ft)**

4 *L. × superbum* **'Mount Everest'** An old-fashioned, wide-eyed, daisy with a bright yellow eye and 10cm (4in) wide flowers.
✿ **White • All summer**
h.&s. **60cm (2ft)**

5 *L. × superbum* **'Horace Read'** Has rounded double flowers, thickly packed with sturdy white petals.
✿ **White • All summer**
h.&s. **60cm (2ft)**

STAR PERFORMER
L. × superbum **'Snowcap'**
An abundant plant which produces a free and easy show. Each large flower is about 10cm (4in) wide with a lemon yellow centre which rises above the snowy petals.

The Essentials

Site demands Will grow in virtually any soil, even slightly heavy clay, as they like quite a bit of moisture. Place in bright sun or lightly dappled shade.
Planting practice Plant out in late spring after the last frost.
Flowering time With a long flowering season, they will brighten up a border all summer long.
Pests and diseases It is highly unlikely that shasta daisies will have any problems with pests.
Bonus point When cut, they will stay fresh for a week or more.

L. × superbum **'Phyllis Smith**

L. × superbum **'Horace Read'**

Limonium

Sea lavender or **statice** is usually found on sea shores or salt marshes and makes an abundant display, usually in shades of lavender but also in brighter hues as well. It can just as easily be grown in gardens, and flowers from the middle of summer.

If you are designing a seaside garden, sea lavender could not be a more authentic plant, but it also does well in the right kind of soil farther inland. With tiny narrow blooms borne in substantial clusters, it creates low spreads of flowers on leafless stems which are a great textural contrast with other border plants.

A variety of beautiful colours are available, from soft pale blues, which look their best in the early evening light, to the different forms of *L. sinuatum* which come in brighter yellows, blues, and pinks.

Most sea lavenders are fully hardy and their ideal soil is free-draining and slightly alkaline. Ensure that you add lime if you want to grow them in a more acid soil. Certain varieties, such as *L. platyphyllum* actively prefer a drier soil so are worth growing if moisture retention can be a problem. For best results plant out younger plants later in the spring when the risk of frost is past.

Once established, sea lavenders need little attention. Deadhead regularly to prolong the show of flowers and cut off the stems once flowering has ended.

L. platyphyllum

L. bellidifolium

STAR PERFORMER

L. sinuatum Mediterranean statice is usually grown as an annual as it flowers best in its first season, bearing large clusters of tiny flowers and deep green leaves with wavy margins. Other varieties include the California Series with strong colours, including purple, and the Petite Bouquet Series with plants up to 30cm (1ft) high.

1 *L. sinuatum*
Strongly-coloured flower clumps contrast with the wavy leaves.
✿✿✿✿✿ Blue, pink, red, white, yellow • Midsummer–early autumn
h. 45cm (1½ft) s. 30cm (1ft)

2 *L. aureum* 'Supernova'
Stiff branches bear greyish green leaves and bright flower sprays.
✿ Orange-yellow • Midsummer–early autumn
h. 30cm (1ft) s. 20cm (8in)

3 *L. platyphyllum*
The thin branching stems are packed with sprays of small lavender-coloured flowers.
✿ Lavender • Midsummer–early autumn
h. 60cm (2ft) s. 45cm (1½ft)

4 *L. bellidifolium*
Ideal for the front of the border. The flowers are offset by the deep green leaves.
✿✿ Blue, pinkish blue Midsummer–early autumn
h. 20cm (8in) s. 10cm (4in)

Site demands Grow it in a seaside garden, or in sandy, free-draining ground in bright sun. If the soil is acid it will need to be treated with lime before planting.
Planting practice Plant out in springtime.
Flowering time Summer into early autumn.
Pests and diseases Sea lavender is remarkably trouble free, but *L. platyphyllum* may suffer from attacks of mildew.
Bonus point Tolerant of wind and salty spray.

Linum

Flax is the ideal plant for a late spring and early summer front-of-border show. Although each flower lasts only one day, there is a constant succession of blooms.

Flaxes thrive where other plants do not, in gravel or scree gardens, and on chalky soil. A small grouping of blue, for example *L. narbonense*, yellow (*L. flavum* 'Gemmell's Hybrid') and white (*L. perenne* 'Diamant') flax makes a superb display. Although some flaxes are short-lived, if you take cuttings from the ends of stems in the summer, they should quickly root to produce vigorous new plants the following season.

STAR PERFORMER

L. narbonense **Quite rightly known as beautiful flax, this is one of the taller varieties, and bears silky, white-eyed flowers.**

Expert's Selection

1 *L. narbonense*
A classic blue flax with an abundance of soft-toned flowers covering its twiggy stems.
✿ **Blue • Midsummer**
h. **50cm (20in)** *s.* **30cm (1ft)**

2 *L. flavum* 'Compactum'
This compact golden flax is ideal in a container. For earlier blooms, try 'Gemmell's Hybrid'.
✿ **Bright yellow • Midsummer**
h.&s. **15cm (6in)**

3 *L. perenne* 'Diamant'
Perennial flax puts on a good show of 2.5cm (1in) flowers.
✿ **White • Summer–early autumn**
h. **40cm (16in)** *s.* **25cm (10in)**

4 *L. arboreum*♀
Originating in Greece and western Turkey, the shrubby flax blooms all summer long.
✿ **Rich yellow • All summer**
h.&s. **30cm (1ft)**

The Essentials

Site demands Ideal for extremely well-drained soil with a place in full sun.
Planting practice Plant out in spring or early summer.
Flowering time Late spring to early autumn.
Pests and diseases Aphids may attack new spring growth.
Bonus point Will thrive even in the driest stony soil.

Liriope

With narrow grape-like flower clusters and elegant, bright green, strap-like leaves, liriopes are excellent clump-forming plants for ground cover in a dry, sheltered site.

Native to China, Japan, Taiwan and Vietnam, liriopes prefer well-drained soil in a warm, sheltered, sunny garden. The flowers come in shades of lavender, mauve and white set off by the grassy foliage and will appear from late summer all the way through the autumn.

The lovely *L. muscari* has several good varieties: 'Monroe White' has white flowers, 'Majestic' taller spikes with soft blue flowers, while 'John Burch' has both tall spikes of violet flowers and variegated leaves.

Expert's Selection

1 *L. muscari*♀
Tall, brightly-toned flower spikes are a smart contrast with the bright green leaves.
✿ **Violet • Late summer–autumn**
h.&s. **45cm (1½ft)**

2 *L. exiliflora* 'Ariaka-janshige' A medium sized plant with smartly variegated leaves that are up to 45cm (1½ft) long.
✿ **Mauve • Late summer–autumn**
h. **25cm (10in)** *s.* **30cm (1ft)**

3 *L. spicata*
This is the spreading version of lilyturf forming clumps as wide as they are high. The flowers can be from pale blue to white, and the leaves are up to 30cm (1ft) long.
✿✿ **Pale blue, white**
Late summer–autumn
h. & s. **45cm (1½ft)**

The Essentials

Site demands They will grow in most garden soils in full sun.
Planting practice Plant in spring.
Flowering time Late summer and autumn.
Pests and diseases Slugs can be a problem.
Bonus point Long-lived or evergreen foliage lasts well after the flowers have died down.

STAR PERFORMER

***L. muscari*♀** **The bright violet, bead-like flowers held in elegant spikes are set off against the evergreen, strap-shaped leaves.**

Lupinus

Lupins, with their spikes of brightly coloured, early summer flowers look sensational in both informal cottage-garden schemes and more elaborate, formal arrangements. These traditional flowers are particularly successful in gardens with slightly acidic, free-draining soil.

In mid May, given good weather, or early June if not, lupins grab the eye with their bright colours. Perennial lupins may need to be replaced every three years or so, but many self-seed too, saving you the trouble. This is also true of the tree lupin, *L. arboreus*, which is a prolific flowerer. But they are still an excellent care-free plant for a light acidic soil, and will add presence and height to give a fantastic multi-coloured show in early summer.

Choosing your colours
Many different colours packed together can look very messy. Instead, choose different shades of lupin to blend into a well-organised colour scheme, and quickly move plants in jarring colours elsewhere in the garden.

STAR PERFORMER
L. **Russell hybrids** Bold, **densely packed spikes appear in a range of sometimes quite unexpected colours, often with duotones, including pink and yellow.**

TAKE A FRESH LOOK
For a late-flowering lupin, plant the shrubby, ground-hugging evergreen, *L. chamissonis*. It forms a spreading mat of silvery grey leaves, from which loosely packed spikes of lovely white and blue flowers rise in August.

The Essentials
Site demands Grows best in free-draining, light, sandy soil that is slightly acidic or neutral, preferably in full sun, though light shade is fine. Avoid copious additions of organic matter, as growth can become soft and floppy when the soil is too rich.
Planting practice Plant out during early spring.
Flowering time Early summer.
Pests and diseases The lupin aphid, which is slightly larger than most aphids, may sometimes attack the underside of leaves and the flower spikes. Prompt spraying gives a quick cure. Also look out for powdery mildew on the leaves.
Bonus point Grows very quickly to produce some of the brightest colours around in early summer.

L. **Band of Nobles Series**

Expert's Selection

1 *L.* **Russell hybrids**
One of the most popular hybrid lupins, it self-seeds freely to produce a range of colours.
✿✿✿✿❀ Assorted colours • Early summer • *h.* 1m (3ft) *s.* 45cm (1½ft)

2 *L.* **Band of Nobles Series**♀ Another hybrid, it produces long-lasting flowers in a number of especially vibrant hues.
✿✿✿✿❀ Assorted colours
Early summer
h. 1m (3ft) *s.* 45cm (1½ft)

3 Named hybrids
Available in many colours. Look for 'Royal Wedding'♀ (white), 'Deborah Woodfield'♀ (cream, pink), 'Olive Tolley'♀ (soft rose), 'The Governor'♀ (blue and white) and 'Troop the Colour'♀ (red).
✿✿✿✿❀ Assorted colours • Early summer • *h.* 1m (3ft) *s.* 45cm (1½ft)

4 *L.* **'Dwarf Lulu'**
Also known as 'Lulu', this is a popular, true-breeding hybrid.
✿✿✿✿❀ Assorted colours
Early summer • *h.&s.* 45cm (1½ft)

Lychnis

Catchflies are available in a bright, snappy range of colours including vivid reds and orange, alongside softer, more muted pinks. One of the classic country plants, they are ideal for any kind of summer scheme, from highly organised borders to more easy-going relaxed designs.

Expert's Selection

1 *L. chalcedonica* ♈
This old cottage-garden favourite looks superb in early summer, when its brilliant scarlet flowers appear.
✿ **Bright red • Early summer**
h. 1m (3ft) *s.* 40cm (16in)

L. viscaria

L. coronaria

2 *L. viscaria*
Provides a wonderful show in May and June, when the mound of stiff stems is topped by abundant clusters of its striking flowers.
✿ **Pinkish purple • Early summer**
h. 45cm (1½ft) *s.* 30cm (1ft)

3 *L. coronaria* ♈
This is one of the most popular catchflies, giving a high-powered display of rich flowers atop tall stems with softly textured silvery grey foliage.
✿ **Dark reddish purple • Midsummer**
h. 60cm (2ft) *s.* 45cm (1½ft)

4 *L. flos-jovis*
If you prefer soft pastels, try planting this, with its tufted downy shoots and silvery-grey leaves.
✿ **Soft pink • Early summer**
h.&s. 45cm (1½ft)

The Essentials

Site demands Any reasonably well-drained site, preferably in full sun, though some shade is fine.
Planting practice Plant in autumn or spring.
Flowering time Early to midsummer.
Pests and diseases Slugs and snails may attack emerging stems. *L. coronaria* is sometimes prone to powdery mildew.
Bonus point Combines brilliant colour with extreme hardiness.

Hardy country plants for sun and shade, catchflies attract butterflies, as well as other insects which may become trapped on the sticky nodes borne on their petals – hence the common name.

Most catchflies look best planted in bold and fairly substantial drifts. They also make a wonderful show when mixed freely with wild flowers.

STAR PERFORMER
L. chalcedonica ♈ **The Maltese cross lives up to its name, with the brightest imaginable scarlet flowers in early summer. Great in cottage gardens, it makes an excellent focal point when surrounded by drifts of paler colours.**

Some varieties such as *L. coronaria*, *L. flos-jovis* and *L. viscaria* are fairly short-lived, lasting only about two seasons. However, as they self-sow, new plants will quickly take over to replace the faded older ones and any unwanted plants can easily be pulled out of the ground.

L. coronaria not only self-seeds very freely but often creates exciting, unexpected colour combinations by itself. It is well worth seeing what occurs naturally before deciding whether to move them to other parts of the garden.

Lysimachia

Loosestrife is a beautiful background plant with tall spires covered by white or yellow, and sometimes pink or purple bell-shaped flowers that are star-shaped on opening. Moisture-loving, they will thrive in damp border soil or near a pond, close to the water's edge.

STAR PERFORMER
L. punctata 'Alexander'
Growing 1m (3ft) tall, this eye-catching plant has green leaves with broad creamy white margins. In mid–late summer, yellow starry flowers grow all the way up the stems. Keep an eye on it to ensure that it does not become invasive.

Expert's Selection

1 *L. punctata* 'Alexander'
Brilliant yellow flowers cluster thickly on the stems to form towering vigorous spires.
✿ **Bright yellow • Mid–late summer**
h. **1m (3ft)** *s.* **60cm (2ft)**

2 *L. ciliata*
A tall loosestrife with star-shaped flowers. New emerging foliage is bronze in spring. 'Firecracker'♀ has vivid, purple-bronze leaves.
✿ **Pale yellow • Mid–late summer**
h. **1.2m (4ft)** *s.* **45cm (1½ft)**

3 *L. ephemerum*
An erect variety, its grey leaves reach up the stems to where the flowers start. Attractive seedheads follow flowering. It is non-invasive.
❀ **White • Mid–late summer**
h. **1m (3ft)** *s.* **60cm (2ft)**

4 *L. clethroides*♀
Somewhat invasive but extremely pretty, with pale flowers borne all the way to the tops of the stems.
❀ **White • Mid–late summer**
h. **1m (3ft)** *s.* **60cm (2ft)**

The Essentials

Site demands If the soil dries out the plants quickly wilt and collapse. All loosestrifes like moist soil, in bright sun or dappled shade.
Planting practice Plant from autumn through to spring.
Flowering time Late summer.
Pests and diseases Slugs and snails that love moist ground can be a problem.
Bonus point Lysimachias flower over a very long season.

L. ciliata

L. clethroides

Spires of yellow or white loosestrife flowers create a beautiful, open effect. They will look marvellous grown around a pond, or beside a stream, because damp soil is the key to their success. *L. ciliata* grows well by streams and in damp woods, and is an ideal choice for bog gardens; *L. ephemerum* likes the damp soil on river banks; and *L. clethroides* can be grown in almost any soils, except for extremely wet or absolutely bone dry.

Controlling the spread
Loosestrife is only a problem if it is grown in the wrong place. Those that are spreaders need to be in a freer, wilder planting scheme and a spare patch of ground can be immediately transformed by their white and yellow star-like flowers. Anything planted too close may quickly get engulfed. Control it by removing fading flowerheads to avoid self-seeding and by cutting clumps back ruthlessly in early spring.

Lythrum

Lythrums are also known as **loosestrife**.
They are superb plants for a garden with damp
conditions and are happiest in boggy places
where they produce long-lasting, tall thin spikes
covered with densely-packed pink or purple
flowers, and often rich yellow autumn colour.

STAR PERFORMER
L. virgatum 'The Rocket'
Tall, thin spires are wonderfully covered with very deep pink flowers from the first half of summer. 'Rose Queen' has a mass of clear pink flowers, and the species has flowers that are more purple-red in tone.

Lythrum, not to be confused with lysimachia, also loves to grow in damp ground. Found naturally in water meadows and damp scrub, as well as in ditches and by the riverside, they have small, star or tube-shaped flowers borne singly or in clusters almost all the way up the stem.

Water lovers
Loostrifes are fully hardy and highly adaptable plants. They will grow submerged under water, in the damp boggy ground by the edge of a stream and in damp border soil. Wherever loosestrife is planted, it is essential not to let the soil dry out completely or the plants will wilt badly.

There are only two species available, but there are several varieties all in varying shades of pinks and purple and all equally care free and easy to grow.

Expert's Selection

1 *L. virgatum* 'The Rocket'
Narrow spires are thickly covered by tiny pink flowers.
✿ **Deep pink • Early–midsummer**
h. 1m (3ft) *s.* 45cm (1½ft)

2 *L. salicaria* 'Feuerkerze' ♀
'Firecandle' is a lovely rose pink.
✿ **Rosy pink • Mid–late summer**
h. 1.2m (4ft) *s.* 45cm (1½ft)

3 *L. virgatum* 'Dropmore Purple' Lush green foliage sets off dark pinkish purple blooms.
✿ **Purple-pink • Early–midsummer**
h. 1m (3ft) *s.* 45cm (1½ft)

4 *L. salicaria*
Large spikes of purple loosestrife gives a terrific late summer show.
✿ **Reddish purple • Mid–late summer**
h. 1.2m (4ft) *s.* 45cm (1½ft)

5 *L. salicaria* 'The Beacon'
Small, dark, rose-coloured flowers are tightly packed together.
✿ **Rose pink • Mid–late summer**
h. 1.2m (4ft) *s.* 45cm (1½ft)

6 *L. salicaria* 'Robert'
Like 'The Beacon' but bright pink.
✿ **Vivid pink • Mid–late summer**
h. 1.2m (4ft) *s.* 45cm (1½ft)

The Essentials

Site demands Full sun or lightly dappled shade, in moist to very damp, even boggy ground.
Planting practice Plant from autumn to spring.
Flowering times Choose a mix of varieties and you should have flowers all summer.
Pests and diseases Slugs and snails may eat new spring growth.
Bonus point A truly care-free plant for boggy ground.

PLANTING IN DAMP PLACES
A collection of moisture-loving plants massed on the banks of a stream can look stunning but you do not have to pack every piece of ground with plants. Leave some space between the plants so that you can stand at the water's edge and watch the wildlife.

L. salicaria 'Robert'

L. salicaria 'Feuerkerze'

Malva

Mallows add a wonderful touch to the garden with soft, open, bowl-shaped flowers in deep and pastel tones, many in lovely shades of blue and magenta with delicate petal veining. Some are showy, some subdued, and all can be easily integrated into the summer garden.

> ### STAR PERFORMER
> *M. sylvestris* **'Primley Blue'** **A delightful, prostrate and rather unusual mallow, it grows much wider than it is high. The rich blue colouring of the open, flat petals which appear abundantly all summer long makes it a delightful addition to a summer border.**

Totally undemanding, mallows tolerate poor and even alkaline soils. The average, well-tended border in a sunny position will be highly suitable for growing mallows successfully. What makes the difference between a good and an average show of flowers is the quality of the drainage. Break up heavy clay soils with additions of organic matter and horticultural grit.

Self-seeding
Perennial mallows grow naturally in Britain and Europe, and many naturally self-seed and will appear suddenly in the border. As they can be short-lived, especially on clay soil, this self-seeding tendency is a bonus, and creates vigorous new plants.

M. moschata f. alba

M. alcea var. fastigiata

Expert's Selection

1 *M. sylvestris* **'Primley Blue'**
Low-growing and long-flowering with delicate blue blooms.
✿ **Blue • Summer–early autumn**
h. **20cm (8in)** *s.* **60cm (2ft)**

2 *M. sylvestris*
A much larger plant which can grow up to 2m (6ft) against a wall. It has dark-veined blue flowers.
✿ **Blue • Summer–early autumn**
h. **1.2m (4ft)** *s.* **50cm (20in)**

3 *M. alcea var. fastigiata*
An erect plant, it is at its best when covered with blooms.
✿ **Bright pink • Summer–early autumn •** *h.* **1.5m (5ft)** *s.* **50cm (20in)**

4 *M. moschata f. alba* ♀
The musk mallow has white blooms and mid-green leaves.
✿ **White • Summer–early autumn**
h. **75cm (2½ft)** *s.* **50cm (20in)**

5 *M. sylvestris* **subsp.** *mauritanica* A stunning deep-coloured mallow which looks good with other colourful plants.
✿ **Magenta • Summer–early autumn**
h. **2m (6ft)** *s.* **50cm (20in)**

The Essentials

Site demands Mallows will grow well in most soils as long as they are well drained. Flowering may be reduced in heavy clay soils.
Planting practice Plant in autumn or spring.
Flowering time The mallows flower right through the summer.
Pests and diseases The main problem to look out for is rust.
Bonus point Mallows regularly replace themselves by self-seeding.

Melissa

Bee balm or **lemon balm** can be grown in herb gardens or right at the front of a border for easy picking. It has a delicious scent, and can also be used in the kitchen.

Expert's Selection

1 *M. officinalis* **'Aurea'**
Bright green leaves with yellow markings on the foliage and tiny white flowers.
❀ **White • Summer** ∅ **Green**
h. **1m (3ft)** *s.* **40cm (16in)**

2 *M. officinali*
'All Gold' Similar to 'Aurea', but with completely yellow leaves.
❀ **White • Summer Yellow**
h. **1m (3ft)** *s.* **40cm (16in)**

The Essentials

Site demands Plant in dryish soil in full sun or very light shade.
Planting practice Plant in spring or autumn.
Flowering time Summer.
Pests and diseases Trouble free.
Bonus point The aromatic foliage can be made into a wonderful tea.

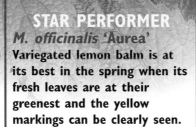

STAR PERFORMER
M. officinalis 'Aurea'
Variegated lemon balm is at its best in the spring when its fresh leaves are at their greenest and the yellow markings can be clearly seen.

Lemon balm can be grown at the front of a spring border, or in the herb garden. Plant it near beehives to ensure that bees remain attracted to the garden.

Fresh leaves
After the first flush of new leaves, the stems often become leggy and leaves may lose their apple green colour. Shearing over the plant in midsummer gets rid of tired leaves and encourages a second crop of foliage. This also stops 'Aurea' from losing its variegation and from self-seeding.

MEDICINE AND COOKERY
Aromatherapists often use the oil of melissa to counter depression. It is also said to cure headaches and nervousness.

The leaves of 'Aurea' have a lemon scent when crushed, and can be used for extra flavouring in fish dishes and salads. It is always best to use fresh leaves. If you dry them they will quickly lose their aroma.

Monarda

Bergamot gives a show of gloriously coloured spiky flowers in a sunny or partly shaded spot in the garden. It looks good in most borders, will grow successfully at the edge of water and is extremely useful in the herb garden.

Expert's Selection

1 *M.* **'Cambridge Scarlet'**♀
Bright red flowers with dark leaves.
✿ **Scarlet • Midsummer–autumn**
h. **1m (3ft)** *s.* **45cm (1½ft)**

2 *M.* **'Beauty of Cobham'**♀
A much quieter and more muted plant with soft coloured flowers.
✿ **Pink • Midsummer–autumn**
h. **1m (3ft)** *s.* **45cm (1½ft)**

3 *M.* **'Schneewittchen'**
'Snow Queen' has white flowers.
❀ **White • Midsummer–autumn**
h. **1m (3ft)** *s.* **45cm (1½ft)**

4 *M.* **'Loddon Crown'**
A favourite bergamot with rich coloured flowers.
✿ **Red-purple**
Midsummer–autumn
h. **1m (3ft)** *s.* **45cm (1½ft)**

Bergamot is grown for its showy flowers and scented leaves, which can be used in salads and stuffings.
To keep plants flowering profusely, dig them up every three years, and discard the worn centre. Newer sections can be replanted about 45cm (1½ft) apart in early spring, before new growth begins.

The Essentials

Site demands They do best in soil that is moist and free-draining, but not at all boggy.
Planting practice Autumn or spring, or summer if pot grown.
Flowering time Late summer, into the beginning of autumn.
Pests and diseases Slugs, snails and powdery mildew may attack.
Bonus point Attractive to bees.

STAR PERFORMER
M. 'Cambridge Scarlet'♀
With brilliantly red spidery flowers and dark brown centres, it blooms from midsummer well into autumn.

Nemesia

Grow nemesias for an abundant display of brightly coloured, small, trumpet-like blooms which will flower from early summer well into autumn. Though not all are able to survive sharp frosts, one species is fully hardy and will grow outside all year.

N. 'Innocence'

N. caerulea

STAR PERFORMER

N. denticulata♀ Sometimes known as **N. denticulata** 'Confetti', this nemesia has scented dark pink summer flowers that are highlighted with bright yellow centres. It is hardy enough to survive outdoors all winter.

Natives of South Africa, nemesias usually grow best in conditions that replicate the sandy soils and sunny climate of their homeland. They will give a vivid show at the front of a border and can also be grown very successfully in containers. The double-lobed blooms, which sometimes have frilled edges, look good as cut flowers.

Choosing the right site

Select a sunny position, with shelter from wind and frost and a well-drained soil. For a plant that can overwinter outdoors, choose **N. denticulata** which will tolerate cold much better than most. If you want more choice use pots – you can bring them indoors for winter. In cooler areas, treat any non-hardy varieties as annuals.

The Essentials

Site demands They like full sun and well-drained soil. They cope best in a warm and sheltered site.
Planting practice Plant out in late spring or early summer, when there is no risk of frost.
Flowering time Prolific flowers throughout summer.
Pests and diseases They should have few problems in the garden.
Bonus point Ideal spreaders in window boxes and hanging baskets.

Expert's Selection

1 N. denticulata♀
This species is the hardiest of the nemesias. Its pinky purple summer flowers have a yellow eye and a very faint scent.
✿ **Pink • Summer**
h. 30cm (1ft) *s.* 75cm (2½ft)

2 N. caerulea
A short-lived perennial, this nemesia has yellow-eyed pastel coloured flowers that will bloom all summer long.
✿ **Lilac • Summer–early autumn**
h. 30cm (1ft) *s.* 75cm (2½ft)

3 N. caerulea 'Woodcote'
A lightly scented hybrid variety that bears an abundance of summer flowers.
✿ **Lavender blue Summer–early autumn**
h. 30cm (1ft) *s.* 75cm (2½ft)

4 N. 'Innocence'♀
With pure white, yellow-eyed flowers it makes a free-flowering clump all summer.
✿ **White • Summer–early autumn**
h. 30cm (1ft) *s.* 75cm (2½ft)

Nepeta

Catmints add a gentle touch as edging or border plants. With a soft haze of light blue flowers, and floppy stems they will droop softly at the front of a bed or over the edge of a pot. The aromatic leaves and flowers are irresistible to cats but also attract plenty of bees.

The Essentials

Site demands Most catmints prefer free-draining soil in full sun. *N. govaniana* however, prefers a cooler, moister soil.

Planting practice Plant out in early spring.

Flowering time Catmints flower in midsummer.

Pests and diseases Powdery mildew can strike during a drought.

Bonus point They attract many beneficial insects into the garden.

N. govaniana

N. 'Six Hills Giant'

Expert's Selection

1 *N.* x *faassenii*
Pale lavender flowers contrast softly with silver-grey leaves.
✿ **Lavender** • **Midsummer**
∅ **Silver-grey** • *h.&s.* **60cm (2ft)**

2 *N.* 'Six Hills Giant'
One of the taller catmints this vigorous plant tones well with pastel colour schemes.
✿ **Lavender-blue** • **Midsummer**
∅ **Dark green** • *h.&s.* **1m (3ft)**

3 *N. sibirica*
The flowers bloom earlier and are slightly larger than most catmints, and contrast nicely with the dark green foliage.
✿ **Lavender-blue** • **Midsummer**
∅ **Dark green** • *h.&s.* **1m (3ft)**

4 *N. govaniana*
More upright and less inclined to flop than many catmints. Unusual pale-coloured flowers are borne on soft, loosely hung spikes.
✿ **Pale yellow** • **Midsummer**
∅ **Dark green** • *h.&s.* **1m (3ft)**

Renowned for its narcotic effect on cats, who will roll on or around the plant in a drug induced haze, catmint is also a most attractive border plant which adds softness to traditional borders and path edgings. As an alternative try growing it in large drifts and clumps in a gravel garden.

Prune shorter catmints hard in July to give a fresh crop of low leaves that will last through the first part of winter, if not affected by frost.

Bee keeping
Plant clumps of catmint to encourage bees to stay in your garden. When growing it in a wild part of the garden clear a 75cm (2½ft) square piece of ground for each plant, to keep out weeds and grass. This gives the catmint a chance to get established without being swamped by invasive neighbours.

STAR PERFORMER
N. x *faassenii* When it spreads – half-flopping over paths in many cottage garden schemes – this nepeta makes an excellent plant for softening the edges of a summer border.

HERBAL REMEDY The true catmint, *N. cataria,* can be grown in herb gardens as a natural remedy for colds and fevers. Cover the leaves with boiling water and leave for 10–15 minutes. Strain and drink as an alternative source of vitamin C.

Oenothera

Evening primroses will add grace and fragrance to a late afternoon with their continuous supply of fresh yellow scented flowers, although some stay open all day. They generally open in the early evening, attracting pollinating moths, and will have closed by the next morning.

O. speciosa 'Siskiyou'

O. fruticosa 'Fyrverkeri'

STAR PERFORMER
***O. perennis* 'Sundrops'** **If your garden is sunny, make room for a cluster of these plants. Their yellow flowers stay open from early morning to dusk, and release a delicious scent that will attract butterflies to your borders.**

Evening primroses bear cup-shaped four-petalled flowers, in delicate and bright shades including the familiar pale and bright yellows as well as whites. Some exquisite flowers are even flushed and veined with pinks, purples and browns. They flower from early summer right into autumn, and although the blooms may last only one day, they are constantly replaced by fresh ones.

In a dry place
Originating in the mountains and deserts of N. and S. America, most evening primroses thrive in light and even stony soils. Avoid damp and heavy soil as it may cause root rot.

Expert's Selection

1 *O. perennis* 'Sundrops'
The large pale yellow blooms borne on dark stalks have a delightful fragrance.
✿ **Light yellow • Early summer–autumn**
h. 40cm (16in) *s.* 30cm (1ft)

2 *O. macrocarpa* ♛
A sprawling, prostrate plant, with fresh green leaves that cover the ground, and set off the large, bright flowers that last until the frosts.
✿ **Light yellow • Early summer–autumn**
h. 15cm (6in) *s.* 18cm (7in)

3 *O. speciosa* 'Rosea'
It spreads well (but sometimes invasively) and the gorgeously scented flowers stay open all day. They have a yellow eye and pink

veins. 'Pink Petticoats' has slightly frilled flowers while 'Siskiyou' is a lovely soft pink.
❀✿ **White, pink • Early summer–autumn**
h. 30cm (1ft) *s.* 45cm (1½ft)

4 *O. fruticosa* 'Fyrverkeri' ('Fireworks') ♛ An upright evening primrose, it has a flashy display of flowers opening from red buds on red stems. *O. f.* subsp. *glauca* has purple leaves.
✿ **Golden yellow • Early summer–autumn**
h. 30cm (1ft) *s.* 40cm (16in)

The Essentials

Site demands Evening primroses need free-draining soil and as much sun as they can get. Do not let them dry out over the summer, and ideally make sure that they are always well watered.
Planting practice Plant in autumn or spring.
Flowering time All summer long, often into the autumn.
Pests and diseases They should be completely untroubled.
Bonus point Evening primrose is an elegant plant to choose for a cottage-garden scheme.

Ophiopogon

Lily turfs form handsome clumps of grassy leaves in striking shades to add interest to the front of the border, and contrast well with taller planting behind.

If you would like a touch of the unusual in your garden, lily turfs are an eye-catching choice. They make excellent foliage plants for both traditional gardens and more modern, minimal planting schemes, and do best in light soils in a relatively warm, sheltered environment.

O. planiscapus 'Nigrescens', is a fashionable architectural perennial that looks like a grass, or giant spider, with black leaves which makes it a popular garden designer's plant. It lends itself to all kinds of lively combinations,

and looks particularly good teamed with yellows and low-growing mat-forming plants. It also adds a strong sculptural element to container displays.

Tiny bell-shaped flowers nestle in among the foliage in summer and are followed by striking blue to black berries.

O. jaburan 'Vittatus'

STAR PERFORMER
***O. planiscapus* 'Nigrescens'**♀
The strap-like foliage is so dark purple that from a distance it looks black. The flowers often have a purple tint, and are followed by tiny, dark blue-black berries. The parent plant, *O. planiscapus*, has dark green, rather than deep purple leaves.

Shiny autumn berries

The Essentials

Site demands A free-draining, soil is ideal for most varieties but *O. japonicus* prefers moister soil.
Planting practice Plant in early autumn or early spring.
Flowering time Flowers appear towards the end of summer.
Pests and diseases Slugs may eat the leaves, otherwise trouble free.
Bonus point Makes a great specimen plant for adding colour and shape to a gravel garden.

Expert's Selection

1 *O.planiscapus* 'Nigrescens'♀ Blackish purple leaves make this an eye-catching addition to any garden.
✐ **Purple-black** ✿ **Purple • Summer**
❦ **Blue-black • Autumn**
h. 25cm (10in) *s.* 30cm (1ft)

2 *O. jaburan* 'Vittatus'
The variegated form of the Jaburan lily has arching leaves, which are blue-green with thick creamy

yellow margins. Protect it in winter with a thick layer of mulch.
✐ **Blue-green and cream** ✿ **White Summer** ❦ **Violet-blue • Autumn**
h. 60cm (2ft) *s.* 30cm (1ft)

3 *O. japonicus*
Used as ground cover in its native Japan, the flowers are sometimes purple, and may get lost amongst the shiny green leaves.
✐ **Green** ✿ **White • Summer**
❦ **Blue-black • Autumn**
h. 30cm (1ft) *s.* 45cm (1½ft)

Paeonia

Peonies are among the most exquisite of the perennials. Their lavish full-bodied blooms, often accompanied by a rich, intense scent and attractive dark green foliage add romance to the late spring garden, and despite their glamour, they are remarkably easy to grow and maintain.

Expert's Selection

1 *P. lactiflora* 'Sarah Bernhardt'♀ A sumptuous, double, fluffy pink peony with ruffled edging and delightful scent.
✿ **Pale pink • Early summer**
h.&s. **1m (3ft)**

2 *P. lactiflora* 'Bowl of Beauty'♀ The delicately scented flowers of this popular Japanese peony form an open cup.
✿ **Pink with cream centre**
Early summer • *h.&s.* 1m (3ft)

3 *P. lactiflora* 'Duchesse de Nemours'♀ Introduced in 1856, the beautiful, large ruffled flowers have a powerful sweet scent.
✪ **White • Early summer**
h.&s. **75cm (2½ft)**

4 *P. lactiflora* 'Kelway's Brilliant' The inner stamens form a mini flower at the heart of the main rich, dark red bloom.
✿ **Dark red • Early summer**
h.&s. **75cm (2½ft)**

5 *P. lactiflora* This superb late-flowering peony is the parent of thousands of cultivars with large, graceful, scented flowers set off by dark green leaves.
✪ **White • Mid–late summer**
h.&s. **60cm (2ft)**

6 *P.* 'America' One of the very best single-flowering reds, with large, bright glossy flowers, yellow stamens and a delicate scent.
✿ **Magenta • Early summer**
h.&s. **1m (3ft)**

7 *P. mlokosewitschii*♀ Better known as 'Molly the Witch', this popular peony bears cool-toned flowers up to 13cm (5in) across, with bright yellow stamens.
✿ **Lemon-yellow • Spring**
h.&s. **75cm (2½ft)**

8 *P. officinalis* 'China Rose' Shorter than most peonies, the cup-shaped flowers are a rich salmon pink, with a blazing mass of orange-yellow stamens.
✿ **Salmon pink • Early summer**
h.&s. **45cm (1½ft)**

Every garden deserves at least one peony to brighten its borders. The choice is now so large, with new cultivars appearing all the time, that it is well worth visiting a reputable specialist nursery in spring before making your choice.

Planting for success
To get the best results, set the plant with its buds about 2.5cm (1in) below the soil surface. Any cultivars (and not species plants) should have three to five buds: avoid those with less.

Do not plant peonies where they have previously grown; this will prevent any possible build-up of disease carriers. Dig up the entire area around where you are intending to plant, and replace with fresh soil, adding plenty of organic matter to give it a boost.

A long show of peonies
A little careful planning will ensure that you have peonies blooming in your garden for months. Start with the lemon-yellow *P. mlokosewitschii* to get an early show of flowers. Follow this with the red 'America' and the pink 'Bowl of Beauty', then

P. 'Duchesse de Nemours'

P. 'Bowl of Beauty'

finish up with the late-season white *P. lactiflora*.

There are also several care-free shrubby peonies (see page 229).

The Essentials

Site demands They prefer rich, moist, well-drained soil in full sun.
Planting practice Plant from autumn through to spring, but do not move them once planted.
Flowering time From mid spring right through into July.
Pests and diseases Few problems although they may wilt and suffer from grey mould.
Bonus point Peonies will flourish happily for years in the same spot.

STAR PERFORMER
P. 'Sarah Bernhardt'♀
The colour of the luscious, round flowerheads is darker in the centre and paler pink on the outside, often turning near white in bright light. It makes an excellent cut flower.

Papaver

Poppies are bright, showy, blowsy and fun, and their unmistakable outline adds instant impact to the border. They look good in any display, and are all the more exciting because their burst of brightly coloured papery petals surrounding a vivid black boss is so intense and brief.

1 *P. orientale* 'Marcus Perry' A classic poppy with cupped orange-red flowers 10cm (4in) across.
❀ **Orange-red • Early summer**
h. 75cm (2½ft) *s.* 60cm (2ft)

2 *P. orientale* 'Black and White' ♀
A black oval mark sits at the base of each pure white petal.
❀ **White • Early summer**
h. 75cm (2½ft) *s.* 60cm (2ft)

3 *P. orientale* 'John III' ♀
The flowers of this true red poppy are smaller than usual.
❀ **Scarlet • Early summer**
h. 70cm (28in) *s.* 60cm (2ft)

4 *P. orientale* 'Mrs Perry' ♀
Each salmon-hued petal has a dark-coloured blotch at its base.
❀ **Pink • Early summer**
h. 75cm (2½ft) *s.* 60cm (2ft)

5 *P. orientale* 'Beauty Queen' A beautiful poppy with a pale, frilled cup.
❀ **Apricot • Early summer**
h. 1m (3ft) *s.* 75cm (2½ft)

6 *P. orientale* 'Picotée'
An unusual flower with an orange edge to its clear-coloured petals.
❀ **White with orange border Early summer**
h. 75cm (2½ft) *s.* 60cm (2ft)

P. orientale 'Black and White'

P. orientale 'Beauty Queen'

7 *P. orientale* 'May Sadler'
The petals of its stunning, unusually coloured flowers grow darker in tone towards the centre.
❀ **Orange-pink • Early summer**
h. 75cm (2½ft) *s.* 45cm (1½ft)

The most care-free varieties of poppy are the oriental ones; many of the others can be short lived. Their summer burst of colour, though still not long-lasting is sensational, and make them well worth growing.

Oriental poppies form vigorous clumps with bristly, deep green leaves and smooth rounded seedpods. They spread by underground runners.

Choose a mainly sunny site, with good drainage and plant early in spring, adding bonemeal or a manure mulch. The glorious blooms will generally appear in June, and though their presence is relatively brief, cutting back after flowering will encourage a second burst of the attractive leaves.

Wild plantings
Oriental poppies will enhance any border, but a lively alternative is to grow them in a more natural setting, as they are found in the wild, with ***Anthriscus sylvestris***, **Geraniums** and **grasses** (see pages 126–7).

Preparation and tidying up
Heavy ground needs to be broken up with additions of horticultural grit and organic matter to improve drainage. If you are digging up unwanted oriental poppies, make sure that you remove all roots, as new ones will grow if large pieces are left.

Site demands Almost any type of site, in sun or light shade.
Planting practice Plant out in early spring.
Flowering time From late May if the weather is good, but usually in June, and sometimes in July.
Pests and diseases Generally trouble free, though young plants may be attacked by slugs and snails.
Bonus point They make good cut flowers, if properly prepared. Simply seal cut ends by holding briefly in a flame.

STAR PERFORMER
P. orientale 'Marcus Perry' One of the many excellent 'Perry' poppies, this is the epitome of an oriental poppy. It has bristly stems and 23cm (9in) long leaves. The flowers open from wonderfully impressive 5cm (2in) long capsules, and they are a truly magnificent sight when in full bloom.

Persicaria

Knotweeds are fully hardy perennials ideally suited to a more informal border or as ground cover. They grow from knee high to head high, bearing small spikes covered with red, pink or white flowers on slender stalks which appear in the second half of summer and into autumn.

Plant knotweeds in a moisture-retaining soil with plenty of sunshine for the best display of fresh green leaves and summer flowers. Taller varieties such as *P. amplexicaulis* particularly prefer damp soil, as does *P. vacciniifolia*. Ensure that the soil does not dry out. To prolong flowering, remove faded flowerheads from taller species.

Knotweeds tend to spread rapidly once established, and for this reason may be more care free in a wild, informal scheme.

STAR PERFORMER
P. bistorta 'Superba'♀
Perfect for a bog garden, it forms tall clumps with large leaves that are up to 20cm (8in) long. The long-lasting stalks of pale pink flowers give a good display all summer.

P. amplexicaulis 'Inverleith'

P. campanulata

Expert's Selection

1 *P. bistorta* 'Superba'♀
The soft pink flower spikes will last throughout summer.
❀ **Pink • Summer–autumn**
h. **1m (3ft)** *s.* **60cm (2ft)**

2 *P. affinis* 'Superba'♀
Erect spikes of pale pink turn rich red at the end of summer, and the leaves turn brown. Other forms include 'Darjeeling Red', with pink-red flowers, and the ground cover 'Donald Lowndes', with light pink flowers that gradually darken.
❀ **Pale pink, then red Summer–autumn**
h.&s. **60cm (2ft)**

3 *P. campanulata*
Good for a medium-sized garden with a damp, wild section, it has bell-like pale pink flowers.
❀ **Pink • Summer–autumn**
h.&s. **1m (3ft)**

4 *P. amplexicaulis* 'Firetail'♀ With big bold clumps, of bright flowers on wiry stems, it is not a plant for small gardens. 'Inverleith' is much lower growing reaching 45cm (1½ft).
❀ **Crimson • Summer–autumn**
h.&s. **1.2m (4ft)**

5 *P. virginiana* 'Painter's Palette' Grow for its patterned foliage splashed with dashes of green, brown and gold.
⊘⊘⊘ **Green, gold, brown • Late summer–autumn**
h. **1.2m (4ft)** *s.* **60cm (2ft)**

6 *P. vacciniifolia*♀
One of the smallest knotweeds, it makes splendid ground cover to edge paving, or spread over walls.
❀ **Pink • Late summer–autumn**
h. **20cm (8in)** *s.* **60cm (2ft)**

The Essentials

Site demands Plant in moist soil in bright sun or very light shade. Do not let it dry out over summer. The ground cover, *P. vacciniifolia* particularly dislikes drought.
Planting practice From autumn to spring. Summer for pot grown.
Flowering time The flowers generally appear towards the end of summer, often lasting well into the autumn.
Pests and diseases Knotweed rarely suffers from any problems.
Bonus point All you need to do is let this plant look after itself.

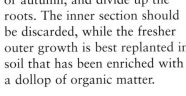

Phlox

Hardy perennial phlox is a North American native that comes in a range of heights from low-growing mat-formers and woodland varieties to stately border plants. There are lots of delightful colours available, including plenty of blues, pinks and reds for the summer garden.

Expert's Selection

1 *P. paniculata* 'Brigadier'♀
A glorious rich pink phlox, the blooms have broad petals tinged with a hint of orange.
✿ Pink • Mid–late summer
h. 75cm (2½ft) *s.* 1m (3ft)

2 *P. maculata*
Meadow phlox, from the eastern USA, is a scented, slender plant.
✿✿❀ Pink, purple, white • Early–midsummer • *h.&s.* 1m (3ft)

3 *P. subulata*
Moss phlox is a very low-growing plant perfect for the front of a border or an alpine garden.
❀✿✿✿✿ White, lilac, pink, violet, purple, red • Spring–early summer
h. 8cm (3in) *s.* 30cm (1ft)

4 *P. divaricata*♀
Blue phlox is a good, low spreader.
✿ Violet blue • Early summer
h. 20cm (8in) *s.* 1m (3ft)

5 *P. douglasii* 'Eva'
A compact evergreen phlox with stiff dark green leaves and lavender flowers with a hint of pink.
✿ Lavender pink • Early–midsummer
h. 8cm (3in) *s.* 30cm (1ft)

P. maculata

P. subulata

The Essentials

Site demands Bright sun and fertile, well-drained soil are ideal.
Planting practice Plant in early spring or autumn.
Flowering time Late spring to the end of summer.
Pests and diseases Slugs and snails, powdery mildew and steel eelworm may affect taller kinds.
Bonus point Pretty, versatile border plants.

Most phloxes require bright sun and fertile soil with good drainage to thrive, but *P. paniculata* and *P. maculata* are also happy in light shade. *P. divaricata* prefers gentle shade. Taller plants will need staking to prevent them getting bent over in heavy winds and rain.

Care-free plants
P. paniculata and its hybrids are the original high-performance, low-maintenance plants. Liven drifts of pale colours with surprises such as the flashier, bolder lipstick pink 'Brigadier'.

Since *P. maculata* and *P. paniculata* have a sweet scent, they are worth planting in large sweeps through a border, or in repeat groups. In early evening, their scent will linger in the air.

Rejuvenation
Some clumps may deteriorate after about four years. If so, dig up the whole clump in spring or autumn, and divide up the roots. The inner section should be discarded, while the fresher outer growth is best replanted in soil that has been enriched with a dollop of organic matter.

STAR PERFORMER
P. paniculata 'Brigadier'♀
There are many excellent varieties of *P. paniculata*. They all flower from July to August and make large clumps of blue, pink, purple or white. 'Brigadier' is a gorgeous shade of rich pink.

Plantago

Plantains are often regarded as weeds, but in the right settings are excellent as a tough ground cover. The varieties recommended here are best grown in wild lawns, in gravel or in rock gardens where they form attractive rosettes of flat leaves with spikes of tiny flowers in summer.

P. major 'Rosularis'

P. nivalis

STAR PERFORMER

P. major 'Rubrifolia' **By far the best looking of all the plantains, this has rounded or heart-shaped veined maroon leaves and greenish purple summer flowers up to 25cm (10in) tall.**

Ask most gardeners what a plantain is and the reply will be 'a weed'. In a showpiece lawn its flat, leathery, ribbed leaves can be an eyesore and it is very difficult to remove except by hand or with a weedkiller.

But in the right situation, its rosettes of leaves and flower spikes make an interesting textural ground cover and it is reliably hardy. Simply plant it where it won't be a nuisance.

Ornamental plantains

Plantains look best in an easy-going corner. Let them emerge between cracks in paving or add a gentle, relaxed touch where the emphasis is on the care free, rather than regimental order.

Polygonatum

Solomon's seal is an ornamental
plant with shiny leaves, arching stems
and hanging, bell-like flowers which appear in
spring and early summer. It is ideal for a shaded
part of the garden planted in a woodland style.

Expert's Selection

1 *P.* x *hybridum* ♀
The dangling, greenish white, bell-
shaped flowers that appear in April
and May will add an elegant touch
to cut flower arrangements.
❀ **White • Late spring**
h. 1.2m (4ft) *s.* 1m (3ft)

2 *P. odoratum var.*
pluriflorum 'Variegatum'
Known as angled Solomon's seal
because the leaves are borne on
angular, arching stems and have
scented flowers with greenish tips.
❀ **White • Late spring**
h. 60cm (2ft) *s.* 30cm (1ft)

3 *P. falcatum*
'Variegatum' *P. falcatum* is
native to Japan and Korea. This is
its variegated form and has small
rounded leaves with a creamy
white margin. The stems have a
gentle pink tint.
❀ **White • Late spring**
h. 1m (3ft) *s.* 45cm (1½ft)

4 *P. biflorum*
A Solomon's seal with a big
difference, it can grow significantly
taller than most other species.
It has solitary, drooping flowers
2cm (¾in) long set against bright
green glossy leaves.
❀ **White • Late spring**
h. 1–2m (3–7ft)
s. 45–75cm (1½–2½ft)

STAR PERFORMER

P. x *hybridum* ♀ **The species most
commonly found in gardens, it grows to 1.2m
(4ft) high, and has arching stems with leaves
to both sides, and delicate hanging mini
clusters of green-tinged spring flowers.**

The Essentials

Site demands Any moist but
well-drained, humus-rich soil, in
either full or partial shade.
Planting practice Plant from
late autumn to early spring.
Flowering time The dainty
flowers open in late spring, with
some still evident in early summer.
Pests and diseases Very few
problems, but watch out for slugs
and snails and the seal sawfly, which
can strip the leaves in days if it is
not controlled.
Bonus point The variegated
plants will brighten shady corners.

TAKE A FRESH LOOK

P. curvistylum, which grows
naturally from Nepal to
western China, is a novel
Solomon's seal that flowers in
early summer. It grows about
45cm (1½ft) high, and the
flowers are lilac or mauve. Try
planting it among low shrubs so
that the flowering stems appear
through them.

If you are looking for
a plant to add grace
and beauty to a shady
part of the garden,
look no further than
the lovely Solomon's seal.

It might seem unlikely that
anything can grow under the
deep shade cast by evergreen
trees, but Solomon's seal will
thrive even in heavy shade
and in cool, moist conditions.
This particularly useful plant
will form attractive clusters,
which can sometimes be
softly scented.

The flowers are usually
white, and carried in groups
of two to four at a time
along a long stem, but a few
varieties have pinkish or lilac
blooms. The elegant leaves
have a glossy sheen and come
in soft and bright greens, that
are often variegated.

P. odoratum 'Variegatum'

Prepare the soil
As well as being beautiful,
Solomon's seal is hardy and care
free. To ensure that the soil is
well prepared for maximum
growth, dig a large hole where
you are planning to plant and
add plenty of organic matter to
boost the fertility. Once in place,
the plant needs only to be lifted
and divided every few years to
keep it at its best.

Potentilla

Cinquefoils, with their clear-toned, often five-petalled blooms, will flower for most of the summer if grown in the sun. They look rather like miniature wild roses and are very attractive when allowed to poke through adjacent plants and shrubs, in a care-free, cottage-garden style.

P. nepalensis 'Miss Willmott'

P. 'William Rollison'

Expert's Selection

1 *P.* 'Gibson's Scarlet'♀
One of the earliest flowering cinquefoils, it has clear scarlet blooms and bright green leaves.
✿ **Bright red • Early summer**
h. **45cm (1½ft)** *s.* **60cm (2ft)**

2 *P.* 'Yellow Queen'
The yellow flowers of this flashy plant make a superb display.
✿ **Yellow • All summer**
h. **45cm (1½ft)** *s.* **60cm (2ft)**

3 *P.* 'William Rollison'♀
Semi-double flowers are dashed with bright yellow highlights.
✿ **Vermilion • All summer**
h. **45cm (1½ft)** *s.* **60cm (2ft)**

4 *P.* x *tonguei*♀
Lovely orange flowers with a touch of apricot suit a more muted planting scheme.
✿ **Orange-yellow • All summer**
h. **15cm (6in)** *s.* **40cm (16in)**

5 *P. nepalensis* 'Miss Willmott'♀ Attractive foliage and dark pink summer flowers make this an excellent choice.
✿ **Dark pink • All summer**
h. **35cm (14in)** *s.* **45cm (1½ft)**

6 *P. alba*
Excellent ground cover with white flowers with yellow eyes.
✿ **White • Midsummer**
h. **10cm (4in)** *s.* **15cm (6in)**

STAR PERFORMER
P. 'Gibson's Scarlet'
Worth searching for, these vivid red flowers start to emerge from May or June. The bright green leaves look just like those of a strawberry, and make a startling contrast to the colour of the blooms.

The Essentials

Site demands Good drainage is important. Break up heavy clay and dig in horticultural grit and organic matter to loosen the texture.
Planting practice Plant out in early spring.
Flowering time Potentillas flower throughout summer.
Pests and diseases They are rarely a problem.
Bonus point Potentillas flower reliably to give colour in the garden over a long season.

Cinquefoils are best known as shrubs, but the long-flowering season of the herbaceous varieties makes them a very attractive proposition for most borders. The brightly coloured flowers are small and round, and bloom for most of the summer. All the herbaceous varieties are hardy and easy to grow if given plenty of sunshine. As well as making care-free border plants there are cinquefoils which will grow in the damp ground around a pond, or as a complete contrast in a free-draining gravel garden.

Pondside planting
Use a pretty cinquefoil to brighten and add shade to the moist ground around a pond. Place it so that the flowers come right up to the water's edge, and give a shady spot for the frogs to hide in during the day. The blue-purple marsh cinquefoil, *P. palustris*, is a larger plant, 45cm (1½ft) high, that is native to pond margins.

ROCK GARDENS Two very small cinquefoils are ideal in rock or gravel gardens. The dark pink *P. nitida* grows just 10cm (4in) high, and spreads barely more than a handspan while the amber-yellow *P.* x *tonguei* has a slightly wider spread.

Primula

Wonderful plants for an informal spring garden, primulas come in a great range of forms and sizes, from the low-growing **primroses** to the tall and striking **candelabra** varieties, in marvellous colours that brighten up streams, hedges and banks, as well as more traditional borders.

Expert's Selection

1 P. denticulata hybrids
The rounded, multi-bloomed flowerheads make a delightful display in a springtime garden.
❀❀ Mauve, white, reddish purple • Mid–late spring
h. 40cm (16in)
s. 20cm (8in)

2 P. pulverulenta♀
The most vigorous and long lasting of the candelabras with distinctive pale stems. The species is bright and dark pink; 'Bartley Hybrids' range from pale pink to purples.
❀❀ Pink, bright pink, purple • Spring
h. 80cm (32in)
s. 20cm (8in)

3 P. rosea♀
A first-rate primrose to grow in shallow water with beautiful 2.5cm (1in) wide flowers.
❀ Red • Early summer
h. 15cm (6in)
s. 20cm (8in)

4 P. vialii♀
A spectacular tall spike packed with tiny flowers.
❀ Lilac-red
Midsummer • *h.* 40cm (16in) • *s.* 15cm (6in)

5 P. veris♀
The native British cowslip thrives in meadows and in drier conditions than many primroses.
❀ Deep yellow • Late spring
h. 25cm (10in) *s.* 20cm (8in)

P. pulverulenta 'Bartley Hybrids'

TAKE A FRESH LOOK

P. **'Wanda'** has dark green leaves and deep reddish purple flowers and is one of many pretty crossbred primrose cultivars now available. They have been created by crossing the European primrose *P. vulgaris* with *P. juliae*, the Caucasian primrose.

6 P. sieboldii♀
Easy to grow, it brightens the ground with its white-eyed blooms.
❀❀❀ White, pink, purple, blue
Late spring • *h.&s.* 20cm (8in)

7 P. florindae♀
Giant cowslips form large-leaved clumps, with several strong stems bearing scented, bell-like flowers.
❀ Yellow • Early summer
h. 80cm (32in) *s.* 30cm (1ft)

8 P. vulgaris♀
The primrose grows in unexpected places in the spring garden.
❀❀ Soft yellow, pale pink, lilac
Spring • *h.* 13cm (5in)
s. 25cm (10in)

Moisture is essential for primroses to thrive so make sure you plant them in a soil which will not dry out.

When growing primroses in a wild garden make sure that the immediate adjacent area is cleared of weeds and grass to give them a chance to establish without any competition.

The Essentials

Site demands Rich, moist soil with plenty of organic matter. All varieties can be grown in dappled shade and in full sun.

Planting practice Plant out in early spring.

Flowering times Most primroses flower in spring, although a few do bloom in early summer.

Pests and diseases Usually trouble free but slugs and snails, and viruses may be a problem.

Bonus point Brilliantly coloured, primulas are a cheap and easy way to brighten up beds in spring. Leave dead heads on the plant and they will seed readily.

STAR PERFORMER

P. denticulata hybrids The drumstick primroses are so called because they have round heads, consisting of several tiny flowers, on top of slender stems in April and May. They usually come in mauve, but there is also a white (var. *alba*, below) and reddish purple ('Ruby') kind.

Prunella

Self heal makes a novel choice for tough, creeping ground cover right at the front of a border. Bees love the small, pink, violet or white flowers that appear all summer.

With its bright little whorls of tube-shaped flowers, self heal will also add a colourful dash planted among smaller shrubs or under trees. When choosing planting companions avoid anything that grows too big or the self heal will soon get dwarfed and overwhelmed.

P. grandiflora is the species with the largest number of varieties. It grows naturally in meadows and open woods, and makes a terrific addition to a wild-flower garden in spring.

STAR PERFORMER
P. grandiflora 'Blue Loveliness' **Growing 23cm (9in) high, and spreading up to 1m (3ft) wide, there is a good spread of dark lilac-blue flowers in summer.**

Expert's Selection

1 *P. grandiflora* '**Blue Loveliness**' The dense spikes of deep-toned flowers also come in white, pink and paler lilac.
✿ **Lilac blue • Summer**
h. 30cm (1ft) s. 1m (3ft)

2 *P. vulgaris*
It forms a flowing carpet of deep-coloured flowers.
✿ **Rich purple • Summer**
h. 23cm (9in) s. 1m (3ft)

3 *P. laciniata*
Similar to *P. vulgaris*, with paler flowers, sometimes tinged pink.
✿ **Cream • Summer**
h. 23cm (9in) s. 1m (3ft)

The Essentials

Site demands Self heal is completely non-fussy. Damp soil and a bright, but not sun scorched, position is ideal.
Planting practice Plant out in early spring.
Flowering time All summer.
Pests and diseases Trouble free.
Bonus point Grows quickly and is great for attracting bees and other pollinating insects.

Pulmonaria

Lungworts give a wonderful show of bell-shaped, early spring flowers and many have attractive leaves spotted with silver or edged with creamy stripes. They are ideal plants for lightly shaded parts of the garden and thrive best in moist, but well-drained soil.

Though it is tempting to place lungworts, especially those with vivid silver-white spots and markings, in full sun, it will be immediately apparent that they dislike hot sunny positions. The thick, rough leaves quickly collapse and wilt.

Make sure instead that they have a shady position, ideally combined with thick, dark, humus-rich soil and you will enjoy their excellent foliage and flowers for months.

Ideal positions
Lungworts can be grown successfully in borders and woodland edges. In borders they mix particularly well with primroses (**Primula**) and hostas. The leaves can be an extremely attractive feature, and once the flowering show has finished the plants can be cut back to promote plenty of fresh new foliage.

Medicinal properties
The name lungwort (the second syllable means 'plant') was given to this plant because the spotted leaves were said to resemble a diseased lung. In the 17th and 18th centuries it was often thought that the medicinal properties of a plant were evident in its appearance and lungworts were used to treat lung disorders. It can in fact aid the lung in various ways by restoring its elasticity, and reducing bronchial catarrh, but must only be taken with medical supervision.

The Essentials

Site demands The key to success is rich, moist soil in shade, whether light or heavy. *P. officinalis* is quite happy in brighter, sunny conditions.
Planting practice Plant out in autumn or spring.
Flowering time Flowers appear in late winter through spring.
Pests and diseases Powdery mildew may occur in dry spells.
Bonus point The flowers and foliage of these long-lived plants make excellent ground cover.

P. mollis

P. saccharata 'Frühlingshimmel'

P. 'Sissinghurst White'

STAR PERFORMER
P. rubra 'David Ward'
Introduced in the mid 1980s, this is one of the best lungworts for silvery foliage: the leaves are pale green with a cream-coloured margin. The red flowers bloom from the end of winter to mid spring.

1 *P. rubra* 'David Ward'
Grow this lungwort for its silver tinged foliage and light red blooms. Another good-looking red lungwort is 'Redstart' which has deeply coloured red flowers on lighter green leaves.
✿ **Red-pink • Late winter–mid spring**
⌀ **Green with cream edges**
h. **45cm (1½ft)** *s.* **1m (3ft)**

2 *P. saccharata*
The Bethlehem sage has many fine varieties. 'Frühlingshimmel' has pale blue flowers with a dark eye and silver spots on the leaves, which are nearly 30cm (1ft) long. The Argentea Group♀ have lovely silvery white leaves and green markings towards the edge, topped by red flowers. 'Pink Dawn' has rich pink flowers, while 'Mrs Moon' has spotted pale green leaves and pink to violet flowers.
✿✿✿✿ **Pale blue, red, pink, violet All spring** ⌀ **Green with silver spots**
h. **30cm (1ft)** *s.* **60cm (2ft)**

3 *P. officinalis*
The small leaves, about 10cm (4in) long, are marked with a plethora of white spots. The pink flowers age to violet-blue. Good alternatives include 'Sissinghurst White'♀ whose pink buds open to white, and the light blue 'Bowles' Blue'. For a more erect plant, try 'Lewis Palmer'♀ with dark blue flowers.
✿✿✿✿ **Dark violet, white, light blue, dark blue • All spring**
⌀ **Green with white spots**
h. **30cm (1ft)** *s.* **45cm (1½ft)**

4 *P. mollis*
One of the largest of the lungworts, it has flowers which start off blue and then fade to purple and pinkish red.
✿ **Blue • Late winter to mid spring**
⌀ **Deep green**
h. **45cm (1½ft)** *s.* **60cm (2ft)**

Ranunculus

The little, rounded blooms of ranunculus are delightful additions to wild-flower and cottage gardens. Let them poke through other plants, to give a fun, relaxed scheme.

Expert's Selection

1 *R. acris* **'Flore Pleno'**
Tall and vigorous with brilliant yellow blooms.
✿ **Yellow • Early summer**
h. **60cm (2ft)** *s.* **25cm (10in)**

2 *R. aconitifolius* **'Flore Pleno'** ♀ It has dark green leaves topped by button-like flowers.
❀ **White • Early summer**
h. **75cm (2½ft)** *s.* **45cm (1½ft)**

3 *R. constantinopolitanu* **'Plenus'** Superb large flowers and jagged leaves.
✿ **Yellow • Late spring**
h. **45cm (1½ft)** *s.* **30cm (1ft)**

Many ranunculus derive from wild, invasive varieties, so if you are planting them in borders they need to be well integrated into the design.

However, in free-flowing gardens they are a marvellous sight, creating fresh, new, unexpected colour combinations with their flashes of white and yellow. To remove any unwanted plants, simply dig them up.

The Essentials

Site demands They generally thrive in moist ground in full sun.
Planting practice Plant from autumn to spring.
Flowering time Most flower during spring and summer.
Pests and diseases Aphids and powdery mildew may be problems.
Bonus point They will grow easily even in areas with poor drainage.

STAR PERFORMER
R. acris **'Flore Pleno' This well-behaved meadow buttercup grows 60cm (2ft) high, and is a real attention grabber in late spring and early summer. Double yellow flowers open on wiry stems.**

Rudbeckia

Coneflowers are big value, bright yellow, late summer plants with daisy-like flowers and tall central cones raised well above the petals. They will lift the look of any border.

Expert's Selection

1 *R.* **'Herbstsonne'**
Tall, strong and sturdy with upward-pointing green eyes.
✿ **Yellow • Midsummer–early autumn**
h. **2m (7ft)** *s.* **60cm (2ft)**

2 *R. fulgida* var. *deamii* ♀
Bright yellow petals surround a black centre.
✿ **Yellow • Midsummer–early autumn**
h. **60cm (2ft)** *s.* **45cm (1½ft)**

3 *R.* **'Goldquelle'** ♀
One of the tallest, it has double flowers with a greenish yellow eye.
✿ **Yellow • Midsummer–early autumn**
h. **1.5m (5ft)** *s.* **1m (3ft)**

4 *R. maxima*
The flowers have downward-angled petals and black eyes set against broad, blue-green leaves.
✿ **Yellow • Midsummer–early autumn • h. 1.2m (4ft)** *s.* **75cm (2½ft)**

The Essentials

Site demands Plant in full sun in soil that never gets too dry.
Planting practice Plant from autumn to mid spring.
Flowering time Late summer into early autumn.
Pests and diseases Trouble free.
Bonus point They are a great draw for butterflies.

The sturdy flowerheads of coneflowers give a reliable display year after year, and the bright yellow gives a lift to any scheme. They can get tall and floppy and may need staking to keep them erect. Allow room for new plants to spread and clump.

STAR PERFORMER
R. **'Herbstsonne' One of the tallest coneflowers, reaching 2m (7ft). The flowers are 13cm (5in) wide, with a prominent green eye.**

Salvia

Grow salvias to add wonderful rich-toned colours to a summer garden scheme, or for their soft, sometimes aromatic leaves. For care-free gardening choose the hardier salvias, which tend to be pale or dark blue, rather than bright rich reds and lipstick pinks.

S. uliginosa

S. guaranitica

The vividly coloured massed spikes of salvias are a vibrant addition to a summer border. The double-lobed tubular flowers are borne in dense whorls along the stems and come in light and deep blues and violets as well as some vibrant pinks and reds.

A very well-drained soil combined with full sun is an essential combination for most salvias. A degree of shelter is also a good idea. S. guaranitica will thrive best in a sheltered, warm position, while you will need to give S. uliginosa some winter protection. A thick mulch will benefit both plants during the winter months.

Cut back the flowering stems once the first flowers have faded and you should get fresh blooms later in summer. Taller plants will need to be staked to give them some support.

Expert's Selection

1 *S. nemorosa* 'Ostfriesland'♀ ('East Friesland') Elegant rich toned spikes for the front of a bed.
✿ **Deep blue • All summer**
h. 45cm (1½ft) *s.* 30cm (1ft)

2 *S.* x *sylvestris* 'Mainacht'♀ A bushy plant that adds a high-quality touch to the border.
✿ **Blue • Midsummer–early autumn**
h. 90cm (3ft) *s.* 60cm (2ft)

3 *S. guaranitica*♀ A tall and distinguished salvia that makes a strong show of colour late in the season. Give it a sheltered position for the best results.
✿ **Deep blue • Late summer–early autumn** • *h.* 1.5m (5ft) *s.* 60cm (2ft)

4 *S. uliginosa*♀ This lofty but less hardy salvia prefers moist soil.
✿ **Light blue • Late summer–early autumn** • *h.* 1.5m (5ft) *s.* 1m (3ft)

The Essentials

Site demands Salvias need very good drainage and plenty of sun.
Planting practice Plant hardy salvias from autumn to spring
Flowering time Summer.
Pests and diseases Beware of slugs and snails.
Bonus point Cut salvias back and you can have two flower shows.

Scabiosa

Pincushion flowers are a magnet for bees and butterflies. The disc-like, rounded flowers, in delicate colours are borne on wiry stems, about knee-high.

These flowers are named for their showy centres with spikey stamens that resemble beaded pins in a pincushion. Their delicate papery petals are a little like those of a poppy and come in soft pastel colours.

Scabious thrive in light, dry, fast-draining soils and do not need constant pampering. They look particularly attractive in the soft colour schemes that work so well in Mediterranean-style gardens. Grow them in decorative pots, or in rock gardens, where they add a gentle, easy-going touch in summer.

Expert's Selection

1 *S. caucasica* 'Clive Greaves'♀ The bushy pale blue blooms have pretty cream centres.
✿ **Lavender-blue • Late summer**
h.&s. **60cm (2ft)**

2 *S. columbaria*
Found growing wild on chalk hills, it has soft pastel coloured flowers.
✿ **Lilac-blue • Late summer**
h. **60cm (2ft)** *s.* **45cm (1½ft)**

3 *S. graminifolia*
A slightly shorter scabious for the front of a fast-draining border.
✿ **Lilac • Late summer**
h.&s. **30cm (1ft)**

STAR PERFORMER
S. caucasica 'Clive Greaves'♀ **A beautiful lavender-blue, it flowers prolifically through late summer. Good alternatives are 'Bressingham White', 'Loddon White' and 'Blausiegel' ('Blue Seal') a rich lavender-blue.**

The Essentials

Site demands Well-drained dry soil ideally in full sun.
Planting practice Plant in spring.
Flowering time Summer.
Pests and diseases Trouble free.
Bonus point Sweetly informal.

Schizostylis

Kaffir lilies add brilliant colours to late summer and autumn gardens.

Though kaffir lilies come from South Africa, they can withstand the chills of a harsh winter, but will always grow best in warmer areas.
A large clump of lilies, especially 'Major' with its vivid red flowers, makes a surprising sight in early autumn on the banks of a stream or by a pond. Clumps can be dug up and divided every few years. Save the newer outer sections and discard the tired inner sections.

Expert's Selection

1 *S. coccinea* 'Major'♀
Big bold flowers make a striking contrast with the long, narrow green leaves.
✿ **Bright red • Late summer**
h. **60cm (2ft)** *s.* **30cm (1ft)**

2 *S. coccinea* 'Sunrise'♀
The pale coloured flowers of this hugely popular variety are very similar to those of 'Major'. 'Viscountess Byng', an excellent salmon colour, is a late flowerer, carrying on into late autumn.
✿ **Pink • Late summer**
h. **60cm (2ft)** *s.* **30cm (1ft)**

3 *S. coccinea f. alba*
When growing a group of kaffir lilies, it is worth including this variety to add contrast.
✿ **White • Late summer**
h. **60cm (2ft)** *s.* **30cm (1ft)**

STAR PERFORMER
S. coccinea 'Major'♀
The top performing kaffir lily, it has big, bold tropical red flowers about 6cm (2½in) wide which open to form star shapes. The flowers appear in clusters at the top of tall and slender stems above the rich green strap-shaped foliage.

The Essentials

Site demands Kaffir lilies like relatively moist ground, in full sun. Though they will grow in a drier soil, damper soil gives best results.
Planting practice Plant in spring or autumn.
Flowering time Late summer and early autumn.
Pests and diseases Watch out for attacks by slugs and snails.
Bonus point These bright, sturdy lilies make great cut flowers.

Scrophularia

Figworts are wild garden plants, but only the decorative water figwort is popularly grown. It has nettle-like leaves, and works well as a pond marginal or in a formal design.

With a minimal amount of help, the water figwort makes a tremendous show in a wild garden. The leaf variegation is quite startling on its own, but when the brownish flowers appear they can, at a stroke, diminish the overall effect. Many gardeners therefore immediately remove the flower spikes. Others also cut them off lest the plants self-seed, creating an abundance of all-green leafed plants without any variegation.

Pond planting

When growing water figwort at the edge of a pond, plant it 15cm (6in) deep in shallow water, amongst plants that root in mud (emergents). Classic companion plants include *Ligularia dentata* 'Othello' with its purple-green leaves and bright orange flowers.

Expert's Selection

1 *S. auriculata* 'Variegata'
With distinctive variegated leaves, it loves a damp position.
🌿 **Blue-green and cream**
Spring–summer
h.&s. **1m (3ft)**

The Essentials

Site demands The variegated water figwort prefers moist soil in lightly dappled shade.
Planting practice Plant from autumn through to early spring.
Flowering time All summer.
Pests and diseases Slugs and caterpillars can be a nuisance.
Bonus point Variegated foliage is a stylish backdrop.

STAR PERFORMER
S. auriculata 'Variegata'
Distinguished by their cream edges, the leaves are the stars on this plant. However, oddly shaped brownish or reddish-maroon flowers appear on square branched stems through summer into early autumn.

Sedum

Stonecrops are free-flowering succulent plants for rock gardens, stone troughs, and even the front of borders. Some are minute, others grow up to 1m (3ft) high.

Expert's Selection

1 *S. spectabile* 'Brilliant' ♀
A vivid pink medium sized stonecrop with blue-grey leaves.
🌸 **Pink • Late summer**
h.&s. **45cm (1½ft)**

2 *S.* 'Ruby Glow' ♀
Dark red flowers complemented by reddish stems and leaves.
🌸 **Red • Late summer**
h. **25cm (10in)** *s.* **20cm (8in)**

3 *S. telephium* subsp. *maximum* 'Atropurpureum' ♀
A magnificent tall plant with purple stems and leaves, and flowers with an orange-red eye.
🌸 **Pink • Late summer**
h. **60cm (2ft)** *s.* **30cm (1ft)**

4 *S. kamtschaticum* 'Variegatum' ♀ Bright yellow variety, with gold-edged leaves.
🌸 **Yellow • Summer–early autumn**
h. **10cm (4in)** *s.* **60cm (2ft)**

S. kamtschaticum 'Variegatum'

The Essentials

Site demands Stonecrops need free-draining soil and sunshine.
Planting practice Spring into summer.
Flowering time Summer into early autumn.
Pests and diseases Aphids, mealy bugs and slugs.
Bonus point Shrugs off drought.

STAR PERFORMER
S. spectabile 'Brilliant' ♀ **One of several excellent pink-flowering varieties. Forms robust clumps topped by a profusion of star-like flowers at the end of summer. 'Iceberg' has white flowers, and 'September' brighter pink flowers.**

Stonecrops look best when planted in large numbers beside paths, where their flowers can put on a superb display. Mixing reds with pinks and yellows gives terrific results. Set stonecrops in the tops of low walls to give them summer colour, and the plants plenty of free-drainage. Do make sure that the planting holes are filled with rich soil to get them off to a good start.

Sempervivum

S. tectorum in flower

Houseleeks, with their fabulous, tight rosettes of leaves, are among the most easily grown and attractive succulents.

Houseleeks are best grown in rock gardens or on the tops of low stone walls, where their beautifully neat leaf rosettes are immediately visible. This also gives ideal growing conditions.

A final flourish
Each rosette lives for a few years before flowering, then dies. But new rosettes appear each summer and the clump continues to grow.

The Essentials

Site demands Dry, shallow soil with fast drainage, and sunshine is ideal. Protect cobwebbed types from excess rain.
Planting practice Plant in spring or early summer.
Flowering time June and July.
Pests and diseases Generally trouble free, but may rot if grown in cool, wet soil, and rust can sometimes be a problem.
Bonus point Also good as pot plants – need little watering.

Expert's Selection

1 *S. tectorum* ♀
A big-leaved houseleek that makes attractive, neat clumps.
✿ **Dark pink • Midsummer**
⊘ **Blue-green**
h. **15cm (6in)** *s.* **30cm (1ft)**

2 *S.* **'Commander Hay'** ♀
The large 20cm (8in) rosettes have red and green pointy leaves.
✿ **Dark pink • Midsummer**
⊘⊘ **Red and green**
h. **10cm (4in)** *s.* **20cm (8in)**

3 *S. arachnoideum* subsp. *tomentosum* ♀ The leaves have tiny white hairs and 'cobwebs' from the tips of the leaves to the crown.
✿ **Red • Midsummer** ⊘ **Light green**
h. **8cm (3in)** *s.* **20cm (8in)**

4 *S.* **'Glowing Embers'**
At the start of summer the tips of the new leaves turn red.
✿ **Pink • Midsummer**
⊘⊘ **Green, then red**
h. **10cm (4in)** *s.* **25cm (10in)**

STAR PERFORMER
S. tectorum ♀ **Broad rosettes, up to 18cm (7in) across, form neat clumps with fleshy, bluish green leaves. Up to a hundred flowers may grow on long stems. 'Red Flush' has red-tinted leaves in spring and summer. 'Nigrum' has red-tipped leaves.**

Sidalcea

Prairie mallows or **checker mallows** resemble small hollyhocks, with their delicate spires bearing pink, purple or white silky flowers, which bloom in midsummer.

Expert's Selection

1 *S.* **'Elsie Heugh'**
The wide, fringed, pale pink flowers are borne above rounded leaves.
✿ **Pale pink • Midsummer**
h. **1m (3ft)** *s.* **45cm (1½ft)**

2 *S.* **'William Smith'** ♀
Vivid, rose pink flowers are tinged with hints of salmon colour.
✿ **Dark pink • Midsummer**
h. **1m (3ft)** *s.* **45cm (1½ft)**

3 *S.* **'Puck'**
A pretty, more compact variety.
✿ **Rich pink • Midsummer**
h. **60cm (2ft)** *s.* **30cm (1ft)**

4 *S. candida*
The best cream-flowered sidalcea.
❀ **White • Midsummer**
h. **1m (3ft)** *s.* **45cm (1½ft)**

The delightful flowering stems of prairie mallows add a touch of grace to the border. The ground-level leaves are also very good at blocking out weeds. Cutting down the stems after the first flowering, gives a fresh flush of blooms later in the summer.

Pretty pastels
Sidalceas are excellent plants for soft, quiet border schemes in cottage gardens. The vertical stems contrast well with a *Gysophila's* open, billowing mass of white flowers, or they can be used in drifts around apple trees.

The Essentials

Site demands Any sunny, fertile site, that is not very dry or wet.
Planting practice Plant from autumn to spring.
Flowering times Midsummer.
Pests and diseases Trouble free.
Bonus point Tall flower spikes offer contrast, at a time when most other flowers are much lower.

STAR PERFORMER
S. **'Elsie Heugh'**
One of the most beautiful sidalceas it bears large, delicate midsummer flowers in an exquisite light pink, carried on a slender stalk above the leaves, which are near ground level.

Sisyrinchium

The strap-shaped leaves often create a fan shape which is a striking contrast to the dainty starry flowers.

Expert's Selection

1 S. striatum 'Aunt May'
Cream and green foliage is topped by taller spires of pale blooms.
✿ **Pale yellow • Midsummer**
h. 30cm (1ft) s. 25cm (10in)

2 S. graminoides
The flowers of blue-eyed grass only open in the afternoon.
✿ **Blue • Midsummer**
h. 45cm (1½ft) s. 30cm (1ft)

3 S. idahoense 'Album'
Clear white flowers with a yellow throat, and strap-shaped foliage.
❀ **White • Early summer**
h. 45cm (1½ft) s. 30cm (1ft)

4 S. 'Quaint and Queer'
A smaller plant with abundant yellow-centred, purple flowers.
✿ **Purple • Early summer**
h.&s. 15cm (6in)

STAR PERFORMER
S. striatum 'Aunt May'
Small bursts of soft creamy flowers are complemented by spikey green leaves striped with cream at their edges.

The Essentials

Site demands Good drainage and full sun are essential.
Planting practice Plant in late spring; water well until established.
Flowering time Summer.
Pests and diseases Trouble free.
Bonus point The strap-like leaves will contrast well with most other herbaceous plants in the border.

Sisyrinchiums are very effective grown round the edges of ponds where their shapes can be reflected in the water. They will create an immediate enclosing mini wall of greenery and the varieties with fan-forming leaves are particularly effective.

Self-seeding
If they are not carefully controlled, sisyrinchiums can prolifically self-seed and spread rapidly. Dead-head finished flowers immediately to avoid this.

S. graminoides

Solidago

Golden rod adds vivid colour to a late summer border with dense sprays of tiny bright yellow flowers. It comes in both dwarf and giant forms, some taller than a man.

Expert's Selection

1 S. 'Goldenmosa'
Makes a bold, high impact clump.
✿ **Bright yellow**
Late summer–early autumn
h. 75cm (2½ft) s. 45cm (1½ft)

2 S. 'Golden Wings'
A giant, that thrives in poor soil.
✿ **Golden yellow**
Late summer–early autumn
h. 1.8m (6ft) s. 1m (3ft)

3 S. rugosa 'Fireworks'
Enlivens any medium-sized border.
✿ **Golden yellow**
Late summer–early autumn
h. 1m (3ft) s. 45cm (1½ft)

4 S. cutleri
Fits perfectly in a rock garden.
✿ **Bright yellow**
Late summer–early autumn
h. 45cm (1½ft) s. 30cm (1ft)

Golden rods will liven up any garden. Taller varieties make a terrific backdrop in a border, and dwarf varieties add splashes of colour to a rockery. They can be planted from mid-autumn to early spring in any relatively moist but well-drained soil. After flowering, deadhead and cut back any dying foliage.

They will look good with end-of-season blues like *Salvia guaranitica* (see page 165) and *Perovskia* **'Blue Spire'** (see page 231), both of which flower in late summer and early autumn.

The Essentials

Site demands Best in moist, well-drained soil, in full sun or light shade.
Planting practice Plant from autumn to spring.
Flowering time Late summer and early autumn.
Pests and diseases Trouble free.
Bonus point Can be cut and dried for 'everlasting' flowers.

STAR PERFORMER
S. 'Goldenmosa' A popular, vigorous variety of medium height, it bears a mass of frothy, bright golden yellow flowerheads throughout August and September.

Stachys

Betony provides both superb foliage plants, with beautiful coloured and textured leaves, as well as some lovely flowering varieties. The two kinds are totally, surprisingly dissimilar. With their liking for well-drained soil and strong sun, a few are real stars in Mediterranean-style gardens.

S. officinalis

Expert's Selection

1 S. byzantina 'Silver Carpet' A superb ground cover with its delightfully textured leaves. Good forms include 'Cotton Boll' with its cotton wool-ball flowers and 'Primrose Heron' with yellow-tinged furry grey leaves and 'Big Ears' with leaves 25cm (10in) long.
⌀ **Silver grey**
h. **60cm (2ft)** *s.* **1m (3ft)**

2 S. macrantha
With dark green foliage, and deep pink or mauve flowers, it grows taller than it is wide.
✿ **Deep pink, rich mauve** ⌀ **Dark green • Early summer–early autumn**
h. **60cm (2ft)** *s.* **30cm (1ft)**

3 S. officinalis
Wood betony grows and self-seeds on dry banks where it produces flowers in a range of colours.
❋✿✿ **White, pink, purple Midsummer** *h.* **60cm (2ft)**
s. **30cm (1ft)**

4 S. coccinea
Scarlet summer blooms are set off by fresh green leaves.
✿ **Bright red** ⌀ **Green • Early summer–autumn • *h.* 60cm (2ft)**
s. **45cm (1½ft)**

STAR PERFORMER
S. byzantina 'Silver Carpet' Often known as 'Lamb's ears' because of its soft, woolly silver-grey leaves which are shown to great effect because 'Silver Carpet' does not flower.

The betonies are grown both for their excellent soft-textured foliage and for their bright summer flowers. They can be used as ground cover, as sculptural edging and in borders. Grow them in a well-drained soil and, once established, they will be very simple to care for.

The most popular betony is *S. byzantina* or one of its many attractive forms. Because the furry grey foliage is so appealing and tempting to touch, grow it either as edging beside a path, or at the front of a border.

S. byzantina 'Cotton Boll' will produce a thick carpet of foliage with small round flowers, while 'Silver Carpet' makes ideal ground cover or a backdrop to white or more colourful planting schemes. 'Primrose Heron' has leaves with an unusual hint of yellow.

In moist soils, *S. macrantha* will develop bright green crinkly leaves with attractive scalloped edges. But if you prefer flowers, grow *S. officinalis* or *S. coccinea*.

Mediterranean gardens
Since many betonies thrive in free-draining ground in full sun, they are ideal for Mediterranean-style gardens. Good companion plants are those with architectural leaves like *Agave parryi* (see page

S. coccinea

337) and *Lychnis coronaria* (see page 145), which has silver-grey leaves topped by bright red summer flowers.

The Essentials

Site demands In general, the betonies like well-drained, even sandy soil, in full sun *S. macrantha* needs damper ground while *S. coccinea* should be grown in a warm, sheltered part of the garden.
Planting practice Plant in early autumn or late spring.
Flowering time Summer.
Pests and diseases Trouble free.
Bonus point Flowering betonies, especially *S. officinalis*, are very good for attracting butterflies and bees into the garden.

Symphytum

Comfrey is a terrific fast-spreading ground cover for gardens with moist soils. Grown for both foliage and flowers, its lush, often variegated leaves and wide range of colourful flowers, including white, pinks, blues and reds are good for informal gardens and in more structured borders.

Expert's Selection

1 *S.* 'Hidcote Pink'
The dainty sprays of bi-coloured flowers stand proud of the leaves.
✿ **Pink and white • Late spring**
h.&s. **45cm (1½ft)**

2 *S. officinale*
Common comfrey is a substantial, thrusting plant with creamy yellow, pink or dull purple flowers and tough, hairy leaves.
✿✿✿ **Yellow, pink or purple Late spring–early summer**
h. **1.2m (4ft)** *s.* **1m (3ft)**

3 *S.* x *uplandicum*
'Variegatum' ⚘ The variegated leaves are grey-green with bold cream markings down the margins, it has bluish purple flowers.
✿ **Bluish purple • Early summer**
h. **1m (3ft)** *s.* **45cm (1½ft)**

4 *S.* 'Rubrum'
A free-flowering ground cover.
✿ **Red • All summer**
h. **60cm (2ft)** *s.* **45cm (1½ft)**

5 *S.* 'Goldsmith'
The dark green leaves have gold and cream coloured markings.
✿ **Blue** ⌀⌀⌀ **Dark green, gold and cream • Late spring**
h. **30cm (1ft)** *s.* **45cm (1½ft)**

The comfreys are no-nonsense, easy-to-grow plants that establish quickly to provide excellent ground cover. With coarse leaves, and small clusters of bright or delicate bell or tube shaped blooms, they are usually grown in wilder gardens but are also a good border decoration. Keep the more invasive kinds to parts of the garden where they can romp freely, as they can smother smaller plants if not controlled. Cut back in early summer to produce a second crop of flowers.

Organic gardening
S. officinale is very effective as a 'green' non-polluting manure. By forking it back into the ground, the soil's fertility is boosted. It can also be used as a compost activator.

Steep the leaves in rain water in a water butt. In about five weeks they produce a solution like strong black tea. Watered down, it is the perfect high-potash feed for tomatoes.

You can also pack the leaves in a plastic box with a hole in the bottom and collect the juice that drips out as they rot: it makes an excellent liquid feed.

The Essentials

Site demands Place in full sun or light shade in moist soil.
Planting practice Plant from autumn to spring.
Flowering time Late spring.
Pests and diseases Tough and vigorous, it is rarely troubled.
Bonus point Comfrey can be left entirely to its own devices.

STAR PERFORMER
S. 'Hidcote Pink' and its sister plant 'Hidcote Blue' produce exceptional sprays of May flowers.

S. x *uplandicum* 'Variegatum'

S. 'Rubrum'

Tanacetum

Tansies, pyrethrums and **feverfews** as they are often known, have button or daisy-like flowers, and silvery, often scented leaves. Feverfew is ideal for herb gardens.

Expert's Selection

1 *T. parthenium* 'Aureum'
Bright yellow leaves with scores of tiny yellow-eyed flowers.
❀ **Yellowish white • Late spring**
h. **45cm (1½ft)** *s.* **30cm (1ft)**

2 *T. coccineum*
Yellow-eyed daisy-like pyrethrums are excellent as cut flowers.
✿✿✿❀ **Red, purple, pink or white**
Midsummer • *h.* **75cm (2½ft)**
s. **60cm (2ft)**

3 *T. vulgare*
A quick spreader with flowers like bright buttons and scented foliage.
✿ **Yellow • Late summer**
h. **1.2m (4ft)** *s.* **60cm (2ft)**

4 *T. densum* subsp. *amani*
In sheltered spots the leaves may be evergreen. Cut off the flowers.
∅ **Grey •** *h.* **20cm (8in)** *s.* **30cm (1ft)**

T. coccineum 'Brenda'

The Essentials

Site demands Free-draining sandy soil in bright sun.
Planting practice Plant in spring.
Flowering time Summer.
Pests and diseases Trouble free.
Bonus point Golden feverfew makes a good foliage plant.

With their abundant flowers and leaves, **Tanacetum** are excellent for a sunny spot. The reds (*T. coccineum* 'Brenda'♀) are striking, while the whites and yellows have a daisy-like charm. Remove the flowers to make the most of the *T. densum* foliage.

Feverfew leaves are a well-known cure for migraine and depression. Eat them in salads or sandwiches.

STAR PERFORMER
T. parthenium 'Aureum'
Bushy golden feverfew self-seeds freely. 'Plenum' and 'Snowball' are also care free.

Tellima

Fringe cups make good ground cover in cool, light woodland shade. All the widely available varieties have attractive foliage and tiny, dangling, late spring flowers.

Expert's Selection

1 *T. grandiflora* 'Purpurteppich' Thin spires of bell-like flowers and rounded foliage with a reddish tinge.
❀ **White-pink • Early summer**
h. **75cm (2½ft)** *s.* **30cm (1ft)**

2 *T. grandiflora*
The leaves remain green while the green-tinged flowers turn pink.
❀ **White • Early–midsummer**
h. **75cm (2½ft)** *s.* **30cm (1ft)**

3 *T. grandiflora* 'Perky'
Red flowers and smaller leaves than 'Purpurteppich'.
✿ **Red • Early–midsummer**
h. **75cm (2½ft)** *s.* **30cm (1ft)**

4 *T. grandiflora* Rubra Group These plants have lovely reddish winter foliage.
❀ **White • Early–midsummer**
h. **75cm (2½ft)** *s.* **30cm (1ft)**

The Essentials

Site demands Grow in dappled shade, out of the summer sun.
Planting practice Plant out in either early autumn or spring.
Flowering time Early summer.
Pests and diseases Trouble free.
Bonus point Provides excellent ground cover, but is not invasive.

STAR PERFORMER
T. grandiflora 'Purpurteppich'
Dangling spires of white-green flowers tinged with pink appear in early summer.

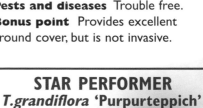

Many woodland plants are thuggish, strapping invaders which quickly overwhelm adjacent plants. Tellima is quite different, and is delicately pretty with bell-like flowers. Extremely easy to grow, it forms compact clumps and looks particularly effective planted beside a path. Grow in moist soil, ideally in light shade, as it will not flower as abundantly in deep shade. Though tellima is generally hardy – even growing as far north as Alaska – exceptionally sharp frosts can cause damage.

Thalictrum

Meadow rues are beautiful plants with a fuzzy aerial haze of summer flowers above lacy, blue-grey foliage. They can be grown both in sunny borders or under light shade. The gorgeous blossoms make excellent cut flowers.

Expert's Selection

1 *T. aquilegiifolium*
The greyish green foliage is topped by delicate fluffy flowers.
✿ Pink • Midsummer
h. 1m (3ft) *s.* 30cm (1ft)

2 *T. delavayi* ♥
Wonderfully elegant, it has an airy show of tiny flowers borne on large panicles with dainty foliage. 'Hewitt's Double' has tightly double, richer-hued flowers and dark stems; 'Album' is white.
✿❀ Lilac • Summer–early autumn
h. 1.5m (5ft) *s.* 60cm (2ft)

3 *T. flavum* subsp. *glaucum* ♥ An airy show of small flowers is complemented by elegant, blue-green divided foliage which looks good in flower arrangements.
✿ Greenish yellow • Midsummer
h. 1.5m (5ft) *s.* 60cm (2ft)

4 *T. diffusiflorum*
A superb plant with relatively large flowers on slender stems, and a mass of small dainty leaves, it prefers a cool, sheltered spot.
✿ Rich lilac • Midsummer
h. 1m (3ft) *s.* 30cm (1ft)

5 *T. rochebruneanum*
Not as dainty as some, but a superb, popular, branching plant.
✿❀ Lavender, white • Midsummer
h. 1.8m (6ft) *s.* 75cm (2½ft)

The Essentials

Site demands Meadow rues need moist, rich soil in sun or light shade. Add leaf-mould for richness.
Planting practice Plant from autumn to spring.
Flowering time Summer.
Pests and diseases Slugs are likely to be the only problem.
Bonus point Tall but sturdy stems require little staking.

CUT FLOWERS Use thalictrum in flower arrangements to surround beautiful scented red roses. When the flowers have finished, the finely divided foliage is a good backdrop in any display.

Meadow rue is not always an immediate, obvious choice for a garden, but the sprays of tiny flowers are quite sensational and they add an extra, delicate, touch to both deep borders and rock gardens.

Planting ideas
Meadow rues look perfect in beds fronting hedges. As they are 'see-through' plants, the view beyond is quite important and you will be able to see between the airy sprays to the green behind. To make sure they are noticed, grow small groups of three to five plants. Some, like *T. delavayi*, may need staking, but bright orange-red climbing nasturtiums can be trained up the stakes to create a vivid contrast.

T. diffusiflorum

STAR PERFORMER
T. aquilegiifolium The sprays of pink flowers look like powder puffs held high on tall stems. It grows naturally in moist meadows and on rocky ravines.

Thymus

Evergreen thymes are beautiful little plants for herb gardens, Mediterranean and gravel schemes and for growing in gaps on terraces and beside paths. They form small flowering clumps which will attract bees, and are a terrific herb for use in cooking.

T. x *citriodorus* 'Bertram Anderson'

T. x *citriodorus*

T. x *citriodorus* 'Silver Queen'

1 *T. pulegioides*
Excellent in cooking but highly attractive as well, it will form small neat clumps of vividly-hued purplish flowers.
✿ **Mauve • Early summer**
h. 8cm (3in) *s.* 20cm (8in)

2 *T. vulgaris* **'Silver Posie'**
An attractive thyme with thin, white-edged leaves, it has a good flavour for cookery.
✿❀ **Pink, white • Early summer**
h. 23cm (9in) *s.* 40cm (16in)

3 *T.* x *citriodorus*
Lemon-scented thyme makes a neat, even clump. The most distinctive kinds are 'Bertram Anderson' with yellow-gold markings on the leaves, and 'Golden King' and 'Silver Queen'♀ which have very good-looking variegated foliage.
✿ **Pink • Midsummer**
h.&s. 15cm (6in)

4 *T. serpyllum* var. *coccineus*♀ Creeping red thyme is a prostrate creeper. It makes a good combination in paving with the white 'Snowdrift'.
✿ **Crimson-pink • Midsummer**
h. 5cm (2in) *s.* 30cm (1ft)

5 *T. herba-barona*
The aptly named caraway thyme makes a low mat of tiny pink flowers that looks appealing grown amidst paving stones. The tiny leaves are dark green.
✿ **Pink • Midsummer**
h. 2cm (1in) *s.* 20cm (8in)

STAR PERFORMER
T. pulegioides Broad-leaved thyme makes an attractively neat mound, thickly covered by spikes of mauve flowers in summer.

For care-free success with thymes, grow them on a light free-draining soil. Because they need such specific conditions it is easiest to group them together where they make a delightful display of low mounds and mats, especially when in flower.

Growing for the kitchen
It is a good idea to have at least two or three different kinds of thymes if they are being used in the kitchen. Variegated forms will help to liven up the display and ensure interest even when the flowers are not in bloom. The group can be encircled by the low-growing mat-forming thymes, which can also be placed in cracks in the paving. *T. pulegioides* is a very good choice for this.

Start taking cuttings in the spring to encourage the plants to bush out. Trim over each clump with a pair of scissors to create oval shapes, and stop the plant from swamping its neighbour.

Rock and gravel gardens
Thymes thrive in the free-draining soil of rockeries. They can also be grown right at the front of gravel gardens and borders. The mat formers quickly spread around and over small rocks, to give a natural look, while the plants also benefit from the reflected heat generated by the stones.

Site demands Thymes like free-draining soil in full sun. Growing them in cold, wet, heavy soil in winter is invariably fatal.
Planting practice Plant in spring or early summer.
Flowering time Summer.
Pests and diseases Thymes rarely suffer any problems.
Bonus point Herb pots are the perfect home for creeping thymes.

Tiarella

Foam flowers have masses of spires of white frothy blossom in the spring, and bright evergreen leaves that make good ground cover in damp, shady places.

Expert's Selection

1 *T. cordifolia*♀
Spreads easily to form a dense mat of pointed leaves with white flowers in spring.
❀ **White • Spring–early summer**
h. 23cm (9In) *s.* 30cm (1ft)

2 *T. wherryi*♀
The ivy-like leaves have dark brown to rich red markings at their best. Cream flowers appear at the start of summer, and may flower twice in one season.
✿❀ **Pink, creamy white**
Early summer
h.&s. 15cm (6in)

3 *T. trifoliata*
The tallest of this trio, it has 25cm (10in) long spires of flowers rising above the foliage.
❀ **White • Late spring–early summer**
h. 45cm (1½ft) *s.* 30cm (1ft)

Foam flowers can be a little fussy, and if not given moist soil in light shade will quickly wither. But in the right place they create a superb spring show with an airy mass of white flowers, and the evergreen leaves are excellent at keeping down weeds.

Bog gardens
One of the best places for growing foam flowers is the bog garden. Try them with primulas, such as the stunning *P. vialii* with its dark red and lilac flowers.

The Essentials

Site demands Give them a cool, damp part of the garden with moist soil and some shade.
Planting practice Plant out in early autumn or mid spring.
Flowering time Late spring and early summer.
Pests and diseases Slugs may attack new shoots.
Bonus point Ground cover that does not take over.

STAR PERFORMER
T. cordifolia♀ It soon builds up quite large, mat-forming colonies, spreading well, to create a marvellous sight in the spring with its white flowers. The leaves are heart-shaped and pointed, with a bronze tint when the winters turn cold.

Tolmiea

Pickabacks are dual-purpose plants, which provide good ground cover in damp shady places and greenish brown flowers in late spring and early summer.

STAR PERFORMER
T. menziesii 'Taff's Gold'♀ The broad green leaves have pale yellow and creamy markings. Small plantlets may sometimes appear where the leafstalk meets the blade.

Pickabacks will fill a shady spot with a mass of good-looking green leaves. They are particularly good at smothering weeds, and in light shade the variegated markings of 'Taff's Gold' really stand out.
They can also be potted up and will thrive on a spare windowsill in a north-facing room, without direct sun, adding a fresh green touch indoors.

The Essentials

Site demands Rich, moist soil in light shade.
Planting practice Plant in autumn or early spring
Pests and diseases Trouble free.
Bonus point An interesting and unusual plant for a hanging basket.

Expert's Selection

1 *T. menziesii* 'Taff's Gold'♀
The speckled leaves are up to 10cm (4in) wide and it bears small delicately scented flowers in spring.
∅ **Green with yellow and cream markings • Late spring**
h.&s. 40cm (16in)

2 *T. menziesii*♀
Very similar in appearance to 'Taff's Gold' but without the variegated leaf markings.
∅ **Greenish brown • Late spring**
h.&s. 40cm (16in)

Tradescantia

Spider lilies are familiar indoor plants, but there are outdoor varieties, too, which are easy to grow and have a long flowering season.

Tradescantias are vigorous and care free. The hardy garden varieties are upright, unlike the well-known trailing houseplants. Plants in the **Andersoniana Group** come in myriad hues and all produce triangular flowers over a long season. Snip off straggly stems in midsummer to keep the clumps looking neat. Some people find that touching the leaves can irritate the skin.

T. **Andersoniana Group 'Iris Prichard'**

Expert's Selection

1 *T.* **Andersoniana Group 'Purple Dome'** Enjoy a succession of solitary, short-lived flowers over a long season.
✿ **Purple • Early summer–early autumn • h. 60cm (2ft) s. 45cm (1½ft)**
Other colours include:
'Iris Prichard' ❀ **White with a bluish tinge**
'Isis' ♀ ✿ **Dark blue**
'Red Grape' ✿ **Cherry red**
'Pauline' ✿ **Lilac pink**
'Innocence' ❀ **White**
'Zwanenburg Blue'
✿ **Royal blue**
'J.C. Weguelin' ♀ ✿ **Pale blue**
'Karminglut' ✿ **Bright red**

STAR PERFORMER
T. **Andersoniana Group 'Purple Dome'** Fleshy strap-like leaves are often tinged purple, like the three-petalled summer flowers.

The Essentials

Site demands Choose a site with well-drained soil in full sun.
Planting Autumn or spring.
Flowering time All summer.
Pests and diseases Trouble free.
Bonus point Truly care free.

Trifolium

Clover is a hugely underrated and subtly scented carpet spreader that will attract bees and liven up a wild-flower lawn with its rounded flowers and three-section leaves.

Expert's Selection

1 *T. repens* **'Green Ice'**
Grown for its large flowers and two-toned leaflets.
❀ **Creamy white • Early summer**
⊘ **Two-tone green • Summer**
h. 15cm (6in) s. 60cm (2ft)

2 *T. repens* **'Purpurascens Quadrifolium'** A low spreader with reddish purple or chocolate leaves edged with green.
❀ **White • Summer** ⊘ **Reddish purple • h. 10cm (4in) s. 60cm (2ft)**

3 *T. pratense* **'Susan Smith'** Leaves veined with gold are studded with dark pink flowers.
✿ **Dark pink • Early summer h. 15cm (6in) s. 45cm (1½ft)**

STAR PERFORMER
T. repens **'Green Ice'** This semi-evergreen clover creeps low and wide in a sunny spot.

If you have a spare patch of ground, for example, in the vegetable garden, where you do not want to leave the soil bare lest it gets taken over by weeds, try making it into a wild lawn.

Clover can also add colour, especially *T. repens* **'Purpurascens Quadrifolium'**, whose striking leaves fade to green at the edges, or the pink-flowered *T. pratense* **'Susan Smith'**.

T. repens **'Purpurascens Quadrifolium'**

The Essentials

Site demands Clover grows in full sun in almost any soil: well-drained ground; heavy clay; and even very alkaline conditions.
Planting practice Plant out in autumn or spring.
Flowering time In summer, generally in the first half.
Pests and diseases Completely trouble free.
Bonus point Clover attracts butterflies and bees to the garden.

Trollius

Globeflowers are an excellent way of brightening up a bog garden or any area with damp soil. They are easy care and very hardy as long as the soil is sufficiently moist. The bright rounded blooms come in a range of yellow tones, some with a dash of orange, others more creamy in colour.

STAR PERFORMER

T. chinensis 'Golden Queen' ♀ **A vibrant globe flower for the height of summer: the multilayered orange flowerheads on tall stems are ideal for flower arrangements.**

T. yunnanensis

Expert's Selection

1 *T. chinensis* 'Golden Queen' ♀ A rich orange bloom with upright, ribbon-like petals on the inside of the flowerhead.
✿ **Orangey yellow**
Early–midsummer
h. **75cm (2½ft)** *s.* **45cm (1½ft)**

2 *T. x cultorum* 'Earliest of All' Bears fresh, flashy yellow, globe-shaped flowers like huge buttercups above the shiny foliage.
✿ **Yellow • Spring and early summer**
h. **75cm (2½ft)** *s.* **45cm (1½ft)**

3 *T. europaeus*
The common globeflower is a British native with sensational flowers. 'Superbus' ♀ is even better, and more free-flowering.
✿ **Yellow • Early summer**
h. **75cm (2½ft)** *s.* **45cm (1½ft)**

4 *T. yunnanensis*
The Chinese form of the globeflower bears just one open flower on each stem. Its leaves are slightly more elegant than those of its European cousins.
✿ **Rich yellow • Early–midsummer**
h. **75cm (2½ft)** *s.* **45cm (1½ft)**

The Essentials

Site demands Globeflowers need rich, damp, even boggy soil in full sun or light shade.
Planting practice Plant from autumn to early spring but not in frosty weather.
Flowering time They flower in spring and the first half of summer. Prompt deadheading can lead to a second batch of flowers.
Pests and diseases Trouble free, although mice enjoy the buds.
Bonus point Leaves provide lush ground cover.

Any garden with a patch of boggy ground can be transformed by planting it with sparkling trollius. Found in Europe, North America and across Asia, globeflowers thrive in moist conditions, and get the garden off to a flying start in the spring. They come in a range of yellow hues, so try mixing and matching, using creamy yellow, bright yellow and orangey yellow varieties. Depending on the species, flowering season ranges from late spring to midsummer.

Lock moisture into the soil
Although their natural habitat is boggy ground, globeflowers can also be grown in the better-drained soil on banks by streams and around natural ponds.

If you wish to grow trollius in a herbaceous border they will need some attention. It is essential to make sure that the soil does not dry out during summer. Give the plants a good soaking then apply a thick mulch to stop the moisture evaporating. Thereafter, water them frequently.

Veronica

Speedwells range in height from small plants for growing in a rockery or wild lawn to tall specimens that need staking in a border. If you like blue, there's one for you.

Expert's Selection

1 *V. gentianoides*♈
Try this powder-blue perennial at the front of a border.
✿ **Blue • Summer •** *h.* **30cm (1ft)** *s.* **40cm (16in)**

2 *V. austriaca* **subsp.** *teucrium* **'Crater Lake Blue'**♈ Striking flowers are an intense cobalt-blue.
✿ **Bright blue • Midsummer** *h.* **20cm (8in)** *s.* **60cm (2ft)**

3 *V. prostrata* **'Rosea'**
Dense spikes of flowers cover this rock plant from late spring.
✿ **Lilac-pink • Early summer** *h.* **10cm (4in)** *s.* **45cm (1½ft)**

STAR PERFORMER
V. gentianoides♈ **Tall spires of hollyhock-like, light blue blooms give this veronica a stately air of elegance.**

TAKE A FRESH LOOK

V. peduncularis **'Georgia Blue'** All veronicas spread, but this variety sprawls wider than most, and forms a low, dense mat of deep blue summer flowers.

4 *V. spicata* **'Icicle'**
Tall white flowers make a contrast with the dark foliage.
❀ **White • Midsummer** *h.&s.* **45cm (1½ft)**

The smallest, low-growing varieties of veronica, such as *V. prostrata*, are perfect plants to grow in scree gardens, where they creep over the rocky ground, untroubled by the dry and impoverished soil. Taller varieties, like *V. spicata* 'Icicle', make good dense clumps of colour in well-drained borders.

The Essentials

Site demands Grow speedwell in light soil in a sunny, sheltered spot.
Planting practice Stake taller varieties on open sites. Deadhead to encourage vigour and a compact habit, and divide every three years.
Flowering time Summer.
Pests and diseases The main problem is powdery mildew.
Bonus point Tolerant of dry and infertile conditions.

Viola

Essential plants for any garden, violas offer a fantastic range of colours from the quietly tasteful to the bold and brash. They make marvellous solid groups, and surprise companions for shrub roses, where they add colour at the base of the plant beneath the bare stems.

Expert's Selection

1 *V. sororia* **'Freckles'**
The sister violet bears speckled flowers on very short stems.
❀ **White and purple • Spring and summer**
h. **10cm (4in)** *s.* **20cm (8in)**

2 *V. cornuta*♈
There are many different kinds of this evergreen horned violet, all with gently scented flowers. Plants in the Alba Group♈ are white.
✿❀ **Lilac or white • Midsummer** *h.* **15cm (6in)** *s.* **30cm (1ft)**

3 *V. odorata*
The English or sweet violet flowers twice a year.
✿❀ **Blue or white • Spring then late summer •** *h.* **8cm (3in)** *s.* **15cm (6in)**

4 *V.* **'Maggie Mott'**♈
An old favourite, this viola has highly scented flowers.
✿ **Silvery mauve • Spring–summer** *h.* **8cm (3in)** *s.* **15cm (6in)**

5 *V.* **'Huntercombe Purple'**♈
Evergreen, compact and very hardy, it has white-eyed flowers.
✿ **Deep purple • Spring–summer** *h.&s.* **15cm (6in)**

6 *V.* **'Jackanapes'**♈
This variety spreads to form flashy evergreen clumps of bright colour.
✿ **Yellow and dark purple • Summer** *h.* **10cm (4in)** *s.* **25cm (10in)**

V. tricolor

7 *V. tricolor*
These flowers are short-lived, but their colours are quite exquisite.
❀✿✿ **White, yellow and purple Spring–late summer** *h.* **10cm (4in)** *s.* **15cm (6in)**

Violas add bright background colour for shrubs and other perennials in a border. The genus also includes pansies, which grow taller and are less likely to be fragrant, and violets. Plant violas in a raised bed to make it easier to bend to smell their scent. Raising them also gives their small flowers greater prominence.

Many violas are treated as annuals (see pages 301 and 302–303), but these selections are hardy evergreens that will flower reliably over a long period with very little care or attention.

STAR PERFORMER
V. sororia 'Freckles' A wonderful self-seeding variety, whose flowers look as though they have been spattered with purple paint.

V. cornuta

V. 'Jackanapes'

The Essentials

Site demands Violas grow best in light-shade to full sun. Avoid ground that is often bone dry.
Planting practice Deadhead the flowers to keep the display going.
Flowering time Most start flowering in spring. By cutting back in midsummer to 8cm (3in), they will put on fresh growth and start flowering again into autumn.
Pests and diseases Slugs and snails may attack new growth.
Bonus point Many varieties have a deliciously sweet fragrance.

Waldsteinia

This bright yellow spring-flowering perennial grows naturally in woodland settings. For a reliably care-free plant, it is surprisingly little known, but easy to find.

Expert's Selection

1 *W. ternata*
This vigorous, low-growing perennial spreads over a wide area and brightens shady corners with its sunny yellow flowers.
✿ Yellow • Late spring–summer
h. 15cm (6in) *s.* 60cm (2ft)

Fast-growing and easy-care, waldsteinia has saucer-shaped flowers which resemble those of a potentilla (see page 234). It makes excellent ground cover, especially in sites with fertile soil and dappled shade, that resemble its woodland habitat.

Waldsteinia creeps on runners close to the surface, and is easy to divide if clumps get too big. Alternatively, snip off rooted shoots and grow them on in pots before planting out.

The Essentials

Site demands Waldsteinia grows in most soils, but it helps if it is reasonably fertile. Light shade is preferable to full summer sun.
Planting practice Divide large clumps in early spring, before they start to flower.
Flowering time The flowers appear in spring or at the very beginning of summer.
Pests and diseases Waldsteinia is invariably trouble free.
Bonus point Spreads wide in dappled shade to make excellent ground cover.

STAR PERFORMER
W. ternata Masses of saucer-shaped yellow flowers bloom in early summer, softening the outline of its spreading, jagged-edged leaves.

climbers, shrubs, sub-shrubs & conifers

Shrubs are among the easiest and most care free of all plants to grow and maintain. They make up the most diverse and useful group of plants in the garden, providing the colour, structure and varied texture that will enhance any design.

Shrubs are woody plants, usually either bushy or climbing and may be either deciduous or evergreen. Sub-shrubs are woody only at the base and often grow and look more like herbaceous perennials.

Whether evergreen or deciduous, shrubs will add a feeling of permanence and continuity to a garden, and provide an enduring backdrop against which to place the more ephemeral elements such as annuals. For this reason it is worth taking a little time over your choice of shrubs, bearing in mind the specific demands of individual plants, and the overall look you want to achieve.

A little groundwork

It is important to prepare the planting site well, to give the plants the best possible start, and to help them become established as quickly as possible. Few shrubs enjoy permanently wet conditions, apart from **willows**, but most are undemanding as to soil, provided it is moderately fertile and not subject to water-logging or drought. However, many **rhododendrons** and their close relatives, including a number of **heathers**, **azaleas** and *Vaccinium*, prefer acid soil and are unlikely to thrive in a shallow, chalky site.

Most shrubs will grow in both sunny and lightly shaded conditions, though a few, such as **lavender**, **tamarisk** and **gorse** need bright strong sunlight, and others, like many **rhododendrons** and **camellias** do better in light or dappled shade.

Setting the scene

Many shrubs can be successfully moved, even when they are well established. However, this can be hard work, so it is worth having in mind a broad outline of your planting design before you start to actually place the plants in the ground.

The ideal is to aim for a balance between the solidity and permanence of evergreens and the seasonal changes of deciduous flowering shrubs. Evergreens come into their own in the winter, when any green foliage is welcome, but too many of them, especially conifers, may look heavy in a summer garden.

In contrast, many deciduous shrubs have more than one season of interest, with flowers in spring or summer, then colourful berries or leaves turning to rich golds and reds in the late autumn. Try to achieve variation in the height, shape, size and texture of foliage for added interest.

Many climbing shrubs are wonderfully showy when in flower, and are invaluable in all gardens. Even in a tiny town plot, well-chosen climbers can be trained across an ugly wall or fence to hide it, or trailed over a small arch or tree stump to offer a fantastic floral display. A number of climbers will even flourish in a pot.

Most shrubs grow well in a variety of soils, but a little preparation and maintenance will help them become established quicker.

Food and water
• Before planting, dig plenty of well-rotted compost or manure into the soil. This will help to conserve moisture as well as providing nutrients for young plants.
• Keep plants well watered, especially in the first year of growth.
• Apply an annual mulch of compost in autumn or early spring, when the ground is moist.

Providing support
• In an exposed site, staking may be necessary to support bushy shrubs, especially young ones.
• Make sure that climbers have something to grow up. Plant those that attach themselves by suckers near a tall, solid object, such as a wall or tree. Train those that climb by twining their shoots or tendrils around a support, either across wire netting or a trellis for the smaller plants, or along a sturdy fence or strong wires fixed horizontally across a wall for larger ones.

Pruning
• Cut out old or unhealthy shoots every two or three years to help maintain vigorous, healthy growth.
• Keep shrubs in good shape by pruning back any that are encroaching on other plants, or have outgrown their allotted space.
• Unless grown as topiary or hedging, try to avoid a light all-over trim. The resulting smooth finish can look very artificial. It is better to prune selectively, using secateurs rather than shears, aiming for a natural, irregular shape.
• Most deciduous shrubs are best pruned after flowering (see pages 16–17), and evergreens in spring.
• Keep conifers in shape with regular, light trims. Few of them can produce sturdy new shoots if they are cut back too hard, down to the really old wood.

Tying a climber to its support will provide extra security.

Abies

Silver firs add an air of maturity to any garden. They are undemanding and reliably hardy, and aftercare could not be simpler. These dwarf varieties are ideal for small gardens and rockeries.

A. koreana 'Silberlocke'

A. balsamea 'Nana'

A. nordmanniana 'Golden Spreader'

1 *A. lasiocarpa* **'Arizonica Compacta'** This little tree is ideal for brightening up a dark damp corner.
⊘ **Silvery blue • *h.* 60cm (2ft)**
***s.* 45cm (1½ft) after 10 years; reaching 2x1m (7x3ft) after 30 years**

2 *A. koreana*
The handsome Korean fir forms a neat pyramid shape. Its glossy needles are silver underneath, and the cones are a bluish purple.
⊘ **Green • *h.* 2–3m (7–10ft)**
***s.* 1.2m (4ft) after 30 years**

3 *A. koreana* **'Silberlocke'**♀ The slowest growing of these firs looks silvery as the pale grey undersides of the needles are visible.
⊘ **Silvery green**
***h.* 1m (3ft) *s.* 60cm (2ft)**

4 *A. balsamea* **Hudsonia Group**♀
Dwarf balsam fir with glossy, aromatic green needles.
⊘ **Green • *h.* 80cm (32in)**
***s.* 1m (3ft) after 20 years**

5 *A. nordmanniana* **'Golden Spreader'**♀ A golden yellow dwarf bush with wide-spreading branches. Protect it from frost.
⊘ **Golden yellow • *h.* 1m (3ft)**
***s.* 1.5m (5ft) after 15 years**

6 *A. balsamea* **'Nana'**
A dwarf balsam fir with densely packed needles, this forms a compact round bush.
⊘ **Dark green • *h.* 80cm (32in)**
***s.* 1m (3ft) after 20–30 years**

With their sweeping branches and silvery trunks, these evergreen conifers make an attractive feature in any garden. Some varieties have the added bonus of silvery needles or colourful cones.

Firs can grow very tall – the giant fir can reach 100m (330ft) or more – but those included here are all dwarf varieties. Neat, slow-growing varieties such as **'Arizonica Compacta'** are especially suitable for the average garden. **'Silberlocke'** is a colourful, very slow-growing variety which would suit the small garden, while the compact dwarf varieties such as the **Hudsonia Group** or **'Nana'** do well in rockeries.

Plant and forget

Silver firs grow best in a cool damp climate, and prefer a moist, acid soil. They are not suitable for inner-city or industrial areas, as they dislike a polluted atmosphere. Varieties with white or gold leaves should be planted in semi-shade, as strong sunlight can scorch the foliage.

Once planted, these firs need little looking after, apart from lopping off the odd unwanted branch. The golden leaved varieties sometimes produce a rogue green branch, and this should be removed.

STAR PERFORMER
A. lasiocarpa **'Arizonica Compacta'** This slow-growing fir looks like a little Christmas tree with silvery blue needles. It is happiest growing in a cool damp spot.

Site demands Deep, moist, acid soils are ideal. They will grow in clay, but few tolerate chalk. Avoid areas of atmospheric pollution. Some need protection from frosts.
Planting practice Plant young trees in autumn or late spring, and avoid disturbing the rootball.
Flowering time Cones are produced in spring and may be red, purple, blue, white or green. Most fruit only after 20 years; the Korean fir produces blue cones after 5–10 years.
Pruning needs Pruning is not necessary. Remove any unwanted branches in winter, and if a golden variety produces a green-leaved branch, cut it out immediately.
Pests and diseases Trouble free, apart from the odd aphid attack.
Bonus point These trees offer year round colour with evergreen foliage and colourful cones.

Akebia

Chocolate vines are attractive climbers whose twining stems will climb and romp over anything. They have unusual deep purple flowers with a spicy scent.

Expert's Selection

1 A. quinata
Evergreen in mild climates, this is a fast growing climber.
✿ Maroon • Spring • *h.&s.* 5m (16ft)

2 A. trifoliata
Deciduous and prone to frost, this is similar to A. quinata, but has the more attractive foliage.
✿ Maroon • Spring • *h.&s.* 5m (16ft)

STAR PERFORMER
A. quinata This substantial climber bears small, cupped, flowers: the female ones are deep purple, the male blooms are paler. On a baking south-facing wall it may also produce sausage-shaped autumn fruits.

Akebias produce both male and female flowerheads with a spicy, vanilla scent. If pollination occurs, they produce purplish sausage-shaped fruit filled with white pulp and black seeds.

When growing it against a wall, train it up wires to keep it neat. This will also mean that the flowers can be more easily seen. The vines can also be grown up pergolas, or even allowed to romp over old tree stumps.

Frost protection
A. quinata is perfectly hardy, but in a cold area a new plant may require protection during its first winter. Mulch around the stem to protect the roots.

The Essentials

Site demands A sunny or lightly shaded position with fertile, moisture-retentive soil is ideal.
Flowering time Spring.
Pruning Retain and tie in six strong shoots on a new plant. Thereafter, remove weak growth. If you wish to restrict its size, cut back stems to one-third their length after spring flowering.
Pests and diseases Trouble free.
Bonus point The flowers have an exotic spicy scent.

Amelanchier

Snowy mespilus is a wonderful showpiece, with its clusters of white flowers and coppery foliage.

Expert's Selection

1 A. canadensis
This shrub forms a thicket of colourful leaves. It grows well in damp conditions.
❀ White • Spring ∅ Copper Autumn • *h.* 1.2m (4ft) after 5 years; ultimately 7m (23ft)

2 A. lamarckii♀
The largest variety has white flowers in spring. Autumn leaves combine brilliant yellows and reds.
❀ White • Spring ∅ Red • Autumn *h.* 1.5m (5ft) *s.* 1.2m (4ft) after 5 years; ultimately 10m (30ft)

3 A. x grandiflora 'Ballerina'♀ The leaves are bronze when young, turning red and brown in autumn.
❀ White • Spring ∅ Red-brown Autumn • *h.* 1m (3ft) after 5 years; ultimately 3m (10ft)

If you have an open space to fill, this bushy shrub will provide a spectacular display from spring to autumn. White spring blossoms are followed by red berries in summer that eventually turn black. The smaller 'Ballerina' is the best for an average garden.

This shrub is truly care free, though you may want to cut it back in winter to keep it in check.

It is sometimes attacked by fire blight at flowering time. Remove and destroy any diseased branches, cutting back beyond the damage by at least 30cm (1ft).

STAR PERFORMER
A. canadensis This multi-stemmed shrub bears white spring flowers and coppery autumn foliage.

The Essentials

Site demands Full sun or partial shade, in moisture-retaining soil.
Planting practice Plant out in early autumn, or plant bare-root shrubs in winter, when dormant.
Flowering time Flowers in spring; copper leaves in autumn.
Pests and diseases Trouble free, but susceptible to fire blight.
Bonus point Profuse spring flowers and lovely autumn colour.

A. lamarckii

Artemisia

Wormwood has long been known for its medicinal properties, and is often grown in herb gardens. However, its silvery feathery foliage looks great in mixed borders and rockeries, and can also be used for ground cover. The leaves are often wonderfully aromatic, too.

A. abrotanum

A. absinthium 'Lambrook Silver'

Expert's Selection

1 *A. arborescens*
One of the prettiest shrubby artemisias, with pale silver, finely cut, aromatic foliage.
⊘ **Silvery grey**
h. **1m (3ft)** *s.* **50cm (20in)**

2 *A. abrotanum*♀
This semi-evergreen shrub is known by several names: Lad's love, Old man and Southernwood. The greenish leaves are sweetly aromatic, with a hint of lemon, and make a refreshing tisane.
⊘ **Grey green**
h. **70cm (28in)** *s.* **50cm (20in)**

3 *A. absinthium* 'Lambrook Silver'♀ This evergreen artemisia looks terrific against contrasting purples. Its foliage is more finely divided than that of the parent plant, which was traditionally used to flavour the liqueur, absinthe.
⊘ **Silver   Pale yellow • Midsummer**
h. **75cm (2½ft)** *s.* **60cm (2ft)**

4 *A. dranunculus*
Better known as tarragon, this sub-shrubby perennial's leaves can be used for seasoning in cookery.
⊘ **Mid–light green**
h. **1.2m (4ft)** *s.* **30cm (1ft)**

STAR PERFORMER
A. arborescens
Delicate silvery leaves on this upright shrub make a feathery evergreen display in a border. Pinch off the dull yellow flowers to encourage bushier foliage.

The Essentials

Site demands Artemisia grows best in an open sunny spot with free-draining soil.
Planting practice Plant out bare root shrubs or rooted cuttings in spring.
Pruning needs Cut back in spring to keep the shrubs in shape and encourage new foliage to sprout.
Flowering time If left on the bush, the flowers open in late summer.
Pests and diseases Aphids and rust may be a problem.
Bonus point Most artemisias have sweetly scented aromatic foliage.

> **ANCIENT HERBAL USES**
> Wormwood was used as a herb by the ancient Greeks and is still used in Chinese herbal medicine. The herbaceous perennial artemesia, mugwort, was once famously known in Europe as the 'mother of herbs'.

Their beautiful silvery grey foliage makes artemesias an asset anywhere in the garden. The herbaceous perennial varieties (see page 94) make good choices for ground cover, while these more upright, shrubby varieties and woody-based perennials look terrific in borders or against a wall – particularly if it is softened with age and silvery lichens.

Sacrifice flowers for foliage
Most varieties of artemisia have small and insignificant yellow flowers, which appear from summer to autumn. If you do not like them, they can be pinched out when they are in bud without harming the plant.

Removing the flowers will also help to produce a growth spurt of the bushy new foliage, which is the plant's main attraction.

Aucuba

Spotted laurel, or *Aucuba japonica,* is a sturdy evergreen, native to Japan, and one of the toughest and hardiest shrubs known. It can be grown almost anywhere, shrugging off even the most difficult conditions, including salt spray, dark shade and atmospheric pollution.

Expert's Selection

1 *A. japonica* 'Crotonifolia' ♀
With its glossy leaves speckled with gold, this female shrub is ideal for giving a splash of winter colour. Grow it near a male plant to see its bright red autumn berries.
⌀ Greeny gold ⏁ Bright red
Autumn • *h.&s.* 2m (7ft)

2 *A. japonica* 'Picturata'
Grow this male plant for its strikingly variegated leaves, with elongated golden splashes.
⌀ Greeny gold ⏁ Bright red
Autumn • *h.&s.* 2m (7ft)

3 *A. japonica* 'Variegata'
The leaves of this variety are wider and more toothed than others, and thickly spotted with gold. Male and female plants are available.
⌀ Greeny gold ⏁ Bright red
Autumn • *h.&s.* 2m (7ft)

4 *A. japonica* 'Nana Rotundifolia' A neat round female shrub with deep green leaves, ideal for containers, or borders in a small garden.
⌀ Dark green ⏁ Bright red
Autumn • *h.&s.* 1m (3ft)

5 *A. japonica* f. *longifolia*
One of the most decorative aucubas, this has narrow pale green leaves with a wavy yellow border.
⌀ Pale green ⏁ Bright red
Autumn • *h.&s.* 2m (7ft)

The Essentials

Site demands Aucubas grow almost anywhere, but variegated varieties do best in open sites.
Planting practice Plant in spring or autumn, positioning male and female plants together for berries.
Pruning advice Cut off unruly shoots in spring. Trim hedges with secateurs to protect the leaves.
Flowering time The purplish flowers grow in spikes in spring.
Pests and diseases Trouble free.
Bonus point Glossy variegated foliage all year round.

Aucubas are understandably popular, since they are so easy to grow. Even problem sites with heavy shade, or polluted inner-city areas with poor soil, won't trouble this tough shrub.

Aucubas are ideal as dense, semi-formal hedging, under trees, or in spots where nothing else will grow. The variegated ones, however, such as **'Crotonifolia'** or **'Variegata'**, may have a better colour in a more open situation.

Berry bonus

Some cultivars of *A. japonica* are male and others female. The bright red berries that appear on the female plant in autumn last for several months.

However, the berries can only develop if the female flowers are pollinated, so grow both sexes close together to enjoy the display. Alternatively, choose just one plant and make the most of its glossy foliage.

A. japonica 'Variegata'

TAKE A FRESH LOOK

A. japonica **'Rozannie'** If you only have space for one aucuba and have your heart set on growing clusters of glossy autumn berries, try this variety. It has bisexual flowers, so can produce fruit on its own.

STAR PERFORMER
A. japonica **'Crotonifolia'** ♀
Large, glossy variegated leaves make this one of the brightest evergreen shrubs. Tiny purple flowers (inset) appear with the fresh new shoots in early spring.
Flowers and new shoots

bamboos

Shapely stalks

Bamboos are woody grasses, growing strong vertical stems that will give shape and structure to the garden, even during winter. They will also add a graceful oriental touch, and are available in some wonderful colours including deep blue-green, black and amber. Bamboos can be used as hedges, screens or focal points, and give much needed height with stems reaching up to 6m (20ft).

Take expert advice before buying a bamboo to ensure that you choose the right plant for your garden. Some are absolute giants, while others are more compact. Some are clump-forming, while others spread, and can eventually become invasive, particularly in a small garden.

A happy medium

The best bamboos for the average garden tend to be quite tall, with thick stems, growing about 3.5m (12ft) high. Bamboos of this size include the eye-catching, unusual yellow-orange stemmed varieties, many of which are species and cultivars of *Phyllostachys*. Allow a minimum space of 1m² (10sq ft) in which to grow any bamboo.

You could also try a solid clump former such as *Fargesia*, which has small leaves and densely packed thinner stems. It will eventually reach 4m (12ft).

Bamboos for containers

When choosing a bamboo for a pot make sure that you choose a clump-former that will not spread too much. Most will eventually require potting on into a half-barrel or 65 litre pot. Besides *Phyllostachys nigra*, there is the new pale green, slender-stemmed

Phyllostachys nigra

Fargesia spathacea 'Simba', which has small leaves and is guaranteed not to exceed 3m (9ft) in height and spread.

The 'see-through' look

You can create an appealing wispy, see-through effect with a bamboo. Gradually remove the lower leaf-bearing branches of a *Phyllostachys*, for example, so that the branches are all above head height and only a group of verticals is left. In time you can also cut out a few of these.

This 'see-through' pruning effect works particularly well in Japanese-style gardens, where there are few plants obstructing the views within.

STAR PERFORMER
Phyllostachys bambusoides 'Allgold'
Known until recently as 'Holochrysa', this is a spectacular plant with rich orange-yellow stems that looks superb in the autumn sun. It grows up to about 5m (16ft) high, with contrasting green leaves. Other good orange-yellow bamboos are *P. aurea* 'Holochrysa' and *P. aureosulcata* var. *aureocaulis*.

Pleioblastus auricomis

P. vivax 'Aureocaulis'

TAKE A FRESH LOOK

Phyllostachys aureosulcata 'Spectabilis' This exceptionally hardy bamboo has blue-green leaves borne on sturdy yellow stems with green grooves that may reach a height of 4m (13ft).

Expert's Selection

Stems and leaves

Bamboos are grown for their architectural stems, which come in exciting colours and interesting patterns, as well as for their abundant foliage.

1 *Phyllostachys bambusoides* **'Allgold'**
Tall and striking, it has richly coloured orange stalks and dark green leaves. The rich colour of the stalks is at its finest in autumn.
Orange-yellow stem ⊘ **Green**
h. 5m (16ft) *s.* 1.5m (5ft)

2 *P. nigra* ♀
The black stems of this popular bamboo are green when young, but they soon change colour.
Green, then black stem ⊘ **Green**
h. 3m (10ft) *s.* 1m (3ft)

3 *P. bambusoides* **'Castillonis Inversa'** ♀
A magnificent tall bamboo with green stems striped with yellow.
Green stem, yellow stripes ⊘ **Green**
h. 5m (16ft) *s.* 1.5m (5ft)

4 *P. vivax* **'Aureocaulis'**
A rich yellow, thick-stemmed bamboo chosen for the random green stripes, some thick, some thin, which appear along the canes.
Yellow stem with green stripes ⊘ **Green**
h. 7.5m (25ft) *s.* 1.5m (5ft)

5 *Pleioblastus auricomus* ♀
One of the best bamboos for a small garden. The slender stems are downy when young and branch from the base.
Purplish stems ⊘ **Bright yellow and green** • *h.* 1m (3ft) *s.* 60cm (2ft)

6 *Chusquea culeou* ♀
One of the most impressive, clump-forming bamboos. Thick stems stand smartly erect, making a dramatic, impenetrable mass.
Yellowy green stems ⊘ **Green**
h. 5m (16ft) *s.* 2m (7ft)

7 *Fargesia spathacea* **'Simba'** A compact, clump-forming bamboo with pale green stems and small leaves.
Pale green stems ⊘ **Green**
h.&s. 3m (10ft)

The Essentials

Site demands Bamboos are easily grown, greedy, thirsty feeders, and will be happy in sun and shade. Give them a spring mulch of compost to make sure that they don't dry out, and add a sprinkling of general-purpose fertiliser in midsummer.
Planting practice Plant in early spring. Before planting add some grit to the soil to improve the drainage if necessary.
Flowering time Most bamboos bloom irregularly, but when they flower it is in early summer.
Pests and diseases Bamboos are remarkably trouble free.
Bonus point Good-looking leaves and attractively patterned stems give shape and structure.

B. x media 'Parkjuweel'

B. darwinii

B. x ottawensis 'Superba'

Berberis

This is a versatile, easily grown shrub which can fulfill many roles – there are dwarf shrubs for rockeries, others for ground cover or clothing a bank, specimen shrubs for show and dense spiny plants for secure hedging.

Expert's Selection

1 B. thunbergii 'Atropurpurea Nana'♀ A deciduous dwarf shrub ideal for a rockery. The similar B. thunbergii f. atropurpurea has dark purple-red foliage, that is bright red in autumn.
⌀ **Purple-red • Autumn ⚘ Bright red** Autumn • h.&s. 60cm (2ft)

2 B. x media 'Parkjuweel'♀ A low mound of bright green leaves turn crimson in autumn.
⌀ **Red • Autumn** ✿ **Yellow • Spring** h.&s. 60cm (2ft) after 5yrs; ultimately 1m (3ft)

3 B. x stenophylla♀ Arching stems form a dense evergreen thicket. In spring it is smothered in scented flowers.
✿ **Yellow • Spring ⚘ Purple • Autumn** h.&s. 2.5m (8ft)

4 B. darwinii♀ A glossy evergreen, it forms a thick hedge, and produces spectacular

clusters of golden flowers in spring and sometimes again in autumn.
✿ **Yellow • Spring ⚘ Purple • Autumn** h. 2m (7ft) s. 1.5m (5ft)

5 B. x ottawensis 'Superba'♀ A deciduous shrub with striking purple foliage.
✿ **Yellow • Spring • h.&s.** 1.5m (5ft) after 5yrs; 2.5m (8ft) after 10yrs

6 B. thunbergii 'Pow-wow' An upright shrub whose bright yellow leaves gradually turn green.
⌀ **Yellow-green • Spring and summer • h.&s.** 1.5m (5ft)

STAR PERFORMER
B. thunbergii 'Atropurpurea Nana'♀
The colourful leaves and berries look striking in autumn, and as it is almost thornless, makes an easily managed low hedge.

---

7 B. thunbergii 'Harlequin' The small purplish leaves of this berberis are mottled with pink.
⌀ **Purple and pink • Spring and summer • h.** 1.5m (5ft) s. 1.2m (4ft)

8 B. thunbergii 'Rose Glow'♀ As the leaves mature they develop a white variegation.
⌀ **Red-purple • Spring and summer** h. 1.5m (5ft) s. 1.2m (4ft)

9 B. 'Rubrostilla'♀ A rounded deciduous shrub with profuse yellow summer flowers and coral-red berries.
✿ **Yellow • Spring ⚘ Red • Autumn** h. 1.5m (5ft) s. 2.5m (8ft)

Colourful leaves, flowers and berries make berberis both versatile and excellent value. The evergreens have dark glossy leaves, spring flowers and blue-black autumn berries. Deciduous varieties also flower in spring and often have bright autumn leaves and clusters of red berries which last well into winter.

The ideal hedge
All except 'Atropurpurea Nana' are covered in spines while larger varieties, such as B. darwinii and B. × stenophylla, make attractive and exceptionally dense hedging.

The Essentials

Site demands Evergreens do well in sun or light shade; deciduous shrubs grown for colour need sun.
Planting practice Plant evergreens in autumn or spring and deciduous shrubs from mid autumn to early spring.
Flowering time Spring.
Pests and diseases Trouble free.
Bonus point Spiny stems make impenetrable hedging.

Brachyglottis

A mound of silvery grey evergreen leaves and a summer sprinkling of small, daisy-like yellow flowers characterise this drought-tolerant shrub. It prefers a sunny position and does not mind the wind, so is ideal for exposed sites.

Expert's Selection

1 B. 'Sunshine' ♀
This New Zealand native loves the sun but will tolerate draughts and strong winds. Its silvery leaves have a white felted underside.
☆ Yellow • Midsummer
h. 1m (3ft) s. 2m (7ft)

2 B. elaeagnifolia
Hardy in coastal areas, this is one of the most vigorous of these shrubs. Narrow dark green leaves are felted white on the other side.
☆ Yellow • Summer
h. 3m (10ft) s. 4.5m (15ft)

3 B. compacta
Small wavy edged leaves emerge white and hairy and become grey and hairless. It forms a dense, neat mound.
☆ Yellow • Midsummer
h. 1m (3ft) s. 2m (7ft)

4 B. monroi ♀
Ideal for a small garden, this has olive green leaves felted white beneath.
☆ Yellow • Midsummer
h.&s. 1m (3ft)

5 B. bidwillii
Slow-growing with unusual colouring – the young shoots and underside of new leaves are chestnut brown; flower clusters are white.
❀ White • Summer
h. 1m (3ft) s. 1.2m (4ft)

6 B. laxifolia
Sprawling variety with unusual scalloped leaves which are white when young, turning dark green.
☆ Yellow • All summer and autumn
h. 1m (3ft) s. 2m (7ft)

The Essentials

Site demands A well drained sunny position.
Planting practice Plant in spring or summer.
Flowering time Summer.
Pests and diseases Trouble free.
Pruning needs Trim to shape after flowering.
Bonus point The felty foliage adds subtle colour all year round.

B. laxifolia

This easygoing evergreen has a quiet charm, with its silver grey foliage and yellow flowers. The colour of the leaves varies from olive to grey green, and the underside is felted densely white.

No problems
These care-free plants need very little looking after. Cut back any straggling growth to keep the rounded shape. Hard pruning improves the leaves, but at the expense of the flowers. While reasonably hardy, the plants may be damaged by frost – if they are affected, cut off the damaged growth. *B. bidwillii* will need protection in colder areas, and is best grown in a sheltered spot.

The compact varieties are ideal for a small garden. Try slow-growing *B. bidwillii*, with its unusual bronze foliage and white flowers, or *B. compacta* with its neat shape. *B. elaeagnifolia* is taller and more eyecatching, and adds colour to the border.

STAR PERFORMER
B 'Sunshine' ♀ The most flamboyant of these shrubs, it produces large clusters of yellow flowers from mid–late summer.

Buddleja

Butterfly bush, as it is often known, is deservedly popular, for it will grow almost anywhere, even in the poorest soil, and still have beautiful flowers. Given the right treatment – hard pruning – it will go on flowering year after year, attracting bees and butterflies to your garden.

Buddlejas flourish in any sunny spot, although they often flower more abundantly in deep, loamy ground. Available in a wide range of flower colours, they grow very fast, so leave plenty of room when planting, and remove flowerheads soon after flowering, as they self seed.

Pruning

Some pruning is essential, or buddlejas become straggly, and eventually produce few flowers. With *B. alternifolia* remove a third of each flower spike, after flowering. Prune the main stems of *B. davidii* to about 45cm (1½ft) high in spring. For all other varieties, cut any previous year's growth to within 5cm (2in) of the old wood.

INSECT 'MAGNET' Buddlejas' nectar-rich flowers will draw large numbers of brightly coloured butterflies.

STAR PERFORMER
B. davidii 'Nanho Blue' The fragrant pale blue flowers last from midsummer to early autumn, attracting nectar loving bees and butterflies.

B. x weyeriana 'Golden Glow'

B. davidii 'White Profusion'

Expert's Selection

1 *B. davidii* **'Nanho Blue'**
The long, scented flower spikes of this fast-growing shrub will give a striking summer show in any sunny corner. For a little variety of colour, mix with 'Nanho Purple'.
✿ **Pale blue • Midsummer–early autumn** ⌀ **Pale green h.&s. 2m (7ft)**

2 *B. davidii* **'White Profusion'**♀ The best white buddleja, it will produce an abundance of sweetly perfumed flower spikes, dense with white, yellow-eyed flowers, right through the summer.
❀ **White • Midsummer–early autumn** ⌀ **Pale green • h.&s. 2m (7ft)**

3 *B. davidii* **'Royal Red'**♀
Give this beautiful shrub a centre stage position in the sun, and it will provide a dramatic display of deep purple-red flowers on plumes up to 50cm (20in) long.
✿ **Purple-red • Midsummer–early autumn** ⌀ **Pale green h.&s. 2m (7ft)**

4 *B. alternifolia*♀
This is known as the 'fountain buddleja', because of its graceful arching stems, covered, in May and June, with clusters of fragrant, lilac flowers. When trained, it makes a lovely weeping tree.
✿ **Lilac • Early summer** ⌀ **Dull green h.&s. 4m (13ft)**

5 *B.* **'Pink Delight'**♀
One of the tallest varieties, though it can be kept in check by pruning. Long, narrow plumes, clustered with pink flowers, will appear throughout August and September.
✿ **Pale pink • Late summer** ⌀ **Pale green • h.&s. 4m (13ft)**

6 *B.* x *weyeriana* **'Golden Glow'** Make a splash with this more unusual variety. A rounded shrub, it bears globular clusters of yellowy orange flowers tinged with lilac at the end of its branches.
✿ **Yellow-orange • Mid–late summer** ⌀ **Pale green • h.&s. 3m (10ft)**

B. 'Pink Delight'

B. davidii 'Royal Red'

Buxus

Box is grown for its shiny, deep green, aromatic leaves – flowers are inconspicious – and is the traditional choice for neat hedging or small, tightly clipped, ornamental shrubs.

Because it grows so slowly, and tolerates endless clipping, box is very easy to keep under control. It is the perfect shrub for topiary, or for planting wherever you require low, dense hedging, or framing for a border. Smaller varieties also grow well in pots.

Keeping in shape
To encourage thick, bushy growth, cut hedge and topiary plants back hard when young. Once mature, they will only need clipping two or three times a year.

The Essentials

Site demands Any soil, in full sun or partial shade.
Planting practice Plant in spring or autumn.
Pruning needs Prune to keep shape, when necessary.
Pests and diseases Trouble free, but insects may damage leaves.
Bonus point Aromatic foliage.

Expert's Selection

1 *B. sempervirens*♀
A bushy, rounded shrub, with glossy, dark green leaves, it makes excellent hedging. 'Aureomarginata', which has a yellow margin to its leaves, would make a colourful, eye-catching addition to any border.
⌀ **Dark green, edged yellow in 'Aureomarginata' • h.&s. 4m (13ft)**

2 *B. sempervirens* **'Suffruticosa'**♀ The smallest variety, with shiny, oval leaves, it is traditionally used for edging flowerbeds in formal gardens.
⌀ **Light green • h.&s. 4m (13ft)**

3 *B. sempervirens* **'Silver Beauty'** The silvery markings on the leaves of this slow-growing box give it a magical quality. It looks wonderful when planted as an ornamental shrub.
⌀ **Silvery green • h.&s. 4m (13ft)**

STAR PERFORMER
B. sempervirens♀ This attractive, glossy leafed evergreen can easily be trimmed into any shape that takes your fancy.

Camellia

Prized for their glossy evergreen leaves and spectacular flowers, set off by yellow-tipped stamens, camellias are truly magnificent shrubs. Though the blooms give an impression of fragility, they are tougher than they look, and all the varieties listed below are fairly hardy and easy to grow.

There are over 200 species of camellia, and because of the differences in hardiness, flowering season and habit, there are plants suitable for almost every type of garden. They are native to Japan, China and India but have been grown in Europe for centuries.

Most, like 'Adolphe Audusson' or 'Donation', are suitable for beds and borders, while a few, such as 'J. C. Williams', and 'Elegant Beauty', have a spreading habit and are ideal for growing against a wall. They can also be trained up a trellis to form an informal screen – good examples for doing this effectively are 'Julia Hamiter', 'J. C. Williams' and 'Dream Boat'. Many camellias, such as 'Nuccio's Jewel', also make fine specimen shrubs for containers, and will create a grand show on terraces or patios.

The Essentials

Site demands Camellias need a well-drained, lime-free soil and a south-west to northern aspect, in light shade or a sheltered spot. To protect from frost damage position away from early morning sun.
Planting practice Plant in early spring to late summer, enriching non-peaty soils with leaf mould or peaty compost. Mulch plants after planting to conserve moisture.
Flowering time Choose carefully and you can enjoy camellias from January to June.
Pruning needs Cut back straggly or unwanted branches.
Pests and diseases Aphids and scale insects can be a problem.
Bonus point In acid conditions, camellias are very easy to grow.

Flowering beauty

Camellias are noted for their spectacular cup-shaped flowers, which can range from 2.5cm (1in) to 20cm (8in) in diameter. The flowers first appear in late winter, and can be single, semi-double, anemone-like, peony-like or rose-like. The colours are most commonly white, pink or red, but may be multicoloured, and even occasionally yellow.

Providing shelter

Most of the varieties listed here will happily survive the winter in a sheltered spot. The ideal position is against a north or south-west facing wall, in filtered shade, although on a south west-facing wall they may need mulching to prevent them from drying out. They are also good in town gardens, which tend to be more sheltered.

Guarantee success

The ideal soil for camellias is moist and lime-free. When planting, enrich non-peaty soils with leaf-mould or peaty compost and mulch well, to help prevent the plants drying out. Continue to water regularly, especially when the plants are coming into bud.

Containers

Camellias grown in containers need a loose, slightly acidic potting soil. A mixture of two parts loam, one part peat and one part sand is ideal, with a little fertiliser added. Be careful when watering containers – the two extremes of overwatering or letting the roots dry out will make the camellias lose their flower buds.

C. x williamsii 'Anticipation'

C. x williamsii 'Donation'

1 *C. japonica* 'Adolphe Audusson'♀ A vigorous upright with large, red, semi-double flowers. The graceful 'Alba Simplex' bears single white flowers and spreads twice as wide.
❀ **Deep red • All spring**
h. **5m (16ft)** *s.* **4m (13ft)**

2 *C. japonica* 'Berenice Boddy'♀ Delicate pink blooms are surprisingly resilient in an exposed plot.
❀ **Pale pink • All spring**
h. **9m (30ft)** *s.* **8m (26ft)**

3 *C. japonica* 'Ballet Dancer'♀ The cream flowers are edged with delicate coral pink.
❀ **Cream • All spring**
h. **9m (30ft)** *s.* **8m (26ft)**

4 *C. japonica* 'Bob Hope'♀ A classic camellia with glorious deep red blooms.
❀ **Dark red • All spring**
h. **3m (10ft)** *s.* **2m (7ft)**

5 *C. japonica* 'Nuccio's Jewel'♀ A lovely small camellia which thrives in containers.
❀ **White • All spring**
h. **3m (10ft)** *s.* **2m (7ft)**

C. japonica 'Berenice Boddy'

6 *C. japonica* 'Mikenjaku' A slow-growing semi-double camellia also known as 'Nagasaki'.
❀ **Red and white • Mid–late spring**
h. **3m (10ft)** *s.* **2m (7ft)**

7 *C. x williamsii* 'Anticipation'♀ Good in containers, with peony-like flowers.
❀ **Deep pink • All spring**
h. **4m (13ft)** *s.* **2m (7ft)**

8 *C. x williamsii* 'Debbie'♀ The peony-like flowers appear in winter. 'Elsie Jury'♀ is a similar size and colour, but flowers later.
❀ **Deep pink • Late winter–late spring** • *h.* **2–3m (7–10ft)** *s.* **1.2–2m (4–7ft)**

9 *C. x williamsii* 'Donation'♀ This camellia is both beautiful and robust, with semi-double flowers.
❀ **Pink • Late winter–late spring**
h. **5m (16ft)** *s.* **2.5m (8ft)**

10 *C. x williamsii* 'Dream Boat' The double blooms are an unusual purplish pink.
❀ **Purple-pink • All spring**
h. **3m (10ft)** *s.* **2m (7ft)**

11 *C. x williamsii* 'Elegant Beauty' A trailing camellia with bronze foliage, and pink blooms.
❀ **Deep pink • All spring**
h. **3m (10ft)** *s.* **2.5m (8ft)**

12 *C. x williamsii* 'J. C. Williams'♀ Good for informally screening a wall or a trellis.
❀ **Blush pink • All spring**
h. **3m (10ft)** *s.* **2.5m (8ft)**

13 *C. x williamsii* 'Julia Hamiter'♀ The double white, pink flushed flowers smother a trellis in spring.
❀ **White • All spring**
h. **3m (10ft)** *s.* **2.5m (8ft)**

Caryopteris

Bluebeards are ideal for the front of the border. These compact little shrubs produce a mass of tiny blue flowers late in summer when many other plants are over.

Bluebeards can be grown in containers or at the front of a border. They also look attractive in the rockery or tumbling over a low wall. In colder areas stems may be killed off in a very hard winter, but protect the roots with a leaf mulch and new shoots appear again in the spring.

1 *C. x clandonensis* 'Dark Night' Choose this plant for its tiny fragrant, dark purple flowers.
❀ **Dark purple • Late summer**
h.&s. **1m (3ft)**

2 *C. x clandonensis* 'Arthur Simmonds' The small mounds of light blue flowers will tumble prettily over a low wall. Ideal for the rockery.
❀ **Light blue • Late summer**
h.&s. **60cm (2ft)**

STAR PERFORMER
C. x clandonensis 'Dark Night' Fragrant grey-green leaves complement the violet blooms of this appealing, scented bluebeard.

TAKE A FRESH LOOK
C. x clandonensis '**Worcester Gold**' is a drought-tolerant bluebeard, with long golden yellow leaves and blue flowers.

The Essentials

Site demands Any well-drained soil in a sunny spot.
Planting practice Plant in autumn or spring.
Flowering time Late summer.
Pruning needs Cut previous growth back to healthy young buds.
Pests and diseases Trouble free.
Bonus point Bluebeards will even grow in chalky soils.

Ceanothus

Californian lilacs make a wonderful show with their dense, showy clusters of stunning blue flowers, which come in a range of hues, from powder-blue to deep lavender. Plant these sun-loving shrubs away from chilly winds, and they will be no trouble at all.

1 *C.* 'Cascade' ♀
A vigorous, trailing evergreen variety which makes a superb show with its dense sprays of powder-blue flowers complemented by glossy dark green leaves.
✿ **Powder-blue • Spring–early summer • h.&s. 3.5m (12ft)**

C. x *pallidus* 'Marie Simon'

C. thyrsiflorus var. *repens*

2 *C.* 'Blue Mound' ♀
Plant this compact version in a sheltered border, to enjoy the contrast of the round clusters of bright blue flowers against the evergreen leaves.
✿ **Bright blue • Late spring h. 1.5m (5ft) s. 1.8m (6ft)**

3 *C.* 'Edinburgh' ♀
Make a dash with this striking evergreen. The leaves are olive-green, and clusters of dark violet-blue flowers appear in late spring.
✿ **Violet-blue • Spring–early summer h.&s. 2m (7ft)**

4 *C. impressus*
This shrub is well named – an impressive sight when trained against a wall to give a magnificent cascade of deep lavender flowers.
✿ **Lavender-blue • Late spring h.&s. 2m (7ft)**

5 *C. thyrsiflorus* var. *repens* ♀ Make a stunning display on a bank or border with this prostrate evergreen, which forms a dense carpet covered with blue flowers in spring.
✿ **Lilac-blue • Spring–early summer h. 45cm (1½ft) s. 2.7m (9ft)**

6 *C.* x *pallidus* 'Marie Simon' Be different and grow this hardy shrub for its conical clusters of pale pink flowers.
✿ **Pale pink • Midsummer–early autumn • h.&s. 1.5m (5ft)**

These splendid shrubs make a magnificent display, the flowers ranging from powder-blue to deep lavender. Rose-pink and white flowers are also available.

Ceanothus are easy going, provided they have a sunny, sheltered site. In colder areas they will do better with the protection of a sunny wall, out of the wind. They will not do well in cold, exposed gardens but are quite happy in coastal areas if sheltered from strong breezes.

An excellent choice
There are ceanothus varieties to suit most situations, from low-spreading ground cover, such as *C. thyrsiflorus* var. *repens* which only reaches 45cm (1½ft), to taller shrubs and climbers. Most are grown as freestanding shrubs or small trees, though spreaders like *C.* 'Cascade' or *C. impressus* look great trained against a wall.

Pruning know-how
Ceanothus is easily pruned but remember that deciduous and evergreen varieties need different treatment. Deciduous ceanothus is pruned in spring: cut back shoots that have flowered to within two or three buds of the previous year's growth.

Prune evergreens that bloom in spring or early summer straight after flowering. Cut back autumn flowering evergreens the following spring to half the previous season's growth.

Do not be tempted to chop off the vigorous outward growing stems of 'Cascade' or you will spoil the charming cascading effect. Just give it plenty of support on trellis or wires.

STAR PERFORMER
C. 'Cascade' ♀
Trained against a sunny wall this makes a wonderful display in late spring with its arching stems covered in powder-blue flowers.

Celastrus

Bittersweet is a jewel of a climber that sprints up walls and posts and saves its star turn for autumn, when yellow berries split to reveal scarlet seeds.

The Essentials

Site demands Free-draining soil in a sunny sheltered position. It dislikes very thin, chalky soils.
Planting time Plant in autumn or spring, avoiding cold weather.
Flowering time The various varieties can provide flowers from early spring to autumn.
Pruning needs Prune in spring.
Pests and diseases Trouble free, though if the soil is too limey the leaves will turn yellow (chlorosis).
Bonus point Fast growing with abundant flowers.

Expert's Selection

1 *C. scandens*
American bittersweet is a deciduous twiner with yellow leaves and insignificant flowers. It will usually fruit only if both male and female plants are grown.
⌀ Yellow • Autumn • *h.* 2.5m (8ft) after 5 years; ultimately 9m (30ft)

2 *C. orbiculatus*
Oriental bittersweet is a hardy deciduous twiner. Its chief glory is the contrast between the bright yellow autumn foliage and the scarlet seeds which are left untouched by the birds. It is available as a hermaphrodite.
⌀ Yellow • Autumn • *h.* 3m (10ft) after 5 years; ultimately 12m (40ft)

3 *C. angulatus*
A climbing, sprawling, woody plant, it has terrific 15cm (6in) long leaves. Both male and female plants are needed for fruit.
⌀ Yellow • Autumn • *h.* 2m (7ft) after 5 years; ultimately 7.5m (25ft)

The Essentials

Site demands Plant in rich, moisture-retentive soil in full sun or partial shade. *C. scandens* is unfussy, even tolerating drought.
Planting time Spring to early autumn.
Flowering time Foliage colours up and berries ripen in autumn.
Pruning needs Trim in winter or early spring after fruits have fallen.

Pests and diseases Trouble free.
Bonus point The stunning three-lobed seedpods with their globular scarlet seeds are ignored by birds.

There are plenty of popular climbers that flower in spring and summer, and many with flamboyant fiery foliage to brighten the autumn garden – but there is nothing quite like a celastrus.

It may be overshadowed by other climbers throughout the growing season, but when its berries (three-lobed, like spindleberries) pop, there is not another climber that can compete. The bright yellow fruits split open revealing brilliant scarlet seeds that persist well into winter.

Let it scramble
This is quite a chaotic climber, making an intricate tangle of branches. It looks best when it is trained to scramble up and over a pergola, fence or wall. It will also effectively smother an old tree stump and looks particularly attractive when dangling out of a tall tree, displaying its seeds.

Guaranteeing fruit
When you buy a celastrus, check whether it is an hermaphrodite (which has both male and female flowers in one plant) or whether you will need to buy a male and female in order to get fruit.

STAR PERFORMER
C. scandens Also known as the staff vine, this is a fast-growing deciduous twiner which eventually reaches about 9m (30ft) in height. The abundant clusters of glossy, orangey yellow, pea-sized fruits appear in autumn, popping open to expose shiny bright red seeds.

C. orbiculatus

Chamaecyparis

False cyprus is an easy to grow and highly popular evergreen. The fast-growing ones can provide almost instant privacy and shelter and there are varieties to suit almost every situation, including dwarf and slow-growing bushes, specimen shrubs, hedging and ornamental trees.

C. lawsoniana 'Minima Glauca'

C. obtusa 'Nana Gracilis'

Expert's Selection

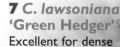

1 *C. lawsoniana* 'Summer Snow' A slow-growing variety with unusual creamy green foliage flecked with white. In spring new growth makes it cream all over.
⌀ **Creamy green**
h. eventually 2m (7ft) *s.* 1.8m (6ft)

2 *C. obtusa* 'Crippsii'♀
A striking shrub with dense foliage forming a cone shape. The new foliage is a bright golden yellow.
⌀ **Greeny yellow**
h. eventually 10m (33ft) *s.* 3m (10ft)

3 *C. obtusa* 'Nana Gracilis'♀ A slow-growing conifer that takes 40 years to reach full height. It is conical, with shell-like sprays of foliage.
⌀ **Dark green**
h.&s. eventually 2m (7ft)

4 *C. lawsoniana* 'Ellwoodii'♀ Narrow and slow-growing, it looks dramatic in the border or in a tub. The grey-green foliage turns steely blue in winter.
⌀ **Grey green**
h. eventually 10m (33ft) *s.* 1m (3ft)

5 *C. lawsoniana* 'Minima Glauca'♀ An attractive feature shrub for a smaller garden with thick sea green foliage that forms a tidy globe shape as it grows.
⌀ **Sea green**
h. eventually 2m (7ft) *s.* 2m (7ft)

6 *C. lawsoniana* 'Van Pelt's Blue'♀ For impact, plant this narrow column of silvery blue foliage so that it stands alone, in a border or on the lawn.
⌀ **Silvery blue**
h. eventually 4m (14ft) *s.* 2m (7ft)

7 *C. lawsoniana* 'Green Hedger'♀
Excellent for dense hedges. Clipping limits the size.
⌀ **Bright green**
h. eventually 24m (80ft) *s.* 4m (14ft)

STAR PERFORMER
C. lawsoniana 'Summer Snow' An easy-to-grow shrub with stunning colour, especially in spring when the new creamy white foliage appears.

From tall, stately trees to dense hedging and dwarf varieties, with striking silvery blue foliage to bright golden hues, these eyecatching, versatile and hardy evergreens are deservedly popular.

Easy to grow, and happy in most conditions, the secret is to choose the right plant for your location. A dwarf or slow-growing variety such as C. 'Nana Gracilis' is perfect for a small garden. For hedging and screens, tree varieties like C. 'Ellwoodii' are ideal, but in an average size garden avoid the larger trees.

For a successful screen, group plants together. Place them singly if you are using them as accents.

The Essentials

Site demands Well-drained acid or neutral soil is best in the sun.
Planting practice Plant in spring and keep well watered until fully established. For hedging, plant 60cm (2ft) apart.
Pruning needs None, although regular trimming controls growth.
Pests and diseases May be attacked by aphids or mites.
Bonus point The coldest winters can bring out the best colours.

Chaenomeles

Japonicas or **flowering quinces** have early, luminous flowers which shine through the gloom of winter.

Japonicas are the ultimate in easy-care wall plants. Simply stretch horizontal wires about 30cm (1ft) apart, then tie in selected branches as the plant grows. The result is a bloom of pink, red, orange or white in early spring. Once the flowers have faded, a japonica makes a natural support for climbing plants, such as the glory vine.

Bring out the best
For a good start, make sure that young plants are well watered for their first two years.

STAR PERFORMER
C. speciosa 'Moerloosei'♀
With its dense clusters of white and pink-tinged flowers, this japonica is also known as 'Apple Blossom'.

The Essentials

Site demands Japonicas grow best in well-drained soil, in a bright sunny position.
Flowering time Early spring.
Pruning needs In May, cut back shoots that have flowered.
Pests and diseases Prone to the occasional aphid attack.
Bonus point Mature japonicas produce aromatic autumn quinces.

Expert's Selection

1 *C. speciosa* 'Moerloosei'♀
This abundant flowering variety is especially easy to train on a wall.
✿❀ Pink and white • Winter–early spring • *h.* 3m (10ft) *s.* 5m (16ft)

2 *C. speciosa* 'Geisha Girl'
Like its name, this long-flowering, neat variety always looks flawless.
✿ Apricot • Winter–early spring
h.&s. 2m (7ft)

3 *C.* x *superba* 'Knap Hill Scarlet'♀ This compact japonica is a good choice for a small space.
✿ Orange-scarlet • Winter–early spring • *h.* 1.5m (5ft) *s.* 2m (7ft)

4 *C. speciosa* 'Simonii'
A low-growing plant with a profusion of blood red flowers.
✿ Bright red • Winter–early spring
h. 1m (3ft) *s.* 2m (7ft)

C. x *superba* 'Knap Hill Scarlet'

Choisya

For a striking but easygoing border shrub, this is the one to choose. The glossy leaves look good all year and clusters of white scented flowers appear from mid spring onwards.

Expert's Selection

1 *C.* 'Aztec Pearl'♀
Exceptionally attractive with pink flushed buds turning to opening white almond-scented flowers.
❀ White • Late spring–autumn
h.&s. 2m (7ft)

2 *C. ternata* 'Sundance'
Though it rarely flowers it gives year-round colour, with the yellow leaves at their brightest in full sun.
Yellow-green • Year-round
h.&s. 1.8m (6ft)

3 *C. ternata*♀
Also known as Mexican orange blossom after the clusters of citrus-scented white flowers.
❀ White • Late spring–autumn
⊘ Dark green • *h.&s.* 3m (10ft)

C. ternata

With shiny evergreen foliage and scented white flowers, choisya makes a wonderful shrub to grow against a wall.

Keeping the cold at bay
Choisyas are usually hardy and generally easy to grow. Protect the plant from frost by growing it against a south or west-facing wall. If frost damage does occur, simply cut off any affected branches in spring, and the plant should recover fully.

Encourage a second flowering in late summer or early autumn by cutting back flowering stems after the first crop has faded. Prune in spring for a neat plant.

The Essentials

Site demands Any well-drained soil in a sunny, sheltered position.
Planting practice Plant in spring.
Flowering time From mid spring.
Pests and diseases Trouble free.
Bonus point A great backdrop for smaller shrubs and flowers.

STAR PERFORMER
C. 'Aztec Pearl'♀ **The exquisite white flowers and narrow dark leaves give an elegant, oriental effect.**

Clematis

Few plants are more undemanding than these deservedly popular climbers. With the right choice of variety and careful planting, they will establish easily, grow quickly and surprise with almost instant interest. They require minimal effort, but will reward you with many years of pleasure.

There are hundreds of types of clematis. Some are scented, some have huge wide flowers and others smallish bells. Colours range from bright whites to rich, silky purple-blues and reds, and some have spectacular silvery seed heads. Large-flowered clematis are excellent subjects for walls, fences, trellises, arches, pergolas and bowers, where the full impact of their showy blooms can be appreciated. Most are trouble free – and the ones chosen here are among the easiest of all to grow and look after.

Planting for success

When planting a clematis, make sure that the base of the stem is 15cm (6in) below the soil surface. This encourages more shoots to emerge from below ground, especially if the top growth is damaged, and reduces the effect of an attack of clematis wilt.

Young plants, especially in their first summer, should be kept well watered. If a clematis is allowed to dry out too much, it will gradually die off. A thick mulch after watering helps keep moisture locked in the ground. In addition to keeping the roots moist, treat plants with a high potash fertiliser, such as a specific rose feed, each spring. A weekly watering with a tomato feed from late spring to late summer will also help.

Supporting a clematis

When growing a clematis up a wall or fence, provide it with strong horizontal wires for the plant to cling on to. If growing one up a post onto a pergola, keep tying it in as you spiral the growth around and up. And when growing one into a tree, train it up a cane angled towards the main trunk, then tie it in to the lowest growth. Once it gets in amongst the branches, the clematis can look after itself, although it will appreciate some pruning (see right).

Clematis may also be grown through border shrubs, or left to intertwine with other climbers, such as **wisteria**, **honeysuckle** and **climbing roses**, provided that they have a moist root run. Stronger-growing clematis will hide eyesores. Herbaceous and rockery varieties can be left to scramble across banks and low obstacles.

Simple to prune

Regular pruning is not necessary, although clematis do eventually become untidy or overgrown and need cutting back. How you do this depends on when they flower. (see **Pruning**, right).

Combating clematis wilt

Young, large-flowered plants may be attacked by clematis wilt, often through lack of water. Late-flowering types are less at risk. If the problem strikes, cut back the stem, into the healthy growth, removing all diseased tissue. Then, once a month, water with a fungicide around the plant. Also feed the plant regularly to help encourage new growth.

C. montana 'Mayleen'

C. 'Général Sikorski'

Early flowers

1 *C. montana* var. *rubens* **'Mayleen'** Planted under a tree, in a couple of years it will be half-way up. The star-shaped flowers open early, filling the air with a rich scent of vanilla and marzipan.
✿ **Pink • Late spring**
h. **8m (26ft)** *s.* **4m (13ft)**

2 *C. armandii*
A distinctive evergreen with long, thin pointy leaves, and a prolific show of creamy white flowers, with a gentle whiff of vanilla.
❀ **Creamy white • Early spring**
h. **9m (30ft)** *s.* **4.5m (15ft)**

Mid-season flowers

1 *C.* 'Henryi' ♀
Stunning, large, 20cm (8in) wide, star-shaped flowers have chocolate brown anthers in the middle.
❀ **White • Early–late summer**
h. **3m (10ft)** *s.* **1m (3ft)**

2 *C.* 'Général Sikorski' ♀
Abundant, large blue flowers grow vigorously on this mid-height plant.
✿ **Mauvish blue • Early–late summer**
h. **3m (10ft)** *s.* **1m (3ft)**

TAKE A FRESH LOOK

C. tubulosa **'Wyevale'** ♀ is a non-climber. It can reach a height of 1.2m (4ft), and will easily scramble over neighbouring border plants, or grow up a wigwam of canes.

Late flowers

1 C. 'Gipsy Queen' ♀
This vigorous late-flowering variety, at its best in August, tolerates cold winds and exposed situations.
✿ **Violet-purple • Late summer–early autumn • *h.* 4m (13ft) *s.* 2m (7ft)**

2 C. 'Madame Julia Correvon' ♀
An exceptionally lovely clematis, with a mass of rich coloured flowers, 6cm (2½in) wide; it grows 2–3m (7–10ft) in a season.
✿ **Wine red • Midsummer–early autumn • *h.* 6m (20ft) *s.* 3m (10ft)**

3 C. 'Paul Farges'
Sometimes known as 'Summer Snow', it will sprint to full height, up a wall or tree, in a season.
✿ **Creamy white • Midsummer–mid autumn • *h.* 6m (20ft) *s.* 3m (10ft)**

4 C. 'Bill MacKenzie' ♀
Dangling, lantern-shaped blooms are spectacular in late summer and early autumn. The flowers are followed by beautiful, spidery, silvery seed heads.
✿ **Yellow • Midsummer–late autumn *h.* 6m (20ft) *s.* 3m (10ft)**

C. 'Madame Julia Correvon'

C. 'Paul Farges'

STAR PERFORMER

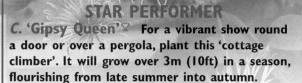

C. 'Gipsy Queen' ♀ **For a vibrant show round a door or over a pergola, plant this 'cottage climber'. It will grow over 3m (10ft) in a season, flourishing from late summer into autumn.**

The Essentials

Site demands Place in rich, moist, but free-draining soil. Roots and the base of stems need shade; the heads require plenty of sun.
Planting practice Spring is the best time to plant clematis. Fix supports first, then plant deep to encourage a large rootball that can support rapid top growth. Feed and water well.
Flowering time From early spring to late autumn, depending on type. Choose a selection, so that you have a clematis in flower from February to November.

Pruning Remove overgrown or untidy growth; if grown into a tree, it will definitely need pruning. *Early flowerers* should be cut back hard after flowering, to encourage new flowering stems. *Mid-season flowerers* should be pruned in February or March: a gentle trim gives flowers high up the stems; pruning lower down gives flowers from head height upwards. *Late flowerers* should be pruned in February or March, to about 30cm (1ft) above the ground.
Pests and diseases Clematis wilt can be a problem, while large, late-flowerers may suffer from mildew.
Bonus point Excellent for hiding an ugly fence, wall or shed.

Cornus

Dogwood is a hardy shrub that provides terrific colour in the garden all year round. Its summer flowers are yellowy green surrounded by large petal-like bracts, its autumn foliage comes in myriad fiery hues and its naked winter stems are often brilliantly colourful.

Planting dogwood is an easy way to provide more all-round colour in the garden. The stem colour ranges from coral pink to dark red, while varieties such as **'White Gold'** or **'Flaviramea'** have yellowy green stems.

Some varieties of cornus are grown as large trees and produce pretty summer flowers and brightly coloured fruits. However, these are generally less care free than the varieties listed here, which are grown primarily for their bright winter stems. Some, such as **'Sibirica Variegata'**, also develop striking autumn foliage.

Dogwoods are remarkably easy to grow in sun or shade, although the flowering varieties are best grown on neutral to acid soil. They will tolerate wet ground, too, and are quite happy growing around the edges of a pond.

Pruning needs
Dogwoods grown for their winter stems should be pruned hard each spring. Do not prune the first year after planting, but the following spring chop all stems back to the ground. Thereafter, each spring cut back to two buds from the previous year's growth. Only prune flowering and variegated varieties if you want to restrict their size.

Some cornus produce suckers that can be used for propagation. Dig them up and replant in winter.

TAKE A FRESH LOOK

C. sanguinea **'Midwinter Fire'** comes into its own in winter. Its naked yellow shoots tipped with orange and red bring a warm flicker to the bare, chilly garden. Plant it in a group for maximum impact.

STAR PERFORMER
C. alba **'Sibirica Variegata'** **Creamy variegated foliage sets off clusters of small green fruits in autumn then falls to reveal dramatic deep red stems in winter.**

Expert's Selection

1 *C. alba* **'Sibirica Variegata'**
Variegated leaves turn crimson. The non-variegated 'Sibirica' ♀ (syn. 'Westonbirt') has coral-pink stems.
⊘ **Crimson • Autumn; deep red stems • Winter • h.&s. 1.5m (5ft)**

2 *C. stolonifera* **'White Gold'** Its bright green stems are yellow when young.
⊘ **Variegated cream and green Spring–summer • h.&s. 1.5m (5ft)**

3 *C. stolonifera* **'Flaviramea'** ♀ Bright yellow-green stems are striking in winter.
⊘ **Red or orange • Autumn h.&s. 2.5m (8ft)**

4 *C. alba* **'Spaethii'** ♀
A colourful variety, with leaves edged with gold, black autumn berries and deep red winter stems.
❧ **Black • Autumn** ⊘ **Red stems Winter • h.&s. 1.5m (5ft)**

5 *C. stolonifera* **'Kelsey'**
This low-growing variety is sometimes called 'Kelseyi Dwarf'.
⊘ **Yellow-green shoots with red tips Autumn • h.&s. 75cm (2½ft)**

6 *C. alba* **'Bailhalo'**
Red winter stems and variegated spring and summer foliage make this good value for colour.
⊘ **Red • Autumn; red stems • Winter h.&s. 1.5m (5ft)**

The Essentials

Site demands Any garden soil, in full sun or light shade.
Planting practice Plant in autumn or spring.
Pruning needs Prune hard in spring for the best winter display of coloured stems (see above).
Pests and diseases Trouble free.
Bonus point Vibrant stem colour brightens up any winter garden. Many have bright autumn leaves.

Corylus

Hazels are sturdy small trees and shrubs grown for their delicate catkins – one of the first harbingers of spring – and their edible nuts, which are known as cobnuts or filberts.

These nut trees can also be grown as an attractive ornamental shrub, especially 'Aurea' and 'Purpurea', the yellow-leaved and purple-leaved forms, while 'Contorta', with its unusual twisted branches, makes a fascinating specimen tree for a container, courtyard or lawn.

Hazel will grow on almost any soil, and being woodland plants by nature they tolerate light shade, although they produce heavier crops of nuts in an open, sunny position.

STAR PERFORMER

C. avellana 'Aurea' This is one of the prettiest of the hazels. Its pale yellow leaves shade into green as summer comes to an end.

Expert's Selection

1 C. avellana 'Aurea'
An attractive variety with woolly catkins and cobnuts if pollination has been good. 'Heterophylla' grows 5m (16ft) tall, with golden autumn leaves and yellow catkins.
◁ **Cobnuts • Autumn**
h. **3m (10ft)** *s.* **2.5m (8ft)**

2 C. maxima 'Purpurea'♀
Plant this for a dramatic spring display of catkins and purple leaves.
✿ **Purple catkins • Late winter–early spring** ⊘ **Purple • h.&s. 6m (20ft)**

3 C. maxima
Grow the Kentish cob as a multi-stemmed shrub for a crop of nuts.
◁ **Filberts • Autumn • h.&s. 6m (20ft)**

4 C. avellana 'Contorta'♀
Twisted corkscrew stems look very striking when bare in winter.
✿ **Yellow catkins • Late winter–early spring • h.&s. 3m (10ft)**

The Essentials

Site demands Any soil in full sun or light shade.
Planting practice Plant a young specimen in late summer.
Pruning needs For best nut crop prune to a bush in late winter. Trim to control growth in winter.
Pests and diseases Usually trouble free, but honey fungus may occur.
Bonus point Easy to grow, with attractive catkins and edible nuts.

Cotoneaster

These easy-to-grow versatile shrubs produce brilliantly coloured berries and rich autumn leaves.

This attractive shrub comes in so many forms it can be grown almost anywhere in the garden – evergreens for hedging and screening, and low-growing creepers for ground cover, or garden walls.

Expert's Selection

1 C. salicifolius 'Gnom'
A low evergreen mound with arching shoots. C. salicifolius is also known as C. floccosus of gardens.
❀ **White • Summer** ◁ **Red • Autumn**
h. **30cm (1ft)** *s.* **up to 2m (7ft)**

2 C. x suecicus 'Coral Beauty' Grow this evergreen as ground cover or up a wall.
❀ **White • Summer** ◁ **Orange Autumn • h. 60cm (2ft) s. 1.5m (5ft)**

3 C. franchetii
Flowers and berries make this semi-evergreen an attractive hedge.
❀ **Pinkish white** ◁ **Orange-red Midsummer–autumn h.&s. 2.7m (9ft)**

4 C. adpressus♀
Prostrate deciduous shrub with scarlet autumn leaves.
❀ **Pinkish white • Summer** ◁ **Red Autumn • h. 30cm (1ft) s. 1.5m (5ft)**

5 C. horizontalis♀
The leaves of the deciduous 'fishbone' cotoneaster turn red in autumn. It is ideal for hiding walls.
❀ **Pinkish white • Late spring** ◁ **Red Autumn • h. 1m (3ft) s. 1.5m (5ft)**

STAR PERFORMER

C. salicifolius 'Gnom' White flowers are followed by bright red berries on this dense, prostrate evergreen.

6 C. divaricatus
A dense rounded deciduous shrub.
❀ **Pinkish white • Summer** ◁ **Red Autumn • h. 2.5m (8ft) s. 3m (10ft)**

7 C. damerii♀
A vigorous prostrate evergreen.
❀ **White • Early summer** ◁ **Red Autumn • h. 20cm (8in) s. 2m (7ft)**

The Essentials

Site demands Most dryish soils.
Planting Spring or autumn.
Pruning needs None.
Pests and diseases Mostly trouble free, but C. horizontalis may suffer from woolly aphids.
Bonus point Adds bright autumn colour, even to a small garden.

Cytisus

Broom is very good value, flowering profusely in late spring, and often into early summer. It is undemanding, will grow almost anywhere, and there is a size to suit every garden, from low prostrate shrubs to small trees.

1 C. x praecox
Great sheets of pale yellow flowers on arching branches. Plant several for a gorgeous massed display.
✿ Pale yellow • Late spring
h. 1.2m (4ft) s. 1m (3ft)

2 C. 'Lena'♥
An upright, compact bush with stunning spring colour and profuse yellow and red flowers.
✿ Yellow and red • Late spring
h. 1.8m (6ft) s. 1.2m (4ft)

3 C. 'Cottage'
A low-growing variety for a small garden or rockery.
✿ Creamy yellow • Late spring
h.&s. 40cm (16in)

4 C. x kewensis♥
A low, spreading shrub, it produces masses of pale sulphur-yellow blooms.
✿ Pale yellow
Late spring
h. 30cm (1ft)
s. 1m (3ft)

5 C. battandieri♥
Plant this tall, sun-loving Moroccan broom by a south-facing wall for its pineapple-scented, golden flowers and silvery leaves.
✿ Golden yellow • Late spring–early summer • h.&s. 4m (13ft)

6 C. 'Hollandia'♥
Tall and spreading, it looks striking in any garden. In late spring its arching branches are heavy with beautiful cerise and cream flowers.
✿ Cerise and cream • Late spring
h.&s. 2.5m (8ft)

C. battandieri

C. 'Hollandia'

A graceful, slender shrub, the broom's brilliantly coloured flowers – yellow, cream, orange or red – appear in late spring and early summer. This is a very easy-going plant which will thrive in full sun in almost any well-drained soil. There are low-growing and prostrate versions for the rockery, shrubs for the border and large specimens for display. Plant the low-growing C. × kewensis in the rockery or to cover a low-lying bank, and for a stunning spring display of abundant pale yellow flowers, plant a long border with C. × praecox. For a bold display, grow the slightly more tender C. battandieri, with its lovely scent, against a south-facing wall. 'Hollandia' is also impressive in a larger garden.

Pruning
Take the time to prune brooms regularly to prevent the plants becoming too leggy. Brooms are rather short-lived, lasting only about ten years. They are weakened by seed production, so to extend their life, cut back immediately after flowering to prevent seeding.

STAR PERFORMER
C. x praecox Plant in the border to bring cheer in spring with its profusion of delightful yellow flowers.

Site demands A sunny site with any well-drained, not too rich soil.
Planting practice Plant in autumn or spring.
Flowering time Late spring and early summer.
Pruning needs Prune as soon as flowering finishes.
Pests and diseases Trouble free.
Bonus point Will flourish, even in the very poorest of soils.

Deutzia

Native to China and the Himalayas, this elegant, flowering shrub looks charming in any garden. Extravagant quantities of starry flowers in sugar pastel shades make a fabulous display in early summer.

Expert's Selection

1 *D. x hybrida* 'Magicien'
The star-shaped flowers grow in clusters 5–8cm (2–3in) across. 'Mont Rose'♀ has deep pink blooms on arching stems.
✿ **Mauve-pink • Early summer**
h.&s. 1.8m (6ft)

2 *D. x elegantissima* 'Rosealind'♀ Scented, carmine-tipped, star-shaped flowers cover arching branches in early summer.
✿ **White and carmine**
Early summer • *h.&s.* 1.2m (4ft)

3 *D. compacta* 'Lavender Time' Suitable for a small bed or border, with cup-like, lilac blooms.
✿ **Lilac, turning to lavender**
Early summer • *h.&s.* 1.5m (5ft)

4 *D. x magnifica*
An elegant arching shrub with double white flowers.
✿ **White • Early summer**
h.&s. 2.5m (8ft)

5 *D. x rosea*
Its bell-shaped rose-pink flowers grow in rounded clusters.
✿ **Rose-pink • Early summer**
h.&s. 1m (3ft)

6 *D. scabra* 'Plena'
Double white flowers are flushed with rosy purple on the outside.
✿ **White with purple • Early summer**
h. 3m (10ft) *s.* 1.8m (6ft)

Deutzia is a charming, hardy shrub, which produces beautiful clusters of pinky purple or white, star-shaped or cup-shaped flowers in early summer. The plants have an upright, sometimes arching habit, and look especially effective when planted beside evergreens. Most are easy to grow, but new shoots may sometimes be damaged by frost.

Plant deutzias in full sun or partial shade, avoiding north facing or cold, windy positions. Mulch with manure or compost in spring. Flowering will be prolonged if there is shade from the sun in the heat of the day.

Plants to suit all plots
A number of deutzias are suitable for the smaller garden, or for growing in containers. *D. x rosea*, with its attractive, bell-shaped flowers, is a compact variety, ideal for a small bed or border. The taller varieties, with elegant, arching branches, make a good focus of attention in the larger garden. Good examples are *D. x magnifica*, with double white flowers, and another white, 'Plena', which will eventually reach 3m (10ft).

D. elegantissima 'Rosealind'

Easy care
This shrub needs little attention, but to encourage new growth, you should prune after flowering, cutting back the old flowering stems down to a strong new shoot. The only problem you are likely to encounter with pests is from snails, which will sometimes munch at the young shoots.

The Essentials

Site demands Any well-drained soil in full sun or partial shade, avoiding exposed north-facing sites.
Planting practice Plant from mid autumn to early spring.
Flowering time Early summer.
Pruning needs After flowering, cut flowered shoots hard back.
Pests and diseases Usually trouble free, but sometimes snails eat the new shoots.
Bonus point Some, like *D. scabra* and *D. compacta*, are scented.

TAKE A FRESH LOOK

D. crenata var. *nakaiana* 'Nikko' is a dwarf deutzia, 1m (3ft) tall, which is ideal for ground cover. With its brilliant white flowers, 'Nikko' also looks very effective in a pot or cascading over a wall.

STAR PERFORMER
D. x hybrida 'Magicien' Plant for display in a sunny, sheltered spot, where the beautiful star-shaped flowers will create a sensation.

Elaeagnus

An attractive shrub that will thrive just about anywhere, including the seaside and in areas of industrial pollution, elaeagnus makes excellent hedges and windbreaks.

Expert's Selection

1 *E.* x *ebbingei* 'Coastal Gold' A variegated evergreen, it is hardy enough for coastal sites.
⌀ **Greeny gold • h.&s. 2.5m (8ft)**

2 *E.* x *ebbingei* 'Gilt Edge'♀
Its glossy, dark green, evergreen leaves have a broad gold edging. 'Limelight' is similar, but with a gold blotch in the centre of its leaves.
⌀ **Green and gold • h.&s. 3m (10ft)**

3 *E. angustifolia*
A deciduous variety, with narrow, silvery leaves and orange fruit.
⌀ **Silvery green** ⁌ **Orange • Autumn h.&s. 3m (10ft)**

4 *E. pungens* 'Goldrim'
The variegated, dark green leaves have striking gold margins.
⌀ **Green and gold • h.&s. 3m (10ft)**

The Essentials

Site demands Any fertile, well-drained soil, except shallow chalk, preferably in full sun.
Planting practice Plant evergreens in spring or early autumn; *E. angustifolia* in autumn.
Pruning needs Remove plain green shoots on variegated plants.
Pests and diseases Trouble free.
Bonus point Although small and insignificant, flowers are scented.

An excellent screening plant, particularly suited to coastal sites, elaeagnus is one of the easiest and most care free of all shrubs. It needs no special care or pruning, and is immune to pests and diseases. The glossy foliage is very attractive, especially on the variegated varieties such as *E. pungens* 'Goldrim' and *E.* × *ebbingei* 'Gilt Edge'.

STAR PERFORMER
E. x *ebbingei* 'Coastal Gold'
The perfect choice for a seaside garden, coping well with salt-laden winds and spray, it has shiny greeny gold leaves.

Escallonia

Grow this handsome, yet hardy shrub for year-round interest. It bears fine, dark winter leaves and brilliant flowers in summer.

Escallonia is both tough and beautiful and, as it can tolerate salty spray and winds, is excellent in coastal gardens. It is often used in seaside gardens for hedging and windbreaks. It prefers a sunny site, and in cold areas is best planted against a south-facing wall for protection.

STAR PERFORMER
E. 'Apple Blossom'♀ **Give this a prominent sunny site in the border or grow as a hedge to enjoy the summer show of pink and white flowers.**

Expert's Selection

1 *E.* 'Apple Blossom'♀
Has shiny, evergreen leaves and stunning, cup-shaped flowers.
✿ **Pink and white • Summer**
⌀ **Dark green • h.&s. 1.5m (5ft)**

2 *E.* 'Red Elf'
Its lovely, crimson flowers contrast strongly with the dark leaves.
✿ **Crimson • Summer**
⌀ **Dark green • h.&s. 2m (7ft)**

3 *E.* 'C. F. Ball'
Is especially tolerant of sea-spray.
✿ **Crimson • Summer**
⌀ **Dark green • h.&s. 3m (10ft)**

4 *E.* 'Silver Anniversary'
The silvery, variegated foliage is edged with cream.
✿ **Pink • Summer**
⌀ **Silvery green • h.&s. 1.8m (6ft)**

5 *E. rubra* 'Woodside'
Sized for a rockery or small bed.
✿ **Crimson • Summer**
⌀ **Dark green • h.&s. 50cm (20in)**

The Essentials

Site demands Any well-drained soil, in sun or shade. In very cold areas grow against a wall.
Planting practice Plant in spring; 30cm (1ft) between hedging plants.
Flowering time Summer.
Pruning needs Prune to keep in shape, if needed, after flowering.
Pests and diseases Trouble free.
Bonus point A long flowering period, right through summer.

E. 'Red Elf'

Euonymus

Spindle trees are wonderfully versatile shrubs, and are available as dwarf, tall, spreading or climbing varieties. Choose deciduous varieties for their colourful fruit and decorative autumn foliage, and use evergreens to create dense hedges or ground cover.

Expert's Selection

1 *E. fortunei* 'Blondy'
This dwarf evergreen suits patios and rockeries, as does the dark green, ground-hugging 'Kewensis'.
⌀ **Green, gold and white**
h.&s. **45cm (1½ft)**

2 *E. fortunei* 'Canadale Gold' A small bush, its has gold-edged leaves. The leaves of 'Emerald Gaiety'♀ have a cream edging, which goes bronze in winter.
⌀ **Dark green and gold**
h. **45cm (1½ft)** *s.* **60cm (2ft)**

3 *E. fortunei* 'Emerald 'n' Gold'♀ Its dazzling foliage is pinkish in winter. Similarly, the dark green 'Coloratus' turn purple-red.
⌀ **Green and gold; pinkish in winter**
h. **3m (10ft)** *s.* **2m (7ft)**

4 *E. europaeus* 'Red Cascade'♀ Gives a glorious multicoloured autumn show.
⌀ **Greeny-red** ✷✷ **Pink, orange Autumn** • *h.&s.* **5m (15ft)**

5 *E. alatus*♀
Is ablaze with reds and purples in autumn. Stems bear corky 'wings'.
⌀ **Greeny-red** ✷ **Reddish purple Autumn** • *h.&s.* **2.5m (8ft)**

6 *E. japonicus* 'Ovatus Aureus'♀ An upright, compact evergreen, ideal for a small space.
⌀⌀ **Green, gold** • *h.&s.* **1.5m (5ft)**

The Essentials

Site demands Any well-drained soil, in sun or light shade. You can grow evergreens in full shade, if it is not too dense.
Planting practice Plant in autumn or spring. For hedges, plant 45–60cm (1½–2ft) apart.
Pruning Prune hedging, and to restrict growth or maintain the shape. Cut out any green shoots that appear on variegated varieties.
Pests and diseases Usually trouble free, but may sometimes be infested by blackfly or caterpillars.
Bonus point Bring attractive, interesting foliage to your garden.

Euonymus will grow almost anywhere, and once it is established, it needs very little looking after. Most species are hardy, though the evergreens are more successful when they are given shelter from cold winds.

Autumnal show
Deciduous varieties such as *E. alatus* and 'Red Cascade' are prized for their decorative foliage and autumn fruits. The four-lobed pink or red open to reveal orange or red seeds hanging from threads. Autumn leaves come in many colours, from yellow to deep red, fiery red or purple.

The evergreens can be grown as freestanding shrubs, climbers or hedges, while compact varieties, such as 'Ovatus Aureus' are ideal for rockeries or the front of the border. 'Kewensis', a prostrate variety, is particularly good for edging, or for as a ground-cover plant.

STAR PERFORMER
E. fortunei 'Blondy' **The variegated good looks of this dwarf variety will brighten a patio or rockery.**

E. europaeus 'Red Cascade'

E. fortunei 'Emerald 'n' Gold'

E. alatus

Exochorda

Plant this elegant shrub in an open, sunny position for its dazzling display of white spring flowers, which resemble wild roses.

As its glorious display of flowers lasts only about a week, exochorda is best grown in a mixed border, with a succession of flowering shrubs. An all white and green colour scheme really suits this shrub. Generally hardy and tolerant of many soils, avoid planting *E. racemosa* on chalky soil as it will not thrive.

STAR PERFORMER

E. x *macrantha* 'The Bride'♀ **Choose a sunny spot and wait for May, when it will be completely smothered in white flowers.**

The Essentials

Site demands Well-drained soil, in full sun or very light shade.
Planting practice Plant out during autumn.
Flowering time Late spring.
Pruning needs Prune lightly after flowering if necessary.
Pests and diseases Trouble free.
Bonus point Pure white flowers are invaluable in a mixed border.

Expert's Selection

1 *E.* x *macrantha* **'The Bride'**♀ This slow-growing plant forms a mound of weeping branches, thickly covered with showy white flowers in spring.
✿ White • Late spring
h.&s. 2m (7ft)

2 *E. racemosa*
An upright, wide-spreading shrub which makes a good specimen plant provided the soil is not chalky. It has snow-white flowers.
✿ White • Late spring
h.&s. 3m (10ft)

3 *E. giraldii* var. *wilsonii*
A tall handsome shrub which produces the largest flowers – 5cm (2in) across – in large clusters on pink stalks.
✿ White • Late spring
h.&s. 3m (10ft)

E. racemosa

Forsythia

The brilliant yellow flowers of forsythia herald the spring. Hardy and easily grown, it includes large and small varieties for hedging and training up a wall.

Expert's Selection

1 *F.* **'Fiesta'**
Bright yellow flowers are followed by beautiful variegated leaves.
✿ Yellow • Early spring
⊘ Greeny gold • Late spring
h.&s. 1.8m (6ft)

2 *F.* x *intermedia* **'Lynwood'**♀ Often used for hedging, with upright arching stems.
✿ Yellow • Early spring
⊘ Dark green • Late spring
h.&s. 3m (10ft)

3 *F.* **'Golden Times'**
Plant this as a specimen shrub, its golden flowers are followed by striking golden leaves.
✿ Yellow • Early spring
⊘ Golden yellow • Late spring
h.&s. 1.8m (6ft)

F. x *intermedia* **'Lynwood'**

STAR PERFORMER

F. **'Fiesta'** **The yellow flowers are worth waiting for, but so too are the bright variegated leaves in shades of green and gold.**

With vivid flowers and foliage, forsythia is superb as a specimen shrub, as hedging, or as wall or trellis cover.

Forsythias benefit from some care, or they may grow long and straggly with a bare base and weak flowerings. Prune flowered shoots to within two buds of old wood. Remove one or two old main stems at the base. After planting, shorten the stems of hedging plants by a third. When shoots are 15cm (6in) long, pinch back for bushy growth.

The Essentials

Site demands Well-drained soil in full sun or partial shade.
Planting practice For hedging plant 60cm (2ft) apart.
Flowering time Early spring.
Pruning needs Once established, prune each year after flowering.
Pests and diseases Birds may attack the flower buds.
Bonus point Cutting back hard limits size, without causing damage.

Fuchsia

Their delicate blooms make fuchsias one of the most popular of the flowering shrubs. The two-tone flowers look stunning on specimen shrubs, and they work very well in pots and hanging baskets. There is a wide variation in habit and hardiness: all the plants selected here are fully hardy.

Expert's Selection

1 *F.* **'Margaret'** ♀
Abundant flowers have crimson sepals and bluish purple petals streaked with scarlet.
✿✿ **Crimson and bluish purple**
Summer–autumn
h. 1.2m (4ft) *s.* 75cm (2½ft)

2 *F.* **'Riccartonii'** ♀
Tall and robust it bears dark crimson sepals and purple petals.
✿✿ **Dark crimson and purple**
Summer–autumn
h. 2m (7ft) *s.* 1.2m (4ft)

3 *F.* **'Lena'** ♀
A compact, arching plant suitable for a small garden. The flowers have pale pink sepals and purple petals.
✿✿ **Pale pink and purple**
Summer–autumn • *h.&s.* 60cm (2ft)

4 *F.* **'Mrs Popple'** ♀
Vigorous, with vibrant red blooms and a spreading, trailing habit, it blooms longer than the other hardy varieties.
✿✿ **Scarlet and purple**
Summer–autumn • *h.&s.* 1.2m (4ft)

5 *F. magellanica*
A bushy shrub and the hardiest of all the fuchsias, which in mild areas can reach 3m (10ft). It makes a good hedge.
✿✿ **Crimson and purple**
Summer–autumn
h.&s. 1.2m (4ft)

6 *F.* **'Lady Thumb'** ♀
A lighter fuchsia for a more pastel colour scheme, it has semi-double flowers with white petals, which are veined with pink and brighter pinky purple sepals.
✿✿ **White and pink**
Summer–autumn
h. 60cm (2ft) *s.* 40cm (16in)

F. 'Lena'

F. 'Mrs Popple'

STAR PERFORMER
F. **'Margaret'** ♀ **Give this fuchsia a sunny position and it will produce stunning flowers in abundance all summer and into mid autumn.**

The Essentials

Site demands Plant in any soil in full sun or partial shade.
Planting practice Plant from mid spring onwards.
Flowering time Early summer to early autumn.
Pruning needs Deadhead regularly for longer flowering.
Pests and diseases Fuchsias may suffer red spider mite, greenfly, rust and bud drop.
Bonus point Many fuchsias attract bees and other insects.

Fuchsias are prized for their beautiful flowers, ease of care and long flowering season. The flowers can be single, double or semi-double, in colours from deep purple to white. Four waxy petals open out below the curved back sepals to form a bell, often in a contrasting colour to the sepals.

Caring for fuchsias
Hardy fuchsias will survive outdoors all year if planted in well-drained soil in a sheltered site. In colder areas, growth above ground may be killed by frost, but new growth will sprout from the base in spring. Cut top growth in autumn to 30cm (1ft) above ground and apply a mulch of bark chips, bracken or straw.

If grown as a hedge, pinch out the tips of young plants to encourage bushy growth. Prune down to healthy buds lower down. Thicken straggly hedging by cutting back in spring.

Garrya

Silk tassel bushes earn their keep with spectacular male catkins, which appear at the start of the year. They grow quickly, are easy going, and will flourish in sun or shade.

Expert's Selection

1 *G. elliptica* 'James Roof' ♀
Showy catkins are 35cm (14in) long, over twice the length of those on its parent plant, *G. elliptica*.
✿ Silver-green catkins • Winter–early spring • *h.&s.* 2.5m (8ft)

2 *G. x issaquahensis* 'Glasnevin Wine' Wine-red catkins turn lime-green in spring.
✿✿ Red, then green catkins Winter–early spring *h.&s.* 2.5m (8ft)

3 *G. x issaquahensis* 'Pat Ballard' Has spectacular, 20cm (8in) long, mauve catkins.
✿ Mauve catkins • Winter–early spring • *h.&s.* 2.5m (8ft)

4 *G. elliptica* 'Evie' Wavy-edged leaves and 30cm (1ft) long catkins add interest.
✿ Grey-green catkins • Winter–early spring • *h.&s.* 2.5m (8ft)

This shrub is a star – easy to grow, with glossy evergreen foliage and dramatic catkins. 'James Roof' has the longest, though 'Pat Ballard' has the most dramatically coloured – mauve.

Garrya bushes may be male or female. All those listed here are male plants, because they are the most easily available, and also have the showiest catkins.

The Essentials

Site demands Any well-drained, fertile soil, in shade, or, for the best catkins, in full sun. Place by wall for shelter in windy, northerly gardens.
Planting practice Plant in autumn or spring.
Flowering time Winter to early spring.
Pruning needs Just remove dead wood, and trim after flowering.
Pests and diseases Trouble free.
Bonus point Thrive even in city pollution and salty, seaside air.

Genista

Broom actually thrives in poor soil, like that on the heaths and moors where it grows naturally. Plant in full sun, and it will reward you with masses of golden yellow flowers.

Expert's Selection

1 *G. lydia* ♀
A spreading shrub with arching stems and clusters of flowers.
✿ Golden yellow • Late spring–early summer • *h.&s.* 60cm (2ft)

2 *G. pilosa* 'Vancouver Gold' Ideal for a rockery, this dwarf variety forms a neat mound.
✿ Golden yellow • Early summer *h.&s.* 45cm (1½ft)

G. hispanica

3 *G. hispanica*
Good as ground cover, the spiny Spanish gorse is especially tolerant of dry, hot sites and poor soil.
✿ Golden yellow • Early summer *h.* 60cm (2ft) *s.* 1m (3ft)

4 *G. tinctoria*
The flowers of 'dyer's greenweed' make a golden yellow dye. The shrub grows erect or prostrate.
✿ Golden yellow • Summer *h.* 30cm–2m (1–7ft) *s.* 45cm–1m (1½–3ft)

Brooms make attractive shrubs, with their wiry stems and masses of golden yellow flowers. They are stars in difficult spots, because they actually flower best in poor soils.

Low-growing varieties such as *G. lydia* can be planted to cascade over a wall or down a bank, while, *G. tinctoria*, when prostrate, will form a low-growing mat, making it ideal in a rockery or to fill gaps in a border.

The Essentials

Site demands Best in a light sandy soil in full sun.
Planting practice Plant in early autumn.
Flowering time Early summer.
Pruning demands Prune lightly in late winter; only trim new wood.
Pests and diseases Trouble free.
Bonus point Bright colour for difficult gardens.

Hebe

Not all hebes are hardy, but these selections are all frost-resistant, and flower over a long season. They range in habit from low ground cover to bushy border varieties.

Expert's Selection

1 *H. pimeleoides* **'Quicksilver'**♀ Silvery leaves set off a mass of violet flowers.
✿ Violet • Mid–late summer ⊘ Silver
h. 60cm (2ft) *s.* 1m (3ft)

2 *H.* **'Autumn Glory'**
This medium-sized bush produces heavenly violet-blue flowers.
✿ Violet-blue • Summer–late autumn
h. 60cm (2ft) *s.* 75cm (2½ft)

3 *H.* **'Nicola's Blush'**
Enjoy two waves of flowers a year.
✿ Pink, fading to white • Spring–midsummer and autumn–winter
h.&s. 75cm (2½ft)

4 *H. cupressoides* **'Boughton Dome'**♀ Rarely flowers, but forms a neat, green dome, packed with scale-like leaves.
⊘ Green • *h.* 60cm (2ft) *s.* 1m (3ft)

5 *H.* **'Red Edge'**♀
The delicate flowers are a subtle violet; the leaves have a red edge.
✿ Pale violet • Summer
⊘ Grey-green with red edge
h.&s. 60cm (2ft)

6 *H.* **'Youngii'**
Also called 'Carl Teschner', its flowers fade as summer wanes.
✿ Violet, fading to white • Summer
h. 20cm (8in) *s.* 60cm (2ft)

7 *H.* **'Wingletye'**
A lilac, low-growing variety.
✿ Lilac • Summer
h. 20cm (8in) *s.* 30cm (1ft)

TAKE A FRESH LOOK

H. ochracea **'James Stirling'**♀ 'Whipcord' hebes, like this one, look similar to cypresses. Its flat top is covered with white flowers in spring.

8 *H. pinguifolia* **'Pagei'**♀
This hardy, prostrate variety makes excellent ground cover.
❀ White • Mid–late spring ⊘ Grey
h. 20cm (8in) *s.* 60cm (2ft)

The Essentials

Site demands Plant in any well-drained soil, preferably in full sun.
Planting practice Plant in autumn or spring.
Flowering time From spring to autumn, depending on variety.
Pruning needs Cut back large or leggy plants in spring.
Pests and diseases Look out for downy mildew in damp autumns.
Bonus point Tolerant of salt-laden winds, they are perfect for providing easy seaside colour.

Hebes are versatile, evergreen shrubs, noted for their stunning flower displays. Many stay in bloom all summer and well into autumn. Mix the pinks, whites and purples of 'Nicola's Blush', 'Pagei' and 'Quicksilver', for a pretty, layered pastel display.

Some of the low-growing hebes, such as 'Youngii' and 'Wingletye', make good ground cover or rockery plants. Another compact variety is 'Boughton Dome', which forms a rounded dome of bright green.

Hardy beauty
Choose a hebe from this list, and you should have no trouble with frost. However, as a general rule of thumb, the larger the leaf, the more tender a hebe will be, so if you live in a very exposed site, choose a 'whipcord hebe', like 'James Stirling'. They are easy to grow and will tolerate gusty, salty winds, making them ideal for seaside gardens.

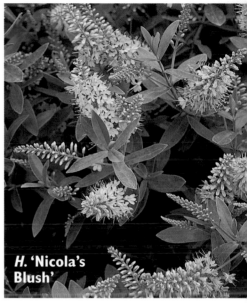

H. **'Nicola's Blush'**

STAR PERFORMER
H. pimeleoides **'Quicksilver'**♀
This open and sprawling shrub will make a show in any summer border.

heaths & heathers

All-year colour

Heaths and heathers are ideal for a low maintenance garden, since they need very little care once established. Botanically, heaths are classified under the genus, *Erica*, although they are also known as bell heathers, while heathers belong to the *Calluna* group; but the term 'heather' is often used to refer to both groups. Given the correct soil conditions, they offer variety in size, colour and habit, and both summer and winter flowers, and can be grown for year-round colour and interest.

As long as you give them the right soil and enough sunshine, heaths and heathers are easy to grow in any garden. Most prefer acid soil, but there are also a large number of lime-tolerant varieties which do well in alkaline soils The bell-shaped flowers range from white, pink or lilac to crimson and purple, while the foliage includes greens, yellow, orange and red, and bronze.

Trouble free
Heathers are generally trouble free if planted in acid soil. If you have a more alkaline soil, ensure that you choose a variety that tolerates lime.

Drifts of frost-tipped E. x darleyensis 'Margaret Porter' make a carpet of delicate colour in a winter heather garden.

Cut back summer-flowering varieties in mid spring to the base of the dead flowers. Winter-flowering varieties should be pruned only to remove straggly growth and keep the shape.

Enhance a mixed bed
Heaths and heathers work well in a mixed bed. *Erica × darleyensis* varieties – such as 'Arthur Johnson', or 'Kramer's Rote' are particularly good for smothering weeds. Use compact and prostrate varieties as low ground cover between shrubs at the front of a bed, or in a rockery.

Large scale effect
For a large area, blend different colours, heights and flowering times to give a variety of interest with a patchwork effect. Tall varieties include 'Elsie Purnell', with striking lavender flowers, and 'Arthur Johnson', which grows to 60cm (2ft) and produces 20cm (8in) long spikes of pink flowers. As a backdrop to shorter varieties, plant a tree heather, such as *E. arborea* var. *alpina*.

MINIATURE HEATHERS There are many dwarf or prostrate varieties, ideal for tubs or containers. Try *E. cinerea* 'Pink Ice'♡, or the mound forming *C. vulgaris* 'Nana Compacta'. *C. vulgaris* 'Sister Anne'♡, with magenta flowers and grey green foliage that turns bronze in winter, is only 10cm (4in) tall, while the dainty, trailing *C. vulgaris* 'White Lawn'♡ is even smaller at 5cm (2in) tall.

Acid soils

Follow these selections if you have an acid soil. You can ensure that your heathers remain care free by planting them in an open position that receives plenty of sunshine.

1 *Calluna vulgaris* 'Beoley Crimson' An excellent heather, particularly for flower arrangers – the crimson flowers appear on elegant, long stems.
❀ **Crimson • Early autumn**
∅ **Dark green**
h. 30cm (1ft) *s.* 45cm (1½ft)

2 *C. vulgaris* 'Gold Haze'♈ Grow this pale yellow heather for year-round colour – it produces white flowers in every season.
❀ **White • All year round**
∅ **Pale yellow**
h. 30cm (1ft) *s.* 45cm (1½ft)

3 *C. vulgaris* 'Elsie Purnell'♈ One of the taller heathers, it produces heavenly, long spikes of double lavender flowers on grey-green foliage.
❀ **Lavender • Autumn** ∅ **Grey-green**

STAR PERFORMER
***Erica carnea* 'Myretoun Ruby'**♈ Thick clusters of deep-toned, urn-shaped flowers will add brilliance to a winter garden.

h. 45cm (1½ft) *s.* 75cm (2½ft)

4 *Erica arborea* var. *alpina*♈ A tree heath with white flowers in dense clusters, it looks striking amid other heathers.
❀ **White • Spring** ∅ **Bright green**
h. 6m (20ft) *s.* 3m (10ft)

5 *E. cinerea* 'C. D. Eason'♈ A good heather for ground cover, its pinkish purple flowers are produced continuously from June well into September.
❀ **Pinkish purple • Early summer–early autumn**
∅ **Bottle green**
h. 25cm (10in) *s.* 45cm (1½ft)

6 *E. cinerea* 'Alba Minor'♈ Good for ground cover, but also compact enough to grow in tubs.
❀ **White • Early summer–early autumn** ∅ **Bottle green**
h. 25cm (10in) *s.* 45cm (1½ft)

7 *E. cinerea* 'Pink Ice'♈ A dwarf heather, it will give colour to the garden all year round.
❀ **Rose-pink • Summer**
∅ **Bronze • Winter**
h. 15cm (6in) *s.* 35cm (14in)

8 *E.* x *griffithsii* 'Heaven Scent'♈ Long sprays of scented lilac-pink flowers adorn this compact variety in the autumn.
❀ **Lilac pink • Autumn** ∅ **Green**
h. 1m (3ft) *s.* 60cm (2ft)

C. vulgaris 'Elsie Purnell'

E. cinerea 'Alba Minor'

E. arborea var. *alpina*

Limy soils

These lime-tolerant heathers should give an excellent display in winter and early spring.

1 *Erica carnea* 'Myretoun Ruby'♈ One of the most striking winter-flowering, red heathers.
❀ **Crimson • Mid-winter–mid-spring**
∅ **Green**
h. 15cm (6in) *s.* 45cm (1½ft)

2 *E.* x *darleyensis* 'Kramer's Rote'♈ A winter heather, with magenta flowers.
❀ **Magenta • Winter–early spring**
∅ **Greeny bronze**
h. 45cm (1½ft) *s.* 60cm (2ft)

3 *E.* x *darleyensis* 'Arthur Johnson'♈ Long, scented flower spikes sit on cream-tipped foliage.
❀ **Pink • Winter–early spring**
∅ **Green**
h. 60cm (2ft) *s.* 75cm (2½ft)

4 *E.* x *darleyensis* 'Margaret Porter' A compact, rounded heather, it is excellent for ground cover and winter colour.
❀ **Lilac • Winter** ∅ **Light green**
h. 20cm (8in) *s.* 45cm (1½ft)

Site demands Except for the winter, lime-tolerant varieties, all require peaty, acid soil. All also prefer an open, sunny position.
Planting practice Plant anytime, away from deciduous trees – fallen leaves can cause fungal problems.
Flowering time All year round, if both summer and winter-flowering varieties are planted.
Pests and diseases Usually completely trouble free.
Bonus point They will give a care-free carpet of colour.

Hedera

Ivy will cover walls, trellises and sheds, form hedges, and can even be left to sprawl as ground cover. There is an amazing range of ivies – more than 300 varieties – so whether you want large leaves or small leaves, perhaps resembling birds' feet or hearts, there will be an ivy to suit.

H. helix 'Glacier'

H. helix subsp. *hibernica* 'Sagittifolia Variegata'

Ivies can be used in all kinds of ways. They make superb evergreen hedges, and provide a quick-growing screen on secure trellis, when you need to block out neighbouring views. They look quite remarkable covering a shed, where they can create a huge evergreen box with holes snipped out for the windows.

Train an ivy up and around 3m (10ft) high poles at the back of a border, or alternatively arrange the poles around a large circular pond to add a sculptural feature to the garden.

Is ivy destructive?

Solid, well-built house walls are safe, because ivy climbs by means of sticky pads which clamp onto a surface. It has no penetrative power, but it can certainly worsen loose woodwork joints or walls with crumbling mortar, and can dislodge roofing tiles.

It can also be grown up non-ornamental, old trees. Ensure that the host tree is stout, because ivy may make it top heavy, and trees with weak roots could then be blown down in a storm.

The Essentials

Site demands Any soil, even poor quality. Variagated foliage needs full sun or loses its markings; over-rich soil can have the same effect.
Planting practice Plant from early autumn to early spring.
Flowering time Autumn.
Pruning needs Trim to control. Restrict heavy pruning to spring.
Pests and diseases Trouble free.
Bonus point Late flowers draw beneficial insects to the garden, at a time when there is little else in bloom to lure them in.

Expert's Selection

1 *H. colchica* 'Sulphur Heart'♀ The large, leathery, leaves are boldly splashed with yellowish-green.
⌀ **Yellowish green**
h. 10m (33ft) *s.* 5m (16ft)

2 *H. colchica* 'Dentata Variegata'♀ A striking plant, its bright green leaves are shaded with grey and rimmed with white.
⌀ **Bright green, grey and white**
h. 10m (33ft) *s.* 5m (16ft)

3 *H. helix* 'Glacier'♀ A cool-toned ivy, its small leaves have a narrow white margin.
⌀ **Silver grey, green and white**
h.&s. 3m (10ft)

4 *H. helix* subsp. *hibernica* 'Sagittifolia Variegata' An excellent ground cover plant, it has deeply-cut, five-lobed, cream and green variegated leaves.
⌀ **Cream and green**
h.&s. 1m (3ft)

5 *H. helix* 'Goldchild'♀ Its mature leaves are blue-green, with a grey-green centre and creamy yellow margins.
⌀ **Blue-green, grey-green and yellow**
h.&s. 1.2m (4ft)

STAR PERFORMER
H. colchica 'Sulphur Heart'♀ A superb ground or wall cover plant. The leaves smell of gin when lightly crushed.

Helianthemum

Rock roses are bright, low-growing shrubs, which flower from late spring all through the summer. They are a cheerful choice for path edgings, terraces or borders.

1 H. 'Fire Dragon' ♀
A striking variety, with vivid flowers and grey-green leaves.
✿ **Orange-scarlet • All summer**
h. **20cm (8in)** *s.* **40cm (16in)**

2 H. 'Raspberry Ripple'
The reddish pink flowers are edged with white and dark green leaves.
✿ **Red-pink • All summer**
h. **20cm (8in)** *s.* **40cm (16in)**

3 H. 'Wisley Primrose' ♀
Primrose yellow flowers contrast with pale grey-green leaves.
✿ **Yellow • All summer**
h. **20cm (8in)** *s.* **40cm (16in)**

These low-spreading, easy-going shrubs are an ideal way to bring colour to a path edge or border. They thrive in warm, sunny spots, producing a succession of open blooms which contrast with their grey-green leaves. Colours range from bright pinks and reds to yellow, white and more delicate pastel shades.

Few problems
Rock roses are generally care free in the right conditions. They will not thrive in over rich or over heavy soils. Add grit to assist drainage in heavy soils. They are hardy, but may need protection if in a cold, open, windy site.

The Essentials

Site demands Any well-drained, sunny site. Avoid anywhere cold and windy.
Planting practice Plant in spring or early summer.
Flowering times Late spring to late summer.
Pruning needs Trim in early spring, or just after flowering.
Pests and diseases Usually trouble free.
Bonus point Drought-tolerant, so will survive dry spells without watering.

STAR PERFORMER
H. **'Fire Dragon'** ♀
Make a striking display in the rockery or along a terrace with these vibrantly coloured flowers.

Hibiscus

This exotic shrub with large, showy flowers belies the delicacy of its blooms. Most varieties are hardy, though some do need protection from cold winds.

1 H. syriacus 'Blue Bird' ♀ Grow in a sheltered border or against a wall. The flowers are a stunning lilac-blue, with a deep red eye.
✿ **Lilac • Midsummer–autumn**
h. **2.5m (8ft)** *s.* **1.8m (6ft)**

2 H. syriacus 'Woodbridge' ♀ Its large, deep pink flowers have a dark eye, and make a good contrast with the dark green foliage.
✿ **Deep pink • Midsummer–autumn**
h. **2.5m (8ft)** *s.* **1.8m (6ft)**

3 H. syriacus 'Diana' ♀
The exquisite, delicate looking white flowers have petals with crinkled edges.
✿ **White • Midsummer–autumn**
h. **2.5m (8ft)** *s.* **1.8m (6ft)**

4 H. syriacus 'Red Heart' ♀
The white flowers have a dramatic, vibrant red centre.
✿✿ **White and red Midsummer–autumn**
h. **2.5m (8ft)** *s.* **1.8m (6ft)**

Give a hibiscus a sunny, sheltered site, and it will prove hardy and easy to grow. A major bonus is that it flowers late in the season, when many other flowers are over. Blooms are not long-lasting, but will appear continuously from July to October. Flowers come in many colours, from white and pink to orange, red, blue and purple.

STAR PERFORMER
H. syriacus **'Blue Bird'** ♀
Give this hibiscus pride of place, and enjoy the glorious flowers late into the summer.

The Essentials

Site demands Any well-drained soil in a sunny position. Place by a south-facing wall in cold areas.
Planting practice Plant in early spring.
Flowering time Late summer to early autumn.
Pruning needs Deadhead to prolong the flowering display.
Pests and diseases Usually trouble free, but aphids may attack.
Bonus point Flower long after most other shrubs have finished.

Humulus

Hops are quick sprinting, twining climbers, grown for their big, bold, fresh green leaves. They make great temporary screening, and will enliven dull hedging.

The best way to take advantage of the hop's vivid, summer foliage is to highlight it against a dark background. Purple-leaved beech hedges (*Fagus sylvatica* **Atropurpurea Group**) provide the perfect backdrop. In autumn, the female flowers add an extra decorative touch, by turning into the papery hops used in brewing.

Pretty on a pergola
You can also grow humulus over pergolas, where its large, bright leaves provide welcome summer shade. If you grow other climbers with hops, they must be robust and kept to the opposite end of the structure, or they will struggle to compete for water and light.

Hydrangea

These handsome shrubs come in a wide variety of sizes and forms, and most are hardy. Flamboyant mophead or delicate lacecap, there is a type to suit almost every location. There are climbing hydrangeas, too, that will clothe a wall in greenery and adorn it with white blooms.

Hydrangeas are easy to grow, and all the varieties listed here are hardy. They are ideal for brightening up a border, since they flower in late summer and early autumn, when many other flowers are over. There are two basic types of flower: lacecap and mophead. Lacecap flowerheads, like '**Bluebird**', are flat and lacy, surrounded by a few florets. The classic mophead, such as '**King George**', is domed and composed entirely of florets. And a few have more unusual conical flowerheads, for example '**Grandiflora**'.

Acid for blue, alkaline for pink
Flower colour is often determined by the soil. A plant that bears blue flowers on acid soil may have pink ones on neutral or alkaline soil, while red flowers on alkaline soil may turn out pale blue on acid soil.

If you want to grow blue flowers on alkaline soil, add a layer of compost or manure in spring, and apply aluminium sulphate (sold as 'blueing compound') during the growing season. To stop red varieties turning blue on acid soil, sprinkle the soil with ground limestone.

Variety
Hydrangeas come in a range of sizes and habits. There are plenty of shrubby examples

suitable for borders in an average sized garden, such as '**Bluebird**' or '**Alpenglühen**', while larger shrubs include '**Grandiflora**' or the colourful '**Quadricolor**'. Dwarf varieties are ideal for containers.

There are also several climbing hydrangeas, the hardiest being *H. anomala* **subsp.** *petiolaris*, with pretty white lacecap flowers.

H. macrophylla 'Quadricolor'

H. macrophylla 'King George'

4 *H. macrophylla* 'Alpenglühen' A crimson mophead (purple on acid soil), with flowerheads up to 23cm (9in) across, and dark green, oval leaves.
✿ Crimson • Mid–late summer
h.&s. 1.5m (5ft)

5 *H. macrophylla* 'Quadricolor' A lacecap variety, it has white or mauve-pink flowerheads, and handsome green, yellow and cream variegated leaves.
✽✿ White or mauve • Late summer
h.&s. 1.8m (6ft)

Expert's Selection

Shrub hydrangeas

1 *H. paniculata* 'Grandiflora'♀ One of the most spectacular varieties, it produces conical flowerheads that are up to 30cm (1ft) long and 10cm (4in) wide at the base. They turn from white to a purplish pink over the summer months.
✽ Whitish pink
Late summer–early autumn
h. 3m (10ft) *s.* 1.5m (5ft)

2 *H. macrophylla* 'King George' This compact mophead variety, with rosy red blooms and good autumn leaf colour, is ideal for the border.
✿ Rosy red • Mid–late summer
h.&s. 1.5m (5ft)

3 *H. serrata* 'Bluebird'♀ Perfect for a smaller garden, its lacecap flowerheads, 15–20cm (6–8in) across, have tiny mid blue flowers, circled by light blue florets. Leaves are coppery red in autumn.
✿ Blue • Early summer–mid autumn
h&s. 1.2m (4ft)

Climbing hydrangeas

1 *H. anomala* subsp. *petiolaris*♀ A vigorous hardy climber, which needs no support. It produces beautiful flat, cream and white, lacecap flowerheads, up to 25cm (10in) across. Avoid placing against a south-facing wall or fence.
✽ Creamy white • Summer
h. 5m (16ft) *s.* 3m (10ft)

2 *H. serratifolia* An excellent self-clinging evergreen, it uses aerial roots to lock on to adjacent material. It thrives on shady walls, clothing them in long, leathery, dark green leaves, and conical, off-white flowerheads, up to 15cm (6in) across, from July to September.
✽ White • Mid–late summer
h. 5m (16ft) *s.* 4m (13ft)

STAR PERFORMER
H. paniculata 'Grandiflora'♀ **Plant this dramatic looking shrub for a show of creamy white flowerheads that is hard to beat.**

STAR PERFORMER
H. anomala subsp. *petiolaris*♀ **Covered in lacy white flowers in summer, this plant's aerial roots grow from its stems, and cling to any surface. It will take about five years to haul itself up to a first floor window.**

The Essentials

Site demands Moist, well-drained soil, with well-rotted compost or manure dug in. Full sun is okay, but prefer partial shade. In cold areas, choose a sheltered position against a wall. Avoid east-facing sites: spring frosts can damage young shoots.

Planting practice Plant in autumn or spring. Feed in early spring, and keep well watered in summer, especially new plants in their first year.
Flowering time Early summer to autumn, depending on variety.
Pruning needs Leave dead flowerheads until spring to protect against frost. Remove weak, spindly shoots, and cut flowered branches, up to 30cm (12in), to strong buds.
Climbers do not need pruning, except for cutting back in spring if growth gets out of hand.
Pests and diseases Generally trouble free but occasionally attacked by aphids.
Bonus point Tough and easy to grow with long-lived blooms.

Hypericum

St John's wort is grown for its bright yellow flowers, which last from June to September. It can make a splendid ground cover, growing readily to suppress weeds, while the taller varieties make a wonderful show in the border or as a specimen plant.

Hypericums are vigorous, hardy and flower throughout summer. Some make effective ground cover, while the taller varieties are attractive shrubs and can even be used as hedging. They are very fast-growing, achieving their ultimate height and spread after five years.

Ground cover

If you want a hypericum for quick ground cover, choose the rose of Sharon (*H. calycinum)* which spreads rapidly and will grow even in shade. It can be somewhat invasive, with a tough, creeping rootstock, so it is important to prune back hard each spring. Less invasive low-growing varieties include *H. x moserianum.*

The taller plants can make splendid border shrubs, particularly the profusely flowering 'Hidcote.'

H. forrestii can also be grown as informal hedging, giving good autumnal colour with its reddish orange leaves.

Easy care

Hypericums are easy to look after: just prune lightly to restrict growth or to train as hedging. The exception is *H. calycinum,* which should be cut back to the ground in spring.

H. calycinum

H. forrestii

STAR PERFORMER
H. **'Hidcote'**♀ **Grow in the border for a wonderful show of spectacular blooms from July through September.**

The Essentials

Site demands Sun or light shade in most soils.
Planting practice Plant in autumn or spring.
Flowering time They bloom from June to September.
Pruning needs Prune in early spring, cutting back to within a few buds of the old wood.
Pests and diseases Powdery mildew and rust may be a problem.
Bonus point Many varieties bear highly decorative autumn berries.

Expert's Selection

1 *H.* **'Hidcote'**♀
It has large golden flowers and dark green semi-evergreen leaves.
✿ **Golden yellow • All summer**
⊘ **Dark green**
h. **1.5m (5ft)** *s.* **1.2m (4ft)**

2 *H. forrestii*♀
Flowers are followed by bronze seedpods and orange-red foliage.
✿ **Golden yellow • All summer**
◗ **Bronze** ⊘ **Orange red • Autumn**
h. **1.5m (5ft)** *s.* **1.2m (4ft)**

3 *H. calycinum*
Also known as rose of Sharon, this low-growing variety makes excellent fast ground cover.
✿ **Bright yellow • All summer**
◗ **Bronze** ⊘ **Green**
h. **30cm (1ft)** *s.* **1m (3ft)**

4 *H.* **x** *moserianum*♀
A semi-evergreen, its golden yellow flowers have reddish anthers.
✿ **Yellow • All summer** ◗ **Purple**
⊘ **Green • h.&s. 75cm (2½ft)**

5 *H. androsaemum*
A semi-evergreen, it can be grown in deep shade. Try f. *variegatum* 'Mrs Gladis Brabazon' as an alternative.
✿ **Golden yellow • All summer**
◗ **Purple** ⊘ **Green • h.&s. 1m (3ft)**

6 *H.* **x** *inodorum* **'Elstead'**
An upright bushy semi-evergreen shrub with small flowers and large fruit which open to a pinkish red.
✿ **Bright yellow • All summer**
◗ **Pinkish red** ⊘ **Green**
h.&s. **1.2cm (4ft)**

7 *H. androsaemum* **'Albury Purple'** Yellow flowers are followed by cone-shaped fruit.
✿ **Bright yellow • All summer**
◗ **Cerise** ⊘ **Green**
h.&s. **1.2cm (4ft)**

Ilex

Holly, with its brilliant berries and sculptural, glossy, often spiky leaves is one of the most care free of all plants. It will grow almost anywhere, tolerating pollution and strong winds. Though classically grown as a tree, small bushes and shrubs can also be planted to give year-round interest.

Grow holly as a beautiful tree, as a bush and as hedging, in even the most unprepossessing situations. It requires very little attention, except for hedges, which must be clipped for shape.

The red berries appear on the female plants, so grow both male and female to ensure a crop. The exception within the selections is *I. aquifolium* 'Pyramidalis', which will self-pollinate.

I. aquifolium, the common holly, is fairly slow-growing, taking 10 years to reach 3m (10ft), though it can eventually reach as high as 20m (66ft).

The glossy green leaves may have a blue tinge, such as *I. x meserveae* 'Blue Angel', and there are many variegated varieties with splashes of silver, cream, or gold such as 'Madame Briot'. These will brighten up a dark corner or provide cheerful winter colour.

I. aquifolium 'Pyramidalis'

The Essentials

Site demands Plant in any soil in sun or shade.
Planting practice Introduce male and female plants from autumn to mid spring.
Pruning needs Cut green shoots from variegated plants as they appear.
Pests and diseases Trouble free.
Bonus point Gives a care-free year-round display.

Expert's Selection

1 *I. aquifolium* **'Madame Briot'** ♀ The mottled green leaves have a gold-yellow margin.
∅ **Greeny gold** ⚜ **Red** • Autumn–winter • *h.* 3m (10ft) *s.* 1.2m (4ft)

2 *I. aquifolium* **'Pyramidalis'** ♀ A glossy green conical tree that self-pollinates.
∅ **Bright green** ⚜ **Red** • Autumn–winter • *h.* 6m (20ft) *s.* 5m (16ft)

3 *I. x altaclerensis* **'Belgica Aurea'** ♀ The mottled grey green leaves have golden yellow margins.
∅ **Grey green** • Ultimately reaches *h.* 12m (40ft) *s.* 5m (16ft)

4 *I. aquifolium* **'Golden Milkboy'** ♀ Long green leaves have central gold markings.
∅ **Green, gold** ⚜ **Red** • Autumn–winter • *h.* 6m (20ft) *s.* 4m (13ft)

5 *I. x meserveae* **'Blue Angel'** ♀ The blue-green leaves turn purple-green in winter.
∅∅ **Blue-green, purple** ⚜ **Red** Autumn–winter
h. 1.8m (6ft) *s.* 1m (3ft)

6 *I. crenata* **'Convexa'** ♀ It has small dark green leaves and black, white or yellow fruit.
∅ **Dark green** ⚜ **Black, white, yellow** • Autumn–winter
h. 5m (16ft) *s.* 4m (13ft)

7 *I. aquifolium* **'Ferox Argentea'** ♀ This male hedgehog holly, named for its spines, has dark green leaves with white margins.
∅ **Dark green and white**
h. 8m (27ft) *s.* 4m (13ft)

TAKE A FRESH LOOK

I. crenata **'Golden Gem'** ♀ is a low, spreading holly, reaching a maximum of only 1.8m (6ft). Its small leaves liberally flecked with gold shine out in a border.

STAR PERFORMER
I. aquifolium **'Madame Briot'** ♀
With its colourful but spiny leaves it makes a hedge that is both decorative and highly efficient as a barrier.

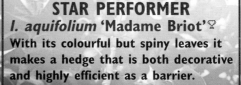

Jasminum

Jasmines grow quickly and easily. Valued for their exotic, often highly perfumed flowers, they can be trained up pillars and around pergolas, or along wires fixed across a wall of your house.

For a stunning, scented summer surround to a doorway or window, or over a garden bench, fix supports around the area to be framed, then plant *J. officinale* (summer jasmine), at the base of one support. Sit back, and watch it effortlessly clamber up and over, then, with a bit of help, down the other side.

Midwinter colour

J. nudiflorum (winter jasmine), is another quick grower. More of a shrub than a climber, it can still reach a height of 4.5m (15ft). Its shoots do not twine, however, so if you wish to train them over a trellis, use plant ties to attach them. Bright yellow flowers will continue to open on its bare branches for months before any leaves appear in early spring. For a cheering mix of winter colour, plant close to a red-berried shrub that holds on to its fruit late into the season. *Pyracantha* 'Mohave' would be an excellent choice.

STAR PERFORMER

J. officinale 'Argenteovariegatum' ♀
Twining and twisting upwards, 'Argenteovariegata' makes a fantastic show, its delicate, white flowers filling the summer garden with their perfume. In warm, sheltered sites, the attractive foliage will linger long into the autumn.

The Essentials

Site demands Well-drained, fertile soil. Position your plant under the hot sun, and you can be sure of a much stronger perfume.
Planting practice At any time.
Flowering time Early to midsummer for *J.* x *stephanense*. Midsummer to early autumn for *J. officinale*. Late autumn till spring for *J. nudiflorum*.
Pruning needs Thin out as required, but only after flowering. Dense, tangled growth can be cut back hard, though it may grow less vigorously the following year.
Pests and diseases Generally trouble free. New shoots are occasionally attacked by aphids.
Bonus point Summer flowers have a rich, powerful fragrance.

Expert's Selection

1 *J. officinale* **'Argenteovariegatum'** ♀
Noted for its distinctive cream-rimmed leaves. Golden patches give 'Aureovariegatum' its striking look.
❀ **White** ∅ **Grey-green and cream**
Midsummer–early autumn
h. **9m (30ft)** *s.* **3m (10ft)**

2 *J. officinale* **f. affine**
Its large, scented flowers are tinged pink on the outside.
❀ **Pinky white • Midsummer–early autumn • h. 9m (30ft) s. 3m (10ft)**

3 *J. nudiflorum* ♀
Yellow flowers bloom all winter.
✿ **Bright yellow • Late autumn–early spring • h. 4.5m (15ft) s. 1.8m (6ft)**

4 *J.* x *stephanense* ♀
Fragrant pale pink flowers nestle amongst olive leaves.
✿ **Pale pink • Early–midsummer**
h. **4.5m (15ft)** *s.* **3m (10ft)**

J. officinale f. affine

Juniperus

Juniper is an easy-going, hardy evergreen. Although some are slow growing, all settle happily in even the poorest conditions, and are particularly good plants for hot, sunny gardens. From the huge variety of shapes and sizes, at least one is bound to fit your garden perfectly.

Junipers are valued for their colourful, evergreen foliage, which ranges from green, gold and yellow to grey and blue. They thrive in almost any type of garden, except where soil is waterlogged, and are more tolerant of drought than most conifers. Some form elegant, architectural columns, while others are ideal as ground cover on slopes and in hollows.

Statuesque shrubs

For care-free, eye-catching shrubs to break up an area of lawn, grow the blue-toned 'Hibernica' or 'Skyrocket' – both will creep slowly, but steadily skywards. Or for something faster-growing, plant a *J. × pfitzeriana*, which gives a glorious, tiered flourish of long, gently drooping branches.

Lying low

For an effective golden ground cover, 'Emerald Spreader' works well. It is very low-growing, but can eventually spread up to 3m (10ft). In the rockery, try 'Repanda', an attractive dwarf creeper, or if you are patient, the slow-growing 'Blue Star', which forms a tight, silvery blue mound.

J. × pfitzeriana 'Gold Sovereign'

J. scopulorum 'Skyrocket'

1 *J. communis* 'Hibernica' Grow this Irish juniper if you are short of space. It forms a narrow column with silver-blue needles, but can take 100 years to reach its final height.
⌀ **Silver-blue**
h. 6m (20ft) *s.* 60cm (2ft)

2 *J. communis* 'Repanda' Forms a dense carpet of branches, bearing grey-green foliage. Leaves may bronze over in winter.
⌀ **Grey-green**
h. 30cm (1ft) *s.* 2m (7ft)

3 *J. × pfitzeriana* 'Gold Sovereign' A semi-prostrate spreader, it is the ideal choice for a splash of eye-catching colour on banks and lawns.
⌀ **Golden yellow**
h. 60cm (2ft) *s.* 1.2m (4ft)

4 *J. horizontalis* 'Emerald Spreader' Short, sharp needles cover the loose network of long branches. Takes to 20 years to reach full size.
⌀ **Bright green**
h. 30cm (1ft) *s.* 3m (10ft)

5 *J. scopulorum* 'Skyrocket' One of the narrowest conifers, the tall pointed column makes a good specimen plant for the lawn.
⌀ **Blue-grey**
h. 7m (23ft) *s.* 30cm (1ft)

6 *J. squamata* 'Blue Star' Another, slow-grower, this Rocky Mountain juniper takes around 30 years to grow into a tight mound, covered in a mass of silvery blue, fleshy, scale-like leaves.
⌀ **Silvery blue**
h. 60cm (2ft) *s.* 1m (3ft)

Site demands Prefer dry soil, in sun or light shade.
Planting practice Plant in autumn or spring.
Pruning needs Can be shaped in spring and autumn if required.
Pests and diseases Fungal root disease can occur in boggy soil.
Bonus point Most are slow growing and easy to control.

STAR PERFORMER

J. communis 'Hibernica' ♛
Perfect for making an impact, this narrow silver blue column will stand elegantly on a lawn or in the midst of a border.

Kerria

A very easy-going shrub, kerria is a member of the rose family. Plant it, then just sit back and enjoy a golden blaze of colour every spring.

Kerria is a highly reliable, care-free shrub that guarantees a good show of golden yellow flowers every spring. It grows well almost anywhere, except in very open and windswept sites. In colder spots, try growing it against a south-facing wall. The tall stems can also be trained up a trellis or fence.

K. japonica 'Pleniflora'

STAR PERFORMER
K. japonica 'Picta'
Prized for its creamy white variegated leaves, this hardy shrub is dotted with delicate, golden flowers in spring.

Expert's Selection

1 *K. japonica* 'Picta'
A shorter, spreading variety, with attractive, variegated foliage.
✿ **Golden yellow • Mid–late spring**
⊘ **Grey-green and cream**
  h. 1.2m (4ft) s. 2m (7ft)

2 *K. japonica* 'Pleniflora' ♀
In April and May, its tall, vigorous, arching stems are thick with golden, pompom-like flowers.
✿ **Golden yellow • Late spring**
h.&s. 3m (10ft)

3 *K. japonica* 'Golden Guinea' ♀ This variety produces large, rose-like flowers.
✿ **Golden yellow • Mid–late spring**
h. 1.8m (6ft) s. 2m (7ft)

The Essentials

Site demands Sunny or lightly shaded site, out of the wind.
Planting practice Plant in spring or autumn.
Flowering time Spring.
Pruning needs After flowering, cut off any old, woody growth.
Pests and diseases Trouble free.
Bonus point Flowers early.

Kolkwitzia

Beauty bush, a hardy, deciduous shrub, is well named – its long arching branches are smothered with stunning pink flowers in spring and early summer.

Kolkwitzia, a member of the honeysuckle family, is a native of China. A tall, tough shrub, its delicate pink flowers resemble foxgloves and grow in thick clusters.

It is very easy to grow, though for the best result, you should place it in a sunny spot. Also, remember to allow plenty of space for it to spread out – it can grow as wide as it is tall.

STAR PERFORMER
K. amabilis 'Pink Cloud' ♀
You can rely on this smaller variety to produce a mass of flowers every summer.

Expert's Selection

1 *K. amabilis* 'Pink Cloud' ♀
Plant on its own, or at the back of the border, and watch it effortlessly produce a profusion of delicate pink flowers, year after year.
✿ **Deep pink • Early summer**
h.&s. 2m (7ft)

2 *K. amabilis*
The long branches of this tall, rounded shrub will be coated in clusters of small flowers, from late spring well into summer.
✿ **Bright pink • Late spring–early summer • h.&s. 3m (10ft)**

The Essentials

Site demands Grows in any soil, except a very wet one.
Planting practice Any time.
Flowering time Late spring to early summer.
Pruning needs After flowering, prune to limit growth or thin out.
Pests and diseases Trouble free.
Bonus point Abundant flowers.

Lavandula

Lavender is a traditional favourite. It has been grown for centuries as an edging or low hedge for paths and borders, and in herb gardens, for its medicinal and culinary qualities. It grows vigorously, making almost no demands. Its only desire is to be placed in a sunny position.

Lavender is valued most for its aromatic flowers and foliage which, being evergreen, provides constant fragrance. The varieties recommended here are truly care free, and will flourish in most sunny, free-draining sites, even in the salty air of the seaside. They are at their most vigorous, however, in poor, stony soil.

A favourite variety is blue-grey *L. angustifolia,* or old English lavender, which also has deeper blue and pink variants, such as 'Hidcote' or 'Miss Katherine'. *L. stoechas* (French lavender) produces densely packed, dark purple spikes twice a year – in early summer, and again in autumn.

Drying lavender
Dried lavender is used to make perfumed sachets and potpourris. Gather stems just as the flowers open, and dry by hanging in an airy place or lying on open trays.

> **STAR PERFORMER**
> *L. angustifolia*
> **'Twickel Purple'**♀
> **Its tall, slender, flower spikes will waft their rich fragrance through the summer air.**

Expert's Selection

1 *L. angustifolia* **'Twickel Purple'**♀ Plant across a bank or border for a tall, scented display of deep purple flowers that lasts all summer.
✿ **Purple • Midsummer** ⌀ **Grey-green • h. 60cm (2ft) s. 45cm (1½ft)**

2 *L. angustifolia* **'Hidcote'**♀
Its deep blue flower spikes make a striking contrast as they begin to appear above the silvery foliage at the start of summer.
✿ **Deep blue • Early–midsummer** ⌀ **Silver-grey • h.&s. 45cm (1½ft)**

3 *L. angustifolia* **'Miss Katherine'** The rich, deep pink colouring of the flowers spikes stand out beautifully against its bright green foliage.
✿ **Deep pink • Early–midsummer** ⌀ **Bright green • h.&s. 75cm (2½ft)**

4 *L. angustifolia* **'Miss Muffet'** A dwarf variety, it forms low, dense bushes of silver foliage, topped with lilac from May to July. It is ideal for low hedging, and in small borders and rockeries.
✿ **Lilac-blue • Early–midsummer** ⌀ **Silver-grey • h.&s. 30cm (1ft)**

5 *L. angustifolia* **'Little Lady'**
Also good for confined spaces, or try it in pots on a balcony or patio.
✿ **Lavender • Early–midsummer** ⌀ **Silver-grey h. 45cm (1½ft) s. 30cm (1ft)**

6 *L. stoechas*♀
This 'French lavender' blooms twice in a year – first from April to June, and again in September.
✿ **Dark purple • Late spring–early summer, and early autumn** ⌀ **Silver-grey • h.&s. 45cm (1½ft)**

The Essentials

Site demands Any well-drained, sunny plot, but is especially happy where soil is poor and stony.
Planting practice Plant in spring.
Flowering time Late spring to late summer. A few varieties have a second autumn flowering.
Pruning needs Trim lightly in the autumn after flowering, then again in April to promote new growth from the base.
Pests and diseases Very few, but can sometimes be attacked by leaf spot or froghopper.
Bonus point The evergreen foliage will continue to fill the garden with perfume, long after the flowers are gone.

L. stoechas

L. angustifolia 'Little Lady'

Lavatera

Tree mallow is one of the easiest of shrubs, and very fast-growing. Give it a sunny spot and it will flower continuously all summer, right up to the first frosts.

Happiest in a sunny position, sheltered from the wind, lavatera seems to spring from its base like a fountain. You may be surprised at how quickly this hardy species grows – shrubs planted in spring will usually flower that same season – so be sure to leave plenty of space for the bush to spread. Alternatively pick one of the smaller varieties available, such as 'Pink Frills'.

Keeping in shape

Prune lavatera hard in spring, cutting out any weak growths, and bring the straight stems to within 30cm (1ft) of ground level. You will then have tidier bushes, plus better displays of the large, saucer-shaped flowers when next summer comes around.

Expert's Selection

1 *L.* **'Barnsley'**♀
Large bold white flowers with a red eye make this tall shrub shine.
❀ **White and red • Summer–autumn**
h.&s. **2m (7ft)**

2 *L.* **'Poynton Lady'**
A new variety with variegated leaves and pinky mauve flowers.
✿ **Pinky mauve**
⊘ **Variegated • Summer–autumn**
h.&s. **2m (7ft)**

3 *L.* **'Burgundy Wine'**♀
Masses of dark pink flowers with darker veins adorn this tall shrub.
✿ **Dark pink • Summer–autumn**
h.&s. **2m (7ft)**

4 *L.* **'Bredon Springs'**
Summer sees a profuse flowering of dusky pink flowers flushed with mauve among grey-green foliage.
✿ **Dusky pink • All summer**
h.&s. **2m (7ft)**

L. **'Burgundy Wine'**

L. **'Pink Frills'**

5 *L.* **'Pink Frills'**
Crinkled pink flowers add interest.
✿ **Pale pink • Summer–autumn**
h. **1m (3ft)** *s.* **75cm (2½ft)**

The Essentials

Site demands Well-drained soil, full sun and shelter from the wind.
Planting practice Allow plenty of room for spreading.
Flowering time Blooms from midsummer until the first frosts.
Pruning needs Prune in spring. Trim in autumn. Prevent splitting by cutting exposed branches in winter.
Pests and diseases Aphids can be a nuisance in spring and summer.
Bonus point Lavatera gives a brilliant show throughout summer.

Leucothoë

Leucothoës are hardy evergreen shrubs, ideal for planting in acid soil. The flowers resemble lily of the valley, while the foliage takes on wonderful hues in autumn and winter.

Expert's Selection

1 *L. fontanesiana* 'Rainbow'
Arching branches of young pinky green leaves turn white and green.
⊘ **Pinky green and white**
h. 1.8m (6ft) *s.* 3m (10ft)

2 *L.* 'Scarletta'
This small variety's leaves bring glorious red hues in winter.
⊘ **Reddish green • Winter**
h.&s. 60cm (2ft)

3 *L. axillaris*
This dwarf mound-shaped evergreen is ideal for the rockery.
⊘ **Dark green**
h.&s. 60cm (2ft)

4 *L. fontanesiana* 'Rollissonii'℣ Dark green leaves turn purple in the winter.
⊘ **Purple • Winter**
h.&s. 1.8m (6ft)

A perfect choice for year-round colour, leucothoë changes its hues from season to season.

Tiny urn-shaped white flowers, hanging on stalks or massed upright among narrow leaves, bring summer cheer, with brilliant red and purple foliage emerging in the colder months.

The Essentials

Site demands Moist, humus-rich, acid soil. Sun or light shade.
Planting practice Add fertiliser suitable for ericaceous plants to encourage vigorous growth.
Flowering time Summer.
Pruning needs Only for neatness.
Pests and diseases Usually trouble free.
Bonus point An effective plant for a peat bed or acid soil setting.

STAR PERFORMER
L. fontanesiana 'Rainbow'
With its graceful fountain shape, white flowers and ever-changing leaf colours it will provide interest all year round.

Leycesteria

Himalayan honeysuckle, or **pheasant berry**, thrives in both sun and shade and makes a tall, unusual shrub.

The only variety of this genus suited to the outdoors, Himalayan honeysuckle is an exotic looking shrub perfect in a woodland setting or at the back of a border. There its most charming feature can easily be seen: long wine-coloured tassels encasing delicate white flowers, that hang between heart-shaped leaves from early summer to early autumn.

Coping with the cold
Tolerant of most soils, and generally hardy, this deciduous shrub has green, bamboo-like stems. Deep mulching in autumn will help to protect the hollow stems from strong winter frosts, and give a sturdy foundation for the following year.

In a windy area grow a Himalayan honeysuckle in the shelter of a wall to protect it from exposure to cold, drying winds.

STAR PERFORMER
L. formosa Intricate oriental-looking flowers give a hint of this shrub's Himalayan and Chinese origins.

Expert's Selection

1 *L. formosa*
A striking upright shrub, with blue-green stems that turn green by the second year. Wine-coloured tassels hang from heart-shaped leaves.
✿ **Wine and white** ❧ **Red-purple**
Summer–early autumn
h. 1.8m (6ft) *s.* 1m (3ft)

The Essentials

Site demands Plant in any well-drained soil, in sun or light shade.
Planting practice Sow seed in autumn; plant in autumn or spring.
Flowering time From early summer to early autumn.
Pruning needs None. Cut some stems to ground level in spring to encourage new growth.
Pests and diseases Trouble free.
Bonus point Established plants will bounce back with new growth in spring even after a hard frost.

Ligustrum

Privet is a traditional choice for hedges, being hardy, fast-growing and able to withstand hard pruning. For a good-looking privet try one of the golden or variegated varieties.

STAR PERFORMER
P. ovalifolium 'Aureum' ♡
This makes a splendid hedge that is both tough and highly attractive. The broad golden green leaves will cheer up the winter gloom.

Privet is a popular choice because of its vigour, hardiness and tolerance of pollution. Most varieties are grown as hedging, but some such as *L. japonicum*, or 'Excelsum Superbum' are decorative enough to be grown as specimen shrubs.

Lonicera

Honeysuckles can be sent flamboyantly twining up into old, stout trees, over walls and up pergolas. There are also highly attractive shrubby varieties which are often used as easily maintained hedging. Both the shrubby and climbing honeysuckles are often beautifully scented.

Climbing honeysuckles are not neat and tidy plants, and tend to create an amazing mass of aerial flowers. But in any garden with a degree of free flow, they will add creamy colours and superb scent.

Plant climbers with their roots to the north side, giving instant shade, and train the new growth round to the sunnier south side, where they will catch the sun. Water well in the first summer, while they are getting established.

Shrub honeysuckles
Certain honeysuckles make splendid easily maintained specimen shrubs, while the small-leaved evergreen varieties make dense formal hedging. The golden varieties, such as 'Twiggy' or 'Baggesen's Gold', are particularly colourful, especially when planted in full sun.

L. periclymenum 'Belgica'

STAR PERFORMER
L. rupicola var. syringantha
**A deciduous shrubby honeysuckle
with an elegant, rounded shape.
The tubular flowers appear
in late spring and early
summer, opening
to form a
star shape.**

Shrubs
The bushy shrub varieties are both
evergreen and deciduous, and many
have highly scented flowers.

**1 L. rupicola var.
syringantha** A graceful shrub
with sweetly scented flowers.
✿✿ Lilac, pink ∅ Grey • Spring–
early summer • **h.&s.** 1.8m (6ft)

2 L. fragrantissima
Plant in a sheltered position for
sweetly scented cream-coloured
flowers which last all winter.
∅ Green ✿ Cream • Winter
h. 2.7m (9ft) **s.** 1.5 (5ft)

**3 L. nitida 'Baggesen's
Gold'**♀ A dense rounded
shrub with small golden leaves.
Greeny gold
h.&s. 2.5m (8ft)

4 L. nitida 'Twiggy'
Plant to make a dense, fast-growing
hedge with golden leaves.
∅ Golden green
h.&s. 1.5m (5ft) if kept trimmed

5 L. pileata
A low dense shrub with dark
green leaves and creamy flowers.
∅ Dark green ✿ White • Late spring
h.&s. 60cm (2ft) **s.** 2.5m (8ft)

**L. nitida
'Baggesen's Gold'**

The Essentials

Site demands Grow in any well-
drained soil. Set the roots in the
shade with the heads in the sun.
Planting practice Plant pot
raised loniceras – often the best –
all year. Plant deciduous shrubs in
winter, evergreens in the spring.
Flowering time Through
summer, into early autumn.
Pruning needs In mild areas
prune in autumn, elsewhere, wait
for spring. Remove excess height
and straggly or diseased branches.
Pests and diseases Keep an eye
out for blackfly, aphids and mildew.
Bonus point Beautiful flowers,
bright berries and glorious scent.

STAR PERFORMER
L. periclymenum 'Graham Thomas'♀ **Common
honeysuckle or woodbine is anything but ordinary. It has
deliciously scented flowers, especially in the evening, right
through summer, and the flowers are followed by sticky
red berries. There are a number of excellent forms: all of
them are equally attractive and vigorous.**

Magnolia

Remarkably hardy despite the beauty of their starry flowers, magnolias are easy to grow and maintain, as long as they are protected against cold winds and late frosts.

1 *M.* 'Jane'♀
Flowers in its first year; dark pink buds open to cup-shaped flowers.
✿ **Deep pink • Mid–late spring**
h.&s. **4.5m (15ft)**

2 *M. liliiflora* 'Nigra'♀
Long, scented, tulip-shaped flowers appear with the unfurling leaves.
✿ **Deep purple • Spring–early summer • *h.&s.* 3m (10ft)**

3 *M. stellata*♀
A good size for small gardens, with masses of fragrant, star-shaped flowers.
❀ **White • Early–mid spring**
h.&s. **3.5m (12ft)**

4 *M.* x *loebneri* 'Leonard Messel'♀
A very hardy shrub, its star-shaped flowers are slightly scented
✿ **Deep pink • Mid spring**
h.&s. **4.5m (15ft)**

5 *M.* x *soulangeana* 'Rustica Rubra'♀
A wide-spreading tree with goblet-shaped flowers.
✿ **Reddish purple • Mid–late spring • *h.&s.* 9m (30ft)**

6 *M. grandiflora*
An intensely fragrant, evergreen variety, it can be trained across a wall.
❀ **White Midsummer–autumn**
h.&s. **15m (50ft)**

Site demands Rich, moist, well-drained soil, in sun or light shade.
Planting practice Plant in autumn or spring.
Flowering time Early spring to late summer, depending on variety.
Pruning needs If needed, trim deciduous types lightly after flowering; evergreens in spring.
Pests and diseases Trouble free.
Bonus point Flower profusely.

STAR PERFORMER
M. 'Jane'♀ **It makes a magnificent sight in spring, with the pink flowers arriving before the leaves.**

Magnolias are one of the first plants to flower in spring, often before the leaves emerge. The flowers can be cup-shaped, tulip-shaped or star-shaped, and range in colour from white and pink to purple. They are available in a wide range of sizes from compact shrubs, which can be grown in containers, to much larger trees, suitable for growing as freestanding specimens

Although they are generally hardy, magnolias do need protection from cold winds, and the very early flowering varieties may suffer frost damage to the buds. Some magnolias can take many years to bloom, so it is best to buy a five-year-old plant.

M. stellata

M x loebneri 'Leonard Messel'

Caring for magnolias
The main thing to bear in mind when planting a magnolia is to choose a reasonably sheltered site. If it is very dry, add a mulch to conserve moisture, and try not to plant or hoe at the base of a magnolia to avoid damaging the roots. Unless it is essential, say to restrict growth or to train the shrub against a wall, do not prune, as many species 'bleed'. Trim lightly, after flowering for deciduous plants, or in spring for evergreens, like *M. grandiflora*.

Where space is limited
The ideal variety for the smaller garden is *M. stellata*, the star magnolia. It is dense and slow-growing, and can even be grown in a tub. It also has the bonus of flowering in its first year.

Mahonia

With its dramatically shaped, long leaves and brightly coloured foliage, mahonia provides a great deal of interest, especially in the winter and spring garden.

These hardy evergreens will brighten up any winter or spring garden with their display of bright yellow flowers which are often sweetly scented. *M. aquifolium*, is often grown as ground cover or a low hedge. The leaves of some varieties, like 'Atropurpurea', turn a reddish purple in winter.

Some of the taller varieties of mahonia, such as 'Winter Sun' or *M. japonica* make splendid monumental plants, with their strongly shaped leaves and flower spikes, which often radiate out like spokes.

Mahonia is trouble free, will grow almost anywhere and rarely needs pruning, except to remove unwanted suckers on the shoots.

The Essentials

Site demands Most soils, in either sun or light shade.
Planting practice Plant in spring.
Flowering time Midwinter to late spring, depending on type.
Pests and diseases Trouble free.
Bonus point Bring fragrance and colour to the winter garden.

Expert's Selection

1 *M. x media* 'Winter Sun' ♥
A tall, upright shrub with dense, erect clusters of fragrant, winter flowers. 'Charity' ♥ is similar, but flowers earlier, from late autumn.
☆ Yellow • Winter ∅ Deep green
h.&s. 3m (10ft)

2 *M. japonica* ♥
Fragrant spikes of lemon flowers radiate out from the centre.
☆ Lemon yellow • Winter
∅ Deep green • *h.&s.* 3m (10ft)

3 *M. aquifolium*
'Atropurpurea' A rounded, spreading shrub, its leaves turn reddish purple in winter. 'Apollo' ♥ has greenish purple, winter leaves.
☆ Golden yellow • Late winter–late spring ∅ Reddish-purple Winter • *h.&s.* 1.8m (6ft)

4 *M. pinnata*
A low shrub, its long leaves are bronze when young.
☆ Bright yellow • Early spring ∅ Bright green *h.&s.* 1m (3ft)

STAR PERFORMER
M. x media 'Winter Sun' ♥
Grow this tall, handsome evergreen in a prime position for the splendid winter display of yellow flower spikes.

Nandina

Sacred bamboo has lovely chameleon-like leaves. They are blue green in summer, but are reddish purple in spring, and a similar or even bright hue in autumn and winter.

With its lacy foliage and cane-like stems, nandina resembles true bamboo, but is not actually related. It is generally hardy, but does best in a sunny, sheltered position, away from cold winds. Once fully established, it is a very tough and adaptable plant, with superb autumn and winter colours. The large creamy white flowers appear in midsummer, and are followed by red berries which can last for months, unless eaten by the birds. Nandina spreads by means of suckers.

The shorter varieties make splendid, colourful ground cover, around a building or along a wall or banking. 'Nana Purpurea', a dwarf form, can be used as ground cover or a low hedge. They can even be grown in tubs or containers on a patio, to give winter colour.

Taller varieties such as 'Richmond' will look dramatic planted against a wall.

The Essentials

Site demands Any fertile, fairly moist but well-drained soil, in a sunny, sheltered position.
Planting practice Plant in early spring.
Flowering time Midsummer.
Pruning needs Prune old shoots in early spring, for denser growth.
Pests and diseases Trouble free.
Bonus point Readily resprouts if shoots are damaged or killed off.

Expert's Selection

1 *N. domestica* 'Fire Power'
A smaller nandina, suitable for ground cover or containers. The leaflets are broader than on other varieties and very brightly coloured in autumn.
❀ Cream • Midsummer
∅ Reddish purple • Autumn/winter
h. 1.2m (4ft) *s.* 60cm (2ft)

2 *N. domestica* 'Richmond'
Its showy, scarlet berries last through the autumn and winter.
❀ Cream • Midsummer
∅ Reddish purple • Autumn/winter
h. 2.5m (8ft) *s.* 1.5m (5ft)

3 *N. domestica* 'Nana Purpurea' A dwarf variety, ideal as a low hedge or as ground cover.
❀ Cream • Midsummer
∅ Reddish purple • Autumn/winter
h. 30cm (1ft) *s.* 60cm (2ft)

STAR PERFORMER
N. domestica 'Fire Power'
The bright foliage shows up well against a white wall or on a patio where it will provide year round colour.

Olearia

Daisy bushes are sun-loving shrubs from New Zealand. They are ideal for seaside gardens, as they will happily tolerate strong winds and salty air.

Expert's Selection

1 *O. x haastii*
Charming clusters of fragrant, daisy-like flowers adorn the bush in summertime.
✿ White • Mid–late summer
⊘ Green and grey • *h.&s.* 1.8m (6ft)

2 *O. macrodonta*♀
Tall and vigorous, with large dark green holly-like leaves with white undersides, it makes great hedging.
✿ White • Mid–late summer
⊘ Green and white • *h.&s.* 6m (20ft)

3 *O. 'Waikariensis'*
A compact variety which bears grey-green leaves and white summer blooms.
✿ White • Mid–late summer
⊘ Grey green • *h.&s.* 1.8m (6ft)

The Essentials

Site demands Plant in any well-drained soil, in sun or light shade.
Planting practice Plant in late summer or early autumn.
Flowering time White flowers appear from mid to late summer.
Pruning Only for shape. Cut back young plants to build thickness.
Pests and diseases Trouble free.
Bonus point Pollution tolerant *O. x haastii* is a great city choice.

These bushy, easy-care shrubs are a godsend for seaside gardens, where they thrive even in strong winds and salty air.

Fast-growing, they are brilliant for hedging, and *O. × haastii* and *O. macrodonta* make particularly fine informal hedges.

STAR PERFORMER

O. x haastii **This hardy shrub gives good value all year round, with evergreen leaves of dark green, with grey undersides, and scented white summer flowers.**

Osmanthus

A large, well-rounded shrub with dark leaves and fragrant white flowers that appear in spring or autumn.

Expert's Selection

1 *O. x burkwoodii*♀
Clusters of scented creamy flowers contrast with elegant shiny leaves.
✿ White • Spring ⊘ Dark green
h.&s. up to 3m (10ft)

2 *O. delavayi*♀
A compact bush with blue-black berries in the autumn.
✿ White • Spring ⊘ Dark green
h. up to 1.8m (6ft) *s.* 2.5m (8ft)

3 *O. heterophyllus*
Holly-like leaves are a fine backdrop to the trumpet-shaped autumn flowers.
✿ White • Autumn ⊘ Dark green
h.&s. 3m (10ft); ultimately 6m (20ft)

4 *O. heterophyllus* **'Variegatus'**♀ A compact variety with variegated leaves, broadly edged with creamy white.
✿ White • Autumn ⊘ Variegated
h.&s. up to 3m (10ft)

The Essentials

Site demands Any well-drained soil, in sun or partial shade.
Planting practice Plant in autumn or spring.
Flowering time Depending on the variety, in autumn or spring.
Pests and diseases Trouble free.
Bonus point These thick shrubs are perfect subjects for topiary.

STAR PERFORMER

O. x burkwoodii♀ **This shrub is useful all year round with its glossy dark leaves – the fragrant, jasmine scented flowers in spring are an added bonus.**

These attractive evergreens are available as shrubs and small trees, with leathery holly-like foliage, which can be both dull-textured and shiny. Attractive leathery foliage, and sweet fragrance add further interest to these shrubs. Some, such as *O. heterophyllus* 'Variegatus' or *O. × burkwoodii* make dense hedging. Prune after flowering to control growth, and clip hedges no later than midsummer.

O. delavayi

Paeonia

Tree paeonies are hardy sub-shrubs which will grow easily in most soils, asking only for a sun and a little shelter. Once established they will bear their delightful rich-hued, layered blooms in late spring for years to come.

P. lutea var. ludlowii

The taller, shrubby deciduous 'tree peonies' such as 'Godaishu' or 'Rock's Variety', may take up to two years to become established but they are worth the wait, with large, extravagant flowers which are often sweet scented. (See page 154 for herbaceous peonies.)

Give them a sunny, sheltered site well away from cold, drying winds. Choose your site carefully – once planted tree peonies don't like being moved. Avoid exposed east-facing positions – young plants dislike frost and early morning sun. The plants will also appreciate extra compost in autumn and a good summer mulch, to retain moisture.

Expert's Selection

1 *P. suffruticosa*
The authentic tree peony, it is very stately, bearing simple cup-shaped, sometimes scented blooms.
❀✿✿✿ **White, pink, red, purple Late spring–early summer**
h. **2m (7ft)** *s.* **1.5m (5ft)**

2 *P. suffruticosa* 'Godaishu'
This tall tree peony is slow-growing, but the spectacular, semi-double white flowers make it well worth waiting for.
✿ **White • Late spring–early summer**
h. **2m (7ft)** *s.* **1.5m (5ft)**

3 *P. suffruticosa* 'Rock's Variety' Large white flowers with a maroon blotch on the inner petals add charm to this peony.
✿ **White • Late spring**
h. **2m (7ft)** *s.* **1.5m (5ft)**

4 *P. lutea var. ludlowii*♀
A vigorous Tibetan variety, it blooms with single golden yellow flowers. In autumn the foliage turns rich shades of yellow and orange.
✿ **Golden yellow • Late spring**
◍◍ **Yellow and orange**
h. **1.8m (6ft)** *s.* **1m (3ft)**

5 *P. delavayi*♀
A shrubby tree peony bearing deep maroon coloured single flowers in late spring.
✿ **Maroon • Late spring**
h. **1.8m (6ft)** *s.* **1m (3ft)**

STAR PERFORMER
P. suffruticosa The Mountain peony makes a dramatic display in spring with huge blooms in white, reds and pinks. Yellow stamens brighten the centres.

The Essentials

Site demands Any fertile, well-drained soil in a sunny sheltered position should be fine.
Planting practice Plant in autumn, digging in well rotted manure or compost. Provide support for large-flowered plants.
Flowering time Peonies flower from late spring to early summer.
Pruning needs Deadhead and cut out old wood on mature plants to encourage bushy growth.
Pests and diseases They may suffer from peony wilt. Remove and burn the affected parts.
Bonus point Huge, eye-catching flowers and bold foliage contrast well with other shrubs.

P. suffruticosa 'Rock's Variety'

Parahebe

A pretty, evergreen shrub, parahebe is a native of New Zealand. Tough and easy going, it is an ideal plant for edging borders and pathways, and deserves to be better known.

This hardy, low-growing shrub can be planted almost anywhere it will catch the sun. All varieties provide excellent ground cover, including the taller *P. perfoliata*, with its vigorous, sprawling branches, although low, ground-hugging varieties, such as 'Pink Parfait', are also good in rockeries and patio containers. Flowers are long-lasting, and are often still seen in early autumn.

Expert's Selection

1 *P. catarractae* 'Delight' ♀
This bushy shrub is covered in violet-blue flowers all summer.
✿ **Violet-blue • Summer–early autumn • h.&s.** 25cm (10in)

2 *P. perfoliata* ♀
Known as digger's speedwell, it has sprawling, wiry branches.
✿ **Violet-blue • Late summer**
h. 1m (3ft) ***s.*** 1.5m (5ft)

3 *P. hookeriana*
Plant this for a patch of strong summer colour in a rockery.
✿ **Lavender-blue • Summer**
h. 15cm (6in) ***s.*** 45cm (1½ft)

4 *P. hookeriana* 'Pink Parfait'
A new variety, its tiny white flowers are flushed with pink.
❀ **Pinky white • Summer**
h.&s. 25cm (10in)

STAR PERFORMER
P. catarractae 'Delight' ♀
This is ideal for a long-lasting splash of colour along the edge of a path in summer.

The Essentials

Site demands Any well-drained soil, in sun or partial shade.
Planting practice Plant anytime.
Flowering time Summer.
Pruning needs Trim off any straggly growth after flowering.
Pests and diseases Mainly care free, but aphids sometimes attack.
Bonus point Gives a delicate and unusual flush of colour all summer.

Parthenocissus

Virginia creepers are grown for their exciting autumn foliage, which erupts into a spectacular blaze of reds, then oranges and yellows, before finally being shed.

Virginia creepers are popular trained up large walls, giving them dense green cover all summer, followed by a thrilling autumn display. But they can also be grown into stout old trees, making an astonishing sight when the burning autumn reds flare out from the branches.

When growing up a wall or tree, place in a large planting hole about 60cm (2ft) from the base. They will shoot up any support, so take care to keep clear of roofs and guttering, by cutting back.

The Essentials

Site demands Almost anywhere.
Planting practice Best to plant between mid autumn and spring. Dig in lots of compost or manure.
Flowering time Inconspicuous, greenish flowers appear in summer.
Pruning needs Thin out and cut off unwanted growth over summer.
Pests and diseases Generally trouble free, but aphids may attack.
Bonus point Gives rapid cover that blazes with colour in autumn.

Expert's Selection

1 *P. tricuspidata* 'Veitchii'
In autumn, its purple-flushed leaves turn a glowing, rich purply red.
⌀ **Purple-red • Autumn**
h. 12m (40ft) ***s.*** 10m (33ft)

2 *P. henryana* ♀
Grow in shade for strong colour in autumn, when the velvety, silver-veined leaves turn deep scarlet.
⌀ **Deep scarlet • Autumn**
h. 10m (33ft) ***s.*** 6m (20ft)

3 *P. quinquefolia* ♀
Gives fantastic rich crimson hues in autumn. Vigorous, so may need to limit growth by cutting back.
⌀ **Crimson • Autumn**
h. 15m (50ft) ***s.*** 9m (30ft)

STAR PERFORMER
P. tricuspidata 'Veitchii'
A wonderfully rampant form of Boston ivy, it rapidly covers walls and tree trunks, clinging on by tiny adhesive pads.

Passiflora

Passion flower plants not only bear amazingly intricate, scented flowers, but may also produce edible, yellow or orange, egg-shaped fruits, that ripen in autumn.

with petals surrounding a distinctive central 'crown' or corona of thread-like filaments.

The key to success is good drainage to prevent roots from rotting in winter. Heavy soils may need the occasional addition of horticultural grit to lighten them.

Expert's Selection

1 *P. caerulea*♀
Fragrant, wide flowers are often followed by orange, egg-sized fruits. 'Constance Elliott'♀ is creamy white, and prefers more shelter.
✿ **White with purple-blue corona Midsummer–early autumn** ✹ **Orange Autumn** • *h.* **10m (33ft)** *s.* **1m (3ft)**

2 *P. incarnata*
Its lightly scented flowers are a beautiful mix of pastel shades.
✿ **Pale purple with purple corona Midsummer** ✹ **Yellow • Autumn** *h.* **7m (23ft)** *s.* **1m (3ft)**

STAR PERFORMER
P. caerulea♀ **A vigorous, tough climber, it will haul itself up walls, and over other shrubs and trees by means of its tightly clinging tendrils.**

Despite origins in the warmer parts of the Americas, some passiflora, such as *P. caerulea* and *P. incarnata,* are hardy and will be perfectly happy in a cooler climate. They are vigorous climbers, that give a flourish of astonishing, summer flowers,

The Essentials

Site demands Any well-drained soil, in a sunny, south or west-facing site, protected from cold wind.
Planting practice Plant out towards the end of spring.
Flowering time Long season, from midsummer, well into autumn.
Pruning needs Shape in spring.
Pests and diseases Generally trouble free, though is sometimes attacked by greenfly.
Bonus point Edible autumn fruit.

Perovskia

Russian sage, with its tall, elegant, winter stems, followed by grey-green, aromatic leaves in spring and a mass of deep blue flower spikes in summer, is a true all-season plant.

Expert's Selection

1 *P.* 'Blue Spire'♀
The flower spikes on this tall quick-growing variety are a beautiful deep blue.
✿ **Deep blue • Midsummer–early autumn** • *h.* **1.2 (4ft)** *s.* **1m (3ft)**

2 *P.* 'Superba'
An especially appealing variety, with silvery leaves and large, showy, violet-blue flowers.
✿ **Violet-blue • Midsummer–early autumn** • *h.* **1.2 (4ft)** *s.* **1m (3ft)**

The Essentials

Site demands Any well-drained soil, in full sun.
Planting practice Plant in spring.
Flowering time Lasts from midsummer to early autumn.
Pruning needs Cut back last year's growth in spring.
Pests and diseases Trouble free.
Bonus point Aromatic leaves.

This tough, truly care-free shrub is also very attractive. It has strong upright growth, and will look good planted in a mixed border or as edging. As long as it is positioned in full sun, it will flower right through to the close of summer.

The hairy, greyish leaves that appear each spring have an aroma similar to that of culinary sage.

STAR PERFORMER
P. 'Blue Spire' **Grow a clump of this aromatic shrub in the border for a dense sweep of deep blue flowers and silvery foliage all summer long.**

Philadelphus

Mock orange is an easy-going shrub grown for its summer show of cup-shaped flowers, which have the heavenly scent of orange blossom.

This deciduous shrub is justifiably popular. Its white or cream flowers emit an exotic musky scent that fills the garden on a warm day. Give it a sunny spot and it will thrive, even in poor soil and polluted air.

STAR PERFORMER

P. x *lemoinei* **Give this shrub pride of place in the border and it will be smothered in scented flowers all summer.**

Expert's Selection

1 *P.* x *lemoinei*
A broad, spreading shrub. 'Erectus' has a close, compact habit.
❀ White • Early–midsummer
h.&s. 1.8m (6ft)

2 *P.* 'Avalanche'
Slender boughs of scented flowers.
❀ White • Early–midsummer
h. 1.5m (5ft) *s.* 75cm (2½ft)

3 *P. coronarius* 'Variegatus'♀ Semi-double flowers and cream-edged leaves.
❀ White • Early–midsummer
h. 1.5m (5ft) *s.* 75cm (2½ft)

4 *P.* 'Belle Etoile'♀
A compact shrub whose heavily scented flowers have fringed petals.
❀ White • Early–midsummer
h.&s. 1.5m (5ft)

The Essentials

Site demands A sunny spot.
Planting practice Plant in autumn or spring.
Flowering time Summer.
Pruning needs Prune after flowering back to a new shoot.
Pests and diseases Leaf spot and aphids may attack.
Bonus point Grows well in gardens on busy roads.

Phlomis

This drought-tolerant evergreen is grown as much for its distinctive silvery grey, fuzzy foliage as for its summer flowers, which come in shades of yellow, pink or purple.

Expert's Selection

1 *P. fruticosa*♀
A sturdy, low-growing shrub with oval or lance-shaped leaves.
✿ Yellow • All summer
h.&s. 1m (3ft)

2 *P. italica*
This variety is more upright and untidy, with dull green leaves.
✿ Purple-pink • Summer
h. 1m (3ft) *s.* 60cm (2ft)

3 *P. chrysophylla*♀
Bears large flowers up to 5cm (2in) long. The grey-green leaves warm to a golden hue with age.
✿ Golden yellow • All summer
h.&s. 1m (3ft)

4 *P. bovei* subsp. *maroccana* A taller variety whose long flowers grow in whorls.
✿ Purple-pink • Summer
h.&s. 1.5m (5ft)

This easy-going shrub will produce dense clusters of snapdragon-like flowers all summer, if given a well-drained soil in a sunny position. It thrives in hot, dry locations and is good for drought conditions.

The Essentials

Site demands A well-drained sunny spot out of cold winds.
Planting practice Plant in spring.
Flowering time All summer.
Pests and diseases Trouble free.
Bonus point Quick to establish.

STAR PERFORMER

P. fruticosa **Plant a clump of Jerusalem sage at the front of the border. Its silvery foliage will be smothered in bright yellow flowers all summer.**

Picea

Spruces look like Christmas trees and are generally much too tall for the average garden. However, the hardy, coniferous evergreens recommended here are small and compact: ideal for providing colour and interest in a restricted space and with very little effort.

1 *P. glauca* var. *albertiana* **'Conica'**♀ A slow-growing conifer, perfectly conical in shape.
⌀ **Bright green needles turning dusky green with age**
h.&s. 1.5m (5ft) after 20 years

2 *P. pungens* **'Lucky Strike'**
A slow-growing dwarf variety. Long reddish brown cones contrast with the brightly coloured needles.
⌀ **Bright green needles**
h.&s. 1.8m (6ft) after 20 years

3 *P. pungens* **'Globosa'**♀
A dome-forming blue variety that is a pretty addition to a rockery.
⌀ **Bright blue needles**
h.&s. 80cm (32in) after 20 years

4 *P. pungens* **'Koster'**♀
A good specimen tree, this forms a tall, slender, conical shape.
⌀ **Silver-blue needles** • *h.* 3m (10ft)
s. 1m (3ft) after 20 years

Site demands A sunny, sheltered, moist site and neutral or acid soil.
Planting practice Plant in late spring.
Pruning needs Pruning will disfigure most spruces.
Pests and diseases Red spider mite attacks many dwarf varieties.
Bonus point Aromatic foliage.

These hardy evergreen conifers will tolerate most conditions, although they prefer a sunny position, sheltered from cold winds. For an average-sized tree try the blue **'Koster'**, which is slow-growing and conical.

Dwarf spruces are often planted in tubs, containers, or in rockeries. One of the prettiest is **'Globosa'**. In a warm spot you will be able to smell the aromatic foliage as you pass by.

Minimum interference
Spruces need very little care and pruning is not necessary – indeed it is more likely to disfigure than enhance the tree. Only remove dead twigs, branches that have reverted to green on coloured varieties, and unwanted branches. Prune in winter to minimise the likelihood of resin bleeding and attracting disease.

P. pungens **'Koster'**

P. pungens **'Globosa'**

> **STAR PERFORMER**
> *P. glauca* var. *albertiana* **'Conica'**♀
> **This little tree looks great in a border. Its new needles emerge vivid yellowy green and soften to a grey-green with age.**

Pinus

Pine trees are available in care-free slow-growing and dwarf varieties, that are ideal for the average-sized garden, and make excellent ornamental shrubs or ground cover.

Pines can be grown almost anywhere, though they prefer an acid soil and good light. Truly hardy, their aromatic, evergreen, needle-like foliage comes in a wide range of attractive shades. They are very easy to look after: just remove the occasional spindly branch to keep the bush in shape.

Male and female flowers appear on each bush, and in many varieties the striking female flowers develop into attractive cones. These gradually change their colour as they ripen, over two to three years.

STAR PERFORMER
P. sylvestris 'Chantry Blue'
With blue needles and bright orange buds in spring, this makes a lovely conical shrub for a border or lawn.

Expert's Selection

1 P. sylvestris 'Chantry Blue'
This slow-growing Scots pine is an especially attractive shrub. Another blue-grey variety, 'Watereri', is even slower to mature. 'Beuvronensis'♀, a dwarf form, only grows to 1m (3ft) and is good in rockeries.
⌀ **Blue-grey** ⚘ **Yellow cones; ripen to brown** • *h.* 4m (13ft) *s.* 2m (7ft)

2 P. heldreichii♀
Another slow-grower, it has very long, stiff, dark green needles. 'Schmidtii'♀, a dwarf variety, takes 100 years to reach 3m (10ft).
⌀ **Dark green** ⚘ **Dark blue cones; ripen to pale brown**
h. 24m (80ft) *s.* 8m (27ft)

3 P. mugo
Striking, red, female flowers appear on the tips of the stems and mature into cones. 'Gnom' is a dwarf variety, only 2m (7ft) high.
⌀ **Dark green** ⚘ **Black-brown cones; ripen to yellow-brown**
h. 3m (10ft) *s.* 9m (30ft)

The Essentials

Site demands Neutral or acid soil, in a sunny position.
Planting practice Plant in mid to late autumn.
Pruning needs Only trim the bush to tidy its shape.
Pests and diseases Usually trouble free, but pine shoot moth caterpillars may attack.
Bonus point Aromatic leaves.

Potentilla

Plant this hardy shrub to bring a splash of long-lasting, vibrant colour to a border or rock garden in summer. There are hundreds of different varieties to choose from, all of them totally care free and easy to grow, as long as you place them in a sunny spot.

STAR PERFORMER
P. fruticosa 'Goldfinger'♀
The large, saucer-like, yellow flowers contrast well with the blue-green foliage. Plant in the border and enjoy a show that will last all summer.

Potentilla flowers resemble small wild roses, and come in various shades of yellow, orange, red, pink or white. Plant a few different varieties in sunny areas around your garden, and you will be able to rely on an effortless abundance of vivid colour from late spring until almost the end of September.

All the varieties suggested here are hardy shrubs, that may need a light trim from time to time to keep them in shape, but are highly unlikely to have any other requirements. However, some may benefit from a spring mulch of organic compost or manure.

Note that there are also herbaceous perennial varieties of potentilla (see page 160).

The Essentials

Site demands Any moderately fertile, well-drained site, in full sun.
Planting practice Plant out from autumn to spring.
Flowering time From early to late summer.
Pruning needs Only trim lightly to tidy the shape of a bush.
Pests and diseases Trouble free.
Bonus point Flowers profusely.

1 *P. fruticosa* 'Goldfinger' ♀
This upright dwarf form is ideal for a glowing summer display.
✿ **Bright yellow • Summer** ∅ **Blue-green • h. 75cm (2½ft) s. 1m (3ft)**

2 *P. fruticosa* 'Red Ace'
A low-spreading variety, it bears wonderful bright red flowers.
✿ **Bright red with yellow centre Summer** ∅ **Bright green h. 75cm (2½ft) s. 1m (3ft)**

3 *P. fruticosa* 'Abbotswood' ♀
Provides a sharp contrast of dark foliage and brilliant white flowers.
❀ **White • Summer** ∅ **Dark green h. 75cm (2½ft) s. 1m (3ft)**

4 *P. fruticosa* 'Manchu'
Its delicate, sparsely scattered white flowers are long-lasting.
❀ **White • Summer** ∅ **Grey-green h. 75cm (2½ft) s. 1m (3ft)**

5 *P. fruticosa* 'Elizabeth' ♀ A low, rounded bush that bears a mass of large, bright yellow flowers.
Canary-yellow • Summer ∅ **Mid green • h. 1m (3ft) s. 1.2m (4ft)**

6 *P. fruticosa* 'Princess'
The pale pink flowers will fade to white in full sun.
✿ **Pale pink • Summer** ∅ **Dark green h. 60cm (2ft) s. 1m (3ft)**

P. fruticosa 'Red Ace'

Prunus

Dwarf versions of these ornamental fruit trees make very attractive, care-free shrubs. Some are grown for their beautiful spring blossom, others for their dazzling autumn foliage.

1 *P. incisa* 'Kojo-no-mai'
The zigzag branches of this slow-growing dwarf cherry are covered in dazzling pink blossom in spring.
✿ **Bright pink • Early–late spring** ∅ **Mid green h.&s 2.5m (8ft)**

2 *P. laurocerasus* 'Otto Luyken' ♀ Plant this evergreen cherry laurel as low hedging or in a small border. 'Schipkaensis' is a little taller, but flowers just as profusely.
❀ **White • Mid spring** ∅ **Dark green h. 1.2m (4ft) s. 1.5m (5ft)**

3 *P.* x *cistena* ♀
An ornamental plum that makes a dense hedge. The glossy red leaves gradually deepen to a copper tone.
❀ **White • Late spring** ∅ **Red h. 2m (7ft) s. 1.5m (5ft)**

4 *P.* x *cistena* 'Crimson Dwarf' Prized for its glorious red leaves and mass of brilliant white, spring blossom.
❀ **White • Early–late spring** ∅ **Red • h.&s. 1.5m (5ft)**

5 *P. tenella* 'Fire Hill' ♀
One of the smallest varieties, the rosy blossom of this dwarf Russian almond makes a stunning display.
✿ **Rosy red • Mid spring** ∅ **Dark green • 1m (3ft)**

P. incisa 'Kojo-no-mai' Enjoy the sumptuous blossoms of this flowering cherry in early spring, before the leaves appear. The leaves change from red to green then orange, as the year progresses.

These dwarf trees demand nothing but the odd trim. They all give an abundance of softly fragrant spring blossom. Some also have spectacularly coloured leaves, and bear edible fruit in autumn.

Site demands Any well-drained, sunny site, except on chalk.
Planting practice Plant from late autumn to mid spring.
Flowering time Spring.
Pruning Trim hedges to shape.
Pests and diseases Rare, but can get canker, silver leaf or spur blight.
Bonus point Spring blossom.

Pyracantha

Firethorns are prized for their rich autumn clusters of bright red, orange or yellow berries that persist well into winter, combined with elegant, glossy evergreen leaves. They look superb planted against walls, and can be easily trained upwards to make dense, colourful hedging.

Expert's Selection

1 *P.* **'Orange Charmer'**
A vigorous, bushy shrub, its dark orange berries are one of the highlights of autumn.
🍂 **Dark orange • Autumn**
❀ **White • Early summer**
h.&s. **3m (10ft)**

2 *P.* **'Teton'**
This colourful, erect shrub has red shoots, glossy, wavy-edged, bright green leaves and an abundance of yellow-orange autumn berries.
🍂 **Yellow-orange • Autumn**
❀ **White • Early summer**
h. **5m (16ft)** *s.* **3m (10ft)**

3 *P.* **'Soleil d'Or'**
A good choice for covering wide walls, it has bright yellow berries.
🍂 **Yellow • Autumn**
❀ **White • Early summer**
h.&s. **3m (10ft)**

4 *P.* **'Mohave'**
The bright red berries will last well into winter.
🍂 **Bright red • Autumn**
❀ **White • Early summer**
h. **5m (16ft)** *s.* **4m (13ft)**

5 *P. coccinea* **'Red Cushion'** Densely leafy, it bears vivid red berries.
🍂 **Bright red • Autumn**
❀ **White • Early summer**
h.&s. **3.5m (12ft)**

P. 'Mohave' in bloom

STAR PERFORMER
P. **'Orange Charmer'** Eventually reaching a height of 3m (10ft), it makes a magnificent sight in autumn, when it is covered with dense bunches of rich orange berries. It will cover a wall completely with its mass of branches.

P. 'Soleil d'Or'

The Essentials

Site demands Any fertile, well-drained soil, that is not too chalky, in sun or shade. They will grow on north and east-facing walls.
Planting practice Plant in autumn or spring.
Flowering time Early summer.
Pruning needs In summer cut back vigorous new shoots on newly planted specimens to three leaves, to promote extra growth. Prune established shrubs in early spring, before flowering, to encourage a substantial show of berries. Subsequent light pruning in summer reduces unwanted growth and exposes the berries. Wear tough, thick gloves when pruning because the thorns are long and sharp.
Pests and diseases Woolly aphids, pyracantha scab and fire blight sometimes cause problems.
Bonus point Birds are attracted into the garden in winter by the red-berried varieties.

Ribes

Flowering currants combine dangling rich-toned spring blossom with attractive autumn foliage. The leaves and flowers of these appealing shrubs are often scented.

Expert's Selection

1 *R. sanguineum* **'Pulborough Scarlet'** The best of the red-flowered varieties. For a lower, spreading form with red blooms, choose the 1.2m (4ft) high 'King Edward VII'.
✿ **Deep red • Mid spring**
h.&s. **2m (7ft)**

2 *R. sanguineum* **'White Icicle'** A tall, elegant variety, its leaves have a spicy fragrance.
✿ **White • Early spring**
h. **3m (10ft)** *s.* **2m (7ft)**

3 *R. odoratum*
Clove-scented flowers are followed by colourful autumn foliage.
✿ **Yellow • Spring** ∅ **Purple Autumn • *h.&s.* 2m (7ft)**

4 *R. speciosum*
Bears a mass of drooping, deep red flower clusters.
✿ **Deep red • Mid–late spring • *h.&s.* 3m (10ft)**

Easy going flowering currants will provide interest in the garden from spring through to autumn with very little attention. The flowers grow in thick grape-like clusters, in a range of colours from white to deep reds. They look good as individual plants, and can also be grown as an informal hedge. To maintain the shape, cut off the flowered shoots after flowering, and cut back old stems to ground level.

STAR PERFORMER
R. sanguineum **'Pulborough Scarlet'** Plant in a sunny spot to enjoy the dense clusters of deep red flowers in spring.

The Essentials

Site demands Any well-drained soil, in sun or light shade.
Planting practice Plant in autumn or spring.
Flowering time Spring.
Pests and diseases Usually trouble free.
Bonus point Brings year-round colour to the garden.

A firethorn will brighten up a shady wall with a mass of deliciously coloured autumn berries. They look good in summer too, covered with masses of soft white flowers. Generally hardy, except in extremely severe winters, they will grow in most soils except chalk, which causes the foliage to turn yellow. The glossy green leaves have sharp thorns, so wear gloves when pruning.

Pyracanthas look fine as freestanding shrubs, but are usually grown as climbers and make excellent hedging.

RESISTANT VARIETIES
Firethorns may be affected by pyracantha scab and occasionally by fire blight. Good disease-resistant varieties to choose from include *P.* **'Teton'**, *P.* **'Navaho'**, and new varieties in the **'Saphyr'** range: **'Saphyr Orange'**, **'Rouge'**, and **'Jaune'**; the colours refer to the berries.

Climbing a wall
Firethorns need to be given strong support while growing up walls. As they are quite sturdy, check that the horizontal support wiring or trellis has been firmly attached to the wall or a strong fence. When growing on walls with windows, ensure that the plant is trained right round to create an attractive effect and avoid blocking light to the house.

Rhododendron

These beautiful flowering shrubs look so exotic that many people assume they must be difficult to grow. They could not be easier, provided you plant them in acid soil. There is an enormous variety. Select for flower colour and size, checking that your choice will not outgrow your garden.

The rhododendrons – a group that include azaleas – ranges from large specimens the size of small trees to dwarf varieties, ideal for growing in rockeries or containers.

Most types are evergreen, some with strikingly attractive leaves. But they are grown mainly for their spectacular flowers, which usually appear in great profusion in spring and early summer. They come in a wide spectrum of often vivid colours, and a few have the bonus of being strongly scented.

Tough beauties
For the average sized garden, the hardiest and easiest of the rhododendrons are the yakushimanum ('yak') hybrids, such as **'Cheer'**, **'Dopey'** or **'Percy Wiseman'**. **'Cheer'** is especially tough, so is useful for adding colour to colder plots.

Taller varieties such as *R. decorum* and **'Pink Pearl'** are suitable only in larger gardens.

Autumn is the best season for planting, as it allows the roots enough time to become well established before growth begins again in spring. Be sure to plant at the correct depth – 2–3cm (1in) down – in well worked and composted soil that the roots can easily penetrate. Only mimimal aftercare is required, but do make sure the soil is kept moist in dry weather, especially during the first season. Mulching with compost or leaf-mould will help conserve moisture and also reduce weeds.

Container planting
Use an acid, free-draining compost, such as peat mixed with composted bark, garden soil, leaf-mould or grit. Hardy dwarf varieties such as **'Bengal'** and **'Ramapo'** are very suitable and evergreen azaleas such as the white **'Palestrina'** are also good for containers, as they are mostly hardy, with an average height and spread of only 60cm–1m (2–3ft).

R. 'Dopey'

STAR PERFORMER
R. **'Cheer'** Plant this in a cold, northern garden, and you will feel like cheering when its flowers open in spring.

Yakushimanum hybrids

1 *R.* **'Cheer'**
An abundance of shell-pink flowers, streaked with red, cover this densely growing shrub throughout spring. It is particularly hardy, so is ideally suited for planting in colder parts of the garden.
✿ **Shell-pink • Spring**
***h.&s.* 1–2.5m (3–8ft)**

2 *R.* **'Dopey'** ♥
From late spring to early summer, neat trusses of long-lasting, glossy, deep red flowers appear on this hardy, upright evergreen.
✿ **Deep red • Late spring–early summer • *h.&s.* 1m (3ft)**

3 *R.* **'Bruce Brechtbill'**
Pink, yellow-tinged flowers open amongst the tough, shiny green foliage between April and May.
✿ **Yellowy pink • Late spring**
***h.&s.* 2m (7ft)**

4 *R.* **'Percy Wiseman'** ♥
A low-growing, compact shrub with pale green leaves, its funnel-shaped peach-pink and cream flowers appear in late spring.
✿ **Peach-pink and cream**
Late spring • *h.&s.* 1.2m (4ft)

R. williamsianum

R. 'Ramapo'

R. 'Satan'

R. 'Palestrina'

Species rhododendrons

1 *R. decorum*
One of the few species with scented flowers, this hardy plant is best suited to larger gardens.
❀✿ **White to pale pink**
Late spring–early summer
h. **6m (20ft)** *s.* **2.5m (8ft)**

2 *R. williamsianum* ♀
A sun-loving, dome-shaped shrub with young leaves of bronze.
✿❀ **Rose-pink and white** ∅ **Bronze and later green** • **Mid–late spring**
h. **1.5m (5ft)** *s.* **1.2m (4ft)**

TAKE A FRESH LOOK

R. ponticum 'Variegatum'
White markings on the leaves of this 6m (20ft) shrub make it one of the more unusual and attractive rhododendron.
R. ponticum is not advised as it will overtake native flora. This variegated form is less intrusive.

Dwarf hybrids

1 *R.* 'Bengal'
A colourful dwarf hybrid, it forms a low, dense mound, making it ideal for the small garden. In April and May, it is covered in a mass of bright red flowers.
✿ **Bright red** • **Late spring**
h.&s. **1m (3ft)**

2 *R.* 'Ramapo' ♀
Exceptionally hardy, the fine grey-blue leaves and pale violet flowers make it strikingly attractive.
✿ **Pale violet** • **Late spring**
∅ **Grey-blue**
h. **1m (3ft)** *s.* **1.2m (4ft)**

Large hybrids

1 *R.* 'Pink Pearl'
Ideally choose a sunny spot for this vigorous shrub, and enjoy the large, brown speckled, pink flowers that appear from late spring onward.
✿ **Pink** • **Late spring–early summer**
h.&s. **4m (13ft)**

2 *R.* 'Crest' ♀
Orange buds open in late spring to create a stunning display of long-lasting primrose-yellow blooms.
✿ **Primrose yellow** • **Late spring**
h.&s. **3.5m (11ft)**

Azaleas

1 *R.* 'Satan' ♀
Grow this bushy azalea for its profusion of striking scarlet flowers and bronze-tinted autumn foliage.
✿ **Scarlet** • **Late spring**
∅ **Bronze** • **Autumn** • *h.&s.* **2m (6ft)**

2 *R.* 'Palestrina' ♀
A medium-sized, Japanese evergreen, its dark, glossy leaves provide the perfect backdrop for its dazzling, spring display of pure white, funnel-shaped flowers.
❀ **White** • **Late spring**
h.&s. **1.2m (4ft)**

R. 'Crest'

The Essentials

Site demands They thrive only in acid soil (see page 8), which should be moist but well-drained. They prefer dappled sun or light shade.

Planting practice Plant in autumn, covering the rootball with just 2–3cm (1in) of soil. Placing too deep can kill or stunt the plant.

Pruning Cut back old or straggly growth in late winter, or just after flowering has finished. Deadheading will help to improve growth and create more flowerheads.

Pests and diseases Few problems, but young shoots in particular may be attacked by caterpillars, slugs and vine weevils. If honey fungus strikes cut it out of the plant at once.

Bonus point A highly spectacular, colourful floral display is virtually guaranteed. Some varieties will fill the garden with their rich fragrance.

Rosa

Roses are unmatched for their variety of size, shape and colour availability, as well as for their glorious fragrance. Many modern varieties are bred specially for health and vigour, so you will encounter few problems. The varieties chosen here are all hardy and resistant to disease.

Roses are the most popular of all the shrubs, and there are thousands of varieties to choose from. All the roses listed here are hardy, and will grow on almost any soil, though some are fussy about their growing conditions.

Most roses generally prefer a rich, heavy soil containing plenty of organic material. They will also benefit from a regular mulch of manure or compost. Waterlogged soils and pure sand, chalk or blue clay are not suitable.

Container-grown roses can be planted at any time, but bare-root roses should be planted over winter. Choose plants with at least three and preferably four sturdy, healthy stems and sound foliage. Do not plant if the soil is very wet or frozen, but keep in a cool place, with their roots moist and covered, until conditions improve.

FRAGRANCE Old roses, such as damask and bourbon roses, are usually sweetly fragrant, but many modern varieties are now also bred for fragrance. Highly-scented plants include 'Gertrude Jekyll', 'Graham Thomas', 'Roseraie de L'Haÿ' and 'Arthur Bell'.

Rose varieties

Whether you are looking for a romantic climber to frame a cottage doorway, substantial bushes for a formal garden or a compact shrub for a patio, there is sure to be a care-free variety to suit. Roses are divided generally into the following categories, and care-free selections are given here for most of them. Species roses, hybrid tea (HT) roses, floribunda roses, shrub roses, patio roses, miniature roses, ground-cover roses, and climbing and rambling roses.

Species roses

All modern roses derive from the original wild roses which are known as species roses. They usually flower once in spring or early summer with five-petalled single flowers and may bear attractive hips in autumn.

Hybrid tea and floribunda roses

Hybrid tea roses have large flowers and are often richly scented. Their upright growth and uniform height make them ideal for planting in formal beds.

Floribunda roses, such as **'Fascination'**, are similar in size and habit to hybrid tea roses, but produce smaller flowers and carry them in larger clusters, some of 20 or more blooms. Floribundas withstand wet weather better than hybrid tea roses and the buds do not open all at once, so, although some hybrid tea roses are repeat flowerers, floribundas may bloom for longer.

Shrub roses

Most modern shrub roses will flower repeatedly if they are deadheaded regularly. Taller ones, such as **'Marguerite Hilling'**, make beautiful specimen plants, while others like **'Fred Loads'** make good hedging.

Old shrub roses, including those that used to be called polyantha roses, are less widely planted. They are mainly hybrids developed in the 19th century and typically have dense double flowers with a lovely scent.

Patio and miniature roses

Modern patio roses such as **'Top Marks'** are larger than miniature roses, but smaller than floribundas. They have an upright bushy growth and form cushions of colour over a long season. They will grow successfully in planters, tubs and containers if given regular feeding.

Climbers and ramblers

Climbing and rambling roses are one of the delights of the summer garden. Train them to cover pergolas, walls and old trees.

To get the best out of a climbing rose on a wall, train its stems along a horizontal wire for the first few years. This will encourage plenty of vigorous sideshoots, which can then be trained upwards. If you do not start the climber horizontally, all the flowers will bloom too high up to be fully appreciated.

Essential tips for pruning

Regularly pruned roses will be more vigorous. Pruning stimulates new shoots to grow from low down the bush, keeping it young. It also removes dead or diseased wood that may weaken the bush, and improves air circulation to keep the rose healthy.

Prune **hybrid tea** roses, **modern shrub** roses and **floribundas** in spring. Remove dead or diseased wood and shorten the previous year's growth by two-thirds. Cut back some old branches hard to encourage new growth.

Species roses are pruned in the same way, but after flowering. Cut back the main shoots of upright shrubs by half to prevent 'legginess'. **Patio** and **ground-cover** roses need minimal pruning.

Climbing roses should be cut back in spring to the next strong bud to produce new sideshoots. Remove the flowered shoots of **rambling roses** immediately after flowering to promote new shoots from the base. Where a wall climber is bare at the base, with all the growth high up, prune some old stems to 30cm (1ft), but not all at once. (For more tips on pruning roses, see page 17.)

Site demands Well-drained, moist, slightly acid soil in full sun or partial shade for part of the day.
Planting practice Plant firmly, with the surface of the soil 2.5cm (1in) above the budding joint. Plant when dormant and shorten all shoots to 15cm (6in) above ground level. Add rose fertiliser.
Flowering time Most roses are now repeat flowering.
Pruning needs See main text.
Pests and diseases Black spot, powdery mildew, canker, rose rust, aphids and caterpillars.
Bonus point Beautiful shape, great colours and lovely perfume.

Hybrid tea and floribunda roses

Hybrid tea roses have large blooms borne singly or in small clusters. Floribundas have smaller blooms, but in clusters of up to 20 flowers. Some are very fragrant.

1 *R.* 'Arthur Bell' ♀
An upright floribunda noted for its strong fragrance with unusually large golden yellow flowers.
✿ **Golden yellow • All summer**
h.&s. 1m (3ft)

2 *R.* 'Fascination'
Plant this floribunda in mixed beds or borders to enjoy its large clusters of shrimp-pink flowers.
✿ **Shrimp-pink • All summer**
h.&s. 45cm (1½ft)

3 *R.* 'Cheshire Life'
A strongly growing hybrid tea rose which bears masses of open, bright red double flowers.
✿ **Bright red • All summer**
h. 75cm (2½ft) s. 60cm (2ft)

4 *R.* 'Peer Gynt'
A hybrid tea rose with round yellow blooms flushed with red.
✿ **Bright yellow • All summer**
h. 75m (2½ft) s. 60cm (2ft)

5 *R.* 'Silver Jubilee' ♀
The beautiful large flowers of this deep pink hybrid tea rose bloom continuously.
✿ **Pink • All summer**
h. 1m (3ft) s. 60cm (2ft)

R. 'Peer Gynt'

R. 'Silver Jubilee'

R. glauca

7 *R. glauca*♀ syn.
R. rubrifolia The short-lived
clusters of flowers on this bluish-
leaved shrub are followed by a
crop of striking red hips.
✿ **Pink • Early summer**
h. **2m (7ft)** *s.* **1.8m (6ft)**

8 *R. rugosa* 'Alba'♀
The single white flowers are
cup-shaped and fragrant. They are
followed in autumn by large hips,
like orange-red tomatoes.
✿ **White • All summer   Orange-red
Autumn • h.&s.** 1–2.5m (3–8ft)

9 *R.* x *jacksonii* 'Max Graf'
A spreading rugosa rose that forms
a mass of glossy foliage. The single
flowers are scented like apples.
✿ **Pink • All summer**
h. 1.2m (4ft) *s.* 2.5m (8ft)

10 *R.* 'Scarlet Fire'
A vigorous rugosa shrub rose with
arching stems. It makes a vivid
scarlet alternative to *R.rugosa* 'Alba'
and each bloom has prominent
golden stamens. Large red hips
provide colour in autumn.
✿ **Red • All summer • h.&s.** 1.8m (6ft)

STAR PERFORMER
R. 'Heritage' The highly structured
blooms are composed of numerous
relatively small petals, intricately
arranged to form an almost
spherical shape.

Species roses

Descended from wild roses, these
hardy species roses and their
hybrids bear single-petalled blooms
along the whole length of their
elegant arching stems. Many are
sweetly scented.

1 *R.* 'Geranium'♀ (syn.
R. moyesii 'Geranium')
A tall arching bush which bears
beautiful crimson flowers and long-
lasting and vibrant orange autumn
hips the shape of long wine flagons.
✿ **Bright red • Early summer**
h. **2.5m (8ft)** *s.* **2m (7ft)**

2 *R. paulii*
This rose grows into a wide
spreading bush with single white
flowers that are up to 10cm (4in)
across, and grey-green leaves with
prominent veins.
✿ **White • Early summer**
h. 1.2m (4ft) *s.* 1.5m (5ft)

3 *R. sericea* subsp.
omeiensis f. *pteracantha*
A spring-flowering rose that reveals
prominent red thorns in winter.
✿ **White • Late spring**
h.&s. **2.5m (8ft)**

4 *R. rubiginosa*♀ syn.
R. eglanteria The eglantine
rose or sweetbriar is a prickly
shrub, which bears single pink
blooms with a white centre
and has fragrant foliage.
✿ **Rose-pink • Midsummer**
h.&s. **up to 2.5m (8ft)**

5 *R.* 'Stanwell
Perpetual' The
voluptuous double pale pink
blooms of this compact shrub
rose will flower repeatedly.
✿ **Light blush pink Midsummer**
h. **1m (3ft)** *s.* **1.2m (4ft)**

6 *R. pimpinellifolia* syn
R. spinosissima A low-growing
dense, prickly shrub with single
white flowers 5cm (2in) across.
✿ **White • Early summer**
h. **1m (3ft)** *s.* **1.2m (4ft)**

'R. Geranium'

R. 'Fred Loads'

R. 'Graham Thomas'

R. 'Nevada'

R. 'Prosperity'

Shrub roses

Free-flowering, versatile and easy to grow, shrub roses have an attractively informal habit.

1 R. 'Heritage'
Dense clusters of sweetly scented petals form big rounded flowers.
✿ **Pale pink • All summer**
h.&s. **1.2m (4ft)**

2 R. 'Ballerina' ♀
A free-flowering shrub rose for a small garden with single pink flowers in mophead clusters.
✿ **Pale pink • All summer**
h.&s. **1m (3ft)**

3 R. 'Fred Loads' ♀
Trusses of large, lightly scented flowers, each with only five petals, weigh down this upright shrub.
✿ **Orange-red • All summer**
h. **1.8m (6ft)** *s.* **1m (3ft)**

4 R. 'Frühlingsgold' ♀
Glorious, large perfumed flowers appear in early summer.
✿ **Primrose-yellow • Early summer**
h. **2.5m (8ft)** *s.* **2m (7ft)**

5 R. 'Frühlingsmorgen'
Vivid pink single blooms are pale primrose at the centre with bright amber stamens, and make a superb springtime display.
✿ **Pink • Late spring**
h.&s. **1.8m (6ft)**

6 R. 'Graham Thomas' ♀
A fragrant English rose with abundant golden yellow flowers 10cm (4in) across.
✿ **Golden yellow • All summer**
h. **1.5m (5ft)** *s.* **1.2m (4ft)**

7 R. 'Marguerite Hilling' ♀
A dense spreading shrub which makes an outstanding early summer show with its profuse scented pink flowers.
✿ **Pink • All summer**
h.&s. **2m (7ft)**

8 R. 'Nevada' ♀
A large, spreading shrub rose which will look good in a border. Its huge, creamy white flowers are lightly scented.
⊛ **Creamy white • All summer**
h.&s. **2m (7ft)**

9 R. 'Roseraie de l'Haÿ' ♀
A tall rose, actually a rugosa hybrid, that looks magnificent in the border with its large, velvety purple flowers. The double blooms are scented. This is a good choice for exposed or seaside gardens.
✿ **Light purple • All summer**
h.&s. **1.8m (6ft)**

10 R. 'Prosperity' ♀
A hybrid musk rose for the border. It has a strong fragrance and semi-double flowers.
⊛ **Creamy white • All summer**
h. **1m (3ft)** *s.* **1.2m (4ft)**

R.'Sweet Dream'

R.'Maigold'

looser as they open. The blooms are particularly sweet-scented.
✿ **Warm pink • Early summer**
h.&s. **4.5m (15ft)**

4 R. 'Danse du Feu'
The brightest scarlet round, double flowers will bloom abundantly right through the summer into autumn.
✿ **Scarlet • All summer**
h.&s. **2.5m (8ft)**

5 R. 'Dublin Bay' ♀
Rich red flowers and glossy foliage are all abundant on this large-flowered climber.
✿ **Rich red • All summer**
h.&s. **2.5m (8ft)**

6 R. 'Gloire de Dijon' ♀
This tall climber makes a gorgeous show with its large flowers and heavy scent.
✿ **Buff yellow • All summer**
h.&s. **5m (15ft)**

Climbing and rambling roses
Most climbing roses send out long shoots to cover walls, trees and fencing and bear small clusters of relatively large repeat-flowering blooms. Rambling roses bear larger clusters of smaller blooms and tend to flower only once during the season.

1 R. 'Compassion' ♀
Beautifully shaped flowers shade from light apricot to a deeper pink at their edges and will bloom continuously for several months.
✿ **Salmon pink • All summer**
h.&s. **3m (10ft)**

2 R. 'Alberic Barbier' ♀
Small clusters of soft orange buds open to beautiful creamy double blooms on this vigorous, almost evergreen rambler.
❀ **Creamy white • Early summer**
h.&s. **4.5m (15ft)**

3 R. 'Albertine' ♀
The open double flowers are large for a rambling rose and become

Patio roses
Short of stature but big on personality, these roses will thrive in tubs or containers on a patio.

1 R. 'Sweet Dream' ♀
One of the modern compact patio roses which flower all summer. This variety has tightly cupped peachy pink flowers.
✿ **Peachy pink • All summer**
h.&s. **45cm (1½ft)**

2 R. 'Top Marks'
Liven up your patio with this dwarf rose which continuously produces masses of bright orange-red flowers.
✿ **Orange-red • All summer**
h. **60cm (2ft)** *s.* **45cm (1½ft)**

TAKE A FRESH LOOK

R. **Penny Lane** is a delightful plant, vigorous and healthy with large flowers which are a gentle honey colour when they open but turn gradually to a light pink. It reaches 2.5m (8ft).

R.'Top Marks'

7 *R.* 'Golden Showers'♀
It bears large, bright yellow double flowers with a strong fragrance and is particularly good when trained up a pillar. The flowers fade quite quickly to a creamy tone.
✿ **Bright yellow • All summer**
h.&s. **2.5m (8ft)**

8 *R.* 'Maigold'♀
The first and most prolific flowering takes place in early spring when the bush bears warm orange double blooms on the stiff thorny stems. After that, flowering is generally more sporadic.
✿ **Orange-yellow • All summer**
h.&s. **2.5m (8ft)**

9 *R.* 'Madame Alfred Carrière'♀ This rose may date back to 1879, but is still one of the best climbing roses available. It is disease-resistant and very strong growing, even in a difficult aspect, and will cover a north-facing wall with masses of pink-tinged flowers. Sweetly scented blooms last through summer into autumn.
❀ **White • All summer**
h.&s. **4.5m (15ft)**

10 *R.* 'New Dawn'♀
Giving a continuous show of flowers all summer long, this rose makes a wonderful climber. Its healthy green foliage also makes it a good choice as a flowering hedge. Grow it where you will appreciate its fresh and fruity scent.
✿ **Blush pink • All summer**
h.&s. **3m (10ft)**

STAR PERFORMER
R. 'Compassion'♀ **An exceptional salmon pink, it grows 3m (10ft) high. The elegantly shaped buds open to sweetly scented flowers right through summer, and the stems are clothed in dark green foliage.**

R. 'New Dawn'

Ground-cover roses
Low and spreading shrub roses with thickly clustered, repeat-flowering blooms, ground-cover roses will not smother weeds, but make a delightful display in a border or covering a wall.

1 *R.* Pink Flower Carpet♀
Beautiful open bright pink double blooms are borne in abundance throughout summer complemented by healthy, glossy leaves.
✿ **Bright pink • All summer**
h. **1m (3ft)** *s.* **1.2m (4ft)**

2 *R.* 'Sunshine Flower Carpet' Very similar to 'Pink Flower Carpet' but with sunny yellow flowers instead.
✿ **Bright yellow • All summer**
h. **1m (3ft)** *s.* **1.2m (4ft)**

R. Pink Flower Carpet

Rosmarinus

Rosemary is a beautiful scented herb, which can be grown as an eye-catching, single shrub, as hedging or as a trailing plant. It will also take pride of place in the herb garden.

Expert's Selection

1 *R. officinalis* 'Miss Jessopp's Upright'♀ For clear blue flowers, choose this variety.
✿ Blue • Early spring–autumn
h.&s. 1.8m (6ft)

2 *R. officinalis* 'Severn Sea'♀ A smaller shrub with spreading, arching branches, it sits perfectly in the border.
✿ Violet-blue • Early spring–autumn
h.&s. 1m (3ft)

3 *R. officinalis* 'Jackman's Prostrate' A low-growing plant, suitable for a small herb garden.
✿ Pale blue • Early spring–autumn
h.&s. 30cm (1ft)

4 *R. officinalis* 'Sissinghurst Blue'♀ Plant in a border or as herb garden hedging.
✿ Deep blue • Early spring–autumn
h.&s. 1.2m (4ft)

The Essentials

Site demands Any sunny, well-drained site, except heavy clay soil.
Planting practice Plant in spring or early summer.
Flowering time Flowers from early spring to early summer, and then intermittently until autumn.
Pruning needs Cut out dead wood and straggly shoots in spring.
Pests and diseases Trouble free.
Bonus point A wonderful culinary herb, especially with lamb.

Long valued as an aromatic herb, rosemary is worth growing on that account alone. It is also a highly attractive evergreen bush, with needle-like leaves and mauve and blue flowers. Rosemary is native to the Mediterranean, and so thrives in full sun and well-drained soil. Some varieties make striking, monumental shrubs, the taller ones, such as 'Miss Jessopp's Upright' reaching 1.8m (6ft). There are smaller plants, more suited to a border, which reach 1–1.2m (3–4ft), as well as low-growing varieties such as 'Jackman's Prostrate'. All are hardy and care free. Prune only to cut out dead wood and keep in shape.

STAR PERFORMER
R. officinalis 'Miss Jessopp's Upright'♀ Planted as fragrant hedging or as a single, bushy shrub, this rosemary will give a marvellous display of blue flowers all summer long.

Ruscus

Butcher's broom is a hardy evergreen with attractive green foliage and bright red berries.

Expert's Selection

1 *R. aculeatus*
Has wiry green stems with small, thick, lance-shaped leaves and shiny bright red berries.
✿ Light green ❧ Bright red • Autumn
h.&s. 1m (3ft)

2 *R. hypoglossum*
Its arching stems bear soft, oval leaves, up to 10cm (4in) long.
✿ Light green ❧ Bright red • Autumn
h. 60cm (2ft) *s.* 1m (3ft)

The Essentials

Site demands Any well-drained soil, in both full sun and shade.
Planting practice Plant out in autumn.
Flowering time In spring or autumn, depending on the weather.
Pruning needs None.
Pests and diseases Trouble free.
Bonus point Cut foliage lasts well in flower arrangements.

R. hypoglossum

STAR PERFORMER
R. aculeatus Perfect for dry shady spots, this will bring a touch of colour all year round, with its bright green leaves and red berries.

Butcher's broom is a natural woodland plant, ideal for planting in dry shady spots where little else will grow. It has sturdy evergreen leaves with distinctive tiny 'leaflets', which grow out of the centre of shoots known as cladodes. Tiny green flowers are borne on the cladodes in both spring and autumn, and the female flowers develop into bright red berries which last into winter. Plant a variety of male and female plants to ensure a good supply of berries.

Salix

Willows bring to mind large, graceful weeping trees (see page 272), but there are many good dwarf willows, suitable for beds or containers, as well as low-growing varieties.

Expert's Selection

1 *S. hastata* 'Wehrhahnii' ♀
Brilliant reddish purple stems and bright woolly catkins.
✿ **Yellow catkins • Spring**
∅ **Reddish purple stems • Autumn**
h.&s. **2m (7ft)**

2 *S. repens var. argentea* ♀
A low spreading bush, its arching stems bear striking, silvery leaves.
✿ **Silver catkins • Late spring**
∅ **Silver-grey**
h. **75cm (2½ft)** *s.* **1.2m (4ft)**

3 *S. cinerea*
The grey willow, with silvery grey down on its branches and leaves.
∅ **Grey leaves and stems**
h. **1.5m (5ft)** *s.* **2.5m (8ft)**

4 *S. gracilistyla*
A spreading shrub grown for its pussy willow buds and the pink catkins that follow them.
✿ **Pink catkins**
Early spring
h.&s. **2m (7ft)**

5 *S. integra* 'Hakuro-nishiki' A graceful shrub that can be grown as a standard.
∅ **Pink and white variegated • Late spring–autumn • *h.&s.* 1.5m (5ft)**

The Essentials

Site demands Heavy, damp soil, in sun or light shade.
Planting practice Plant in spring.
Pruning needs If grown for stem colour, cut shoots to ground level in winter, removing half of them in alternate years.
Pests and diseases Trouble free.
Bonus point Stems and catkins look good in flower arrangements.

The smaller willows are grown for their woolly catkins and coloured stems. Pussy willow buds appear briefly in late winter or early spring, then open out into male catkins, usually long and yellow, or silvery female ones.

STAR PERFORMER
S. hastata 'Wehrhahnii' ♀
Plant in a border or large container, and enjoy the wonderful winter display of reddish purple stems, with white catkins in spring that turn yellow as they mature.

Salvia

Sages are mainly grown for their aromatic, decorative foliage, in shades of purple, pink and green, though some also have attractive, colourful flower spikes.

Expert's Selection

1 *S. officinalis* 'Purpurascens' ♀ The soft purple leaves gradually darken in colour throughout summer.
✿ **Purple • Summer** ∅ **Purpley-green**
h. **60cm (2ft)** *s.* **1m (3ft)**

2 *S. officinalis* 'Icterina' ♀
Grow this for its lovely aromatic leaves, that are marbled with primrose yellow and gold.
∅ **Green, yellow and gold**
h. **60cm (2ft)** *s.* **1m (3ft)**

3 *S. officinalis* 'Kew Gold' ♀
The glorious leaves are sometimes flecked with dots of green. Produces very few flowers.
∅ **Golden yellow**
h. **60cm (2ft)** *s.* **1m (3ft)**

4 *S. officinalis* 'Tricolor' ♀
The variegated white, deep pink and purple leaves grow darker as summer progresses.
∅ **White, pink and purple**
h. **60cm (2ft)** *s.* **1m (3ft)**

STAR PERFORMER
S. officinalis 'Purpurascens' ♀
Plant in a border or herb garden, for its lovely purple flowers, as well as the colourful, aromatic leaves.

These hardy, shrubby sages are very easy to grow, provided they have a sunny position. They give year-round interest with their aromatic, often highly colourful, evergreen leaves, plus, in some varieties, attractive flower spikes. For some unusual hues in a border or herb garden, grow a variegated form of *S. officinalis*, such as 'Tricolor' ♀.

The Essentials

Site demands Any well-drained soil, in full sun.
Planting practice Plant in spring.
Flowering time Midsummer. Cut back after the first flowers to encourage a second, later flourish.
Pests and diseases Usually trouble free, but may be attacked by powdery mildew or capsid bugs.
Bonus point It is a powerfully aromatic culinary herb.

Sambucus

Common elder grows wild, but there are also cultivated varieties, which are just as easy to grow but more colourful, with foliage that ranges from deep purple to gold.

S. racemosa 'Plumosa Aurea'

S. nigra 'Aurea'

Expert's Selection

1 *S. nigra* 'Black Beauty'
An exciting new variety, with large flowerheads and rich purple leaves.
✿ **Rose-pink • Early summer**
⊘ **Deep purple • h.&s. 6m (20ft)**

2 *S. racemosa* 'Sutherland Gold'♈ Place in full sun for its feathery, golden foliage to develop the richest colour.
✿ **Yellow • Early summer**
⊘ **Gold • h.&s. 4m (13ft)**

3 *S. nigra* 'Guincho Purple'♈
The young foliage is green, turning to purple-black in summer, then finally red in autumn.
✿ **Pinkish • Early summer**
⊘ **Purple-black, turning to red**
Summer–autumn
h. 6m (20ft) s. 4m (13ft)

4 *S. nigra* 'Aurea'♈
Again, a sunny site will help to develop the best colour in its glowing golden leaves.
✿ **White • Early summer**
⊘ **Gold • h. 6m (20ft) s. 4m (13ft)**

5 *S. racemosa* 'Plumosa Aurea' Another golden-leaved variety, with rich yellow blooms.
✿ **Rich yellow • Early summer**
⊘ **Gold • h.&s. 4m (13ft)**

6 *S. nigra* 'Marginata'
Ideal for a small plot, this has pretty, lacy cream-edged leaves.
✿ **Creamy white • Early summer**
⊘ **Green with cream edges**
h. 1.2m (4ft) s. 1.5m (5ft)

If you have a bare patch in need of some instant colour, the wild hedgerow plant, European elder, fits the bill, with its coarse, green leaves and white flowerheads. There are also several more colourful varieties, worth growing for their decorative foliage and flowers: try 'Black Beauty' or 'Guincho Purple'. They are just as hardy and easy to grow as the wild version.

Elder also bear attractive, edible, autumn berries. They are black on *S. nigra* varieties, and on *S. racemosa,* bright red.

Keeping in shape
Prune elder hard to keep it in check and enhance the decorative foliage. In winter, when the shrub is dormant, cut half the stems to the ground and shorten the rest.

The Essentials

Site demands Well-drained soil in sun or light shade. Golden forms need full sun for best colour.
Planting practice Plant in spring.
Flowering time Early summer.
Pruning needs They may be pruned to the ground in winter.
Pests and diseases Rare, but aphids and mosaic virus may attack.
Bonus point Both the flowers and berries can be used to make wine and cordial drinks.

STAR PERFORMER
S. nigra 'Black Beauty'
Plant this new variety in a prime position for its amazing show of glossy dark purple foliage and pink flowers.

Santolina

Cotton lavender is a dwarf evergreen that forms a mound of fine leaves and button-like flowers. It is ideal as a low hedge or perhaps towards the front of a border.

Expert's Selection

1 *S. chamaecyparissus* 'Lambrook Silver'
A neat shrub ideal for hedging, with silver, thread-like foliage. 'Lemon Queen' has grey-green foliage and, despite its name, cream flowers.
✿ **Deep yellow • Mid–late summer**
h.&s. 60cm (2ft)

2 *S. pinnata*
Its smooth leaves are mid green. 'Sulphurea' has feathery grey-green foliage and pale yellow flowers.
❀ **White • Mid–late summer**
h. 60cm (2ft) *s.* 30cm (1ft)

The Essentials

Site demands Any well-drained soil in full sun.
Planting practice Plant in spring or early autumn.
Flowering time From mid to late summer.
Pruning needs Neaten in spring.
Pests and diseases Trouble free.
Bonus point The foliage gives off a spicy aroma.

Cotton lavender thrives on neglect, growing in beds, borders or rockeries, or as low hedging, which can easily be kept in shape by shearing just once a year after flowering. These hardy, little evergreens are very undemanding. Small button-like flowers appear any time from mid to late summer, and those with silvery grey foliage are particularly attractive.

STAR PERFORMER
***S. chamaecyparissus* 'Lambrook Silver'** **Grow this variety as a pretty edging for a path or border.**

STAR PERFORMER
***S. hookeriana* var. *digyna*♀** Clusters of flowers with spiky stamens bloom at the point where several of the bright green leaves join the stem.

Sarcococca

These small evergreen shrubs are perfect for edging in the front of a border or along a garden path. Fragrant white or creamy flowers cheer up the garden in midwinter.

Expert's Selection

1 *S. hookeriana* var. *digyna*♀
Glossy green leaves are dotted with white and pink winter flowers.
❀ **White, with pink • Winter**
🍒 **Black • Summer • *h.&s.* 1.2m (4ft)**

2 *S. ruscifolia*
Plant this species in front of the border for its dark foliage and fragrant flowers.
❀ **Ivory • Late winter to early spring**
🍒 **Blood red • Summer**
h.&s. 1.2m (4ft)

3 *S. hookeriana* var. *humilis*
A low-growing variety that makes attractive ground cover.
❀ **White, tinged with pink • Winter**
🍒 **Black • Summer • *h.&s.* 60cm (2ft)**

4 *S. confusa*♀
Slightly taller, but less invasive than the others as it has no suckers. Its winter flowers bloom alongside the previous year's berries.
❀ **Cream** 🍒 **Black • Winter**
h.&s. 1.5m (5ft)

The Essentials

Site demands Moist but well-drained, loamy soil, in partial shade.
Planting practice Plant in early spring, anywhere it can spread.
Flowering time Winter.
Pruning needs Not necessary except to restrict spread.
Pests and diseases Trouble free.
Bonus point Winter scent.

These hardy evergreen shrubs spread by suckers, and will soon provide attractive ground cover or edging for a border. The clusters of fragrant flowers appear in midwinter, followed by attractive red or black berries.

All varieties, except *S. confusa*, can be invasive, so plant where you are happy for it to spread.

SAFETY WARNING Do not plant sarcococca if you have small children, as the berries are poisonous if eaten.

Skimmia

Skimmia is the perfect winter shrub, with its glossy leaves and clumps of bright red berries. Clusters of star-like flowers add their own summer charm.

With its dark evergreen leaves and glinting red berries, a skimmia will bring a shine to winter. It makes a useful addition to town gardens, as it is very tolerant of air pollution, and is also hardy in harsh seaside plots.

Most varieties are happy in any moist soil; only *S. japonica* subsp. *reevesiana* dislikes chalky sites. Plant them in partial shade, or, for a skimmia that likes a sunny spot, choose 'Kew Green'.

Some varieties are male, such as 'Rubella', and others female, like 'Vetchii'. Only *S. japonica* subsp. *reevesiana* is bisexual. Plant both male and female varieties close together, so that the female flowers can be pollinated, if you want to enjoy winter berries.

STAR PERFORMER
S. japonica 'Rubella' ♀
Grow this male variety for its outstanding winter colour, with long, bright green leaves and large sprays of pink buds which last all winter.

The Essentials

Site demands Moist, well-drained soil, in partial sun or light shade.
Planting practice Plant anytime, ideally in early autumn or spring.
Flowering time Spring.
Pruning needs None, except to cut out whitened foliage in spring.
Pests and diseases Usually trouble free. Cold, heavy or very limy soil can cause leaves to yellow.
Bonus point Some varieties bear strongly scented summer flowers.

Expert's Selection

1 *S. japonica* 'Rubella' ♀
This dense male shrub is noted for its long sprays of pink buds on coppery stalks. The buds last throughout winter, opening in early spring into richly scented flowers. The striking red-rimmed leaves are over 10cm (4in) long.
✿ **Pink • Winter–late spring**
∅ **Bright green with red margins**
h.&s. **1.5m (5ft)**

2 *S. japonica* 'Veitchii'
This is a vigorous upright female shrub. Fragrant creamy white flowers add their scent in late spring, and large bunches of bright red berries can be found throughout the winter.
✿ **White • Late spring** ❦ **Bright red Winter** ∅ **Bright green**
h.&s. **1.5m (5ft)**

3 *S. x confusa* 'Kew Green' ♀
Plant this small, neat male variety in full sun, where it will thrive. The creamy, off-white flowers, in clusters up to 10cm (4in) long, are elegantly highlighted by the rich green of the leaves.
✿ **Cream • Spring**
∅ **Deep green**
h.&s. **1m (3ft)**

4 *S. japonica* 'Nymans' ♀
Grow this female variety for the large quantities of big red berries it produces. The open spreading nature of this shrub and the red tinged stalks make it a popular choice.
✿ **Off white • Late spring** ❦ **Bright red Winter** ∅ **Bright green**
h.&s. **1.2m (4ft)**

TAKE A FRESH LOOK

S. japonica subsp. *reevesiana* is the skimmia to choose if you only have room for one bush, but want to be sure of a crop of glossy red berries. This is the only bisexual variety of the shrub, and bears creamy star-like white flowers among the glossy, tapered leaves in late spring. The flowers are pollinated from others on the same bush and are soon followed by a clutch of deep red berries, which ripen towards the end of summer.

S. x confusa 'Kew Green'

Solanum

Charming solanums twine and scramble. An explosion of small, yellow-eyed flowers throughout summer turns one into a dense spread of either whites, blues or purples.

Expert's Selection

1 *S. crispum* 'Glasnevin' ♀
A quick growing, semi-evergreen with a very productive flowering season, sometimes from late spring until the end of October.
✿ **Blue-purple • Late spring–autumn**
h. 4m (13ft) *s.* 1m (3ft)

2 *S. laxum* 'Album' ♀
More tender than 'Glasnevin', its long-lasting, brilliant white flowers sparkle against the purple-hued leaves well into autumn.
✿ **White • Midsummer–autumn**
h. 3m (10ft) *s.* 60cm (2ft)

Although it is usually trained to grow up walls, if left alone solanum soon becomes an impressive, sprawling flowery mound. Whichever style you like, you will have a beautiful display.

Wires or a trellis will make a good climbing support, and give extra warmth for the winter.

Don't despair if your plant disappears over winter, as long as the roots survive, new growth will appear.

The Essentials

Site demands Any free-draining soil, in a sunny, sheltered site.
Planting practice Plant in spring; insulate roots with a winter mulch.
Flowering time From early summer, sometimes into winter.
Pruning needs Trim for shape only, in spring.
Pests and diseases Trouble free.
Bonus point Mixing with red and purple plants gives a riot of colour.

STAR PERFORMER
S. crispum 'Glasnevin' ♀
The Chilean potato tree brims with a mass of deep blue-purple flowers, followed by tiny white berries. It makes an exceptional display if grown with or through other plants, such as Citronella lilies.

STAR PERFORMER
S. tomentosa var. *angustifolia* ♀
This handsome shrub deserves pride of place for its masses of large flower clusters which appear from mid to late summer. The red stems of this new variety bring out the green of the leaves.

Sorbaria

Sorbarias are tall, fast-growing shrubs, planted for their elegant feathery branches and long clusters of tiny white flowers, which appear at midsummer.

These hardy, impressive shrubs are perfect in a large garden. The slightly drooping habit, the elegantly long leaves, and large flower clusters make a stunning summer display. If you have a small garden opt for *S. sorbifolia*.

The Essentials

Site demands Most moist, well-drained soils, preferably in full sun.
Planting practice Plant from mid autumn to mid spring.
Flowering time Mid and late summer.
Pruning needs Prune in late winter or early spring.
Pests and diseases Trouble free.
Bonus point A thicket-forming shrub, ideal for woodland settings.

Expert's Selection

1 *S. tomentosa* var. *angustifolia* ♀ Red stems support long feathery leaves and flowers.
✽ **White • Mid–late summer**
h.&s. 3m (10ft)

2 *S. kirilowii*
Arching leaves and white blooms.
✽ **White • Midsummer**
h.&s. 4.5m (15ft)

3 *S. tomentosa*
Creamy flowers and elegant foliage.
✽ **Cream • Mid–late summer**
h.&s 4.5m (15ft)

4 *S.sorbifolia*
Smaller, with erect flower clusters.
✽ **White • Mid–late summer**
h. 1.8m (6ft) *s.* 3m (10ft)

Spartium

Spanish broom is a tall, slender shrub which looks its best at the back of the border. It is hardy, versatile and, since it thrives in sandy soil, ideal for seaside gardens.

Expert's Selection	The Essentials

1 *S. junceum*♀
There is only one variety. Fragrant yellow flowers cluster in soft, loose sprays up to 45cm (1½ft) long.
✿ **Yellow • Early summer–early autumn • h.&s. 3m (10ft)**

Site demands Plant in light or sandy soil, in a sunny position.
Flowering time Early summer to early autumn.
Pruning needs Prune to avoid it becoming top-heavy and prolong the flowering season (see below).
Pests and diseases Trouble free.
Bonus point An especially good choice for seaside gardens.

STAR PERFORMER
S. junceum♀ **Lofty, adaptable and hardy, with delightful sunny blooms, Spanish broom loves the lightest soil and is ideal as an informal hedge on a dry bank.**

For best results it is essential to prune broom after flowering. In the first two years cut back the main stems by half to encourage a bushy growth. Thereafter cut back to the base of the flowering shoots, to within 2.5cm (1in) of the old wood.

Spiraea

An attractive and versatile shrub, spiraea is deservedly popular for being quick-growing and easy to cultivate, suitable for both hedging and ground cover. Masses of tiny saucer-shaped flowers in shades of white, pink, yellow and purple are borne in globes or looser clusters.

S. 'Arguta'

Spiraea is hardy and easily grown. It comes in two forms: early-flowering varieties bloom in spring and early summer, while the late-flowering kinds display from midsummer onwards. Some are tall, with graceful arching branches and make handsome specimen shrubs.

There are also small kinds ideal for the border or a small garden. These are short and twiggy, often with colourful foliage. All grow quickly into a dense bush or hedge.

Pruning
Early-flowering varieties are best pruned just after flowering. Cut back the flowered stems to strong

STAR PERFORMER
S. x *vanhouttei*♀ **Bushy and vigorous, it bears dense clusters of bowl-shaped flowers on graceful arching shoots and is ideal for hedging.**

buds and remove any weak growth. On established plants, cut back some of the oldest stems to ground level each year. Prune late-flowering plants in early spring, cutting all growth back hard. Clip dwarf varieties to maintain shape after flowering.

S. japonica 'Goldflame'

The Essentials

Site demands Plant in any reasonably fertile soil, in sun or partial shade.

Flowering time Plant a combination of early and late flowering varieties to enjoy the blooms from May to September.

Pruning needs Annual hard pruning is essential to keep these shrubs in shape and maintain flowering. Prune early-flowering varieties after flowering and late-flowering ones in early spring.

Pests and diseases Trouble free.

Bonus point Tolerant of a wide range of growing conditions.

green in spring to soft green edged with cream then orange in autumn.
❀ **White • Early spring** ⊘ **Variegated**
h.&s. **1m (3ft)**

4 *S. japonica* **'Candlelight'**
Buttery yellow foliage makes the perfect foil for pink flowers. 'Anthony Waterer'♀ is red.
✿ **Pink • Mid–late summer** ⊘ **Yellow**
h.&s. **1m (3ft)**

5 *S.* **'Arguta'**
Clusters of early flowers smother arching sprays.
❀ **White • Mid-spring–early summer**
⊘ **Bright green •** ***h.&s.*** **1.8m (6ft)**

6 *S.* x *pseudosalicifolia*
'Triumphans' Grow this for its showy plumes, but not on chalk.
✿ **Purplish pink • Mid–late summer**
⊘ **Mid green •** ***h.&s.*** **1.8m (6ft)**

7 *S.* x *cinerea* **'Grefsheim'**♀
An early-flowerer, with long downy leaves and dense flower clusters.
❀ **White • Mid-spring** ⊘ **Grey-green**
h.&s. **1.8m (6ft)**

8 *S. prunifolia*
Small double flowers bloom early.
❀ **White • Mid–late spring** ⊘ **Yellow**
Autumn • ***h.*** **1.2m (4ft)** ***s.*** **1m (3ft)**
in five years; ultimately 1.8m (6ft)

S. japonica **'Nana'**♀ is one of a number of very attractive compact varieties of *S. japonica*. It forms a compact mound 45cm (1½ft) high and 1.2m (4ft) across with pink flowerheads and pale green leaves that turn coppery red in autumn. Other appealing miniatures include 'Bullata', with pinky red flowers, and 'Gold Mound', which only reaches 25cm (10in) and has bright gold foliage.

S. japonica 'Nana'

Expert's Selection

1 *S.* x *vanhouttei*♀
A tall early-flowering variety, its white flowers have yellow centres and creamy stamens.
❀ **White • Early summer** ⊘ **Dark green •** ***h.&s.*** **1.8m (6ft)**

2 *S. japonica* **'Goldflame'**♀
A late-flowerer with orange foliage that fades to yellow as it ages.
✿ **Dark pink • Mid–late summer**
⊘ **Reddish orange •** ***h.&s.*** **1m (3ft)**

3 *S. thunbergii* **'Mount Fuji'**
Leaves change colour from pinkish

Syringa

Lilacs are easy to grow in a sunny position. These deciduous shrubs produce a glorious display of scented plumes in late spring and early summer. They tolerate city pollution, and will be excellent for creating an eye-catching centrepiece, or in a border, in any town garden.

S. x josiflexa 'Bellicent'

STAR PERFORMER
S. vulgaris 'Charles Joly' ♀
Plant this tall, upright shrub in a sunny site near the house, so you can see its magnificent display of richly coloured, double flowers, and enjoy their heavenly scent.

Grow lilacs for their superb scented flowers. They are hardy and easy to grow, requiring only a sunny position for the best show of flowers in spring.

The larger varieties, such as 'Charles Joly' and 'Bellicent', look splendid, but there are also smaller shrubs suitable for the average border or small garden, such as the highly scented, pink 'Congo'. Lilac does not need pruning until it becomes old and

leggy, when it can be given a new lease of life by cutting back hard, to within 60cm (2ft) of the ground in early winter. New growth will take two to three years to flower. Pull off any suckers found close to the roots.

The Essentials

Site demands Any well-drained soil, including chalk, in full sun.
Planting practice Plant bare-rooted plants in autumn; pot-grown at any time.
Flowering time From mid spring to early summer.
Pruning needs Deadhead after flowering. Pull off suckers.
Pests and diseases Watch for willow scale and lilac blight.
Bonus point Just one spray of flowers in a vase will scent a room.

S. vulgaris 'Madame Lemoine'

Expert's Selection

1 *S. vulgaris* 'Charles Joly' ♀
Tall shrub with double flowers.
✿ **Dark purplish red • Mid–late spring • h. 3.5m (12ft) s. 3m (10ft)**

2 *S. vulgaris* 'Madame Lemoine' ♀ Bears heavenly scented compact flowers.
❀ **Pure white • Mid–late spring h.&s. 3.5m (12ft)**

3 *S. vulgaris* 'Congo'
Compact bush with small flowers.
✿ **Deep pink • Late spring–early summer • h. 1.8m (6ft) s. 1.5m (5ft)**

4 *S. x josiflexa* 'Bellicent' ♀
Has striking, long flower plumes.
✿ **Rose-pink • Late spring–early summer • h. 5m (16ft) s. 3.5m (12ft)**

5 *S. x prestoniae* 'Elinor' ♀
Slow grower with slender plumes.
✿ **Pale lilac • Late spring–early summer • h. 5m (16ft) s. 3.5m (12ft)**

6 *S. microphylla* 'Superba'
Fragrant flowers often appear for a second time in early autumn.
✿ **Rosy pink • Late spring; often again in autumn • h.&s 1.8m (6ft)**

Tamarix

This delicate-looking shrub, with its slender flower plumes, is tougher than it looks: the fine feathery branches bend in the strongest winds without breaking.

A row of tamarix makes an attractive windbreak for less robust plants in open gardens. They grow particularly well at the seaside, where they shrug off salty air as well as any strong blasts.

Tamarix does not like heavy soil, but in the right place it grows fast and responds well to regular pruning.

STAR PERFORMER

***T. tetranda*♀** In spring and early summer, this bush is a haze of pale pink, when its sprays come into bloom. And the arching branches, clothed in tiny pale green leaves, look just as pretty for the rest of the season.

Expert's Selection

1 *T. tetranda*♀
A loose, open bush with arching branches, its feathery, pink flower sprays, up to 5cm (2in) long, appear before the tiny, pale green leaves.
✿ **Pale pink • Spring–early summer**
h.&s. **4m (13ft)**

2 *T. ramosissima* 'Rubra'♀
For a colourful display even out of the flowering season, try this quick-growing variety, with its red-brown branches and pale grey-green leaves. The deep pink flowers appear in late summer.
✿ **Deep pink • Late summer**
h. **5m (16ft)** *s.* **6m (20ft)**

3 *T. ramosissima* 'Pink Cascade' Its spectacular display of fluffy pink flowers can obscure all the green foliage in late summer.
✿ **Pink • Late summer**
h. **5m (16ft)** *s.* **6m (20ft)**

The Essentials

Site demands Any well-drained, light soil, preferably in full sun.
Planting practice Plant from late autumn to early spring.
Flowering time Spring to late summer, depending on variety.
Pruning needs Spring-flowering plants should be pruned just after the flowers have faded. Prune summer-flowerers in spring.
Pests and diseases Trouble free.
Bonus point Makes a pretty and unusual windbreak.

STAR PERFORMER
***T. baccata* 'Summergold'**
This golden spreader looks great in a tub or rockery.

Taxus

Yew trees are often found in churchyards, but as well as stately specimens, yew can also be dwarf or spreading. The varieties listed here are all suitable for small gardens.

Expert's Selection

1 *T. baccata* 'Summergold'
A broad flat shrub, good for ground cover. It likes full sun.
⌀ **Gold •** *h.* **50cm (20in)** *s.* **1.5m (5ft)**

2 *T. baccata* 'Ivory Tower'
Forms a column, creamy white in winter, golden yellow in summer.
⌀ **Gold •** *h.* **1m (3ft)** *s.* **50cm (20in)**

3 *T. baccata* 'Fastigiata'♀
The Irish yew has almost vertical branches and forms a column.
⌀ **Dark green**
h. **1.5m (5ft)** *s.* **50cm (20in)**

SAFETY WARNING All parts of a yew, including berries and leaves, are poisonous if eaten.

T. baccata 'Fastigiata'

The Essentials

Site demands Any well-drained soil, in full sun or deep shade.
Planting practice Plant with roots only just below ground level.
Pruning needs Not necessary.
Pests and diseases Root rot and die-back may affect yews.
Bonus point Good for topiary.

Slow-growing and long-lived, yew is very undemanding. Columnar or prostrate, it can be planted anywhere, except in waterlogged soil. Yew trees do not need pruning, but the shrub is also traditionally used for hedging, in which case it should be clipped to shape twice a year, in spring and late summer.

Thuja

With their soft sprays of colourful evergreen foliage, thujas are perfect for providing year-round colour and interest without any effort. Tall conical trees will suit a large garden, or can be used for hedging, while the rounded dwarf ones are ideal for rockeries, containers and small gardens.

T. occidentalis 'Hetz Midget'

Expert's Selection

1 *T. occidentalis* 'Smaragd'♀ As it grows, this variety makes an elegant olive green column that looks good in the middle of a lawn.
⌀ **Olive green • *h.* 2.5m (8ft)**
s. **50cm (20in) after 10 years**

2 *T. occidentalis* 'Rheingold'♀ Grows slowly to form a tidy conical bush. The golden-green foliage develops a bronze tint in cold weather.
⌀ **Golden green • *h.* 2m (7ft)**
s. **1.5m (5ft) after 15 to 20 years**

3 *T. occidentalis* 'Holmstrup'♀ A rich green column with a pointed spire. It makes a good specimen for the lawn.
⌀ **Dark green • *h.* 2.5m (8ft)**
s. **50cm (20in) after 20 years**

4 *T. plicata* 'Stoneham Gold'♀ Gradually forms a narrowly conical tree, but is so slow-growing that it also makes a good container plant. Bright gold new leaves age to a darker green.
⌀ **Gold to dark green**
h.&s. **2m (7ft)**

5 *T. plicata* 'Atrovirens'♀ This eventually makes a tall conical tree, but is best grown as a dense, easily controlled hedge.
⌀ **Dark shiny green • *h.* 8m (26ft)**
s. **2m (7ft) after 20 years**

6 *T. occidentalis* 'Hetz Midget' This rounded dwarf plant is the smallest thuja. It makes a neat ball or dome and can be grown in a tub or a rockery.
⌀ **Bright green • *h.&s.* 25cm (10in)**

The Essentials

Site demands Moist, well-drained soil in sun or light shade. Thujas grow best in acid or neutral soil.
Planting practice Plant trees from late autumn to early spring.
Pruning needs Not necessary, but clip hedging in early spring.
Pests and diseases Honey fungus and canker rot may attack. Cut out any foliage that looks affected and burn it.
Bonus point The foliage, which reaches to the ground, is aromatic when crushed.

Thujas are hardy, easy-going conifers, ideal for almost any location – although they prefer a moist, acid well-drained soil. They will tolerate light shade, though the foliage of colourful versions will be less bright.

Larger thujas, such as 'Holmstrup' and 'Smaragd', make ideal specimen shrubs, while the tall, dense 'Atrovirens' makes good thick hedging.

Thujas are also ideal for the rockery or patio. Dwarf versions include 'Hetz Midget'.

Care-free conifers
Thujas need very little attention. To create an evergreen hedge, plant trees 60cm (2ft) apart and clip once a year. Cut out and burn any sign of disease that turns the foliage brown.

STAR PERFORMER

T. occidentalis 'Smaragd'♀ **This attractive column-shaped shrub could not be easier to grow: plant it in a prominent position and leave it alone.**

Ulex

Gorse is a spiny yellow-flowered shrub, ideal for growing in poor soil, such as on a dry sunny bank. It is a plant that thrives on neglect, needing no pruning or watering.

STAR PERFORMER

U. europaeus 'Flore Pleno'♀ **This compact gorse bears honey-scented blooms.**

Gorse could not be easier, provided you avoid rich moist soils. It likes poor soils and sandy coastal conditions and enjoys a site in full sun. The golden yellow flowers have their most impressive flush in spring, then appear from time to time over the year. On warm days they give off a sweet scent.

Expert's Selection

1 *U. europaeus* 'Flore Pleno'♀ A small bush with stunning double flowers.
✿ Yellow • Early–late spring
h.&s. 60cm (2ft); ultimately 1m (3ft)

2 *U. europaeus*
The common gorse of heathland.
✿ Yellow • Early–late spring
h.&s. 1m (3ft); ultimately 1.8m (6ft)

The Essentials

Site demands Most well-drained soils in a sunny position. It prefers soil that is not too rich.
Planting practice Plant young bushes in spring or early autumn.
Flowering time Spring.
Pruning needs None required.
Pests and diseases Trouble free.
Safety warning Gorse catches fire easily. Site away from buildings.
Bonus point Butterflies love it.

Vaccinium

Blueberries or **bilberries**, grown as small shrubs, are ideal for moist acid soils. A plus is the edible berries of some species which also include cranberries.

Expert's Selection

1 *V. vitis-idaea* Koralle Group♀ A dwarf, creeping evergreen cranberry.
❧ Red, edible • Late summer
h. 30cm (1ft) *s.* 50cm (20in)

2 *V. myrtillus*
The bilberry bush has green stems.
✿ Pink • Early summer ❧ Blue-black
Late summer • *h.&s.* 60cm (2ft)

3 *V. nummularia*
Dwarf evergreen with shiny leaves.
✿ Pink • Early summer ❧ Black
Autumn • *h.&s.* 40cm (16in)

4 *V. corymbosum*♀
The best blueberry for wet ground.
⊘ Orange ❧ Blue-black, edible
Autumn • *h.&s.* 1.5m (5ft)

The Essentials

Site demands Permanently moist rich acid soil, in light shade.
Planting practice Plant in autumn or spring. *V. nummularia* needs shelter in very cold areas.
Pruning needs Trim in spring if necessary to keep the shape.
Pests and diseases Birds will eat berries; rabbits and deer like leaves.
Bonus point Several varieties have edible berries.

Shrubs in this family love moist acid soils, even tolerating exceptionally peaty or sandy sites. There are both evergreens, and deciduous plants that give a good show of autumn colour before the leaves fall. The many-seeded berries are usually cooked and used in jams, desserts and sauces.

STAR PERFORMER

V. vitis-idaea Koralle Group♀ **The mountain cranberry is great for giving year round colour in a small garden.**

Viburnum

Viburnum is hardy, easily grown and suitable for almost every location. It will make a handsome feature in a border, on a lawn, as hedging or as ground cover and will provide year-round colour and interest: many varieties have brilliant autumn foliage and colourful berries.

V. tinus

Viburnums provide an enormous range of foliage, flowers and berries for year-round interest. Hardy and easy to grow, they come in both deciduous and evergreen varieties. Plant one on a lawn, in a border or as hedging. Some varieties, such as 'Compactum', are grown for their brilliant autumn foliage as well as for their flowers and berries.

The low growing varieties such as *V. davidii* can be planted as specimen shrubs or ground cover. To maintain a ground covering habit, clip off any vertical shoots that will spoil the shrub's tiered horizontal shape.

One of the best shrubs for lifting the dark days of winter is *V.* x *bodnantense*, which bears a succession of pink blossoms, even when there is snow on the ground.

Expert's Selection

1 *V. opulus* 'Compactum' ♀
A dense shrub with large flower-heads and bright leaves and berries.
✿ **White • Early summer** ❦ **Bright red • Late summer–autumn**
∅ **Red • Autumn • h.&s. 1.5m (5ft)**

2 *V.* x *bodnantense* 'Charles Lamont' ♀ A sweetly scented winter-flowering variety. 'Deben'♀ has pink buds that open to white.
✿ **Pink • Winter**
h. **3m (10ft)** *s.* **1.8m (6ft)**

3 *V. davidii* ♀
A low-growing evergreen shrub ideal for a small border.
✿ **White • Early summer** ❦ **Iridescent blue • All winter • h.&s. 1.5m (5ft)**

4 *V. lantana*
The wayfaring tree has white flowers and black autumn fruit.
✿ **White • Late spring–early summer**
❦ **Black • Autumn**
h. **5m (16ft)** *s.* **4m (13ft)**

5 *V. farreri* 'Candidissimum'
Erect, twiggy, winter-flowering shrub with scented flower clusters.
✿ **Pink • Winter**
h. **1.8m (6ft)** *s.* **1.5m (5ft)**

6 *V. tinus*
An evergreen shrub with shiny leaves and pinky white flowers.
✿ **Pinky white • Winter–early spring**
∅ **Dark green • h.&s. 3m (10ft)**

V. farreri 'Candidissimum'

STAR PERFORMER
V. opulus 'Compactum' ♀
Known as the Guelder rose, it is a must in the border with its display of beautiful white flowers followed by the brightest red berries.

The Essentials

Site demands Most soils, except for shallow or very wet ones.
Planting practice Plant in autumn or spring.
Flowering time Winter or summer, depending on variety.
Pruning needs Prune after flowering.
Pests and diseases Look out for signs of aphid attack.
Bonus point Winter flowering viburnums are sweetly scented.

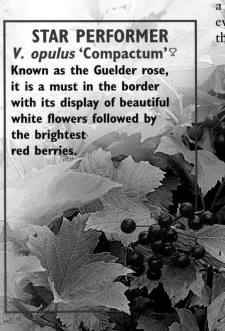

Vinca

Periwinkle is a vigorous flowering creeper. It grows well in shade and is useful under trees and shrubs or to edge mixed beds.

STAR PERFORMER
V. major 'Maculata'
Evergreen leaves are perfect for covering banks or bare ground under trees.

The Essentials

Site demands Any well-drained soil in sun or shade.
Planting practice Plant in autumn or spring, mulch in spring.
Pruning needs None, except to control the size of the plants.
Pests and diseases Trouble free.
Bonus point Can be trained up trellis as an unusual climber.

Expert's Selection

1 *V. major* 'Maculata'
A tall variety, it has yellowy green leaves and large flowers.
✿ **Pale blue • All summer**
h. 35cm (14in) *s.* indefinite

2 *V. major* var. *oxyloba*
The flowers have narrow petals.
✿ **Dark violet • Spring–early summer**
h. 35cm (14in) *s.* indefinite

3 *V. minor* 'Alba Variegata'
A smaller evergreen with yellowish foliage. Try 'Argenteovariegata' and 'Variegata' for different effects.
✿ **White • Spring–early summer**
h. 20cm (8in) *s.* indefinite

4 *V. minor* 'Atropurpurea'
Another small version with dark green leaves and purple flowers.
✿ **Purple • Spring–early summer**
h. 20cm (8in) *s.* indefinite

5 *V. major*
Glossy evergreen trailing creeper.
✿ **Bright blue • Spring–early summer**
h. 35cm (14in) *s.* indefinite

Provided the soil is not too dry, periwinkles are very easy to grow, and will produce flowers in spring and summer. They make great ground cover, thrive in sun or shade and produce masses of pretty flowers in blue, purple and white. All periwinkles will spread indefinitely on rooted stems if allowed to, but smaller varieties, such as 'Atropurpurea', are less invasive and can be happily grown in borders.

Weigela

Among the easiest and most popular of all the summer-flowering shrubs, weigelas are hardy, have attractive foxglove-shaped flowers, and grow more or less anywhere.

Expert's Selection

1 *W.* 'Victoria'
Purple tinged leaves and clusters of showy, funnel-shaped flowers.
✿ **Red • Summer**
h.&s. 1m (3ft); ultimately 1.8m (6ft)

2 *W.* 'Bristol Ruby'
The branches are upright, not arching. 'Bristol Snowflake' has white flowers; 'Briant Rubidor' has yellow leaves and red flowers.
✿ **Crimson • Summer**
h.&s. 1.8m (6ft)

3 *W.* 'Florida Variegata'
Pretty cream edged leaves.
✿ **Rose pink • Summer**
h.&s. 1m (3ft); ultimately 1.8m (6ft)

4 *W.* 'Nana Variegata'
A dwarf weigela with unusual yellow-edged leaves.
✿ **Rose pink • Summer**
h. 1m (3ft) *s.* 1.2m (4ft)

The Essentials

Site demands Plant in any well-drained soil, in sun or light shade.
Planting practice Mulch after planting.
Pruning needs Prune flowering stems immediately after flowering.
Pests and diseases Trouble free.
Bonus point Grows anywhere.

STAR PERFORMER
W. 'Victoria' With its red flowers and purple leaves, this makes an outstanding show in a small garden.

Weigela is deservedly popular, being so easy and trouble-free. Give the arching stems space to show off their long, funnel-shaped flowers, or choose a dwarf variety, such as 'Nana Variegata', for a small garden. This shrub is usually undemanding, but will appreciate mulching in dry weather. It flowers on last season's wood, so prune after flowering for the best display the following year.

Wisteria

Wisterias are in the top list of spectacular plants, with their thick, coiling, snake-like stems and gorgeously scented dangling flowers in white, pinks, lilacs and blues. They can be grown up walls and pergolas, or as free-standing trees, but need plenty of room.

The sinuous branches of wisteria will readily climb in twists and turns around anything in their path. They can form stout trees, but their flowers are best seen cascading down a wall or hanging from a pergola. On a wall, aim for a vertical central stem, and fix sturdy horizontal wires along which to train the branches. Don't let any climbing up a house wall reach the roof tiles; they will dislodge them.

Vigorous and tough

All wisteria have pretty feathery foliage, and produce long, elegant, scented trails of typically pea-family shaped flowers.

W. floribunda is a Japanese native, and *W. sinensis* comes from China. An intriguing difference is that the former twine clockwise and the latter anti-clockwise. Both are tough, but *W. sinensis* tends to flower in late spring, so avoid it if your garden gets severe late spring frosts, as these will prevent flowering. The Chinese varieties, however, generally grow more vigorously and are taller than *W. floribunda* with larger, more highly scented flowers, of which there is often a second, late summer flush.

Patience rewarded

A wisteria is unlikely to flower within its first couple of years, but thereafter, and as each year goes by, the show will be more prolific. Be sure to ask the nursery for a grafted plant, easily distinguished because the base of the stem is slightly darker than the wood above it.

STAR PERFORMER
W. floribunda 'Multijuga' Grow this vigorous climber for its beautiful early summer display of violet-purple flowers.

W. floribunda 'Alba'

Expert's Selection

1 *W. floribunda* 'Multijuga'
Beautiful, long trails of violet-purple flowers appear in early summer on this hardy deciduous climber. These are followed in autumn by distinctive bean-like seedpods.
✿ **Violet • Early summer**
h.&s. **up to 9m (30ft)**

2 *W. sinensis* 'Alba'
White wisterias are a total joy especially when grown in rows, or even better over arches making long tunnels to walk through in late spring.
✿ **White • Late spring**
h. **12m (40ft)** *s.* **up to 9m (30ft)**

3 *W. floribunda* 'Alba'
Fragrant snowy white flowers and feathery pale to mid green foliage characterise this Japanese wisteria.
✿ **Pure white • Early summer**
h.&s. **up to 9m (30ft)**

The Essentials

Site demands Rich soil in full sun gives best results; avoid wet clay.
Planting practice Plant in spring or in autumn.
Flowering time *W. floribunda* flowers in early summer and *W. sinensis* earlier, in late spring.
Pruning needs Whether trained over a pergola or along wires fixed to a wall, long shoots should be trimmed back to about six buds in midsummer, and then to three buds in late winter.
Pests and diseases Largely trouble free, although birds may eat flower buds. Treat aphids, thrips and leaf spot if they arise.
Bonus point Although the flowering season is short, the foliage is long lasting, and also exceptionally pretty.

Yucca

These large, spiny evergreens are grown for their striking sword-like leaves and tall, eccentric flower spikes. The varieties listed here are all hardy, despite their exotic looks. Just choose a sunny position for your yucca, then forget about it; this plant is truly care free.

Expert's Selection

1 *Y. filamentosa* 'Bright Edge'♀ Also known as Adam's needle, the erect green leaves have yellow edges. 'Variegata' leaves have cream streaks and pinkish edges.
❀ Creamy white • Late summer
∅ Emerald green, edged with yellow
h.&s. 1m (3ft)

2 *Y. flaccida* 'Ivory'♀
Forms a low clump, with curving leaves and creamy white flowers with a green stain.
❀ Greenish white • Late summer
∅ Mid green • *h.&s.* 75cm (2½ft)

3 *Y. gloriosa*♀
Also known as Spanish dagger, this tall variety has fiercely spiny leaves. The flowers are creamy white tinged with red, though it may take up to five years to bloom.
❀ White tinged red • Late summer
∅ Dark green • *h.&s.* 1.5m (5ft)

4 *Y. flaccida* 'Golden Sword'♀ A shorter variety, its leaves are banded with pale yellow.
❀ Creamy white • Late summer
∅ Green with yellow banding
h.&s. 75cm (2½ft)

5 *Y. recurvifolia*♀
For the larger garden, it has long leaves and 2.5m (8ft) high stems.
❀ Cream • Late summer
∅ Blue-green
h.&s. 2.5m (8ft)

Y. flaccida 'Golden Sword'

Y. gloriosa

The Essentials

Site demands Any well-drained soil, in full sun.
Planting practice Plant in spring.
Flowering time Late summer.
Pruning needs None.
Pests and diseases Rarely any but leaf spot can occur.
Bonus point Hardy, despite their exotic appearance.

Plenty of sunshine and a well-drained plot are all yuccas need to thrive. Most are hardy and, as they tolerate air pollution, are ideal for town gardens. Native to Central America and Mexico, these dramatic looking, evergreen shrubs are grown mainly for their spiky foliage, but the flowers, if they appear, are an added bonus. Tall, exotic-looking stems, densely covered in creamy, bell-shaped flowers, shoot up above the rosettes or clumps of leaves. Some varieties can take several years to flower.

The shorter types of yucca, such as 'Bright Edge', 'Golden Sword' or 'Ivory' can be grown in the average sized garden, where they will make splendid specimen plants. But keep in mind when planting any of these that the flower stems sometimes stand up to 1.8m (6ft) high.

Some of the taller varieties definitely need more space, and are suitable only for a large garden, where they can occupy a commanding position – examples are *Y. recurvifolia* or *Y. gloriosa*. Sometimes the flower stems of *Y. gloriosa* reach a height of 2m (7ft), making a dramatic display, but it may not flower for five or more years after planting.

No pruning is necessary. The only care required is to simply slice off the spent flower spikes in spring, cutting them as close as possible to the centre of the rosette of leaves.

STAR PERFORMER
Y. filamentosa 'Bright Edge'♀ Give this impressive plant a prime site in full sun, and enjoy its brilliant foliage all year round and a dramatic display of tall flower stems in late summer.

trees

Trees bring a sense of permanence to a garden and their longevity makes them central to any planting plan. Not all trees are of a mighty stature, so even in a small space they can be used to add an extra dimension – height.

Because it is not practical to move established trees, it makes sense to place any trees first when designing a new plot. It is also vital to consider likely growth rate and size after, say, ten years, and the potential ultimate size of the tree.

Few trees look their best when pruned hard, even if this is sensitively done, which emphasises the importance of choosing the right tree to fit your site. Large forest trees, however majestic, are inappropriate in the average-sized garden, but there is a huge range of small and medium-sized trees which provide strong focal points.

Living with the neighbours

There are a few other crucial points to bear in mind when deciding where to plant a tree. Linked to its size, and often equally important, is the amount of shade a tree will cast – and where – as this will restrict what can be planted around it.

Remember, too, that some trees have fairly shallow roots that may inhibit the growth of other plants placed close by.

It is a good idea to bear in mind when you are planning your garden that the root-spread of most trees will be much wider than that of their branches when the tree is mature.

Keeping up appearances

A tree is such a conspicuous feature that it makes sense to select one that can offer an attractive display all year round. This does not mean, however, that you should only plant evergreens.

Although keeping their foliage through winter is a bonus, evergreens often lack the charm and interest provided by the ever-changing appearance of deciduous species. The ideal is to include a mixture of both: deciduous to reflect seasonal change, and evergreens for continuity.

Place versatile trees at centre stage

Try to give trees that have more than one season of interest, such as many of the **flowering cherries (*Prunus*)** and some **maples (*Acer*)**, a more prominent position than others whose display is confined to a few weeks each year. *Laburnums* are a truly glorious sight when they are in flower, but can look fairly nondescript during other seasons.

Trees that are usually grown for their fruit or rich autumn colours have a longer period of display, and some, such as *Malus* and *Sorbus*, offer a seasonal flow of eye-catching features: a profusion of spring blossom, followed by clusters of jewel-like berries accompanied by the warm reds, oranges and browns of their autumn foliage.

Most trees are surprisingly easy to grow and will tolerate a wide range of conditions. But it does pay to choose your plants and site carefully.

Plant choice

• Semi-mature trees are available, at a price. But unless an instant effect is essential, they are rarely worth the expense. Smaller specimens will establish much more quickly, and soon attain a good size.
• Trees sold in containers can be planted at any time, as long as the ground is neither dry nor frozen, but winter to early spring is best.
• Some nurseries only supply bare-rooted trees. Plant these between autumn and early spring.

Site essentials

• Almost all trees do best with some space around them. Planting a tree close to existing large trees or near a high wall may lead to lop-sided growth.
• Even in a sheltered garden, stake newly planted trees (see page 17) to protect them from wind rock.

Root troubles

• Shrinkable clay soils contract considerably in dry weather and this can damage buildings that are sited on them. The amount of water drawn up by tree roots exacerbates this problem. On such soils, a rule of thumb is not to plant any tree closer to a building than two and a half times its ultimate height.
• To avoid damage from spreading roots, do not plant a potentially large tree immediately next to a building or close to drains.

Plant no deeper than the rootball.

Acer

Maples offer finely cut foliage in myriad hues, which often produces a fabulous fiery autumn display. Ornamental bark gives several varieties winter interest as well. These easily grown deciduous trees come in all sizes, including dwarf varieties, so you can enjoy a maple in the smallest garden.

Maples are decorative and easy to grow. Smaller ones thrive in a shady, sheltered spot where young foliage is unlikely to be damaged by frost. This is especially true of the beautiful Japanese maples, *A. japonicum* and *A. palmatum,* prized for their spectacular autumn colours and delicate appearance. They also prefer neutral or slightly acid soil.

Maples make ideal focal points in small gardens; good examples are **'Aconitifolium'** and the **Dissectum Atropurpureum Group**. Small and slow-growing, they reach only 4m (13ft) after 20 years.

There are a number of maples prized specially for their colourful or patterned bark, which can enhance any winter garden. That of **'George Forrest'** is stripey, while the trunk of the snake bark maple **'Erythrocladum'** turns a striking pinky red in winter.

STAR PERFORMER
A. pseudoplatanus **'Brilliantissimum'** ♀
The pinky yellow spring foliage of this tree is outstanding.

Expert's Selection

1 *A. pseudoplatanus* **'Brilliantissimum'** ♀ A small, slow-grower with pinky yellow young leaves. 'Prinz Handjéry' has leaves with a red-purple underside.
⌀ **Pinky yellow • Spring**
h.&s. **3m (10ft)**

2 *A. grosseri var. hersii* ♀ An upright tree, the smooth green bark has white stripes.
⌀ **Orange • Autumn**
h. **4m (13ft)** *s.* **2m (7ft) after 20 years; ultimately 10m (33ft) tall**

3 *A. pensylvanicum* **'Erythrocladum'** ♀ The snake bark maple has green bark striped with white that turns pinky red.
⌀ **Bright yellow • Autumn**
h. **5m (16ft)** *s.* **3m (10ft)**

4 *A. davidii* **'George Forrest'** ♀ An elegant weeping tree with distinctive striped bark.
⌀ **Reddish gold • Autumn**
h. **4m (13ft)** *s.* **2m (7ft) after 20 years; ultimately 10m (33ft) tall**

5 *A. platanoides* **'Drummondii'** ♀ A relative of the Norway maple, its small shiny green leaves have white margins.
⌀ **Variegated • Spring and summer**
h. **10m (33ft)** *s.* **5m (16ft)**

6 *A. negundo* **'Flamingo'** ♀ A beautiful box elder it has leaves edged with white and pink.
⌀ **Variegated • Spring and summer**
h. **6m (20ft)** *s.* **4m (13ft)**

7 *A. pseudoplatanus* **'Nizetii'** Streaky leaves of pale green and white are red-purple underneath.
⌀⌀ **Green, white and purple Spring and summer**
h.&s. **12m (40ft)**

A. platanoides **'Drummondii'**

A. japonicum **'Aconitifolium'**

CHANGING SEASONS Autumnal acers can simply dazzle. *A. japonicum* 'Aconitifolium' ♀ and *A. tataricum* subsp. *ginnala* ♀ blaze in scarlet. *A. rubrum* 'Red Sunset' bursts into fiery orange-red, while trees in the *A. japonicum* Dissectum Atropurpureum Group turn a rich crimson.

The Essentials

Site demands Maples need a well-drained but rich moist soil.
Planting practice Plant in autumn or spring.
Pests and diseases Trouble free, but watch for honey fungus.
Bonus point Pretty trees of manageable size that add interest to a garden all year round.

Betula

Birches are graceful, elegant trees grown for their silvery white bark, greeny yellow catkins and radiant autumn foliage. They are hardy and easy to grow.

Most birches are completely hardy in Britain. They look good in all seasons, from winter, when the bark – from silver through gold, pink and brown – is the main attraction; in spring with a full head of bright green leaves; and again in autumn when the leaves glow bright gold and yellow. Birch trees are excellent in more enclosed spaces because they do not grow too large and the roots are not invasive. As they do not create dense shade, grass and a number of herbaceous plants can be grown under a birch canopy.

The Essentials

Site demands Plant in any soil in a sunny situation. *B. nigra* will thrive best in wet soil.
Planting practice Timing is not critical when planting out containerised trees.
Pests and diseases Honey fungus may attack.
Bonus point The spring catkins attract early beneficial insects to the garden.

Expert's Selection

1 B. utilis var. jacquemontii
The Kashmir birch is the whitest of all birches with pure white bark.
⊘ **Yellow • Autumn**
h. 14m (46ft) *s.* 4m (13ft)

2 B. nigra♀
Happiest in wet ground near water, this has dark grey peeling bark.
⊘ **Yellow • Autumn**
h. 10m (33ft) *s.* 5m (16ft) after 20 years. Ultimately 24m (80ft) tall.

3 B. pendula♀
The traditional silver birch has a graceful slightly weeping habit.
⊘ **Yellow • Autumn**
h. 14m (46ft) *s.* 5m (16ft) after 20 years; ultimately 20m (65ft).

STAR PERFORMER
B. utilis var. *jacquemontii* If you have space, plant a group of these elegant trees to highlight the stunning bark.

Caragana

Pea trees have an attractive feathery appearance with dainty yellow flowers. Native to central Asia and very hardy, they make excellent specimen trees.

The pea tree, so-called because the flowers resemble those of the sweet pea, is relatively uncommon in Britain. But if you are seeking a hardy tree for a smaller garden, they are a terrific choice.

The tree that likes a hard time
Having evolved in the dry environment of central Asia: hot, dry summers and bitter, dry winters, pea trees are well adapted to harsh conditions, and in fact do best in drier soils. The milder, moister conditions found in most British gardens may lead to a less profuse display of leaves and flowers.

C. arborescens is the species most commonly available. It rarely grows more than 3m (10ft) tall and is available in both upright and weeping varieties.

STAR PERFORMER
C. arborescens 'Walker' Delicately drooping branches bear tiny pale yellow blooms in late spring and summer.

Expert's Selection

1 C. arborescens 'Walker'
An elegant weeping variety of its upright parent, *C. arborescens*, with feathery delicate foliage. This pretty little tree is ideal in small gardens.
⊘ **Green • Spring and summer**
✿ **Yellow • Late spring**
h. 1.5m (5ft) *s.* 1.2m (4ft)

The Essentials

Site demands Plant in any well-drained soil in full sun.
Pruning None required, except to remove dead wood.
Pests and diseases Trouble free.
Bonus point They are a manageable size for most gardens.

Crataegus

Hawthorn is well known as a care-free hedging plant, but it can also be grown as a small tree. Plant one, and watch birds flock to your garden in autumn, drawn by the berries.

1 *C. laevigata* 'Paul's Scarlet'♀ Makes an attractive, small tree, the magnificent double red flowers contrasting beautifully with the glossy, dark green leaves. Berries are red, but often fail to appear. 'Rosea Flore Pleno'♀ bears a mass of bright pink double flowers in spring.
✿ **Red • Spring** ∅ **Dark green**
h.&s. 5m (16ft)

2 *C. persimilis* 'Prunifolia'♀ Abundant autumn berries appear as the leaves turn scarlet and orange.
❀ **White • Early summer** ∅ **Dark green** ❧ **Dark red • Autumn**
h.&s. 3m (10ft)

3 *C.* 'Autumn Glory' Noted for its berries and richly coloured autumn foliage.
❀ **White • Spring** ∅ **Dark green**
❧ **Bright red • Autumn**
h.&s. 6m (20ft)

STAR PERFORMER
C. laevigata 'Paul's Scarlet'♀
Plant for its wonderful show of large red flowers every spring.

Site demands Any soil, in full sun.
Planting practice Plant from late autumn to early spring.
Flowering times Spring and early summer.
Pruning needs None, but can clip hedging after leaves have fallen.
Pests and diseases Trouble free.
Bonus points Scented flowers.

Clusters of fragrant flowers, followed by bright berries and often a golden blaze of autumn leaves, make hawthorn a very popular garden choice. It is exceptionally care free and hardy, only needing attention if it is grown as hedging. Then all it needs is the occasional trim.

Eucalyptus

Gum trees are prized for their glossy, aromatic, leaves, and colourful, peeling bark in shades of cream, pinky grey and green. Most also have a summer show of tiny, cream flowers.

1 *E. gunnii*♀
A very hardy variety, with attractive peeling, grey and pale green bark. It is popular to keep it cut well back, so that it grows as a shrub, only ever producing the lovely, silvery juvenile foliage.
∅ **Silvery blue-grey; later blue-green**
h. 15m (50ft) s. 6m (20ft)

2 *E. dalrympleana*♀
A fairly fast grower, if left uncut it will evenually form a tall, slender tree with peeling white, grey and pinkish bark and a crown of orange-red twigs.
∅ **Blue-grey; later blue-green**
h. 20m (66ft) s. 8m (26ft)

3 *E. pauciflora* subsp. *niphophila*♀ This extremely hardy variety is noted for its brilliant white bark and long grey-green, young leaves, which are borne on red twigs.
∅ **Grey-green; later mid green**
h. 15m (50ft) s. 6m (20ft)

4 *E. coccifera*♀
A relatively low, shrubby tree, it has smooth, brilliant white bark. The young leaves are mid-green, while mature leaves take on a greyish hue, and smell strongly of peppermint.
∅ **Mid green; later grey**
h. 8m (26ft) s. 4m (13ft)

5 *E. parvifolia*♀
A slow-growing tree, it is ideal for the average-sized garden. Can be kept as short as 2m (7ft) with annual pruning.
∅ **Blue-green; later grey-green**
h. 12m (40ft) s. 4m (13ft)

6 *E. perriniana*
Another slow-growing variety that suits the smaller garden. The young foliage is a lovely purply blue, with paired leaves encircling the stem.
∅ **Purple-blue; later blue-green**
h. 10m (33ft) s. 5m (16ft)

E. perriniana

STAR PERFORMER

***E. gunnii*♀ Grow this as a rounded, silvery bush by pruning regularly, or leave it to shoot up into a tall, elegant tree, with peeling, greeny grey bark and blue-green leaves.**

Native to Australia, there are hundreds of varieties of eucalyptus, many of them very hardy and care free, like those listed here. The only point to note is to avoid planting one too near a building, as the roots run wide, and could damage a wall.

A eucalyptus can be used to suit most sizes of garden. You could just leave it, and let it grow slowly into a tall, elegant tree, or cut it back hard each year, for a bushy shrub. This also stops the attractive, silvery, young leaves from maturing to a duller tone.

Once a tree is about five years old, strips of its colourful bark will start to peel back, revealing contrasting patches beneath.

The Essentials

Site demands Any moist, well-drained soil, in full sun. They do best sheltered from cold winds.
Planting practice Plant from early to midsummer.
Flowering times Summer.
Pruning needs Prune hard after the winter frosts, to keep to any desired size. For constant juvenile foliage, cut back all shoots to ground level each year in early spring, before new growth starts.
Pests and diseases Generally trouble free, but silver leaf disease may strike.
Bonus point Aromatic foliage will scent the air all year round.

Gleditsia

Honey locust is grown for its glorious, annual flourish of brightly coloured leaves. Flowers are inconspicuous, but give rise to pendulous seedpods, that last well into winter.

Expert's Selection

1 *G. triacanthos* **'Sunburst'**♀
New leaves are a dazzling, bright yellow. They will gradually turn to a pale green, before being shed late in the autumn.
Bright yellow • Spring–autumn
***h.* 12m (40ft) *s.* 3m (10ft)**

2 *G. triacanthos* **'Rubylace'**
A more compact tree, its spring leaves are deep bronze red, fading gently as the season progresses.
Bronze red • Spring–autumn
***h.* 10m (33ft) *s.* 3m (10ft)**

3 *G. triacanthos* **'Elegantissima'** A shrubby variety, its leaves eventually turn a clear yellow.
Golden green
Spring–autumn
***h.* 10m (33ft)**
***s.* 3m (10ft)**

The Essentials

Site demands Any well-drained soil, in sun or light shade.
Planting practice Plant from late autumn to early spring.
Pruning needs Just cut off any dead wood in spring.
Pests and diseases Trouble free.
Bonus point Colourful foliage.

For a marvellous, display of richly coloured, feathery leaves, that subtly change shade as autumn draws near, plant this hardy tree. It is utterly care free, needing only the odd, light trim.

STAR PERFORMER

***G. triacanthos* 'Sunburst'**♀

A very good choice for the average-sized garden, it gives an impressive display, with its tiered branches and feathery, yellow leaves.

Laburnum

Fast-growing and hardy, the light, graceful laburnum makes a wonderful focal point in a sunny garden. It comes in both upright and weeping varieties, all of which bear the characteristic pendulous clusters of golden yellow flowers, which appear in late spring and early summer.

Expert's Selection

1 *L. x watereri* 'Vossii' ♀
A spectacular variety, also called the golden chain tree, it has tassels of yellow flowers up to 38cm (15in) long with glossy pale leaves.
✿ **Yellow** • **Early summer**
⊘ **Pale green**
h. **6m (20ft)** *s.* **4m (13ft)**

2 *L. alpinum* 'Pendulum'
Known as Scotch laburnum, this tree is slow-growing with weeping branches. The golden yellow flowers grow in clusters 25cm (10in) long and are slightly fragrant.
✿ **Yellow** • **Early summer**
⊘ **Dark green**
h. **3m (10ft)** *s.* **2m (7ft)**

3 *L. anagyroides* 'Pendulum'
A weeping variety, its flower clusters are shorter than average.
✿ **Yellow** • **Early summer**
⊘ **Dark green**
h. **4m (13ft)** *s.* **3m (10ft)**

The Essentials

Site demands Any well-drained soil in full sun.
Planting practice Plant in autumn. May need staking.
Flowering time Early summer.
Pruning needs Remove dead or damaged branches after flowering.
Pests and diseases Trouble free.
Bonus point Easily trained to form spectacular archways.

Laburnum is a splendid and untemperamental tree, which puts on a great show in late spring. Most varieties are fast-growing, except for *L. alpinum* 'Pendulum', and provided it is planted in a position with full sun, it is very easy to grow, needing no special care.

Some varieties, such as *L. anagyroides* 'Pendulum' and *L. alpinum* 'Pendulum', have drooping branches, and there is even a weeping version of the upright *L.* × *watereri* 'Vossii'.

The golden yellow flower clusters vary in length from 25cm (10in) to a dramatic 60cm (2ft).

Training a laburnum
Laburnum can be trained up a pergola or over an arch, where the long trailing flowers are shown to great advantage. Plant one or two-year-old trees, and train over the framework of the arch, tying in early while the wood is still supple. Once the framework is established, prune at the end of the growing season to reduce the density of growth and produce flowering spurs.

L. alpinum 'Pendulum'

TAKE A FRESH LOOK

+ *Laburnocytisus* 'Adamii' is a hybrid of laburnum and broom, which bears a mixture of yellow, pink and purple flowers on the same tree. The long flower sprays, up to 18cm (7in), appear in early summer.

Malus

Crab apples make a gorgeous sight in spring with their clouds of pink blossom, and again in autumn with colourful fruit and foliage. They are hardy, easy to grow, and small enough to suit the average garden.

M. transitoria

Expert's Selection

1 *M.* x *schiedeckeri* **'Red Jade'** A small elegant tree with slender weeping branches.
❀ **White • Spring** ∅ **Bright green**
❧ **Red • Autumn**
h. 3m (10ft) *s.* 2m (7ft)

2 *M. rockii* **'Rudolph'**
A stunning tree, its leaves, flowers and fruit are all richly coloured.
✿ **Rose red • Spring** ∅ **Bronze red**
❧ **Orange-yellow • Autumn**
h. 6m (20ft) *s.* 4m (13ft)

3 *M.* **'Laura'**
The fruit of this dwarf tree makes excellent crab apple jelly.
❀✿ **White, pink • Spring** ❧ **Maroon**
Autumn • *h.&s.* 1.8m (6ft)

4 *M.* x *robusta* **'Red Siberian'**♀ Its red autumn fruits stay on the tree well into winter.
❀✿ **White, pink • Spring**
❧ **Red flushed with yellow • Autumn**
h. 6m (20ft) *s.* 4m (13ft)

5 *M.* x *purpurea*
It has purplish green leaves, dark purple flowers and purple red fruit.
✿ **Purple • Spring** ∅ **Purple green**
❧ **Purple red • Autumn**
h. 4m (13ft) *s.* 3m (10ft)

6 *M. transitoria*♀
An upright, spreading tree, it is noted for its lovely autumn foliage.
❀ **White • Spring** ∅ **Yellow/red**
❧ **Light yellow • Autumn**
h. 7m (23ft) *s.* 4m (13ft)

7 *M. hupehensis* **'John Downie'**♀ Brightly hued fruits make a striking autumn display.
❀ **White • Spring** ❧ **Orange-red**
Autumn • *h.* 1.5m (5ft) *s.* 1m (3ft)

8 *M. floribunda*♀
A profusion of pale pink blossom opens from crimson buds in spring.
✿ **Pale pink • Spring** ❧ **Yellow**
Autumn • *h.* 1.5m (5ft) *s.* 1.2m (4ft)

Berries of *M.* x *robusta* **'Red Siberian'**

The Essentials

Site demands Any soil, except very dry or waterlogged.
Planting practice Plant in autumn or early spring.
Flowering time Spring.
Pruning needs Remove dead or damaged shoots in winter.
Pests and diseases Generally trouble free, but honey fungus or fireblight may occur.
Bonus point Attractive all year.

M. x purpurea

Crab apples are well worth growing for the ornamental value of their spring flowers and autumn fruit. They are also very easy to care for.

Flower colour ranges from white or pink to deep red, while the fruit, which ripens in early autumn, can be yellow, red, or green, flushed with red or purple. The trees can vary in height from 9m (30ft) to 3m (10ft), so it is possible to grow one even in a small or average-sized garden. The elegant weeping 'Red Jade' and the new compact dwarf crab apple 'Laura' both make excellent additions to an oriental-style garden.

Outstanding trees for autumn colour include *M. transitoria*, with its yellow and red leaves and yellow fruit, and 'John Downie', with orange and red fruit.

Caring for crab apples
Very little pruning is necessary. Simply remove any dead or damaged branches in winter, when the tree is dormant. If the tree is attacked by fireblight, remove and destroy the affected shoots, cutting back beyond the damage by at least 30cm (1ft). If a tree is attacked by honey fungus, and is dead or dying, it should be destroyed.

STAR PERFORMER
M. x *schiedeckeri* **'Red Jade'**
Add Japanese-style elegance to the garden and enjoy the splendid display of pink blossom followed by cherry-sized red fruit.

Prunus

Flowering cherries, plums and **almonds** are grown for their dazzling spring display, with clouds of exquisite blossom which range from pure white or pink to deep red. These ornamental fruit trees are easy to grow, and all the varieties selected here are hardy.

The blossom-laden branches of these trees are one of the delights of spring. They come in an enormous choice of varieties, and can be spreading, weeping or upright in habit.

Height and spread sizes given are after 10 years, but some varieties can ultimately reach 6m (20ft) or more. In a small garden plant one of the compact varieties, such as 'Alba Plena', or one of the *Prunus* shrubs from page 235.

These beautiful trees need little looking after. If any pruning is necessary, trim in late summer, after flowering. This reduces the risk of diseases like silver leaf.

TAKE A FRESH LOOK

P. serrula, a flowering cherry, is grown for its high-gloss, deep reddish brown bark.

Expert's Selection

1 *P.* 'Taihaku' ♀
A Japanese flowering cherry with large white flowers.
❀ White • Spring ∅ Coppery green
h. 2.7m (9ft) s. 1.5m (5ft)

2 *P.* x *yedoensis* ♀
A pretty cherry with almond-scented flowers.
❀ Pinky white • Spring
∅ Dark green
h. 3m (10ft) s. 2.5m (8ft)

3 *P. padus* 'Purple Queen'
Noted for its purple shoots and coppery leaves, tinged with purple.
✿ Pale pink
Late spring
∅ Coppery
purple-green
h. 6m (20ft) s. 3m (10ft)

4 *P. glandulosa* 'Alba Plena' ♀ A flowering almond, this domed shrub blooms in late spring.
❀ White • Late spring
∅ Coppery green
h.&s. 1.5m (5ft)

5 *P. tenella*
This dwarf Russian flowering almond is really a shrub, but a good choice for a small garden.
❀ Bright pink • Mid spring
∅ Coppery green • h.&s. 1m (3ft)

The Essentials

Site demands Any well-drained site, except where soil is very dry. An open, sunny location is ideal.
Planting practice Plant in spring or autumn, avoiding frosty spells.
Flowering time Spring.
Pruning needs Rarely needed.
Pests and diseases Usually trouble free, but may suffer from leaf or spur blight.
Bonus point Many also have brilliantly coloured autumn foliage.

P. glandulosa 'Alba Plena'

P. tenella

ZSTAR PERFORMER

P. 'Taihaku' ♀ **Known as the great white cherry, this looks stunning in spring, when its huge white flowers contrast well with the coppery green foliage.**

Pyrus

Ornamental pears are unusual, but well worth seeking out for their fluffy white blossom, decorative 'felted' young foliage and appealing shapes.

1 *P. salicifolia* 'Pendula'♀
A beautiful weeping tree with masses of spring blossom.
❀ **Creamy white** • **Mid-spring**
h. 5m (16ft) *s.* 2.7m (9ft)

2 *P. calleryana*
'Chanticleer'♀ A narrow, pyramid-shaped tree with lovely red autumn leaves.
❀ **Creamy white** • **Mid spring**
⊘ **Green, turning red in autumn**
h. 5m (16ft) *s.* 2.5m (8ft)

3 *P. nivalis*
The snow pear, its leaves are white and attractively felted when young.
❀ **White** • **Late spring**
⊘ **White, later turning green**
h. 5m (16ft) *s.* 2.7m (9ft)

The foliage is also appealing: the young leaves of 'Pendula' and *P. nivalis* are white and felted when young, while 'Chanticleer' has vibrantly ruddy autumn foliage.

The Essentials

Site demands Any well-drained site, except where soil is very dry, in either full sun or partial shade.
Planting practice Plant from mid autumn to early spring.
Flowering time Spring.
Pruning needs Prune after flowering to restrict growth or to tidy up straggly branches.
Pests and diseases Trouble free.
Bonus point They are particularly hardy, and will also tolerate urban air pollution.

STAR PERFORMER
P. salicifolia 'Pendula'♀ **A beautiful feature tree for a larger garden, with its willow-like weeping branches and creamy white flowers.**

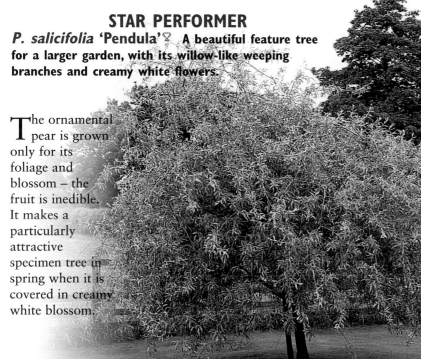

The ornamental pear is grown only for its foliage and blossom – the fruit is inedible. It makes a particularly attractive specimen tree in spring when it is covered in creamy white blossom.

Robinia

False acacia will add grace to any garden with its light airy foliage and hanging flower clusters.

1 *R. pseudoacacia* 'Frisia'♀
Bright golden yellow foliage turns orange yellow in the autumn. 'Bessoniana' and 'Coluteoides' have green leaves and smaller, but still abundant, flowers.
❀ **White** • **Late spring** ⊘ **Golden yellow** • *h.* 9m (30ft) *s.* 8m (26ft)

2 *R. pseudoacacia* 'Lace Lady' Also called 'Twisty Baby', it has contorted branches and leaves.
❀ **White** • **Late spring** ⊘ **Lime green**
h. 2.5m (8ft) *s.* 3m (10ft)

3 *R.* x *slavinii* 'Hillieri'♀
An elegant small tree with long clusters of pale pink flowers.
✿ **Pink** • **Early summer** ⊘ **Green**
h. 1.2m (4ft) *s.* 60cm (2ft)

These elegant trees are hardy and easy to grow. Avoid windy sites, however, as the thorny branches can be brittle and tend to break in high winds.
'Lace Lady' can also be grown as a bonsai-like shrub, so that it only reaches 1.2m (4ft).

STAR PERFORMER
R. pseudoacacia 'Frisia'♀ **Grow in an open, sunny position and watch the colour change from golden to orange yellow in autumn.**

The Essentials

Site demands Any well-drained site, in sun or partial shade.
Planting practice Plant in spring.
Flowering time Spring.
Pruning needs Generally not necessary, but cut back hard to grow as shrubs if space is limited.
Pests and diseases Trouble free.
Bonus point Dainty leaves contrast well with those of other ornamental trees and shrubs.

R. pseudoacacia 'Bessoniana'

Salix

Willows are a family of hardy, mainly deciduous trees that include the classic weeping willow, as well as many upright varieties. They may be grown for their slender branches, coloured bark or shoots, fluffy catkins or attractive foliage. The smallest will fit in a patio pot; the largest are huge.

1 *S. aegyptiaca*
The musk willow is native to the Middle East. Its long, fragrant catkins make it a haze of soft yellow in late winter.
✿ **Grey furred, yellow catkins • Late winter • h. 6m (20ft) s. 4m (13ft)**

S. alba subsp. *vitellina* 'Britzensis'

S. caprea 'Kilmarnock'

2 *S. alba* subsp. *vitellina* 'Britzensis'♀ Grown for its orange red stems, obtained by cutting down every two years to encourage new, young stems.
⌀ **Orange red stems • Late autumn until leaves hide shoots in late spring • h. 1.5m (5ft) s. 3m (10ft)**

3 *S. caprea* 'Kilmarnock'♀ A slow-growing, compact, weeping willow suitable for a small garden or container.
✿ **Greeny yellow catkins Spring**
h. 1.5m (5ft) s. 2m (7ft)

4 *S. babylonica* 'Tortuosa'♀ A fast-growing tree noted for its twisted, contorted branches.
✿ **Greeny yellow catkins Early spring**
h. 10m (33ft) s. 7m (23ft)

5 *S.* x *pendulina* var. elegantissima The cascades of bright green foliage look spectacular, especially when a pond catches their reflection.
⌀ **Bright green • Spring–summer h. 8m (26ft) s. 6m (20ft)**

6 *S. alba* 'Liempde'
A narrow tree with slender, upright branches. Hairs on the leaves give this tree a silvery appearance.
⌀ **Silver grey • Spring–summer h. 12m (40ft) s. 5m (16ft)**

These striking, hardy trees are very easy to grow. There are male and female trees, the males with larger, more showy catkins.

Some weeping willows need a lot of room for both branches and wide-spreading roots, but smaller varieties, such as the diminutive **'Kilmarnock'**, will suit the smallest garden or even a tub.

You need to cut out about half of this tree's branches every year, and shorten the rest, to form an open umbrella-like framework. Varieties like **'Britzensis'** are grown for their colourful young stems. These are obtained by regularly cutting the tree down to ground level so that new stems grow from the base. Do this in winter, cutting only half the stems each time. Then you will still get catkins which only appear on wood of at least a year old.

Site demands Heavy damp soil, in sun or light shade.
Planting practice Plant in spring or autumn.
Pruning needs Trim 'Kilmarnock' to keep in shape and, in late winter, cut down those grown for their stem colour.
Pests and diseases Usually trouble free, but look out for aphids, moths, beetles and weevils.
Bonus point Colour may appear as catkins, winter shoots or leaves.

STAR PERFORMER
S. aegyptiaca **Plant this tree in a prominent position: the fragrant grey catkins with their yellow fuzzy anthers will bring a haze of colour to the late winter garden.**

Sorbus

Whitebeams and **mountain ash** or **rowan** are elegant, deciduous trees, that provide a glorious display of autumn foliage, along with dense clusters of colourful berries.

Expert's Selection

S. cashmiriana

1 *S. aucuparia* **'Sheerwater Seedling'** ♀ A narrow tree with abundant white flowers followed by orange-red fruit. The vigorous 'Cardinale Royal' is similar, but taller.
✿ **White • Late spring**
🍂 **Orangey red • Autumn**
h. 8m (26ft) s. 3m (10ft)

2 *S. cashmiriana* ♀
The Kashmir rowan, its soft pink, spring flowers are followed by white or pink-tinged berries.
✿ **Pale pink • Spring**
🍂 **Pink or white • Autumn**
h. 4m (13ft) s. 3m (10ft)

3 *S. sargentiana* ♀
Bears distinctive large, sticky, red leaf buds in winter.
🍂 **Brilliant orange-red • Autumn**
🍂 **Scarlet • Autumn**
h.&s. up to 10m (33ft)

4 *S. aria* **'Lutescens'** ♀
In spring, the purple shoots are clothed in downy white leaves.
🍂 **Red and brown • Autumn**
🍂 **Orangey red • Autumn**
h. 6m (20ft) s. 4.5m (15ft)

5 *S. x hostii*
A blaze of autumn colour follows pink flowers in May.
🍂 **Red, orange and yellow** 🍂 **Bright red • Autumn** 🍂 **Pink • Early summer**
h. 4m (13ft) s. 1.5m (5ft)

6 *S. 'Joseph Rock'* ♀
Gives outstanding autumn colour, both from its multi-hued foliage and its striking berries.
🍂 **Red, orange and yellow • Autumn**
🍂 **Creamy yellow turning orange-yellow • Autumn**
h. 6m (20ft) s. 2.5m (8ft)

The Essentials

Site demands Any well-drained soil, in sun or partial shade.
Planting practice Plant young trees from autumn to spring.
Pruning needs None required.
Pests and diseases Usually trouble free, but are sometimes attacked by fire blight.
Bonus point Truly care free and hardy, even in polluted areas.

These attractive trees can be grown in almost any garden, since they are hardy and range in size from dwarf shrubs to tall, statuesque trees. The foliage often has outstanding autumn colour, in shades of orange, red and yellow, and clusters of orange, pink, scarlet, yellow or white berries.

Choose the right sized tree
Because these trees come in a wide range of sizes, you are likely to find one that will be suitable for your garden. Where space is limited, the ideal varieties are *S. cashmiriana* and *S. × hostii*, or the narrow 'Sheerwater Seedling'. Medium-sized trees for an average garden include the conical 'Lutescens', the vividly-coloured 'Joseph Rock', or one of the native mountain ash varieties such as *S. aucuparia* 'Cardinale Royal'.

If you are lucky enough to have a large, open space, you could plant *S. sargentiana*. This large, rounded tree not only has highly decorative, large, red buds all winter, but also gives a glorious autumn display of brilliant orange-red leaves.

S. 'Joseph Rock'

STAR PERFORMER
S. aucuparia **'Sheerwater Seedling'** ♀ **An elegant rowan tree, this is ideal in a town garden where space is limited. It also has the advantage of tolerating air pollution.**

annuals,
biennials, bedding &
container plants

With their wide range of often brilliant colours, abundant flowers and ease of cultivation, annuals – plants that flower and die within a year – are deservedly popular. Biennials, which flower in the year after the seed is sown are also great care-free choices.

The bedding and container plants readily available from nurseries are mostly either annuals or perennials. Most are too tender to plant out until the risk of frost has passed, but you can raise these plants in a greenhouse from seeds or cuttings taken in early autumn, or if you wish, simply buy a new selection each year.

A cheap and cheerful display

Their short-lived nature makes these plants wonderfully versatile. Give them a bed of their own, or dot them casually among established perennials. They are very useful too, as cheerful gap-fillers among other perennials or shrubs in a recently planted bed, where the permanent planting has not yet reached maturity.

Their sometimes garish colours mean that annuals and bedding plants do not always blend happily with hardy perennials, so choose more subtly-coloured and small-flowered species,

such as *Argyranthemum*, *Bidens*, *Brachyscome*, *Limnanthes*, *Sutera* and *Verbena*, for planting in mixed beds.

Grown in a block, annuals can make a real splash of colour. Unless you are restrained, using a mixture of colours or types can create an overly rigid or clashing effect but a mass planting of a single variety can be really striking.

The seeds and plants of annuals and biennials may be bought in single colour varieties or mixed for a random display. Make your choice depending on the situation and your desired effect. Compact annuals are ideal for edging, or a formal effect. Plant them among late spring bulbs including tulips, either to flower at the same time, or to follow on.

Pack colour into a pot

Many of the smaller annuals, biennials and bedding plants are ideal for planting in containers including large decorative pots, window boxes and hanging baskets. Compact, bushy varieties towards the centre with trailing plants nearer the sides will give a really good and vigorous show for much of the summer in return for regular watering and an occasional feed.

For smaller containers, plants such as *Sutera*, **Million Bells** petunias, *Glechoma hederacea*, *Brachyscome*, *Diascia*, *Felicia*, *Lobelia* and *Scaevola* are ideal. A really large pot or urn with *Argyranthemum* underplanted with *Bidens* 'Golden Goddess', and perhaps also some violet or purple **Million Bells** or **Surfinia petunias** will create a splendid focal point on a terrace or patio.

Grow annuals in a sunny spot and plant them in well-drained soil for the brightest display.

Annuals for cold spots
• In exposed or coastal sites choose low-growing varieties.

Improve the soil
• Improve heavy soil by working in plenty of organic matter in the autumn or winter prior to planting.
• Do not overfeed with nitrogen-rich fertilisers or farmyard manure which will encourage lax growth.
• Apply potash-rich tomato feed for the best display of flowers.

Sowing seed
• Sow hardy annuals in early autumn or early spring in the bed where they are to flower.
• Make a series of parallel drills (shallow trenches), 10–20cm (4–8in) apart, to help you to distinguish seedlings from weeds.
• Thin out the young seedlings if they germinate too thickly.
• Sow half hardy annuals in a greenhouse and plant out after the risk of frost has passed.
• Biennials are sown in early summer, for planting out in autumn to flower the following spring.

Easy aftercare
• As most annuals set seed freely, it is worth deadheading every week. Then the plants will put all their energy into producing fresh flowers.
• In dry weather, water annuals generously, especially those in containers. Water-retaining gels are a useful addition to container compost, especially in hanging baskets, which dry out quickly.
• Plants in containers will benefit from an occasional feed: once a month from midsummer onwards.

Try something different
• Because annuals and bedding plants give their show within a year of planting, it is easy to experiment with different combinations from one year to the next.
• Although most annuals flower from late spring to autumn, they can provide pleasure in winter for the armchair gardener. Enjoy browsing through catalogues or web sites to plan next year's display.

Deadheading petunias will prolong the flowering season

Argyranthemum

Marguerites or **Paris daisies** have beautiful flowers in soft colours, complemented by attractively cut foliage. The blooms are borne throughout summer and into autumn.

Marguerites are commonly grown as summer bedding plants, although they are tender perennials. Their compact habit, good foliage, and freely produced flowers in a range of colours make them hard to beat, and they also provide long-lasting colour in large containers.

A. 'Jamaica Primrose'

Expert's Selection

1 A. 'Qinta White' ♀
Double flowers make this variety a popular choice.
✿ **White • Early summer–autumn**
h. 50cm (20in) **s.** 60cm (2ft)

2 A. Courtyard Series
Compact and long flowering.
✿✿ **White or yellow • Early summer–autumn • h.&s. 40cm (16in)**

3 A. gracile 'Chelsea Girl' ♀
Finely-cut, grey-green foliage is a perfect foil for the single daisies.
✿ **White with yellow centre • Early summer–autumn • h.&s. 60cm (2ft)**

4 A. 'Jamaica Primrose' ♀
Long branching stems are topped by primrose yellow flowerheads.
✿ **Yellow • Early summer–autumn**
h.&s. 1m (3ft)

STAR PERFORMER
A. 'Qinta White' ♀ These double white daisies love to soak up the summer sun.

The Essentials

Site demands Marguerites need only sun and a well-drained soil.
Planting practice Plant in early summer.
Flowering time Summer–autumn.
Pests and diseases Aphids and leaf miners may damage the plants.
Bonus point Makes a long-lived perennial if protected from frost.

Begonia

The fibrous-rooted Semperflorens begonias, with their abundant displays of flowers throughout the season, give great value summer bedding. Unlike many bedding plants, begonias perform well in some shade and do equally well whether in containers or garden beds.

Expert's Selection

1 B. 'Dragon Wing'
A large fibrous-rooted begonia, that bears clusters of vivid flowers above its lop-sided, but very large light green leaves. It looks good massed in a bed or in a pot.
✿ **Scarlet • Summer**
h.&s. 30–35cm (12–14in)

2 B. Olympia Series
A particularly weather-resistant series of compact begonias with vivid yellow centres, they may have green or bronze leaves.
✿✿ **Pink, white • Summer**
h.&s. 20cm (8in)

3 B. Excel Series
These large-flowered plants includes both green and deep bronze leaved varieties in pale and bright colours.
✿✿✿ **White, pink, red • Summer**
h.&s. 20cm (8in)

4 B. Cocktail Series
The rounded bronze foliage on this series of small begonias makes a great contrast with the wide range of flower colours.
✿✿ **White, pink, red • Summer**
h.&s. 15–20cm (6–8in)

B. Olympia Series 'Salmon Scarlet'

5 *B.* Organdy Series
Harsh weather conditions are no problem for the single flowers of this dwarf series.
✿✿✿ **White, pink, rose, scarlet**
Summer • *h.&s.* 15cm (6in)

The Semperflorens begonias are ideal bedding plants for a summer-long display. The small to medium-sized flowers are carried just above rounded, often bronze-tinted leaves.

They have fibrous roots, and grow well in both sun and partial shade, in a humus-rich soil which is neutral or slightly acid. It is difficult to raise good plants from seed, and most gardeners prefer to buy small plants from a nursery in late spring, planting out after all risk of frost is past.

Flowers and leaves may suffer in prolonged periods of drought so water your plants freely during any dry spell. Deadheading the plants regularly will help to encourage new flowers to form.

Each year sees the introduction of new varieties, so it is worth looking out for them in nurseries and catalogues. All the varieties listed here have single flowers, but varieties with double flowers are also occasionally available.

Begonias are susceptible to attack by vine weevils and aphids, while botrytis and mildew may damage the plants in wet weather.

The Essentials

Site demands A well-drained soil and a sunny or partially shaded site will satisfy these easy begonias.
Planting practice Plant out when there is no risk of frost.
Flowering time Pretty flowers appear all through summer.
Pruning needs Regular deadheading will prolong the display.
Pests and diseases Vine weevils, aphids, botrytis and mildew are frequent problems.
Bonus point Unlike many summer bedding plants, begonias will thrive in the shade.

STAR PERFORMER
B. 'Dragon Wing' **With its unusual foliage and brilliant red flowers, this variety will add drama to any planting scheme. It tolerates dry spells well, making it a great care-free choice for containers.**

Bidens

With their golden flowers and prettily-cut foliage, these vigorous plants are ideal for borders or larger containers, where they will create thick, long-blooming mats.

Expert's Selection

1 *B. ferulifolia* 'Golden Goddess' This large flowered variety will form a broad lacy mound which blooms for months on end. The species is equally attractive but has smaller flowers.
✿ **Golden yellow • Summer–autumn**
h. 30cm (1ft) *s.* 1m (3ft)

2 *B. aurea*
The abundant starry flowers are borne above dissected leaves, on plants that may be either spreading or trailing
✿ **Yellow • Early summer–autumn**
h.&s. 30cm–1m (1–3ft)

These free-flowering plants form wide mats, with the starry golden-yellow daisies held just above the lacy foliage. They are best grown in large baskets or containers, which allow the long stems to trail elegantly. Although they are perennials, they are not hardy and are best treated as half-hardy annuals.

Bidens are easily grown in most reasonably well-drained soils, and require a sunny position. The seed can be sown in a warm greenhouse in early spring, but small plants are readily available from nurseries. These should be planted out after the risk of frost has passed. Flowering starts in early to mid summer and continues until the autumn frosts. Regular deadheading keeps plants looking tidy.

STAR PERFORMER
B. ferulifolia 'Golden Goddess' **An abundance of vivid flowers and beautiful, finely divided foliage make this variety a star in pots and beds.**

The Essentials

Site demands Bidens tolerates most soils, but needs plenty of sun.
Planting practice Plant out in late spring when there is no risk of further frosts.
Flowering time These plants are studded with bright yellow blooms from early summer to autumn.
Pests and diseases Plants may be damaged by aphids or slugs.
Bonus point Bidens makes a pretty yellow alternative to lobelia or ivy trailing from hanging baskets.

Brachyscome

Swan River daisies with masses of small vibrant flowers displayed over compact, ferny foliage are ideal for the front of a border or in a container.

STAR PERFORMER
B. Bravo Series
Small, bright daisies over a cushion of ferny foliage bring a splash of colour to the borders in summer.

The Essentials

Site demands Swan River daisies prefer a sunny position in almost any fertile soil.

Planting practice Plant out in beds or containers when there is no danger of frosts.

Flowering time Flowers appear from midsummer until mid autumn.

Pruning needs Deadhead regularly and trim straggly plants.

Pests and diseases Trouble free.

Bonus point The annual varieties listed here are delicately fragrant.

Expert's Selection

1 *B.* **Bravo Series**
A mixture of white, violet-blue or purple flowers with dark centres are produced in abundance.
✿✿✿ **White, blue or purple**
Midsummer–mid autumn
h. **25cm (10in)** *s.* **30cm (1ft)**

2 *B.* **Splendour Series**
These compact plants have white, pink or purple flowers with dark or yellow centres.
✿✿✿ **White, pink or purple**
Midsummer–mid autumn
h. **20cm (8in)** *s.* **25cm (10in)**

3 *B.* **'Blue Star'**
The deep yellow eyes of these flowers make a stunning contrast with the rich purple-blue petals.
✿ **Blue • Midsummer–mid autumn**
h. **30cm (1ft)** *s.* **40cm (16in)**

With a winning combination of abundant flowers in a range of colours, a compact habit and lacy foliage, Swan River daisies are a popular choice. Their neat habit also makes them ideal for containers.

Although they can be bought as young plants ready for bedding out after the spring frosts, Swan River daisies are easily raised from seed sown in early spring in a cool greenhouse.

Diascia

There is a dainty diascia in almost every shade of pink. Their long flowering season makes them great value in beds and tubs and some will overwinter in sheltered spots.

D. **'Coral Belle'**

The diascias bring shades of salmon and coral pink to the garden throughout the summer months. Most are perennials of borderline hardiness, and so are ideal for bedding out as annuals.

A sunny position in a humus-rich, well-drained soil that does not dry out in summer will satisfy their needs. Most are best bought from nurseries or grown from cuttings, but a few, such as **'Apricot Queen'**, can be raised from seed.

You can easily increase your stock from cuttings taken in summer and overwintered in a frost-free greenhouse.

STAR PERFORMER
D. **barberae** '**Ruby Field**'♀ **Dense sprays of rich pink flowers on slender stems last all summer long.**

1 *D. barberae* 'Ruby Field' ♀
Plant this fairly hardy perennial in large drifts to appreciate the full effect of its rich pink flowers.
✿ **Rich pink • Summer**
h. 25–60cm (10–24in)
s. 40cm (16in)

2 *D.* 'Coral Belle'
Delicate, two-spurred flowers are borne on elegant stems.
✿ **Deep salmon pink • Summer**
h. 25–35cm (10–14in) *s.* 40cm (16in)

3 *D.* 'Iceberg'
This striking white variety makes a dramatic contrast if grown alongside the pink shades of the other diascias.
❀ **White • Summer**
h. 25–35cm (10–14in)
s. 40cm (16in)

4 *D. rigescens* ♀
The flowers of this distinctive species are borne in dense erect spikes above a mat of dark foliage.
✿ **Pink • Summer**
h. 50cm (20in) *s.* 40cm (16in)

The Essentials

Site demands A sunny, fairly moist and sheltered position.
Planting practice Plant out in late spring when there is no further risk of frosts.
Flowering time Diascias flower all summer long.
Pruning needs Regular deadheading will encourage the plants to produce more flowers.
Pests and diseases Trouble free apart from the risk of damage by slugs and snails.
Bonus point Cut back the first flush of flowers once they are over and a second flush will follow.

Erysimum

Wallflowers have long been a favourite among gardeners for their early, fragrant blooms. With a wide range of colours available, there is one to suit every garden.

Expert's Selection

1 E. Tom Thumb Series
These compact plants carry flowers in fiery shades of yellow, orange and red.
✿✿✿ **Yellow, orange or red • Early summer • h.&s. 20cm (8in)**

2 E. My Fair Lady Series
The flowers in this mixture are in more subtle shades of cream, pale orange and red.
❀✿✿ **Cream, light orange and red Late spring–early summer h.&s. 35cm (14in)**

3 E. 'Blood Red'
As its name suggests, this plant bears ruby-coloured flowers. They are also deeply fragrant.
✿ **Deep red • Late spring–early summer • h.&s. 30cm (1ft)**

4 E. Bedder Series
This mixture produces plants with an excellent compact habit and flowers in shades of yellow, orange and light red.
✿✿✿ **Yellow, orange and light red • Late spring–early summer • h.&s. 30cm (1ft)**

5 E. 'Primrose Bedder'
The richly fragrant flowers of this dwarf variety are a gentle primrose yellow – a pleasing change from the strident colours of the majority of wallflower varieties.
✿ **Primrose yellow • Late spring–early summer h.&s. 25cm (10in)**

The Essentials

Site demands Wallflowers will tolerate any well-drained soil if they are given a position in full sun.
Planting practice Plant out young plants in autumn to flower the following spring. Wallflowers will also self-seed.
Flowering time Late spring to early summer.
Pests and diseases Wallflowers can be affected by bacterial and fungal disease, and cabbage root fly.
Bonus point Wallflowers will fill the garden with their sweet scent from late spring.

Familiar residents of cottage garden borders and public parks, wallflowers are timeless favourites. They bring a variety of bright colours, and a rich, sweet fragrance, that are most welcome in late spring.

Wallflowers are easily grown in almost any soil, provided it is well-drained and not too rich. In wet or recently manured soil they tend not to flower so freely. Sheltered sites are best and the plants prefer to be in full sun. A south facing wall is ideal.

Young wallflower plants are available from garden centres and nurseries in autumn. Plant them where they are to flower. Large blocks or drifts look stunning and this will also concentrate the fragrance. Plant dwarf varieties densely in pots and, to make the most of their fragrance, move them to where you like to sit.

STAR PERFORMER
E. Tom Thumb Series This compact mixture is well suited to containers as well as for bedding out, producing a reliable display of colourful blooms.

Eschscholzia

California poppies produce a succession of vibrant flowers during summer. All they need is low-nutrient soil and plenty of sunshine.

California poppies are easily grown annuals which ask little in return for a summer-long display. They need a poor, well-drained soil in a sunny position.

Sow the seeds thinly in early spring or autumn, in the site where they are to flower. They commonly self-seed.

STAR PERFORMER
E. californica 'Dali' ♀ **Scarlet flowers held above ferny, grey foliage will accentuate a sunny corner of the garden.**

2 E. californica 'Mission Bells' This variety has semi-double or double flowers and is available in a wide range of colours.
❀✿✿✿ **Cream, yellow, orange or pink • Summer**
h. **25–30cm (10–12in)** *s.* **15cm (6in)**

Expert's Selection

1 E. californica 'Dali'♀
A compact, single-coloured variety.
✿ **Scarlet • Summer**
h. **25cm (10in)** *s.* **20cm (8in)**

3 E. californica 'Buttermilk'
Another compact variety with attractively fluted petals.
✿ **Creamy yellow • Summer**
h. **20–25cm (8–10in)** *s.* **15cm (6in)**

4 E. californica 'Thai Silk'
This exotically coloured mixture is aptly named.
✿✿✿ **Orange, pink or red • Summer**
h. **25–30cm (10–12in)** *s.* **15cm (6in)**

E. californica 'Mission Bells'

The Essentials

Site demands A poor, well-drained soil and plenty of sun.
Planting practice Sow in spring or autumn where they will flower.
Flowering time All summer.
Pests and diseases Trouble free.
Bonus point Excellent for cutting and arranging indoors.

Felicia

Kingfisher daisies are South African plants that flower all summer and into autumn. They need little attention and thrive in dry conditions.

Expert's Selection

1 F. amelloides 'Read's Blue' Vivid blue petals are set off by bright yellow eyes.
✿ **Violet-blue • Summer–autumn • h. 15–30cm (6–12in)** *s.* **25cm (10in)**

2 F. amelloides 'Santa Anita Variegated'♀
The boldly cream and green variegated leaves provide a striking background to the large flowers of this very vigorous variety.
✿ **Violet-blue • Summer–autumn**
h. **30cm (1ft)** *s.* **25cm (10in)**

3 F. bergeriana
The common kingfisher daisy is well suited to window boxes or other small containers.
✿ **Bright blue • Summer–autumn**
h. **15–20cm (6–8in)** *s.* **25cm (10in)**

STAR PERFORMER
F. amelloides 'Read's Blue'
Large flowers and compact habit make this variety perfect for growing in pots.

These vivid blue daisies are half-hardy annuals and perennials and are very easily grown where their simple requirements can be provided.

A well-drained soil, not too rich, is important and, as the flowers close in dull weather, a position in full sun. A sheltered spot will prevent the stems from being broken by gusts of wind.

Sow seeds in pots in early spring, keeping in a cool greenhouse. Or buy new young plants once there is no risk of severe frost. Throughout summer, remove the fading flowers to encourage new buds to form.

Varieties of *F. amelloides* such as **'Read's Blue'** and **'Santa Anita Variegated'**, can be propagated by cuttings taken in late summer and overwintered in a frost-free greenhouse.

The Essentials

Site demands A sheltered, sunny site and well-drained soil.
Planting practice Plant out when all risk of frost has passed.
Flowering time From early summer to autumn.
Pruning needs Regular deadheading will keep the flowers coming over a long season.
Pests and diseases Largely trouble free once planted out.
Bonus point Even in dry spots on hot days these low-maintenance daisies will not need watering.

Fuchsia

Fuchsias are among the most easy care and popular of all plants. Their pendulous, jewel-like flowers range in colour from the purest of whites to the gaudiest shades of purple and pink. There are trailing types for hanging baskets, pots and raised beds, or upright varieties for the borders.

The great popularity of fuchsias is easy to understand: the combination of easy cultivation, long flowering season, and elegant habit is difficult to match. As well as making a splendid show in the open garden, most are very suitable for containers.

Fuchsias vary considerably in hardiness, and both hardy and half-hardy varieties are recommended here. The former can, in most areas, be planted and left in the ground throughout winter. In mild regions they may be evergreen, but in most gardens they die back each winter, and throw up new shoots from soil level in late spring. Half-hardy types and plants in containers need to be kept under cover.

Shrubby fuchsias (see page 207) are also available, and provide a more long-term feature in the garden.

Expert's Selection

1 *F.* '**Eva Boerg**'
Low-growing and hardy in many areas, this variety is well suited to containers. Its flowers have pale pink sepals and rosy purple petals.
✿✿ **Pale pink and purple • Summer–autumn • h.&s. 75cm (2½ft)**

2 *F.* '**Golden Marinka**'♈
This spreading half-hardy variety has leaves variegated with yellow, and an abundance of flowers.
✿ **Crimson • Summer–autumn h. 30–45cm (1–1½ft) s. 50cm (20in)**

3 *F.* '**South Gate**'
A half-hardy variety, which forms a bushy plant bearing sumptuous double flowers.
✿ **Light pink • Summer–autumn h.&s. 45cm (1½ft)**

4 *F.* '**Heidi Ann**'♈
The large double flowers, with crimson sepals and lilac petals, are borne on a compact, bushy plant. It is only half-hardy.
✿✿ **Crimson and lilac • Summer–autumn h. 45cm (1½ft) s. 30cm (1ft)**

5 *F.* '**Winston Churchill**'♈
This compact, half-hardy variety bears flowers with pink sepals and violet-blue petals that gradually fade to purple.
✿✿ **Pink and violet • Summer–autumn • h.&s. 45cm (1½ft)**

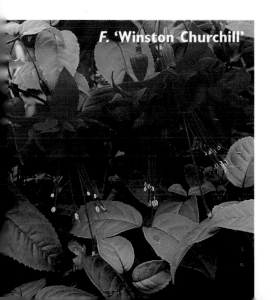
F. 'Winston Churchill'

TAKE A FRESH LOOK

F. '*Thalia*'♈ bears clusters of narrowly trumpet-shaped flowers, accentuated by large oval-shaped leaves. Growing to 1m (3ft) tall, this upright half-hardy variety deserves to be given space in the garden.

The Essentials

Site demands Happy in almost any soil, in sun or light shade.
Planting practice Plant out half-hardy fuchsias when the risk of hard frosts have passed.
Flowering time From summer to late autumn.
Pruning needs As bedding plants, fuchsias need no pruning.
Pests and diseases Largely trouble free.
Bonus point In mild areas, fuchsias can make dazzling hedges.

hardy annuals

Summer specials

For sheer impact, hardy annuals take a lot of beating. They are easily grown, thrive in poor soils and are truly one of the best ways of providing an abundance of colour in the shortest possible time. Because they need minimal ground preparation they are particularly useful for gardeners who have just moved into a new house, and who want a quick and reliable show with minimum time and effort.

Annuals are plants that flower in the same year the seed is sown, after which they usually set seed and ultimately die. Most are brash, showy and free-flowering, and there are few gardens to which annual plants cannot make a colourful contribution throughout the summer months.

Prairie beauties

The great majority of annuals originate from meadows, prairies and similar open places, which gives a clue to their requirements in the garden. Many are at their best in poor soils, provided these are reasonably well-drained and have access to full sun.

Sowing the seeds

Most hardy annuals can be sown direct in the garden, where they are to flower. Sow seeds where you want them to bloom early in spring. Most can also be sown in autumn to flower in spring and early summer, but this does carry the risk that you will lose some plants over winter.

Sow seeds in straight lines so it is easier to distinguish the annuals from weed seedlings. Once the plants are fully grown, the lines will not be visible. If necessary, thin out the seedlings before they become too large, to avoid disturbing them later.

Supporting taller plants

Most of the taller annuals, such as cornflowers, need support. Push twigs 30–45cm (1–1½ft) long in among the seedlings (birch twigs are ideal). The plants will grow through the twigs, and they will be hidden once the plants reach flowering size.

Centaurea cyanus **'Blue Diadem'**

Pick and mix

Many annuals, including *Limnanthes* and *Nigella*, will self seed freely. Others produce seed, that can be collected and stored over winter for sowing in spring. Remember that selected varieties, and especially 'F1 hybrids', will rarely come true to type from such home-collected seeds. But there is little to lose from saving and sowing such seeds, provided you are prepared to take a gamble on what comes up.

The Essentials

Site demands Most hardy annuals thrive in a wide range of conditions, especially in poor soils, and do best in full sun.
Planting practice Sow seed in early spring, where it is to flower.
Flowering time A selection of hardy annuals sown in succession will give flowers from late spring, well into autumn.
Pests and diseases Hardy annuals are generally trouble free.
Bonus point Great plants for introducing children to gardening.

STAR PERFORMER
Calendula 'Fiesta Gitana' **Thickly packed sunshine yellow and brilliant orange blooms on this low-growing marigold will boost any summer scheme.**

Papaver rhoeas Shirley series

Consolida ajacis Dwarf Rocket series

Limnanthes douglasii

Convolvulus tricolor 'Royal Ensign'

Hardy winners

Choose from our sure fire selection for the easiest ever summer garden.

1 *Calendula* 'Fiesta Gitana' A compact marigold with large, fully double orange and yellow flowers borne over a long season.
✿✿ Yellow, orange • Late spring–late summer • h.&s. 30cm (1ft)

2 *Iberis amara* 'Pinnacle' A fragrant candytuft with densely clustered flowers.
✿ White • Summer • h.&s. 30cm (1ft)

3 *Convolvulus tricolor* 'Royal Ensign' This beautiful trailing variety is excellent for containers or bedding.
✿ Blue with white and yellow centre Summer • h.&s. 15–50cm (6–20in)

4 *Consolida ajacis* Dwarf Rocket series These dwarf larkspur have a lovely informality when boldly massed together.
✿✿✿✿ Blue, pink, white, lavender Summer
h. 45cm (1½ft) s. 20cm (8in)

5 *Lavatera trimestris* 'Silver Pink' A compact plant which bears large, attractively veined flowers.
✿ Light pink • Summer–autumn
h. 60cm (2ft) s. 50cm (20in)

6 *Helianthus annuus* 'Teddy Bear' A dwarf sunflower with long-lasting fully double flowers.
✿ Yellow with green centre Summer • h. 1m (3ft)

7 *Clarkia unguiculata* Royal Bouquet Series Bright double flowers resemble carnations.
✿✿✿ Pink, mauve, red • Summer
h. 60cm (2ft) s. 25cm (10in)

8 *Phacelia campanularia* A bushy annual with vividly hued flowers that are attractive to bees.
✿ Blue • Late spring–summer
h.&s. 15cm (6in)

9 *Papaver rhoeas* Shirley series The popular Shirley poppies have single flowers, some picotee, in a wide range of colours.
✿✿✿✿ White, pink, lilac, crimson Summer • h. 60cm (2ft)

10 *Centaurea cyanus* 'Blue Diadem' Large cornflowers that look good in a border and make excellent cut flowers.
✿ Rich blue • Summer
h. 75cm (2½ft)

11 *Limnanthes douglasii* The well-named poached egg plant, makes a wonderful bright edging.
✿ White with yellow centre Summer–autumn • h. 20cm (8in)

12 *Nigella* Persian Jewels Series Love-in-a-mist has airy foliage and attractive seed capsules when the flowers finish.
✿✿✿✿ White, pink, lilac, crimson Summer • h. 25–40cm (10–16in)

Glechoma

Ground ivy isn't an ivy at all, but a trailing plant grown mainly for its attractive white-splashed foliage and small lavender-blue flowers.

Expert's Selection

1 *G. hederacea* 'Variegata'
The slender trailing stems bear brightly white-variegated leaves, making this an ideal filler for a hanging basket. Its small lavender-blue flowers are an added feature.
✿ **Lavender-blue • Summer**
⌀ **Variegated • h. 1m (3ft)**
s. **20cm (8in)**

Ground ivy gets its name from its creeping habit, but it is more closely related to mint than to ivy. It is completely trouble free, and is equally suitable for ground cover between taller plants, or as a trailing specimen in a container or hanging basket. In pots it is best planted among other plants, for which its neatly variegated leaves provide a pleasing complement.

Ground ivy thrives in sun or shade and is tolerant of almost any soil that is not too dry. It can be divided in autumn or early spring, prior to replanting.

STAR PERFORMER
G. hederacea 'Variegata'
With its pretty foliage, the variegated ground ivy is not so much a star as a valuable backing artist.

The Essentials

Site demands Ground ivy tolerates almost all soil types.
Planting practice Plant out in early spring.
Flowering time Summer.
Pests and diseases None.
Bonus point An easy-to-please care-free plant that spreads to make excellent ground cover.

HERBAL REMEDY Ground ivy is also known as field balm, relating to its medicinal use in curing fevers, coughs and sore eyes. It was also used to sharpen the taste of ale.

Helichrysum

The greyish felted foliage of helichrysum is at its most effective when contrasted with more colourful bedding plants.

H. petiolare 'Limelight'

Although the flowers are less than special, *H. petiolare* and its varieties have wonderful foliage, providing the perfect backdrop to brightly coloured annuals and bedding plants. The plants will grow quickly, giving a lush display.

Like most grey, woolly leaved plants, helichrysum demands sunlight and a well-drained soil. Combined with its semi-trailing habit, this makes it a good choice for growing in containers.

Take cuttings in late summer and overwinter in a frost-free greenhouse. Plant out in spring, after frost has passed.

Expert's Selection

1 *H. petiolare* ♀
This vigorous plant makes a mound of silvery grey foliage.
⌀ **Grey-felted • h. 50cm (20in)**
s. **1m (3ft)**

2 *H. petiolare* 'Limelight' ♀
This variety is grown for the softly hairy, lime-green leaves.
⌀ **Lime-green • h. 50cm (20in)**
s. **1m (3ft)**

3 *H. petiolare* 'Variegatum' ♀ Grown for its cream-edged leaves.
Cream-edged • h. 50cm (20in)
s. **1m (3ft)**

The Essentials

Site demands Sun and light soil.
Planting practice Plant out after the danger of frost has passed.
Flowering time Summer–autumn.
Pruning needs Remove the flowers if you prefer.
Pests and diseases Completely trouble free.
Bonus point Can be kept from year to year if protected from frost.

STAR PERFORMER
H. petiolare ♀ **Long trailing stems of grey felty foliage provide a leafy backdrop for more colourful annuals and bedding plants.**

Impatiens

Busy lizzies produce a profusion of colourful flowers throughout summer. They are particularly good for brightening up a shady corner of the garden and, if regularly deadheaded, will carry on flowering right into autumn when many other bedding plants have faded.

Expert's Selection

1 *I.* Super Elfin Series
For a block of dense colour, these plants are perfect. They come in a wide range of colours, including pink, red, orange, violet and pastel shades, often with delicate picotee effects on the petals.
✿✿✿✿ **Pink, red, orange or violet Summer–early autumn**
h.&s. **25cm (10in)**

2 *I.* Carousel Series
This mixture has fully double flowers like miniature roses in white, pink and red shades.
✿✿✿ **White, pink or red • Summer–early autumn • *h.&s.* 25cm (10in)**

3 *I.* 'Stardust'
The white speckling in the centre of each flower gives this variety its distinctive appearance. Flowers are pink or red, all with white centres.
✿✿ **Pink or red • Summer–early autumn • *h.&s.* 25cm (10in)**

4 *I.* 'Mega Orange Star'
This variety is more compact than most. It has large orange flowers with a white central star.
✿ **Orange with white central star Summer–early autumn**
h.&s. **20cm (8in)**

5 *I.* Tempo Series
The mixture with the widest colour range available, including bicolours and picotees.
✿✿✿✿✿ **White, pink, orange, red or violet Summer–early autumn**
h.&s. **23cm (9in)**

6 *I.* Blitz 2000 Series This fairly tall variety has dark foliage that shows up its colourful flowers beautifully. The flowers can be white, pink, orange, red or shades of purple.
✿✿✿✿ **White, pink, orange, red or purple Summer–early autumn**
h.&s. **35cm (14in)**

I. **Carousel Series**

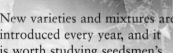

Few bedding plants give more colour per square foot than busy lizzies, and they are equally happy growing in sun or partial shade, in any fertile, well-drained soil that does not dry out too much in summer. Neat and compact in habit, they can be used in large drifts to spectacular effect, either in a single colour or random mixture, but are equally suitable for containers.

Trays of young plants appear in garden centres in early summer, ready for planting. Alternatively, you can buy small plants or 'plugs' in early spring. These may be better value for money, but they require some nurturing. You will need to grow them on in larger pots in a greenhouse before hardening them off in late spring and planting out when all risk of frost has passed.

New varieties and mixtures are introduced every year, and it is worth studying seedsmen's catalogues to review the latest selections before you buy.

The Essentials

Site demands Busy lizzies will tolerate most fertile, well-drained soils, in sun or partial shade.
Planting practice Plant out after the risk of frost has passed.
Flowering time Summer to mid autumn.
Pruning needs Regular deadheading prolongs the display.
Pests and diseases Vine weevil grubs from late summer, and red spider mite can be a problem.
Bonus point Even if they dry out, busy lizzies will recover quickly when watered.

Lobelia

With their delicate habit and an abundance of flowers appearing over a long season, lobelias are a mainstay of many bedding schemes. They are also popular in container plantings and hanging-basket designs.

Although they are perennials, lobelias are short-lived and are usually grown as annuals. Their flowers may be small, but they are produced in profusion from early or midsummer until late autumn.

Let trailing varieties tumble over a retaining wall to show off their elegant habit. Bushy, non-trailing sorts may be used to underplant taller annuals or shrubs. Single colours and mixtures are available and all are easily grown given a moderately fertile moist soil in full sun. In the ground or in containers, they will need watering during dry spells.

The Essentials

Site demands Moist, fertile soil in sun or partial shade.
Planting practice Plant out in late spring, when safe from frost.
Flowering time Early summer to late autumn.
Pruning needs Deadheading encourages further flowers.
Pests and diseases Trouble free, but look out for slugs and snails.
Bonus point Trailing lobelias have a long flowering season if kept well watered.

Expert's Selection

1 *L. richardsonii* ♀
A trailing species that flowers over a long period.
✿ Lilac-blue and white • Summer–autumn • *h.&s.* 10–30cm (4–12in)

2 *L. erinus* Cascade Series
A neatly trailing variety that looks its best when grown in a container.
✿✿❀✿ Red, pink, white or blue Summer–autumn • *h.* 15cm (6in) *s.* 30cm (1ft)

3 *L. erinus* 'Kathleen Mallard' A compact upright variety with long-lasting large double flowers.
✿ Blue • Summer–autumn *h.&s.* 10–20cm (4–8in)

4 *L. erinus* 'White Lady'
A bushy white variety that does not trail.
❀ White • Summer–autumn *h.&s.* 10–15cm (4–6in)

5 *L. erinus* 'Crystal Palace' ♀
Grows into a compact dome, ideal for edging a border.
✿ Dark blue • Summer–autumn *h.&s.* 10–15cm (4–6in)

STAR PERFORMER
L. richardsonii ♀
With larger flowers than most trailing varieties, this makes a showy hanging-basket plant.

L. erinus 'Kathleen Mallard'

L. erinus 'White Lady'

Lobularia

Sweet alyssum is a classic cottage-garden bedding plant. Its profuse honey-scented flowers bloom all summer and are available in an ever-growing range of colours.

1 *L. maritima* 'Snow Crystals' One of the taller mound-forming varieties.
✿ White • All summer
h.&s. 25cm (10in)

2 *L. maritima* Aphrodite Series A wide range of good colours, all produced over a long period. 'Pastel Carpet' grows a little taller and comes in delicate shades of white and pink.
✿✿✿ White, pink and red • All summer • *h.&s.* 10–15cm (4–6in)

3 *L. maritima* 'Oriental Night' A particularly well-scented variety.
✿ Rich purple • All summer
h.&s. 10–25cm (4–10in)

With its profuse flowers and summer-long season, sweet alyssum, also called sweet Alison, is a long-time favourite among hardy annuals. Its low growth and compact habit make it ideal for a formal edging, yet it also looks just right in containers, in planting pockets in a retaining wall, or on a rock garden.

This is an easy-to-grow annual, that is happy positioned in full sun in most soils that are reasonably free draining.

The Essentials

Site demands Any well-drained soil in full sun.
Planting practice Plant out in late spring or sow seeds in situ in early summer.
Flowering time Sweet alyssum flowers all through summer.
Pruning needs Occasional dead-heading will help prolong flowering.
Pests and diseases Young plants may be attacked by flea beetles.
Bonus point Sweet alyssum thrives in seaside conditions.

STAR PERFORMER
***L. maritima* 'Snow Crystals'** This variety forms a dense cushion of tiny snowy white flowers that will last all summer long.

Lysimachia

Creeping Jenny is aptly named, spreading its mats of shiny foliage, studded with small bright yellow flowers, wherever it can.

Lysimachia can be a rampant spreading perennial, but those recommended here are superb when treated as bedding plants for brightening tubs or beds – even in shade. Variegated plants, such as 'Outback Sunset', will colour best in good light.

Expert's Selection

1 *L. nummularia* This vigorous spreader covers the ground in shady places with prostrate mats of bright foliage. 'Aurea' has golden leaves from spring to autumn
✿ Yellow • Early summer
h. 2.5cm (1in) *s.* 1m (3ft)

2 *L. congestiflora* This creeping perennial forms mats of foliage above which each stem ends in a cluster of flowers.
✿ Yellow with a reddish centre
Early summer–early autumn
h. 10cm (4in) *s.* 45cm (1½ft)

The Essentials

Site demands Moist humus-rich soil in sun or partial shade.
Planting practice Plant out in autumn or spring.
Flowering time Summer.
Pests and diseases Trouble free.
Bonus point Complements many hanging basket colour schemes.

STAR PERFORMER
L. nummularia Bright carpets of glossy foliage, studded with yellow flowers, will brighten up any rocky spot or container.

TAKE A FRESH LOOK
***L. congestiflora* 'Outback Sunset'** This striking new variety forms lush mats of boldly variegated leaves beneath clusters of yellow flowers with a reddish centre.

Matthiola

Stocks have long been associated with cottage gardens. They add colour to the border and make good cut flowers, filling a room with their outstanding sweet fragrance. Most varieties have dense upright spikes of rosette-like double flowers, in a wide range of pastel and vivid colours.

Stocks are grown as much for their fragrance as for the flowers, although many modern varieties make colourful and versatile bedding plants. The larger flowering sorts, derived from *M. incana*, are grown mostly in long-lasting, double flowered varieties, and these are also useful for cutting for the house. The night-scented stock is a different species, *M. longipetala*.

Stocks are easily grown, provided that you give them a fertile and fairly moist soil. They also enjoy a position that is either in full sun or partial shade. You can grow them from seed, sowing thinly where they are to flower, in late spring. Otherwise, buy young plants, also to put out late in the spring. Always remember that stocks dislike drought, and must be well watered during dry spells.

**M. incana
Ten Week Mixed**

M. longipetala

> ### STAR PERFORMER
> *M. incana* 'Apple Blossom' **With its pretty pink and white double flowers and compact habit, this variety can flower into early autumn.**

Mimulus

Monkey flowers are so called because their flower markings look like monkey's faces. They give a jolly display all summer long.

Expert's Selection

1 M. Magic Series
A showy variety, bearing small flowers, mostly in bright tints.
✿✿✿ **Cream, yellow, orange and red • Summer**
h. 20cm (8in) *s.* 30cm (1ft)

2 M. Calypso Series
These come in a lively mix of brilliant colours, some of them being two-toned.
✿✿ **Yellow, red and bicoloured Summer**
h.&s. 15-25cm (6-10in)

3 M. Shade Loving Mixed
This mixture yields plants with a range of bright, fiery colours, ideal for warming up a cool border.
✿✿✿ **Yellow, orange and scarlet, sometimes speckled • Summer**
h. 25-30cm (10-12in) *s.* 40cm (16in)

4 M. naiandinus♀
(syn. M. 'Andean Nymph')
A uniquely coloured variety that is a must for any damp garden.
✿✿ **Cream and pink, spotted with red • Summer**
h. 20cm (8in) *s.* 30cm (1ft)

STAR PERFORMER
M. Magic Series With their flowers mostly in clear, bright colours, this variety has a striking purity of effect.

Traditionally thought of as plants for a bog garden, mimulus has been developed into a highly successful and very easily grown bedding plant.

They thrive in most fertile soils, as long as they remain moist through the summer months.

Plant out in late spring, and divide and replant the best plants in the autumn.

The Essentials

Site demands Any rich, moist, ideally slightly acidic, site, in full sun or light shade.
Planting practice Plant in spring.
Flowering time Summer.
Pests and diseases Largely trouble free, but may be damaged by slugs or aphids.
Bonus point The flowers are a great attraction for bees.

Myosotis

Forget-me-nots are just about the easiest of hardy biennials, producing the prettiest spring haze of sky-blue flowers in sun or shade.

Forget-me-not is a biennial plant, flowering in the spring after it is sown. It is easily grown in almost any soil, in sun or, preferably, in partial shade. You can sow the seeds outdoors where you want them to flower, or plant out young plants in the autumn.

In dry weather, the leaves may be affected by powdery mildew, but this is less of a problem in a moist soil or in light shade. If the faded flowers are left on, the plants will self-seed quite freely, but normally the plants are scrapped after flowering.

Expert's Selection

1 M. sylvatica 'Blue Ball'♀
Rounded plants bear a profusion of richly coloured flowers.
✿ **Bright blue • Late spring–early summer • h.&s.** 15cm (6in)

2 M. sylvatica 'Royal Blue'
A taller variety with darker blue flowers.
✿ **Deep blue • Late spring–early summer • h.&s.** 30cm (1ft)

3 M. sylvatica 'Rosylva'
A compact variety, it has lovely clear pink flowers.
✿ **Clear pink • Late spring–early summer • h.&s.** 15cm (6in)

4 M. sylvatica 'Snowball'
Another compact plant, it is perfect for pots or as bedding.
✿ **White • Late spring–early summer h.&s.** 15cm (6in)

The Essentials

Site demands Any well-drained soil, in sun or light shade.
Planting practice Sow seeds in summer, or plant out young plants in the autumn.
Flowering time From late spring to early summer.
Pests and diseases Mainly trouble free, but powdery mildew may occur in dry weather.
Bonus point M. sylvatica varieties have fragrant flowers.

STAR PERFORMER
M. sylvatica 'Blue Ball'♀
Well named for its compact and rounded habit, this is a popular variety for edging a border, for containers, or for bedding.

Nicotiana

Tobacco plants bloom for long periods during summer and autumn. Some open only to give off their scent in the evening; others are open all day but are less strongly fragrant. The flowers offer a range of harmonious colours and all are excellent for bedding.

The slender-tubed flowers of ornamental tobacco plants are borne in open clusters, held well above the rather large leaves. The wide range of colours lacks any strident tones, and they look as good planted in mixed colours as they do in single shades. However, they harmonise better with perennials than with their more gaudy fellow annuals.

Tobacco plants do best in a reasonably fertile, moist but well-drained soil and grow in full sun or partial shade. The taller varieties may need staking in an exposed site, while the dwarf varieties are deservedly valued for their weather resistance.

As the scent of tobacco plants is strongest in the evening, plant them near a seating area, where you can enjoy their fragrance.

TAKE A FRESH LOOK

N. 'Avalon Bright Pink'
With starry flowers on compact plants, growing to just 25cm (10in) tall, this variety tolerates hot conditions better than most, and is ideal for use on a sun-baked patio.

Expert's Selection

1 *N.* x *sanderae* **Domino Series** Bushy, compact plants, in a wide range of colours, are suitable for containers or bedding out.
❀❀❀❀❀ **White, lime-green, pink, salmon-pink, red, purple • Early summer–autumn • h.&s. 30cm (1ft)**

2 *N.* x *sanderae* **Nicki Series** Dwarf variety ideal for growing in containers. The flowers are weather-resistant, too.
❀❀❀❀ **White, pink, red or mauve Early summer–autumn h.&s. 30cm (1ft)**

3 *N. alata* '**Lime Green**' ♀
This well-known variety is admired for the unusual colour of its weather-resistant flowers.
❀ **Lime-green • Summer–autumn h. 75cm (2½ft) s. 40cm (16in)**

4 *N.* x *sanderae* **Sensation Series** This fragrant variety is taller than most.
❀❀❀ **Red, pink and white • Early summer–autumn h. 60–75cm (2–2½ft) s. 30cm (1ft)**

SAFETY WARNING All parts of ornamental tobacco plants are toxic if eaten.

N. alata 'Lime Green'

STAR PERFORMER
N. x *sanderae* **Domino Series** Upward-facing flowers on compact bushy plants look terrific in containers.

The Essentials

Site demands Fertile, fairly moist soil in sun or light shade.
Planting practice Plant out after the risk of frost has passed.
Flowering time Early summer until mid autumn.
Pests and diseases Aphids and slugs may damage young plants.
Bonus point Choose *N. alata* varieties for amazing evening scent.

Osteospermum

With large, colourful daisy-like flowers borne from late spring until autumn, it is no wonder that these showy plants have become so popular for bedding and containers. They like a sunny spot in any well-drained soil, and in mild areas some may even survive into winter.

Expert's Selection

1 O. **Springstar Series**
Each large flower on these bushy plants has a dramatic dark blue central eye.
✿✿❀ **Pink, purple and white with striking deep blue centres**
Late spring–autumn
h.&s. 45cm (1½ft)

TAKE A FRESH LOOK

O. Starshine Series Most osteospermums are best bought as young plants from the garden centre and planted as soon as you get home. If you enjoy the thrill of cultivating plants yourself, choose from the pink, carmine, red and white varieties in the long-flowering Starshine Series, which are all best raised from seed.

2 O. **Symphony Series**
The yellow-eyed flowers in this mixture are carried on neat, compact plants.
✿✿❀ **Lemon-yellow, orange or cream with yellow centres**
Late spring–autumn
h.&s. 50cm (20in)

3 O. **'Starlight Vega'**
A compact variety particularly well-suited to being grown in pots and containers.
✿ **Purple with a darker eye**
Late spring–late summer
h.&s. 45cm (1½ft)

4 O. **'Silver Sparkler'**♀
Variegated cream and green leaves pick out this plant from the rest.
❀ **White with purple eye**
Late spring–late summer
h.&s. 60cm (2ft)

The Essentials

Site demands Any light, well-drained soil in full sun.
Planting practice Plant out osteospermums in late spring.
Flowering time Their bright daisies appear continuously from early summer to autumn.
Pruning needs Regular dead-heading extends flowering season.
Pests and diseases Look out for aphids and downy mildew.
Bonus point There are colours available to suit every scheme.

STAR PERFORMER
O. **Springstar Series With their compact, bushy growth and large, neatly formed flowers in a good range of colours, this variety is one of the best for bedding in a sunny border or rock garden.**

Each year brings new varieties of osteospermum, as their popularity increases. None is reliably hardy in Britain, but those listed here are more hardy than most. They all look terrific massed in a border, used as fillers in a rockery or planted in tubs.

Osteospermums vary in habit from bushy and upright to spreading mounds, and have a long flowering season from late spring or early summer until the first autumn frosts.

The plants will grow well in any well-drained soil. Although they survive happily in some shade, a position in full sun will give the best show of blooms. The flowers tend not to open at all in deep shade or dull weather, but this helps to protect them from rain.

Young plants from nurseries should be planted out in late spring, when flowering will often start almost immediately. Remove old flowerheads regularly to encourage new buds to develop.

Pelargonium

Bedding geraniums, as pelargoniums are commonly called, make excellent, easy-care bedding plants and look great in containers too. Their ability to withstand drought makes them perfect for containers, and they are available in a range of colours, leaf shapes and habits.

Pelargoniums can be grown in containers or in the garden, where they put on an impressive display of flowers from early to late summer, and sometimes into autumn. These robust plants are well suited to people who do not have a lot of time to spend in the garden, since they will forgive the occasional lapse in watering.

Although pelargoniums are often referred to as geraniums, they are only distantly related to the genus *Geranium*, which includes mostly hardy perennials. Perennial pelargoniums are invariably frost-tender and somewhat shrubby when mature.

Infinite variety

Plant breeders have developed a huge number of varieties which are classified into several groups. The zonal and ivy-leaf groups are the most useful for bedding and the most care free. Thin, rounded and slightly hairy leaves, usually patterned with zones of contrasting colour, characterise **zonal pelargoniums**, such as 'Maverick'. Most have a purplish band on a green leaf, but a few varieties have striking variegated green and cream, yellow, red or maroon foliage.

Zonal pelargoniums are upright and bushy in growth, and look splendid bedded out in the open garden, either massed together or used as gap fillers, or in large containers.

In the ivy league

Ivy-leaf pelargoniums, such as the Decora Series, have strongly lobed leaves, which are slightly fleshy, and smooth and glossy.

These varieties also tend to have a trailing habit which makes them ideal for hanging baskets and window boxes.

Pelargoniums can be raised from cuttings, or bought in spring as young plants ready for bedding out. All varieties grow best in a moderately fertile, well-drained soil, that is ideally neutral or slightly alkaline. They are happiest in full sun, but zonal types tolerate some shade. All pelargoniums benefit from having the old flowers and any faded leaves removed regularly.

In early autumn, the plants can be lifted for winter and stored in dry, frost-free conditions. In early spring cut them back by half and pot them up to restart growth. Cuttings taken in midsummer will root easily to provide young plants for the following year.

STAR PERFORMER

P. 'Maverick' **This variety will produce large, vividly coloured flowerheads throughout summer and until the first of the ground frosts.**

P. 'Fantasia'

FRAGRANT FOLIAGE Some pelargoniums have scented leaves, though the flowers tend to be small. The downy leaves of *P. tomentosum* smell of peppermint, while *P. graveolens*, the source of oil of geranium, has deeply lobed leaves with a fresh, lemony scent. Plant scented leaf varieties in pots for the patio or alongside paths where the foliage will release its delicious aroma as people brush past.

The Essentials

Site demands Pelargoniums need a well-drained, fertile soil in full sun or partial shade.

Planting practice Plant out in late spring, after all risk of frosts has passed.

Flowering time Summer–autumn.

Pruning needs Deadhead regularly for continuous flowering.

Pests and diseases Usually trouble free, but look out for rust.

Bonus point For plants that are frequently used in containers and baskets, their resistance to drought is a major plus.

Expert's Selection

1 *P.* 'Maverick'
The striking flowers of this zonal variety appear earlier than many others and last just as long.
❀ **White with a pink centre**
Summer • **h.&s. 30cm (1ft)**

2 *P. tomentosum*
Known as the peppermint geranium, this variety has large, mint-scented leaves and tiny white flowers. Its scrambling stems can be trained up a pillar or wall, preferably in partial shade.
❀ **White** • **Summer**
h. 1m (3ft) s. 60cm (2ft)

3 *P.* Decora Series
These ivy-leaf pelargoniums look good in window boxes or hanging baskets, where their dainty flowers are displayed to full advantage.
❀✿✿ **White, pink, lilac or red**
Summer
h. 30cm (1ft) s. 50cm (20in)

4 *P.* Orbit Series
Zonal pelargoniums that make lush and bushy plants with rounded and patterned leaves.
❀✿✿ **White, pink, orange or red**
Summer • h. 35cm (14in)
s. 30cm (1ft)

5 *P.* Pulsar Series
This series of zonal pelargoniums stand out, because of their particularly boldly marked foliage.
❀✿✿ **White, pink, red or bicolour**
Summer • h.&s. 30cm (1ft)

6 *P. graveolens*
The deeply lobed, lemon-scented leaves are carried on strong stems. Its star-shaped flowers are pink with darker markings.
✿ **Pink • Summer**
h. 1m (3ft) s. 60cm (2ft)

7 *P.* Cascade Series
These ivy-leaf pelargoniums produce single flowers on compact, trailing stems, making them an ideal choice for summer containers.
✿✿✿ **Pink, lilac or red • Summer**
h. 30cm (1ft) s. 50cm (20in)

8 *P.* 'Fantasia'
Semi-double flowers in vivid shades of red or pink are enhanced by dark green foliage. This zonal pelargonium has an upright habit.
✿✿ **Red or pink • Summer**
h.&s. 25cm (10in)

TAKE A FRESH LOOK

P. 'Evka' The rich red flowers of this ivy-leaved pelargonium look stunning as they tumble out of a hanging basket. Its pretty white-edged leaves give added interest.

P. Pulsar Series

P. Orbit Series

P. Decora Series

Petunia

For sheer quantity and variety of colour, from classic white to fluorescent pinks, allied to a graceful habit, petunias are hard to beat. The newest, smaller flowered, varieties are more weather-resistant than their predecessors and continue flowering well into autumn.

The range of petunias has never been wider, leaving gardeners spoilt for choice when it comes to colour, size and habit. With a growing number of varieties available that are resistant to poor weather, there is no excuse for ignoring these vibrant plants.

A range of habits

Petunias are divided into three broad groupings. The **Grandiflora group** consists of the traditional large-flowered varieties, which are now also available in shades of yellow. These are very showy but susceptible to damage by wind and heavy rain, so are best grown in a sheltered position.

This is especially true of double-flowered varieties. The flowers are up to 10cm (4in) across and the plants vary from bushy to moderately spreading.

The **Multiflora group** consists of plants with smaller but more abundant flowers, about 5cm (2in) across. They vary from bushy plants to vigorously trailing and most are suitable for hanging baskets and other containers.

A more recent development is the **Milliflora group,** of which the **Million Bells Series** is typical. These plants have small flowers, about 3cm (1½in) across. Most are strongly trailing and best suited to containers or for bedding out as ground cover.

Plants in the Multiflora and the Milliflora groups are much more resistant to bad weather than the larger flowered varieties.

Raising your plants

Petunias are perennials, but are only half-hardy, so are invariably grown as annuals. They do best in poor, well-drained soil in full sun and perform particularly well in seaside gardens.

Though plants in the Grandiflora group are easy to grow from seed, most varieties in the Multiflora and Milliflora groups are easiest bought as young plants from a reputable garden centre.

Regular deadheading will prolong flowering and you can trim straggly plants at any time.

STAR PERFORMER

P. **Surfinia Series** **These petunias have proved themselves in the most unpredictable weather of a British summer. They can be relied upon to produce masses of flowers come rain or shine.**

The Essentials

Site demands In full sun and poor, well-drained, but not dry soil, petunias produce abundant flowers.
Planting practice Plant out when the risk of frosts has passed.
Flowering time All summer and well into autumn.
Pruning needs Regular deadheading prolongs the display.
Pests and diseases Greenfly, slugs, and various viral diseases.
Bonus point Many petunias have a delicious scent in the evening.

Multiflora Group

1 *P.* Surfinia Series
Trailing plants which are especially weather resistant. The flowers are often marked with darker veins.
❀✿✿ **White, pink, red, purple or violet • Summer–autumn**
h. 30cm (1ft) *s.* 50cm (20in)

2 *P.* Cascadia Series
Tough trailing petunias, ideal for an exposed hanging basket.
✿✿ **Yellow, lavender or pink Summer–autumn**
h. 30cm (1ft) *s.* 50cm (20in)

3 *P.* 'Surfinia Pink Ice'
A trailing variety with leaves boldly variegated with creamy-yellow. Pink flowers have darker veins.
✿ **Pink • Summer–autumn**
h. 20–40cm (8–16in) *s.* 50cm (20in)

4 *P.* Duo Series
Something a little different, with its double or semi-double flowers.
✿ **Various • Summer–autumn**
h. 30–60cm (1–2ft)
s. 50cm (20in)

Milliflora Group

1 *P.* 'Million Bells Cherry' Blooms with an abundance of small, yellow-eyed, cherry-red flowers.
✿ **Red • Summer–autumn**
h. 15–40cm (6–16in)
s. 30cm (1ft)

2 *P.* 'Million Bells Terra Cotta' An appealing small-flowered petunia which will trail prettily from a basket or container.
✿ **Yellow and red • Summer–autumn • *h.* 15–40cm (6–16in)**
s. 30cm (1ft)

3 *P.* 'Prism Candy'
It is easy to raise this variety from seed and enjoy its large flowers.
✿✿✿ **Yellow, pink, purple or violet Summer–autumn**
h.&s. 30cm (1ft)

4 *P.* 'Moonshine'
Cream variegated foliage is the perfect contrast to rich, deep purple flowers.
✿ **Deep purple • Summer–autumn**
h.&s. 30cm (1ft)

5 *P.* Frenzy Series
Freely flowering petunias with good weather resistance. Some have veined petals.
✿ **Various • Summer–autumn**
h. 30cm (1ft) *s.* 50cm (20in)

Grandiflora Group

1 *P.* Supercascade Series
Easy-to-grow, they spread fast to form an unusual ground cover.
✿ **Various • Summer–autumn**
h. 30cm (1ft) *s.* 50cm (20in)

P. **'Supercascade Lilac'**

P. **'Duo Series'**

P. Frenzy Series **'Lavender Vein'**

P. **'Million Bells Cherry'**

P. **'Million Bells Terra Cotta'**

Plectranthus

Grow these tender perennials for their long trailing stems and beautiful heart-shaped leaves, which will complement the flowers of more colourful plants in a hanging basket.

Although they tend to be bushy when young, bedding plectranthus later develop long trailing stems bearing pairs of heart-shaped leaves, which are often variegated or attractively coloured. The small white or pale blue flowers are insignificant, but appear sporadically throughout summer and autumn.

These plants are ideal for mixed plantings and look great in hanging baskets or containers, where their trailing habit is shown off to its best advantage. Site the pot or basket in a light position, but shaded from the strongest midday sun.

Expert's Selection

1 *P. forsteri* 'Marginatus'
Variegated scallop-edged leaves grow on prostrate trailing stems.
❀✿ **White or pale mauve but insignificant • Summer**
⊘ **Green edged with cream or yellow Summer • h. 20cm (8in) s. 60cm (2ft)**

2 *P.* 'Nico'
Trailing stems are covered in dark, heart-shaped leaves.
⊘⊘ **Dark green and deep reddish purple underneath • Summer h. 20cm (8in) s. 60cm (2ft)**

The Essentials

Site demands Any soil-based potting compost in light shade.
Planting practice Plant out in early summer, after all risk of frost.
Pruning needs Pinch out shoot tips for a bushier plant.
Pests and diseases These plants are usually trouble free.
Bonus point Attractive foliage complements any colour scheme.

STAR PERFORMER
P. forsteri 'Marginatus'
With its bold cream or yellow variegation and trailing habit, this makes a perfect hanging basket plant.

Sanvitalia

Creeping zinnia is a trailing or mound-forming plant clothed with small, yellow or orange flowers from summer to autumn.

STAR PERFORMER
S. 'Mandarin Orange' **The bright orange flowers and compact growth of this variety make it a terrific choice for colourful ground cover.**

Creeping zinnias are hardy annuals native to Mexico. They enjoy a position in full sun, and will thrive in any well-drained soil. They have a low, spreading habit and are ideal in containers, especially hanging baskets, or bedded out as annual ground cover.

You can sow the seed where it is to flower in early autumn, or plant out from late spring.

Expert's Selection

1 *S.* 'Mandarin Orange'
This variety is fairly compact and low growing, and has unusually coloured flowers.
✿ **Bright orange with a black eye Summer–autumn h. 10cm (4in) s. 35cm (14in)**

2 *S.* 'Little Sun'
With its starry flowers and compact habit, this variety is ideal for smaller containers.
✿ **Deep yellow with a dark eye Summer–autumn h. 20cm (8in) s. 40cm (16in)**

3 *S.* 'Sunbini'
Narrower leaves and fuller flowers with shorter petals make this variety different from the others.
✿ **Golden yellow with a green eye Summer–autumn h. 25cm (10in) s. 45cm (1½ft)**

The Essentials

Site demands Any well-drained soil in full sun.
Planting practice Plant out in late spring or early summer.
Flowering time A succession of flowers all summer and autumn.
Pruning needs Regular dead-heading prolongs flowering.
Pests and diseases Trouble free.
Bonus point Sanvitalia blooms on, when many annuals are over.

Scaevola

Fan flowers are aptly named after the shape of their profuse blooms. The trailing growth of these long-flowering tender perennials makes them perfect for baskets and pots.

1 *S. aemula* 'Blue Wonder'
A vigorous trailing variety. 'New Wonder' has lavender-blue flowers and grows twice as tall.
✿ Lilac-blue • Summer–autumn
h. 15cm (6in) *s.* 60cm (2ft)

2 *S. aemula* 'Blue Ice'
Makes a bushy display in a pot.
✿ Violet-blue • Summer–autumn
h.&s. 30–45cm (1–1½ft)

3 *S. aemula* 'Alba'
A less vigorous variety that provides a contrast in colour.
✾ White • Summer to autumn
h.&s. 30–40cm (12–16in)

Fan flowers, originally from Australia, are tender perennials, usually grown as annuals. They have a long flowering season and attractive trailing habit, and are especially effective in raised containers or hanging baskets where the long stems come into their own.

They thrive in almost any well-drained soil, but in containers they require a good loam-based compost and a sunny position.

Site demands Any well-drained soil in sun or very light shade.
Planting practice Plant out in late spring or early summer.
Flowering time Summer and autumn.
Pests and diseases Trouble free.
Bonus point These tender perennials can be overwintered in a frost-free greenhouse.

STAR PERFORMER
S. aemula 'Blue Wonder'
The white-eyed blooms of this free-flowering variety can be twisted up the wires of a hanging basket.

Senecio

Commonly known by its synonym, *Cineraria maritima*, this white-leaved foliage plant is an old favourite, valued as a foil for many brightly coloured flowering bedding plants.

1 *S. cineraria* 'Cirrus'
This variety has broad, coarsely toothed leaves.
⌀ White • Late spring to first frosts
✿ Yellow • Summer (best removed)
h.&s. 30cm (1ft)

2 *S. cineraria* 'Silver Dust' ♀
Giving a very different effect, the dazzlingly white-felted leaves are deeply lobed in this compact variety.
⌀ White • Late spring to first frosts
✿ Yellow • Summer (best removed)
h.&s. 30cm (1ft)

These easily grown perennials are usually planted as annual foliage plants. In summer they produce small bright yellow daisies which, although quite showy, are best snipped off as soon as they appear, to allow the best display from the foliage.

The more compact varieties can be grown in large pots, but come into their own when they are planted among colourful flowering annuals. They can be used to edge a border or as dots of light colour in formal bedding schemes, but are equally useful for more relaxed plantings, where their soft felty foliage invites you to bend down and touch it.

Senecio cineraria is very unfussy but will do best in a well-drained, not-too-rich soil in full sun. Plant out after all risk of frost has passed.

Site demands Any well-drained soil in full sun.
Planting practice Plant out in late spring after the last frosts.
Pruning needs Cut off any flower buds as they appear.
Pests and diseases Trouble free.
Bonus point The silver felty foliage complements all colours.

STAR PERFORMER
S. cineraria 'Cirrus' **Dramatic white felty foliage provides a spectacular contrast to the 'hot' colours of summer bedding plants.**

Solenopsis

Also known as *Isotoma* or *Laurentia*, these tender perennials bear starry flowers over a long period, and give an exotic look to bedding displays or containers.

Expert's Selection

1 *S. axillaris* 'Blue Star'
This compact bushy plant is suitable for containers or for bedding out. Its flowers are borne singly on slender stems.
✿ Lavender blue • Summer–late autumn • h.&s. 30cm (1ft)

2 *S. axillaris* 'White Star'
A dome-shaped plant with white starry flowers and a slightly lax trailing habit.
✿ White • Summer–late autumn h.&s. 30cm (1ft)

STAR PERFORMER
S. axillaris 'Blue Star'
Add an exotic sparkle to beds, tubs or baskets over a long flowering season with this dainty blue variety.

The Essentials

Site demands Tolerates most well-drained soils.
Planting practice Plant out after the risk of frost has passed.
Flowering time Early summer to late autumn.
Pruning needs Deadhead regularly for longer flowering.
Pests and diseases Greenfly may attack the plants in dry conditions.
Bonus point The starry flowers are fragrant.

Solenopsis are tender perennials, grown as annuals for summer bedding. They can be planted in the open garden, but also look good in containers, which show off their slightly trailing habit. Choose a sunny or lightly shaded spot with moderately fertile, well-drained soil. Use a soil-based potting compost in containers and water freely in dry spells.

Sutera

More commonly known as *Bacopa*, these neat trailing plants are perfect in pots, with a profusion of small flowers over a long season.

Expert's Selection

1 *S.* 'Blizzard'
A vigorous variety that withstands hot conditions particularly well.
✿ White • Summer–autumn h.&s. 45cm (1½ft)

2 *S.* 'Candy Floss'
This profuse variety makes a compact mat of tidy foliage smothered with flowers.
✿ Deep lilac-pink • Summer–autumn h.&s. 50cm (20in)

3 *S.* 'Olympic Gold'
A less vigorous variety, this has boldly yellow-variegated foliage.
✿ White • Summer–autumn h.&s. 25cm (10in)

4 *S.* 'Lavender Storm'
Relatively large flowers and a vigorous habit.
✿ Lavender blue • Summer–autumn h.&s. 50cm (20in)

STAR PERFORMER
S. 'Blizzard' Tiny white flowers give the effect of a blizzard and make a pretty gap filler for beds or baskets.

Sutera is a native of South Africa, and is much valued for summer bedding. Its trailing habit and neat little flowers makes it especially pretty in containers.

The plants will do well in most reasonably fertile, well-drained soils (in containers, use a soil-based compost) and thrive in full sun or light shade.

Too much shade will result in leafier plants with fewer flowers. They form a spreading or trailing mound of foliage spangled with small, often yellow-throated flowers for most of the summer and autumn.

The Essentials

Site demands Any well-drained fertile soil, in sun or light shade.
Planting practice Plant out after all risk of frost has passed.
Flowering time Continuously from early summer into autumn.
Pests and diseases Apart from greenfly, usually trouble free.
Bonus point Has a particularly long flowering season.

Tagetes

French and **African marigolds** give great value throughout their long flowering season. With their fiery hued flowers, marigolds can bring a feeling of warmth to a cool summer. Most are compact plants with large double flowers, and are just as happy in pots as in borders.

Marigolds have long been popular bedding plants, partly for their brilliantly coloured flowers and long season of interest and partly because they are so easy to grow. Most modern varieties offer large, long lasting double flowers.

Marigolds will grow happily in any well-drained garden soil, but avoid rich soils which encourage leafy growth at the expense of flowers. Sow the seed where it is to flower once the soil has warmed up after winter.

T. erecta 'Vanilla'

T. patula 'Naughty Marietta'

Expert's Selection

1 *T.* **Boy o' Boy Series**
This French marigold has carnation-like double flowers.
✿✿✿ **Yellow, orange or reddish brown • Late spring–early autumn**
h.&s. **20cm (8in)**

2 *T.* **Bonita Series**
A French marigold that bears large flowers, some bicoloured, in abundance.
✿✿✿ **Yellow, orange and red Late spring–early autumn**
h.&s. **30cm (1ft)**

3 *T. erecta* 'Vanilla'
An African marigold; its large, fully double flowers have unique colouring.
✿✿ **Creamy white, tinged yellow Late spring–early autumn**
h.&s. **35cm (14in)**

4 *T. patula* 'Naughty Marietta' Strikingly marked bi-coloured flowers make this French marigold really stand out.
✿✿ **Yellow with bold deep red markings • Late spring–early autumn**
h.&s. **30cm (1ft)**

5 *T.* **Excel Series**
The large double flowers of this African marigold may measure up to 12cm (5in) across.
✿✿ **Light to deep yellow or orange Late spring–early autumn**
h.&s. **30cm (1ft)**

TAKE A FRESH LOOK

T. **Zenith Series** is a double-flowered variety of an Afro-French hybrid marigold. It is bushy and grows to 30cm (1ft) tall, with large yellow, orange or bi-coloured blooms.

STAR PERFORMER
T. **Boy o' Boy Series**
Large flowers in a wide range of colours make a stunning summer show.

The Essentials

Site demands Any well-drained, not too rich soil, in full sun.
Planting practice Plant out after the risk of frost has passed.
Flowering time Late spring until early autumn.
Pruning needs Deadhead regularly to prolong the display.
Pests and diseases Slugs may devour young plants.
Bonus point Marigolds can be sown in situ in late spring and early summer, when the soil is warm.

Tropaeolum

Nasturtiums are hard to match for sheer flower power. Easily grown, they come in upright and bushy or trailing forms.

Expert's Selection

1 *T.* Alaska Series♀
Bushy variety with marbled foliage. Whirlybird Series is slightly smaller and has single or semi-double flowers in mixed colours.
✿ ✿✿ **Cream, yellow, orange, red**
Summer–autumn • h.&s. 45cm (1½ft)

2 *T.* Gleam Series
A semi-trailing variety, with semi-double flowers, ideal for baskets and other containers.
✿✿✿ **Yellow, orange, scarlet and pastels • Summer–autumn**
h.&s. 60cm (2ft)

3 *T.* 'Peach Melba'
A bushy variety with unusually coloured semi-double flowers.
✿✿ **Creamy yellow marked with red**
Summer–autumn • h.&s. 45cm (1½ft)

STAR PERFORMER
T. Alaska Series♀ **With its profuse, vibrantly coloured flowers, this variety makes arresting summer bedding. Use the edible petals as a colourful addition to a summer salad.**

The Essentials

Site demands Any moist, well-drained soil, in full sun.
Planting practice Plant out after the last frosts.
Flowering time From summer to autumn.
Pests and diseases May be attacked by aphids and caterpillars.
Bonus point Great for covering a trellis, and in patio pots.

Nasturtiums remain one of the most popular annuals, grown for their vivid colours and long flowering season. The trailing varieties are best grown in baskets and other containers, while the more bushy types are excellent for bedding out.

They are easily grown, requiring a sunny position in a well-drained, moderately fertile soil that does not dry out in hot weather. Sow the seeds in mid spring where they are to flower, or plant out seedlings when the risk of frost has passed.

Verbena

With their bright colours, long flowering season and neat habit, it is easy to understand the popularity of verbenas. Some varieties are best suited to bedding out and are ideal fillers at the front of a border; others, especially the trailing ones, are tailor-made for baskets and other containers.

Expert's Selection

1 *V.* x *hybrida* Tapien Series
A trailing variety with clusters of small flowers. The similar Temari Series also produces white flowers.
✿✿✿ **Pink, red, rose and purple**
Summer–autumn
h.&s. 40cm (16in)

2 *V.* 'Peaches and Cream'
This variety has unusually coloured flowers, which have an almost antique quality.
✿✿ **Coral-pink, aging to creamy yellow • Summer–autumn**
h.&s. 35cm (14in)

3 *V.* x *hybrida* Sandy Series
A compact and upright plant.
✿✿✿ **White, pink, magenta and scarlet • Summer–autumn**
h.&s. 25cm (10in)

4 *V.* x *hybrida* Novalis Series The varieties in this series are bushy and erect, and are among the best choices for bedding out.
✿✿✿ **White, pink, scarlet and violet • Summer–autumn**
h.&s. 25cm (10in)

The Essentials

Site demands A warm sunny position in well-drained, fertile soil.
Planting practice Plant out after the last frosts have passed. Trailing varieties will tumble over a wall or from a container, or can be trained up a wigwam support.
Flowering time Early summer into autumn.
Pests and diseases Slugs and aphids may be a problem.
Bonus point Vivid colours and long flowering season make for terrific container displays.

V. 'Peaches and Cream'

V. x *hybrida* Novalis Series

Viola

Violas are among the best-loved of cottage-garden plants, and are especially pretty in window boxes. Those listed here are short-lived and treated as half-hardy annuals.

The *Viola* genus also includes pansies, see pages 302–303.

Expert's Selection

1 *V.* 'Magnifico'
These violet-tinged white flowers are ideal for containers.
❀❀ **White with violet border Spring and summer h.&s. 15–30cm (6–12in)**

2 *V.* Penny Series
A prolific viola, great for bedding.
❀❀❀❀ **Yellow, orange, blue and cream and bicoloured • Spring and summer • h.&s. 15–30cm (6–12in)**

3 *V.* Miniola Series
Distinctive two-toned flowers.
❀❀ **Blue or purple with large orange 'face' • Spring and summer h.&s. 15–30cm (6–12in)**

Violas are easily grown in almost all gardens. Most moderately fertile soils suit them, and they thrive in full sun; in light dappled shade they may flower a little less freely.

Plant out from mid to late spring and deadhead regularly to promote continuous flowering.

The Essentials

Site demands Any fairly fertile, well-drained soil, in a cool position.
Planting practice Plant in spring.
Flowering time From spring, well into summer.
Pruning needs Deadhead often for continuous flowering.
Pests and diseases May be attacked by aphids and slugs.
Bonus point Although small, the flowers are usually sweetly scented and are edible.

STAR PERFORMER
V. 'Magnifico' A delicate violet edge gives these pretty flowers definition – and the appeal of sugared almonds.

STAR PERFORMER
V. x *hybrida* Tapien Series
This trailing verbena, in mixed or single colours, has a compact habit and will make a magnificent hanging basket display.

The verbenas grown for bedding are all half-hardy perennials but are treated as annuals. With their range of different growth habits, neat and attractive foliage, and clusters of small, brightly coloured flowers, they are among the more versatile bedding plants. Some are bushy and upright in growth, and these can be bedded out in the garden, either massed or individually, or used to provide a focal point in containers. Others are more or less trailing in habit, and lend themselves to use in containers, and especially hanging baskets, either mixed with other plants or by themselves.

Verbenas like a warm, sunny position in a fertile, well-drained soil. Plant out in late spring or early summer, after the risk of frost has passed. If planting them in containers, use a soil-based potting compost such as John Innes No.2.

Keep the soil moist, watering containers particularly generously during any dry periods. Keep an eye open in wet weather, when newly planted verbenas will tempt slugs and snails. Discard plants in autumn once flowering is over.

Viola

Pansies are both tactile and visually striking, with velvety blooms available in the widest range of colours. With a careful choice of varieties, you can enjoy them almost all year. Their semi-trailing style of growth makes them suitable for containers or as bedding plants at the front of borders.

These most appealing and versatile plants are treated as hardy or half-hardy annuals, being discarded when their display fades. There are varieties that flower throughout the summer, as well as the popular winter-flowering pansies.

Plant a bold display

Pansies have larger and more flamboyant flowers than the rest of the violas. They look particularly showy when bedded out in drifts, where they will make a colourful carpet beneath bulbs such as tulips. They also look beautiful in containers, following on from small, early spring bulbs. Summer-flowering pansies are useful for filling in gaps in a border with long-lasting colour.

Easy to grow, easy to please

Care free and among the easiest plants to grow, pansies thrive in any reasonably fertile soil that does not dry out excessively in summer. Flowering is most prolific on plants grown in full sun, but you will still enjoy a good display from those growing in light or dappled shade.

Garden centres stock trays of single or multicoloured pansies whenever they are in season, but they are also easy to raise from seed. Sow winter pansies in pots or trays in summer, to plant out in autumn. For summer-flowering pansies, sow in early spring, and plant out in late spring or early summer. To ensure a continuous succession of flowers, the plants should be regularly deadheaded throughout the flowering season.

Although various fungal diseases may affect pansies, they are generally reliable and trouble free. In damp weather, slugs and snails can be a nuisance and in dry weather, pansies can sometimes be infested by aphids.

V. Clear Crystal Series

V. Universal Plus Series

V. Turbo Series

Expert's Selection

1 *V.* **Ultima Series** ♀
This winter pansy comes in a wide range of colours which are sometimes blotched. 'Ultima Sherbet' has white flowers with markings that are nearly black.
❀ ✿✿✿ **White, yellow, red, blue or purple • Winter–spring**
h.&s. **25cm (10in)**

2 *V.* **Universal Plus Series**
A popular winter pansy that will also flower in summer.
❀ ✿✿✿ **White, yellow, orange, blue, purple or red • Winter–spring or summer • *h.&s.* 20cm (8in)**

3 *V.* **Turbo Series**
This variety offers an unusually wide colour range, as well as bicoloured blooms.
❀ ✿✿✿✿ **White, cream, yellow, orange, pink, red, blue or purple Summer • *h.&s.* 25cm (10in)**

4 *V.* **Can Can Series**
Large, wonderfully ruffled flowers, mostly boldly blotched, create an attractive effect.
❀ ✿✿ **Cream, yellow, pink or red • Summer**
h.&s. **20cm (8in)**

5 *V.* **Clear Crystal Series** Flowers of the varieties in this series have no central blotch, and come in a range of clear colours.
❀ ✿✿ **White, yellow, red, mauve or purple Summer**
h.&s. **20cm (8in)**

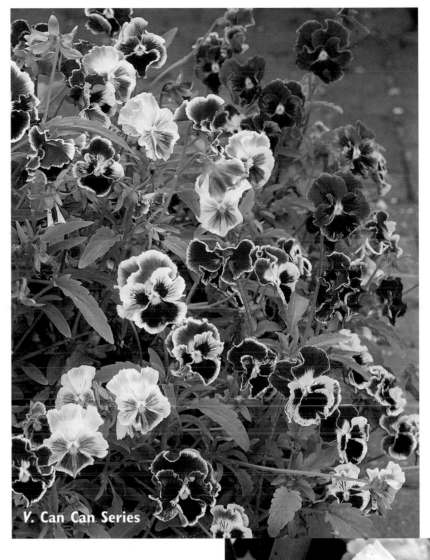

V. **Can Can Series**

The Essentials

Site demands Any fairly fertile, well-drained site, ideally in full sun.
Planting practice Plant out in autumn or late spring.
Flowering time A good selection of different varieties will give flowers for most of the year.
Pruning needs Will flower for longer with regular deadheading.
Pests and diseases Generally trouble free, but look for slugs, aphids and various fungal diseases.
Bonus point Will self-seed, if left, to produce attractive new variants.

V. **'Ultima Sherbet'**

bulbs, corms, tubers & rhizomes

For care-free gardening, bulbs, corms, tubers and rhizomes are hard to beat. Just bury them and leave them, and a selection of bulbs will provide flowers throughout the year. They are particularly welcome for their cheerful colour in early spring.

Although the term 'bulbs' is used for most of the plants in this section, the plants and their flowers may also grow from corms, tubers or rhizomes. Bulbs are made up of the fleshy leaf bases of plants such as **daffodils**, while corms are swollen stems with buds at the top – **crocus** grow from corms, for example. Rhizomes are fat stems that spread horizontally from plants like some **irises**. **Dahlias** grow from tubers, or thickened roots. All these natural devices provide underground stores of energy for the growing plant.

Choices for sun and shade

Bulbs are the mainstay of most spring gardens, but they can also make a valuable contribution to the garden in summer. Not all bulbs are right for every section of the garden, but with a little simple planning you will be sure to have the right plant for a particular site.

Most bulbs dislike cold and wet, or stagnant soils, so good drainage is key. Heavier soils can be improved – ideally over the whole bed, not just in each single planting hole – by working in plenty of good, fibrous compost and coarse grit before you start to plant.

Many bulbs enjoy a sunny position, and a few such as *Dahlia* and *Gladiolus* will only flower well if they receive a real baking in summer. Others, including many lilies, are happier in light shade or a dappled woodland setting.

Follow a natural planting plan

Almost all bulbs have an informal charm, and look best when planted in natural-looking drifts or clumps.

Woodland bulbs, such as **bluebells** (*Hyacinthoides*) and **snowdrops** (*Galanthus*) thrive beneath trees, where they make the most of the dappled light that filters through before the canopy is in full leaf. *Crocus* naturalise well in a lawn, giving the grass a jewel-studded effect when they bloom in early spring. Bedding tulips are the exception to this rule: with their glossy petals and sentry-like upright habit, they work brilliantly planted in ranks or blocks in a formal context.

Plant bulbs for a parade of colour

There is much to be said for thinking of the garden in terms of compartments, or 'rooms', each of which peaks at a different time of year. Bulbs, with their predictable flowering season, can help to create this effect, which helps to give an increased sense of scale and perspective to even the smallest garden, and is far more interesting than a single-season scheme that can be taken in at a glance.

Plant bulbs in early autumn for spring colour

Easy-going and low maintenance, bulbs require little attention once they are planted. These few simple jobs will help to keep them blooming.

Root out weeds
• Like most plants, bulbs prefer not to have to compete for light and nutrients, so pull out weeds as the bulb shoots start to nudge through.

Remove fading flowers
• Deadheading bulbs as the flowers finish will prevent them from wasting energy producing seeds.
• The best way to deadhead bulbs is to snap off the spent flowers at the top of the stalk.

Dealing with dying leaves
• Once bulbs have finished flowering, the leaves may become unsightly. Resist the temptation to cut them off or tie them in knots: the leaves must be left to die down naturally, in order to replenish the bulbs for the following year's display.
• After six to eight weeks, dying leaves can be cut off at ground level.
• If bulbs are naturalised in grass, mow round the leaves until they have died back, then mow them off.
• Plant bulbs among deciduous ground-cover plants or beneath open-branched small shrubs to disguise the dying leaves.

Winter care for tender bulbs
A few plants in this section, notably dahlias and gladioli, may only be fully hardy in warm inner-city sites.
• In sheltered gardens, these plants can be left in the ground all year.
• In exposed sites, lift the tubers for winter after the first frost. Cut off the stems, dust the tubers with fungicide, then dry them and store in a cool, airy, but frost-free place.

Increasing and dividing
• Most bulbs will increase, either by seeding or by producing offsets (small additional bulbs).
• When clumps become congested, flowering may be affected, or even stop altogether. To prevent this, lift clumps, split them and replant the bulbs every few years.
• Snowdrops will flower freely for many years with no attention but you can encourage a better display by separating the clumps after flowering and replanting the bulbs over a larger area.

Allium

Ornamental onions provide a range of colour and form, from short varieties that find a foothold in a craggy spot to the more stately blooms of the herbaceous border. These easy-going bulbs ask little in return for their summer display: just a sunny spot and fertile well-drained soil.

Expert's Selection

1 *A. moly* ♀
A fast-spreading, free-flowering allium for a bright splash of colour.
✿ **Yellow • Early summer**
h. 15–25cm (6–10in)

2 *A. hollandicum* ♀
This tall allium is good for cutting, or adding height to a border and is also listed as *A. aflatunense*. 'Purple Sensation' ♀ is a very dark purple.
✿ **Purple • Early summer**
h. 1m (3ft)

3 *A. christophii* ♀
Huge globes of starry flowers are followed by spectacular seed heads. Also called *A. albopilosum*.
✿ **Purple • Midsummer**
h. 30–60cm (1–2ft)

4 *A. cyaneum* ♀
This rock-garden species has grassy leaves and hanging blooms.
✿ **Violet-blue • Midsummer**
h. 10–25cm (4–10in)

5 *A. oreophilum* 'Zwanenburg' ♀ These add vibrant colour to a rock garden.
✿ **Pink to purple • Midsummer**
h. 10–20cm (4–8in)

6 *A. cernuum*
The lady's leek or nodding onion has loose, drooping flowerheads.
✿ **Rosy purple • Early summer**
h. 30–60cm (1–2ft)

7 *A. karataviense* ♀
Grow this allium for its handsome blue-green and purple leaves.
✿ **Cream • Late spring–early summer**
⊘ **Blue-green and purple**
h. 15–20cm (6–8in)

8 *A. ursinum*
Ramsons, or wild garlic, prefer some shade. A woodland setting beneath a deciduous tree is ideal.
✿ **White • Late spring**
h. 10–45cm (4–18in)

Be bold with bulbs and plant in groups for a better effect than dotting solitary specimens here and there. Alliums are a great choice for a sunny garden, where established plants will thrive for several years with minimal effort. Leave the seed heads to develop and some may spread, or increase clumps by lifting and dividing.

Flower clusters may be blue, pink, purple, white or yellow and some, like *A. christophii*, also develop ornamental seed heads. Foliage varies from bold, strap-like leaves, to the fine leaves of some of the rock garden varieties.

A scented family clue
Ramsons (*A. ursinum*) spread rampantly, and carpet a shady woodland spot with broad green leaves massed with heads of pure white flowers in late spring.

Be warned, like many alliums, this 'wild garlic' has a strong garlic scent when the leaves are bruised. Others give off a hint of onion.

The Essentials

Site demands Fertile, well-drained soil and full sun. In wet sites the bulbs will rot.
Planting practice Plant bulbs in autumn, or transplant from containers after flowering.
Flowering time Spring to autumn, but mostly summer.
Pruning needs Deadhead to prevent prolific self-seeding.
Pests and diseases Watch for white rot, fusarium and rust. Onion fly grubs may damage the bulbs.
Bonus point The ornamental seed heads of some varieties can be dried for arranging.

A. cernuum

A. christophii

STAR PERFORMER
A. moly ♀ With its clusters of vivid yellow flowers, the golden garlic is a guaranteed star performer for rock garden or border.

Begonia

With only a little attention, a collection of flamboyant tuberhybrida begonias will bring an exotic look to your garden in high summer. Mix the bushier varieties with other border plants, or make a real show by picking varieties in a palette of pastel shades and planting them in drifts.

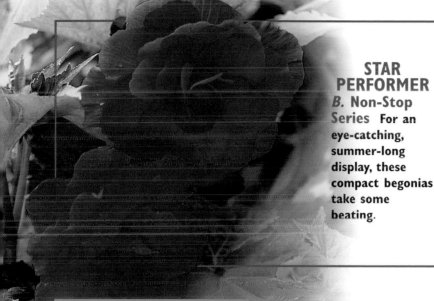

STAR PERFORMER
B. **Non-Stop Series** For an eye-catching, summer-long display, these compact begonias take some beating.

The Essentials

Site demands Well-drained, fertile soil. Shelter them from the strongest sunlight.
Planting practice Start the tubers in pots, and then plant out.
Flowering time Blooms from summer to early autumn.
Pests and diseases Aphids, vine weevils, mealy bugs and grey mould are all worth looking out for.
Bonus point Tubers can be divided in spring when the shoots start to sprout.

Get the best from your begonias by starting them in pots in early spring. Plant the tubers hollow-side up, and keep them in a light, frost-free place until the weather improves. Then move them to an open site that is sheltered from the midday sun, and has a free draining soil, rich in humus. In warmer areas, tubers can be planted directly outside once the frosts have passed, but will flower later than plants started inside.

A fortnightly liquid feed with a balanced general fertiliser will help to prolong the display, but avoid watering over the foliage.

Winter care
To keep the tubers for another year, lift them in early autumn. Dry them carefully in a cool, airy place out of the sun, while the top growth dies down, then store them for winter in boxes of nearly dry sand or peat.

B. grandis subsp. *evansiana* grows as a perennial in sheltered sites. In late summer, small bulbils are produced where the leaf joins the stem. These can be detached, stored like tubers, and potted up in spring for a fresh display.

B. **Illumination Series**

B. **'Pin-Up'**

B. **'Roy Hartley'**

Expert's Selection

1 *B.* Non-Stop Series
Bushy plants bear medium-sized double flowers all summer.
✿✿✿✿❀ **Red, pink, orange, yellow or white • Summer • h. 30cm (1ft)**

2 *B.* 'Flamboyant'
A neat upright variety ideal for a display of summer bedding.
✿ **Red • Summer • h. 20cm (8in)**

3 *B.* 'Helene Harms'
Very weather-resistant, this small sized variety has profuse flowers.
✿ **Coppery yellow • Summer h. 15cm (6in)**

4 *B.* Illumination Series
Their floppy habit suits these small-flowered begonias to hanging baskets, or window boxes.
Pink or orange • Summer h. 45cm (1½ft)

5 *B.* 'Pin-Up'
This compact variety has pretty, single, white flowers with a broad frilly edging of deepest pink.
✿❀ **Pink and white • Summer h. 25cm (10in)**

6 *B.* 'Roy Hartley'
This is one of the larger bedding varieties; its frilly, double pink flowers are almost rose-like.
✿ **Pink • Summer • h. 60cm (2ft)**

7 *B. grandis* subsp. *evansiana* Pink flowers bloom above coppery foliage.
✿ **Pink • Late summer–early autumn h. 60cm (2ft) s. 30cm (1ft)**

TAKE A FRESH LOOK

Cascade Series begonias are pendulous, and best appreciated in a hanging basket, where their small double flowers hang close to eye level. *B. sutherlandii*, which has single orange flowers, can be trained up a frame or left to sprawl.

Chionodoxa

Glory of the snow is among the easiest of early-flowering dwarf bulbs to grow and provides a welcome pastel contrast to the bright yellows of so many spring flowers.

Expert's Selection

1 *C. forbesii* 'Pink Giant'
Several flowers on each stem mark out this free-flowering variety.
✿❀ **Pink and white • Spring**
h. 10–20cm (4–8in)

2 *C. luciliae*♀
This will bring colour to bare ground beneath deciduous shrubs.
✿❀ **Blue and white • Early spring**
h. 10–15cm (4–6in)

3 *C. sardensis*♀
Deep blue starry flowers set this *Chionodoxa* apart from the rest.
✿ **Deep blue • Early spring**
h. 15cm (6in)

STAR PERFORMER
C. forbesii 'Pink Giant'
With its large blooms, 'Pink Giant' stands out on dull days.

The Essentials

Site demands Place in sun or light shade, with fairly rich, free-draining soil that does not dry out.
Planting practice Plant bulbs in autumn, or move pot-grown plants to the border after flowering.
Flowering time Early spring.
Pests and diseases Slugs and snails may shred the flowers.
Bonus point They are a delicate addition to indoor decorations.

Starry blue or pink flowers, each with a bright white 'eye', make a welcome appearance on dull late winter and early spring days, and earn chionodoxa its name, 'Glory of the snow'.

Plant the bulbs in autumn, in any good garden soil and forget about them. These bulbs are truly care free, and will slowly increase by offsets from the bulbs, as well as by seeding.

Splashes of winter colour
The sky blue and white flowers of *C. forbesii* and *C. luciliae* are popular and reliable, although an attack by slugs or snails can wipe them out overnight (see page 19). 'Pink Giant' introduces a warmer shade.

Chionodoxas are perfect under small deciduous shrubs, where their flowers can be enjoyed before the shrub leaves emerge. They will often naturalise there.

C. sardensis

Colchicum

Autumn crocus, or **meadow saffron** flowers look frail, but are unexpectedly hardy. Their curvaceous goblet shape may be the source of their alternative name, naked ladies.

Expert's Selection

1 *C. byzantinum*♀
Each bulb in this vigorous, easy species may bear up to 20 flowers.
✿ **Lilac-pink • Late summer–autumn**
h. 15cm (6in)

2 *C. speciosum* 'Album'♀
Large flowers with rounded petals shrug off blustery autumn weather.
❀ **White • Autumn • *h.* 23cm (9in)**

3 *C. agrippinum*♀
For a striking flower choose this, with its chequered patterning on pointed petals.
✿ **Purplish pink • Early autumn**
h. 10cm (4in)

4 *C.* 'The Giant'
This truly giant colchicum is vigorous and naturalises freely.
✿ **Purplish pink Autumn • *h.* 20cm (8in)**

The Essentials

Site demands Colchicums thrive in a sunny, well-drained, fertile spot.
Planting practice Wear gloves when planting corms in summer.
Flowering time The flowers bloom in autumn, before the leaves.
Pests and diseases Slugs are attracted to the flowers and leaves.
Bonus point An unplanted bulb will flower dry if given enough sun.

STAR PERFORMER
C. byzantinum♀ The flowers may be smaller than some, but they make an impact through their sheer abundance.

SAFTEY WARNING
All parts of the autumn crocus are poisonous if eaten.

Autumn crocuses are not related to crocuses at all, despite a very similar shape. Their giant crocus-like flowers appear in autumn.

The one drawback to these plants, is their floppy, strap-like leaves, which emerge after the flowers die down and become large and rather coarse by spring.

In the right soil autumn crocuses will soon form clumps. Lift them in summer and take offsets from the corms to spread around the garden.

For a more unusual look, try 'Waterlily', with its flamboyant, many-petalled, pink flowers. For best effect, plant it amongst other low plants that will support the heavy flowerheads.

Convallaria

Lily of the valley with its dripping chains of flowers, makes a fragrant carpet beneath a tree or shrub.

Lily of the valley is a real 'plant and forget it' perennial. Give it a deep, moist soil with plenty of humus and it will spread and flower reliably. Most varieties prefer full or partial shade, but the variegation of the leaves of 'Albostriata' is brighter where it gets a little sun.

Plant rhizomes just beneath the surface of the soil in autumn, and they will branch out and spread freely. You may find the rhizomes growing up out of the ground, but a top dressing of autumn leaf-mould will soon cover them. You can lift and separate the rhizomes in autumn and relocate them.

STAR PERFORMER
C. 'Fortin's Giant'
With large flowers and leaves and just as much scent, this lily-of-the-valley is tempting to pick for a vase indoors.

Expert's Selection

1 *C.* 'Fortin's Giant'
The large scented blooms of this variety appear quite late.
✿ White • Mid–late spring
h. 30cm (1ft)

2 *C. majalis* 'Albostriata'
Leaves with veins of gold are the main attraction on this convallaria.
✿ White • Spring • *h.* 23cm (9in)

3 *C. majalis* ♀
Easy to find and grow, plant this common variety and watch it go.
✿ White • Spring • *h.* 23cm (9in)

The Essentials

Site demands Moisture and shade suit the needs of this plant.
Planting practice Plant the rhizomes in autumn.
Flowering time Enjoy the flowers' lovely fragrance in spring.
Pests and diseases Lily of the valley is generally trouble free.
Bonus point Warmth, light and repotting give rhizomes new life.

Pick a posy from the garden
The deliciously fragrant flowers are perfect in posies and small flower arrangements. Lift plants in autumn and to enjoy their scent out of season, keep them in a frame or cool greenhouse.

TAKE A FRESH LOOK
C. majalis var. *rosea* For a woodland carpet with an unusual hue, try this lily of the valley with its fragrant dusky pink flowers.

Crocosmia

Montbretia's vivid flowers, rising in sprays out of lance-like foliage, embody the heat of summer.

Expert's Selection

1 *C.* 'Lucifer' ♀
Small, but bright red flowers light up this hardy modern variety.
✿ Vivid red • Summer • *h.* 1m (3ft)

2 *C.* x *crocosmiiflora* 'Solfatare' ♀ Unusual bronze leaves complement apricot flowers.
✿ Apricot-yellow • Summer
h. 60cm (2ft)

3 *C. masoniorum* ♀
Striking pleated leaves and arching flower spikes draw a crowd.
✿ Orange-red • Summer
h. 1.2m (4ft)

4 *C.* 'Spitfire'
This brilliant modern hybrid has small, but fiery flowers.
✿ Orange-red • Summer
h. 75cm (2½ft)

5 *C.* 'Emberglow'
Dark red flowers glow on deep reddish brown stems.
✿ Deep red • Early summer
h. 60cm (2ft)

STAR PERFORMER
C. 'Lucifer' ♀ The brilliant red flowers of this new montbretia make it as fiery as its devilish name suggests.

The smaller flowered varieties of montbretia listed here are the best choice for the care-free gardener. Their lance shaped leaves rustle in the breeze from spring onwards, while yellow, dramatic orange or red flowers create a stunning summer display.

Try to plant crocosmias in good-sized clumps, so that their bold colours create maximum impact. Most varieties increase quickly, so lift and divide large clumps every four years or so.

In cold areas, applying a mulch of leaf litter in early winter will help to protect the more tender varieties. But no such effort is required for the common montbretia, *C.* × *crocosmiiflora*: a tough and showy perennial that thrives in a semi-wild corner.

The Essentials

Site demands Moist but well-drained soil in sun or light shade.
Planting practice Plant corms 10cm (4in) deep in early spring.
Flowering time Summer.
Pests and diseases Look out for red spider mites in hot weather.
Bonus point Seed heads can be easily used in dried arrangements.

Crocus

Their goblet-shaped flowers will brighten even the gloomiest late winter day, making crocuses welcome in any garden. In a well-drained soil and a sunny spot they will open and bask in the weak but warming rays. Let them spread across the lawn and enjoy their blooms into spring.

Expert's Selection

1 *C. cartwrightianus* **'Cream Beauty'** ♀ Plant dense clumps of this creamy crocus in the grass to resemble pools of milky sunlight.
❀ **Clotted cream • Late winter** *h.* 10cm (4in)

2 *C. ancyrensis*
With up to five golden flowers a corm this variety is terrific value.
❀ **Golden yellow • Late winter** *h.* 5cm (2in)

3 *C. tommasinianus* ♀
This species comes in several hues. It spreads rapidly and is great for naturalising in grass under a tree.
❀ **Purple • Early spring** *h.* 10cm (4in)

4 *C. pulchellus* ♀
The delicately veined flowers of this vigorous autumn flowering species pop up before the leaves.
❀ **Pale lilac • Mid–late autumn** *h.* 18cm (7in)

5 *C. vernus* **'Pickwick'**
Distinctive 'beach hut' stripes and vivid yellow stamens give this rounded crocus a bright and cheery air.
❀ **Purple and white • Late winter– early spring** • *h.* 13cm (5in)

6 *C.* x *luteus* **'Golden Yellow'** ♀ Also known as 'Dutch Yellow', this vibrant golden crocus will naturalise easily in grass.
❀ **Rich yellow • Late winter–early spring** • *h.* 13cm (5in)

7 *C. cartwrightianus* **'Zwanenburg Bronze'** ♀ For unusual colour, this is an excellent choice, with its rusty blooms.
❀ **Red-brown and yellow • Early spring** • *h.* 10cm (4in)

8 *C. cartwrightianus* **'Gipsy Girl'** Large yellow flowers are striped brown on the outside.
❀ **Yellow and purple • Late winter** *h.* 10cm (4in)

9 *C. cartwrightianus* **'Ladykiller'** ♀ Slender pure white flowers have a purple splash.
❀ **White and deep purple • Late winter** • *h.* 10cm (4in)

When crocuses start to bejewel the lawn or push through the bare ground beneath a tree, you know that spring is just around the corner.

The flowers usually appear just before, or with, the narrow green leaves, which have a silvery midrib and go on growing after the honey-scented flowers fade.

Crocuses grow from small, slightly flattened corms, each producing at least one funnel-shaped flower. In most varieties, the flowers open wide in bright sunlight, but some remain half closed and goblet shaped.

Plant them and sit back
Crocus are easy to grow and most will increase rapidly by offsets. Some, such as *C. tommasinianus*, will also self-seed.

Lift congested clumps in summer or autumn, separating and replanting the corms. Early flowering varieties are best planted in autumn, about 10cm (4in) deep and 5cm (2in) apart. Some less commonly grown species flower in late autumn: plant these in late summer.

C. vernus 'Pickwick'

C. tommasinianus

Chase away hungry pests
Mice, voles or grey squirrels may nibble young corms, making for a disappointing first year display. Shredded flowers, especially yellow ones, have probably been pecked at by house sparrows.

If your crocuses are naturalised in grass, do not mow the lawn until the leaves have died down and the seeds have been scattered.

The Essentials

Site demands Most well-drained soils, preferably in full sun.
Planting practice Plant dormant corms in late summer to autumn.
Flowering time From late winter to early spring, though some varieties flower in autumn.
Pests and diseases The corms may be eaten by voles and mice, and birds may peck the flowers.
Bonus point The flowers of most crocuses have a sweet honey scent. Bring them inside to enjoy it.

STAR PERFORMER
C. cartwrightianus **'Cream Beauty'** ♀
The luscious rounded cream flowers have yellow bases and orange styles. Plant in large clumps for maximum impact.

Cyclamen

Forget the familiar and brightly coloured, large-flowered indoor cyclamen, and dot the ground beneath a spreading tree with these delicate-looking hardy varieties. Their flowers are held on almost invisibly slender stems and bob about like butterflies hovering in the breeze.

1 *C. hederifolium* ♀
Worth growing for the patterned leaves, which appear after the pale to deep pink flowers.
✿ **Pink • Autumn • h. 13cm (5in)**

2 *C. coum* **Pewter Group** ♀ Silvery green leaves with a green centre show off the small flowers.
✿ **Pink • Winter–early spring h. 8cm (3in)**

3 *C. coum* 'Album'
Each of these white flowers seems to have been dipped in purple ink.
✽ **White • Winter–early spring h. 8cm (3in)**

4 *C. purpurascens* ♀
A limey soil best suits this delightful fragrant species.
✿ **Purple • Summer • h. 10cm (4in)**

5 *C. repandum*
In this scented species, the ivy-like leaves are shot through with silver.
✿ **Purplish pink • Spring h. 13cm (5in)**

C. coum 'Album'

C. repandum

In nature, hardy cyclamen are woodland plants. They do well in any moderately fertile, well-drained site, but a few varieties, like *C. repandum*, prefer a limey soil. Cyclamen will tolerate sun or light shade as long as they are not bone dry in summer: spread them on a bank beneath a tree, where they may naturalise, or in a shady part of a rock garden.

Varieties like *C. repandum* and *C. purpurascens* have strongly fragrant flowers; in others, like *C. hederifolium* and *C. coum*, marbled leaves are the draw. The flowers are generally purplish pink, but there are attractive white forms to be had, too.

Try to avoid buying dry tubers. The initial outlay might be greater for plants, but it is a far more reliable option. An annual mulch of leaf-mould, applied as the leaves fade, will keep the soil cool and moist, but otherwise, cyclamen are best left alone.

Spreading their seed

Some hardy cyclamen self-sow, so do not deadhead them: watch the stalk coil up to be nearer the soil as the seedpod ripens.

Alternatively, you can collect the seed and sow it in pots. Keep the pots in a dark place until germination begins. After a year, the small tubers can be potted up individually for growing on and eventually planting out.

Site demands Cyclamen like a well-drained soil with plenty of humus, and partial shade.
Planting practice Plant the tubers about 5cm (2in) deep and 15–30cm (6–12in) apart. Or collect seed and sow in pots.
Flowering time Different species of cyclamen flower in spring, summer, autumn and winter.
Pests and diseases Grey squirrels, mice and voles may dig up and eat the tubers.
Bonus point In some species the butterfly shaped flowers are deliciously fragrant.

STAR PERFORMER
C. hederifolium ♀ **Once it is established this autumn-flowering cyclamen will give a fine show of delicate blooms every year.**

Dahlia

Although dahlias have a reputation as specialist plants needing lots of care from the dedicated gardener, many, including this expert's selection, are remarkably trouble free and easy to grow. They will reward you with a fabulous array of late summer and early autumn colour.

The huge range of dahlias now available – there are perhaps as many as 20,000 varieties – is mostly derived from just two of the 30 species that grow wild in Mexico and Central America. These original species themselves are rarely grown, but hybrid dahlias remain very popular with gardeners. Happily, they are relatively easy to grow, with those varieties recommended here being the most trouble free.

Myriad shapes and sizes

Dahlias are conveniently classified according to flower shape and size. Waterlily and Anemone flowered dahlias have flat petals, the latter with smaller, tubular central petals. Pompons, and the larger Ball dahlias have very regular and formal double flowers, whilst Decorative and Cactus dahlias have a softer shape and, in some varieties, very large flowers.

Peony-flowered dahlias have flat, semi-double flowers. The single varieties have a less artificial appearance, and blend most easily with other plants in the border. The unusual Collerette dahlias have single flowers, but they are ornamented with a ruff of much shorter petals, often of a contrasting colour.

The rather formal appearance of many dahlias means that they are often grown in a bed by themselves. In fact, massing them in this way gives the most spectacular display, and makes it far easier to prepare the site for planting than when they are grown among other plants.

D. 'Yellow Hammer'

D. 'Chimborazo'

STAR PERFORMER

D. 'Arabian Night' Fabulous full flowers on long stems make this striking plant great for cutting, while it also looks dramatic planted as a clump among border perennials.

Where to plant

Thoughtful use of some of the more informal types of dahlia, especially the single flowered ones like **'Bishop of Llandaff'** and **'Yellow Hammer'**, can provide a dramatic accent in a mixed border. These also have the bonus of handsomely coloured foliage – the first, reddish purple, the second, bronze. Shorter varieties look effective planted in large pots or tubs, to brighten up a corner of a patio or sitting area.

Dahlias require a rich, fertile soil with a high humus content. They prefer a position in full sun but will grow reasonably well in partial shade, though they are likely to flower less freely. Good

The Essentials

Site demands Dahlias like a fertile, well-drained soil in full sun.
Planting practice Plant the tubers in well-prepared soil with plenty of humus in late spring.
Flowering time Dahlias bloom from midsummer to autumn.
Pests and diseases Slugs and snails, aphids and caterpillars may damage dahlias.
Bonus point Dahlias have a great range of colours and several also have strikingly coloured foliage.

drainage is important, but dahlias should not be allowed to dry out. In mid spring, fork a general purpose granular fertiliser into the top few inches of soil at the recommended rate. Plant the dormant tubers about 10–13cm (4–5in) deep. If you are massing them, then space them at about 30–60cm (1–2ft) apart to allow for subsequent growth.

Alternatively, you can start dahlia tubers off in a frost-free greenhouse or a cool spare room and plant them out once the risk of frost has passed.

Dwarf bedding varieties do not need staking but should be kept bushy by pinching out the growing tip when the shoot is about 15cm (6in) tall. For all other types, push canes into the soil when planting and tie in the shoots as they grow. Again, pinch out the growing tip once to encourage bushier growth.

Feeding and watering

You can add more quick release granular fertiliser in midsummer, watering it in (unless you do the job when it is raining). Water plants freely during dry spells. A thick mulch applied when the soil

D. 'Bishop of Llandaff'

D. 'Hillcrest Royal'

D. 'Pearl of Heemstede'

is really damp will help to retain moisture and reduce the need for future watering. But don't be tempted to put down a mulch onto dry soil as this will effectively hinder the rain from reaching the roots. If you want extra large blooms, you can disbud plants: the flower buds develop in threes, and disbudding simply involves removing the two side buds and leaving the central one. Once flowering is underway, disbudding can be continued if you wish. All old flowerheads should be removed regularly.

Winter care

With the first frosts, the colourful foliage will turn black. This is traditionally the time when the tubers are lifted out of the ground, treated and stored in a dry, frost-free place. However, for the most part, they will be fine if left where they are for winter, especially if deeply planted and in areas with mild weather.

In early summer, slugs and snails will feast on young shoots, so try to keep them at bay. Once flowering begins, watch out for aphids, capsid bugs and earwigs.

Eranthis

Winter aconites dot the winter earth beneath deciduous trees or shrubs, where their rich golden yellow-cup flowers epitomise the optimism of early spring.

STAR PERFORMER
E. hyemalis ♀
Let this plant spread freely beneath a tree.

Hardy winter aconites are easily grown in almost any sunny or lightly shaded situation. The bright yellow flowers are most welcome in late winter and early spring. They look especially pretty massed under deciduous shrubs or trees, and some varieties will spread freely. They need little more than a reasonably fertile, well-drained soil that does not dry out in summer.

Choose growing plants
Dry, dormant tubers are often sold for autumn planting, but these do not always establish well, and you are better off buying growing potted plants and planting them in spring. Sink the small, knobbly tubers about 5cm (2in) deep in the soil. Most types set plenty of seed which can be collected and sown, but it is simpler to leave this to nature and allow aconites to naturalise.

Expert's Selection

1 *E. hyemalis* ♀
Ideal for naturalising under a tree.
Yellow • Early spring
h. 5–8cm (2–3in)

2 *E. hyemalis* Tubergenii Group 'Guinea Gold' ♀
Charming free-flowering clumps.
Yellow • Early spring
h. 8cm (3in)

3 *E. hyemalis* Cilicica Group
Large flowers and dissected leaves mark these out as a bit special.
Yellow • Early spring
h. 10cm (4in)

The Essentials

Site demands Provide fertile soils in sun or light shade.
Planting practice Plant tubers 5cm (2in) deep in autumn.
Flowering time Early spring.
Pests Snails and slugs.
Bonus point Can be grown indoors as a house plant.

Galanthus

Snowdrops must be among the most beloved of winter flowers. Many will naturalise in slightly shaded spots, where their bell-shaped heads nod in a gentle breeze.

Expert's Selection

1 *G. elwesii* ♀
This robust species snowdrop will always make an impression.
❀ White • Late winter
h. 23cm (9in)

2 *G. 'S. Arnott'* ♀
A vigorous and elegant variety, this has large, rounded flowers.
❀ White • Late winter
h. 20cm (8in)

3 *G. nivalis* 'Flore Pleno' ♀
This cultivar of the wild snowdrop has generous double flowers.
❀ White • Late winter
h. 10–15cm (4–6in)

Drifts of snowdrops beneath bare trees are a cheering vision in late winter. You can re-create this effect even in a small garden by planting beneath a hedge or deciduous shrub.

Snowdrops are easy-going bulbs, and grow well in most soils, provided they do not dry out. Most will naturalise and spread steadily over the years. Congested clumps can be lifted just after flowering, and the bulbs separated for replanting.

Although dry bulbs are often sold, they are unreliable, and it is far better to buy bulbs 'in the green', in early spring. These should be planted about 10cm (4in) deep, either in a border or in grass, provided it is not mown until the leaves have died down.

The Essentials

Site demands Most snowdrops will thrive in any well-drained, fairly moist soil.
Planting practice Plant or divide growing bulbs just after flowering.
Flowering time Most snowdrops flower in late winter.
Pests and diseases Grey mould and narcissus bulb fly may occasionally attack the plants.
Bonus point The flowers of many snowdrops have a delightful honey-like scent.

STAR PERFORMER
G. elwesii ♀ Large flowers contrast beautifully with unusual broad grey leaves.

Gladiolus

Gladioli look spectacular in a florist's display, but there are several less well-known elegant species and miniatures that are not only far easier to grow than the taller varieties, but will also harmonise better with perennials in a mixed garden border.

G. 'The Bride'   G. 'Robinetta'

Expert's Selection

1 *G. communis* subsp. *byzantinus* ♀ This species is fairly hardy in sheltered southern Britain and the corms need not be lifted for winter.
✿ **Magenta • Early summer**
h. 1m (3ft).

2 *G. callianthus* ♀
Better known as *Acidanthera bicolor*, this has highly fragrant flowers.
✤ **White with purple throat • Late summer–early autumn • h. 1m (3ft)**

3 *G.* 'The Bride' ♀
A shorter variety ideal for bedding out in a sunny border.
✤ **White • Early summer**
h. 60cm (2ft)

4 *G.* 'Robinetta' ♀
A small bedding variety with short, dense spikes of vivid flowers.
✿ **Purplish red marked with cream**
Early summer • h. 60cm (2ft)

5 *G.* 'Nova Lux'
The golden blooms of this large-flowered hybrid make a real show.
✿ **Golden yellow • Midsummer–early autumn • h. 1.2m (4ft)**

6 *G. imbricatus*
This sturdy gladiolus will survive in the ground through winter in the warmer parts of the country.
✿ **Rose-red • Late spring**
h. 30–75cm (1–2½ft)

STAR PERFORMER
G. communis subsp. *byzantinus* ♀ With its tall spikes of vivid magenta-pink flowers, this relatively hardy species is excellent for cutting as well as for the border.

For a spectacular show, the large-flowered gladiolus hybrids, such as 'Nova Lux', make dramatic bedding displays. However, they need staking and a little care, so the smaller sorts recommended in the rest of this list are a more care-free choice.

Plant the corms in groups in spring, about 10–15cm (4–6in) deep. A little sharp sand beneath each corm will help drainage and stop them rotting in very wet weather. Dusting the corms with fungicide will also help.

Most gladioli are not fully hardy, and the corms are best lifted in autumn for winter. Remove any offsets, and dry them thoroughly before storing in a cool, dry and frost-free place.

In warmer gardens, the tougher species gladioli, such as *G. communis* subsp. *byzantinus*, can be left in the ground, where they will often spread rapidly.

RING THE CHANGES A huge range of gladioli is available and new ones are introduced each year. Try *G. tristis*, a slender, but tender species bearing cream flowers lightly marked with purple, that are very fragrant in the evening.
G. papilio is moderately hardy, with bell-shaped yellow flowers marked with purple. It spreads underground by runners. Other dainty varieties include the salmon pink 'Amanda Mahy' and 'Elvira', whose pale pink flowers are splashed with red on the lower petals.

The Essentials

Site demands Gladioli like a sunny position and grow best in rich and fertile soil.
Planting practice Plant the corms in well-drained soil in spring.
Flowering time Late spring until early autumn depending on type.
Pests and diseases Gladioli may be vulnerable to aphids, thrips, slugs and corm rot.
Bonus point A few species are delightfully fragrant.

Hyacinthoides

Bluebells carpeting a wood in spring are a magical sight. In the garden, too, they can be naturalised under deciduous trees or shrubs to equally stunning effect.

The needs of bluebells are minimal: moderately fertile soil that is fairly moist, and a position in dappled shade. Plant the bulbs in autumn, about 8cm (3in) deep, where they are to become naturalised; they need no further attention. However, they will seed freely, and in some situations it is wise to remove the spent flowerheads straight after flowering, to restrict their spread. Established clumps can be dug up in autumn, and the bulbs separated for replanting.

Bluebells can be picked for the house without harming the bulbs. Indoors their scent is more noticeable, but any buds that open will tend to be much paler.

Expert's Selection

1 *H. hispanica* 'Excelsior'
A tall, robust plant with striking dark-striped light blue bells carried all round the stem.
✿ **Light blue with darker stripe on each petal • Spring • h. 45cm (1½ft)**

2 *H. non-scripta*
The native bluebell bears its narrow flowers along one-sided, nodding heads.
✿ **Violet-blue • Spring**
h. 30cm (1ft)

3 *H. non-scripta alba*
The graceful white bluebell is often more vigorous than the traditional wild blue form.
✿ **White • Spring • h. 40cm (16in)**

STAR PERFORMER
H. hispanica 'Excelsior'
This selection of the Spanish bluebell forms splendid, free-flowering clumps and will grow freely in any situation.

The Essentials

Site demands Bluebells will grow in most moist soils.
Planting practice Plant the bulbs during autumn.
Flowering time Carpets of bluebells are a spring delight.
Pests and diseases These easy bulbs are quite trouble free.
Bonus point *H. non-scripta* has a sweet light scent.

Hyacinthus

Hyacinths, with their combination of wonderful fragrance and showy flowers in a wide range of colours, will really brighten up the garden in spring.

Expert's Selection

1 *H. orientalis* 'Jan Bos'
These vivid and robust spikes of flowers will flourish in the garden.
✿ **Cerise-red • Early spring**
h. 20–30cm (8–12in)

2 *H. orientalis* 'Delft Blue'♀
The soft tones of this variety are sure to make it a favourite.
✿ **Lilac-blue • Early spring**
h. 20cm (8in)

3 *H. orientalis* 'City of Haarlem'♀ This yellow is a beautiful contrast to blue varieties.
✿ **Primrose yellow • Mid spring**
h. 20cm (8in)

4 *H. orientalis* 'Pink Pearl'♀
The petals of this variety have paler edges, giving a picotee effect.
✿ **Pink • Early spring**
h. 20cm (8in)

Hyacinths will grow in almost any moderately fertile, well-drained soil, in sun or light shade. Although they are often grown in containers, the bulbs will not withstand freezing, so they are safer in open ground. Plant out indoor-grown hyacinths after flowering, although they may not bloom so well again.

SAFETY WARNING Wear plastic gloves when handling hyacinth bulbs: they can cause an allergic reaction.

The Essentials

Site demands Hyacinths will flourish in any well-drained soil.
Planting practice Plant the bulbs about 10cm (4in) deep and 15cm (6in) apart in summer or autumn.
Flowering time A selection of varieties will give flowers from early to mid spring.
Pests and diseases Hyacinths are generally trouble free.
Bonus point Delicious fragrance, best enjoyed by planting hyacinths in pots or raised beds.

STAR PERFORMER
H. orientalis 'Jan Bos'
Rich red blooms will add vibrancy in early spring.

Iris

When raised from bulbs, irises offer sophisticated colour, and often fragrance too. Unlike the familiar rhizomes, bulbous irises come in both dwarf and tall varieties.

Expert's Selection

1 I. 'Harmony'
A fine dwarf iris with large flowers held well above the leaves.
✿ Blue • Early spring • *h.* 15cm (6in)

2 I. danfordiae
A delicate dwarf iris with sweetly fragrant blooms.
✿ Yellow • Late winter–early spring
h. 10cm (4in)

3 I. 'George'
Sumptuously coloured purple flowers adorn this dwarf species.
✿ Purple with darker falls
Early spring • *h.* 15cm (6in)

4 I. histrioides
Short-stemmed plants carry a wonderful large flowerhead.
✿ Blue • Early spring
h. 10–15cm (4–6in)

5 I. 'Katharine Hodgkin'
Unusual greeny blue flowers have yellowish green falls.
✿ Green-blue and yellow
Early spring • *h.* 13cm (5in)

6 I. 'Professor Blaauw'♀
A tall Dutch iris with velvety blooms. Good for a sunny spot.
✿ Dark blue with yellow stripe
Early summer • *h.* 60cm (2ft)

7 I. latifolia♀
The tall English iris will flourish when naturalised in grass on moist soils. 'Mont Blanc' is white.
✿✿ Blue or violet • Early summer
h. 60cm (2ft)

The Essentials

Site demands Well-drained soils in a sunny position are ideal. Reticulata irises prefer alkaline soil.
Planting practice Plant the bulbs fairly deep in autumn.
Flowering time Dwarf varieties flower in spring, Dutch and English irises a little later.
Pests and diseases Slugs and a fungal disease may damage bulbs.
Bonus point Dutch irises are wonderful in cut-flower displays.

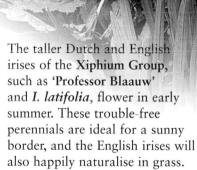

STAR PERFORMER
I. 'Harmony'
The plant may be short, but the blue flowers are large and luxuriant.

The dwarf irises listed here belong to the **Reticulata Group**, and flower in late winter and early spring. These include 'Harmony', *I. danfordiae*, 'George', *I. histrioides* and 'Katharine Hodgkin'.

Reticulata irises are ideal for a rock garden or at the front of a sunny border. The flowers open before the leaves are fully developed, giving the blooms the chance to shine. The leaves then elongate when the flowers fade.

The taller Dutch and English irises of the **Xiphium Group**, such as 'Professor Blaauw' and *I. latifolia*, flower in early summer. These trouble-free perennials are ideal for a sunny border, and the English irises will also happily naturalise in grass.

Some large irises grow from spreading woody rhizomes and are usually treated as herbaceous perennials in the border (see pages 136–137). Those listed here all grow from bulbs.

Planting and growing
Iris bulbs should be planted in autumn at a depth of twice their own height. Sometimes, especially with Reticulata irises, the bulbs split into many offsets, resulting in few flowers the following year. If this happens, wait until the flowers have faded then feed the bulbs every couple of weeks with a high potash liquid fertiliser until the leaves die down. This should encourage larger bulbs and better flowering the following year.

I. danfordiae *I. 'George'* *I. latifolia*

Lilium

Lilies bring a touch of glamour to any garden, but despite their exotic allure, they are surprisingly easy to grow. While tall lilies are gorgeous amidst a herbaceous border, shorter varieties look splendid grown in containers on a patio or in a conservatory.

Few flowers add more drama to the garden than lilies and in spite of their exotic appearance, most are easy to grow. Their tall and stout stems are well suited to planting among shrubs or medium-sized perennials. Flower-shapes vary from star-like to funnel-shaped and Turk's-cap lilies, such as *L. martagon*, have distinctive curled-back petals.

A sunny situation will encourage free-flowering, but most lilies will do equally well in partial shade and a few, such as *L. speciosum*♀, actually prefer some shade. The ideal position is among shrubs, where their roots will be cool and shaded while their heads are in the sun.

Planting and cultivating lilies

With most lilies, the bulbs should be set at a depth two to three times their height. The stem-rooting lilies, which include *L. speciosum*♀, *L. martagon* and *L. regale*♀, produce roots from the base of the stem, as well as from the bulb, and should be planted 15–20cm (6–8in) deep.

The bulbs will produce offsets, which can be detached to grow on to full flower. If you carefully peel the outer scales from dormant bulbs and place them in trays of damp compost, they will form small bulblets which can be potted up and grown on for eventual planting out.

Choosing for scent and display

Lilies make spectacular cut flowers, but the brilliant orange or yellow pollen can stain skin, clothes and soft furnishings. The **Kiss Series**, which mostly have double flowers, all lack stamens, so are particularly well suited to flower arranging or growing in pots on a small patio or balcony.

STAR PERFORMER
L. 'Enchantment'♀ **Bright orange flowers produced with vigour and freedom make this compact variety a perennial favourite.**

The Essentials

Site demands Lilies tolerate most aspects, but do best in well-drained, fertile soils. Avoid deep shade or very wet ground.
Planting practice Plant in humus-rich soil between late autumn and early spring.
Flowering time Pick a selection of lilies for a constant display from late spring to early autumn.
Pests and diseases Squirrels may dig up and eat the bulbs; slugs and snails enjoy young shoots; check too for aphids and red lily beetle.
Bonus point If planted in tubs and regularly fed, lilies thrive for several years without repotting.

L. speciosum var. *album*

LILIES FOR ALKALINE SOILS
If your garden is on chalk, try the white Madonna lily, *L. candidum*, the robust yellow *L. pyrenaicum*♀ and the orange *L. testaceum*♀, all of which tolerate neutral to alkaline soils.

L. Asiatic Group Kiss Series

Expert's Selection

1 *L.* 'Enchantment' ♈
This vigorous lily's star-shaped
flowers are ideal for cutting.
✿ **Orange • Early summer**
h. **75cm (2½ft)**

2 *L. speciosum* var. *album*
The large, pristine flowers of this
variety are strongly fragrant.
❀ **White • Late summer**
h. **1.2m (4ft)**

3 *L.* Asiatic Group Kiss
Series   The flowers have no
stamens, making these small lilies
an ideal cut flower.
❀✿✿ **White, yellow, orange or pink**
Early summer • *h.* 60cm (2ft)

4 *L.* 'Connecticut King'
Large, starry, upward-facing flowers
are well suited to the open garden.
✿ **Yellow • Early summer**
h. **1m (3ft)**

5 *L.* Pink Perfection Group ♈
Highly scented pink flowers are
borne on long, stout stems.
✿ **Pink • Late summer**
h. **1.2m (4ft)**

6 *L. martagon*
Long stems bear up to 50 waxy,
scented Turk's-cap flowers.
✿ **Purplish pink • Midsummer**
h. **1.5m (5ft)**

7 *L. regale* ♈
The regal lily is tall and elegant,
with heavily fragrant white blooms
that have a purple flush.
❀ **White and purple • Late summer**
h. **1.5m (5ft)**

8 *L. auratum*
The golden-rayed lily is highly
fragrant with bowl-shaped flowers.
❀ **White and gold • Late summer**
h. **1.5m (5ft)**

L. 'Connecticut King'

L. Pink Perfection Group

L. martagon

9 *L. cernuum*
The nodding lily is small but sweet.
✿ **Pale lilac, pink or purple • Early–
midsummer • *h.* 2m (7ft)**

10 *L. davidii* ♈
This Turk's-cap lily bears up to 20
pendulous flowers on each stem.
✿✿ **Red or orange • Mid–late
summer • *h.* 1m (3ft)**

Muscari

Grape hyacinths, an easy-going dwarf species, get their
name from the tiny clusters of globular flowers resembling
a bunch of grapes, which form their blooms.

Expert's Selection

1 *M. armeniacum*
'Blue Spike'   This showy variety
has dense clusters of deep blue
double flowers.
✿ **Blue • Spring**
h. **15–20cm (6–8in)**

2 *M. botryoides* 'Album'
For a contrast of colour, try this
dainty but hardy bulb.
❀ **White • Spring • *h.* 15cm (6in)**

3 *M. neglectum*
Slightly fragrant, richly coloured
blue flowers adorn this species.
The most common muscari, it
multiplies rapidly.
✿ **Deep blue • Spring • *h.* 15cm (6in)**

4 *M. comosum* 'Plumosum'
One of the taller muscari, this
curious variety, known as a tassel
hyacinth, bears a large cluster of
thread-like florets.
✿ **Purple-blue • Late spring**
h. **30cm (1ft)**

The Essentials

Site demands Grape hyacinths
tolerate most soils and all but the
deepest shade.
Planting practice Plant the bulbs
in autumn.
Flowering time Grape hyacinths
flower for several weeks in spring.
Pests and diseases These are
trouble-free bulbs.
Bonus point Most muscari are
very hardy and easy to grow.

These easy-to-grow little spring
bulbs give a charming display
from early to mid spring. For best
effect they should be allowed to
form carpets or large clumps.
They are also happy in tubs, pots
or window boxes.

Grape hyacinths will grow
in most soils, though they are
happiest in a well-drained
position in full sun or partial
shade. Plant the bulbs about 5cm
(2in) deep in autumn. They will
gradually increase each year.
Invasive or congested clumps can
be lifted when dormant and the
bulbs separated and replanted.

STAR PERFORMER

M. armeniacum 'Blue
Spike' **The large heads
of minute dark blue double
flowers are tipped with
greenish yellow.**

Narcissus

Daffodils are a delightful sign of spring. The range of sizes, flower shapes and colours is far wider than many gardeners realise, from vibrant trumpets to delicate dwarf varieties. There is one for every location: in a rock garden or formal border, amongst shrubs or growing freely amid grass.

STAR PERFORMER
N. 'Spellbinder' ♛
This reliable daffodil is a real multi-purpose variety, suitable for pots, borders or simply naturalised in grass.

Expert's Selection

1 *N.* 'Spellbinder' ♛
A tall and vigorous Trumpet daffodil with sulphur-coloured flowers.
✿ **Yellow • Mid spring**
h. **45cm (1½ft)**

2 *N.* 'Tête-à-Tête' ♛
This graceful Dwarf daffodil carries one to three flowers per stem.
✿ **Yellow • Early spring**
h. **15cm (6in)**

3 *N.* 'Bridal Crown'
Sweetly fragrant, with several double flowers on each stem.
❋ **White with orange segments**
Early spring • *h.* **40cm (16in)**

4 *N.* 'Hawera' ♛
This dwarf Triandus daffodil has several multiflowered stems each with small, nodding flowers.
✿ **Light yellow • Late spring**
h. **40–60cm (16in–2ft)**

5 *N. cyclamineus* ♛
Easily naturalised in damp grass, this species has long-tubed flowers with reflexed outer petals.
✿ **Yellow • Early spring**
h. **23cm (9in)**

6 *N.* 'Mount Hood' ♛
The large pale trumpet flowers are a welcome contrast to yellow.
❋ **Creamy white • Mid spring**
h. **40–60cm (16in–2ft)**

7 *N.* 'Geranium' ♛
A fragrant Tazetta bearing three or four flowers per stem.
✿ **Pure white with orange cup • Late spring •** *h.* **40cm (16in)**

8 *N.* 'Vulcan' ♛
A large-cupped daffodil with shapely and colourful flowers.
✿ **Yellow with vivid orange cup**
Mid spring • *h.* **45cm (1½ft)**

N. 'Tete-à-Tete'

N. cyclamineus

9 *N.* 'Cassata'
A split-Corona daffodil with the lemon-yellow inner petals held flat against the outer white ones.
✿ **Lemon yellow and white**
Mid spring • *h.* **40cm (16in)**

10 *N.* 'Telamonius Plenus'
A long-lived, old-fashioned variety, with double flowers.
✿ **Greenish yellow • Early spring**
h. **40cm (16in)**

11 *N. triandrus* ♛
The angel's tears daffodil tolerates dry conditions well and can be naturalised on dry, acid soil.
❋ **Cream • Mid spring**
h. **10–20cm (4–8in)**

Wonderfully versatile and always eye-catching, narcissi are easily grown in a wide range of settings from natural drifts to windowsill pots.

Although they are commonly known as daffodils, this term strictly only applies to the classic trumpet-shaped flowers, such as 'Spellbinder'. Other narcissi are correctly classified by flower shape, such as the large cupped 'Vulcan', or the species from which they are derived, such as 'Hawera' and 'Geranium'.

Daffodils need a reasonably well-drained soil, but should not dry out during the growing season, as this may prevent free-flowering. They will tolerate some shade, or full sun, but seldom flower well in deep shade.

Knee-deep in daffodils

Plant narcissi in informal drifts: blocks of a single variety look especially effective. An easy way to achieve a natural look is to toss the bulbs over an area, and plant each wherever it lands.

Each bulb will increase by division, but congested clumps may no longer flower freely. If this happens, lift the clump as the leaves fade, then separate the bulbs for immediate replanting.

Leave the leaves

Because seed production depletes the bulbs, fading flowers should be broken off. However, true-breeding species, such as *N. cyclamineus*, can be left to self-sow if you wish.

Resist the temptation to tidy up foliage after flowering, either by cutting it off or by tying it into a knot, as this will weaken the bulbs. Let the leaves die down naturally: this takes about eight weeks from the end of flowering.

The Essentials

Site demands Daffodils tolerate a range of soils and aspects. Most thrive in acid and alkaline soils, but some need acid conditions.

Planting practice Plant the bulbs in autumn. The hole should be three times the depth of the bulb.

Flowering time A selection of varieties will give flowers from winter to late spring.

Pests and diseases Largely trouble free, bulbs may rot in wet soils, or be eaten by narcissus eelworm or grubs of the narcissus fly. Fungal rot can be a problem.

Bonus point Many daffodils have sweetly fragrant flowers.

N. 'Mount Hood'

N. 'Geranium'

Nerine

Guernsey lilies bloom in autumn, to finish the year with a flourish. Although they are slightly tender in some gardens, nerines thrive in a place in the sun.

Expert's Selection

1 *N. bowdenii* ♀
Each tall stem carries up to eight funnel-shaped flowers.
✿ **Pink • Autumn • h. 45cm (1½ft)**

2 *N. bowdenii* 'Mark Fenwick' A hardy choice of a delicate-looking plant, which bears flowers on contrasting dark stalks.
✿ **Rose • Autumn • h. 50cm (20in)**

3 *N. bowdenii* 'Alba'
The ice-blue blooms make a cool contrast to the usual pink.
✿ **Bluish white • Autumn**
h. 50cm (20in)

STAR PERFORMER

N. bowdenii **The elegant rose-pink flowers, borne in small clusters, are a delight as the garden year winds down.**

The Essentials

Site demands Any soil as long as it is well drained, and in the sun.

Planting practice Plant the bulbs in early spring.

Flowering time Autumn.

Pests and diseases Slugs and snails are a common problem.

Bonus point Adds a splash of colour to the autumn border.

Native to South Africa, nerines are mostly rather tender in Western Europe, but the delicate blooms of *N. bowdenii* and its varieties are hardy enough to survive in the right conditions.

Well-drained soil, and a position in full sun are essential for a good display. The ideal site is in a narrow bed or border at the foot of a south or west-facing wall, where they will benefit from reflected heat and light. Plant the bulbs with their tips just below the soil surface.

Newly planted bulbs may not flower for a year of two; in fact they flower best when the bulbs have divided to form a slightly congested clump, so they should be left undisturbed. Very congested clumps can be lifted and separated in the summer.

In all but the warmest areas, it is wise to cover the bulbs with a thick dry mulch for added protection from frost in winter.

Ornithogalum

Star-of-Bethlehem appears in late spring and early summer. In most of these trouble-free species, the backs of the white petals are striped with green.

Expert's Selection

1 *O. umbellatum*
Short stems carry broad white flower clusters.
❀✿ White and green • Late spring–early summer • *h.* 30cm (1ft)

2 *O. narbonense*
Masses of starry flowers form a slender cluster on this tall plant.
❀ White • Late spring–early summer
h. 60cm (2ft)

3 *O. nutans*♀
An elegant species with one-sided clusters of slightly nodding flowers.
❀✿ White and green • Late spring–early summer • *h.* 45cm (1½ft)

4 *O. pyrenaicum*
This tall species is worth growing for its unusual flower colour.
✿✿ Pale yellow and green • Late spring–early summer • *h.* 1m (3ft)

The easy-going bulbs of ornithogalum can be planted and forgotten. They are easily satisfied by almost any soil and a sunny or partially shaded position, in which some will readily naturalise.

Plant bulbs in autumn or early spring, at a depth about the same as the bulb's height. They increase by seed and by offsets, and clumps can be lifted and divided in autumn. *O. umbellatum* may seed quite freely, its vigour making it suitable for naturalising in grass or under shrubs.

The Essentials

Site demands Suitable for any soil in sun or light shade.
Planting practice Plant the bulbs in autumn or spring.
Flowering time Late spring to early summer.
Pests and diseases Trouble free.
Bonus point Most are very hardy and thrive on neglect.

STAR PERFORMER
O. umbellatum **As tough as it is beautiful, this is perfect for a naturalistic setting.**

Oxalis

Bright, showy flowers in summer and autumn add style and colour to a border or rock garden.

Expert's Selection

1 *O. purpurea* 'Ken Aslet'
Vivid yellow flowers contrast with the dark green silky leaves.
✿ Yellow • Autumn and winter (with shelter) • *h.* 10cm (4in)

2 *O. adenophylla*♀
Large pink flowers with a deeper pink centre grow on short stems.
✿ Pink • Late spring
h. 10cm (4in)

3 *O. tetraphylla* 'Iron Cross'
This species takes its name from the striking purple-marked leaves.
✿ Reddish purple • Summer
h. 15cm (6in)

4 *O. bowiei*
Loose clusters of funnel-shaped flowers on a taller stem.
✿ Pink, with white or yellow eye
Summer • *h.* 20cm (8in)

The bulbous species of oxalis vary from perfectly hardy to rather tender, but all are easily grown, undemanding plants for a rock garden or the front of a border. All varieties require a sunny position and a well-drained soil. The more tender ones, like *O. tetraphylla* and *O. purpurea* need a very sheltered position, or can be grown in pots in a cold greenhouse.

Plant the bulbs in spring at a depth equal to their height. Bulbs grown in pots under glass should be kept almost dry in winter.

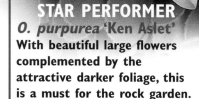

STAR PERFORMER
O. purpurea 'Ken Aslet'
With beautiful large flowers complemented by the attractive darker foliage, this is a must for the rock garden.

Most of the bulbous species increase by producing offsets, which can be separated if the clump is lifted for dividing in early spring.

The Essentials

Site demands Though hardy, oxalis needs full sun and a well-drained soil.
Planting practice Plant the bulbs in spring.
Flowering time Flowers tend to open in sunlight, from late spring to early autumn.
Pests and diseases Oxalis may be susceptible to rust disease.
Bonus point These low-growing free-spreading perennials will cover a bare patch in a border.

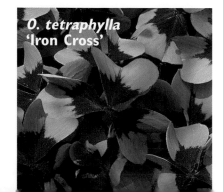
O. tetraphylla 'Iron Cross'

Puschkinia

Small spikes of pale blue flowers bring their own charm to any sunny position. Puschkinias grow happily in dry soils and will spread freely in a rock garden or between shrubs.

Closely related to the scillas, and sharing the common name, squills, puschkinias will grow in almost any soil as long as it is not waterlogged. However, they flower more freely in a sunny spot. Their diminutive size makes them ideal for a rock garden or for pots, and they will happily naturalise in the sunny spaces between deciduous shrubs.

Plant the bulbs 2.5–5cm (1–2in) deep, in autumn. Old congested clumps can be divided in summer, as the leaves die back. Puschkinias will often self-seed, so do not deadhead the plants.

Expert's Selection

1 *P. scilloides*
The hardiness of these bulbs is belied by their delicate-looking flowers, striped with a darker blue.
✿ **Pale blue with deeper blue stripe**
Spring • h. 15cm (6in)

2 *P. scilloides* var. *libanotica*
This white form can be grown on its own or mixed with the blue.
✿ **White • Spring • h. 15cm (6in)**

The Essentials

Site demands Any soil, but ideally well drained in full sun.
Planting practice Plant bulbs in autumn, about 5cm (2in) deep.
Flowering time The stubby flower spikes appear in spring.
Pests and diseases Trouble free.
Bonus point This pretty bulb grows happily in dry soils.

STAR PERFORMER
P. scilloides This dwarf bulb will enliven the ground beneath deciduous shrubs in springtime.

Scilla

Squills bring a touch of summer to the early spring garden with their luminous blues.

Expert's Selection

1 *S. siberica* 'Spring Beauty'
A vigorous variety with richly coloured flowers in short clusters.
✿ **Vivid blue • Early spring**
h. **15cm (6in)**

2 *S. bifolia* ♀
The violet starry flowers of this species have a delicate fragrance.
✿ **Violet-blue • Early spring**
h. 15cm (6in)

3 *S. mischtschenkoana*
The pale flowers with a dark stripe open almost at ground level.
✿ **Pale blue • Late winter–early spring • h. 10cm (4in)**

4 *S. peruviana*
This taller plant has broad conical heads, but needs sun and warmth.
✿ **Deep violet • Early summer**
h. **30cm (1ft)**

5 *S. autumnalis*
Starry flowers bloom in autumn.
✿ **Pinky lilac • Early autumn**
h. **25cm (10in)**

The Essentials

Site demands Any well-drained soil in sun or light shade.
Planting practice Plant in early autumn about 5cm (2in) deep.
Flowering time Late winter to summer, and autumn.
Pests and diseases Trouble free.
Bonus point Scillas look lovely naturalised under trees or in grass.

STAR PERFORMER
S. siberica 'Spring Beauty'
With its intensely blue flowers, this easy variety really lives up to its name.

Different scillas provide colour from late winter into summer; one, *S. autumnalis*, even flowers in autumn. They really come into their own when they are allowed to naturalise in drifts beneath shrubs and trees or in grass, but are also very effective planted in containers.

Most species thrive happily in any well-drained, fertile soil in sun or dappled shade, although *S. peruviana* needs full sun and a warm site to survive. Plant bulbs in autumn, preferably in loose drifts. Most scillas self-seed, so do not deadhead them and in time they may spread over a wide area. You can lift and divide established clumps in summer or early autumn.

Tulipa

Tulips are unmatched for a glorious springtime display of grace. They come in a huge range of colours, from pure white to a purply black, with most shades in between. The most care-free tulips of all are the many small species, which can be simply planted and left undisturbed.

Expert's Selection

1 *T. praestans* 'Fusilier'♥
This colourful variety is vigorous and long-lived in the garden.
✿ **Brilliant red • Early spring**
h. **30cm (1ft)**

2 *T. saxatilis*
A fragrant and long-stemmed tulip that spreads by runners.
✿ **Lilac-pink with yellow centre**
Late spring • *h.* 35cm (14in)

3 *T. turkestanica*♥
Up to 10 flowers are borne on each stem of this vigorous species.
❀ **Creamy white • Winter–early spring • *h.* 30cm (1ft)**

4 *T. greigii*
All the greigii tulips have large attractive, purple-marked leaves. 'Toronto'♥ flowers rose-red, while 'Zampa'♥ is a primrose-yellow.
✿ **Yellow, pink or red • Mid–late spring • *h.* 15–35cm (6–14in)**

T. sprengeri

STAR PERFORMER

T. praestans 'Fusilier'♥ **With up to four vivid red blooms on each stem, this variety will add impact to any garden.**

5 *T. urumiensis*♥
This appealing dwarf species has large star-shaped flowers.
✿ **Yellow, tinged lilac on outside**
Early spring • *h.* 15cm (6in)

6 *T. 'Red Riding Hood'*♥
The vivid flowers contrast with striking maroon-mottled leaves.
✿ **Red with black base inside**
Early spring • *h.* 20cm (8in)

7 *T. sprengeri*♥
A dainty tulip with fiery heads, *T. sprengeri* spreads by seeds, so there is no need to deadhead.
✿✿ **Red or orange-red • Early summer • *h.* 30cm (1ft)**

8 *T. tarda* ♥
Starry flowers carried on short stems open wide in full sun.
✿ **Yellow petals with white tips**
Mid spring • *h.* 15cm (6in)

9 *T. humilis*
Large rounded flowers grow above a rosette of grey-green leaves.
✿ **Purplish pink • Late winter–early spring • *h.* 15cm (6in)**

10 *T. sylvestris*
These fragrant starry flowers do best in light tree shade.
✿ **Yellow • Mid spring • *h.* 30cm (1ft)**

There is so much more to tulips than the tall hybrid varieties seen in parks and gardens. Though easily grown, such plants are often short-lived, and for this reason tend to be treated as bedding plants.

For an interesting and care-free selection, choose from the smaller varieties: those listed on these pages are especially trouble free, as well as being vigorous and long-lived. Simply plant them, and then leave them undisturbed. Several will naturalise, increasing by offsets, runners or bulbs.

The flowers of many species tulips are cup-shaped like the traditional cultivars, but some have star-shaped flowers that open wide in bright sun. They might have a big splash of a second colour inside, like *T. tarda* with its bright yellow zone.

In certain species, such as *T. turkestanica*, one stem may bear several flowers, giving a delightfully informal look. A number of varieties, including *T. saxatilis*, have a sweet fragrance, most noticeable on a still, warm spring day.

When and where to plant

All tulips need a fertile soil that drains readily: waterlogged bulbs will simply rot. If you have heavy soil, adding some coarse grit and humus will help enormously.

All the species listed here need a site in full sun, in which they will flower most freely, and the flowers will open more widely.

Plant the bulbs nice and deep in autumn – November is the best time – at about 15–20cm (6–8in), and even deeper in light sandy soils. You will achieve the most natural effect by placing the bulbs in small, irregular groups, with 10–15cm (4–6in) between them. Once planted, the bulbs should be left undisturbed.

Unless you have planted *T. sprengeri*, which spreads by seed, it is best to deadhead immediately after flowering. Well-established clumps will slowly increase by offsets from the bulbs. Unusually, *T. saxatilis* spreads by runners.

Growing tulips in containers

Though tulips are easily grown in the open garden, they also flourish in containers. Large pots planted with these and other bulbs can brighten the smallest patio in spring. Plant the bulbs in a well-drained, soil-based compost and after they have flowered, plant them out in the garden for another year.

Pests and other problems

Most dwarf tulips are trouble free, but slugs are especially partial to the flowers of greigii tulips. Tulip fire is a common fungal disease, leaving brown spots on the petals. Some people develop an allergy to tulips, so handle bulbs with care.

T. turkestanica

T. tarda

T. greigii

The Essentials

Site demands All of these tulips grow easily in a fertile, well-drained soil and full sun.

Planting practice Plant the bulbs deeply in mid to late autumn.

Flowering time Tulips provide some of the most brilliant colours throughout spring.

Pests and diseases Slugs damage some tulips and fungal diseases can be a problem.

Bonus point Tulips, especially those with a sweet scent, are a great addition to an alpine garden.

T. saxatilis

care-free

features

Designing a lawn for easy care

Its shape and style, and your choice of grass mixture can help to make
your lawn care free. If your site is not well suited to growing grass,
make life easier for yourself by choosing an alternative to the conventional
lawn, such as a wild-flower meadow, a paved area or a gravel garden.

Make mowing easy

Sweeping curves Designing a lawn with curves
rather than straight lines will minimise the number
of times you will have to stop and turn the mower.
A perfect circle of grass in a small garden will look
striking, be quick to mow and leave deep beds in the
corners of the garden for planting.

Remove obstacles Island beds or trees growing
in the lawn will slow you down as you mow. Make
sure that any paths or steppingstones are at a level
slightly lower than the grass, so that the mower can
pass over the top without damaging the blades.

Lay a mowing strip Edge the lawn with bricks
or paving, laid lower than the grass, to cut down
on time spent trimming the lawn edges. Make it
wide enough to double as a wet-weather path.

Choose grass that will thrive

For the most care-free lawn, avoid the finest grass
mixes, which need constant mowing, feeding,
watering and weeding to look good. If in doubt
about the best mixture to choose, ask your garden
centre for advice, or ring the customer services
department of the firm supplying the seed – look
for the number on the bag or box.

Everyday grass A utility mix is quite satisfactory
for most lawns. It will remain healthy with the
minimum of care and will cope well with heavy
use in every season. Modern grass mixes contain
species that are attractive, hard wearing and require
minimal maintenance.

A lawn in shade Choose a special shade mixture
for areas of lawn in light or dappled shade. These
grasses will tolerate lower light levels and often drier
soil conditions than others. Some are also drought
resistant and suitable for areas of low rainfall.

Lay steppingstones
lower than the grass

Consider all the alternatives

In some situations, such as in dense dry shade, grass
will never grow well. It is easier to try something
different than to persevere in trying to make a lawn.

Wild-flower meadows Turn over a section of your
garden to nature, by choosing wild flowers that suit
your soil and allowing them to spread.

Hard landscaping It is hardly worth buying a
mower for a tiny garden, so consider laying paving
or decking and using pots for colour and interest.

Gravel In a hot dry garden, gravel makes an
attractive complement for sun-loving plants.

*Lawns with
smooth curves
and brick edges
(above) are quick
and easy to cut.*

*For truly care-free
ground cover, a
pretty wild-flower
meadow (right) is
hard to beat.*

In dry gardens, gravel with low plants growing through it (left) may be more care-free than a lawn of grass.

Paving and planted pots decorate a small dark corner (below), where grass would struggle to survive.

Making the care-free lawn

A lawn pristine enough for playing croquet may be beyond the reach of most amateur gardeners, but it is perfectly possible to have a good-looking lawn without becoming a slave to it. All that is needed is some careful preparation at the outset and a little regular maintenance.

Planning for the perfect lawn

Careful preparation of the ground before you lay a new lawn will pay dividends in time saved later on maintenance. A smooth, level surface is important for achieving a professional finish, but will also make mowing the lawn easier. Equally, removing perennial weeds from a bare site is far less work than digging them out of an established lawn.

Seed or turf? Sowing seed is the most cost effective and least backbreaking way to create a lawn. It is also the best method if you need a particular kind of grass for your site. However, laying turf gives faster results, needs little attention to get established and is ready to walk on much sooner than seed.

Some turf suppliers sell treated meadow turf, which is very popular, because it is fast to establish. However, it contains coarse and quick-growing species that can make a lawn difficult to maintain and keep in good condition; also it often introduces pests and diseases to the garden, so is best avoided.

Timing The best time to lay a lawn is in early September, when the ground is moist and warm, and there is enough rain to encourage seeds to germinate quickly and turf roots to develop. Grass seed will not germinate during hot, dry weather or between the end of September and April, but turf can be laid at any time except during drought, frost and snow.

Preparing the ground It is important to remove all perennial weeds, particularly grassy ones, such as couch grass (twitch), before laying a lawn. The easiest way of doing this is to allow the weeds to grow to a height of 30cm (1ft), then treat them with a glyphosate-based weedkiller. Once all the weeds are dead, remove them from the lawn area.

If you prefer not to use chemicals, dig out the weeds, being careful not to leave any small pieces of root behind, as these may grow back and prove very difficult to eradicate from a new lawn.

Laying turf A turfed lawn gives an instant effect and, if laid correctly, should need no more maintenance than regular mowing. Follow these six steps to success.

Before you start, dig the area to around 20cm (8in) deep, breaking up hard sub-soil that might hinder drainage. Allow the soil to settle for a week or so.

1 Buy turf no thicker than 1.6 cm (⅝in). The roots will have been trimmed to encourage new roots to develop and help the lawn to establish quickly.

2 Rake the ground level, picking out any large stones.

3 Firm the soil with your heels, making sure not to leave any bumps or hollows that will make mowing difficult.

4 Work off a plank to protect the level soil and carefully unroll the turf.

5 Stagger the joints, row by row, to avoid 'fault lines', where the grass will be vulnerable to cracking.

6 Tamp down the grass using firm strokes applied with the back of a spade.

1 Thin turf establishes quickly

2 Rake the ground level

3 Firm the soil

4 Unroll the turf

5 Stagger joints

6 Tamp down with a spade

Easy lawn maintenance

A well-prepared and carefully laid lawn will need very little work to keep it looking good. Follow this simple advice for a professional look.

Mowing Cut your lawn regularly – a quick trim twice a week is better for the grass than a scalping every ten days. Use the highest setting for the first and last cuts of the season, but never cut a lawn too short, as this will encourage moss to grow and give weed seeds a chance to take hold. Leave the grass at least 2.5cm (1in) long in summer and 3.8cm (1½in) in spring and autumn.

Leave clippings If the lawn is not cut short, grass should easily grow through the clippings, which will break down to form humus in the top layer of soil. In hot, dry periods the cuttings make a protective mulch for the grass. If the clippings matt together to form a thatch of dead grass, remove it with a scarifier attached to your mower or manually, with a spring-tined rake.

Feeding A new lawn should not need feeding for the first season, but thereafter, use a lawn fertiliser. For low maintenance, avoid feeds that encourage sudden bursts of growth, but a tired-looking lawn can be boosted with a fast-acting liquid feed. Slow-release fertilisers feed throughout the growing season and provide maximum results with minimum effort. Apply the fertiliser in spring, again in midsummer and follow up with a special autumn feed to toughen up the grass.

Weeding A perfectly weed-free lawn demands constant maintenance, but a regularly cut, properly fed lawn can contain a few weeds without looking

Rake out thatch

Lawn protector helps in areas with heavy wear

Spike wet ground

Leave grass clippings on the lawn

unkempt. However, if broad-leaved, perennial weeds become a problem, dig them out with a sharp blade, or spot-treat them with a lawn weedkiller. A combined feed and weed may seem an attractive option, but it is usually more efficient to apply each separately, where they are needed most.

Moss If the surface of the lawn is compacted, the soil unusually moist, or the grass is cut too short, moss can develop. Spiking the lawn with shoe attachments (left) or a fork will let in air and help to reduce moss growth. Moss under trees can be alleviated by raising the crown of the tree or thinning the branches to let light in. If moss continues to be a problem, it is probably better to replace the lawn with suitable shade or moisture-tolerant plants.

Heavy wear Children playing on a wet lawn, or people or pets walking across a lawn all year round, particularly on poorly drained soil, can wear down the grass. Laying strips of lawn protector – a wire mesh that the grass grows through and hides – will help to keep the lawn in good condition.

Planning the care-free pond

Many gardens are suitable for a pond or other water feature, and these are hard to beat as a source of tranquillity, especially during the warm summer months. Plan, plant and stock thoughtfully and you will discover that it is quite possible to have a pond without a lot of hard work.

Size, shape and position

Size A medium sized pond is the easiest to maintain. Very large ponds can be hard to access, while small ones of less than 3.5m² (40sq ft) require constant attention to keep them in check.

Construction Modern ponds are often constructed with a pre-formed rigid liner, or a flexible sheet. Concrete ponds are hard work to build and may crack and leak, particularly on soft soils. Rigid liners offer a range of designs, but the hole must be accurately dug and back-filled. With a flexible liner you can create a pond to your own requirements, but without the need for such precision. Always use a guaranteed long-life liner – never polythene which quickly becomes brittle and starts to leak in sunlight.

Position Choose an open position, out of dense shade and away from any tree canopy. Trees constantly shed bits which will rot and pollute the water if not removed. Ideally the pond should be positioned where leaves will not blow into it in autumn, but in all but the largest gardens, this is not usually possible. A successful pond will need at least some sunshine during the day.

Don't dig too deep To accommodate the range of plants needed for a balanced pond (right), the water at its deepest point should be 45cm (1½ft), but have shelves at different depths. Shallow ponds require frequent topping up, and very deep ones are difficult to clean, can be dangerous, and restrict the species of plant that can be grown.

Water for pleasure Water gardens do not have to be planted or include fish. A shallow rill, perhaps with a pump to move the water, will add a feeling of tranquillity to any garden, and needs very little maintenance. Alternatively, a raised tank with a wide brick surround provides a place to sit and dip your hands on a hot day.

Splash through a shallow rill

A small pond (above) in an ideal situation sports a wide range of planting. A tiny alpine bed makes an interesting contrast just above the pond.

Glorious rose red water lilies (Nymphaea 'Attraction') thrive on the surface of this large pond but do not overwhelm it (left). The pond is edged with reeds.

Choosing the plants

Select plants with a restrained growth habit for easy care. Rampant ones, while quickly giving a mature effect, soon outgrow their space.

To keep the water clear, always include at least one submerged oxygenating plant, which will release vital oxygen into the water. Cover about half the surface with floating flat-leaved plants, such as water lilies, to stop the water turning green in bright sun. To finish, choose a few marginal plants for the edges.

Oxygenators

- **Callitriche hermaphroditica** Tiny, dark green leaves stay active even in winter.
- **Ceratophyllum demersum** (hornwort) Like a tiny bottle-brush when in leaf, it sinks to the bottom as buds in winter.
- **Fontinalis antipyretica** (willow moss) With dark green feathery foliage, it is an excellent spawning ground for fish.

Floating aquatics

- **Hydrocharis morsus-ranae** (frog-bit) Round, bright green, leaves are dotted with tiny white flowers. Sinks in winter.
- **Stratiotes aloides** (water soldier) Foliage like a pineapple top surfaces in summer.

Water lilies

- **Nymphaea 'Albatross'** Milky white flowers and bronze-tinted leaves with red undersides.
- **N. 'Pink Sensation'** Bears lots of clear pink flowers. Bright green leaves have red undersides.
- **N. 'Paul Hariot'** Clear yellow flowers, shaded coppery red.

Other deep water aquatics

- **Nymphoides peltata** (floating heart, water fringe) Bright yellow flowers and tiny floating leaves. Plant in a crate of its own.
- **Aponogeton distachyos** (water hawthorn) Produces fragrant white flowers nearly all year round. Leaves are shaped rather like elongated water lily leaves.

Marginals

- **Alisma plantago-aquatica** (water plantain) Thrives in shallow water but it is best suited to large ponds, because the flower spikes grow to 1m (3ft).
- **Caltha palustris** (marsh marigold) Gold, starry blooms for the water's edge. (See page 102).

Nymphaea 'Pink Sensation'

Stratoites aloides

Caltha palustris

Nymphoides peltata

- **Hypericum elodes** (marsh St John's Wort) Good for softening hard edges. Has yellow flowers.
- **Veronica beccabunga** Bright green, glossy foliage and vivid blue summer flowers.
- **Acorus calamnus 'Variegatus'** (variegated sweet flag) Produces stiff, grassy, cream and green, aromatic leaves 1m (3ft) tall, from pink and cream spring shoots.

Planting & pond maintenance

With the right planting and an open site your pond will thrive with the minimum of care. Very often, the best way to look after a pond is to leave it alone: just skim off any stray leaves or petals, turn on a pump to move the water around and it should be fine.

Planting practice The best time to plant a pond is between May and September. At this time the water is at its warmest and the plants are growing strongly.

Put plants in planting crates for easy maintenance. Each crate can be removed from the water and the plants in it divided and replanted when necessary, without the need to drain the entire pond.

Most aquatic centres supply water plants in individual plastic crates that are suitable for putting straight into a pond, but larger crates are available and make it easier to achieve attractive and natural-looking mixed plantings.

Traditional planting crates have large holes in their sides and should be lined with hessian before planting to contain the soil or compost.

Modern planting crates have fine mesh sides. This means you can plant straight into them without lining the container first. However, in practice it is a good idea to line the inside with old tights or something similar, to help prevent fine soil particles escaping and clouding the water.

❶ **Use a heavy garden soil**

❷ **Put in the plants**

❸ **Gravel weighs down the soil**

❹ **Lower into the water**

❺ **Make sure the crate is at the correct depth**

Follow these simple steps for planting a mixed crate.

❶ **Use a heavy garden soil** or specially formulated aquatic compost. These will encourage water plants to root firmly.
❷ **Place the plants in the crate** at the same depth as they were in their original crates.
❸ **Cover the compost with gravel** to prevent the water washing off the surface soil.

❹ **Lower the crate** into the water. Long plastic pond gloves are useful, particularly in deep water.
❺ **Make sure that the crate is at the correct depth** for the plants and that it is firm and level on the bottom or pond shelf. Marginal plants, such as *Acorus calamus* and *Caltha palustris* need their foliage to be just above the water's surface, while other water plants prefer to be completely submerged (see page 333).

Moving water stays clean longer

Fish add a flash of bright colour

Maintaining your pond

The two biggest problems in ponds are algae, which turn the water green, and blanket weed.
• **Algae** can be avoided by siting your pond away from full sun. However, it is rarely a problem once a pond is established.
• **Blanket weed** can be inadvertently introduced on new aquatic plants. Buy blocks of barley straw and float on the water's surface to reduce it.

Moving water Algae and blanket weed are rarely a problem in moving water. Fit a pump with a filter (connected to the mains via a RCD, see page 11) and a fountain or waterfall to keep the water moving. This should be kept running throughout the brighter months of the year.

Raking Clear blanket weed by raking it off the surface. Another effective technique is to twirl it round a cane, like candyfloss, and lift it out.

Scoop up fallen leaves

Green water A newly filled pond may be green for a few days, or even weeks, until the water has become 'aired', but the problem nearly always rights itself automatically.

Water level Regular rainfall normally compensates for water lost through evaporation, but in very long periods of dry weather you may need to top up your pond with fresh tap water to keep plants and fish alive.

Cleaning out It is usually only necessary to clean a pond if it has become so polluted with decaying organic material for it to be a danger to fish, or if it begins to look unsightly. This should be done either in spring or summer. Cutting back water plants as they start to die off and removing leaves from the water's surface (see below) will help to prevent the water becoming polluted.

Autumn care Falling leaves will invariably blow into the pond during autumn and early winter, however hard you try to site your pond away from overhanging trees. If a lot of leaves fall on the water, scoop them off in a daily trawl with a net to stop them sinking to the bottom, where they will rot, and give off gases which may harm wildlife and fish. A simple way to reduce your work in subsequent years is to cover the surface of your pond with mesh netting for autumn. Lift it off periodically and clear away the leaves.

Fish and wildlife Let a new pond settle for a few weeks to reduce chlorine levels and allow plants to root in well before introducing fish.

• **Choose fish** with few special needs for a care-free pond. Ask an aquatic centre for advice.
• **Summer is the best time** to introduce fish, when the water is at its warmest.
• **Do not overstock** at the beginning, because healthy fish will soon start to breed.
• **If the pond ices over** fish will survive for short periods near the bottom, the pool is deep enough, and the water is clean. Float a ball in the water in winter and remove it in a freeze, leaving a hole in the ice, which will allow air to reach the water.
• **Small ponds** may benefit from a heater to keep the water just above freezing for the fish.
• **Wildlife** is attracted to a pond with sloping sides. Frogs might move in if there are places to shelter, though they are wary of fish, which may eat them; mating frogs, by contrast, can harm fish.

Creating a container garden

With containers you can grow a garden full of interest in every season without a lot of hard work. Plant a series of pots to bloom at different times, keep them in an out-of-the-way corner, feed and water them occasionally, then bring them to centre stage when their moment of glory arrives.

Tips for successful containers

Plain pots, glazed bowls, window boxes, hanging baskets, chimney pots, and even wheelbarrows – the range of plant containers is vast. Pots can give small plants prominence, add colour to paved areas or walls and keep plants safe from slugs and snails.

Size and site Large containers are generally more care-free than small ones, which dry out fast in hot weather, but position can also minimise the attention pots require. Baskets and tubs next to the house may be in a rain shadow and need watering more than those in the open and those standing on slabs can be baked by reflected heat at the height of summer.

Grouped together Single containers can be very effective when planted with something sculptural (see box) or attention-grabbing, but pots also work in groups. Try to keep to a simple colour scheme in the plants or containers, and introduce variety with shapes and textures, as you would in a bed. Grouping pots can also create a microclimate, providing wind protection and increasing humidity.

Create a focal point Whether you are planting a single pot or a group, aim to include a mix of plants with different growth habits. Erect or bushy plants work best in the centre of a display, with spreading or trailing ones towards the edge. If the containers are to be grouped, choose a single large shrub as the centrepiece, with a mix of complemenary lower growing and trailing plants around it.

In the borders Pots do not have to be confined to the patio: a blooming container is the perfect way to fill a gap in the border when something has finished flowering. Growing bulbs in pots and dropping them into place when they flower keeps your borders free for bedding plants, reduces the likelihood of spiking your bulbs with a fork as you work and keeps them safe from digging squirrels.

Plant requirements Be careful to group only plants that share the same requirements. Plant a shade-loving fern or hosta with heat-demanding annuals, and one or other will always be unhappy, whether the pot is positioned in sun or shade.

Group containers to create a 'border' effect

Grasses spray out of straight-sided pots

Sculptural plants look great in pots that emphasise their sharp silhouettes. Go for hard edges, straight lines and try stone or metals.

Palms and succulents that will not survive winter in the ground can be protected in pots. Wrap the pot in bubble polythene or move it indoors until the frosts have passed. Try these plants for a little drama.

- ***Agave filifera*** ♀ Spiny grey-green fleshy lances. *h.* 45cm (1½ft) *s.* 60cm (2ft)
- ***Aloe vera*** ♀ Succulent grey-green foliage. *h.&s.* 60cm (2ft)
- ***Chamaerops humilis*** ♀ Dwarf fan palm. *h.&s.* 1m (3ft)
- ***Cordyline australis*** ♀ Sprays of green to purple lance-like leaves. *h.&s.* 1.8m (6ft)
- ***Cortaderia selloana* 'Pumila'** ♀ Dwarf pampas grass with cream feathery plumes. *h.&s.* 1.5m (5ft)
- ***Dicksonia antarctica*** ♀ Tree fern. *h.* 6m (20ft) *s.* 2.4m (8ft)
- ***Echeveria elegans*** ♀ Fleshy alabaster white rosettes. *h.* 15cm (6in) *s.* 30cm (1ft)

Recipes for success

Try these combinations of plants in containers or experiment with groupings of your own.

A tub for a shady corner
Elegant lilies will rise above a collar of white *Impatiens* and soft green *Alchemilla mollis*. Choose a medium height white lily from the Asiatic Group Kiss Series (see page 318).

Baking in the sun Hot colours suit hot sites. Fill a large tub with yellow, sun-loving annuals, such as *Helichrysum petiolare*, *Bidens* and *Tagetes*. Add a splash of red with a *Begonia*.

A hanging basket Keep it simple with just one type of plant, such as trailing petunias, in differing shades of a colour to give your baskets a touch of sophistication. Solid sides will help a basket to retain moisture.

In an open site A combination of white *Antirrhinums*, *Limonium* and *Pelargoniums* shrug off a battering by wind and rain. Silver foliage plants, such as *Stachys*, reflect the harsh rays of the sun and help to keep the plant cool.

A window box for winter Brighten your outlook on a dull day with a trough of bright winter pansies mixed with early-flowering dwarf *Narcissus*.

Solid baskets mean less watering

Lilies light up a shady corner

Tough flowers stand up in an open site

Planting a care-free container

Putting together container displays can be great fun, as you can be more adventurous with these short-term plantings than in an established border. Pick a suitable pot, fill it with the right compost and follow these simple planting tips, and you can create a wonderful easy-care container display.

Choosing the right pot

If you are planning an all-year display, choose a robust pot. Frost-proof terracotta is long-lasting, will keep the root-ball cool and moist in summer, and is unlikely to be blown over in wild weather.

Watering (see far right) is crucial to keep your containers looking good, but your choice of pot can lighten the load. Less water will evaporate from glazed terracotta than from an unglazed pot and plastic retains water even better – so well that over-watering can be a risk. Solid-sided hanging baskets, rather than wire, will also reduce water loss.

Choose heavy, frost-proof terracotta

Container composts

For easy-care container gardening, choose compost that is specially formulated with additional elements for container-grown plants.

Moisture is vital, and many container composts contain water-retaining crystals which swell up when wet (below) to keep the compost moist.

Plant food will help to ensure a good display, so buy compost containing a slow-release fertiliser. If you make your own compost, add some to the mix.

Pest control is included in some container composts. Look for one that will protect from vine weevils: the most common container pest.

Crystals swell to a gel with added water

Planting tips

Good drainage Make sure that there are several drainage holes in the bottom of the pot, then put a generous layer of drainage crocks in the base – to about one tenth of the pot's height. Use bits of old pot, gravel, broken up polystyrene plant trays or anything similar that will prevent the compost from blocking the drainage holes.

Start with crocks for good drainage

Choose plants with the container in mind If you are shopping for both together, choose the pot first and wheel it around the garden centre with you as you select the plants to go in it.

Annuals and bedding plants The traditional choices for containers are short-lived, but many shrubs and even small trees also make excellent container plants. For example, purple-leaved heucheras or many fuchsias, will grow well in pots and can be surrounded by a few 'cheap and cheerful' annuals, such as *Nigella* or petunias. Shrubs grown for foliage such as *Buxus*, which is often clipped into a formal shape, and some dwarf conifers, can also make excellent long-term planting in suitable containers, but will need an annual feed.

A dense display Plants can be grouped more closely in pots than borders because they are often intended only as temporary displays, but resist the temptation to cram the pot with plants. Congested pots will need constant watering and feeding and the cramped conditions will encourage pests and disease.

Plan to keep pots care-free Minimise the attention your containers require by choosing the plants carefully. For containers on a hot and sunny patio, drought-resistant varieties such as lavender or *Sisyrinchium* are a good choice and will reduce the need for watering in dry weather. Similarly, plants that do not need regular dead-heading have an advantage over those, such as pansies and violets, whose flowering soon suffers if the spent blooms are not frequently removed.

Position plants carefully Put plants in compost at the same depth as they were in their original pots. Place tall plants in the centre of the pot and floppy or trailing varieties around the edge.

Finish off with a decorative mulch

Finish with a mulch A 2.5cm (1in) thick layer of mulch will reduce water loss from the surface and make weeds easy to pull out. Gravel is ideal, but be imaginative (left) with shells, bark, small pieces of broken crockery, recycled glass chippings or painted pebbles.

Raise containers off the ground Stand pots on feet, gravel or pieces of broken pot to allow water to drain away from the holes in the base. This will also discourage insects and worms from burrowing into the compost.

Feeding and watering

Even easy-care containers will need some attention if they are to look their best all season. Food and water are their main requirements.

Slow-release fertiliser is incorporated in most container composts and should sustain the plants for a season, but a weak liquid feed of general purpose fertiliser, given once a fortnight when the plants are in flower, will help to sustain the display.

Permanent displays need to be fed in spring. Scatter on a top-dressing of slow-release feed or push fertiliser pellets (top) into the compost.

Large containers require less water than small pots, which dry out fast and need watering at least once a day in summer. Soak them until water emerges from the holes in the base of the pot. Hanging baskets will benefit from an occasional thorough wetting: simply sit them in a bucket of water.

Self-watering containers (right) help to minimise watering in summer. However, they are less suitable for use in autumn and winter, when they tend to make the compost too wet.

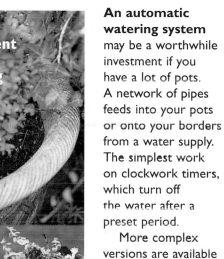

Feed permanent displays in spring

Give baskets a good drink

An automatic watering system may be a worthwhile investment if you have a lot of pots. A network of pipes feeds into your pots or onto your borders from a water supply. The simplest work on clockwork timers, which turn off the water after a preset period.

More complex versions are available with an electronic programmer. However, none of the systems makes any allowance for the weather, and the same amount of water is delivered on a hot dry day as during a storm.

Self-watering pots make for easy care. A reservoir in the base holds water and a layer of matting draws the moisture up into the compost. Many incorporate a tube for easy watering.

Seasonal directory

If a gap in your garden needs a splash of summer pink or you want to add winter colour, this directory of plants will help to narrow your search for a solution. Pick a season, look for flowers, foliage, berries or bark, choose a colour, then turn to the pages indicated for more information.

Spring

Flowers

Herbaceous perennials

Ajuga ❀ Blue ➤p.89
Aquilegia ❀ White, pink, violet, blue, red and two tones ➤p.93
Bergenia ❀ Pink ➤p.100
Brunnera ❀ Shades of blue ➤p.101
Caltha ❀ Yellow ➤p.102
Dicentra ❀ White, pink, red and two tones ➤p.108
Doronicum ❀ Shades of yellow ➤p.109
Epimedium ❀ Shades of yellow ➤p.112
Euphorbia ❀ Green, yellow, orange ➤pp.118–119
Helleborus ❀ White, pink, purple, violet ➤pp.130–131
Iris ❀ White, pink, blue, purple, yellow two tones ➤pp.136–137
Knifophia ❀ Yellow, orange, red, greeny yellow ➤p.138
Paeonia ❀ White, yellow, shades of pink, red, magenta ➤p.154
Phlox ❀ White, pink, purple, white, violet-blue ➤p.157
Primula ❀ White, lilac, mauve, purple, pink, yellow, blue, two tones ➤p.161
Pulmonaria ❀ White, pale blue, pink, violet, red, dark blue ➤p.163
Symphytum ❀ Yellow, pink, purple, white ➤p.171
Tiarella ❀ White, pink ➤p.175
Waldsteinia ❀ Yellow ➤p.179

Climbers and shrubs

Akebia ❀ Maroon ➤p.182
Amelanchier ❀ White ➤p.183
Camellia ❀ White, pink, red ➤pp.192–193
Ceanothus ❀ Blue, pale pink ➤p.194
Chaenomeles ❀ Pink and white, apricot, shades of red ➤p.197
Choisya ❀ White ➤p.197
Clematis ❀ White, shades of pink, blue, purple, red and yellow ➤pp.198–199
Corylus ❀ Purple and yellow catkins ➤p.201
Cytisus ❀ White, shades of yellow, two tones, red-orange ➤p.202
Escallonia ❀ Pink, crimson ➤p.204
Exochorda ❀ White ➤p.206
Forsythia ❀ Yellow ➤p.206
Garrya ❀ Silver, red, purple and green catkins ➤p.208
Heaths and heathers ❀ White, pink, lavender, crimson ➤pp.210–211
Jasminum ❀ Yellow ➤p.218
Kerria ❀ Golden yellow ➤p.220
Kolkwitzia ❀ Shades of pink ➤p.220
Lonicera ❀ White, yellow, pink ➤pp.224–225
Magnolia ❀ White, shades of pink and purple ➤p.226
Osmanthus ❀ White ➤p.228
Paeonia ❀ White, pink, red, purple, maroon, yellow ➤p.229
Philadelphus ❀ White ➤p.232
Phlomis ❀ Yellow ➤p.232
Prunus ❀ White, pink, red ➤p.235
Ribes ❀ White, pink, yellow, red ➤p.237
Rhododendron ❀ White, cream, yellow, pink, red, purple, violet ➤pp.238–239
Rosa ❀ Huge variety of colours ➤pp.240–245
Rosmarinus ❀ Blue, grey ➤p.246
Salix ❀ Yellow, pink, black catkins ➤p.247
Sarcococca ❀ Ivory ➤p.249
Skimmia ❀ White, cream, pink ➤p.250
Spiraea ❀ White, pink ➤pp.252–253
Syringa ❀ White, pink, lilac, shades of deep pink and red ➤p.254

Tamarix ❀ Two-toned pink and green, deep pink and reddish brown ➤p.255
Ulex ❀ Yellow ➤p.257
Vinca ❀ White, blue, purple ➤p.259
Weigela ❀ White, pink, red ➤p.259

Trees

Crataegus ❀ White, red, pink ➤p.266
Malus ❀ White, pink, rose-red, purple ➤p.269
Prunus ❀ White, shades of pink ➤p.270
Pyrus ❀ White, creamy white ➤p.271
Robinia ❀ White, pink ➤p.271
Salix ❀ Grey and greeny yellow catkins ➤p.272
Sorbus ❀ White, pale pink ➤p.273

Annuals

Erysimum ❀ Cream, orange, red, yellow ➤p.249
Myosotis ❀ White, blue, pink ➤p.289
Osteospermum ❀ White, pink, purple, yellow, orange ➤p.291
Tagetes ❀ Yellow, orange, red ➤p.299
Viola ❀ Multi tones in shades of yellow, white, violet, blue, cream ➤p.301

Bulbs

Chionodoxa ❀ Pink, white, blue, two tones ➤p.308
Convallaria ❀ White, pink ➤p.309
Cyclamen ❀ Pink, white, purple ➤p.311
Eranthis ❀ Yellow ➤p.314
Hyacinthoides ❀ White, shades of blue, pink, violet ➤p.316
Hyacinthus ❀ White, pink, shades of blue, yellow, red ➤p.316
Iris ❀ Blue, purple, yellow ➤p.317
Muscari ❀ Blue, white ➤p.319
Narcissus ❀ White, yellow ➤p.320
Oxalis ❀ Yellow, pink, purple ➤p.322
Puschkinia ❀ White, pale blue ➤p.323
Scilla ❀ Shades of blue ➤p.323
Tulipa ❀ White, shades of pink, red, yellow ➤pp.324–325

Foliage

Herbaceous perennials

Artemesia ∅ Grey, silver, yellow, green ➤p.94
Epimedium ∅ Bronze, copper, orange, shades of green ➤p.112
Euphorbia ∅ Green, red, blue-green ➤pp.118–119

Ferns ∅ Shades of green and brown ➤pp.116–117
Grasses ∅ Various ➤pp.126–127
Hosta ∅ Shades of green, grey, blue, variegated ➤pp.134–135
Houttuynia ∅ Red, yellow, dark green, blue-green ➤p.135
Lamium ∅ Green, silvery, variegated ➤p.139
Ophiopogon ∅ Purple-black, variegated, green ➤p.153
Pulmonaria ∅ Variegated green with silvery spots and stripes ➤p.163
Sempervivum ∅ Blue-green, red and green, light green ➤p.168
Stachys ∅ Green, grey ➤p.170

Climbers and shrubs

Abies ∅ Green, silvery blue, golden yellow ➤p.182
Akebia ∅ Green ➤p.182
Amelanchier ∅ Copper, red ➤p.183
Artemesia ∅ Silvery grey, grey-green deep green ➤p.184
Aucuba ∅ Greeny gold, dark green ➤p.185
Bamboos ∅ Green, bright yellow and green variegated ➤pp.186–187
Berberis ∅ Red, purple-red, yellow-green ➤p.188
Brachyglottis ∅ Silvery and felted, dark green, olive-green ➤p.189
Celastrus ∅ Yellow ➤p.195
Chamaecyparis ∅ Creamy green, greeny yellow, dark green, grey-green, silvery blue ➤p.196
Choisya ∅ Green, yellow ➤p.197
Clematis ∅ Green, bronze ➤pp.198–199
Cornus ∅ Pinky red, orange, variegated green and cream, crimson ➤p.200
Eleagnus ∅ Greeny gold, greeny yellow, silvery green ➤p.204
Escallonia ∅ Dark green, silvery green ➤p.204
Euonymus ∅ White, gold-green, greeny red, green and gold ➤p.205
Exochorda ∅ Shades of green ➤p.206
Forsythia ∅ Greeny gold, dark green, golden yellow ➤p.206
Heaths and heathers ∅ Green, yellow, grey-green, bronze ➤pp.210–211
Hedera ∅ Yellow-green, silver-grey, variegated ➤p.212
Ilex ∅ Blue, green, purple, gold ➤p.217

Jasminum ⌀ Grey-green, green, variegated ➤p.218

Juniperus ⌀ Silver-blue, grey-green, golden yellow, bright green ➤p.219

Kerria ⌀ Green, variegated ➤p.220

Lavandula ⌀ Silver-grey, grey-green, bright green, variegated ➤p.221

Leucothoë ⌀ Pinky green and white, reddish green, dark green, purple ➤p.223

Ligustrum ⌀ Golden green, variegated, dark green ➤p.224

Lonicera ⌀ Grey, green, greeny gold ➤pp.224–225

Mahonia ⌀ Deep green ➤p.227

Olearia ⌀ Dark green, grey-green ➤p.220

Osmanthus ⌀ Dark green, variegated ➤p.228

Phlomis ⌀ Silvery, green ➤p.232

Picea ⌀ Bright green, bright blue, silver-blue ➤p.233

Pinus ⌀ Blue, blue-grey, dark green ➤p.234

Salvia ⌀ Greeny gold, purply green, variegated ➤p.247

Sambucus ⌀ Greeny purple, golden, variegated ➤p.248

Santolina ⌀ Silver, grey-green ➤p.249

Skimmia ⌀ Bright green ➤p.250

Taxus ⌀ Gold, dark green ➤p.255

Thuja ⌀ Shades of green, gold ➤p.256

Vinca ⌀ Dark green, greeny yellow, variegated ➤p.259

Weigela ⌀ Purple, yellow, variegated ➤p.259

Yucca ⌀ Green, variegated ➤p.261

Trees

Acer ⌀ Shades of yellow, gold, orange, purple, dark green, scarlet ➤p.264

Betula ⌀ Green ➤p.265

Caragana ⌀ Shades of green ➤p.265

Crataegus ⌀ Shades of green ➤p.266

Eucalyptus ⌀ Silvery green, grey-green, blue-grey ➤p.267

Gleditsia ⌀ Bright yellow, bronze-red, golden green ➤p.267

Laburnum ⌀ Shades of green ➤p.268

Malus ⌀ Green, bronze, purple-green ➤p.269

Prunus ⌀ Copper-green, purple ➤p.270

Pyrus ⌀ Green, white ➤p.271

Robinia ⌀ Yellow, lime green ➤p.271

Salix ⌀ Shades of green ➤p.272

Sorbus ⌀ Shades of green ➤p.273

Summer

Flowers

Herbaceous perennials

Acanthus ❀ White-mauve, pink-white, deep pink and green ➤p.88

Achillea ❀ White, yellow, purple ➤p.88

Ajuga ❀ Blue, purple ➤p.89

Alchemilla ❀ Yellow-green ➤p.90

Anaphilis ❀ White ➤p.90

Anemone ❀ White, blue, pink ➤p.91

Anthemis ❀ White, yellow, orange ➤p.92

Anthriscus ❀ Creamy white ➤p.92

Aquilegia ❀ White, pink, violet, blue, red and two tone ➤p.93

Armeria ❀ White, bright pink, purple, red ➤p.94

Artemesia ❀ Yellow, white ➤p.94

Arum ❀ Cream, yellow, purple ➤p.96

Aruncus ❀ Creamy white ➤p.95

Astilbe ❀ White, pink, red ➤p.98

Astrantia ❀ White, pink, red ➤p.99

Aurinia ❀ Shades of yellow ➤p.99

Campanula ❀ White, pink, blue, lavender, violet ➤p.103

Centaurea ❀ Yellow, pink, blue ➤p.104

Centranthus ❀ White, pinky red ➤p.104

Chaerophyllum ❀ White, lilac ➤p.106

Corydalis ❀ Yellow, pink, blue ➤p.106

Dianthus ❀ White and pink, red, yellow and red ➤p.107

Dicentra ❀ White, yellow, pink, red and two tone ➤p.108

Echinacea ❀ Cream, pink, purple ➤p.110

Echinops ❀ White, blue ➤p.111

Erigeron ✿ White, pink, orange, purple, violet ➤p.113

Eryngium ❀ Shades of blue ➤p.114

Eupatorium ❀ White, cream, pink, purple ➤p.115

Euphorbia ❀ Green, yellow, orange ➤pp.118–119

Filipendula ❀ White, pink, red ➤p.120

Fragaria ❀ White, pink, red ➤p.120

Gaillardia ❀ Yellow, red, orange ➤p.121

Geranium ❀ Pink, blue, white, violet, magenta, lavender ➤pp.122–123

Geum ❀ Yellow, orange, red ➤p.124

Globularia ❀ Shades of blue ➤p.125

Gypsophila ❀ White, pink, red ➤p.125

Grasses ❀ Various ➤pp.126–127

Helenium ❀ Yellow, orange, red, copper ➤p.128

Helianthus ❀ Shades of yellow ➤p.129

Hemerocallis ❀ Yellow, pink, orange, red ➤p.132

Heuchera ❀ Yellow, shades of pink and red, white ➤p.133

Hosta ❀ White, mauve, lavender ➤pp.134–135

Houttuynia ❀ White ➤p.135

Iris ❀ White, pink, blue, purple, yellow two tone ➤p.136–137

Knifophia ❀ Cream, yellow, orange, red, greeny yellow ➤p.138

Lamium ❀ White, pink, yellow, copper-pink ➤p.139

Lathyrus ❀ Pink, blue, purple ➤p.140

Leucanthemum ❀ White ➤p.141

Limonium ❀ White, pink, blue, yellow, orange, lavender ➤p.142

Linum ❀ White, yellow, blue ➤p.143

Liriope ❀ White, blue, mauve ➤p.143

Lupinus ❀ White, yellow, pink, red, blue, purple ➤p.144

Lychnis ❀ Pink, red, white ➤p.145

Lysimachia ❀ White, yellow ➤p.146

Lythrum ❀ Shades of pink ➤p.147

Malva ❀ White, pink, blue ➤p.148

Melissa ❀ White ➤p.149

Monada ❀ White, pink, scarlet ➤p.149

Nemesia ❀ White, pink, lavender, lilac ➤p.150

Nepeta ❀ Yellow, lavender-blue ➤p.151

Oenothera ❀ White, pink, yellow ➤p.152

Ophiopogon ❀ White ➤p.153

Paeonia ❀ White, yellow, shades of pink, red, magenta ➤p.154

Papaver ❀ White, pink, apricot, scarlet, orange-red ➤p.155

Persicaria ❀ Shades of pink, red ➤p.156

Phlox ❀ White, pink, purple, white, violet-blue ➤p.157

Potentilla ❀ Yellow, orange, shades of red, white ➤p.160

Primula ❀ White, lilac, mauve, purple, pinks, yellow, blue, two tone ➤p.161

Prunella ❀ Cream, lilac blue, lavender ➤p.162

Ranunculus ❀ White, yellow ➤p.164

Rudbeckia ❀ Yellow ➤p.165

Salvia ❀ Shades of blue ➤p.165

Scabiosa ❀ Purplish blue ➤p.166

Schizostylis ❀ White, pink, red ➤p.166

Sedum ❀ Yellow, pink, red ➤p.167

Sempervivum ❀ Pink, red ➤p.168

Sidalcea ❀ White, shades of pink ➤p.168

Sisyrinchium ❀ White, yellow, blue, purple ➤p.169

Solidago ❀ Yellow ➤p.170

Stachys ❀ White, pink, red, purple ➤p.170

Symphytum ❀ Yellow, pink, purple, white ➤p.171

Tanacctum ❀ White, pink, red, yellow, purple ➤p.172

Tellima ❀ White, pink, red ➤p.172

Thalictrum ❀ Pink, lilac, greeny yellow ➤p.173

Thymus ❀ White, pink, mauve ➤p.174

Tiarella ❀ White, creamy white, pink ➤p.175

Tradescantia ❀ White, lilac, blue, red ➤p.176

Trifolium ❀ White, pink ➤p.176

Trollius ❀ Shades of yellow ➤p.177

Veronica ❀ Blue, lilac-pink, white ➤p.178

Viola ❀ White, purple, blue, yellow, bi and tri-colours ➤p.178

Waldsteinia ❀ Yellow ➤p.179

Climbers and shrubs

Brachyglottis ❀ White, yellow ➤p.189

Buddleja ❀ White, blue, red, pink, lilac ➤pp.190–191

Caryopteris ❀ Blue, purple ➤p.193

Ceanothus ❀ Blue, pale pink ➤p.194

Choisya ❀ White ➤p.197

Clematis ❀ White, shades of pink, blue, purple, red and yellow ➤pp.198–199

Cotoneaster ❀ White ➤p.201

Deutzia ❀ White, pink, red, lilac ➤p.203

Escallonia ❀ Pink, crimson, white ➤p.204

Fuchsia ❀ Two-tone pink and purple, scarlet and purple, white and pink ➤p.207

Genista ❀ Yellow ➤p.208

Hebe ❀ Pink and white, violet, lilac, white ➤p.209

Heaths and heathers ❀ White, pink, shades of lavender, crimson ➤pp.210–211

Helianthemum ❀ Yellow, scarlet, pink ➤p.213

Hibiscus ❀ White, pink, lilac, white and red ➤p.213

Hydrangea ❀ White, cream, blue, red, mauve ➤p.215
Hypericum ❀ Shades of yellow ➤p.216
Jasminum ❀ White, yellow ➤p.218
Kolkwitzia ❀ Shades of pink ➤p.220
Lavandula ❀ Shades of blue, purple and lilac ➤p.221
Lavatera ❀ White, pink ➤p.222
Lonicera ❀ White, cream, yellow, pink, dark red, two tone ➤pp.224–225
Mahonia ❀ Yellow ➤p.227
Nandina ❀ Cream ➤p.227
Olearia ❀ White ➤p.228
Paeonia ❀ White, pink, red, purple, maroon, yellow ➤p.229
Parahebe ❀ Pinky white, lavender-blue, violet-blue ➤p.230
Passiflora ❀ White, pale purple ➤p.231
Perovskia ❀ Blue ➤p.231
Phlomis ❀ Yellow, pinky purple ➤p.232
Potentilla ❀ White, yellow, pink, red ➤p.234
Pyracantha ❀ White ➤p.236
Rhododendron ❀ White, pink, red, purple, violet, yellow ➤pp.238–239
Rosa ❀ Huge variety of colours ➤pp.240–245
Rosmarinus ❀ Shades of blue ➤p.246
Salvia ❀ White, pink, purple ➤p.247
Sambucus ❀ White, pink ➤p.248
Santolina ❀ Cream, yellow ➤p.249
Solanum ❀ White ➤p.251
Sorbaria ❀ White ➤p.251
Spartium ❀ Yellow ➤p.252
Syringa ❀ White, pink, lilac, red ➤p.254
Tamarix ❀ Two-toned pink and green, deep pink and reddish brown ➤p.255
Vaccinium ❀ Pink ➤p.257
Viburnum ❀ White, pink ➤p.258
Vinca ❀ White, blue, purple ➤p.259
Weigela ❀ White, pink, red ➤p.259
Wisteria ❀ White, violet ➤p.260
Yucca ❀ White, cream ➤p.261

Trees
Laburnum ❀ Yellow ➤p.268

Annuals
Argyranthemum ❀ White, yellow ➤p.276
Begonia ❀ White, pink, red ➤p.276
Bidens ❀ Yellow ➤p.277
Brachyscome ❀ White, pink, blue, purple ➤p.278
Diascia ❀ White, shades of pink ➤p.278

Erysium ❀ White, cream, yellow, orange, red ➤p.279
Eschscholzia ❀ Cream, yellow orange, pink, scarlet ➤p.280
Felicia ❀ Bright and violet-blue ➤p.280
Fuchsia ❀ Two tone with pink and purple, red, pink ➤p.281
Hardy annuals ❀ Various ➤pp.282–283
Glechoma ❀ Lavender-blue ➤p.284
Impatiens ❀ White, pink, orange, red, violet ➤p.285
Lobelia ❀ White, pink, red, blue ➤p.286
Lobularia ❀ White, pink, red, purple ➤p.287
Lysimachia ❀ Yellow ➤p.287
Matthiola ❀ Two tone, white, pink red, purple, lilac ➤p.288
Mimulus ❀ Cream, yellow, pink, orange, red, two tone ➤p.289
Myosotis ❀ White, pink, blue ➤p.289
Nicotiana ❀ White, lime-green, pink, red, purple, mauve ➤p.290
Osteospermum ❀ White, pink, yellow, purple, orange ➤p.291
Pelargonium ❀ White, pink, lilac, orange, red, bi-colours ➤pp.292–293
Petunia ❀ White, pink, red, purple, violet, yellow ➤pp.294–295
Sanvitalia ❀ Yellow, orange ➤p.296
Scaevola ❀ White, shades of blue ➤p.297
Solenopsis ❀ White, lavender-blue ➤p.298
Sutera ❀ White, lilac-pink, lavender blue ➤p.298
Tagetes ❀ Cream, yellow, orange, red, reddish brown ➤p.299
Tropaeolum ❀ Cream, yellow, orange, red and pastels ➤p.300
Verbena ❀ White, shades of pink and red, purple ➤p.300
Viola ❀ Multi tones in shades of yellow, white, violet, blue, cream ➤p.301
Viola (pansy) ❀ White, cream, yellow, orange, blue, red, purple, mauve ➤pp.302–303

Bulbs
Allium ❀ Yellow, pink, violet, purple ➤p.306
Begonia ❀ White, yellow, orange, pink, red ➤p.307
Colchicum ❀ White, shades of pink ➤p.308

Crocosmia ❀ Yellow, orange, red ➤p.309
Dahlia ❀ Yellow, shades of pink, orange, red, magenta ➤pp.312–313
Gladiolus ❀ White, magenta ➤p.315
Iris ❀ Blue, yellow, purple ➤p.317
Lilium ❀ White, yellow, orange, pink ➤p.318
Ornithogalum ❀ White, white and green, pale yellow and green ➤p.322
Oxalis ❀ Yellow, pink, purple ➤p.322
Tulipa ❀ White, shades of pink, red, yellow ➤pp.324–325

Foliage

Herbaceous perennials
Artemesia ⊘ Grey, silver, yellow green ➤p.94
Epimedium ⊘ Bronze, copper, orange, shades of green ➤p.112
Euphorbia ⊘ Green, red, blue-green ➤pp.118–119
Ferns ⊘ Shades of green and brown ➤pp.116–117
Grasses ⊘ Various ➤pp.126–127
Heuchera ⊘ Green, brown, purple, red, coppery, pink, yellow ➤p.133
Houttuynia ⊘ Red, yellow, dark green, blue-green ➤p.135
Ophiopogon ⊘ Purple-black, variegated, green ➤p.153
Persicaria ⊘ Green, gold, brown ➤p.156
Plantago ⊘ Cream, grey, maroon, purple ➤p.158
Sempervivum ⊘ Blue-green, red and green, light green ➤p.168
Stachys ⊘ Green, grey ➤p.170
Tradescantia ⊘ Green, yellow, purplish ➤p.176

Climbers and shrubs
Abies ⊘ Green, silvery blue, golden yellow ➤p.182
Akebia ⊘ Green ➤p.182
Amelanchier ⊘ Copper, red ➤p.183
Artemesia ⊘ Silvery grey, grey-green deep green ➤p.184
Aucuba ⊘ Greeny gold, dark green ➤p.185
Bamboos ⊘ Green, bright yellow and green variegated ➤pp.186–187
Berberis ⊘ Red, purple-red, yellow-green ➤p.188

Brachyglottis ⊘ Silvery and felted, dark green, olive-green ➤p.189
Buddleja ⊘ Shades of green ➤pp.190–191
Celastrus ⊘ Yellow ➤p.195
Chaemaecyparis ⊘ Creamy green, greeny yellow, dark green, grey-green, silvery blue ➤p.196
Choisya ⊘ Shades of green, yellow ➤p.197
Clematis ⊘ Green, bronze ➤pp.198–199
Cornus ⊘ Variegated, green ➤p.200
Cotoneaster ⊘ Shades of green ➤p.201
Elaeagnus ⊘ Greeny gold, greeny yellow, silvery green ➤p.204
Escallonia ⊘ Dark green, silvery green ➤p.204
Euonymus ⊘ White, gold-green, greeny red, green and gold ➤p.205
Exochorda ⊘ Shades of green ➤p.206
Forsythia ⊘ Greeny gold, dark green, golden yellow ➤p.206
Heaths and heathers ⊘ Shades of green, pale yellow, grey-green, bronze ➤pp.210–211
Hedera ⊘ Yellow-green, silver-grey and green variegated, cream and green ➤p.212
Hypericum ⊘ Shades of green, orange-red ➤p.216
Ilex ⊘ Blue, green, purple, gold ➤p.217
Jasminum ⊘ Grey-green, green, variegated ➤p.218
Juniperus ⊘ Silver-blue, grey-green, golden yellow, bright green ➤p.219
Kerria ⊘ Green, variegated ➤p.220
Lavandula ⊘ Silver-grey, grey-green, bright green ➤p.221
Lavatera ⊘ Green, variegated ➤p.222
Leucothoë ⊘ Pinky green and white, reddish green, dark green, purple ➤p.223
Ligustrum ⊘ Golden green, variegated, dark green ➤p.224
Lonicera ⊘ Grey, green, greeny gold ➤pp.224–225
Mahonia ⊘ Deep green ➤p.227
Nandina ⊘ Reddish purple ➤p.227
Olearia ⊘ Dark green, grey-green ➤p.228
Osmanthus ⊘ Dark green, variegated ➤p.228
Philadelphus ⊘ Shades of green, variegated ➤p.232

Phlomis ⌀ Silvery, green ➤p.232
Picea ⌀ Bright green, bright blue, silver-blue ➤p.233
Pinus ⌀ Blue, blue-grey, dark green ➤p.234
Prunus ⌀ Shades of green, red ➤p.235
Ribes ⌀ Shades of green ➤p.237
Salvia ⌀ Greeny gold, purpley green, white, pink and purple variegated ➤p.247
Sambucus ⌀ Greeny purple, golden, variegated ➤p.248
Santolina ⌀ Silver, grey-green ➤p.249
Sarcocca ⌀ Shades of green ➤p.249
Skimmia ⌀ Bright green ➤p.250
Taxus ⌀ Gold, dark green ➤p.255
Thuja ⌀ Shades of green, gold, yellow-green ➤p.256
Vinca ⌀ Dark green, greeny yellow ➤p.259
Weigela ⌀ Purple, yellow, variegated ➤p.259
Yucca ⌀ Green, variegated ➤p.261

Trees

Acer ⌀ Shades of yellow, gold, purple, dark green ➤p.264
Betula ⌀ Green ➤p.265
Caragana ⌀ Shades of green ➤p.265
Crataegus ⌀ Shades of green ➤p.266
Eucalyptus ⌀ Silvery green, grey-green, blue-grey ➤p.267
Gleditsia ⌀ Bright yellow, bronze-red, golden green ➤p.267
Laburnum ⌀ Shades of green ➤p.268
Malus ⌀ Green, bronze, purple-green ➤p.269
Prunus ⌀ Coppery green ➤p.270
Pyrus ⌀ Green, white ➤p.271
Robinia ⌀ Yellow, lime-green ➤p.271
Salix ⌀ Shades of green, silver-grey ➤p.272
Sorbus ⌀ Shades of green ➤p.273

Annuals

Lysimachia ⌀ Green, gold ➤p.287
Pelargonium ⌀ Shades of green, variegated, scented ➤pp.292–293
Plectranthus ⌀ Variegated green and cream, dark green and reddish purple ➤p.296
Senecio ⌀ White ➤p.297
Tropaeolum ⌀ Green, variegated ➤p.300

Autumn

Flowers

Herbaceous perennials

Anaphilis ❀ White ➤p.90
Anemone ❀ White, blue, pink ➤p.91
Aster ❀ Lilac, cerise, violet, lavender-blue, purple and white ➤p.97
Chrysanthemum ❀ Amber, pink, red, yellow, white ➤p.105
Dicentra ❀ White, yellow, pink, red and two tone ➤p.108
Echinachea ❀ Cream, pink, purple ➤p.110
Fragaria ❀ White, pink ➤p.120
Gaillardia ❀ Yellow, red, orange ➤p.121
Geranium ❀ Pink, blue, white, violet, magenta, lavender ➤pp.122–123
Helenium ❀ Yellow, orange, red, copper ➤p.128
Helianthus ❀ Shades of yellow ➤p.129
Knifophia ❀ Cream, yellow, orange, red, greeny yellow ➤p.138
Limonium ❀ White, pink, blue, yellow, orange, lavender ➤p.142
Liriope ❀ White, blue, mauve ➤p.143
Malva ❀ White, pink, blue ➤p.148
Monada ❀ White, pink, scarlet ➤p.149
Nemesia ❀ White, pink, lavender, lilac ➤p.150
Oenothera ❀ White, pink, yellow ➤p.152
Persicaria ❀ Pink, red ➤p.156
Rudbeckia ❀ Yellow ➤p.165
Salvia ❀ Shades of blue ➤p.165
Solidago ❀ Yellow ➤p.169
Stachys ❀ White, pink, red, purple ➤p.170
Tradescantia ❀ White, lilac, blue, red ➤p.176

Climbers and shrubs

Brachyglottis ❀ White, yellow ➤p.189
Buddleja ❀ White, blue, red, pink, lilac ➤pp.190–191
Choisya ❀ White ➤p.197
Clematis ❀ White, shades of pink, blue, purple, red and yellow ➤pp.198–199
Fuchsia ❀ Two-tone pink, purple, scarlet, white ➤p.207
Hebe ❀ Pink, white, violet, lilac ➤p.209
Heaths and heathers ❀ White, pink, lavender, crimson ➤pp.210–211

Jasminum ❀ White, yellow ➤p.218
Lavatera ❀ White, pink ➤p.222
Lonicera ❀ White, cream, yellow, pink, dark red, two tone ➤pp.224–225
Perovskia ❀ Shades of blue ➤p.231
Rosmarinus ❀ Shades of blue ➤p.246
Ruscus ❀ Light green ➤p.246
Sorbaria ❀ White ➤p.251
Vaccinium ❀ Pink ➤p.257

Annuals

Argyranthemum ❀ White, yellow ➤p.276
Bidens ❀ Yellow ➤p.277
Brachyscome ❀ White, pink, blue, purple ➤p.278
Felicia ❀ Bright and violet-blue ➤p.200
Fuchsia ❀ Two tone with pink and purple, red, pink ➤p.281
Hardy annuals ❀ Various ➤pp.282–283
Impatiens ❀ White, pink, orange, red, violet ➤p.285
Lobelia ❀ White, pink, red, blue ➤p.286
Lysimachia ❀ Yellow ➤p.287
Nicotiana ❀ White, lime-green, pink, red, purple, mauve ➤p.290
Osteospermum ❀ White, pink, yellow, purple, orange ➤p.291
Petunia ❀ White, pink, red, purple, violet, yellow ➤pp.294–295
Sanvitalia ❀ Yellow, orange ➤p.296
Scaevola ❀ White, blue ➤p.297
Solenopsis ❀ White, blue ➤p.298
Sutera ❀ White, lilac-pink, blue ➤p.298
Tagetes ❀ Cream, yellow, orange, red, reddish brown ➤p.299
Tropaeolum ❀ Cream, yellow, orange, red and pastels ➤p.300
Verbena ❀ White, shades of pink and red, purple ➤p.300
Viola ❀ White, cream, yellow, orange, blue, red, purple, mauve ➤pp.302–303

Bulbs

Colchicum ❀ White, pink ➤p.308
Crocus ❀ Cream, rich yellow, lilac, purple ➤p.310
Cyclamen ❀ White, pink, purple ➤p.311
Dahlia ❀ Yellow, pink, orange, red, magenta ➤pp.312–313
Nerine ❀ Bluish white, pink ➤p.321
Oxalis ❀ Yellow, pink, purple ➤p.322

Foliage

Herbaceous perennials

Epimedium ⌀ Bronze, copper, orange, shades of green ➤p.112
Ferns ⌀ Shades of green and brown ➤pp.116–117
Geranium ⌀ Green, grey-green, variegated ➤pp.122–123
Grasses ⌀ Various ➤pp.126–127
Heuchera ⌀ Brown, purple, dark green ➤p.133
Hosta ⌀ Shades of green, grey and blue, variegated, yellow ➤pp.134–135
Houttuynia ⌀ Red, yellow, dark green, blue-green ➤p.135
Ophiopogon ⌀ Purple-black, variegated, green ➤p.153
Persicaria ⌀ Green, gold, brown ➤p.156
Stachys ⌀ Green, grey ➤p.170
Tradescantia ⌀ Green, yellow, purplish ➤p.176

Climbers and shrubs

Abies ⌀ Green, silvery blue, golden yellow ➤p.182
Akebia ⌀ Green ➤p.182
Amelanchier ⌀ Copper, red ➤p.183
Artemesia ⌀ Silvery grey, grey-green deep green ➤p.184
Aucuba ⌀ Greeny gold, dark green, variegated ➤p.185
Bamboos ⌀ Green, bright yellow and green variegated ➤pp.186–187
Berberis ⌀ Red, purple-red, yellow-green ➤p.188
Brachyglottis ⌀ Silvery and felted, dark green, olive-green ➤p.189
Buddleja ⌀ Green ➤pp.190–191
Celastrus ⌀ Yellow ➤p.195
Chamaecyparis ⌀ Creamy green, greeny yellow, dark green, grey-green, silvery blue ➤p.196
Choisya ⌀Green, yellow ➤p.197
Clematis ⌀ Green, bronze ➤pp.198–199
Cornus ⌀ Pinky red, orange, variegated green and cream, crimson ➤p.200
Corylus ⌀ Pale yellow, green ➤p.201
Cotoneaster ⌀ Shades of green ➤p.201
Eleagnus ⌀ Greeny gold, greeny yellow, silvery green ➤p.204

Escallonia ∅ Shades of green ➤p.204

Euonymus ∅ White, gold-green, greeny red, green and gold ➤p.205

Exochorda ∅ Shades of green ➤p.206

Forsythia ∅ Greeny gold, dark green, golden yellow ➤p.206

Hebe ∅ Shades of silvery green ➤p.209

Heaths and heathers ∅ Green, yellow, grey-green, bronze ➤pp.210–211

Hedera ∅ Yellow-green, silver-grey and green variegated, cream and green ➤p.212

Hypericum ∅ Green, orange-red ➤p.216

Ilex ∅ Blue, green, purple, gold ➤p.217

Jasminum ∅ Grey-green, green, variegated ➤p.218

Juniperus ∅ Silver-blue, grey-green, golden yellow, bright green ➤p.219

Kerria ∅ Green, variegated ➤p.220

Lavatera ∅ Green, variegated ➤p.222

Leucothoë ∅ Pinky green, white, reddish, dark green, purple ➤p.223

Ligustrum ∅ Golden green, variegated, dark green ➤p.224

Lonicera ∅ Grey, green, greeny gold, variegated ➤pp.224–225

Olearia ∅ Dark green, grey-green ➤p.228

Osmanthus ∅ Dark green, variegated ➤p.228

Parthenocissus ∅ Shades of red ➤p.230

Philadelphus ∅ Green, variegated ➤p.232

Phlomis ∅ Silvery, green ➤p.232

Picea ∅ Bright green, bright blue, silver-blue ➤p.233

Pinus ∅ Blue, blue-grey, dark green ➤p.234

Prunus ∅ Shades of green, red ➤p.235

Pyracantha ∅ Dark green ➤p.236

Ribes ∅ Green, purple ➤p.237

Rhododendron ∅ Shades of green ➤pp.238–239

Salix ∅ Shades of green, purple, grey, variegated ➤p.247

Sarcococca ∅ Shades of green ➤p.249

Skimmia ∅ Bright green ➤p.250

Taxus ∅ Gold, dark green ➤p.255

Thuja ∅ Shades of green, gold and copper, yellow-green and purple ➤p.256

Viburnum ∅ Shades of green ➤p.258

Vinca ∅ Dark green, greeny yellow ➤p.259

Weigela ∅ Purple, yellow, variegated ➤p.259

Yucca ∅ Green, variegated ➤p.261

Trees

Acer ∅ Orange, yellow, scarlet ➤p.264

Betula ∅ Yellow ➤p.265

Crataegus ∅ Scarlet, orange ➤p.266

Eucalyptus ∅ Grey ➤p.267

Gleditsia ∅ Bright yellow, bronze-red ➤p.267

Malus ∅ Bronze, yellow, red ➤p.269

Pyrus ∅ Red ➤p.271

Robinia ∅ Orange, yellow ➤p.271

Sorbus ∅ Red, orange, yellow, brown ➤p.273

Annuals

Senecio ∅ White ➤p.297

Berries

Herbaceous perennials

Arum ⚘ Red ➤p.96

Iris ⚘ Orange seeds ➤pp.136–137

Ophiopogon ⚘ Violet-blue, blue-black ➤p.153

Climbers and shrubs

Akebia ⚘ Purplish ➤p.183

Aucuba ⚘ Bright red ➤p.185

Berberis ⚘ Bright red, purple ➤p.188

Celastrus ⚘ Yellow ➤p.195

Cornus ⚘ Green, black ➤p.200

Corylus ⚘ Cobnuts and filberts ➤p.201

Cotoneaster ⚘ Red, orange ➤p.201

Euonymus ⚘ Pink, orange, purple ➤p.205

Hypericum ⚘ Bronze, purple, red, cerise ➤p.216

Ilex ⚘ Red, black, white, yellow ➤p.217

Passiflora ⚘ Orange, yellow ➤p.231

Pyracantha ⚘ Red, orange, yellow ➤p.236

Ruscus ⚘ Red ➤p.246

Vaccinium ⚘ Red, black, blue-black ➤p.257

Viburnum ⚘ Red, blue ➤p.258

Trees

Crataegus ⚘ Shades of red ➤p.266

Malus ⚘ Orange-yellow, red, purple-red, yellow ➤p.269

Sorbus ⚘ Orange-red, orange-yellow, pink, white, scarlet ➤p.273

Winter

Flowers

Herbaceous perennials

Helleborus ❀ Green, white, purple-red ➤pp.130–131

Pulmonaria ❀ Red, blue ➤p.163

Climbers and shrubs

Chaenomeles ❀ Pink and white, apricot, shades of red ➤p.197

Garrya ❀ Silver, red, purple and green catkins ➤p.208

Heaths and heathers ❀ White, pink, lavender, crimson ➤pp.210–211

Hibiscus ❀ Shades of green ➤p.213

Jasminum ❀ Yellow ➤p.218

Lonicera ❀ Cream ➤pp.224–225

Mahonia ❀ Yellow ➤p.227

Sarcocca ❀ White ➤p.249

Bulbs

Crocus ❀ Cream, rich yellow, lilac, purple ➤p.310

Cyclamen ❀ White, pink, purple ➤p.311

Galanthus ❀ White ➤p.314

Oxalis ❀ Yellow, pink, purple ➤p.322

Tulipa ❀ Cream, purplish pink ➤p.322

Foliage

Herbaceous perennials

Epimedium ∅ Bronze, copper, orange, shades of green ➤p.112

Ferns ∅ Shades of green and brown ➤pp.116–117

Heuchera ∅ Brown, purple, dark green ➤p.133

Pulmonaria ∅ Green, variegated with cream and silver ➤p.163

Climbers and shrubs

Abies ∅ Silvery blue, golden yellow, shades of green ➤p.182

Akebia ∅ Shades of green ➤p.182

Artemesia ∅ Green, grey, silver ➤p.184

Bamboos ∅ Green ➤pp.186–187

Chamaecyparis ∅ Creamy green, greeny yellow, dark green, grey-green, silvery blue ➤p.196

Choisya ∅ Shades of green, yellow-green ➤p.197

Elaeagnus ∅ Shades of greeny gold and silver-green ➤p.204

Escallonia ∅ Shades of green ➤p.204

Euonymus ∅ Shades of green, golden green, red, variegated ➤p.205

Heaths and heathers ∅ Green, bronze, yellow, grey ➤pp.210–211

Hedera ∅ Yellow-green, silver-grey and green variegated, cream and green ➤p.212

Ilex ∅ Blue, green, purple, gold ➤p.217

Jasminum ∅ Grey-green, green ➤p.218

Juniperus ∅ Silver-blue, grey-green, golden yellow, bright green ➤p.219

Leucothoë ∅ Pinky green and white, reddish green, dark green, purple ➤p.223

Ligustrum ∅ Golden green, variegated, dark green ➤p.224

Lonicera ∅ Grey, green, greeny gold ➤pp.224–225

Mahonia ∅ Shades of green ➤p.227

Osmanthus ∅ Dark green, variegated ➤p.228

Picea ∅ Bright green, bright blue, silver-blue ➤p.233

Pinus ∅ Blue, blue-grey, dark green ➤p.234

Sarcococca ∅ Shades of green ➤p.249

Skimmia ∅ Bright green ➤p.250

Taxus ∅ Gold, dark green ➤p.255

Thuja ∅ Green, gold, copper, yellow-green and purple ➤p.256

Berries

Climbers and shrubs

Ilex ⚘ Red, black, white, yellow ➤p.217

Sarcoccca ⚘ Black, red ➤p.249

Skimmia ⚘ Dark pink, bright red ➤p.250

Bark

Climbers and shrubs

Cornus ∅ Pink, green, yellow, red ➤p.200

Trees

Acer ∅ Striped, pinky red ➤p.264

Betula ∅ White, grey ➤p.265

Prunus ∅ Reddish brown ➤p.270

acknowledgments

The following abbreviations have been used throughout the picture credits:
t top; **c** centre; **b** bottom; **l** left; **r** right
SC Sarah Cuttle
DP Debbie Patterson
JS Jason Smalley
© RD images that are copyright of The Reader's Digest Association Ltd.
PL pictures from the Reader's Digest Plant Library, which may previously have appeared in Reader's Digest *New Encyclopedia of Garden Plants and Flowers*.
GPL Garden Picture Library
PHPL Photos Horticultural Picture Library
Other photographs in the book came from the sources listed below.

Cover Shutterstock, inc/Lijuan Guo **1** © RD/SC **2–3** © RD/DP **4–5** © RD/DP **6 t** PHPL **b** © RD/Artist, Ian Sidaway **6–7** © RD/JS **7 l** GPL/John Glover **tr** PHPL **c** John Glover **cr** John Glover **bl** © RD/PL **br** PHPL **8 tl** © RD/DP **8–9** PHPL **9 tr** © RD/DP **br** © RD/DP **10** © RD/DP **10–11** © RD/DP **11** © RD/DP **12 tl** © RD/DP **cl** © RD/DP **bl** © RD/DP **br** PHPL **12–13** © RD/DP **13** © RD/DP **14** © RD/DP **14–15** © RD/DP **15 tr** © RD/DP **cr** PHPL **br** © RD/DP **16 tl** © RD/DP **tr** © RD/DP **cl** Ardea, London/Ian Beames **bc** Holt Studios Ltd./Nigel Cattlin **17 t** Holt Studios Ltd./Alan & Linda Detrick **l** © RD/ Artist, Rudi Vizi **c** © RD/Artist, Rudi Vizi **cr** PHPL **b** © RD/DP **18 tr** © RD/DP **cr** © RD/DP **bl** Ardea, London/Steve Hopkin **bc** Holt Studios Ltd./Nigel Cattlin **br** © RD/DP **19 tl** © RD/DP **tr** Holt Studios Ltd./Nigel Cattlin **cr** Holt Studios Ltd./Nigel Cattlin **bl** PHPL **br** Holt Studios Ltd./Nigel Cattlin **20–21** GPL/Ann Kelley **22** © RD/Daphne Ledward **23 t** GPL/Howard Rice **b** GPL/Sunniva Harte **24 tl** © RD/Richard Surman **r** © RD/Artist, Ian Sidaway **24–25** Jerry Harpur/John Brookes – Design for Mr & Mrs Mulville, Argentina **26 t** © RD/PL **b** © RD/Artist, Ian Sidaway **26–27** © RD/JS **28 l** © RD/SC **28–29** Clive Nichols/Cambridge Botanic Garden **29** © RD/Artist, Ian Sidaway **30** © RD/PL **30–31** © RD/DP **31** © RD/Artist, Ian Sidaway **32 tl** PHPL **br** © RD/Artist, Ian Sidaway **32–33** © RD/JS **34 tl** © RD/Richard Surman **br** © RD/Artist, Ian Sidaway **34–35** Sheila & Oliver Mathews **36 l** Flower-photos **36–37** GPL/Christi Carter **37** © RD/Artist, Ian Sidaway **38 l** GPL/John Glover **38–39** © RD/JS **39** © RD/Artist, Ian Sidaway **40 l** PHPL **40–41** GPL/Tim Griffith **41** © RD/Artist, Ian Sidaway **42 tl** © RD/Richard Surman **b** © RD/Artist, Ian Sidaway **42–43** Jerry Harpur/The Garden House **44** © RD/PL **44–45** © RD/DP **45** © RD/Artist, Ian Sidaway **46** © RD/Artist, Ian Sidaway **46–47** © RD/JS **48 tl** © RD/PL **tr** © RD/Artist, Ian Sidaway **49** Andrew Lawson **50 l** GPL/John Glover **50–51** GPL/Brigitte Thomas **51** © RD/Artist, Ian Sidaway **52** © RD/DP **52–53** © RD/JS **53** © RD/Artist, Ian Sidaway **54 l** © RD/Richard Surman **54–55** Clive Nichols **55** © RD/Artist, Ian Sidaway **56** © RD/Artist, Ian Sidaway **56–57** © RD/JS **58** © RD/Artist, Ian Sidaway **tl** © RD/DP **58–59** © RD/DP **60 tl** Jerry Harpur **b** © RD/Artist, Ian Sidaway **60–61** © RD/DP **62** © RD/Artist, Ian Sidaway **62–63** © RD/JS **64 tl** © RD/Richard Surman **b** © RD/Artist, Ian Sidaway **64–65** © RD/JS **66 tl** © RD/JS **b** © RD/Artist, Ian Sidaway **66–67** © RD/SC **68 tl** © RD/RDPL **b** © RD/Artist, Ian Sidaway **68–69** © RD/DP **70 tl** © RD/PL **b** © RD/Artist, Ian Sidaway **70–71** © RD/DP **72 tl** © RD/PL **br** © RD/Artist, Ian Sidaway **73** © RD/DP **74 tl** © RD/PL **74–75** GPL/Ron Evans **75** © RD/Artist, Ian Sidaway **76** © RD/Artist, Ian Sidaway **76–77** GPL/Ron Sutherland **78 tl** © RD/PL **78–79** GPL/Jacqui Hurst **79** © RD/Artist, Ian Sidaway **80 l** © RD/PL **80–81** GPL/JS Sira **81** © RD/Artist, Ian Sidaway **82–83** © RD/SC **84–85** © RD/DP **85 tr** © RD/DP **b** © RD/Daphne Ledward **86–87** © RD/SC **87** © RD/DP **88 l** © RD/PL **r** © RD/ PL **89 tl** Clive Nichols **bl** © RD/Richard Surman **br** GPL/Chris Burrows **90 l** © RD/DP **r** © RD/PL **91 tl** GPL/Mayer/Le Scanff **tr** PHPL **bl** © RD/Richard Surman **br** Derek St Romaine **92 l** © RD/JS **r** © RD/Richard Surman **93 tl** GPL/John Glover **tc** GPL/Howard Rice **tr** PHPL **br** PHPL **94 tr** Andrew Lawson **bl** Harry Smith Collection **br** © RD/JS **94–95** © RD/Richard Surman **95** © RD/Richard Surman **96 tr** PHPL **cr** GPL/Howard Rice **bl** PHPL **br** GPL/John Glover **97 tl** © RD/PL **tr** GPL/Sunniva Harte **bl** PHPL **br** GPL/Howard Rice **98 l** © RD/Richard Surman **tr** © RD/PL **br** © RD/PL **99 l** © RD/Richard Surman **r** © RD/Richard Surman **100 tl** PHPL **tr** PHPL **b** John Glover **101 tl** PHPL **r** © RD/JS **bl** GPL/Sunniva Harte **102 tr** © RD/PL **bl** PHPL **br** © RD/Richard Surman **103 r** © RD/Richard Surman **bl** © RD/SC **bc** Jerry Harpur/Marcus Harpur **104 l** © RD/PL **r** © RD/ Richard Surman **105 tl** Harry Smith Collection **tc** Derek St Romaine **br** A–Z Botanical Collection **106 l** © RD/JS **r** © RD/PL **107 tl** GPL/Mayer/Le Scanff **tr** Derek St Romaine **bl** PHPL **br** © RD/PL **108 t** © RD/Richard Surman **bl** PHPL **br** © RD/JS **109 tl** © RD/PL **tr** © RD/PL **br** Andrew Lawson **110 tr** PHPL **bl** GPL/JS Sira **br** © RD/PL **111 t** GPL/JS Sira **b** © RD/PL **112 tr** Derek St Romaine **bl** PHPL **br** © RD/DP **113 t** © RD/PL **bl** © RD/JS **br** Jerry Harpur/Beth Chatto **114 tl** GPL/JS Sira **tr** Neil Holmes **bl** © RD/JS **br** © RD/SC **115 tr** © RD/PL **bl** PHPL **br** PHPL **116** Harry Smith Collection **117 tl** © RD/JS **tc** Harry Smith Collection **tr** Derek St Romaine **bl** © RD/PL **br** © RD/JS **118 bl** PHPL **118–119 r** PHPL **119 tc** PHPL **c** Harry Smith Collection **r** © RD/Richard Surman **bl** © RD/Richard Surman **120 l** © RD/Richard Surman **r** © RD/PL **121 l** © RD/PL **r** © RD/PL **122 t** © RD/SC **b** © RD/JS **123 l** PHPL **tc** Neil Holmes **tr** © RD/Richard Surman **bc** Derek St Romaine **124 tc** © RD/JS **tr** PHPL **bl** PHPL **125 l** A–Z Botanical Collection/Bruno Petriglia **r** A–Z Botanical Collection/Sam Ke Tran **126 tr** PHPL **bl** Harry Smith Collection **br** Harry Smith Collection **127 t** PHPL **bl** Harry Smith Collection **br** Neil Holmes **128 tr** PHPL **bl** © RD/PL **br** © RD/PL **129 tr** © RD **br** GPL/JS Sira **130 tl** GPL/Howard Rice **tr** Flower-photos **br** Photography © Andrea Jones/Garden Exposures Photo Library **131 r** Andrew Lawson **bl** Neil Holmes **bc** Jerry Harpur/Marcus Harpur **132 tr** © RD/JS **bl** © RD/JS **br** Derek St Romaine **133 tl** PHPL **tr** © RD/JS **br** Neil Holmes **134 tl** © RD/DP **tr** Clive Nichols **bl** © RD/JS **135 tl** © RD/JS **tr** © RD/JS **br** © RD/Richard Surman **136 bl** © RD/PL **bc** © RD/JS **br** © RD/JS **136–137** © RD/Richard Surman **137 tr** © RD/Richard Surman **br** John Glover **138 l** GPL/Howard Rice **r** John Glover **139 l** GPL/JS Sira **c** © RD/JS **r** © RD/JS **140 tl** © RD/PL **tr** John Glover **br** © RD/PL **141 t** John Glover **bl** Neil Holmes **br** © RD/PL **142 t** © RD/PL **cr** © RD/PL **bl** Harry Smith Collection **143 bl** © RD/SC **br** Harry Smith Collection **144 tc** PHPL **tr** © RD/PL **bl** PHPL **145 tl** GPL/Bjorn Forsberg **bl** © RD/JS **br** © RD/SC **146 l** © RD/SC **bc** PHPL **br** © RD/JS **147 l** © RD/DP **tr** PHPL **148 tr** © RD/JS **bl** © RD/Richard Surman **br** © RD/PL **149 l** © RD/PL **r** PHPL **150 tl** Harry Smith Collection **tr** GPL/Howard Rice **bl** © RD/DP **151 tl** Harry Smith Collection **tr** © RD/PL **bl** © RD/JS **152 tc** PHPL **tr** Derek St Romaine **bl** Derek St Romaine **153 t** © RD/PL **cr** © RD/PL **bl** PHPL **154 tr** PHPL **bl** Flower-photos **br** © RD/JS **155 tl** © RD/JS **bl** PHPL **br** PHPL **156 tc** © RD/SC **tr** PHPL **bl** © RD/JS **157 tl** © RD/DP **bl** Neil Holmes **br** Neil Holmes **158 tl** © RD/SC **tr** Harry Smith Collection **bl** PHPL **159 t** © RD/PL **b** © RD/PL **160 tl** © RD/JS **tr** © RD/PL **bl** © RD/PL **161 tl** © RD/Richard Surman **bl** © RD/Richard Surman **br** © RD/PL **162 l** © RD/Richard Surman **br** Derek St Romaine **163 tl** GPL/Sunniva Harte **tr** PHPL **b** Derek St Romaine **164 l** PHPL **r** PHPL **165 l** PHPL **c** GPL/John Glover **r** PHPL **166 l** © RD/PL **r** PHPL **167 tr** © RD/PL **bl** © RD/PL **br** © RD/PL **168 tl** Flowerphotos **bl** GPL/Rex Butcher **br** © RD/Richard Surman **169 tl** © RD/DP **bl** PHPL **br** © RD/PL **170 tr** © RD/PL **bl** © RD/PL **br** PHPL **171 bl** PHPL **bc** PHPL **br** © RD/Richard Surman **172** PHPL **173 tr** Andrew Lawson **b** © RD/PL **174 tl** PHPL **tr** © RD/Richard Surman **c** Derek St Romaine **bl** PHPL **175 l** GPL/John Glover **r** PHPL **176 t** © RD/PL **cl** John Glover **cr** © RD/PL **b** © RD/PL **177 l** © RD/PL **r** PHPL **178 tl** PHPL **tr** Andrew Lawson **bl** © RD/JS **178–179** © RD/Richard Surman **179 bl** Andrew Lawson **bc** Neil Holmes **br** Andrew Lawson **180–182** © RD/DP **181** © RD/DP **182 tl** John Glover **tr** PHPL **cr** John Glover **bl** GPL/Juliette Wade **183 tl** John Glover **tr** PHPL **br** Jerry Harpur **184 tl** © RD/PL **tr** PHPL **bl** © RD/PL **185 tr** GPL/Neil Holmes **c** GPL/JS Sira **br** © RD/PL **186 l** Harry Smith Collection **186–187** Neil Holmes **187 tl** Neil Holmes **tc** PHPL **tr** GPL/Neil Holmes **188 tl** © RD/Richard Surman **tc** Neil Holmes **tr** Neil Holmes **br** © RD/PL **189 r** © RD/SC **bl** GPL/Andrea Jones **190 tr** Ardea, London/Jack A.Bailey **bl** PHPL **bc** © RD/PL **br** PHPL **191 r** © RD/JS **bl** GPL/Neil Holmes **bc** GPL/Neil Holmes **192 t** PHPL **bl** GPL/Lamontagne **br** PHPL **193 tr** © RD/PL **bl** PHPL **br** GPL/ Jerry Pavia **194 tl** GPL/Jerry Pavia **bl** Clive Nichols **194–195** PHPL **195** GPL/David Cavagnaro **br** PHPL **196 tl** PHPL **tr** Harry Smith Collection **b** PHPL **197 tl** GPL/Christopher Fairweather **tr** Harry Smith Collection **bl** GPL/Brian Carter **br** © RD/DP **198 tl** PHPL **tr** PHPL **bl** Picturesmiths Limited **br** GPL **198–199** Harry Smith Collection **199 tr** © RD/PL **br** PHPL **200 tr** PHPL **c** © RD/Richard Surman **bl** © RD/PL **201 tr** PHPL **bl** GPL/Brian Carter **202 tl** John Glover **tr** PHPL **bl** © RD/PL **203 t** PHPL **b** GPL/Juliette Wade **204 tr** GPL/John Glover **bl** PHPL **br** © RD/PL **205 tr** PHPL **bl** John Glover **bc** PHPL **br** Clive Nichols **206 tl** PHPL **tr** © RD/PL **bl** © RD/PL **br** © RD/PL **207 tr** PHPL **cl** GPL/Neil Holmes **bl** PHPL **208 tl** GPL/John Glover **tr** John Glover **br** © RD/PL **209 tl** John Glover **tr** PHPL **br** PHPL **210** John Glover **211 t** © RD/PL **cr** Harry Smith Collection **bl** Neil Holmes **br** PHPL **212 l** © RD/Richard Surman **c** © RD/PL **r** John Glover **213 tr** PHPL **bl** © RD/Richard Surman **214 l** © RD/Richard Surman **214–215** © RD/Richard Surman **215 tl** PHPL **tc** PHPL **tr** © RD/Richard Surman **216 t** © RD/JS **c** © RD/Richard Surman **bl** © RD/Richard Surman **217 tl** PHPL **tr** PHPL **b** PHPL **218 l** PHPL **r** © RD/PL **219 tl** PHPL **r** © RD/DP **bl** PHPL **br** © RD/DP **220 tl** PHPL **tr** © RD/PL **bl** GPL/Howard Rice **221 bl** © RD/PL **bc** GPL/Howard Rice **br** Neil Holmes **222 l** PHPL **tr** GPL/Christopher Fairweather **cr** © RD/PL **223 l** GPL/Lamontagne **r** © RD/PL **224 tl** www.osf.uk.com/Geoff Kidd **bl** © RD/PL **br** PHPL **224–225** PHPL **225 tr** GPL/Sunniva Harte **br** GPL/John Glover **226 tr** Clive Nichols **cr** PHPL **bl** © RD/PL **227 l** © RD/Richard Surman **r** PHPL **228 tr** © RD/PL **bl** © RD/PL **br** © RD/PL **229 tl** PHPL **tr** GPL/Howard Rice **br** PHPL **230 l** © RD/Richard Surman **r** © RD/Richard Surman **231 l** © RD/JS **r** © RD/PL **232 l** PHPL **r** © RD/JS **233 tl** PHPL **r** PHPL **bl** © RD/PL **234 bl** PHPL **234–235** PHPL **235 r** Neil Holmes **bl** Neil Holmes **236 t** PHPL **b** PHPL **236–237** GPL/Mel Watson **237 br** PHPL **238 tr** GPL/John Glover **bl** © RD/PL **239 tcl** PHPL **tcr** PHPL **tl** © RD/PL **tr** PHPL **b** © RD/PL **240–241** PHPL **241 tr** GPL/David Askham **br** Neil Holmes **242 tl** PHPL **tc** GPL/Howard Rice **242–243 br** PHPL **243 tl** GPL **tr** PHPL **bc** © RD/PL **br** PHPL **244 tl** PHPL **tr** Dorling Kindersley **bl** PHPL **br** GPL/Laslo Puskas **245 tr** GPL/Mayer/Le Scanff/Le Baque France **bl** PHPL **br** GPL/Densey Clyne **246 tr** PHPL **bl** Neil Holmes **br** PHPL **247 tr** © RD/Richard Surman **bl** © RD/PL **248 tl** Neil Holmes **tr** © RD/DP **bl** PHPL **br** © RD/DP **249 l** © RD/PL **r** GPL/Christopher Fairweather **250 tl** © RD/PL **tr** PHPL **br** GPL/JS Sira **251 tr** © RD/PL **c** © RD/PL **bl** PHPL **252 tc** PHPL **bl** © RD/SC **252–253** PHPL **253 tr** © RD/PL **br** © RD/PL **254 l** © RD/PL **tr** PHPL **br** © RD/PL **255 tr** PHPL **bl** © RD/PL **br** GPL/JS Sira **256 l** GPL/Jerry Pavia **r** PHPL **257 tl** © RD/PL **cl** © RD/PL **bl** © RD/PL **br** PHPL **258 tl** Neil Holmes **tr** PHPL **br** Neil Holmes **259 tl** PHPL **r** © RD/RDIG **260 l** © RD/DP **r** GPL/David Askham **261 tl** GPL/Jerry Pavia **tr** © RD/Richard Surman **br** GPL/John Glover **262–263** © RD/DP **263** © RD/DP **264 tr** © RD/PL **cr** © RD/PL **bl** Clive Nichols **265** PHPL **266 c** PHPL **bl** PHPL **br** © RD/Richard Surman **266–267** © RD/PL **267 c** PHPL **br** © RD/PL **268 t** © RD/PL **cr** PHPL **269 t** GPL/Howard Rice **c** GPL/Rex Butcher **bl** Clive Nichols **br** © RD/Richard Surman **270 tr** PHPL **cr** GPL/Sunniva Harte **bl** © RD/DP **b** GPL/John Miller **271 tr** PHPL **bl** © RD/JS **br** © RD/PL **272 tl** © RD/PL **c** GPL/Howard Rice **bl** PHPL **br** Harry Smith Collection **273 tl** Clive Nichols **tr** © RD/Richard Surman **br** © RD/PL **274–275** © RD/DP **275** © RD/DP **276 t** © RD/PL **bl** © RD/PL **bc** GPL/Jerry Pavia **276–277** Colegrave Seeds Ltd. **277 r** © RD/JS **278 tl** Colegrave Seeds Ltd. **tr** © RD/JS **br** PHPL **279** Harry Smith Collection **280 tl** Colegrave Seeds Ltd. **tr** Harry Smith Collection **bl** PHPL **281 tr** PHPL **c** Derek St Romaine **bl** Harry Smith Collection **282 l** PHPL **r** Harry Smith Collection **283 tl** GPL/Didier Willery **tr** GPL/Brian Carter **bl** PHPL **br** GPL/Mark Bolton **284 tl** GPL/Jerry Pavia **tr** Harry Smith Collection **br** GPL/Chris Burrows **285 tr** GPL/Jerry Pavia **bl** Colegrave Seeds Ltd. **286 t** © RD/JS **bl** Harry Smith Collection **br** PHPL **287 tr** GPL/John Glover **bl** © RD/Richard Surman **br** Colegrave Seeds Ltd. **288 tc** PHPL **tr** GPL/Howard Rice **bl** PHPL **289 l** PHPL **r** © RD/PL **290 tr** PHPL **bl** Colegrave Seeds Ltd. **br** © RD/DP **291 l** Harry Smith Collection **r** Harry Smith Collection **292 bl** © RD/Richard Surman **292–293** www.gardenworldimages.com/Gilles Delacroix **293 tr** Harry Smith Collection **bl** Harry Smith Collection **bc** Harry Smith Collection **br** GPL/Eric Crichton **294 bl** © RD/Richard Surman **294–295** PHPL **295 tc** PHPL **tr** © RD/PL **cr** PHPL **bc** Colegrave Seeds Ltd. **bc** PHPL **br** PHPL **296** PHPL **297 l** Harry Smith Collection **r** PHPL **298** PHPL **299 tl** Harry Smith Collection **tr** PHPL **bl** Harry Smith Collection **br** PHPL **300 tl** Derek St Romaine **bc** Derek St Romaine **br** PHPL **300–301** PHPL **301 br** PHPL **302 tl** PHPL **tr** Harry Smith Collection **bl** Colegrave Seeds Ltd. **302–303** PHPL **303** PHPL **304–305** © RD/DP **305** © RD/DP **306 tl** © RD/Richard Surman **r** © RD/Justyn Wilsmore **bl** © RD/PL **307 tl** Harry Smith Collection **tr** PHPL **cr** Derek St Romaine **br** Harry Smith Collection **308 tl** © RD/PL **bl** © RD/PL **br** © RD/PL **309 tl** www.gardenworldimages.com/MAP/Arnaud Descat **tr** Clive Nichols **b** PHPL **310 tr** PHPL **bl** © RD/PL **br** Derek St Romaine **311 tl** © RD/PL **bl** Harry Smith Collection **br** © RD/Richard Surman **312 tl** © RD/PL **tr** Clive Nichols/Hadspen Garden, Somerset **bl** GPL/JS Sira **313 t** Clive Nichols **bl** © RD/PL **br** © RD/PL **314 l** © RD/PL **r** © RD/PL **315 l** Clive Nichols **tc** Harry Smith Collection **tr** PHPL **316 l** Andrew Lawson **r** Andrew Lawson **317 tr** GPL/Howard Rice **bl** PHPL **bc** PHPL **br** Harry Smith Collection **318 tl** PHPL **cr** PHPL **br** Harry Smith Collection **319 tl** Andrew Lawson **cl** Andrew Lawson **bl** PHPL **br** © RD/PL **320 l** © RD **tr** Andrew Lawson **br** Harry Smith Collection **321 tl** PHPL **tr** Harry Smith Collection **bl** Clive Nichols **322 tr** © RD/PL **bl** Andrew Lawson **br** © RD/PL **323 l** Clive Nichols **r** www.gardencollection.com/John Glover **324 tr** Harry Smith Collection **bl** GPL/John Glover **325 tr** Harry Smith Collection **cr** John Glover **bl** Harry Smith Collection **br** Sheila & Oliver Mathews **326–327** © RD/DP **328 l** GPL/Tommy Candler **328–329 t** GPL/John Glover **b** GPL/Juliette Wade **329 tr** GPL/Sunniva Harte **br** GPL/Marie O'Hara **330** © RD/DP **tl** GPL/Jane Legate **331 t** GPL/Alec Scaresbrook **cl** © RD/PL **cr** © RD/DP **b** © RD/DP **332 tl** GPL/Georgia Glynn–Smith **332–333 t** GPL/Lamontagne **b** GPL/Gary Rogers **333 tr** GPL/John Glover **cl** GPL/Michael Howes **cr** GPL/Mark Bolton **br** GPL/Howard Rice **334** © RD/DP **335 tl** GPL/JS Sira **tr** GPL/Gary Rogers **b** © RD/DP **336 l** GPL/Linda Burges **r** © RD/Joanna Walker **337 l** © RD/DP **tr** © RD/DP **br** © RD/Joanna Walker **338** © RD/DP **339** © RD/DP

635·9

Project team

Editor
Lisa Thomas

Art editor
Julie Bennett

**Senior
assistant editor**
Alison Candlin

Assistant editors
Helen Spence
Cécile Landau
Celia Coyne

Designers
Kate Harris
Heather Dunleavy
Sailesh Patel

Editorial assistant
Rachel Weaver

Picture researcher
Rosie Taylor

Proofreader
Barry Gage

For Vivat Direct

Editorial director
Julian Browne

Art director
Anne-Marie Bulat

Managing editor
Nina Hathway

Trade books editor
Penny Craig

**Picture resource
manager**
Sarah Stewart-
Richardson

**Pre-press technical
manager**
Dean Russell

**Product production
manager**
Claudette Bramble

**Production
controller**
Jan Bucil

**The Reader's Digest
Association, Inc. would
like to thank the following
for their contribution
to this book.**

**For their help with
planning and producing
the book:**
Martin Bennett
Ian Brownhill
Colegraves Seeds Ltd
Julian Hunt
MacKnade Garden Centre,
  Faversham
Notcutts Garden Centre,
  Maidstone
The Royal Horticultural
  Society

**For allowing us to
use their gardens
for photography:**
The Beth Chatto
  Gardens Ltd
Gail Boucher
Dr and Mrs Edeleanu
The Garden House,
  Buckland, Devon
Mona Gude
Gillian Hill
Christopher Holiday
Mr and Mrs A. Hutchinson
Kay Jefferson
Ray O'Brien
The Royal Horticultural
  Society Gardens,
  Wisley, Surrey and
  Rosemoor, Devon
Mr and Mrs Richard Tite
Westdean College,
  Sussex

Care-free Plants Published in 2011 in the United Kingdom
by Vivat Direct Limited (t/a Reader's Digest),
157 Edgware Road, London W2 2HR

Care-free Plants is owned and under licence from
The Reader's Digest Association, Inc. All rights reserved.

First published in 2002

Reprinted in 2011

We are committed both to the quality of our products and the
service we provide to our customers. We value your comments
so please do contact us on 0871 351 1000 or via our website
at **www.readersdigest.co.uk**

If you have any comments or suggestions about the content of
our books, email us at gbeditorial@readersdigest.co.uk

Origination: FMG
Printed in China

Concept code US/3958/IC
Book Code 400 559 UP0000 1
ISBN 978 1 78020 056 9